PUBLIC OPINION and PUBLIC POLICY
Models of Political Linkage

329.05
L97p   64969

DATE DUE			
Mar 24 '69			
Feb 9 '70			
Jan 21 '72			
Jan 29 '72			
Nov 27 '72			
Dec 11 '72			
Apr 24 '74			
Apr 22 '75			
May 3 '78			
Apr 30 '82			

GAYLORD M-2   PRINTED IN U.S.A.

THE DORSEY SERIES IN POLITICAL SCIENCE

EDITOR NORTON E. LONG *Brandeis University*

MACRIDIS & BROWN *The De Gaulle Republic*

MACRIDIS & BROWN (eds.) *Comparative Politics: Notes and Readings* rev. ed.

DRAGNICH *Major European Governments* rev. ed.

ROBINSON *Congress and Foreign Policy-Making: A Study in Legislative Influence and Initiative* rev. ed.

JACOBINI *International Law: A Text* rev. ed.

MANGONE *The Elements of International Law* rev. ed.

GRIPP *Patterns of Soviet Politics* rev. ed.

MINAR *Ideas and Politics: The American Experience*

MEEHAN *The Theory and Method of Political Analysis*

EDELMANN *Latin American Government and Politics*

JACOB & ATHERTON *The Dynamics of International Organization: The Making of World Order*

SPIRO *World Politics: The Global System*

BROWN & WAHLKE *The American Political System: Notes and Readings*

ROELOFS *The Language of Modern Politics: An Introduction to the Study of Government*

MEEHAN *Contemporary Political Thought: A Critical Study*

FROHOCK *The Nature of Political Inquiry*

MEEHAN *Explanation in Social Science: A System Paradigm*

LUTTBEG (ed.) *Public Opinion and Public Policy: Models of Political Linkage*

PUBLIC OPINION and PUBLIC POLICY

Models of Political Linkage

Edited by

NORMAN R. LUTTBEG

TEMPLE UNIVERSITY

1968
THE DORSEY PRESS, HOMEWOOD, ILLINOIS
IRWIN–DORSEY LIMITED, Nobleton, Ontario

*To the memory of
my father,
an inspiration*

PREFACE

This collection of readings grows out of various classes and seminars in community politics and public opinion. As such, it is not specifically directed to any commonly offered course in political science, but rather reflects what I find to be a useful ordering of many important findings on the relationship between public policy and public opinion. This is one of the most difficult-to-research areas within public opinion and, probably for that reason, receives little attention in readers on public opinion and propaganda. This reader will probably be of most interest to those concerned with public opinion; but for reasons which should be obvious on reading the table of contents, it also concerns political parties and pressure groups.

Being a reader rather than a monograph, this work is largely the product of other men's creativity; and I must thank them for permitting me to reprint their work. I owe a special debt to Professor Harmon Zeigler who contributed an article on the relationship between legislators and lobbyists, thus filling a large void in the section on pressure groups. Also, Professors Melvin Kahn, Steven Wasby, John Baker, Joann Paine, and Joseph Zikmund provided invaluable comments and criticism resulting in a much improved reader. Finally, I must thank Mrs. Kay Myers and Mr. William O'Neill who shared with me the arduous task of assembling the materials.

April, 1968   N. R. L.

TABLE OF CONTENTS

INTRODUCTION

POLITICAL LINKAGE IN A LARGE SOCIETY

Norman R. Luttbeg

Probably the most widely held conception of the ideal society for participant democracy is one sufficiently small to allow everyone's participation in making decisions of societal importance. The New England town meeting exemplifies such an ideal situation. In such circumstances clearly not all will choose to participate, since some will not find the issue important or salient, and others will bow to those who are better informed, and will not actively participate in any decisions. But nothing precludes any individual from participating to his own satisfaction. Such total participation, however, becomes cumbersome when the society gets too large. In such large societies political leaders, the specialists in policymaking, must act for all, and given their importance in making societal decisions these political specialists always have the opportunity to act contrary to the public's opinion on the issue and to be unresponsive to the public's demands and wants.

An extensive literature describes the role the public should play in a democratic government and the necessary functions of representation in a large democratic society. Most of this discussion emphasizes the importance of the individual's participation in his government.[1] But a parallel literature, originating with Mosca and Pareto, warns of the potential dangers of extensive public participation in government. This literature emphasizes the desirability of a stable society and the need for rational, well-conceived, foresightful direction in the affairs of government.

The increasingly numerous empirical studies of citizen participation in politics in both the United States and other democratic societies paint a picture that totally satisfies neither of these schools of thought. On one hand the public shows a tendency to vote their party identification, which they learn from their parents; thus the flow of decisions made in the country little affects their votes. Their vote is insensitive to political decision making. Also they show a substantial degree of apathy and disinterest in the acts of government.[2] If few are politically involved and the few activists are insensitive to the performance of leaders, as these findings would indicate, leaders must be substantially autonomous and free of public interference in their decision making. The elite theorists might draw satisfaction from this conclusion, while those who encourage full-scale participation in decision making might express pessimism about the chances for a

---

[1] A valuable summary and critique of this literature is Peter Bachrach, *The Theory of Democratic Elitism* (Boston: Little, Brown and Co., 1967).

[2] Angus Campbell, Philip E. Converse, Warren E. Miller, and Donald E. Stokes, *The American Voter* (New York: John Wiley & Sons, Inc., 1960).

1

desirable democracy under these conditions. But nevertheless the devices of democracy remain, and the public shows some capability of using them in coping with unresponsive leadership, as unpopular leaders are defeated and some decision alternatives are precluded because of their unpopularity. Also the public seems to be confident that if it wanted to act against a leader it would be successful.[3] Moreover, the occasional critical elections, in which the voters change their party loyalty, thrusting the previously unpopular party into power, would indicate some capability on the part of the public to cope with their political environment.[4]

Many of those who study mass participation in politics have stressed the desirable balance between citizen participation and leadership discretion present in the United States and several of the more advanced European democracies.[5] With this happy balance the public feels capable of participating in and having an effect on government, but at the same time their lack of participation, along with extensive satisfaction with the actions of their government, allows the leaders great autonomy.[6] Such authors emphasize the stability of these democratic governments in the last 100 years as evidence of the virtue of the status quo. But this happy conclusion

is not shared by all; its critics stress the importance of participation in a development of the individual. Jack Walker makes this point in this reader.[7]

Political linkages, the subject of the reader, loom more important within the context of democracy conceived as a method of decision making than as a form of government maximizing participation. This concept of political linkage stresses the impact of public opinion on public policy. A linkage between the public and its leaders is the mechanism that allows public leaders to act in accordance with the wants, needs, and demands of their public. The better read student will immediately discover that at least several of the models are commonly discussed in our discipline, but they have seldom been conceived as the set of linkages that, in conjunction, explain how leaders act consistently with their constituents. My intent in organizing this reader is to gather from diverse sources conceptual frameworks and pertinent data that will allow some assessment of the explanatory power of various models. I intend to make no statements about their desirability but merely to indicate their effectiveness. The difficulty of recommending one method of linkage over another is, in my opinion, sufficiently important to offer an end section on the difficulties of policy recommendations.

But what is a political linkage? I have already described it as a mechanism that allows public leaders to act in accordance with their public. This focus encourages the consideration of various linkage models, which differ greatly in their operating characteristics. Some authors have conceived of a leader–public linkage as a two-way communications channel whereby the leader is aware of public sentiments and the public is aware of their leader's sentiments. Conceiving of linkage as com-

---

[3]Gabriel A. Almond and Sidney Verba, *The Civic Culture* (Princeton, N.J.: Princeton University Press, 1963), chap. 8.

[4]V. O. Key, Jr., "A Theory of Critical Elections," *Journal of Politics,* Vol. XVII (February 1955), pp. 3–18. See also Campbell *et al., op. cit.,* pp. 531–58.

[5]Almond and Verba, *op. cit.,* pp. 493–94.

[6]Throughout this article I have referred to the public. In using this concept I do not want to imply that the public is any more than the sum of all its members. Clearly, as I noted in the New England town meeting, on any given issue some people may feel the issue is irrelevant; they have no opinion; they choose not to participate. Public opinion in such cases is the opinion of those who have preferences and choose to participate. The saliency of the issue to a given individual and his resulting intense participation might well cause his opinion to weigh more heavily in some linkage processes.

[7]Jack L. Walker, "A Critique of the Elitist Theory of Democracy," *American Political Science Review,* Vol. LX (June 1966), pp. 285–95.

munication certainly suffices for understanding the first three models presented. But the last two—the belief-sharing model and the role-playing model—depend on leader characteristics. No communication is involved unless one stretches the concept of communication to include the socialization of children, some of whom will become leaders. The process of leadership recruitment or selection is important in the operational effectiveness of these last two linkage models. Two variables for differentiating among several linkage models—the degree of leadership coercion available to the public and the distinction between personal opinion and perceptions of others' opinions—will be useful in classifying the various models offered.

A SCHEMA FOR POLITICAL LINKAGE MODELS

Many theorists have stressed the importance of a corrective mechanism whereby the public may exchange or remove from office those leaders who fail to respond to their wants and demands, i.e., throw the rascals out.[8] Possibly leaders will act to satisfy the public's demands and expectations even in the absence of a corrective or coercive mechanism. Many linkage models, however, include coercive elements.

To decision making, leaders bring numerous propensities to action. For one thing they have their own attitudes—what they see as desirable, necessary, and so on. Additionally they have perceptions about what the public will prefer. Of course the most desirable situation for the leader exists when he thinks both sets of attitudes are in agreement, that his desires are shared by his constituents. There is some indication that leaders strongly desire

their preferences and their constituents' preferences to be reconcilable, and discrepancy, if perceived, can be sufficiently traumatic to cause the leader to resign.[9] Few of the more carefully articulated models have distinguished between whether the leader acts on the basis of his own preferences or those he perceives his constituents to hold, but consideration of this distinction may cause us to conceive of alternative models.

By use of these two conceptions, four alternative means by which leaders can satisfy the public's expectations and desires are offered in Figure 1; only two posit a need for a functioning means of public coercion. Notably, these four alternatives deal only with the means for individual leaders to give expression to the public's desires. They explain only how a certain cross section of personal preferences and perceptions of public preferences might exist in a group of leaders. A second process whereby these profiles of opinion are converted into public policy is not considered, but certainly the second process depends largely on the first, since it is difficult to conceive of any interaction among leaders in policymaking that would result in a policy consistent with public opinion if no linkage process were functioning. If the leaders were against Medicare and perceived that the public shared this opinion while indeed the public favored Medicare, it is difficult to conceive of any process of interaction among leaders in policymaking that would result in a policy consistent in public sentiment. On the other hand if there were perfect consensus in the society, namely all leaders perfectly shared the values and preferences of the public, this secondary process of leadership interaction would be trivial since there would be little possibility of

---

[8]Preferences are beliefs held by individuals, which may or may not be expressed or articulated to anyone. Demands however are expressed preferences that carry an expectation of fulfillment. In making a demand an individual expects that it will be satisfied.

---

[9]Norman R. Luttbeg and Harmon Zeigler, "Attitude Consensus and Conflict in an Interest Group; An Assessment of Cohesion," *American Political Science Review*, Vol. LX (September 1966), pp. 655–66.

FIGURE 1

Means by Which Leaders Can Serve the Preferences of the Followers

	Coercion of Some Sort Used to Assure Performance	No Means of Coercion Necessary to Assure Performance
Leader acts consistently with his personal preferences	Men whose preferences are preferred by the followers are made leaders. A	Because leaders and followers share many experiences and preferences, leaders in voting their own preferences also vote the preferences of the followers. C
Leader acts on what he believes to be the preferences of those he leads	Leaders vote the preferences of their followers in fear of being removed from leadership. B	Leaders vote what they believe to be the preferences of their followers and even anticipate their preferences because the leaders believe they should do so. D

their policy's running contrary to popular support.

MODELS OF POLITICAL LINKAGE

The English language, like all languages, contains vague and inadequate terms, at least when contrasted with the rigor of mathematical statements. This vagueness, along with the length of a prose presentation of an argument, makes self-contradiction possible at different times in the presentation. Schematically this would be comparable, for example, to saying early in an article that A alone explains B and at a later point saying that non-A explains B.[10]

For this reason I have chosen not to paraphrase the writing of a given theorist for each of these areas, but rather have attempted to portray the various models as simply and succinctly as possible. Since most of the authors undoubtedly saw the crux of their writing as offering an explanation of observed behavior rather than the articulation of a hypothetical linkage model, one would undoubtedly be hard

put to find any author who has presented the models as unguardedly as I will. The selections included in the reader contain brief statements by exponents of the various models. Therefore, the correctness of my interpretation can to some degree be judged by the reader.[11]

The Rational-Activist Model

This model merely takes the desirable activities on the part of individuals in a small, ideal, democratic society where everyone would weigh equally in making decisions, and introduces the element of representation made necessary by the larger size of the present century's nation-states. The individual is expected to be politically informed, involved, rational, and, above all, active. On the basis of an informed and carefully reasoned set of personal preferences and an accurate perception of the various candidates' positions, the voter is expected to vote for those candidates who best reflect his per-

---

[10]It is this logical fallacy that Rothman believes he detects in Truman's writings. See Rothman in Section III.

[11]In the choice of exponents for the given models I in no way mean to criticize these authors. Their work was chosen because of the brevity and completeness of their statement of the model as I perceived it.

sonal preferences. Thus, if an officeholder or a candidate neglects the public's wants and demands, the public will sense it and may well deny him support in the next election. Of course all actions that subvert the meaning of the elections, such as not allowing the electorate a choice or not allowing those elected to take office, violate the spirit of this model.

The means of coercion in this case clearly is the electoral process. There is little distinction between whether the official acts on the basis of his own preferences or those he perceives the electorate to hold. His career rests on his satisfying them; thus the distinction between cell A and cell B is irrelevant.

Although few authors would state that this model substantially accounts for leaders' ability to act consistently with public demands, it frequently is treated as a last-ditch method by which the public controls its leaders.

The Political Parties Model

The political parties model focuses on an intermediate institution—the political party—which because of its desire to be victorious and to have its candidates elected provides a link between leaders and their public. This model's first stage, the public's relationship with the parties, utilizes the mechanism of the rational-activist model. Once again a rational-activist citizen is asked to make his selection at the polls, but he selects the party that most closely reflects his personal preferences. Thus rather than a candidate-by-candidate selection on the ballot, the voter merely chooses that party whose platform and candidates' speeches he found most acceptable.

The second stage in this model is the mechanism whereby the party enacts its platform into policy with the aid of its elected members. The party must possess sufficient control over its elected candidates to ensure their aid in enacting the platform. The public in turn assesses the party's performance while in control of government; as in the rational-activist model, if dissatisfied they vote the rascals out, or in this case they vote the party out, electing the other party's candidates.

Because the institution of government normally necessitates that a party have a majority of the positions in the government to ensure its control, the preference is usually for a two-party system, which, it is assumed, facilitates this majority control. This of course is done at the expense of the party's ideological purity. If only two parties exist, achieving consistency within the party's platform will be more difficult because the range of opinion that must be tolerated is far greater. Thus there is some debate within the literature about the relative virtues of the multiple-party system versus the two-party system, but this debate is essentially irrelevant to the model as presented here.

The political parties model is clearly a coercive-type model, and at least in the first stage the link between the party platform and the public entails perceptions of public wants and desires. Thus it constitutes a B-type model.

The Pressure Groups Model

Even as the political parties model was developed from an awareness of an institution active in politics (the political party) so the political pressure groups model has derived from a sudden awareness—developed about the turn of the century—of the role of pressure groups in American government. The model argues that very little individual opinion exists within a modern society apart from group attitudes. Either groups are the source of all opinions, or all opinions of importance are expressed by groups. This greatly reduces the number of actors whose opinions must be considered in democratic policy decisions, since there are far fewer groups than individuals; thus it permits a reversion to an ideal democracy in which all participate in making decisions for the society and none serve as leaders. This aggregation conclusion converts modern nation-states into the revered town meeting democracy of New England, but two major problems exist. First, not all the actors weigh equally as would the individuals in the New England town meeting. Some groups are enormous in size; others while vocal are quite small. Clearly the model necessitates some weighting of opinion. Second, these groups cannot directly make policy but must act through elected officials. A vote of all group opinion cannot be taken and the result enacted into policy. Rather the groups must act through elected public officials. Not surprisingly the elected official plays a small role in this model, since his role is analogous to that of a leaf being pushed about by the winds; in this case the winds are the pressure groups.

Actually I am aware of no author who expresses the pressure groups model in pure form. Most accept political parties and discuss the pressure groups' activities to make candidates and parties responsive to their needs. Since the pressure groups primarily rely on offers of support and threats to deny support in their relations with parties, there is debate about the best strategy for dealing with public leaders. If the pressure group strongly identifies with a political party that proves victorious, the pressure group of course is in a far better position to enact its preferences. But if the party loses, the political leaders elected from the other party will feel no need to respond to their demands, and the group loses its access.

Ideally the political pressure groups model necessitates no linkage because all actors participate in making governmental policy. Thus it does not fit anywhere in the presented schema. But in its accommodation of the political parties model it fits into cell B, since coercion is implied and political leaders succeed by being responsive to public demands expressed by pressure groups.

Although I can think of no literature that emphasizes the pressure groups model without including important functions for political parties, there has been a rather polemic discussion on the role of the political pressure groups model among those who are confident of the effectiveness of the political parties model. Some theorists and researchers have argued that the mix of political parties and pressure groups operates to optimize the linkage between public and leaders. Thus any alteration of the status quo in the United States to better reflect the nature of the competitive two-party model, as exemplified by the British party system, would potentially threaten the American political system.[12] Other theorists have argued that the activity of political pressure groups at least partially causes ideological impurity of the American party system.[13] They argue that a competitive political party system functions best when independent of pressure groups. This amounts to saying the political parties model will not operate properly in the presence of a functioning pressure groups model.

The Pluralist Nonmodel

Each of the preceding models clearly has coercive elements, a public capability of seeing that those in office will not be returned if they fail to do the public's bidding. But the question of the effectiveness of such models becomes even more acute in the modern American community where numerous studies have shown that men of economic and social status have undue influence in decisions that affect the community. On the basis of this research one might well conclude that democracy does not function in most American communities. Certainly none of the preceding three models can explain how the public's

---

[12]Pendleton Herring, *The Politics of Democracy* (New York: Rinehart & Co., Inc., 1940).

[13]Committee on Political Parties of the American Political Science Association, "Toward a More Responsible Two-Party System," *American Political Science Review*, Vol. XLIV (September 1950), supplement.

interest might be served when decisions are made by noncoercible economic and social leaders. Of course the public may express its growing disenchantment with the policies of such an elite by refusing to shop in their stores, by not selling their houses through them, and so on, but such methods are cumbersome at best and may be unavailable when an economic leader's industry dominates the community. Such a leader is invulnerable to public coercion within the limits of the law.

Indeed many researchers of modern American communities have concluded that democracy functions only in name. But other researchers find this conclusion unsatisfactory. They stress the importance of the difference between a single elite that dominates all decisions in the community and subsets of leaders from social, economic, and political influence bases who make decisions in different areas.[14] These researchers, labeled pluralists, hasten to note the important role played by coercible political leaders in communities they have researched. Of course the importance of political leaders in a community's decision making indicates the degree to which the political parties model of linkage can operate. But this is but small measure of comfort to those who question the effectiveness of democracy in the modern American community.

The pluralists offer a rather complex model for the functioning of the modern American community, which at least in one case has been generalized to apply to behavior in nation-states.[15] In addition to the importance of leaders' specialization in certain decision areas and the important role played by the political leader, they stress the importance of consensus within the society and the desire on the part of the political leader to give expression to public preferences in his policymaking. They note that, like other persons

in society, the political leader has been socialized to believe in the desirability of leaders' acting democratically.

Thus the pluralists suggest the final two models I will present—the sharing model and the role-playing model. The process the pluralists claim operates in American communities lacks conceptual usefulness in that it claims that the mix of all these various elements—shared rules of the game adhered to by both public and leaders, importance of the political leader, specialization of concern into certain areas of policymaking, and so on—fortuitously leads to a democratic expression. No statement is made about the relative importance of the various elements, circumstances in which one will predominate, or the effects of inoperative linkages, and most unfortunately researchers are not directed on how to demonstrate the superiority of this model over the others. Finally the model ultimately rests on the effectiveness of the rational-activist model; that is, when worse comes to worse the public, aware of its own perceptions, rational in its deductions, and aware of the leaders' stands on the various issues, will elect leaders most closely expressing its personal preferences.[16] Despite its conceptual ambiguities the pluralist model suggests two more rigorous models of political prestige.

The Sharing Model

The sharing model is quite simple. If the society were totally homogeneous in its opinions on policies—an instance of total consensus—it would not matter which members of the society actually participated in policymaking. Thus to some degree leaders give expression to public wants and demands merely because they share preferences with the public. No coercive element is present here; as a result, no correction is possible if the leaders do not share the public's attitudes. But we

---

[14]See Floyd Hunter's review of Dahl, *Who Governs?, Administrative Science Quarterly,* Vol. 7 (March 1966).

[15]Almond and Verba, *op. cit.,* chap. 15.

[16]Robert A. Dahl, *Who Governs?* (New Haven, Conn.: Yale University Press, 1961), pp. 92 and 322.

must assess the necessity of coercive models and the degree to which the leaders satisfy public preferences even in the absence of such coercion.

The concept of sharing is not new, as indicated by the discussions of consensus and rules of the game. Both concern the sharing of attitudes between leaders and the public. Sharing is a type C model.

The Role-Playing Model

As in other positions played in a complex society, the position of the leader has an associated role, and the controversy over which role the leader should play is a rather important historical conflict. Edmund Burke's statement that the leader should act on the basis of his own preferences and that the public elects a man be-

cause of his wisdom essentially urges the political leader to play the role of the trustee in contrast to perceiving himself as the voice of his constituents. The role-playing model merely states that one possible political linkage is by way of the leader's feeling he should give expression to public sentiment, wants, desires, and so on.

The public has no coercive function in this model, and the leader would undoubtedly rely on his perception of his constituents' attitudes in trying to reflect their desires. The role-playing model is clearly a D type model in terms of the schema.

CONCLUSIONS

Without a systematic conceptual distinction between the alternative models

FIGURE 2
Linkages

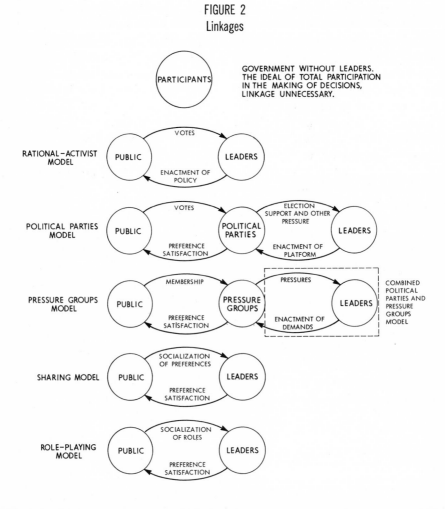

that might explain leader–follower linkage in a democratic society, it is unlikely that we will proceed to an evaluation of the relative effectiveness of the various models and to a consideration of the circumstances in which each best applies. I hope that my effort at differentiating the five models, schematically presented in Figure 2, will in some way contribute to this ultimate development of a political linkage theory. Furthermore I hope that the presentation of materials in this reader will in some way remove the aura of "proven" theories from the political parties and pressure groups models. Certainly there is substantial evidence to question their validity.

The reader includes eight sections; the first three contain presentations by adherents to each of the first three models and empirical assessments of their effectiveness. The fourth section includes two selections by pluralists, from which the sharing and role-playing models are derived. This section is followed by two sections that give empirical assessments of the accuracy and effectiveness of these two new models. The seventh section of the reader includes a discussion of possible effects of linkage failure in a system. Finally I have included an exchange between two theorists, which highlights the difficulties in making policy recommendations on the basis of empirically observed facts.

SECTION I

The Rational-Activist Model

Bernard Berelson, in our first selection, strives to systematically present the requisites of the rational-activist model. Then noting the distinction between theory and fact, he stresses the public's inability to fulfill the requirements of this model and suggests that were the public to be rational and active in politics, society's stability might well be endangered. He hypothesizes a political man who is neither strongly ideological nor totally apolitical. Such men, he claims, are present in American society and help to maintain the balance between conflict and consensus so necessary for a stable society. We will repeatedly see this idea of balance throughout the literature on political linkage.

Walter Berns accuses Berelson and his coauthors Lazarsfeld and McPhee of ". . . sacrific[ing] . . . political relevance on the altar of methodology," because he finds serious fault with Berelson's statements of "traditional democratic theory" and doubts the desirability of the balance political man alternative. These first two selections highlight in this area of political behavior the thin line between empirical research and the question of what is desirable.

The great outpouring of research in voting behavior, of which Berelson, Lazarsfeld, and McPhee's *Voting* was an important milestone, has thrown into question the ability of the average citizen to utilize the institution of elections to control his leaders. Although it is impossible to present all the relevant findings here, the two included selections represent this literature in the sense that they challenge the effectiveness of the model. Using a statistical technique that permits assessment of the relative importance of the various attitudes that influence an individual's vote, Stokes shows that it is candidate appeal—his sincerity, honesty, attractiveness, and so on—which fluctuates most between elections and has the greatest impact on election outcomes. The rational-activist voter in contrast would be swayed more by the issues, both domestic and foreign, and by party performance.[1]

The second selection pertaining to voting behavior, a chapter from *The American Voter*, considers the turnout of voters for Presidential elections. Apart from the fact that few Americans (60–65 percent) vote in even this most exciting election in sharp contrast to the expectations under the rational-activist model, those who do vote have several desirable characteristics. They are more concerned with the outcome of the election, more interested in the campaign, and

---

[1]The reader might want to read Philip Converse, "The Nature of Belief Systems in Mass Publics," from Section V for additional data on the average individual's ability to cope with the issues that currently affect governmental decisions.

11

feel it is their civic duty to vote; but they are also the more partisan members of our society. Indeed if there is one most supported finding in the study of voting, it is the importance and permanence of identification with political parties and its major impact on how people vote.[2] A partisan voter, especially one whose political party is so likely to be that of his parents, is not likely to fulfill the expectations of the rational-activist model. How are public leaders to be controlled if the most informed and active voters vote their fathers' parties and others respond primarily to the attractiveness of the candidates?

The late V. O. Key, Jr. was unconvinced by these pessimistic findings. In *The Responsible Electorate* he argues that American voters are responsive to the issues of the day. Having demonstrated the importance of young voters just entering the electorate as well as those who vote the party opposite the one they voted in the previous election, Key here seeks to show that both the standpatters— those who stay with their political party—and the switchers seek consistency between their vote and their political attitudes on important issues.

It certainly is too early to conclude that voters are incapable of conceiving of important issues and utilizing the institutions of elections to affect their implementation. Many are loyal partisans for at least the short run, but the occasional critical election, such as 1932, may reflect the average man's achievement of consistency between his party identification and his attitudes on important issues.

---

[2]Again the reader may want to look ahead to Arthur Goldberg's "Discerning a Causal Pattern among Data on Voting Behavior," which depicts the central importance of our consideration of whether we are Democrats or Republicans.

DEMOCRATIC PRACTICE AND DEMOCRATIC THEORY*

Bernard R. Berelson

There is always a terrible gulf between the fine and elevating theories about democracy which we read in books on political theory and the actual facts of politics.—Lord Lindsay

---

*Reprinted from *Voting* by Bernard R. Berelson, Paul F. Lazarsfeld, and William N. McPhee by permission of the University of Chicago Press. Copyright 1954.

The senior author is particularly indebted to his friend and colleague, Edward Shils, for stimulation and instruction on this topic in general and for advice on this chapter in particular.

I

What does all this mean for the political theory of democracy? For we have been studying not how people come to make choices in general but how they make a political choice, and the political content of the study has broad ramifications beyond the technical interests. In the end, of course, we must leave such theoretical questions to the political theorists and the political philosophers. But the fact that they would not be at home in our empirical material has encouraged us to speak at least briefly to their concerns. Both theory and facts are needed. As Schumpeter says in *Capitalism, Socialism and Democracy*: "The question whether [certain] conditions are fulfilled to the extent required in order to make democracy work should not be answered by reckless assertion or equally reckless denial. It can be answered only by a laborious appraisal of a maze of conflicting evidence."

With respect to politics, empirical-analytic theory and normative theory have only recently become truly separated—and often to their mutual disadvantage and impoverishment. In a recent essay a British scholar comments on "The Decline of Political Theory." That there has been and is now a "decline" seems to be generally accepted. Why? Because, says Alfred Cobban, the theory of the great political thinkers of the past was written "with a practical purpose in mind. Their object was to influence actual political behavior. They wrote to condemn or support existing institutions, to justify a political system or persuade their fellow citizens to change it: because, in the last resort, they were concerned with the aims, the purposes of political society." He points out that John Stuart Mill tried to reconcile the demands for state action with established ideals of individual liberty, Bentham to establish a theoretical basis for the legislative and administrative reforms that were then urgently needed, Burke to provide an alternative to the new democratic principle of the sovereignty of the people, Locke to provide a political theory for a generation that had overthrown divine right and established parliamentary government, Hobbes to maintain the primacy of sovereignty in an age of civil wars, etc. From being "formerly the work of men intently concerned with practical issues," the study of political theory

has become instead an academic discipline written in various esoteric jargons almost as

though for the purpose of preventing it from being understood by those who, if they did understand it, might try to put it into practice. . . . Political theory has in this way become disengaged from political facts. Even worse, it has become disengaged on principle, as it has seldom if ever been in the past.

Here, it seems to us, lies one potential use of our data. If the political theorists do not engage directly in politics, they might explore the relevance, the implications, and the meaning of such empirical facts as are contained in this and similar studies. Political theory written with reference to practice has the advantage that its categories are the categories in which political life really occurs. And, in turn, relating research to problems of normative theory would make such research more realistic and more pertinent to the problems of policy. At the same time, empirical research can help to clarify the standards and correct the empirical presuppositions of normative theory. As a modest illustration, this concluding chapter of the volume turns to some of the broad normative and evaluative questions implied in this empirical study.

REQUIREMENTS FOR THE INDIVIDUAL

Perhaps the main impact of realistic research on contemporary politics has been to temper some of the requirements set by our traditional normative theory for the typical citizen. "Out of all this literature of political observation and analysis, which is relatively new," says Max Beloff, "there has come to exist a picture in our minds of the political scene which differs very considerably from that familiar to us from the classical texts of democratic politics."

Experienced observers have long known, of course, that the individual voter was not all that the theory of democracy requires of him. As Bryce put it:

How little solidity and substance there is in the political or social beliefs of nineteen persons out of every twenty. These beliefs, when examined, mostly resolve themselves into two or three prejudices and aversions, two or three prepossessions for a particular party or section of a party, two or three phrases or catch-words suggesting or embodying arguments which the man who repeats them has not analyzed.

While our data do not support such an extreme statement, they do reveal that certain requirements commonly assumed for the successful operation of democracy are not met by the behavior of the "average" citizen. The requirements, and our conclusions concerning them, are quickly reviewed.[1]

Interest, Discussion, Motivation

The democratic citizen is expected to be interested and to participate in political affairs. His interest and participation can take such various forms as reading and listening to campaign materials, working for the candidate or the party, arguing politics, donating money, and voting. In Elmira the majority of the people vote, but in general they do not give evidence of sustained interest. Many vote without real involvement in the election, and even the party workers are not typically motivated by ideological concerns or plain civic duty.

If there is one characteristic for a democratic system (besides the ballot itself) that is theoretically required, it is the capacity for and the practice of discussion. "It is as true of the large as of the small society," says Lindsay, "that its health depends on the mutual understanding which discussion makes possible; and that discussion is the only possible instrument of its democratic government." How much participation in political discussion there is in the community, what it is, and among whom—these questions have been given

answers in an earlier chapter. In this instance there was little true discussion between the candidates, little in the newspaper commentary, little between the voters and the official party representatives, some within the electorate. On the grass-roots level there was more talk than debate, and, at least inferentially, the talk had important effects upon voting, in reinforcing or activating the partisans if not in converting the opposition.

An assumption underlying the theory of democracy is that the citizenry has a strong motivation for participation in political life. But it is a curious quality of voting behavior that for large numbers of people motivation is weak if not almost absent. It is assumed that this motivation would gain its strength from the citizen's perception of the difference that alternative decisions made to him. Now when a person buys something or makes other decisions of daily life, there are direct and immediate consequences for him. But for the bulk of the American people the voting decision is not followed by any direct, immediate, visible personal consequences. Most voters, organized or unorganized, are not in a position to foresee the distant and indirect consequences for themselves, let alone the society. The ballot is cast, and for most people that is the end of it. If their side is defeated, "it doesn't really matter."

Knowledge

The democratic citizen is expected to be well informed about political affairs. He is supposed to know what the issues are, what their history is, what the relevant facts are, what alternatives are proposed, what the party stands for, what the likely consequences are. By such standards the voter falls short. Even when he has the motivation, he finds it difficult to make decisions on the basis of full information when the subject is relatively simple and proximate; how can

---

[1] A somewhat more general statement is contained in Bernard Berelson, "Democratic Theory and Public Opinion," *Public Opinion Quarterly*, Vol. XVI (fall, 1952), pp. 313–30.

he do so when it is complex and remote? The citizen is not highly informed on details of the campaign, nor does he avoid a certain misperception of the political situation when it is to his psychological advantage to do so. The electorate's perception of what goes on in the campaign is colored by emotional feeling toward one or the other issue, candidate, party, or social group.

Principle

The democratic citizen is supposed to cast his vote on the basis of principle—not fortuitously or frivolously or impulsively or habitually, but with reference to standards not only of his own interest but of the common good as well. Here, again, if this requirement is pushed at all strongly, it becomes an impossible demand on the democratic electorate.

Many voters vote not for principle in the usual sense but "for" a group to which they are attached—their group. The Catholic vote or the hereditary vote is explainable less as principle than as a traditional social allegiance. The ordinary voter, bewildered by the complexity of modern political problems, unable to determine clearly what the consequences are of alternative lines of action, remote from the arena, and incapable of bringing information to bear on principle, votes the way trusted people around him are voting. A British scholar, Max Beloff, takes as the "chief lesson to be derived" from such studies:

Election campaigns and the programmes of the different parties have little to do with the ultimate result which is predetermined by influences acting upon groups of voters over a longer period. . . . This view has now become a working hypothesis with which all future thinking on this matter will have to concern itself. But if this is admitted, then obviously the picture of the voter as a person exercising conscious choice between alternative persons and alternative programmes tends to disappear.

On the issues of the campaign there is a considerable amount of "don't know"—sometimes reflecting genuine indecision, more often meaning "don't care." Among those with opinions the partisans *agree* on most issues, criteria, expectations, and rules of the game. The supporters of the different sides disagree on only a few issues. Nor, for that matter, do the candidates themselves always join the issue sharply and clearly. The partisans do not agree overwhelmingly with their own party's position, or, rather, only the small minority of highly partisan do; the rest take a rather moderate position on the political considerations involved in an election.

Rationality

The democratic citizen is expected to exercise rational judgment in coming to his voting decision. He is expected to have arrived at his principles by reason and to have considered rationally the implications and alleged consequences of the alternative proposals of the contending parties. Political theorists and commentators have always exclaimed over the seeming contrast here between requirement and fulfillment. Even as sensible and hard-minded an observer as Schumpeter was extreme in his view:

Even if there were no political groups trying to influence him, the typical citizen would in political matters tend to yield to extra-rational or irrational prejudice and impulse. The weakness of the rational processes he applies to politics and the absence of effective logical control over the results he arrives at would in themselves suffice to account for that. Moreover, simply because he is not "all there," he will relax his usual moral standards as well and occasionally give in to dark urges which the conditions of private life help him to repress.

Here the problem is first to see just what is meant by rationality. The term, as a recent writer noted, "has enjoyed a long history which has bequeathed to it a legacy of ambiguity and confusion. . . . Any man may be excused when he is puzzled by the question how he ought to use the word and particularly how he ought to use it in relation to human conduct and politics." Several meanings can be differentiated.

It is not for us to certify a meaning. But even without a single meaning—with only the aura of the term—we can make some observations on the basis of our material. In any rigorous or narrow sense the voters are not highly rational; that is, most of them do not ratiocinate on the matter, e.g., to the extent that they do on the purchase of a car or a home. Nor do voters act rationally whose "principles" are held so tenaciously as to blind them to information and persuasion. Nor do they attach efficient means to explicit ends.

The fact that some people change their minds during a political campaign shows the existence of that open-mindedness usually considered a component of rationality. But among whom? Primarily among those who can "afford" a change of mind, in the sense that they have ties or attractions on both sides—the cross-pressured voters in the middle where rationality is supposed to take over from the extremes of partisan feeling. But it would hardly be proper to designate the unstable, uninterested, uncaring middle as the sole or the major possessor of rationality among the electorate. As Beloff points out: "It is likely that the marginal voter is someone who is so inadequately identified with one major set of interests or another and so remote, therefore, from the group-thinking out of which political attitudes arise, that his voting record is an illustration, not of superior wisdom, but of greater frivolity."

The upshot of this is that the usual analogy between the voting "decision" and the more or less carefully calculated decisions of consumers or businessmen or courts, incidentally, may be quite incorrect. For many voters political preferences may better be considered analogous to cultural tastes—in music, literature, recreational activities, dress, ethics, speech, social behavior. Consider the parallels between political preferences and general cultural tastes. Both have their origin in ethnic, sectional, class, and family traditions. Both exhibit stability and resistance to change for individuals but flexibility and adjustment over generations for the society as a whole. Both seem to be matters of sentiment and disposition rather than "reasoned preferences." While both are responsive to changed conditions and unusual stimuli, they are relatively invulnerable to direct argumentation and vulnerable to indirect social influences. Both are characterized more by faith than by conviction and by wishful expectation rather than careful prediction of consequences. The preference for one party rather than another must be highly similar to the preference for one kind of literature or music rather than another, and the choice of the same political party every four years may be parallel to the choice of the same old standards of conduct in new social situations. In short, it appears that a sense of fitness is a more striking feature of political preference than reason and calculation.

II

If the democratic system depended solely on the qualifications of the individual voter, then it seems remarkable that democracies have survived through the centuries. After examining the detailed data on how individuals misperceive political reality or respond to irrelevant social influences, one wonders how a democracy ever solves its political problems. But when one considers the data in a broader perspective—how huge segments of the society adapt to political conditions affecting them or how the political system adjusts itself to changing conditions over long periods of time—he cannot fail to be impressed with the total result. Where the rational citizen seems to abdicate, nevertheless angels seem to tread.

The eminent judge, Learned Hand, in a delightful essay on "Democracy: Its Presumptions and Reality," comes to essentially this conclusion.

I do not know how it is with you, but for myself I generally give up at the outset. The simplest problems which come up from day to day seem to me quite unanswerable as soon as I try to get below the surface. . . . My vote is one of the most unimportant acts of my life; if I were to acquaint myself with the matters on which it ought really to depend, if I were to try to get a judgment on which I was willing to risk affairs of even the smallest moment, I should be doing nothing else, and that seems a fatuous conclusion to a fatuous undertaking.

Yet he recognizes the paradox—somehow the system not only works on the most difficult and complex questions but often works with distinction. "For, abuse it as you will, it gives a bloodless measure of social forces—bloodless, have you thought of that?—a means of continuity, a principle of stability, a relief from the paralyzing terror of revolution."

Justice Hand concludes that we have "outgrown" the conditions assumed in traditional democratic theory and that "the theory has ceased to work." And yet, the system that has grown out of classic democratic theory, and, in this country, out of quite different and even elementary social conditions, does continue to work—perhaps even more vigorously and effectively than ever.

That is the paradox. *Individual voters* today seem unable to satisfy the requirements for a democratic system of government outlined by political theorists. But the *system of democracy* does meet certain requirements for a going political organization. The individual members may not meet all the standards, but the whole nevertheless survives and grows. This suggests that where the classic theory is defective is in its concentration on the *individual citizen*. What are undervalued are certain collective properties that reside in the electorate as a whole and in the political and social system in which it functions.

The political philosophy we have inherited, then, has given more consideration to the virtues of the typical citizen of the democracy than to the working of the *system* as a whole. Moreover, when it dealt with the system, it mainly considered the single constitutive institutions of the system, not those general features necessary if the institutions are to work as required. For example, the rule of law, representative government, periodic elections, the party system, and the several freedoms of discussion, press, association, and assembly have all been examined by political philosophers seeking to clarify and to justify the idea of political democracy. But liberal democracy is more than a political system in which individual voters and political institutions operate. For political democracy to survive, other features are required: the intensity of conflict must be limited, the rate of change must be restrained, stability in the social and economic structure must be maintained, a pluralistic social organization must exist, and a basic consensus must bind together the contending parties.

Such features of the system of political democracy belong neither to the constitutive institutions nor to the individual voter. It might be said that they form the atmosphere or the environment in which both operate. In any case, such features have not been carefully considered by political philosophers, and it is on these broader properties of the democratic political system that more reflection and study by political theory is called for. In the most tentative fashion let us explore the values of the political system, as they involve the electorate, in the light of the foregoing considerations.

REQUIREMENTS FOR THE SYSTEM

Underlying the paradox is an assumption that the population is homogeneous socially and should be homogeneous politically: that everybody is about the same in relevant social characteristics; that, if something is a political virtue (like interest in the election), then everyone should have it; that there is such a thing as "the" typical citizen on whom uniform requirements can be imposed. The tendency of classic democratic literature to work with an image of "the" voter was never justified. For, as we will attempt to illustrate here, some of the most important requirements that democratic values impose on a system require a voting population that is not homogeneous but heterogeneous in its political qualities.

The need for heterogeneity arises from the contradictory functions we expect our voting system to serve. We expect the political system to adjust itself and our affairs to changing conditions; yet we demand too that it display a high degree of stability. We expect the contending interests and parties to pursue their ends vigorously and the voters to care; yet, after the election is over, we expect reconciliation. We expect the voting outcome to serve what is best for the community; yet we do not want disinterested voting unattached to the purposes and interests of different segments of that community. We want voters to express their own free and self-determined choices; yet, for the good of the community, we would like voters to avail themselves of the best information and guidance available from the groups and leaders around them. We expect a high degree of rationality to prevail in the decision; but were all irrationality and mythology absent, and all ends pursued by the most coldly rational selection of political means, it is doubtful if the system would hold together.

In short, our electoral system calls for apparently incompatible properties—which, although they cannot all reside in each individual voter, can (and do) reside in a heterogeneous electorate. What seems to be required of the electorate as a whole is a *distribution* of qualities along important dimensions. We need some people who are active in a certain respect, others

in the middle, and still others passive. The contradictory things we want from the total require that the parts be different. This can be illustrated by taking up a number of important dimensions by which an electorate might be characterized.

Involvement and Indifference

How could a mass democracy work if all the people were deeply involved in politics? Lack of interest by some people is not without its benefits, too. True, the highly interested voters vote more, and know more about the campaign, and read and listen more, and participate more; however, they are also less open to persuasion and less likely to change. Extreme interest goes with extreme partisanship and might culminate in rigid fanaticism that could destroy democratic processes if generalized throughout the community. Low affect toward the election—not caring much—underlies the resolution of many political problems; votes can be resolved into a two-party split instead of fragmented into many parties (the splinter parties of the left, for example, splinter because their advocates are *too* interested in politics). Low interest provides maneuvering room for political shifts necessary for a complex society in a period of rapid change. Compromise might be based upon sophisticated awareness of costs and returns—perhaps impossible to demand of a mass society—but it is more often induced by indifference. Some people are and should be highly interested in politics, but not everyone is or needs to be. Only the doctrinaire would deprecate the moderate indifference that facilitates compromise.

Hence, an important balance between action motivated by strong sentiments and action with little passion behind it is obtained by heterogeneity within the electorate. Balance of this sort is, in practice, met by a distribution of voters rather than by a homogeneous collection of "ideal" citizens.

Stability and Flexibility

A similar dimension along which an electorate might be characterized is stability-flexibility. The need for change and adaptation is clear, and the need for stability ought equally to be (especially from observation of current democratic practice in, say, certain Latin-American countries).

How is political stability achieved? There are a number of social sources of political stability: the training of the younger generation before it is old enough to care much about the matter, the natural selection that surrounds the individual voter with families and friends who reinforce his own inclinations, the tendency to adjust in favor of the majority of the group, the self-perpetuating tendency of political traditions among ethnic and class and regional strata where like-minded people find themselves socially together. Political stability is based upon social stability. Family traditions, personal associations, status-related organizational memberships, ethnic affiliations, socioeconomic strata—such ties for the individual do not change rapidly or sharply, and since his vote is so importantly a product of them, neither does it. In effect, a large part of the study of voting deals not with why votes change but rather with why they do not.

In addition, the varying conditions facing the country, the varying political appeals made to the electorate, and the varying dispositions of the voters activated by these stimuli—these, combined with the long-lasting nature of the political loyalties they instil, produce an important cohesion within the system. For example, the tendencies operating in 1948 electoral decisions not only were built up in the New Deal and Fair Deal era but also dated back to parental and grandparental loyalties, to religious and ethnic cleavages of a past era, and to moribund sectional and community conflicts. Thus, in a very real sense any particular election is a composite of various elections and various political and social events. People vote for a President on a given November day, but their choice is made not simply on the basis of what has happened in the preceding months or even four years; in 1948 some people were in effect voting on the internationalism issue of 1940, others on the depression issue of 1932, and some, indeed, on the slavery issues of 1860.

The vote is thus a kind of "moving average" of reactions to the political past. Voters carry over to each new election remnants of issues raised in previous elections—and so there is always an overlapping of old and new decisions that give a cohesion in time to the political system. Hence the composite decision "smooths out" political change. The people vote *in* the same election, but not all of them vote *on* it.

What of flexibility? Curiously, the voters least admirable when measured against individual requirements contribute most when measured against the aggregate requirement for flexibility. For those who change political preferences most readily are those who are least interested, who are subject to conflicting social pressures, who have inconsistent beliefs and erratic voting histories. Without them—if the decision were left only to the deeply concerned, well-integrated, consistently-principled ideal citizens—the political system might easily prove too rigid to adapt to changing domestic and international conditions.

In fact, it may be that the very people who are most sensitive to changing social conditions are those most susceptible to political change. For, in either case, the people exposed to membership in overlapping strata, those whose former life-patterns are being broken up, those who are moving about socially or physically, those who are forming new families and new friendships—it is they who are open to adjustments of attitudes and tastes. They may be the least partisan and the least interested voters, but they perform a valuable function for the entire system. Here again is an instance in which an individual "inadequacy" provides a positive service for the society: The campaign can be a reaffirming force for the settled majority and a creative force for the unsettled minority. There is stability on both sides and flexibility in the middle.

Progress and Conservation

Closely related to the question of stability is the question of past versus future orientation of the system. In America a progressive outlook is highly valued, but, at the same time, so is a conservative one. Here a balance between the two is easily found in the party system and in the distribution of voters themselves from extreme conservatives to extreme liberals. But a balance between the two is also achieved by a distribution of political dispositions through time. There are periods of great political agitation (i.e., campaigns) alternating with periods of political dormancy. Paradoxically, the former— the campaign period—is likely to be an instrument of conservatism, often even of historical regression.

Many contemporary campaigns (not, however, 1952) must be stabilizing forces that activated past tendencies in individuals and reasserted past patterns of group voting. In 1948, for example, the middle-class Protestants reaffirmed their traditional Republican position, the working-class Protestants reverted toward their position of the 1930's and the working-class Catholics toward their position not only of the 1930's but of a generation or more earlier. In this sense the campaign was a retreat away from new issues back toward old positions.

Political campaigns tend to make people more consistent both socially and psychologically; they vote more with their social groups and agree more with their own prior ideas on the issues. But new ideas and new alignments are in their in-

fancy manifested by inconsistency psychologically and heterogeneity socially; they are almost by definition deviant and minority points of view. To the extent that they are inhibited by pressure or simply by knowledge of what is the proper (i.e., majority) point of view in a particular group, then the campaign period is not a time to look for the growth of important new trends.

This "regressive tendency" may appear as a reaction to intense propaganda during decisive times. The term "regressive" need not imply a reversion to less-developed, less-adaptive behavior; in fact, one might argue that the revival of a Democratic vote among workers was functional for their interests. What it refers to is simply the reactivation of prior dispositions— dispositions in politics that date back years and decades, often to a prior political era.

Its counterpart, of course, is what we believe to be an important potential for progress during the periods of relaxed tension and low-pressure political and social stimuli that are especially characteristic of America between political campaigns. The very tendency for Americans to neglect their political system most of the time—to be "campaign citizens" in the sense that many are "Sunday church-goers"—is not without its values. Change may come best from relaxation.

Again, then, a balance (between preservation of the past and receptivity to the future) seems to be required of a democratic electorate. The heterogeneous electorate in itself provides a balance between liberalism and conservatism; and so does the sequence of political events from periods of drifting change to abrupt rallies back to the loyalties of earlier years.

Consensus and Cleavage

We have talked much in the text, and perhaps implied more, about consensus and cleavage. Although there were certain clusters of political opinion in Elmira, at the same time there were a number of opinions that did not break along class or party lines. American opinion on public issues is much too complex to be designated by such simple, single-minded labels as *the* housewife opinion or *the* young people's opinion or even *the* workers' opinion. If one uses as a base the central Republican-Democratic cleavage, then one finds numerous "contradictions" within individuals, within strata and groups, and within party supporters themselves. There are many issues presented, cafeteria-style, for the voter to choose from, and there are overlaps in opinion in every direction.

Similarly there are required *social* consensus and cleavage—in effect, pluralism—in politics. Such pluralism makes for enough consensus to hold the system together and enough cleavage to make it move. Too much consensus would be deadening and restrictive of liberty; too much cleavage would be destructive of the society as a whole.

Consider the pictures of the hypothetical relationships between political preference (e.g., party support) and a social characteristic as presented in this chart:

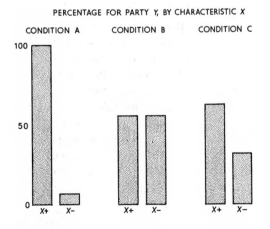

PERCENTAGE FOR PARTY Y, BY CHARACTERISTIC X

In Condition A there is virtual identity between the characteristics and political preference; all the people of type $X+$

vote one way, and all the people of $X-$ vote the other way. In Condition B the opposite is the case, and there is no relationship between vote and the characteristic; both parties are supported equally by people of the two types. In Condition C there is neither a complete relationship nor a complete absence; more $X+$'s than $X-$'s are partisans of a given side, but there are some members of each type in each political camp.

Now a democratic society in which Condition A was intensified would probably be in danger of its existence. The issues of politics would cut so deeply, be so keenly felt, and, especially, be so fully reinforced by other social identifications of the electorate as to threaten the basic consensus itself. This might be called "total politics" —a conception of politics, incidentally, advanced by such leading theorists of National Socialism and communism as Carl Schmitt and Lenin. This involves the mutual reinforcement of political differences and other social distinctions meaningful to the citizen. The multiplication of Condition B, on the other hand, would suggest a community in which politics was of no "real" importance to the community, in which it was not associated with special interests. Condition C is a combination of Conditions A and B—that is, a situation in which special interests are of some but not of overriding importance. It portrays neither the extremist or fanatical community like A nor the "pure" or utopian community like B.

There is nothing in Elmira that represents Condition A; the closest approximation would be the relationship between vote and religion or minority ethnic status, and even here there are group overlaps in vote amounting to from a quarter to a third of the members. The nearest approximation to Condition B is the relationship between vote and sex, which is another way of saying that there is little relevance of this characteristic to political matters, at least so far as party preference is concerned. The relationships between vote and socioeconomic status or vote and occupation are examples of Condition C.

The social and political correlations we find in places like Elmira (that are not a priori meaningless) are of the C type to a greater or less extent. What this means is that there is a good deal of cross-group and cross-party identification and affiliation within the community. The political lines are drawn in meaningful ways but are not identical with the lines of social groupings. The same social heterogeneity that produces self-interest also produces a cross-cutting and harmonious community interest.

Thus again a requirement we might place on an electoral system—balance between total political war between segments of the society and total political indifference to group interests of that society—translates into varied requirements for different individuals. With respect to group or bloc voting, as with other aspects of political behavior, it is perhaps not unfortunate that "some do and some do not."

Individualism and Collectivism

Lord Bryce pointed out the difficulties in a theory of democracy that assumes that each citizen must himself be capable of voting intelligently:

Orthodox democratic theory assumes that every citizen has, or ought to have, thought out for himself certain opinions, i.e., ought to have a definite view, defensible by argument, of what the country needs, of what principles ought to be applied in governing it, of the man to whose hands the government ought to be entrusted. There are persons who talk, though certainly very few who act, as if they believed this theory, which may be compared to the theory of some ultra-Protestants that every good Christian has or ought to have . . . worked out for himself from the Bible a system of theology.

In the first place, however, the information available to the individual voter is not limited to that directly possessed by him.

True, the individual casts his own personal ballot. But, as we have tried to indicate throughout this volume, that is perhaps the most individualized action he takes in an election. His vote is formed in the midst of his fellows in a sort of group decision—if, indeed, it may be called a decision at all—and the total information and knowledge possessed in the group's present and past generations can be made available for the group's choice. Here is where opinion-leading relationships, for example, play an active role.

Second, and probably more important, the individual voter may not have a great deal of detailed information, but he usually has picked up the crucial *general* information as part of his social learning itself. He may not know the parties' positions on the tariff, or who is for reciprocal trade treaties, or what are the differences on Asiatic policy, or how the parties split on civil rights, or how many security risks were exposed by whom. But he cannot live in an American community without knowing broadly where the parties stand. He has learned that the Republicans are more conservative and the Democrats more liberal—and he can locate his own sentiments and cast his vote accordingly. After all, he must vote for one or the other party, and, if he knows the big thing about the parties, he does not need to know all the little things. The basic role a party plays as an institution in American life is more important to his voting than a particular stand on a particular issue.

It would be unthinkable to try to maintain our present economic style of life without a complex system of delegating to others what we are not competent to do ourselves, without accepting and giving training to each other about what each is expected to do, without accepting our dependence on others in many spheres and taking responsibility for their dependence on us in some spheres. And, like it or not, to maintain our present political style of life, we may have to accept much the same interdependence with others in collective behavior. We have learned slowly in economic life that it is useful not to have everyone a butcher or a baker, any more than it is useful to have no one skilled in such activities. The same kind of division of labor—as repugnant as it may be in some respects to our individualistic tradition—is serving us well today in mass politics. There is an implicit division of political labor within the electorate.

III
CONCLUSION

In short, when we turn from requirements for "average" citizens to requirements for the survival of the total democratic system, we find it unnecessary for the individual voter to be an "average citizen" cast in the classic or any other single mold. With our increasingly complex and differentiated citizenry has grown up an equally complex political system, and it is perhaps not simply a fortunate accident that they have grown and prospered together.

But it is a dangerous act of mental complacency to assume that conditions found surviving together are, therefore, positively "functional" for each other. The apathetic segment of America probably has helped to hold the system together and cushioned the shock of disagreement, adjustment, and change. But that is not to say that we can stand apathy without limit. Similarly, there must be some limit to the degree of stability or nonadaptation that a political society can maintain and still survive in a changing world. And surely the quality and amount of conformity that is necessary and desirable can be exceeded, as it has been in times of war and in the present Communist scare, to the damage of the society itself and of the other societies with which it must survive in the world.

How can our analysis be reconciled with the classical theory of liberal political democracy? Is the theory "wrong"? Must it be discarded in favor of empirical political sociology? Must its ethical or normative content be dismissed as incompatible with the nature of modern man or of mass society? That is not our view. Rather, it seems to us that modern political theory of democracy stands in need of revision and not replacement by empirical sociology. The classical political philosophers were right in the direction of their assessment of the virtues of the citizen. But they demanded those virtues in too extreme or doctrinal a form. The voter does have some principles, he does have information and rationality, he does have interest—but he does not have them in the extreme, elaborate, comprehensive, or detailed form in which they were uniformly recommended by political philosophers. Like Justice Hand, the typical citizen has other interests in life, and it is good, even for the political system, that he pursues them. The classical requirements are more appropriate for the opinion leaders in the society, but even they do not meet them directly. Happily for the system, voters distribute themselves along a continuum:

SOCIABLE MAN   POLITICAL MAN   IDEOLOGICAL MAN
(Indifferent to   (Absorbed in
public affairs,   public affairs,
nonpartisan,   highly partisan,
flexible. . .)   rigid. . .)

And it turns out that this distribution itself, with its internal checks and balances, can perform the functions and incorporate the same values ascribed by some theorists to each individual in the system as well as to the constitutive political institutions!

Twentieth-century political theory—both analytic and normative—will arise only from hard and long observation of the actual world of politics, closely identified with the deeper problems of practical politics. Values and the behavior they are meant to guide are not distinctly separate or separable parts of life as it is lived; and how Elmirans choose their governors is not completely unrelated to the considerations of how they are *supposed* to choose them. We disagree equally with those who believe that normative theory about the proper health of a democracy has nothing to gain from analytic studies like ours; with those who believe that the whole political tradition from Mill to Locke is irrelevant to our realistic understanding and assessment of modern democracy; or with those like Harold Laski who believe that "the decisions of men, when they come to choose their governors,

are influenced by considerations which escape all scientific analysis."

We agree with Cobban: "For a century and a half the Western democracies have been living on the stock of basic political ideas that were last restated toward the end of the eighteenth century. That is a long time. . . . The gap thus formed between political facts and political ideas has steadily widened. It has taken a long time for the results to become evident; but now that we have seen what politics devoid of a contemporary moral and political theory means, it is possible that something may be done about it."

A CRITIQUE OF BERELSON, LAZARSFELD, AND McPHEE'S VOTING*

Walter Berns

The classical theorists of democracy, according to Berelson, Lazarsfeld, and McPhee, set down certain requirements of citizenship in a democratic regime: interest and participation in political affairs; a "capacity for and . . . practice of discussion"; and a knowledge of the issues, "what their history is, what the relevant facts are, what alternatives are proposed, what the party stands for, what the likely consequences are." The democratic citizen, furthermore, is "supposed to cast his vote on the basis of principle . . . with reference to standards not only of his own interest but of the common good as well." He "is expected to exercise rational judgment in coming to his voting decision." Finally, the population is supposed to be socially and politically homogeneous (see pp. 13–15 this text).

But Elmirans gave no evidence of sustained interest, many voted "without real involvement in the election," even party workers were not "typically motivated by . . . civic duty." There was "little true discussion between the candidates, little in the newspaper commentary, little between the voters and the official party representatives, some within the electorate." The citizen was not well informed on the issues in the campaign; he misperceived the political situation; his perception was "colored by emotional feeling." Many voted out of habit or for their groups, unthinkingly. In short, the authors of *Voting* conclude, people's decisions as consumers are more carefully calculated than their decisions as voting citizens (see pp. 13–16 this text).

One cannot be certain whether these conclusions (although they may be true) are meant to be taken seriously here. It is impossible to say that the voters are uninformed without some conception of what a voter ought to be informed about,

*From *Essays on the Scientific Study of Politics* edited by Herbert J. Storing. Copyright © 1962 by Holt, Rinehart & Winston, Inc. Reprinted by permission of Holt, Rinehart & Winston, Inc.

just as it is impossible to say that there is little "true discussion" without knowing what a political discussion ought to be. (As we pointed out above, the authors seldom bother to tell the reader what was actually said in the discussions that took place.) These assertions show again that the authors of *Voting*, despite their methodological commitment, are not altogether successful in suppressing the question of the common good; on some occasions they permit their common sense to break through the crust of their methodology.[1]

Nevertheless, a pre-"scientific" observer of politics would have counseled severe remedial measures or might even have despaired if his study revealed a situation similar to the one here described by the authors of *Voting*. They do neither. They do neither because if the "democratic system depended solely on the qualifications of the individual voter, then it seems remarkable that democracies have survived through the centuries."[2] They neither despair nor counsel severe remedial measures because the American democracy, despite the character of the American citizen whose decisions in front of the soap counter are said to be more carefully calculated than his decisions in the voting booth, is a healthy system, one that "survives and grows" (pp. 16, 17). It does not require the qualities prescribed by

"traditional normative theory," and what it does require America possesses in abundance.

Berelson, writing in *The Public Opinion Quarterly*, tells us what he means by political health.[3]

Does community interest refer to agreement on procedures, or to an outside criterion (and if so, what), or to the residual decision after the various self-interests have balanced themselves out, or to genuine concern for other groups, or to restraint upon self-interest, or to deviation from the predominant vote of one's group? The more one looks into the matter, the more it appears that one man's self-interest is another man's community interest, and that many people sincerely identify the one with the other. . . .

In a current study of opinion formation (the Elmira study), we concluded that it is more satisfactory to analyze this question in terms of the forces making for political cleavage and political consensus within the community. The health of a democratic order depends on achieving a nice balance between them: enough cleavage to stimulate debate and action, enough consensus to hold the society together even under strain.

In *Voting* the point is made as follows:

Similarly there are required *social* consensus and cleavage—in effect, pluralism—in politics. Such pluralism makes for enough consensus to hold the system together and enough cleavage to make it move. Too much consensus would be deadening and restrictive of liberty; too much cleavage would be destructive of the society as a whole [p. 21].[4]

With this as a background the authors go on to assert that classical democratic theory is in error in demanding too many qualities from the individual citizen; it overlooks that certain qualities, if present in the electorate as a whole, will conduce to the public interest even if individual citizens are unintelligent, disinter-

---

[1]Thus, they also refer to "the obvious political importance of elections"; but their social science does not permit them to make this statement. The importance of neither voting nor the study of voting can be established by the scientific method—as this is understood in modern social science. The scientific method merely assures them that the answer to a question will be scientifically correct given certain conditions; it does not guarantee that the right questions will be asked or the important subjects studied. What is it that gives elections their "obvious political importance"? To answer this question, these social scientists would be required to engage in *political* discourse.

[2]Anyone with even a cursory acquaintance with history is forced to wonder what democracies they have in mind in this statement. Democracies have come into being for centuries, but how many of them have survived for centuries?

---

[3]Fall 1952, p. 328.

[4]For a critique of this "social" conception of pluralism see Burdick, "Political Theory and the Voting Studies," *American Voting Behavior*, pp. 141–44.

ested, and unwilling to participate in politics. What is decisive to political health is neither political institutions nor the individual citizen, the chief objects of concern to former theorists, but certain "social" characteristics that "form the atmosphere or the environment in which both operate" (p. 18). Whereas the classical democratic theorists might have despaired at the picture of the democratic voter drawn by modern social science, the authors of *Voting* find nothing incompatible between the American electorate and a revised and reasonable understanding of the qualities needed to constitute a healthy democracy. Disinterestedness, even apathy, are valuable if not carried to extremes; heterogeneity permits a balance between progress (defined merely as movement or change) and conservatism; neglect of politics is not without value: "Change may come best from relaxation" (pp. 20, 21). It is interesting to note that there is nothing "scientific" or "empirical" about the way they arrive at this changed (and lowered) conception of political health, yet it is on the basis of it that they draw this *decisive* conclusion.

What is implicit throughout the book suddenly becomes explicit here in the last chapter. It is unnecessary to consider the question, what is opinion? It is unnecessary to evaluate the voters' explanations of their behavior. It is unnecessary to pay attention to that human faculty that makes the generation of dispositions possible. It is, in short, unnecessary and wrong to study voting from the point of view of the common good as understood by classical democratic theory. Despite its incapacity to deal with such matters as these, indeed, precisely because of its avoidance of them, the methodology of *Voting* cuts through to the conditions of a healthy democracy, truly and newly defined. This methodology permits them to describe voting behavior from the point of view of the elements that really produce a healthy democracy, which is defined as a balance between the "forces making for political

cleavage and political consensus." The healthy democracy, they say, is the consequence of sociological (and irrational) forces, and consists in pluralism, because pluralism makes "for enough consensus to hold the system together and enough cleavage to make it move." The classical theorists of democracy from "Mill to Locke" (!) (p. 24), to whom we might otherwise have looked for guidance in our study of politics, are refuted.

Unfortunately, it is difficult to be certain whom the authors of *Voting* regard as a theorist of democracy, because, except in the awkward fashion indicated above, they fail to specify the men whose teachings they claim to have refuted. This is to be regretted especially because the democratic credentials of some of these theorists are much disputed, for example, in the case of Rousseau. But we know that the question to which Rousseau directs his attention is one that all classical democratic theorists deal with; and if Rousseau teaches that democracy requires racial, economic, and religious homogeneity,[5] it is not sufficient merely to assert that a healthy democracy, even of the "moving cohesiveness" type, does not require racial, economic, and religious homogeneity. Before we would be justified in discarding Rousseau's teachings, it would be—or one might think it would be—necessary to show that this understanding of political health is superior to Rousseau's, or that we have reached the state where homogeneity is no longer so important to a healthy democracy.

No discussion of this question is to be found in *Voting*, yet the question concerns the very possibility of a profoundly heterogeneous but healthy democracy. Have the problems of heterogeneity been solved only at the price of the conformism and uniformity of a mass technological society? How important is religion in the United States? What will be the effect of the potentially explosive racial differences,

---

[5]Rousseau, *The Social Contract*, iii, 4; iv, 8.

which will probably remain important for some time? To what extent is the wealth that is the product of our technological society responsible for the apathy that mitigates the dangers of heterogeneities? If the apathy we need is the result of the wealth, what, if anything, had to be sacrificed in order to attain the wealth and what is the relation of the sacrificed element to a healthy democracy?[6] In the light of the evidence of a lack of public spirit in the United States, was Rousseau writing utter nonsense when he wrote:

It is through the hustle of commerce and the arts, through the greedy self-interest of profit, and through softness and love of amenities that personal services are replaced by money payments [and] as soon as public service ceases to be the chief business of the citizens and they would rather serve with their money than with their persons, the State is not far from its fall.[7]

And what is the effect of the wealth (needed for the apathy needed to mitigate the heterogeneities) on religion, and what is the relation of religion to a healthy democracy?[8] None of these questions is even raised in the last chapter of Voting. Yet we are assured that the American democracy is healthy. No doubt instability

and stagnation are to be avoided if possible, and perhaps pluralism is superior to the unity advocated by such men as Rousseau, but this too requires an argument it does not get in Voting.

To refute the teachings of John Stuart Mill, to continue, is it really sufficient to argue that what Mill and others had to say "is defective . . . in its concentration on the individual citizen [while ignoring] certain collective properties that reside in the electorate as a whole . . ."? Berelson, Lazarsfeld, and McPhee assert that the actual political system, even without the traditionally prescribed qualities—or perhaps because of the lack of these qualities—not only continues to work, but does so "perhaps even more vigorously and effectively than ever" (p. 16). But is it not essential before dismissing the old teaching, to wonder why someone like Mill would disagree? Consider what Mill had to say about voting:

But the exercise of any political function, either as an elector or as a representative, is power over others. Those who say that the suffrage is not a trust but a right will scarcely accept the conclusions to which their doctrine leads. If it is a right, if it belongs to the voter for his own sake, on what ground can we blame him for selling it, or using it to recommend himself to any one whom it is his interest to please? . . . His vote is not a thing in which he has an option; it has no more to do with his personal wishes than the verdict of a juryman. It is strictly a matter of duty; he is bound to give it according to his best and most conscientious opinion of the public good. Whoever has any other idea of it is unfit to have the suffrage; its effect on him is to pervert, not to elevate his mind. Instead of opening his heart to an exalted patriotism and the obligation of public duty, it awakens and nourishes in him the disposition to use a public function for his own interest, pleasure, or caprice; the same feelings and purposes, on a humbler scale, which actuate a despot and oppressor.[9]

---

[6]See Joseph Cropsey, Polity and Economy: An Interpretation of the Principles of Adam Smith (The Hague: Martinus Nijhoff, 1957), esp. pp. 88ff.

[7]Rousseau, op. cit., iii, 15. Cf. "A Reporter at Large," The New Yorker, October 26, 1957, pp. 114–69.

[8]Rousseau, op. cit., iv, 8. See also Washington's Farewell Address: "Of all the dispositions and habits which lead to political prosperity, religion and morality are indispensable supports. In vain would that man claim the tribute of patriotism who should labor to subvert these great pillars of human happiness, these firmest props of the duties of men and citizens. The mere politician, equally with the pious man, ought to respect and to cherish them. A volume could not trace all their connections with private and public felicity. . . . And let us with caution indulge the supposition that morality can be maintained without religion. Whatever may be conceded to the influence of refined education on minds of peculiar structure, reason and experience both forbid us to expect that national morality can prevail in exclusion of religious principle."

[9]J. S. Mill, Considerations on Representative Government (On Liberty and Considerations on Representative Government), (Oxford: Basil Blackwell, 1948), pp. 231–32.

What is the understanding of political health implicit in these remarks on voting? Consider whether, on the basis of the following excerpts, Mill would agree to the understanding of a healthy democracy as a moving cohesiveness.

[Except under representative government] the public at large remain without information and without interest on all the greater matters of practice; or, if they have any knowledge of them, it is but a *dilettante* knowledge, like that which people have of the mechanical arts who have never handled a tool. Nor is it only in their intelligence that they suffer. Their moral capacities are equally stunted. . . . Let a person have nothing to do for his country, and he will not care for it. . . . Religion remains: and here at least, it may be thought, is an agency that may be relied on for lifting men's eyes and minds above the dust at their feet. But religion, even supposing it to escape perversion for the purposes of despotism, ceases in these circumstances to be a social concern, and narrows into a personal affair between an individual and his Maker, in which the issue at stake is but his private salvation. Religion in this shape is quite consistent with the most selfish and contracted egoism, and identifies the votary as little in feeling with the rest of his kind as sensuality itself.[10]

Mill argues that the active character is superior to the passive, because it is the active character that promotes the "three varieties of mental excellence, intellectual, practical, and moral"; and, because of "the influence of the form of government upon character," this becomes an argument in favor of representative government. Had they read Mill with even a modicum of care, the authors of *Voting* would have learned that the emphasis of his argument is not on these excellences as prerequisites of representative government, but rather on representative government as a means of promoting these excellences! In addition, they might then have seen the distance separating a "moving cohesiveness" from Mill's "Ideally Best Polity."

It is of course possible, even likely, that our modern problems are not satisfactorily solved by such classical democratic theorists as Rousseau and Mill, and no one would argue that they merit close study merely on atiquarian grounds. But even the few examples given here are sufficient to show that they raised questions that are relevant, indeed crucial, to the discussion in the last chapter of *Voting*, and therefore to the whole enterprise. The authors' failure to take classical democratic theory seriously in their haste to suggest its "revision . . . by empirical sociology" (p. 23) is only an aspect of their failure even to begin a penetrating consideration of the problems of modern democracy. Ignoring these older thinkers and the questions they raise, the authors of *Voting* confine their discussion to trivialities and present conclusions that might very well be wholly false.[11]

In an earlier chapter the authors flirt with another explanation of cleavage and consensus, and something of the mood (for it is impossible to put it more exactly) of that earlier discussion seems to have

---

[10]*Ibid.*, pp. 137–38.

[11]Indeed, they do not seem to take seriously any writing on political theory. Their chapter begins with a reference to, and purports to take its bearings from, an article by Alfred Cobban entitled, "The Decline of Political Theory" (*Political Science Quarterly*, September 1953, pp. 321–37). They are only partly correct in saying that Cobban attributes this decline to the fact that modern theorists, unlike the theorists of the past, do not write with a practical purpose in mind, because they are concerned with the "aims" of political society. Cobban also says: "If political theory *has* become generally disengaged from practice, and if this is one cause of its decline, it will be worth while asking why this has happened" (p. 332). And what does account for this disengagement, this theory filled with artificialities, dealing with "arbitrarily" chosen issues, and written in "various esoteric jargons"? Cobban says: "What I want to do is to suggest that modern political theory has largely ceased to be discussed in terms of what ought to be; and the reason, I believe, is that it has fallen under the influence of two modes of thought which have had a fatal effect on its ethical content. These, and they have come to dominate the modern mind, are history and science" (p. 333). Had they read Cobban with, again, even a modicum of care, they would have seen the inappropriateness of using him as they do.

carried over into the last chapter. Addressing themselves to the question of "how the political system as a whole handles the resolution of issues," the authors suggest in Chapter 9 that issues have a characteristic "life history," moving from their introduction by a small vanguard through the "political gateway" where they hang in the balance, to their near-unanimous acceptance. Political cleavage turns on the issues at the "political gateway." The authors conclude that "to understand the process of cleavage on the issues, one must understand the broader historical trends on which the cleavage is based and of which the campaign issues are topical manifestations." Yet in the final chapter we are instructed that political health is "enough consensus to hold the system together and enough cleavage to make it move," with no reference at all to these historical trends.

In the earlier discussion, in Chapter 9, the authors argued that as "events and the needs of society push such [specific] proposals into, through, and beyond the political gateway of decision, party dispositions facilitate or inhibit not so much the final decision as the speed of acceptance." This suggests that the political theory of *Voting* depends upon a notion—a largely implicit and wholly unexplored notion—of "historical trends." However it may appear to the actors, political activity does not really affect the question of what is to be done, but only the question of when? The decisions themselves are determined by some historical process. As public housing and social security have passed through the gateway, so compulsory health insurance, new (Brannan-type) farm plans, and new controls on corporations (the authors' examples of issues not yet at the gateway) will do so, and political activity will determine only whether this is sooner or later.

If we examine the last chapter of *Voting* with this notion of "historical trends" in mind, the authors might be understood as arguing that a political system should

(and that the American system does) adopt a posture that invites history to act upon it, not so suddenly as to do violence to the system and not so slowly as to fail to "adapt" altogether, but steadily following its determined course. Two points must be emphasized. First, it is impossible to examine this theory, or even to say with any confidence that it is the one on which the authors rest, because we are provided with nothing but the barest, formal outline of what the theory is, in spite of the absolutely crucial character of the questions it raises for the whole study of voting. Second, whether the basis of the authors' "revision" of classical democratic theory is some notion of historical trends or whether they finally rest (as they seem to do in Chapter 14) on nothing more than a moving cohesiveness, the revision is not made by "empirical political sociology," but by another political theory or theory of history. Either one of these theories serves the authors' purpose in this last chapter, because either justifies their approach to the study of voting. The significance of this chapter is missed if it is regarded as nothing more than an incidental essay in political theory, unconnected with the rest of the book. It is, on the contrary, the essential political ground on which is built their whole social psychological enterprise. Only if this ground is tenable can they argue, as they must, that our criticism (that their approach ignores the political in voting) is based on an outmoded notion of political health.

However, their own notion of "the health of a democratic order" would be more convincing if it were supported by reasonable argument—which they make no effort to supply—and if, when speaking of the "forces making for enough consensus to hold the system together and enough cleavage to make it move," they were to pay some attention to the character of the system cohering and the direction in which it is moving. It would also be more convincing if, when assuring us that the apathy, unintelligence, and heterogeneity in Elmira are actually conducive to political health, they were to do more than hint that the ability to deal with its political problems might have some relation to the health of a political system. The un-"scientific" student of politics would say that one way to measure American voting behavior today is by the requirements of survival in the face of the Soviet Union, the most urgent political fact of our time, and that a democracy is not healthy if incapable of adopting measures reasonably calculated to provide for the common defense.[12] He would argue that it makes a difference whether, when the United States is faced with the decision of whether to spend billions of dollars for missile development, the voter thinks only of the taxes he would have to pay to support such a program without regard to the requirements of defense. Not only do the authors of *Voting* deny this implicitly, and explicitly too when they say that to insist "at all strongly" that a citizen vote with reference to the common good is to make "an impossible demand" (p. 15), they assert such behavior to be unnecessary for a healthy democracy. Without it our democracy is better than ever. Still, the question is of critical importance. Can a healthy democracy be the consequence of merely sociological forces, depending in no way on citizens capable of rational thought and action? They assure us it can be and is. But this assurance is not supported with an argument. In-

---

[12]The authors are not entirely successful in suppressing questions of this kind, in spite of their conclusion that a discussion confining itself to political cleavage and consensus is "more satisfactory." When they wonder "how a democracy ever solves its political problems," they suggest that there are problems to be solved more or less well. When they assert that "somehow the system not only works on the most difficult and complex questions but often works with distinction," they suggest a standard of distinction beyond stability and change. When they assert that "too much consensus would be deadening and restrictive of liberty," they suggest that a healthy democracy has the substantive aim of protecting individual liberty.

stead, they introduce into their analysis at this point (and not by chance) what it does not require an Arthur Bentley to call a "spook." "Where the rational citizen seems to abdicate," they conclude, "nevertheless angels seem to tread" (p. 16). *Their* healthy democracy cannot be preserved in any other way.

Suppose there was a voter—one of the authors of *Voting*, for example—who appreciated the virtues of this democracy and decided to vote with a view to its preservation, perhaps out of the fear that the angels, following the example of the rational citizen, might decide to abdicate too. How would such a voter proceed? His problem would be to vote in such a way as to maintain the balance between cleavage and consensus. This, of course, would depend on how others intend to vote. If the others think only of their selfish interests, and he knows the strength of these interests, he might be able to calculate how they are going to vote, then act accordingly; but this one vote would have very little effect in maintaining the pluralistic balance. On the other hand, to the extent that others think and act as he does, with a view to preserving the balance, it becomes difficult to know how they will (and therefore how he should) vote; in fact, the more citizens there are who try to vote with a view to the public interest (that is, with a view to preserving the balance), the more difficult such a vote becomes. The way out of this dilemma is a pre-election meeting (or meeting of *minds*) of all those who, whatever their substantive political ideas—left or right, labor or capital, farm or city—and whatever their positions on the issues—civil rights or anti-civil rights, a small and balanced budget or greater defense spending, federal aid to education or state independence of federal subventions—agree nevertheless to cast their ballots with a view only to maintaining the pluralistic balance.

Such a thing is not impossible in the real

world, but it depends on factors that are not present in the world of Berelson, Lazarsfeld, and McPhee. It depends on a community of interest brought into being not by a similarity of social characteristics or psychological drives, but by the willingness of some members of the community to forego their narrow selfish interests in order to protect the broader community interest. Now even if one were to say that such voters would be foregoing merely a short-range selfish interest in order to protect a long-range selfish interest, the decisive thing is that they would have to *think* about this, they would have to calculate, they would have to act on the basis of a rational consideration of the whole political (or, as the authors of *Voting* would say, social) situation. In the absence of the angels, the preservation of the healthy democracy would depend on a community of rational citizens, willing to forego voting on the basis of the substantive political issues in order to preserve the balance between cleavage and consensus. Since, according to the authors of *Voting*, the rational citizen seems to have abdicated and, therefore, plays no part in keeping the democracy healthy; since the authors implicitly deny the existence of citizens, or perhaps one should say persons, capable of voting on any basis other than that of their selfish class interest; since in fact one promise of this kind of research is the impossibility of rational action, they are driven to the suggestion of the band of angels. The democracy is maintained in health by some inexplicable ghostly agency, providentially guarding the selfish, blind citizenry from any harm. Readers of *The Governmental Process* will recall that David Truman solves the same problem with a spook labelled "potential groups."[13]

According to *Voting*, it does not matter whether the political campaign is charac-

terized by "true discussion." It does not matter whether the party workers are motivated by civic duty. It does not matter whether social groups are inactive in the campaign. It does not matter whether citizens have any interest in the election or whether they are ignorant of the issues. It does not matter whether there are political leaders or merely junction points in a brainless system. No part of the system is critical (except perhaps the angels?); no part is any closer to the *reason* for the system than any other part; no part is governing. Our institutions do not do what they are supposed to do according to the older understanding of politics, our citizens lack the qualities they are supposed to have, but we have a healthy democracy nevertheless: we move and we cohere.

Indeed, despite their reference to "the obvious political importance of elections" (which must be seen as one of their common-sensible asides), if it does not make any difference how people vote, are we entitled to conclude that for Berelson, Lazarsfeld, and McPhee voting itself is not important? Rossi tells us that Lazarsfeld began studying voting not because he thought it was important, but because he could not get the money for a panel study of consumer preferences. "Despairing of obtaining financial support for a panel study of consumer preferences, Lazarsfeld hit upon the idea of studying the impact of a presidential campaign upon a panel of voters. . . . With this less commercial focus, finanical support was obtained from the Rockefeller Foundation for a panel study of the 1940 presidential campaign" (*American Voting Behavior*, pp. 15–16).[14] It would be of interest to learn whether the authors of *Voting* reject the implications of this revealing, but not surprising, disclosure.

---

[13]David B. Truman, *The Governmental Process: Political Interests and Public Opinion* (New York: Alfred A. Knopf, Inc., 1951), ch. 16.

[14]See also Brodbeck, *American Voting Behavior*, p. 123: "It is an 'accident' that Professor Lazarsfeld chose to study these questions in terms of voting decisions. They could have been answered in many other areas of applied social science."

CONCLUSION

Democratic elections are one way of deciding the political question of who should rule and of what should be the character of that rule. One test of an electoral system is the extent to which it is democratic, that is, the extent to which everyone is permitted to participate in the choice. Another test, and perhaps the decisive one, is the quality of the men elected to office, for the primary purpose of elections is to choose these men; and the quality of the men chosen depends, in part, on the individual voters who choose them. The study of voting behavior is altogether proper, provided the purpose of voting is not forgotten in the formulation of the questions asked in the study.

Why people vote as they do, or what motivates the voters, is a question related to the purpose of voting. Asking it might enable the political scientist to determine the extent to which voters act with a view to the common good and the extent to which they act intelligently. The simplest way of determining why people vote as they do would be to ask them directly, but to do this, and to pursue the question to the point where it would be possible to distinguish a genuine from a spurious concern for the common good, would pose problems the modern social scientist feels he must avoid. His response is to ask questions the respondents can, and perhaps do, answer accurately (such as their age, sex, education, religion, and voting choice) and to report their answers with statistical exactitude. The result is the sacrifice of political relevance on the altar of methodology. The questions asked and pursued are determined by the limits of the scientific method rather than by the subject matter, which is voting or, more specifically, the purpose of voting. They prefer exact, statistical answers to less exact, politically relevant answers. As Morton Grodzins has said, "The scientist who defines his technique first and his problem second has placed second things first."[15]

Are voters intelligent, do they act wisely, do they make a genuine effort to evaluate candidates and their stands on issues in terms of what is required by the political situation? Intelligent observers of the political scene, here and elsewhere, have despaired at the lack of intelligence and the extent of selfishness; the authors of *Voting* claim to confirm this by showing, for example, the extent of ignorance on issues, but they do not despair because of their peculiar notion of political health. Now, it may be true that the average voter is even ignorant of how the presidential candidates stand on the issues, but before we can draw conclusions from this information we have to know from their own lips why they voted as they did, for they may have voted for reasons remote from the particular issues discussed by the candidates. Before we could condemn this, we should have to decide whether the issues on which the voters were misinformed were the important issues in the election, whatever their status in the campaign. For example, it is doubtful that price control and the Taft-Hartley Act were as important in the 1948 election as the authors of *Voting* claim they were. Union officials described the latter as a "slave-labor act," but perhaps the mass membership of the unions recognized this for the gross exaggeration it was. This is suggested by Senator Taft's huge plurality in his re-election to the Senate in 1950. Moreover, as the authors themselves say at one point, "the political genius of the citizenry may reside less in how well they can judge public policy than in how well they can judge the people who advise them how to judge policy." Even a relatively high degree of ignorance regarding

---

[15] *Ethics*, April 1959, p. 200. The self-imposed restraints of the psychologically oriented social scientist are of a different kind, but the effect is the same. He may ask his subject why he votes as he does, but he does not take the reply seriously, using it instead as a vehicle into the subject's unconscious motivations.

the particular policy questions facing the country may be offset if the citizens show good sense in choosing whom to trust, both in their primary groups and in the national government.[16]

Are we told in defense of these voting studies that whereas previously our knowledge of the determinants of voting was based at best on the shrewd guesses of intelligent observers, we now have, or will have, scientific knowledge of these determinants? We have no such thing. *The*

---

[16]Deciding who should constitute the government in power is a consideration distinct from determining what should be the appropriate policy on the many major issues that public opinion and legislative judgment must decide during any one party's tenure of office." Avery Leiserson, *Parties and Politics: An Institutional and Behavioral Approach* (New York: Alfred A. Knopf, Inc., 1958), p. 163.

Voter Decides tells us that Eisenhower was elected in 1952 because a large number of former Democrats voted for him, and they voted for him because they were attracted by him, or oriented "toward" him. *Voting* tells us that "intentions supported by . . . social surroundings are more predictably carried out than are intentions lacking such support." But the determinants of voting are by no means identified precisely; what is known is that a host of factors are related to vote. In the words of Avery Leiserson: "there are any number of indices of *group affiliation* in the sense of interpersonal association and contact, as well as subjective identification and class consciousness, that are correlated with political attitudes.[17]

---

[17]Leiserson, *op. cit.*, p. 153.

SOME DYNAMIC ELEMENTS OF CONTESTS FOR THE PRESIDENCY*

Donald E. Stokes

Despite the measured pace of American elections, there have now been a number of presidential campaigns since the advent of survey studies of voting. However sparingly, political history slowly has added to the set of distinct configurations of men and events which comprise a contest for the Presidency. The set is still small, whatever the impression created by massed thousands of interviews or by the accompanying files of election returns. Yet it is now large enough to be pressed hard for evidence about the sources of electoral change.

---

*Reprinted from the *American Political Science Review*, Vol. LX (March 1966), pp. 19–28. Copyright 1966, The American Political Science Association.

A primary virtue of measurements extended over a series of elections is that they can throw light on the problem of change. So long as the earliest voting studies were confined to cross-sectional relationships, they could deal only very inadequately with changes superimposed on these relationships or with changes in the relationships themselves. In the case of Lazarsfeld's enormously influential Erie County study in 1940, the natural limitations of a single-election study were compounded by the investigators' misfortune in choosing a campaign whose dominant personality and principal issues differed little from those of preceding elections. I have often wondered whether the static social determinism of *The People's Choice* would have emerged from a campaign in which the tides of short-term change were more nearly at flood.[1]

I shall examine here some sources of change which are richly evident in the presidential elections of the last two decades. In doing so I shall utilize several time series which can be extracted from the Survey Research Center's interview studies of the American electorate. The presidential contest of 1964 marked the fourth occasion on which the Center's national electoral studies have recorded the public's response to the issues and personalities of a presidential campaign.

This lengthening interval of electoral history contains material enough for the analyst of change. From the Eisenhower victories of the early 1950's, the high-point of presidential Republicanism since the Great Depression overwhelmed Hoover's party, the strength of Eisenhower's successors ebbed away in 1960 and sank in 1964 to a level which can only be regarded as one of the extreme lows of American national party competition. I shall examine some of the attitudinal factors in this extraordinary decline, focusing especially on the importance of changes in the issues and leaders which the electorate is asked to appraise. The relation of these "inputs" to the "output" of the presidential vote is exceedingly complex, but the moral of my piece is that this relationship introduces more dynamism into contests for the Presidency than the stability of party identification or of the social bases of party preference might lead us to expect.

In the course of the discussion I shall

utilize a statistical model which has proved useful for measuring various attitudinal forces on the nation's vote. Dealing with a type of behavior which is notoriously subject to multiple influences, this model seeks to discern the relative importance of several dimensions of attitude both for individual choice and for the nation's collective decision.[2] The model treats the behavior of the individual voter as governed in an immediate sense by the direction and strength of his attitudes toward the several political objects he is asked to appraise, attitudes which we have probed in these presidential elections by asking a series of free-answer questions about the parties and presidential candidates. Since a presidential campaign confronts the voter with four main objects—the two parties and the two candidates—it is natural to place each respondent along four dimensions of attitude, and many of the findings reported below will rely on such a four-dimensional model. For other purposes, however, it is more revealing of the content of political attitude to place each respondent along six attitudinal dimensions: (1) attitude toward the Democratic candidate as a person; (2) attitude toward the Republican candidate as a person; (3) attitude toward the parties and candidates which relates to the benefit of various groups; (4) attitude toward the parties and candidates which relates to domestic policy; (5) attitude which relates to foreign policy; and (6) attitude which relates to the general performance of the parties in the nation's affairs. A detailed account of the procedure by which respondents are assimilated to these several dimensions appears in the appended note.

The appendix also describes the statistical operations by which we obtain definite estimates of each dimension's contri-

[1]Paul F. Lazarsfeld, Bernard Berelson, and Hazel Gaudet, *The People's Choice* (New York: Duell, Sloan and Pearce, 1944). It is paradoxical that Lazarsfeld and his associates should have come to so static a view of party preference, since the desire to observe changes of preference was so central to their original intentions. Had they worked within the context of an election such as that of 1952 it is entirely unlikely that they could have ignored the presence of massive inter-election change, overlaid on the social bases of preference summarized in the Index of Political Predisposition.

[2]For a report of the application of this model to the Eisenhower elections see Donald E. Stokes, Angus Campbell, and Warren E. Miller, "Components of Electoral Decision," *American Political Science Review*, Vol. LII (June 1958), 367–87.

bution to the winning majority—the means by which, in effect, the nation's collective decision is resolved into a set of attitudinal components. These methods must of course be regarded as approximate, for reasons of sampling if no other, and I advance no claim to exact measurement; none is really necessary to the central conclusion which I shall draw from the analysis. Nevertheless, the model's success in estimating the direction and size of the winning majority in each of a series of elections does increase our confidence that we have measured dimensions of popular feeling which are deeply involved in changes of party fortune.

The several dimensions of attitude, however, have by no means been equally involved in electoral change. Just as the various components of electoral decision can be very different in their direction and strength at a given point in time, they can exhibit a very different tendency to change over time. In the period of our research some have been relatively stable, others not. By examining the role of each attitude component over twelve years we form several time series which are extraordinarily suggestive of the sources of change during this interval of our national politics.

THE ATTITUDINAL COMPONENTS OVER TIME

The curves described by the components of the six-dimensional model arrange themselves into three interesting pairs. The first of these is a pair whose values have consistently favored the Democrats over the entire period. As shown by Figure 1, partisan evaluations relating to domestic issues and to group benefits have uniformly helped the Democrats more than the Republicans, although the extent of this aid has fluctuated from year to year.[3] To an unusual degree these ele-

---

[3]The vertical coordinate of Figure 1, as well as of Figures 2 and 3, gives the value of the quantity

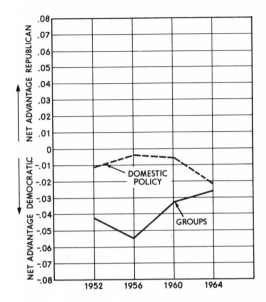

FIGURE 1
Continuing Democratic Advantage:
Groups and Domestic Policy

ments of the party images have roots in the past, extending back at least to the Roosevelt New Deal. Indeed, the benefit to the Democrats from their party's sponsorship of disadvantaged elements of American society is an antique theme of our party politics. Even in the mid-1950's and the early 1960's the volume of comment approving the Democrats and disapproving the Republicans in terms of the interests of the common man was impressive. In the two most recent elections, however, these class-related comments were diminished somewhat and were accompanied by references to religious and racial groups in which the arithmetic of group size was less favorable to the Democrats. For these reasons the group curve in Figure 1 shows

$$b_i(\overline{X}_i - X_i{}^0)$$

defined in the appendix. As explained there, this quantity may be interpreted either at the individual level as the average amount by which a given dimension has increased (or lessened, in the case of negative values) the probability of the individual's voting Republican or at the level of the whole electorate as the proportion of the total two-party vote by which a given dimension has increased (or lessened) the Republican share.

the party's advantage to be somewhat less in 1960 and 1964.

It will be apparent that the concept of "group" is defined here in a very inclusive manner. Likewise, our net has been cast very widely in coding references relating to domestic issues. In particular, many of the comments giving substance to the domestic issue dimension are "valence" or "image" issues, in which the parties or candidates are linked with something which is uniformly approved or disapproved ("the Republicans are the party of depression") rather than "position" issues on which there are genuine differences of party policy. The leading image issue of domestic politics throughout this period was the association of Democrats with good times, the Republicans with bad. This association, which probably had weakened steadily from the height of the Great Depression to the election of 1952, was further attentuated by the prosperity of Eisenhower's first term. But it revived again in the recession of 1958, before the Republican administration had left office, and it has been given fresh substance by the rising prosperity of the Kennedy and Johnson years.

The domestic issue dimension has not, however, been altogether lacking in genuine position issues. One of the peculiar qualities of the Goldwater candidacy is that it converted into position issues a number of image issues on which a broad consensus had hitherto existed between the parties. This fact was not lost upon the general public. Under the Goldwater challenge, the Democrats were rewarded more generously in 1964 than in any of the three prior elections for their sponsorship of social security and of the circle of other social and economic welfare policies which had wide popular approval. Primarily for this reason the domestic issue curve of Figure 1 shows a greater Democratic advantage in 1964 than in the years before.

A second pair of curves is traced by the movement of two components in

which a strong initial Republican advantage is seen to have vanished over these four elections. As shown by Figure 2, the

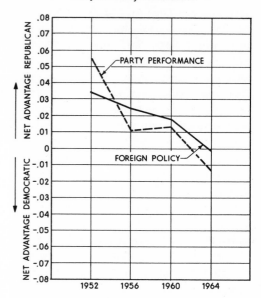

FIGURE 2
Decaying Republican Advantage: Foreign Policy and Party Performance

Republican party under Eisenhower enjoyed a substantial lead over the Democrats on foreign affairs—preeminently in terms of the great image issue of peace and war. This lead was not greatly lessened when Eisenhower's deputy sought the Presidency in 1960, but Nixon's legacy dissolved altogether in the contest of Goldwater and Johnson. It would be a misreading of the 1964 value, however, to suppose that widely-held foreign policy beliefs consistent with Goldwater's were nicely balanced by widely-held beliefs consistent with Johnson's. According to our evidence, foreign affairs did intrude on the public's consciousness in the 1964 campaign more than in any election since 1952, but popular references to foreign issues in 1964 still had only about a fourth the frequency of references to domestic issues. The loss of Republican advantage on this dimension was due to the final collapse of the belief that the party under

Goldwater was more likely to bring peace than were the Democrats under Johnson.[4]

The loss of Republican advantage in foreign affairs is paralleled by the decay of the party's advantage in popular assessments of party performance. The Republicans began this series of elections immensely aided by the mood for a change in 1952. There is no more striking element in all of our attitudinal materials than the public's anger and frustration with the outgoing Democratic administration in that year. Whatever the validity of the public's grievance, it was real enough in motivational terms and contributed handsomely to Eisenhower's first victory. The force of this feeling was easily spent, however, once the Democrats had been driven from office. Yet in 1956 and again in 1960 the Republicans still enjoyed an edge in terms of the electorate's general evaluations of current party performance, a fact which is the more remarkable in view of the stronger hold of the Democrats on the nation's underlying party identifications.[5] By 1964, however, this lingering advantage had been swept away, and the Democrats by a modest margin were now seen as the party better qualified to conduct the country's affairs.

The third pair of curves is traced by the components having to do with popular reactions to the personal attributes of the candidates. As shown in Figure 3, there has been remarkable variety in the appeal of the Republican candidates. The values of this component in 1952 and 1956 attest to General Eisenhower's personal hold on the electorate, an attraction which, if anything, was even more wholly per-

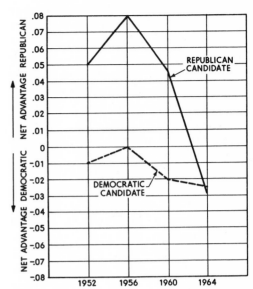

FIGURE 3
Greatest Variation: Appeal of Candidates

sonal after Eisenhower had served four years as President. Mr. Nixon's appeal in 1960 was somewhat less, although his personal appeal to the electorate, especially the sense of his broad experience, was marked. If the eventual account given by the political histories is that Nixon was a weak candidate in 1960, it will be largely myth.

The response to Goldwater, however, was something else again. Whereas Nixon's personal stature helped bring his party to the verge of a third presidential victory against a party enjoying a clear advantage in the country's partisan identifications, popular reaction to Goldwater contributed to his party's electoral ruin. The detailed references to Goldwater are an impressive amalgam of doubts—a wild and erratic campaigner, muddled and unclear, unstable, poorly educated, and so on—with these themes very little offset by references to the advertised qualities of integrity, sincerity, and decisiveness. If our estimates are right, the transition from Nixon to Goldwater cost the Republicans something like 7 percent of the total vote.

Despite immense differences of person-

[4]For direct additional evidence on this point see Philip E. Converse, Aage R. Clausen, and Warren E. Miller, "Electoral Myth and Reality: The 1964 Election," *American Political Science Review*, Vol. LIX (June 1965), p. 332.

[5]For evidence on the distribution of party identification in this period see "The Concept of the 'Normal Vote'," in A. Campbell, P. Converse, W. Miller, and D. Stokes, *Elections and the Political Order* (New York: John Wiley and Sons, Inc., 1966), Ch. 1.

al style, the appeal of three successive Democratic candidates was much more nearly equal. And except for Stevenson's second campaign, the response to each of these candidates added to his strength at the polls. Certainly the movement of the Democratic curve in Figure 3 shows Johnson to have been an asset to his own candidacy in 1964: the response to Johnson's attributes apparently did the Democrats about as much good as the response to Goldwater's did. The combined effect of both appears to have moved the two-party vote roughly 5 percentage points toward Johnson.

To emphasize the dynamic implications for party competition of pairing successive candidates for President, Figure 4 com-

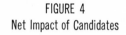

FIGURE 4
Net Impact of Candidates

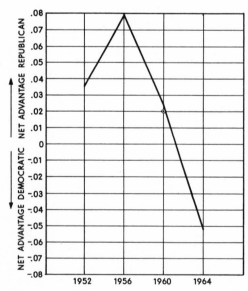

bines the effect of the personal appeals of the two men seeking the office in each of these elections.[6] The variation of this sum-

6The individual and aggregate interpretations of the quantity represented by the vertical coordinate of Figure 4 are the same as before, but the quantity itself is the sum of the components measuring the increment or decrement to Republican strength due to personal attributes of the Republican and Democratic candidates.

mary curve is impressive indeed. From a maximum Republican advantage of nearly 8 percent in the rematch of Eisenhower and Stevenson, the curve falls through more than 13 percentage points to a maximum Democratic advantage of more than 5 percent in the contest of Johnson and Goldwater. A more eloquent statistical comment on the personal contribution which candidates for President can make to electoral change could hardly be given.

It would be a mistake to read into these figures too simple an explanation of the impact of candidate personality on the mass public. Certainly it would be grossly wrong to suppose that the properties of these "stimulus objects" are somehow immediately and directly impressed on the electorate's response. The relation of stimulus and response is remarkably complex, involving an interplay of several quite different factors. Before drawing some general conclusions about the problem of change, it would be well to consider the interaction of the "actual" properties of the stimuli to which the electorate responds, certain response dispositions which the electorate has already learned, and some properties of the communication processes by which the electorate is informed of the objects of presidential politics.

STIMULUS PROPERTIES AND RESPONSE DISPOSITIONS IN THE ATTITUDE COMPONENTS

Although the comments below extend to the full range of stimuli to which the public is exposed, some of the subtleties of electoral response can most readily be observed in connection with candidate effects. The men seeking the Presidency bring to a campaign certain "real" properties as stimulus objects. Some of these belong to the past—the candidate's role as war hero, his success as governor or senator, his marital difficulties, and so on—although the communication of these things to much of the public may lie ahead. Other properties have to do with appearance, behavior, and personal style— the candidate's smile, the timbre of his voice, his smoothness in dealing with the teleprompter, his willingness to suffer fools gladly—knowledge of which can reach the electorate in numberless ways.

Impressions of these things, however, do not fall on wholly unprepared ground. Voters display a variety of response dispositions as they form their evaluations of the candidates. One type of response disposition is so evident as to require little comment. A wealth of research evidence, as well as familiar observation, attests the profound influence which partisan loyalties may have on the voter's perceptions of the men seeking office. The stronger the voter's party bias, the more likely he is to see the candidate of his own party as hero, the candidate of the other party as villain. No one who has talked with a sample of voters during a presidential campaign can have failed to note at every hand the processes by which cognitive balance is achieved.[7]

The voter's perceptual predispositions are not, however, limited to party bias. We are confronted at times by striking evidence of other identifications exerting a like influence on candidate images. A vivid example of these is the influence of religion on perceptions of John F. Kennedy during the 1960 election campaign.

---

[7]Certainly evidence of it is plentiful enough in the Center's studies. See, for example, Angus Campbell, Philip E. Converse, Warren E. Miller and Donald E. Stokes, *The American Voter* (New York: John Wiley and Sons, 1960), pp. 120–45. An excellent general review of the achievement of cognitive congruence in political attitudes is given by Robert E. Lane and David O. Sears in their *Public Opinion* (Englewood Cliffs, N.J.: Prentice-Hall, 1964). An interesting application of these concepts to attitude change may be found in Denis G. Sullivan, "Psychological Balance and Reactions to the Presidential Nominations in 1960," in M. Kent Jennings and L. Harmon Zeigler (eds.), *The Electoral Process* (Englewood Cliffs, N.J.: Prentice-Hall, 1966), pp. 238–64.

Because Kennedy was the Democratic candidate, voters identifying with the Democratic party tended to view him more favorably than did voters identifying with the Republican party. But Kennedy was seen by the electorate not only as a Democrat; he was seen as a Catholic as well. As a result, at every point along the party identification continuum, Catholics tended to perceive Kennedy in a more favorable light than did Protestants.

A demonstration of the joint biasing effects of religion and party in 1960 may be found in Figure 5. In that campaign we

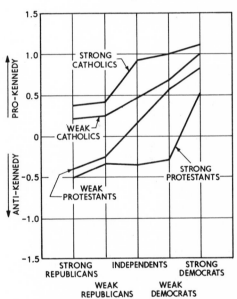

FIGURE 5

Influence of Party and Religious Identifications on Perceptions of Kennedy

placed each of our sample respondents along a standard party identification scale, represented here by five ordered groups: Strong Republicans, Weak Republicans, Independents, Weak Democrats, and Strong Democrats. At the same time we placed each of our Protestant and Catholic respondents on a scale of religious identification defined here by four ordered groups: persons strongly identified with a Protestant Church, persons weakly identified with such a church, persons weakly identified with the Catholic Church, and persons strongly identified with the Catholic Church. These two forms of psychological identification are moderately correlated in American society (that is, Catholics are more likely than Protestants to be Democratic) but not more than moderately so. Crossing the two here yields twenty groups defined by religion and party at once in which we may examine the distribution of attitude toward Kennedy. Figure 5 displays the mean attitude toward Kennedy within each of these twenty groups.[8]

The means exhibit a remarkable pattern. The fact that the curve for each religious group slopes upward to the right shows that, whatever the voter's religious identification, he is more likely to have perceived Kennedy favorably the closer he was to the Democratic end of the party identification dimension. And the march of the four religious curves up the figure shows that, whatever the voter's party identification, he is more likely to have perceived Kennedy positively the closer he was to the Catholic end of the religious dimension. There is even a pattern to the partial discontinuities: the regularity of the curves for weak Protestants and weak Catholics suggests that the biasing tendencies of party identification were generally effective among the mildly religious while the irregularity of the curves for strong Protestants and strong Catholics suggests that party loyalty could have a marked impact on the strongly religious only if a party faith were itself strongly held.

Figure 5 is so rich in evidence of selec-

[8]In order to standardize the metric used in these comparisons, I have divided each of these means by the sample standard deviation of attitude toward Kennedy. Because the sample contained only seven Weak Catholic Weak Republicans and only seven Weak Catholic Independents the means for these two groups have been adjusted to reduce the probable effect of sampling error.

tive perception that we may easily miss what it has to say about the element of Kennedy's image which was not the result of response disposition based on religion and party. The fact that this element was a favorable one ought not to be obscured by the strong pattern of the figure. Any reasonable operation by which we might seek to reconstruct a mean attitude among persons who are religiously and politically neutral would show that Kennedy was likely to be positively seen when his image did not fall prey to strong negative bias. For example, persons who were politically independent perceived Kennedy favorably even if they were weakly identified with a Protestant church.

We ought not to conclude from this that partisan and religious dispositions were the only response biases involved in the electorate's response to Kennedy or that, these dispositions aside, Kennedy was in some absolute sense an attractive candidate. In 1960, as any campaign year, many other kinds of response dispositions underlay the private impressions of the candidates formed by tens of millions of voters. We have identified two of the most important. It would not be difficult to suggest other factors which may have predisposed voters to react positively or negatively to something in the youthful, vigorous, Ivy-educated, Boston-accented stimulus which Kennedy presented.

Perhaps this point can be stated even more forcefully in terms of popular reaction to General Eisenhower, the most attractive presidential candidate since Franklin Roosevelt. The point is simply that "attractive" implies more than something about the candidate himself; it also implies something about the response dispositions of the electorate. Given the dominant values of contemporary American society, Eisenhower was enormously appealing. But we can at least imagine his having done very badly before an electorate less resonant to the military conqueror and less susceptible to the charm of a supremely other-directed personality who nevertheless evoked many of the traditional virtues. We might suppose, for example, that Eisenhower would have done very badly indeed before an electorate whose dominant values are those of American university faculties of social science.

Attitudes already formed toward some political objects are of course among the dispositions which can influence response to others. This seems especially true in the case of attitudes toward the candidates. When one rival for the Presidency already is well known, as an incumbent President will always be, the public's attitude toward his opponent will inevitably be colored by its response to the established figure. Thus, in 1940, Roosevelt-haters were quick to discover the virtues of Wendell Willkie when he was thrust onto the presidential stage, as Roosevelt's partisans were quick to discern Willkie's vices. And in the early 1950's, Adlai Stevenson had the misfortune to be paired with a much better established rival who already enjoyed the highest public regard.[9]

Of course the complex relation of candidate stimulus to the public's response also involves important communication factors. In a sense, the only real candidate stimuli are those which reach the voter via the mass media and interpersonal conversation, stimuli which only rarely are complemented by direct voter contact with the candidate. Therefore, the benefit or harm done to a candidate's cause by his actual personal attributes is mediated not only by the response dispositions of the electorate; it is mediated as well by the manner in which these attributes are communicated to the electorate. It is not hard to believe that some of the disarray of Goldwater's popular image was due to his

extraordinarily bad press. The candidate properties communicated to the public are not a pure fiction of the media. But neither are they a pure reflection of the candidate himself, as he might have been seen at home in the desert.

What has been said of candidates can be said of any object which has electoral effects. Certainly the political role of domestic and foreign issues involves a similar interplay of stimulus properties, response tendencies, and communication processes. The Korean War's immense profit for the Republicans in 1952, for example, depended on much more than a set of objective events in the Far East and the parties' stand on those events. It depended too on a welter of response dispositions in the electorate—general isolationist or internationalist attitudes, hostility to communism, latent militarist tendencies, the anxieties of farmers over having sons away at harvest time, and the like—as well as the way in which the public was informed by the communications media of what was happening half a world away.

If the political effects of issues and personalities in the wider environment depend partly on what the electorate hears and how it is disposed to react to what it hears, it follows that changes in communication and response tendencies can at times alter the political effects of a stimulus which has not itself changed. A clear example of this is the rapid build-up of a candidate by the mass media when he steps into the charmed circle of leading contenders—or the opposite experience, which many potential candidates have had, of falling through the medias' trap door to oblivion. Instances of marked change of response dispositions while political objects remain unchanged are more difficult to discern, but they undoubtedly occur. Herbert Hoover's high starched collars, a symbol of middle class prosperity in the booming twenties, probably looked quite different from the bread-lines of 1932.

---

[9]The voter's attitude toward a given political object may be influenced by the presence of other objects in his perceptual field even when no question of order is involved in the formation of attitude. In such a case, however, it is more reasonable to think of these effects as belonging to the configuration of stimulus objects, rather than to the voter's response dispositions.

Although changes of communication and of response dispositions can alter the electorate's response to a given political object, it is nevertheless true that a turnover of objects—of the personalities, issues, and events of national politics—is the more important source of short-term electoral change. This is the more true since a stimulus object can affect communication and response dispositions themselves. For example, quite apart from the sort of man he "really" is, a candidate can have wide influence on his treatment by the mass media. If the newspapers gave Mr. Goldwater extraordinarily rough treatment for a Republican candidate, Goldwater's own posture toward the press was part of the reason. Similarly, different candidates engage different response dispositions in the mass public. Unlike any Democratic candidate since Al Smith, Kennedy activated response dispositions based on Catholic and Protestant religious identifications, as we have seen. And candidates can lead the electorate to learn new dispositions, as Kennedy helped make the country receptive to a whole new generation of youthful, vigorous candidates for national and state office.

This type of change is vividly mirrored in the components of electoral decision given here for the past four presidential elections. The evidence of the changing personal impact of the candidates is especially impressive. Yet in a presidential system the turnover of candidates has implications reaching beyond sheer personal appeal. A candidate for the nation's great office is a focus for popular feeling about issues and questions of group benefit as well, and our measurements should be extended to take this fact into account.

RELATIVE CHANGE IN CANDIDATE AND PARTY ATTITUDE

It is hardly surprising that candidates for the Presidency should attract attitudes which are somewhat distinct from those attaching to the parties themselves. The platforms adopted by the nominating conventions are much less binding than the election manifestoes of a British party, for example, and a presidential candidate is notoriously at liberty to take his own stands on major issues and the problems of major social groupings. Equally, on matters requiring congressional action he is free to contradict positions taken by his party in the Senate and House. And on matters of foreign policy, the country is largely dependent on the candidate's record and views to know what his administration would be likely to do in the world. This is the stuff of which a presidential system is made.

Therefore, it is of interest to compare the variability of attitudes toward the parties and their presidential candidates. Neither has been constant over the period of our research, but the two have shown vastly different propensities to change. When we turn from a six- to a four-dimensional model, summarizing popular feeling according to the party or candidate toward which it is directed whether or not it concerns domestic or foreign issues, questions of group benefit, or other matters, the candidate components are found to have moved much more strongly from Republican to Democratic advantage.

This contrast is shown by Figure 6, in which each pair of party and candidate components of the four-dimensional model is added together at each election. The combined party curve has not by any means stood still. The public's full assessment of the parties showed a marked Republican advantage in the mood of 1952. But by 1956 the comparison of parties had moved to the Democrats' benefit, and this trend continued over the later two elections.

The combined candidate curve, however, describes a very much greater change. The public's full assessment of Eisenhower and Stevenson, including issue and group perceptions as well as percep-

FIGURE 6

Variation of Party and Candidate Components

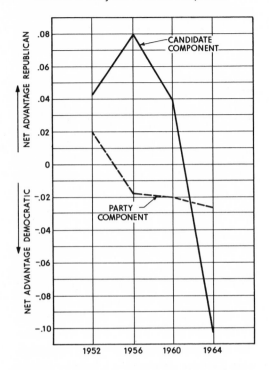

tions of personal qualities, was strongly Republican in 1952 and even more decisively so four years later. In the 1960 election, the comparison of candidates still favored the Republicans, although much more moderately. But between the Kennedy-Nixon campaign and the Johnson-Goldwater campaign the combined candidate component moved a most remarkable distance to the Democrats' advantage. In each contest the candidate curve was the farther removed from the zero-point: indeed, its average displacement from the neutral point has been more than 6 percent, whereas the average displacement of the party curve has been about 2 percent. But the really arresting comparison has to do with relative change: over these elections the variance of the candidate curve has exceeded that of the party curve by more than 10 to 1.

It is therefore evident that the dynamism of popular attitude is peculiarly tied to the emergence of new candidates for the Presidency. The attitudes toward the parties are not inert. The shift in the relative assessment of the parties over the period of this research has been enough to alter the parties' strength by something like six million votes on a turnout equal to that of 1964. But this change, impressive as it is, nevertheless is moderate by comparison with the change induced by succeeding pairs of candidates. The fluctuations of electoral attitudes over these elections have to a remarkable degree focused on the candidates themselves.

All of this is quite out of keeping with the static perspective of the earliest studies of voting. Even if our findings are no more than approximately true, they argue strongly the dynamic implications of changes of the stimulus objects of national politics. This source of change has in fact brought spectacular shifts of presidential voting despite the fact that over the same period there has been almost no perceptible shift in the single most important type of response disposition, the electorate's enduring party loyalties. It may also be noted that the variations of attitude recorded here have been largely independent of secular changes in the structure of American society, although, as we have seen, a turnover of stimulus objects can alter dramatically the facts of social structure which are relevant to political choice. Taken together, changes in the several stimulus objects of presidential politics in this span of years have been quite enough to bring a change of party control, indeed to have induced a drastic transformation of party fortune in the contest for the Presidency.

APPENDIX: A NOTE ON THE STATISTICAL MODEL

Since the number of positive and negative comments which a given voter makes about a given political object depends on the direction and strength of his feeling toward the object, we have placed a respondent on any given attitude dimension by forming the arithmetic difference of his pro-Republican and pro-Democratic responses whose content relates to the dimension. A pleasing variety of evidence can be marshaled to support the assumptions involved in this technique. That the resulting scales measure the intensity of attitude is borne out by the monotonic (indeed linear) relationships they exhibit with a host of other partisan variables, including the vote itself. That the neutral point is correctly located is indicated by the fact that a majority of those placed at the first scale position to the pro-Democratic side of the zero-point of each dimension do in fact vote Democratic; a majority of those at the first scale position to the pro-Republican side, Republican. The correct location of the neutral point is also attested by the model's success in estimating the direction and magnitude of the winning majority, as explained below. That the distances between scale positions are roughly equal (an assumption necessary to the further statistical operations) is also supported by the linearity of the relationship between the attitude scales and individual voting choice. Indeed, the proportion of the variance of the vote explained when individual choice is treated as a linear regression (as measured by the square of the product moment correlation) is almost identical with the proportion of the variance due to differences between the scale classes (as measured by the correlation ratio). That only a modest amount of error is involved in forming these relative-frequency measures of the direction and intensity of attitude is indicated by the success of the scales in accounting statistically for voting choice. Interestingly, the possibility that large errors have resulted from differences of verbal behavior can be partially discounted on the basis of experimental permutations of the order in which respondents were invited to comment on the two parties and the two candidates. Despite the reasonableness of the suspicion that either

"warm-up" or "fatigue" effects might produce large differences in the volume of response according to the order in which the parties and candidates were presented, changes of order in fact seem not to make a particle of difference.

A linear probability model is used to describe the relation of these scales to voting choice, with a Republican vote scored 1 and a Democratic vote 0. If the probability of voting Republican, $\Pr(R)$, is expressed as a linear regression on the dimensions $X_1, \cdots, X_I$:

$$\Pr(R) = b_0 + b_1 X_1 + \cdots + b_I x_I, \quad (1)$$

where I is either four or six according to the model used, the coefficients $b_1, \cdots, b_I$, of this linear combination measure the relative dependence of partisan choice on each of the dimensions. For some purposes it is useful to standardize these coefficients by measuring each attitude dimension in terms of sample standard deviations, yielding a new set of coefficients $b_1^*, \cdots, b_I^*$, as defined in a manner:

$$b_i^* = b_i s_i \quad (i = 1, \cdots, I) \quad (2)$$

which removes the effect of differences in the extent of variation along each of the dimensions. These standardized coefficients are not, however, the familiar beta coefficients of a regression equation in which both the dependent and independent variates are measured in sample standard deviations about their respective means. Scoring the dependent variable 0 and 1 is necessary to the probability interpretation of estimated scores. And each attitude scale is measured about its neutral point since this constitutes a theoretically meaningful origin.

The multiple correlation of the several predictors with partisan choice has varied in the range of .72 to .75 over the four presidential elections studied. There is reason to believe that most of the remaining "error" variance is due to the dichotomous nature of the dependent variate and that the multiple correlation of the attitude dimensions with some underlying *propensity* to vote Republican or Democratic would be substantially higher. Of the alternative ways of describing this relationship, I have given most attention to a multivariate probit model under which the probability of voting Republican varies according to the cumulative normal ogive. Such a model has aesthetically pleasing formal properties, especially the fact that it will never give probability estimates less than zero or exceeding unity. In practice, however, its performance differs little from that of the model used, since the relation of voting choice to the several dimensions is so nearly linear over the range of attitude actually found in our samples. The distribution of the electorate along an attitude dimension is much more easily summarized under the linear model, a fact which counts greatly in its favor.

To estimate the average amount by which a given dimension has increased (or lessened) the probability of the individual's voting Republican, we combine the information about its relation to voting choice, as measured by the multiple regression coefficient, with information about the mean location of voters on the dimension, as measured by the displacement of the observed mean from the theoretical neutral point, forming for each attitude dimension the product

$$b_i(\overline{X}_i - X_i{}^0) = b_i{}^* \frac{\overline{X}_i - X_i{}^0}{s_i} \qquad (3)$$

where b_i and $b_i{}^*$ are as defined above and $X_i{}^0$ is the neutral point of the ith dimension. If the neutral point is taken as

the origin, this product of course simplifies to

$$b_i\overline{X}_i = b_i{}^* \frac{\overline{X}_i}{s_i}. \qquad (4)$$

It is these quantities which I have called "attitudinal components" of the vote. The rationale for taking account of the mean's displacement from the neutral point is of course that a given dimension will benefit one party or the other only as its mean departs from the neutral point.

On the assumption that a dead heat would be the outcome of an election in which neither party was advantaged along any of the dimensions of attitude, the test of the model's ability to estimate the winning majority consists in seeing how well this relation is satisfied by the actual vote:

$$P_R - .5 = \sum_{i=1}^{I} b_i\overline{X}_i \qquad (5)$$

where P_R is the proportion of the two-party vote actually polled by the Republican candidate for President and each attitude factor X_i is measured about its theoretical neutral point. Over the four elections studied the maximum departure of this relation from equality has been about two percent, despite the fact that the Republican proportion of the two-party vote has varied over an interval from 58 percent to less than 40 percent. Indeed, the correlation of estimated and actual majorities over these four contests is .98, a figure which increases our confidence that we have faithfully measured many of the immediate attitudinal forces on the electorate's decision.

VOTING TURNOUT*

Angus Campbell, Philip E. Converse, Warren E. Miller, and Donald E. Stokes

The act of voting requires the citizen to make not a single choice but two. He must choose between rival parties or candidates. He must also decide whether to vote at all. Since a partisan decision can be effective only if it is expressed at the polls, people's decisions whether or not to vote have great influence on party fortunes. Indeed, the dramatic turns of our electoral history have been accompanied as much by wide changes in turnout as they have by shifts in relative party strength. In percentage terms, the change in turnout between the 1948 and 1952 elections was greater than the change in relative party strength.

Citizen participation at the polls is highly valued in American society, and every national election campaign brings its spate of exhortations to vote. Because of the high value placed on turnout, a good deal of the attention given it in popular discussion has to do with why so many people fail to vote. Despite the great public interest aroused by a presidential contest, our national elections bring less than two thirds of the adult population to the polls.[1] Of course, in any year a great many people are kept from voting by legal barriers—most commonly, in a nation of movers, by the requirements of minimum

residence in a state and its lesser divisions.[2] And many others are kept from voting by political or personal obstacles they could not reasonably overcome. But in each of our national elections millions of people whose way toward registering and voting is relatively clear fail to do so, and this fact has excited wide comment.

Although accounting for nonvoting is important in understanding the turnout decision, we will conceive the problem of explanation too narrowly if we concentrate solely on failures to vote. The really extraordinary aspect of our presidential elections is that tens of millions of people *do* expend the energy required to reach their polling-places and register their votes. If we are to explain this type of behavior we must find the patterns of motivation that lead these people to vote, as we must find the conditions that keep others from doing so. The explanatory problem is just that of finding what it is that distinguishes the voter from the nonvoter, and we will see as the discussion proceeds that the deviant voter—the person we "expect" *not* to vote yet who does—is somewhat more difficult to explain than is the person we expect to vote who fails to do so.

We assume that the decision to vote, no less than the decision to vote for a given party, rests immediately on psychological forces, although nonpsychological barriers to action are more prominent among the

*Reprinted from Campbell, *et al.*, *The American Voter: An Abridgement* (New York: John Wiley & Sons, 1964), Chap. 4.

[1] For example, the 61,522,000 people who voted for President in 1952 constituted 62.7% of the 97,574,000 people the Census Bureau estimated to be civilians of voting age on November 1 of that year. In 1956, 62,027,000 voters comprised 60.4% of an estimated 102,179,000 civilians of voting age.

[2] A comparison of reported length of current residence with state and local residence requirements indicates that these requirements have prevented at least 3 per cent of our respondents from voting.

TABLE 1
Popular Participation in Politics, 1952 and 1956*

	1952	1956
"Do you belong to any political club or organizations?"	2%	3%
"Did you give any money or buy tickets or anything to help the campaign for one of the parties or candidates?"	4%	10%
"Did you go to any political meetings, rallies, dinners, or things like that?"	7%	7%
"Did you do any other work for one of the parties or candidates?"	3%	3%

*Entries are proportions of total samples answering affirmatively.

causes of turnout than they are among the causes of partisan choice. Hence, our quest of understanding begins with an examination of motivational forces, and this chapter will describe a number of psychological influences that affect the likelihood the individual will vote. Yet we assume that the proximate causes of turnout, like the immediate determinants of partisan choice, are intervening variables that express the influence of a wide array of antecedent factors.

MODES OF POLITICAL PARTICIPATION

For most Americans voting is the sole act of participation in politics. Table 1 shows for the two Eisenhower elections the proportion of the electorate that was politically active in each of four elementary ways. The percentages of this table make clear that only small fractions of the public are connected with a party apparatus or help with the work and expense of a campaign. Moreover, since the groups in our samples who did report engaging in these activities are widely overlapping, the percentages cannot be added together to reach an estimate of the total number who were active.

Beyond these modes of participation there are several informal, less well-defined ways in which large numbers of people become "engaged" in a presidential contest. One of the most important of these is informal political discussion. In

each of the Eisenhower elections about a fourth of the electorate reported having talked to other people and having tried to persuade them to vote a given way.[3] The casual nature of this behavior should not conceal its importance either as an expression of individual motivation or as a means by which the final distribution of partisan preference in the electorate is achieved. Discussion of this sort is undoubtedly one of the most significant forms of political behavior by a mass public, even if it does not draw the individual directly into organized political activity.

Although it requires still less personal energy, following the campaign through the mass communications media might also be described as a type of informal participation. For some individuals, gleaning the political content of newspapers and magazines and of radio and television is a principal means of relating to politics. For others—presumably for a great majority of Americans—following the campaign in the mass media is a much more passive activity. Yet since the audiences of the media screen out vast amounts of their content, the individual plays at least a minimal role in deciding what he will and will not attend, and in this sense following an election campaign in the media may be

[3]The question "Did you talk to any people and try to show them why they should vote for one of the parties or candidates?" was answered "yes" in 1952 by 27% of our respondents; in 1956 by 28%.

called a form of participation.[4] In the Eisenhower elections only about one person in twenty said that the campaign had failed to reach him through any of the principal media of communication.

Since this book is concerned primarily with the act of voting itself, we will fix our attention on turnout rather than on other types of participation in politics. Yet in assessing the determinants of the voting act we are assessing factors which may underlie other modes of behavior by which the individual may participate in the political process. In one other respect the act of voting in a given election can be interpreted as an element of a broader dimension of behavior. It is plausible to think of voting as a type of conduct that is somewhat habitual and to suppose that as the individual develops a general orientation toward politics he comes to incorporate either voting or nonvoting as part of his normal behavior. Certainly we have found a pronounced association between what people tell us their past behavior has been and whether they vote in the elections we have studied. From this viewpoint our inquiry into the determinants of voting turnout is less a search for psychological forces that determine a decision made anew in each campaign than it is a search for the attitude correlates of voting and nonvoting from which these modes of behavior have emerged and by which they are presently supported. As the inquiry proceeds we will find that some of the dimensions of attitude that are most helpful in accounting for turnout appear to have the character of orientations to politics much more than they do the character of forces acting on a present decision.[5]

---

[4]See Angus Campbell, Gerald Gurin, and Warren E. Miller, "Television and the Election," *Scientific American*, Vol. CLXXXVIII (May 1953), p. 47.

[5]For a discussion of the causal relation of participation behavior and various psychological dimensions see Heinz Eulau and Peter Schneider, "Dimensions of Political Involvement," *Public Opinion Quarterly*, Vol. XX (Spring 1956), pp. 128–42.

However useful it may be to distinguish turnout and partisan choice analytically, we ought not to suppose that these dimensions of the voting act appear distinct to the individual citizen. It is natural for the individual to perceive that he votes because he wants to make his preference between parties or candidates count, or that he fails to vote because he does not have a clear preference between partisan objects that he feels are equally appealing, unappealing, or without any affective content at all. Almost certainly this perception of the motives for voting overreaches the facts: we will see that the strength of preference only partially accounts for turnout. Yet the perception catches a clear element of motivation, and the relation of turnout to the intensity of preference is the first important fact we should establish in seeking to explain why some people have voted and others have not.

The evidence for this relation is readily seen if we classify people according to the intensity of their preference, and observe what proportion has voted at each level of intensity. Data of this sort from our combined samples of 1952 and 1956 are arrayed in Figure 1. The pattern seen in the

FIGURE 1

Relation of Intensity of Partisan Preference to Voting Turnout, 1952 and 1956

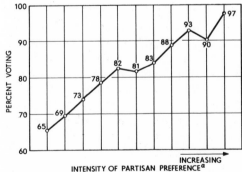

figure shows that the probability that a person will vote depends on the strength of his partisan preference. Across virtually

TABLE 2
Relation of Perceived Closeness of Election and Intensity of
Partisan Preference to Voting Turnout, 1956

| | Election Perceived to Be | | | | | |
| | One sided Intensity of Preference | | | Close Intensity of Preference | | |
	Weak	Medium	Strong	Weak	Medium	Strong
Voted	70%	71%	73%	71%	79%	89%
Did not vote	30	29	27	29	21	11
	100%	100%	100%	100%	100%	100%
Number of cases	130	170	88	301	360	226

the entire range of intensity found in these samples, the greater the strength of the individual's preference, the greater the likelihood he would vote. And the rate of voting at the highest levels of intensity shows that the individual's preference virtually insures his turnout.

Intensity of preference affects not only whether the individual votes; it affects how "strongly" he votes as well. A common observation is that people go to the polls with different degrees of concern about voting. For some the act is imbued with strong positive affect, whereas for others it is much more neutrally toned. To measure these differences we have asked each person who voted how much he cared about having voted, and we have used the answers to this question to identify people who cared a great deal and those who voted in a much more perfunctory way. The strength of voting is plainly associated with the intensity of preference; among those of low preference intensity, the proportion of perfunctory voters is a good deal larger than it is among those whose strength of preference is high.

This sketch of the influence of preference intensity is in one respect overly simple and needs to be complicated by the addition of a perceptual factor. Despite the immediacy of the impact that we would expect strength of preference to have on turnout, its motivational force seems to depend on how close the individual perceives the election to be. The interaction of these factors in the motivation of turnout is shown in Table 2 for the election of 1956. In this table, the levels of intensity in Figure 1 are combined into three broad categories, and the proportion voting in each of these categories is given separately for those who expected the election to be one sided and those who expected it to be close. What the entries of the table have to say about the motivation of turnout is quite clear. The person who thinks the outcome of the election is a foregone conclusion is not more likely to vote if his preference is strong. But the person who thinks the outcome is in doubt is more likely to vote if the intensity of his partisan preference is high. The power of partisan choice to motivate turnout evidently is contingent on the individual feeling, at least in some diffuse way, that his vote may "count."[6] To put the matter another way, the turnout behavior of a person of weak preference is not affected by

[6]The questions we have used to classify respondents according to their expectations about the election have referred to the contest *in the nation as a whole*. Because presidential electors are chosen by states and because all of a state's electors are usually awarded to a single party, we might suppose that how close a person feels the presidential candidates are running in his own state would be of greater importance. But the analysis of answers to a question referring to the presidential race within the respondent's state indicates that it is the election *as a whole* that has cognitive and motivational significance, despite the existence of the Electoral College.

whether he thinks the election will be close. But the behavior of someone of stronger preference is affected a good deal by his perception of how close the election will be.

The relation between strength of preference and turnout that is seen in our data needs to be interpreted with a greater time perspective. If our measures spanned a broader interval in the life of the individual we would expect to find that the strength of his preference in prior elections has an effect on the likelihood of his voting in later elections. In showing the relation of turnout to the strength of preference in single elections, our data undoubtedly understate the full impact of preference intensity on the decision to vote. A strong commitment to one side or the other in any election tends to involve the individual psychologically more deeply in politics. As a result, the probability of his participating in subsequent elections increases, even though his preference may be substantially less strong in the later campaigns. In this sense, the influence of partisan choice on turnout transcends that shown by the data we have presented here. Yet this secondary effect plainly involves intervening factors. The effect of intensity of preference in time past must be transmitted through forces that act on the individual at the moment of his present behavior.

The need to identify additional psychological forces on the turnout decision is strongly reinforced by a realistic appraisal of how well the intensity of current preference can explain this type of behavior. The findings we have given demonstrate that in a single election someone of strong preference is more likely to vote than is someone of weaker partisan dispositions. Yet Figure 1 should dispel altogether the idea that the strength of partisan choice can by itself fully explain why some people go to the polls and others do not. The inadequacy of strength of preference in accounting for turnout is perhaps most

clearly seen in its failure to explain the behavior of those of minimum partisan disposition. Although the proportion voting is lowest in the group having the slightest degree of preference, nearly two-thirds even of these people were found to have cast a vote.

TURNOUT AND POLITICAL INVOLVEMENT

The partial dependence of turnout on preference is of theoretical importance in large part because it implicates everything that may influence the intensity of preference as a possible influence on the disposition to vote. The fact that one basic dimension of voting is related to the other means that any element in the array of factors leading to partisan choice may lead to turnout as well. The truth of this is recognized at least implicitly in a number of discussions that have explained the disposition to vote in terms of what may strengthen or weaken the disposition to vote a given way.[7] Furthermore, many discussions of the antecedents of partisan choice can throw light on the causes of turnout as well.

Our concern for the moment is not with the antecedents of the intensity of preference but rather with psychological influences on turnout that act apart from the effect of a disposition to vote a given way. In pressing this aspect of our research our major effort has been to relate turnout behavior to what we will call the individual's psychological involvement in politics. We have felt that the individual develops a characteristic degree of interest and involvement in political affairs, which varies widely among individuals but which exhibits a good deal of stability for the same person through successive election cam-

---

[7] It is of central importance, for example, in the discussion of turnout appearing in Seymour M. Lipset et al., "The Psychology of Voting: An Analysis of Political Behavior," Handbook of Social Psychology, ed. Gardner Lindzey (Cambridge, Mass.: Addison-Wesley Publishing Co., 1954), Vol. II, pp. 1124–1175.

TABLE 3
Relation of Degree of Interest in Campaign to Voting Turnout, 1956

	Degree of Interest in Campaign		
	Not Much Interested	Somewhat Interested	Very Much Interested
Voted	58%	72%	87%
Did not vote	42	28	13
	100%	100%	100%
Number of cases	540	695	520

paigns. Postulating a dimension of this sort leads naturally to the hypothesis that the stronger the individual's psychological involvement the more likely he is to participate in politics by voting. We have sought to design measures that would catch several aspects of the individual's psychological involvement in politics; in particular, we have measured two sorts of attitudes that describe the individual's orientation to a specific election and two additional attitudes that characterize his orientation to politics and elections more generally.

Interest in the Campaign

The first aspect of involvement we have sought to measure is the degree of a person's interest in the campaign. The presidential contest holds the attention of different people quite unequally, and the degree of interest has varied widely among the individuals we have interviewed in several election campaigns. The importance of this aspect of involvement for voting turnout is demonstrated by Table 3 with data drawn from the election of 1956. The entries of the table show that the rate of turnout among persons of high interest exceeded that among persons of low interest by nearly 30 per cent. What is more, the incidence of nonvoting among the third of the electorate that is lowest in interest is appreciably greater than it is among the third that is lowest in strength

of partisan preference, as shown by Figure 1. Our measure of interest carries us further than the measure of partisan intensity in finding the conditions of nonvoting, although we still need to learn what brought to the polls more than half of those who tell us they are not much interested in the campaign.

Concern over the Election Outcome

A person's orientation to a specific election can be described also in terms of his concern over its outcome. Some people are deeply involved, psychologically speaking, in the electoral result, whereas others are relatively indifferent. Concern over the election result would seem intuitively to be somewhat distinct from political interest, and in our data it is by no means perfectly correlated with interest. Yet the association of the two suggests the influence of a more general involvement factor and leads us to concur in Lane's observation that "questions on 'interest' and 'concern' tend to select out the same populations and to be related to behavior in roughly the same way."[8] The relation we have found between the individual's concern over the outcome and the probability of his voting is shown in Table 4 for 1956. Here again, the effect of involvement on voting turnout seems very clear.

—————

[8] Robert E. Lane, *Political Life* (Glencoe, Ill.: The Free Press, 1959), p. 134.

TABLE 4

Relation of Degree of Concern about Election Outcome to Voting Turnout, 1956

	Degree of Concern over Election Outcome			
	Don't Care at All	Don't Care Very Much	Care Somewhat	Care Very Much
Voted	52%	69%	76%	84%
Did not vote	48	31	24	16
	100%	100%	100%	100%
Number of cases	230	367	627	459

Sense of Political Efficacy

Our measures of interest and of concern over the election outcome refer explicitly to the election at hand. As such, they are likely to catch important short-term fluctuations of the individual's political involvement. These measures may tap more enduring orientations to politics as well. The individual does not react *de novo* to each election but tends rather to respond to the stimuli of a new campaign in terms of stable attitudes and dispositions he has toward politics generally. His social environment, immediate and distant, is composed of a number of areas that compete for his emotional energy and in which he comes to have a characteristic level of emotional involvement. Politics is such an area, and most adults have a relatively fixed degree of involvement in it, although their commitment to political affairs, as to work, family, religion, or sports, may vary somewhat over time. This characteristic level of involvement differs widely among people. A really intense

commitment to politics probably is limited in American society to a small fraction of political activists, but even in the wider electorate we find substantial differences in the extent of emotional involvement in political affairs.

An important aspect of the individual's response to politics as a general area is the degree to which this response is passive in character. To some people politics is a distant and complex realm that is beyond the power of the common citizen to affect, whereas to others the affairs of government can be understood and influenced by individual citizens. We have assessed the effectiveness the individual feels in his relation to politics by using answers to several questions probing attitudes of this sort to develop a cumulative scale, on which we could array our samples. The influence this dimension of attitude has on the turnout decision is shown by Table 5 for the election of 1956. The rate of voting turnout was found to increase uniformly with the strength of the individual's sense of political efficacy, and more than 40 percentage points separated those

TABLE 5

Relation of Sense of Political Efficacy to Voting Turnout, 1956

	Sense of Political Efficacy				
	Low				High
Voted	52%	60%	75%	84%	91%
Did not vote	48	40	25	16	9
	100%	100%	100%	100%	100%
Number of cases	263	343	461	501	196

TABLE 6
Relation of Sense of Citizen Duty to Voting Turnout, 1956

	Sense of Citizen Duty				
	Low				High
Voted	13%	42%	52%	74%	85%
Did not vote	87	58	48	26	15
	100%	100%	100%	100%	100%
Number of cases	89	78	146	639	812

whose sense was least developed from those whose sense of effectiveness was strongest.

Sense of Citizen Duty

The final aspect of involvement we have sought to measure also transcends a single election. Wide currency in American society is given the idea that the individual has a civic responsibility to vote. When this norm becomes a part of the value system of the individual, as it has for most of our citizens, it may be regarded as a force acting directly on the turnout decision. Of course its strength is not the same for everyone, and the degree to which the individual feels an obligation to vote is an important aspect of his orientation to politics. We have measured the strength of this attitude by constructing a cumulative scale from several questions about the responsibility to vote and classifying those we have interviewed into the categories of the scale. When the proportion voting is shown for each category, as it is in Table 6 for the election of 1956, it is clear that the strength of a person's sense of citizen duty has a very great influence on the likelihood of his voting.

The most striking entries in Table 6 are those indicating that voting is rare among people whose sense of citizen duty is least strong. In those whose sense of citizen duty is weakest we have found a small group whose motivation to participate in politics is so near zero that other forces in-

ducing them to vote only rarely bring them to the polls.

Despite the evidence that the four aspects of political involvement we have measured share an important common component, we have considered separately their relation to turnout because each aspect contributes a distinctive element. However, we can assess how well involvement accounts for behavior only if we examine the joint relation to turnout of the four measures. In order to make entirely clear what we have *added* to our ability to account for the turnout decision by measuring these aspects of involvement, we will include strength of partisan preference among the explanatory variables so that their *combined* power to account for behavior may be compared directly with that of the intensity of preference alone, as shown in Figure 1.

Such a comparison attests the fundamental role of involvement in motivating turnout behavior. As is seen in Figure 2, the rate of turnout increases steadily with political involvement and partisan preference, and differs by more than 75 per cent from one extreme to the other, whereas the proportions voting at the extremes of low and high intensity of preference alone differed by less than half this much. The fact that persons of the highest involvement are more nearly unanimous in voting than are those of lowest involvement in not voting suggests that we are still beset more by the problem of the deviant *voters* than we are with that of the deviant *non-*

FIGURE 2
Relation of Intensity of Political Involvement to
Voting Turnout, 1956

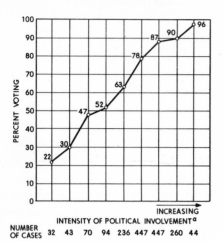

We are better prepared, by the popular lore about voting, for error at the extreme of high involvement. Located here is the person of strong motivation who is kept from voting by personal circumstances he could not reasonably overcome, as the individual who was prevented from voting by a flat tire on his way to the polls. We doubt that this specific factor, which we would unhesitatingly declare exogenous, has had a very high incidence in American politics, but it suggests well the sort of barrier that may keep a highly motivated person from voting. An inspection of our interview protocols provides a number of such cases.

Located here, too, are the individuals of strong motivation who are barred from voting by legal disabilities. Some of our respondents living in states that make no provision for absentee balloting have been away from their homes on election day. Others have changed their residences too recently to satisfy the requirements of minimum residence. Nonregistration ought generally to be regarded as a legal barrier only with caution, since the failure to register may simply reflect the same motivational factors as the failure to vote. Yet in certain cases the impossibility of registering has stood as a clear barrier for those who were motivated to perform the voting act.

voter. And the existence of any group of similar motivation whose behavior is not homogeneous invites us to push further the quest for explanation.

Divergent Cases

Most of the variability in turnout that political involvement fails to explain is found in the middle categories of Figure 2, where the psychological forces we have measured are neither so weak that the individual is highly unlikely to vote nor so strong that he is highly unlikely *not* to vote. In these middle categories other factors, some of them undoubtedly exogenous to our theoretical concerns, have determined whether the individual will vote. But the "error" in Figure 2 that is most interesting is found at the extremes of political involvement, where we would expect to be able to predict with higher confidence whether the individual will in fact vote. The presence of error of this sort leads naturally to an intensive examination of divergent cases to learn why it is that our expectations have proven wrong.

Deviant cases of the opposite sort, in which a person of slight motivation has voted, are less familiar in the common lore, except perhaps for what is known of party machines that have voted the dead. An analysis of interviews with people of very low motivation who have gone to the polls indicates that the most important force on their behavior is interpersonal influence, as we have found it to be in inducing deviant partisan behavior. Personal influence seems particularly important within the family group. Of the twelve voters in 1956 who had the least reason for going to the polls in terms of the psychological factors we have measured, nine

TABLE 7
Postelection Preference of Nonvoters, 1948 to 1956*

	1948	1952	1956
Would have voted Democratic	82%	52%	28%
Would have voted Republican	18	48	72
Total	100%	100%	100%
Number of cases	192	417	429

*Among nonvoters giving a preference between major-party candidates.

were women who appeared to respond to the wishes of husbands or of other men in their immediate families.

It is the preferences of those who vote that are of primary importance in the wider political system. But the preferences of those who do not are by no means of trivial importance; indeed, in recording substantial shifts over time they prove to be of considerable theoretical interest. Let us examine the partisan preference of nonvoters, as they have been assessed over a twenty-year period.

With the rise of public opinion polls in the 1930's, the first systematic evidence began to appear that nonvoters—or at least people who expected not to vote—were more Democratic than the electorate as a whole. This evidence accumulated through the latter years of the New Deal and the Fair Deal until the generalization that nonvoters tend to be Democrats had worked itself into the popular understanding of politics. Since it was well known that both partisan preference and voting turnout were related to social class, an explanation of the strongly Democratic color of nonvoters was easily supplied.

The report of partisan preferences we obtained from a national sample interviewed after the election of 1948, the high-water mark of the Fair Deal, was consistent with this description of nonvoters. Whereas the preferences reported by voters were divided very nearly evenly between the parties, the preferences reported by nonvoters favored the Democrats

by a margin of more than 4–1. Were it not for the fact that the Truman vote exceeded the advance expectations, the closeness of the Democratic victory in 1948 relative to earlier years would probably have been explained in terms of the lower level of turnout.

If the report taken from those who failed to vote in 1948 supported the contention that nonvoters tend to be Democrats, the postelection reports of 1952 and 1956 dealt this notion severe blows. In our interviews following the election of 1952 only about half of the nonvoters indicating a preference said they would have voted Democratic; in our interviews following the election of 1956 little more than a quarter of the nonvoters giving a preference said they would have voted Democratic. The extreme nature of this shift in the Democratic proportion over an eight-year period is shown by Table 7. Few statistics in all of our studies have shown so violent a change over time as this one.

What can explain so great a shift among nonvoters? Over a period in which the division of preference changed by little more than ten per cent among voters it changed by more than 50 per cent among nonvoters. How are we to account for the difference? Undoubtedly a number of factors have been at work, but we believe that much of the observed change can be explained by a few central ideas. The major key to understanding is supplied by what we have found to distinguish non-

TABLE 8

Relation of Degree of Political Involvement to Change in
Partisan Preference of Nonvoters*

	1952 Election		1956 Election	
	Before	After	Before	After
Very much interested 51%	51%	54%	43%	37%
Somewhat interested 56%	56%	57%	40%	37%
Not much interested 63%	63%	52%	42%	24%

*Entries are percentages favoring Democrats of those giving a preference.

voters from voters: the nonvoter tends to be a person of lower involvement whose emotional investment in politics and its partisan decisions is on the average much less than that of the voter. As a result, we would expect the nonvoter to be less stable in his partisan inclinations than the voter and more responsive to the massive political stimuli that produce shifts of popular attitude over time. And we have little doubt that for the nonvoter a stimulus of great importance in this period, as in any other, was the fact of who was winning elections. For at least part of the way between his position of 1948 and his position of 1956 the nonvoter was riding a psychological bandwagon.

Several kinds of evidence can be marshalled in support of this general view. First of all, if we are right in thinking that the outcomes of these elections were stimuli of relatively greater importance for the nonvoter, we ought to find evidence of the fact in a comparison of the reported preference of nonvoters before and after each election. We do not have the data to make this comparison for the election of 1948, but for each of the Eisenhower elections we may examine the nonvoter's report of preference in the first and second interviews of our brief panel studies spanning the elections. The division of preference among nonvoters shifted in the direction of the winner in each of these years; indeed, the postelection shift toward Eisenhower in 1956 (from 58% to 72%) was 14 percentage points—as great as

the shift of preference among voters over the entire period from 1948 to 1956. We would suppose that the Truman victory had much the same effect on the preference of nonvoters—although in the opposite direction—as the Eisenhower victories had in each of the elections that followed.

The most telling evidence for our characterization of change, however, is obtained by further dividing nonvoters according to the degree of their involvement in politics. In any election some individuals whose involvement is high and whose motivation is strong fail to vote. If we can separate these people from individuals who are weakly involved, we should have a clearer sense of the forces inducing change in preference over time. Table 8 makes such a separation for each of the Eisenhower elections by classifying nonvoters according to the extent of their interest in the campaign. Several observations that are important for our formulation of change can be based on this table. First, it is clear for both the 1952 and 1956 elections that change in the Republican direction between the pre- and postelection interviews occurred more among the slightly involved than it did among those of greater involvement. Only the group least interested in the campaign shifted toward Eisenhower in his first victory; hence, the shift seen among nonvoters as a whole rests on the fact that most nonvoters are people of little involvement. Second, the fact that the Democratic percentage prior to the 1952 election was highest among those of slightest interest suggests that these people were most under the influence of past Democratic victories. Yet is it this same group that responded most strongly to the Eisenhower victories and shifted far enough that by the postelection interview of 1956 less than one-fourth of their number favored the Democrats.[9]

This unbroken swing in the Republican

[9]Of course we have repeated measurements of the preferences of the same persons only within a single election and not over two or more elections. The assumption that the composition of the several involvement groups would be fairly stable over time cannot be validated with these data, and comparisons of their preferences between elections ought to be treated with caution.

direction dissolves the generalization that nonvoters are pro-Democratic and calls attention in the most dramatic way to the importance of psychological involvement in explaining political behavior. We have treated in some detail the shifts of preference among those who fail to vote because these changes suggest the far-reaching effects on behavior of the low involvement that is the nonvoter's primary quality. Yet voters and nonvoters are by no means the only groups within the electorate that differ in the extent of their political involvement, and we shall have occasion in later chapters to examine the behavior of other groups as well for which involvement supplies a key to understanding.

THE RESPONSIBLE ELECTORATE*

V. O. Key, Jr.

The apparent stability of the popular support of the political party dominant at the moment excites the curiosity of students of American politics. For relatively long periods one party or the other commands so consistently the votes of a majority that the country is said to be either normally Republican or normally Democratic. From 1932 to 1952 elections appeared to be only reassertions by the standing majority of its continued faith in Democratic leadership. In 1932 Franklin D. Roosevelt drew 59.1 per cent of the two-party vote and in 1936, in an extraordinary expression of popular confidence, 62.5 per cent. The Democratic proportion of the vote declined in succeeding elections bit by bit: 55.0 per cent in 1940; 53.8 per cent in 1944; and 52.3 per cent in 1948. Yet it seemed as if each election was but an occasion for the New Deal to muster again its phalanxes only in slightly diminished strength, march them to the polls, and thereby record its claim to power for another four years.

Elections such as these, in which the party pattern of the preceding election prevails, Angus Campbell calls "maintaining" elections.[1] While this characterization serves happily in a conceptual system for the differentiation of broad types of elections, it tells us nothing about the pro-

cesses by which a majority party maintains—or does not maintain—its dominance. A satisfactory explanation of those processes would move us toward a better understanding of popular government. Such evidence as can be mustered suggests that the popular majority does not hold together like a ball of sticky popcorn. Rather, no sooner has a popular majority been constructed than it begins to crumble. The maintenance of a supportive majority requires governmental actions, policies, and gestures that reinforce the confidence of those who have placed their faith in the Administration. Yet to govern is to antagonize not only opponents but also at least some supporters; as the loyalty of one group is nourished, another group may be repelled. A series of maintaining elections occurs only in consequence of a complex process of interaction between government and populace in which old friends are sustained, old enemies are converted into new friends, old friends become even bitter opponents, and new voters are attracted to the cause—all in proper proportions to produce repeatedly for the dominant party its apparently stable and continuing majority.

The unbroken series of Democratic victories in the 1930's and 1940's occurred against a background of marked and abrupt innovations in governmental policy. To the extent that interactions between governmental action and public attitudes can be traced, this epoch should be instructive about the processes involved in the maintenance and renewal

---

*Reprinted by the permission of the publishers from V. O. Key, Jr., *The Responsible Electorate*, Cambridge, Mass.: The Belknap Press of Harvard University Press. Copyright 1966 by the President and Fellows of Harvard College.

[1] Angus Campbell, P. E. Converse, W. E. Miller, and D. E. Stokes, *The American Voter* (New York: John Wiley & Sons, 1960), ch. 19.

of a dominant popular coalition. And, thereby, we may also enlarge our information on the behavior of the supposedly errant voter. To speak of these interactions, though, we must recall some of the principal governmental actions of the 1930's. For a substantial part of the population they are by now only vague episodes in a dim and distant history.

The federal government underwent a radical transformation after the Democratic victory of 1932. It had been a remote authority with a limited range of activity. It operated the postal system, improved rivers and harbors, maintained armed forces on a scale fearsome only to banana republics, and performed other functions of which the average citizen was hardly aware. Within a brief time it became an institution that affected intimately the lives and fortunes of most, if not all, citizens. Measures of recovery and of reform—as the categorization of the time went—contributed to this fundamental alteration of federal activities. Legislative endeavors to achieve economic recovery from the Great Depression shaded over into steps toward basic reform; both types of policy touched the interests and hopes of great numbers of people and ignited the fiercest political controversy.

Large-scale measures for the relief of the unemployed made federal policy highly perceptible to millions of destitute persons. Administered at first as direct relief —a dole—by state relief administrations, the program soon came to be conducted by the Works Progress Administration, a federal agency which employed people on projects as diverse as theatricals, road construction, and leaf raking to the accompaniment of a spirited criticism not noticeably shared by those who relied on the WPA for sustenance. Another numerous class of persons received federal assistance through the Home Owners' Loan Corporation, an agency which had $3,000,000,000 to refinance home mortgages to tide necessitous debtors over until a better day.

Hard-pressed banks and other business enterprises received infusions of government capital often in the form of loans. Expenditures on a new scale for public works pumped money into the economy. By the Agricultural Adjustment Act, Congress attempted to alleviate the lot of the farmer who had been especially hard hit by the depression. The National Recovery Administration sought, oddly enough, to activate industry by something of a system of legalized cartels, with the inclusion in the cartel agreements (or industry codes) of standards with respect to minimum wages, maximum hours, collective bargaining, and other aspects of the employer–employee relationship.

Only a hazy line divided measures of recovery from those of reform; yet some actions clearly contemplated permanent and often drastic changes in public policy. Some of these new policies had effects of marked visibility. The Social Security Act of 1935 established a system of federal grants to states for programs of assistance to the aged, to the blind, and to dependent children, but it also instituted a system of contributory old-age annuities and a scheme of unemployment compensation, the first national steps into the field of social insurance. The Wagner Labor Relations Act assured to labor the right to organize and imposed on employers an obligation to bargain with employees collectively, an act of fundamental significance in the definition of the structure of the industrial order. In another area the government hoped by the Public Utility Holding Company Act to prevent a recurrence of financial abuses that had been notable, and the Tennessee Valley Authority and various power projects were regarded by the electrical utilities as an entering wedge for a socialism that would ultimately destroy them. Other legislation restrained sharp operators in the securities business who had bilked a goodly number of their fellow men in the halcyon days of the new era of the 1920's.

The merits or demerits of all these actions—and many others—are not our concern. The relevance of their mention is to suggest the considerable range of novel governmental actions with a widespread impact upon the fortunes and aspirations of voters. What kinds of interactions between government and electorate occurred in consequence of this revolution —as American revolutions go—in public policy? The broad effect was, of course, obvious. By 1936 the innovation period of the New Deal had pretty well run its course, and in that year the voters responded with a resounding ratification of the new thrust of governmental policy. Or, if one wishes to be cautious, the electorate resoundingly rejected the Republican alternative, which, as the campaign of 1936 developed, appeared to be a hysterical plea to return to the pre-1932 status quo lest the American system become a dictatorship.[2]

To portray the processes of the maintenance of the New Deal coalition, though, one must go beyond the broad electoral verdict and examine the detailed movements in voter sentiment underlying the grand totals. The maintenance and switching of party positions reflected in part responses to specific and concrete actions of government; they also reflected the responses of voters to the political oratory of the time. As campaigns developed, the commotion over individual policies seemed to be transmuted into the grand abstractions of political debate. The political discussion of the 1930's was heavily tinged with the rhetoric of the conflict of class and interest, and the battle seemed to take the shape of a competition between rich and poor, or between the American constitutional system and some alien alternative. On the left, evangels, such as Huey Long, preached a doctrine of "share the wealth," while those who had somewhat more than a modicum of

wealth organized the Liberty League and other such societies to defend the American system. In 1936 the Republican national committee gloomily forecast that the "American plan of government might be lost forever," if Roosevelt were kept in office.

How might voters be expected to respond to the actions of government and to the campaign oratory of this era? American parties have had historically a multiclass following. Doubtless in 1932, though the data are not available, persons of all classes deserted the Republicans to vote for Franklin D. Roosevelt and a change. The result was that the 1932 Democratic vote probably included large numbers of persons who would not be regarded as "Democratic" in disposition. At any rate, it would be plausible to expect that as the New Deal unfolded, persons of upper-class status and of conservative disposition would be drawn from their Democratic posture to the Republican ranks. Moreover, it might be supposed that a countertendency would also operate as 1932 Republican voters in the lesser economic categories moved over to the Democratic side of the fence. In short, the impact of governmental actions and political rhetoric would be expected to heighten polarization along class and occupational lines.

Some such movement of voters occurred, evidently on a fairly large scale. Many upper-class Democratic voters defected, while relatively fewer working-class Democrats left the ranks. Scarcely any information is available for the election of 1936, but in the elections of 1940, 1944, and 1948 these differentials in party switching existed. Persons at all economic levels at each election moved away from the Democratic party but at rates varying with level of economic status. The differentials in party defection among economic levels, as estimated from Gallup polls of presidential preference, appear in Table 1. The rankings from "wealthy" to "poor" assigned by the interviewers are doubtless

---

[2] For the tenor of the politics of the time, see A. M. Schlesinger, Jr., *The Politics of Upheaval* (Boston: Houghton Mifflin, 1960).

TABLE 1
Patterns of Vote Switching in Presidential Elections, 1936–1948,
in Relation to Economic Status*

Status	1936–40†		1940–44‡		1944–48§	
	% of 1936 D's, D–R	% of 1936 R's, R–D	% of 1940 D's, D–R	% of 1940 R's, R–D	% of 1944 D's, D–R	% of 1944 R's, R–D
Wealthy	46	2	35	4	‖	0
Average + ...	30	1	27	5	47	1
Average	28	4	24	7	32	3
Poor + ...	20	5	¶	¶	¶	¶
Poor	18	7	19	8	22	6
Old-age assistance	19	4	13	5	18	‖
On relief	14	7	11	‖	‖	‖

*The table entries are the percentages of those with a recall of a vote for a major-party candidate at the first election of the pair of years who expressed a preference for a major-party candidate in surveys in October just prior to the election of the second year of each pair. In each instance several surveys are combined to obtain larger samples in the individual cells. Economic status was that assigned to the respondent by the AIPO interviewer.

†A consolidation of the following AIPO surveys: 215K, 216T, 217, 218K. Roper 22, October 1940, yielded the following percentages of switchers, D-R, in the indicated economic levels: A, 25; H, 24; C, 20; D, 12. The corresponding R-D switches were: 2, 3, 5, 9.

‡A consolidation of AIPO 330, 331, 332, 333, 334.

§A consolidation of AIPO 430 and 431.

‖Less than 50 cases.

¶Data obtained from low-income respondents in 1944 and 1948 were coded only in terms of a "poor" category. There was no "poor +" category.

not measures of precision; nevertheless, of the "wealthy" 1936 Democratic voters, in the neighborhood of four out of ten deserted to the Republicans in 1940. At the other extreme, less than one in seven persons on relief took that step.

The countermovement, from Republican in 1936 to Democratic in 1940, was relatively small, yet it had a class bias in that relatively more of the poor than of the better-off 1936 Republicans switched to Democratic in 1940. In 1944 involvement in World War II gave the stimuli of the campaign a less class-oriented tone; yet in lesser degree than in 1940 the same class-tinged pattern of party switching prevailed. In 1948, with the war out of the way, the political battle assumed its older form with a more marked difference in switching among economic levels. Though the rates of switching in party preference shown by the pre-election polls analyzed in Table 1 may

exceed the switch in the actual vote, they suggest the existence of quite large movements across party lines in these elections which brought voting alignments toward a closer congruity with income classes.[3]

Another test of our expectations about how voters might have responded to the impact of the New Deal appears in Table 2, which shows the switches from Demo-

[3]For the technician it should be noted that the differences in switching rates that appear, for example, in the first column of Table 1 could be attributable in part to a variant of the Maccobyean effect, so called for its identification by Eleanor Maccoby, "Pitfalls in the Analysis of Panel Data: A Research Note on Some Technical Aspects of Voting," *American Journal of Sociology*, LXI (1956), 359–62. The effect may result in an overstatement of differences in rates of change between large and small samples. Random errors in recording responses and in punching data into cards may inflate the rates of change for small N's more than for large N's. The odds are that the potential of the effect is negligible for most of our tables, but comparisons between cells with large and with extremely small N's should be regarded with some wariness.

TABLE 2

Percentages within Occupational Categories Switching from Democratic to Republican Presidential Preference from Election to Election, 1936–1948, as Measured by Pre-Election and Post-Election Polls*

Group	1936–40†		1940–44‡		1944–48§	
	Pre	Post	Pre	Post	Pre	Post
Business and professional	33	35	25	18	57	26
White-collar	28	24	22	16	39	21
Skilled and semiskilled	22	19	18	14	23	11
Unskilled	17	15	19	12	23	10
Farmers and farm laborers	23	24	24	16	18	13

*The percentages for the pre-election columns were computed in the same way as the comparable percentages in Table 1. The post-election percentages are derived from surveys conducted during the month after the presidential election; they rest, thus, on reported votes in November as compared with the reported vote of four years before.

†The pre-election column rests on a consolidation of AIPO 216T, 217, 218K, 220, 221. The post-election column represents a consolidation of AIPO 224 and 225. Roper's October 1940 survey produced the following D-R percentages: business and professional, 29; white-collar, 26; wage earners, 15; farmers and farm laborers, 15. The occupational categories were not exactly the same as those of the AIPO.

‡The pre-election column rests on a consolidation of AIPO 331, 332, 333, 334; the post-election column on AIPO 335 and 336K.

§The pre-election column rests on a consolidation of AIPO 429, 430, and 431; the post-election column on AIPO 432.

cratic to Republican within broad occupational groups at the same series of elections. Business and professional Democratic voters at one election were far more likely to defect to the Republican candidate at the next election than were unskilled workers. Nevertheless, defections occurred at all occupational levels, a matter not easily explained if one attributes voting behavior largely to the effect of objective economic interest. If one's concern as an unskilled worker governs his voting, by what conceivable reason should an unskilled Democrat of 1936 have become a Republican voter in 1940? The explanation, which will occupy us later, is not immediately apparent; nevertheless, about one in seven of the group in question made that switch. Table 2 incidentally illustrates some of the characteristics of the data with which we work; it shows switching as measured both by a pre-election expression of preference and by a post-election report of the vote. Except for the election of 1940, a fairly wide difference exists between the two sets of figures. Probably the "true" figures fell somewhere between the two

sets of percentages; the data serve better as indicators of contrasting shifts in attitude of groups of voters than as measures of their absolute rates of switching in the voting.[4]

[4]Several factors contribute to the differences between the pre-election and post-election findings. The two figures are about alike for 1940, probably the result of the practice in that year of screening many prospective nonvoters from the sample at the interview stage. Beyond that, the pre-election figures rest on a consolidation of several surveys during the campaign, a factor that would tend to overestimate switching since during this era the Democratic vote seemed to reach more complete activation as the campaign progressed. The inclusion of potential nonvoters also probably inflates switching rates; the impression develops that this class of persons has a sharp sensitivity to the winds of the moment and would be especially prone under the circumstances of these campaigns to report a switch in preference. The odds also are that, given the tendency for the popular majority to be inflated in surveys reporting past votes, the post-election surveys understate the actual defection rates. The differences between the pre-election and post-election data for 1948 are especially wide, a factor which lends credence to the supposition that in this campaign quite marked shifts in sentiment occurred in the last ten days or so of the campaign. In this campaign the pre-election polls forecast a Republican victory, much to the glee of the critics of the polls whose forecasts were, incidentally, no better.

TABLE 3
Democratic Percentage of Presidential Preference of New Voters, within Occupational Categories, as Measured by Pre-Election and Post-Election Polls*

Group	1940		1944		1948	
	Pre	Post	Pre	Post	Pre	Post
Business and professional	46	42	49	46	39	48
White-collar	53	54	53	66	44	58
Skilled and semiskilled	68	65	59	64	61	75
Unskilled	68	67	63	59	67	69
Farmers and farm laborers	56	48	42	45	48	61

*Based on same surveys as Table 2. New voters are defined as those who did not vote in the preceding presidential election, either because they were too young or for some other reason.

The pattern of recruitment of new voters into the Democratic ranks resembled the patterns of switching among old voters. Democratic losses among old voters decreased from step to step down the ladder of occupational status; the proportion of new voters preferring the Democratic candidate increased from step to step down the ladder. These variations in the voting inclinations of new voters, that is, those who either were too young or simply failed to vote four years earlier, are shown in detail for each of the elections in Table 3. A significant factor in the maintenance of the position of the "normal" majority probably consists in its success in attracting new voters to its banner. As has been shown (in Table 4), the new voters make up a relatively large proportion of the vote, and a failure to capture the loyalties of a majority of them could within a few elections change the balance of power between the parties. Of greatest importance, of course, is the recruitment of young persons who, once they form partisan attachments, may be expected to remain with the party with fair consistency for many years. Yet the older "new voters" are also a numerous, if heterogeneous, category, not without unimportance in the vote.[5]

5Over the elections 1940–1960, as shown by Table 4, the Democrats drew a somewhat larger proportion of the "new voters" than of the

So far our analysis follows conventional forms and yields findings that depend upon our reading into the data plausible assumptions about voter motivation. The data suggest that the issues and alternatives of the time tended to sharpen the class cleavage between the parties and in the process produced voter switching on a scale whose magnitude is not commonly suspected. Yet the analysis also generates persistent doubts. It rests on an assumption that voting can best be understood as an expression of motivations induced by the impact of campaign alternatives on short-range, individual economic interest which we assume to be associated with occupation or status. We impute motives to types of individuals, run the cards through the sorter, and, lo and behold, upper-status persons switch in differing degrees

"old" voters, as measured by expressions of pre-election preference. This Democratic advantage in the recruitment of new support doubtless contributed to the maintenance of its position as the party with the larger number of loyal followers. When the new voters at these elections were grouped into age categories, 21–39, 40–59, and 60 and over, the usual pattern over the period was for the Democratic proportion of the pre-election preference to be highest in the 21–39 age group, which suggested uniformly greater Democratic success in recruiting young voters. The notable exception occurred in 1940 when the Democratic proportion among those 60 and over exceeded the Democratic proportion among those under 40, probably a consequence of the special impact of the old-age security issue on the old folks.

and directions than do lower-status persons. Yet the embarrassing fact remains that in the elections examined many lower-status persons also switched preferences from Democratic to Republican; moreover, many lower-status persons maintained a standpat Republican position from election to election. And many well-to-do persons, strange though it may seem, remained steadfast Democrats from election to election.

What would we find if we proceeded directly to motive or attitude and ascertained the relation between vote switching and views on policy? What kinds of relations would be found if we assumed that the voter was a fairly reasonable fellow who voted to promote or to discourage public policies he approved or disapproved, insofar as he could perceive the consequences of his vote? Obviously, all kinds of motives, attitudes, and concerns enter into the voting decision; yet analyses of the available information indicate quite marked correlations between policy attitudes and vote switching. In short, the data make it appear sensible to regard the voter as a person who is concerned with what governments have done or not done and what they propose to do rather than one guided, perhaps unaware, by the imperatives of economic status or the tricks of Madison Avenue.

Our information on the relation of voter switching to policy preferences is not as comprehensive as we might wish. The information on the election of 1936, which was evidently an event of great significance in the reshaping of the American pattern of party loyalties, is especially limited. Nevertheless, in that year the old-age annuity provisions of the Social Security Act turned out to be a major issue. Republicans attacked the act. All citizens would soon be wearing dog tags carrying their social security numbers and less restrained campaign orators treated the system as a fraud. Voters responded with an expression of opinion startling in its clarity. In the neighborhood of four out of ten 1932

Democratic voters who opposed the legislation shifted over to the Republican candidate while about three out of ten of those 1932 Republicans who favored the plan moved to the support of Roosevelt. The details appear in Table 4.* Had the social security issue been the only influence on the vote these switches would have been closer to ten out of ten in each direction. It was not, of course, the only issue.† Nevertheless, an impressive relation between voting behavior and policy preference on this question prevailed, which raises a presumption that the social security issue had a notable power to

_____

*Editor's note: Key intended to elaborate at some length on the relationship in Table 4 between voters' 1936 presidential preference and their attitude toward the old-age insurance program. Attitudes on the social security issue may have had two broad effects on the 1936 voting. In addition to making voters whose position on the issue was not congruent with their previous presidential vote more likely to switch parties in 1936, it also may have made individuals whose previous presidential vote and policy attitude on the social security question were mutually consistent more inclined to stick with the party they had previously supported. Among 1932 Democratic voters, although four in ten of those who opposed the old-age insurance plan switched to the G.O.P. in 1936, only one in eight of the 1932 Democrats who supported federal old-age pensions left the Democratic party at the next presidential election. On the other hand, 1932 Republican voters who supported the insurance plan were much more likely to switch to the Democratic presidential nominee in 1936 than were 1932 Republican voters who opposed the Social Security pension plan. Three in ten of the 1932 Republican voters who supported the plan switched to Roosevelt in 1936; only 7 per cent of the 1932 Republican voters who opposed the plan deserted the G.O.P. in 1936.

†Editor's note: The data in Table 4 do not indicate how important or visible the social security issue was to the members of Dr. Gallup's sample. Some voters, for example, may have duly registered their approval or disapproval of the old-age insurance scheme without really caring very much about its inclusion in the Social Security Act; and Key intended to emphasize that undoubtedly the social security issue was more salient for some voters than for others during the 1936 campaign. Either a lack of concern over the social security question or a greater concern with other issues among some voters could help explain why the relation between policy attitudes on social security and 1936 voting behavior was not even stronger than it was.

TABLE 4

Switches in Presidential Voting Preference, 1932–1936, in Relation to
Response to Question: "Do you favor the compulsory old-age
insurance plan, starting January first, which requires employers
and employees to make equal monthly contributions?"*

Response	% of 1932 D's, D-R	% of 1932 R's, R-D	% of New Voters, D†
Yes, favor	12 (1,630)	30 (643)	61 (626)
No	40 (483)	7 (535)	45 (245)
No opinion	13 (315)	16 (175)	71 (170)

*AIPO 53, 9-26-36. This is the only surviving deck of cards for a 1936 survey with a recall of the 1932 vote. Data on the characteristics of the sample are nonexistent, but the addition of the N's to produce a national sample would probably be even more perilous than to the use here made of the data. The N's appear in parentheses. As in Table 1 and other tables, N is the total number of respondents on which the percentage is based. Thus, the figure 1,630 in the first column means that there were 1,630 respondents who recalled having voted for the Democratic candidate in 1932 and who favored the compulsory old-age insurance plan in 1936. Of these 1,630 persons, 12 per cent reported that they intended to support the Republican candidate in 1936.

†New voters are respondents who had not voted in 1932, either because they were too young or for other reasons.

wrench voters from their 1932 party positions to a vote in accord with their policy preferences.

As the election of 1940 approached, newspaper headlines tended to focus on the threat of war; yet voters seemed to be more concerned with the grand issues of domestic politics. Those issues turned broadly around the place and power of business in the American system, and the Democratic Administration occupied the role, in the eyes of business, as the enemy of business and, in the eyes of others, as the protagonist of the generality. The tolerant attitude of government toward the sitdown strikes in the automobile industry in 1937 symbolized the situation. As the 1940 polling neared, however, business protests became sharper as earlier New Deal legislation, made temporarily ineffective by constitutional litigation, began to make its effects felt. The defeat of Roosevelt's plan for the rejuvenation of the Supreme Court heartened business only temporarily. The Court found ways and means to hold major New Deal legislation constitutional, contrary to the opinions of most of the corporation lawyers in the country. Employers, thus, began to

feel the bite of the Wagner Labor Relations Act. Wendell Willkie, an erstwhile Democrat and former president of a utility corporation that had had to sell out to the Tennessee Valley Authority, won the Republican nomination and led the forces of protest against the New Deal.

How did the voters respond to the campaign alternatives? Did their response proceed from their preferences about governmental policy? Or did voters react in a random fashion as the winds of the campaign blew them about? To an astonishing degree (that is, a degree astonishing to persons with experience in the analysis of polling data) voters in their movements to and fro across party lines and from an inactive to an active voting status behaved as persons who made choices congruent with their policy preferences. In a sense, the question of more or less government control of business bundled up most of the lesser domestic questions of the campaign into a single great issue. Of those 1936 Democratic voters who felt that there should be less government regulation of business, about half expressed an intent to defect to Willkie in 1940. Of the 1936 Republican voters who

TABLE 5

Switches in Presidential Voting Preference, 1936–1940, in Relation to Response
to Question: "During the next four years do you think there should be more
or less regulation of business by the Federal government than at present?"*

Response	% of 1936 D's, D-R	% of 1936 R's, R-D	% of New Voters, D†
More regulation	10 (856)‡	15 (161)	73 (187)
About same	10 (712)	16 (122)	76 (124)
Less regulation	50 (841)	2 (1,263)	32 (229)
No opinion	14 (637)	8 (158)	68 (148)

*A consolidation of AIPO 215K-T, 10-9-40, and 219K-T, 10-24-40.

†New voters consist of those respondents who had not voted in 1936, either because they were too young or for other reasons.

‡Here is an illustration of how to read the table entries: these two figures mean that, of the 856 poll respondents in 1940 who said they had voted for Roosevelt in 1936 and who wanted more regulation in the 1940's, 10 per cent expressed an intent to defect to Willkie.

thought there should be less business regulation, 98 per cent remained steadfastly Republican (and the 2 per cent desertion to the Democrats is not in excess of error that could have been produced in recording interviews and in processing the data). Few 1936 Republican voters favored the existing level of business regulation or more regulation, but those who did succumbed far more frequently to Democratic blandishments; about 15 per cent of them favored Roosevelt. Table 5 contains the details.[6]

An even more marked association pre-

---

[6]For the nontechnical reader, it should be explained that the probability of divergence between the sample percentages in the tables and the true percentages in the sampled population is higher with small samples. Hence, the fact that a poll estimates fairly closely the percentage division of the two-party vote of the nation does not mean that percentages for subdivisions of the sample, for instance, Negroes or unskilled workers, are equally near the true percentages. The chances are high for greater sampling divergencies, on both the high and low sides, for sub-samples. Further, the technicians judge that recent polls are superior to earlier ones in their sampling techniques, in their interviewing practices, and in their administration. For the technician, it should be said that the N's of the tables cannot usually be added to produce the total N of a specific survey or combination of surveys; no attempt has been made to account for all the miscellaneous categories of respondents not relevant to our main purpose. The N's may be used, though, to compare the size of the various cells as defined.

vailed between voter attitudes on farm policy and shifts across party lines. About seven out of ten Democrats of 1936 who became disillusioned about the farm program had a 1940 preference for Willkie. Republican defectors were not numerous but about one out of five 1936 Republicans who approved the Democratic farm program looked favorably on Roosevelt in 1940. Those with the appropriate policy outlooks stood pat in remarkable degree. Only 1 per cent of the 1936 Republicans who disapproved the Administration farm program threatened to vote Democratic. This relationship between policy outlook and vote (shown in detail in Table 6) doubtless reflected to a degree the tendency of a voter on a specific question to improvise policy views that seem to be consistent with the way he planned to vote for other reasons entirely. A steadfast Democratic partisan might have been expected to opine that the "Roosevelt administration has done a good job in handling the farm problem," if the question were put to him in that form. Yet, however such opinions come into being, their supportive function in the political system should be the same.

By 1940 the Supreme Court had held the Wagner Labor Relations Act constitutional; nevertheless, many employers remained hopeful of the ultimate repeal or

TABLE 6

Switches in Presidential Voting Preferences, 1936–1940, in Relation to
Views on Roosevelt Administration's Program for Helping Farmers*

View	% of 1936 D's, D-R	% of 1936 R's, R-D	% of New Voters, D
Approve†	7 (978)	23 (131)	83 (242)
Disapprove	69 (202)	1 (529)	16 (134)
No opinion	22 (269)	6 (170)	60 (130)

*AIPO 215K&T, 10-9-40.

†In this survey the schedule was split and the question was put in a slightly different form in the K and T versions. One question form was: "Do you think the Roosevelt administration has done a good job, or a poor job, in handling the farm problem in this country?" The other was: "In general do you approve or disapprove of the Roosevelt administration's program for helping farmers?" The "approve" version drew 50 per cent approval; the "good" version found only 42 per cent who thought the administration had done a good job. The two surveys are consolidated in this analysis.

TABLE 7

Switches in Presidential Voting Preference, 1936–1940, in Relation to
Response to Question: "Do you think the Wagner Labor Act
should be revised, repealed or left unchanged?"*

Response	% of 1936 D's, D-R	% of 1936 R's, R-D	% of New Voters, D
Revised	24 (193)	3 (258)	59 (90)
Repealed	52 (42)	3 (77)	†
Left unchanged	12 (376)	12 (91)	64 (106)
No opinion	22 (497)	5 (283)	59 (192)

*AIPO 215K&T, 10-9-40. The analysis is limited to those who said they had "heard of" the Wagner Act.

†Only 9 respondents fell in this cell; one reported a Democratic preference.

modification of the act. The only way to fulfill that hope was to defeat Roosevelt. The electorate responded predictably to the impact of the issue. Of the 1936 Democrats who had come to believe that the act should be repealed (which, in the context of the times, was an antilabor move) about one out of two expressed a 1940 Republican preference. Those who thought it should merely be revised defected only about half as frequently. Similarly, Republican loyalties were maintained most steadfastly by those who stood for repeal or revision of the act. Interestingly, in our sample of 1936 nonvoters only nine respondents turned up favoring the repeal of the act; eight of the nine preferred Willkie. Withal, vote switches occurred in

directions consistent with the assumption that voters were moved by a rational calculation of the instrumental impact of their vote. The detailed data are in Table 7.[7]

Roosevelt's candidacy in 1940 ran counter to the two-term tradition, a fact that agitated the citizenry, especially those who opposed him on other grounds any-

[7]The labor issue had begun to take its toll of 1936 Democratic voters by the time of the congressional election of 1938. A survey during the congressional campaign asked: "Do you think the National Labor Relations Board is fair to businessmen and other employers?" Among 1936 Democratic presidential voters who thought the board unfair, 31 per cent favored Republican congressional candidates; among those who thought it fair, only 14 per cent did so. AIPO 135, 10-8-38.

TABLE 8

Switches in Presidential Voting Preference, 1936–1940,
in Relation to Views of Third-Term Question*

Views	% of 1936 D's, D-R	% of 1936 R's, R-D	% of New Voters, D
Silly and outworn tradition	5 (521)	14 (56)	83 (98)
Not good, but exceptions	8 (1,390)	20 (243)	15 (369)
Under no condition	88 (332)	0.3 (989)	5 (189)
Don't know	15 (59)	4 (23)	68 (28)

*Based on Roper survey, October 1940. The question was:
"With which of these statements concerning a third term do you come closest to agreeing?
"a) The idea that a President should not hold office for three terms is a silly and outworn tradition.
"b) While it may not generally be a good idea for a President to serve three terms, there should be no rule at a time of national crisis.
"c) Never under any conditions should a President hold office for three terms."

way. And probably those who supported him on other grounds declined in an especial degree to become exercised about the third-term question. In any case, the great shifts of the electorate had a close relationship to attitude on the third-term question, as may be seen from Table 8. Of the 1936 Democrats who felt that under no condition should a President serve three terms, nearly 90 per cent moved over to a Republican preference in 1940. On the other hand, 1936 Republicans who became 1940 Democrats tended to hold moderate views on the third-term matter. They could see the necessity for exceptions. These relations do not, of course, establish that persons opposed to a third term in principle defected from the Democracy [sic] for that reason. An alternative assumption is that they adopted that position because they chose to defect from the Democracy [sic]. Whatever its origin, the congruence of outlook on the constitutional issue and the direction of the vote is of importance, and it is not unreasonable to suppose that a goodly number of persons may very well have been governed in their candidate choice by their policy outlook.

The opinion surveys during the campaigns of 1944 and of 1948 included few inquiries suitable for the identification of policy-related movements of voters in those elections. From the behavior of persons of different economic and occupational status (presented earlier in Tables 1 and 2) it is a fair assumption that patterns quite similar to those of 1940 prevailed in 1948 and probably to a lesser extent in 1944 when war muted to some extent the divisive issues of domestic policy.[8] One relevant analysis from the 1948 election appears in Table 9, which presents our familiar pattern of switching in its relation to views on the question whether the laws governing labor unions were too strict or not strict enough. By 1948 the Wagner Act had been revised by the Taft-Hartley Act to the disadvantage of unions. The AFL and CIO exerted themselves in

[8]Unhappiness with wartime economic controls doubtless contributed to Democratic defections in 1944. In a 1944 survey the following question was put: "After the war in Europe is over, should the following government controls be continued or discontinued? a) Food rationing? b) Gasoline rationing? c) Price ceilings on things people buy?" The D-R percentages among "continued" and "discontinued" groups of 1940 Democratic voters were: a) 15 and 20; b) 12 and 21; c) 16 and 21. AIPO 331, 10–6–44.

TABLE 9

Switches in Presidential Vote, 1944–1948, in Relation to Response to Question:
"As things stand today, do you think the laws governing labor unions
are too strict or not strict enough?"*

Response	% of 1944 D's, D-R	% of 1944 R's, R-D	% of New Voters, D
Too strict	8 (304)	22 (76)	74 (80)
About right	15 (357)	9 (218)	68 (118)
Not strict enough	27 (232)	6 (318)	51 (87)
No opinion	15 (181)	10 (101)	64 (58)

*Based on AIPO 432, 11-1-48. Interviews were conducted after the election; the date is the "send-out" date.

support of Harry S Truman who urged repeal of the act, a position which by now had become a prolabor position. The evidence from this question supports the conventional view that the campaign of 1948 shaped antagonisms along New Deal and anti-New Deal lines. Those few Dewey supporters of 1944 who felt that labor laws were too strict deserted to Truman at a rate of about one of five in 1948. On the other hand, 1944 Roosevelt supporters who thought the labor laws not strict enough switched to Dewey with somewhat higher frequency, as the table indicates.

As the campaign of 1940 approached, the threat of war preoccupied the pundits and the commentators, who doubtless communicated their anxieties to the public. Yet the promises made and expectations raised by the candidates with respect to foreign policy seemed to have far less bearing on the vote than did questions of domestic policy. For a time foreign policy seemed to have been taken out of the campaign, but as the election neared, Willkie, under the prodding of the Republican professionals, stirred up the issue by his forecasts that war would soon come if Roosevelt were re-elected. Democratic campaigners probably became more worried about these charges than did the electorate generally.[9] At any rate, the data in-

dicate a comparatively mild relation between attitudes on foreign policy and vote shifting.

The question whether it was more important to keep out of war ourselves or to help England even at the risk of getting into war should have separated persons into the two conflicting camps of the time. Though more of those who thought that we should keep out of war deserted to Willkie, the difference between this figure and the rate of desertion of those who thought we should help England win (Table 10) was not wide enough to indicate that this difference in attitude contributed nearly so heavily to vote switching as did the impact of domestic issues. Similarly, a person's views on the question whether we should have gotten into World War I might be expected to segregate those of isolationist sentiment from their opponents. Those 1936 Democrats who thought our World War I venture was a mistake shifted to Willkie more frequently than did those who held an opposing view; yet again the difference (Table 11) was relatively small.

This is not to say that foreign policy questions invariably command less attention than do domestic questions. Rather in 1940 this seemed to be the case. Probably the more general rule is that the electorate responds most markedly and most clearly to those events it has experienced and observed, vicariously or directly. Voters had enjoyed or not enjoyed eight

---

[9] On this aspect of the 1940 campaign, see R. E. Sherwood, *Roosevelt and Hopkins* (New York: Bantam, 1950), ch. 8.

TABLE 10

Switches in Presidential Voting Preference, 1936–1940, in Relation to Opinions
on Whether More Important to Keep Out of War or to Help England Win*

Attitude	% of 1936 D's, D-R	% of 1936 R's, R-D	% of New Voters, D
Keep out of war	31 (1,975)	3 (1,127)	56 (724)
Help England win	19 (2,426)	5 (1,211)	61 (653)
No choice	25 (166)	0 (76)	72 (68)

*A consolidation of AIPO 217, 10-22-40; 220, 10-22-40; 224, 11-19-40.
Note that a post-election survey is combined with two pre-election surveys. The
question was: "Which of these two things do you think is the more important
for the United States to try to do: 1. To keep out of war ourselves, 2. To help
England win, even at the risk of getting into war." The schedules carried the
"no choice" box, though the meaning of this response is unclear.

TABLE 11

Switches in Presidential Vote, 1936–1940, in Relation to Response to Question:
"Do you think it was a mistake for the United States
to enter the last World War?"*

Response	% of 1936 D's, D-R	% of 1936 R's, R-D	% of New Voters, D
Yes, mistake	28 (511)	4 (382)	49 (140)
No	18 (636)	5 (322)	64 (154)
No opinion	20 (258)	6 (118)	67 (108)

*AIPO 224, 11-19-40.

years of domestic policy of the New Deal
and they reacted demonstrably to those
experiences. The prospects for the future
may generally tend less to engage the
voter or to govern his actions. Those prospects tend to be hazy, uncertain, problematic. Voters may respond most assuredly
to what they have seen, heard, experienced. Forecasts, promises, predicted disaster, or pie in the sky may be less moving.

A kind word needs to be said for that
supposedly benighted fellow, the standpatter, the consistent party voter. So far
our attention has centered on the switcher.
The evidence indicates that the shifting
voter is far more numerous than is commonly supposed. Moreover, his reports of
his actions and attitudes indicate that as
he navigates his way from party to party
he moves in a manner that is sensible in
the light of his policy preferences. To be
sure, partisan loyalties invest the electoral

mass with a degree of inertia and not all
voters follow their policy inclinations by
moving from candidate to candidate.[10]
What of these voters who remain in the
party ranks from election to election? Are
they obtuse diehards who swallow their
principles to stick by their party?

Almost all the analyses of the preceding pages throw light on the question.
On issue after issue those with views consistent with the outlook of their party

[10]The data used in this study permit no analyses to ascertain the relation between consistent
party support and the sense of party identification
which has been extensively examined by Angus
Campbell and his associates of the Survey Research Center of the University of Michigan.
Doubtless the standpatters of our tables who resist the pull of their policy inclinations toward
the opposite party include large numbers of
"strong" party identifiers, that is, persons who
regard themselves as "strong" Republicans or
Democrats in their responses to interviewers of
the Survey Research Center.

stood pat in their voting preference. Notably few Republican defections occurred among those who subscribed to sound Republican doctrine. Democratic deserters were uniformly fewest among those who concurred with the pure and orthodox Democratic tenets of the time. No doubt some Republicans and some Democrats adjusted their views to make them conform with their perceptions of the positions of their party. Yet it is the parallelism of vote and policy view that is significant for our analysis, not its origin.

The facts seem to be that, on the average, the standpatters do not have to behave as mugwumps to keep their consciences clear; they are already where they ought to be in the light of their policy attitudes. Tables 12, 13, and 14 demonstrate this point in another way.* Those who vote consistently from one election to the next, the data of those tables indicate, adhere to the party doctrine in high degree. Though partisan groupings of voters are not models of ideological purity, the standpatters of each party manifest fairly high agreement with the party positions as popularly perceived. Thus, well over half of the 1936–1940 D-D's felt that there should be during the next four years about the same degree or more government regulation. Similarly, the Administration's

---

*Editor's note: At this point Key planned to comment further on Tables 12, 13, and 14, and to stress how they differ from Table 11 and some of the other tables presented earlier in this chapter. These earlier tables focused attention on the percentages of persons interviewed who switched parties between two consecutive elections and the presidential preferences of new voters in relation to their position on specified policy questions. The earlier tables emphasized the policy preferences of voters who switched parties from one election to the next. Tables 12, 13, and 14 present data for all voters in each major party camp—new voters, standpatters, and switchers. They indicate the distribution of given policy preferences among each group of voters. Data presented in this form highlight the degree to which the standpatters tend to endorse doctrinal positions usually associated with the party they support.

farm program found favor with three fourths of the 1936–1940 D-D's, while only a little more than 10 per cent of the R-R's could bring themselves to approve it. Again far fewer of the 1944–1948 D-D's than of the 1944–1948 R-R's thought that the laws governing labor unions were too strict.[11]

Party switchers move towards the party whose standpatters they resemble in their policy views, a proposition made apparent by the tables. The D-R's are divided in their policy views in about the same fashion as the R-R's with whom they join in the election, and the R-D's resemble the D-D's to which they attach themselves for the voting. The nonvoters at the preceding election who join the D-D's or the R-R's also have an attitudinal resemblance to the standpatters with whom they ally themselves. Yet, as the tables also indicate, the switchers bear earmarks of their origin. The D-R's are not in quite the same degree as the R-R's attached to the party policy position, and the R-D's also bore traces of their Republican origin. Nevertheless, on balance each of these groups bore far greater resemblance to the standpatters of the party of their destination than to the faithful of the party of their origin.

One major problem remains to be touched on, if not disposed of. That is the

---

[11]Standpatters, the evidence suggests, acquire their policy attitudes in at least two ways. Some persons more or less deliberately affiliate with the party whose policy emphases appear to parallel their own. Other persons, psychologically identified with a party, adopt those policy outlooks espoused by the more prominent spokesmen of their party. In the course of party life, the acceptance of the cues of party leadership may result in alteration of the attitudes of party followers. This flexible conformity with shifting party doctrine probably occurs most markedly among those strongly identified psychologically with the party. See Angus Campbell and Homer C. Cooper, *Group Differences in Attitudes and Votes* (Ann Arbor, Mich.: Survey Research Center, 1956), pp. 102–4.

TABLE 12
Pattern of Presidential Preference, 1936–1940, in Relation to Distribution of Responses to Question: "During the next four years do you think there should be more or less regulation of business by the Federal government than at present?"*

Response	D-D	R-D	O-D†	O-R†	D-R	R-R
More regulation	32%	28%	34%	18%	13%	8%
About same	27	23	23	10	11	7
Less regulation	18	34	18	55	63	76
No opinion	23	15	25	17	13	9
	100	100	100	100	100	100
N‡	(2,386)	(85)	(403)	(285)	(660)	(1,619)

*A consolidation of AIPO 215K-T, 10-9-40, and 219K-T, 10-24-40 (as in Table 5).
†New voters, i.e., nonvoters in 1936.
‡As in all tables, the figures in parentheses, technically known as N, are the numbers of survey respondents on which the percentages are based. For example, 2,386 of those interviewed were Democratic standpatters (according to their replies) and 1,619 were Republican standpatters. Of these 1,619, only 8 per cent wanted more regulation of business.

TABLE 13
Patterns of Presidential Preference, 1936–1940, in Relation to Distribution of Views on Roosevelt Administration's Program for Handling Farm Problem*

Response	D-D	R-D	O-D†	O-R†	D-R	R-R
Approve	76%	64%	66%	19%	26%	13%
Disapprove	5	13	7	55	51	66
Don't know	18	21	26	25	22	20
No answer	1	2	1	1	1	1
	100	100	100	100	100	100
N	(1,191)	(47)	(305)	(207)	(274)	(795)

*Based on AIPO 215K&T, 10-9-40, as in Table 6, which see for the form of the question.
†Nonvoters in 1936.

TABLE 14
Patterns of Presidential Preference, 1944–1948, in Relation to Distribution of Responses to Question: "As things stand today, do you think the laws governing labor unions are too strict or not strict enough?"*

Response	D-D	R-D	O-D	O-R	D-R	R-R
Too strict	31%	26%	27%	17%	15%	9%
About right	33	31	36	31	31	31
Not strict enough	19	28	20	35	38	46
No opinion	17	15	17	17	16	14
	100	100	100	100	100	100
N	(909)	(65)	(220)	(123)	(165)	(648)

*Based on AIPO 432, 11-1-48, a post-election survey (interviews were conducted after the election; the date is the "send-out" date).

problem of the role of personality in the maintenance of the Democratic following during the 1930's and 1940's. How do we cope with the assertion that the series of Democratic victories reflected the massive appeal of the personality of Franklin Delano Roosevelt and nothing more? Even the most cursory reflection destroys this

TABLE 15

Switches in Presidential Voting Preference, 1936–1940, in Relation to
Response to Question: "If the U.S. should get into the war, which
man would you prefer to have as President—Roosevelt or Willkie?"*

Response	% of 1936 D's, D-R	% of 1936 R's, R-D	% of New Voters, D
Roosevelt	4 (1,158)	47 (59)	93 (341)
Willkie	97 (329)	† (717)	4 (157)
Undecided	51 (71)	0 (54)	45 (44)

*Based on AIPO 220, 10-22-40.
†Less than one half of 1 per cent; one respondent in this cell reported a shift to Roosevelt.

type of explanation in its crude form. It becomes ridiculous immediately if one contemplates what the fate of Franklin Delano Roosevelt would have been had he from 1933 to 1936 stood for those policies which were urged upon the country by the reactionaries of the day. Before 1932 acute political observers had seen him as only a pleasant country gentleman of the Hudson Valley who had a yearning to be president. He became, though, a formidable and wicked opponent to his enemies and a savior to those who regarded him as their champion. His position derived not so much from the kind of a man he was as from the kinds of things for which, and against which, he fought. His personal qualities may have intensified both hatred and love for him. And the popular image of Roosevelt doubtless enabled many persons to support and to oppose him without detailed knowledge of what policies he was for or against; they could accurately regard him as for or against their kind of people.

Neither our data nor the analytical tools of social science permit completely satisfactory appraisals of the place of personality in the determination of the vote. Nevertheless, some wisps of evidence—more or less tautological in nature—have a relevance to the question. In 1940 Dr. Gallup's interviewers asked the respondents in his sample: "If the United States should get into the war, which man would

you prefer to have as President—Roosevelt or Willkie?" To ask such a question might be thought to be about the same as to ask, "For whom, as of today, do you plan to vote?" Yet the question raised a perfectly legitimate problem, one to which the citizen should address himself if he is to perform his classical role of recording relevant and responsible decisions as he votes. What did the response to the vote indicate? Some, but not many, 1936 Landon voters opined that Roosevelt would, indeed, be the better man if we got into war, and about half of them, probably reluctantly, had decided to defect from the Republican ranks to support Roosevelt. On the other hand, a goodly number of 1936 Democratic voters liked what they saw in Willkie as a potential wartime leader; 97 per cent of them moved to the Republican side, as Willkie himself had done only a short time before. For the details see Table 15.

In 1944 the National Opinion Research Center put questions to a national sample which showed somewhat similar patterns of voter movement. At the time of this campaign one popular concern was the successful conclusion of World War II; moreover, some people were beginning to worry about the shape of public policy when peace came again. The NORC asked in October 1944: "Sometimes one man does a better job of handling certain problems than another man. Do you think

TABLE 16

Switches in Presidential Voting Preference, 1940–1944, in Relation to Response to Question: "Sometimes one man does a better job of handling certain problems than another man. Do you think Roosevelt or Dewey would do a better job of winning the war?"*

Response	% of 1940 D's, D-R	% of 1940 R's, R-D	% of New Voters, D
Roosevelt	6 (828)	35 (114)	87 (144)
Dewey	90 (29)	0 (257)	3 (29)
No difference	44 (100)	3 (335)	12 (48)
Don't know	45 (29)	0 (56)	21 (14)

*NORC 30/229, October 1944.

TABLE 17

Switches in Presidential Voting Preference, 1940–1944, in Relation to Response to Question: "Sometimes one man does a better job of handling certain problems than another man. Do you think Roosevelt or Dewey would do a better job of providing jobs after the war?"*

Response	% of 1940 D's, D-R	% of 1940 R's, R-D	% of New Voters, D
Roosevelt	3 (747)	52 (63)	93 (124)
Dewey	82 (88)	1 (556)	1 (69)
No difference	25 (73)	12 (92)	42 (19)
Don't know	24 (74)	2 (49)	41 (22)

*NORC 30/229, October 1944.

Roosevelt or Dewey would do a better job of winning the war?" A very few 1940 Democrats had arrived at the conclusion that Dewey could do a better job of winding up hostilities; most of them switched to Republican in 1944. A much larger number of Willkie voters of 1940 felt obliged to concede that Roosevelt was a better man for this particular job. About a third of them had decided to vote for him, while their fellow Republicans who saw merit in Mr. Dewey stood almost to a man with the G.O.P. The exact figures appear in Table 16. The same survey put a question on whether Dewey or Roosevelt would do better at "providing jobs after the war." The familiar movements and countermovements in consonance with voter judgments on this issue occurred, as Table 17 indicates.

For those who have persevered to this point, a few preliminary reflections on the significance of the information so far assembled are in order. We have established patterns of movement of party switchers from election to election and the patterns of stability of the standpatter that lead us to a conception of the voter that is not often propounded. From our analyses the voter emerges as a person who appraises the actions of government, who has policy preferences and who relates his vote to those appraisals and preferences. One may have misgivings about the data and one can certainly concede that the data also indicate that some voters are governed by blind party loyalty and that some others respond automatically to the winds of the environment of the moment. Yet the obtrusive feature of the data is the large number of persons whose vote is instrumental to their policy preferences.

These parallelisms of voting patterns and policy preferences may be dismissed as the meaningless result of the disposition of people to adopt consistent sets of views on interrelated matters. A survey respondent, bedeviled by an interviewer, may express a preference for a Democratic candidate and then, to keep things tidy, adopt a favorable attitude toward Democratic policy positions. He would, though, in our analysis fit into the same pigeonhole of the IBM sorter as the person who arrived at the same consistent constellation of attitudes by a process of anguished thought and reflection. Doubtless both kinds of respondents are encountered by poll interviewers. Yet, however these patterns of consistent voting preferences are formed, they can scarcely be regarded as without political significance. Our correlations, though, should not be taken to mean that the policy attitudes correlated with changes and continuities in voting preference necessarily cause those changes or continuities. Rather they demonstrate the tendency of persons to build up combinations of outlooks and to adopt voting preferences that make sense in the light of those outlooks.

In another direction our data throw light on the interactions between government and public and on the functions of the electorate in the democratic process. A notable element of our tables is the extent to which an Administration seems to lose the votes of its erstwhile supporters who dissent from actions it has taken. The tables seem to verify the journalistic superstition that the people only vote against; never, for. That appearance results in part from the manner in which the facts have been presented; an equally strong case could be made for the proposition that the standpatters stand pat because they are for what has been done. Nevertheless, the fact remains that some

erstwhile supporters do vote against and they tend to disagree with actions that have been taken. Few erstwhile enemies are attracted to a dominant party by its actions, though some are. A president may, with justification, be anxious lest a projected action draw down his reservoir of popular good will. He cannot proceed on the assumption that inaction will maintain the loyalty of the faithful by antagonizing no one. Yet to govern he must be prepared to expend some of his good will. And to continue to govern he must attempt to offset those losses by policies that attract support from the opposition or from among the new voters. *

The patterns of flow of the major streams of shifting voters graphically reflect the electorate in its great, and perhaps principal, role as an appraiser of past events, past performance, and past actions. It judges retrospectively; it commands prospectively only insofar as it expresses either approval or disapproval of that which has happened before. Voters may reject what they have known; or they may approve what they have known. They are not likely to be attracted in great numbers by promises of the novel or unknown. Once innovation has occurred they may embrace it, even though they would have, earlier, hesitated to venture forth to welcome it.

These tendencies of the electorate, as they obtrude from our many tables, make plain how completely the minority party is a captive of the majority—and of the situation. Critics of the American party system fret because the minority party does not play the role of an imaginative advocate heralding the shape of a new world. In truth, it gains votes most notably

*Editor's Note: At this point Key intended to elaborate on this "maintenance process"—stressing both the importance to the governing party of maintaining the loyalty of its previous supporters and its need to win converts from the opposition and additional new support among the new voters.

from among those groups who are disappointed by, who disapprove of, or who regard themselves as injured by, the actions of the Administration. The opposition can maximize its strength as it centers its fire on those elements of the Administration program disliked by the largest numbers of people. Thus, as a matter of practical politics, it must appear to be a common scold rather than a bold exponent of innovation, though it may propose new (or old) approaches to old questions. The misfortunes of the Republicans over the period 1932–1952 sprang essentially from the simple fact that they could not lay their hands on an issue on which the Democrats had outraged enough people to vote them out of office.

SECTION II

The Competitive Political Parties Model

In the first selection of this section R. M. MacIver gives an excellent summary of the dynamics of the competitive political parties model. If this model accounts for the proper functioning of government, several relationships must hold; and the included selections assess one or more of these relationships. Thus, if the political parties do serve as organizers of opinion, as MacIver suggests, and the voter only needs to find the party whose positions are most in line with his own and then vote for that party's candidates, there should be consistency of opinion within the party and between these opinions and the votes of the elected members of the party. V. O. Key, Jr. shows a strong relationship between the ideological direction of a congressman's vote, whether it is liberal or conservative, and his political party. He also roughly assesses the agreement between constituency opinion and its congressman's opinion, which would be expected if the linkage were functioning.

Like the rational-activist model, the competitive political parties model expects the public to be attentive to the decisions made by their representatives and to vote their satisfaction or dissatisfaction. But in seeking to assess the public's possession of ". . . basic information about the parties and their party program" Donald Stokes and Warren Miller find the congressman generally need not concern himself with his constituency's reaction to his votes because ". . . his constituency isn't looking."

Certainly, if competition between political parties is vital to the performance of government, we would expect that policies enacted in a political system with competing political parties would differ from those enacted in a system dominated by one party. But Richard Hofferbert shows ". . . the nature of the party system and its operation do not seem to go very far toward explaining the kind of policies produced in the states." If the presence or absence of the dynamics of the model leave policy largely unaffected, the model must be of little relevance.

The competitive political parties model conceives of the parties as marketing policy positions in hope of public support. We know from the various voting studies that the average Democrat does differ from a Republican in the policies he supports and that a child generally adopts the party of his parents. But do people become Democrats because they support the policies of that party; do they take the party of their parents because they share the opinions of their parents; or, more disturbingly, do they take the label Democrat and then adopt the policy positions of that party? Arthur Goldberg's causal analysis stresses the

77

seminal importance of political party identification.[1] Although people do vote their political attitudes to some degree, their party identification causes them to have these attitudes and independently causes them to vote as they do. The political parties can hardly be called the summarizers of opinion but seem primarily to be the formulators of opinion; as such, the public is afforded little control of their leaders by way of choosing among political parties.

[1]This technique may be beyond the technical competences of many readers, and I can hardly expect to give a complete understanding in so brief a space, but the idea underlying this analysis is not too difficult. Perhaps we are concerned with peoples' political party identification, their political attitudes, and their vote. If the nature of one's political party identification causes him to have certain political attitudes and in turn to vote for a certain party as shown below, rather than political party directly causing him to vote as he does, removing the effects

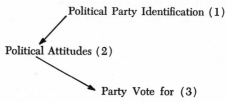

of political attitudes on how people vote should result in no relationship between their party identification and their vote. In other words if we look only at persons of liberal persuasion we should not find that those who are Republicans vote less for the Democratic party (more technically $r_{13.2}$ should equal 0). If the data do not yield such results, we must conclude that the model as shown is incorrect in some respect.

THE IMPORTANCE OF POLITICAL PARTIES*

Robert M. MacIver

ORGANIZATION OF OPINION

It is not our purpose in this book to discuss the mechanics of government, except where the discussion is of primary importance for the understanding of its functioning or its development. On this ground it is desirable to examine certain features of the democratic structure. Democracy differs from all other forms of government in that it postulates the free organization of opposing opinions. This

*Reprinted with permission of The Macmillan Company from *The Web of Government* by Robert M. MacIver. Copyright © Robert M. MacIver 1965.

kind of organization presents some peculiar features and has to solve some peculiar problems. The organization of opinion is a very different matter from the organization of power.

When we speak here of the organization of opinion we are not referring to the way in which governments, by the control of propaganda, by intimidation, and by various other devices, seek to maintain political orthodoxy and to suppress criticism. Such methods are anti-democratic. We are referring to the modes by which variant opinions find political expression, to the systems under which conflicting opinions are elicited, registered, channeled, and brought to bear on government, and to the devices by which government is made responsive to the trends and tides of opinion.

In every modern democracy the major political vehicle of opinion is the party. Although party is often "extra-constitutional" it is an essential organ of every large-scale democracy. Until quite recently the role of party in democracy was curiously ignored. David Hume wrote two interesting short essays on parties, in one of which he distinguished parties from *interest,* parties from *affection,* and parties from *principle,* remarking that "parties from *principle,* especially abstract speculative principle, are known only to modern times, and are, perhaps, the most extraordinary and unaccountable *phenomena* that have yet appeared in human affairs." But he was content merely to deplore the portentous phenomenon, and generally, until near the end of the nineteenth century, the treatment of parties by writers on government was casual, curt, and rather derogatory. Mill could write, in 1861, a work, *Representative Government,* in which he paid not the slightest attention to the party system. There was no systematic study devoted to the subject until Ostrogorski published in 1902 a fine analysis of parties in the United States.

Are political parties then so modern an invention? Were there not parties in Ancient Greece, such as the parties respectively of the mountain, of the plain, and of the coast in Attica? What of the patricians and plebians of Rome, and later its democrats and republicans? What of the medieval Guelphs and Ghibellines, the Catholic and Protestant parties in France, the English cavaliers and roundheads, and so forth? Opposing groups of this sort have existed everywhere at all times, but they are not properly denominated political parties. The old word "faction" is more applicable to them. They were not groups organized for electoral purposes within a political framework that recognized and provided for their existence. Under the

Athenian democracy there were groups which rallied to the principles and policies of a leader, but these groups did not establish any continuous organizations and therefore can hardly be called parties in our sense. There was no party-system. The first clear development of a party-system occurred in England in the eighteenth century, though there were approaches to it in the seventeenth, and it was not until the nineteenth century that party-systems took their characteristic forms.

.   .   .   .

Those who, in the name of democracy, have deplored the existence of parties or even advocated their abolition, from Madison to such modern writers as Herbert Croly in his *Progressive Democracy,* have failed to realize that the party-system is an essential mechanism of democracy. Public opinion is too variant and dispersive to be effective unless it is organized. It must be canalized on the broad lines of some major division of opinion. Party focuses the issues, sharpens the differences between the contending sides, eliminates confusing cross-currents of opinion. Each party formulates its platform, grooms and selects its candidates, enables the public to make its choice between sufficiently distinct alternatives. The party educates the public while seeking merely to influence it, for it must appeal on the grounds of policy. For the same reason it helps to remove the inertia of the public and thus to broaden the range of public opinion. In short the party, in its endeavors to win the public to its side, however unscrupulous it may be in its modes of appeal, is making the democratic system workable. It is the agency by which public opinion is translated into public policy.

At the same time the party-system maintains the responsibility of the government to the people. Here the distinctive quality of democracy is most apparent. For the democratic government not only suffers the opposition to express itself and to organize its forces but provides it with particular facilities, sometimes even, as in the British and Canadian systems, giving a quasi-ministerial status—and a salary—to the leader of the opposition. There could be no more signal illustration of the difference between the oligarchical and the democratic spirit. The opposition is an ever vigilant critic of the government, searching out the weaknesses of its hold on the public and forever compelling it to defend and justify its policies before the court of public opinion.

In this way the party-system brings political issues down to the man in the street. No doubt it does so at a price. Often it debases the issues and raises false ones. The object of the party is to persuade or to cajole the voter. On some levels it stoops to the pettiest tricks and does not shrink from direct or indirect corruption. In every community there are many people who are so engrossed in their private interests or problems that they give no heed to larger affairs; others again have no understanding of political situations, and their emotions are responsive to the cheap appeals of those who play on them. The votes of morons count equally with the votes of the discerning. This fact is sometimes made the ground of an indictment of democracy. A more balanced judgment would recognize that this defect is not overcome by other systems of government, since they too must hold the allegiance of the multitude and since by suppressing criticism they stifle the educational process that raises the general level of political intelligence. The dangers arising from mass ignorance and prejudice reach their height not under democracy but under the totalitarian "one-party" system, where the monopoly of indoctrination exercises a hypnotic influence that for a time affects not only the morons but all except the hardiest and most independent spirits.

In order that the party-system may work effectively it must reduce the multitudinous differences of opinion to rela-

tively simple alternatives. This is done most easily under the two-party system, where the voters must choose between two ostensibly antithetical platforms. The party-system originated in the opposing fronts of two parties, but while this type prevailed for centuries in England it has been superseded or greatly modified, except in the United States of America and a few other countries, by a more elaborate diversification. One main reason for the change has been the growth of left-wing parties, which in turn tend to split into separate units. Under certain conditions, particularly where there is a strong and relatively prosperous middle class, this process has been held in check, so that there exist usually three main parties, as in England, in Canada, in Australia, in Belgium, and elsewhere. In most European countries the process has gone much further, resulting in a multiple party-system which differs in very important respects from either the dual or the triple party structure.

The multiple-party system works through the agreement of blocs to set up a coalition government, since no one party can claim a majority. The blocs are unstable, their components readily enter into new combinations, and consequently governments based on them are less securely established than under the two-party system. Under the latter system the alternative to the existing government is clearly known in advance. Under the multiple-party system it frequently remains uncertain, depending on last-hour deals between the various groups. The two-party system consequently gives to the government a more unified authority and a greater concentration of responsibility. On the other hand, where there are only two parties to choose between, it is more difficult for public opinion to formulate and express 'itself on new or changing issues. And the party "machine" is likely to exercise greater control. It has greater influence over candidates, over appointments, and over the spoils of office.

ROLL-CALL VOTES AND CONSTITUENCY OPINION*

V. O. Key, Jr.

Most of the time the elegant prose spilled over the question of whether a legislator should be a man and vote his mature convictions in the national interest or be a mouse and bow abjectly to the parochial demands of his constituents is irrelevant to the realities. Few of his constituents have even the slightest awareness of most of the questions on which the legislator must stand up and be counted. On those few issues about which awareness is widespread among his constituents, he usually has no trustworthy estimate of the distribution of opinions of his constituents. In some districts on some issues the legislator may know well enough what opinion is. A southern congressman from a predominantly Negro district may have no doubt that his supporters—that is, the whites—oppose federal intervention in race relations. Such instances of clarity of opinion, however, are relatively few among all the questions a legislator must consider. On the same issue, the congressman from a northern, white constituency may vote in the opposite way from his southern colleague, though usually he has no reliable information on the attitudes of his constituency. Generally, a legislator may hear from a few people on a few issues. He must always, as he votes, assume the risk of antagonizing some constituents, but he is rarely faced by the difficult choice of rejecting or accepting the mandate of his constituency, for he does not know what it is. And, indeed, there may be none.

LEGISLATIVE VOTES AND IMPUTED CONSTITUENCY ATTITUDES

The sketchiness of knowledge about constituency opinion creates its embarrassments for any discussion of the relation between the voting of legislators and the attitudes of the people of their districts. Sampling the opinions of a congressional district—so strange are the properties of survey methods—amounts to almost as great a task as sampling the people of the nation. Hence, given the data now available, any treatment of how any representative links opinion in his constituency to the governing process must be less than exact. Political analysts approach the problem chiefly by indirection. They ascertain demographic characteristics of legislative districts. They reason that people of specified characteristics—industrial workers, for example—ought to have a specified outlook toward a given legislative issue. Therefore, it is concluded, a representative reflects the opinion of his district if he takes a position in harmony with the opinion imputed to a majority of his constituents. The frailty of the analysis rests in the fact that people's opinions often are not the same as those imputed to them. Nevertheless, on some kinds of issue this type of analysis yields plausible results and is, in reality, about the only sort of information that is available on the relation between representative and constituency.[1]

*From *Public Opinion and American Democracy* by V. O. Key, Jr. (pp. 482–86). Copyright © 1961 by V. O. Key, Jr. Reprinted by permission of Alfred A. Knopf, Inc.

[1]Warren E. Miller, of the Survey Research Center of the University of Michigan, has under way an analysis of the relation between legislators' roll-call votes and attitudes of their constituents as measured by a 1958 national survey.

One method to check the relations between constituents and representatives without the necessity of imputing opinions to constituents is to make global comparisons of party groups in the electorate and in the representative body. That method has its obvious shortcomings because we cannot connect representative A with constituency A'. Yet it has its uses. Opinion surveys show that, on the average, Democrats and Republicans in the country as a whole differ on questions of domestic economic policy. If the voting records of members of the House of Representatives resemble the outlook of the people who elected them, we should expect Republican legislators to differ from Democratic legislators in their voting records on issues of domestic economic policy. In fact, given the tendency for leadership echelons to espouse group doctrines in an especially pure form, we should expect wider differences to prevail between the two groups of legislators than between their supporters in the electorate.

Such comparisons of the voting records of Republicans and of Democrats in the House of Representatives are commonplace; they show the expected concentration of Republicans toward the conservative end of the scale and of Democrats toward the opposite end. A specimen of this type of distribution appears in Figure 1, which arrays Democratic and Republican members of the House on an index built of their votes on ten roll calls in 1955 and 1956. The *New Republic* characterized the votes on each of these roll calls by a plus or a minus, depending on whether it coincided with that journal's position. While the resulting index is not a work of psychometric art, it is a serviceable separator of persons of contrasting political outlooks.[2] The distribution of House members on the scale in Figure 1

---

[2]For its use in this context the index is also marred by the fact that it includes three roll calls on foreign policy and one on civil rights. For the items included in the index, see the compilation in *New Republic*, October 15, 1956.

FIGURE 1
Distribution of House Members, by Party, on Roll-Call Index Constructed from 1956 Votes Rated by New Republic

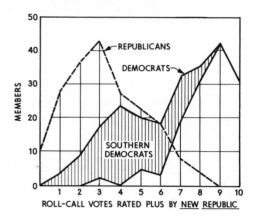

conforms to expectations built on the assumption that legislators will differ as their constituencies differ. In another respect, though, the relations diverge from such expectations. In the figure, southern Democrats are shown separate from Democrats generally, and they manifest a less-liberal average record than do nonsouthern Democrats, which results in part from the inclusion in the index of a roll call on civil rights. Southerners, as was shown earlier, do not have a markedly more conservative outlook than people elsewhere. The divergence of southern Democratic members may have a partial explanation in the low levels of political participation of persons disposed to be liberal in outlook; these legislators may lean toward their politically active constituents rather than toward their constituents generally.

Such a contrast between groups of voters and groups of legislators does not tell us much about the relation between representative A and his own constituents in district A'. A second stage in the analysis, which involves the imputation of opinions to types of constituents, will take us a step nearer to the demonstration of communion between representative and constituent. In Figure 1 Republican Representatives are spread rather widely along the index of liberalism. What kinds of districts do the more liberal Republicans come from? The *Congressional Quarterly Almanac* has obligingly fitted the census data to congressional districts and classified them into these four groups:

I, primarily rural districts with no city of over 25,000;

II, small-town districts, with no city over 50,000;

III, mid-urban districts, "substantially influenced" by a city of from 50,000 to 200,000; and

IV, metropolitan districts, with cities of 200,000 or over or within such cities.

These categories cannot be related to our opinion data, but earlier tabulations of survey data indicated that a cutting point of 50,000 tended to mark fairly sharp differences in opinion beween places of different population size. If Republican Representatives resemble their constituents, we should expect the Republicans from metropolitan districts to rank higher, on the average, on the index in Figure 1 than Republicans from rural districts, and that is in fact the case. The percentages of those Republicans from each type of district with index scores of four or more are as follows:

District Type	*Per Cent of Representatives with Score of 4 or More*
I	22%
II	24
III	43
IV	57

Expectations about the relations of the voting records of Democratic Representatives and the character of the constituency would be the same—namely, that Representatives from metropolitan districts would rank higher on the index more frequently than would Democrats from rural districts. Though this is true, the contrast is more marked among nonsouthern Democrats than among all Democrats. The percentages of nonsouthern Democrats from each of the types of district with scores of eight or more on the index are as follows:

District Type	*Per Cent of Representatives with Score of 8 or More*
I	59%
II	59
III	81
IV	90

These tabulations make the relationship between the constituency and the vote of its Representative in Congress far more simple than it is. The limitations of constituency characteristics in the explanation of the vote are apparent in the figures themselves. If we had a measure of determinative constituency opinion, we should expect, for example, all our rural Democrats to rank at 0 on the scale and all the metropolitan Democrats to place at 10. From the data we have, however, about all that can be concluded is that constituency opinion—as inferred from the particular demographic characteristics—is only one of a complex of factors that bear on a legislator's vote.

PARTY GOVERNMENT AND THE SALIENCY OF CONGRESS*

Donald E. Stokes and Warren E. Miller

Any mid-term congressional election raises pointed questions about party government in America. With the personality of the President removed from the ballot by at least a coattail, the public is free to pass judgment on the legislative record of the parties. So the civics texts would have us believe. In fact, however, an off-year election can be regarded as an assessment of the parties' record in Congress only if the electorate possesses certain minimal information about what that record is. The fact of possession needs to be demonstrated, not assumed, and the low visibility of congressional affairs to many citizens suggests that the electorate's actual information should be examined with care.

How much the people know is an important, if somewhat hidden, problem of the normative theory of representation. Implicitly at least, the information the public is thought to have is one of the points on which various classical conceptions of representation divide. Edmund Burke and the liberal philosophers, for example—to say nothing of Hamilton and Jefferson—had very different views about the information the public could get or use in assessing its government. And the periods of flood tide in American democracy, especially the Jacksonian and Pro-

gressive eras, have been marked by the most optimistic assumptions as to what the people could or did know about their government. To put the matter another way: any set of representative institutions will work very differently according to the amount and quality of information the electorate has. This is certainly true of the institutional forms we associate with government by responsible parties. A necessary condition of party responsibility to the people is that the public have basic information about the parties and their legislative record. Without it, no institutional devices can make responsibility a fact.

To explore the information possessed by those who play the legislative and constituent roles in American government, the Survey Research Center of the University of Michigan undertook an interview study of Congressmen and their districts during the mid-term election of Eisenhower's second term. Immediately after the 1958 campaign the Center interviewed a nationwide sample of the electorate, clustered in 116 congressional districts, as well as the incumbent Congressmen and other major-party candidates for the House from the same collection of districts.[1] Through these direct interviews

*From *Public Opinion Quarterly*, Vol. XXVI (Winter 1962) pp. 531–46. Reprinted by permission of the Princeton University Press, copyright owners.

The research from which this report is drawn was supported by grants of the Rockefeller Foundation and the Social Science Research Council. The authors also gratefully acknowledge the skilled assistance of Ralph Bisco, Jon Faily, Julie Crowder, and Arthur Wolfe.

[1]The 116 districts are a probability sample of all constituencies, although the fact that the study was piggy-backed onto a four-year panel study of the electorate extending over the elections of 1956, 1958, and 1960 made the design of the 1958 representation sample unusually complex. In particular, since metropolitan areas and nonmetropolitan counties or groups of counties, rather than congressional districts, were used as primary sampling units when the panel sample

with the persons playing the reciprocal roles of representative government, this research has sought careful evidence about the perceptual ties that bind, or fail to bind, the Congressman to his party and district. We will receive some of this evidence here for the light that it throws on the problem of party cohesion and responsibility in Congress.

THE RESPONSIBLE-PARTY MODEL AND THE AMERICAN CASE

What the conception of government by responsible parties requires of the general public has received much less attention than what it requires of the legislative and electoral parties.[2] The notion of responsibility generally is understood to mean that the parties play a mediating role between the public and its government, making popular control effective by developing rival programs of government action that

are presented to the electorate for its choice. The party whose program gains the greater support takes possession of the government and is held accountable to the public in later elections for its success in giving its program effect.

Two assumptions about the role of the public can be extracted from these ideas. *First,* in a system of party government the electorate's attitude toward the parties is based on what the party programs are and how well the parties have delivered on them. The public, in a word, gives the parties *programmatic* support. And, in view of the importance that legislative action is likely to have in any party program, such support is formed largely out of public reaction to the legislative performance of the parties, especially the party in power.

Second, under a system of party government the voters' response to the local legislative candidates is based on the candidates' identification with party programs. These programs are the substance of their appeals to the constituency, which will act on the basis of its information about the proposals and legislative record of the parties. Since the party programs are of dominant importance, the candidates are deprived of any independent basis of support. They will not be able to build in their home districts an electoral redoubt from which to challenge the leadership of their parties.[3]

How well do these assumptions fit the behavior of the American public as it

---

was originated in 1956, the districts represented in our 1958 sample did not have equal probability of selection and the efficiency of the sample of districts was somewhat less than that of a simple random sample of equal size. Descriptions of the sample design may be obtained from the Survey Research Center.

[2]For example, the 1950 report of the American Political Science Association's Committee on Political Parties, the closest approach to an official statement of the responsible-party view as applied to American politics, concentrates on the organization of Congress and the national parties and deals only very obliquely with the role of the public. See *Toward a More Responsible Two-party System* (New York: Rinehart), 1950. In general, theoretical and empirical treatments of party government have focused more on the nature of party *appeals*—especially the question of whether the parties present a real "choice"—than on the cognitive and motivational elements that should be found in the *response* of an electorate that is playing its correct role in a system of responsible-party government. For example, see the excellent discussion in Austin Ranney and Wilmoore Kendall, *Democracy and the American Party System* (New York: Harcourt, Brace, 1956), pp. 151–52, 384–85, 525–27.

It should be clear that the data of this report are taken from a particular election of a particular electoral era. We would expect our principal findings to apply to most recent off-year elections, but they are of course subject to modification for earlier or later periods.

---

[3]This assumption does not imply that pressures toward party cohesion come *only* from the mass public. Other sanctions against party irregularity are of equal or greater importance, especially those available in the nominating process and within the legislative parties themselves. To cite the most celebrated empirical case, the cohesiveness of the British parliamentary parties is not enforced primarily, if at all, by the British electorate. Nevertheless, the public ought not to give aid and comfort to the legislative party irregular; the idea of the candidate building a local bastion of strength from which he can challenge the party leadership is clearly contradictory to the party-government model.

TABLE 1

1958 Vote for House Candidates,

by Party Identification

(in per cent)

	Party Identification*			
	Democratic	Independent	Republican	Total
Voted Democratic	53†	2	6	61
Voted Republican	5	3	31	39
Total	58	5	37	100

*The Democratic and Republican party identification groups include all persons who classify themselves as having some degree of party loyalty.

†Each entry of the table gives the per cent of the total sample of voters having the specified combination of party identification and vote for the House in 1958.

reaches a choice in the off-year congressional elections? A first glance at the relation of partisan identifications to the vote might give the impression that the mid-term election is a triumph of party government. Popular allegiance to the parties is of immense importance in all our national elections, including those in which a President is chosen, but its potency in the mid-term congressional election is especially pronounced. This fact is plain—even stark—in the entries of Table 1, which break down the vote for Congress in 1958 into its component party elements. The table makes clear, first of all, how astonishingly small a proportion of the mid-term vote is cast by political independents. Repeated electoral studies in the United States have indicated that somewhat fewer than 1 American in 10 thinks of himself as altogether independent of the two parties.[4] But in the off-year race for Congress only about a twentieth part of the vote is cast by independents, owing to their greater drop-out rate when the drama and stakes of the presidential contest are missing.

Table 1 also makes clear how little deviation from party there is among Republicans and Democrats voting in a mid-term

year. The role of party identification in the congressional election might still be slight, whatever the size of the party followings, if partisan allegiance sat more lightly on the voting act. But almost 9 out of every 10 partisans voting in the off-year race support their parties. Indeed, something like 84 per cent of *all* the votes for the House in 1958 were cast by party identifiers supporting their parties. The remaining 16 per cent is not a trivial fraction of the whole—standing, as it did in this case, for 8 million people, quite enough to make and unmake a good many legislative careers. Nevertheless, the low frequency of deviation from party, together with the low frequency of independent voting, indicates that the meaning of the mid-term vote depends in large part on the nature of party voting.

THE SALIENCY OF THE PARTIES' LEGISLATIVE RECORDS

If American party voting were to fit the responsible-party model it would be *programmatic* voting, that is, the giving of electoral support according to the parties' past or prospective action on programs that consist (mainly) of legislative measures. There is little question that partisan voting is one of the very few things at the bottom of our two-party system; every serious third-party movement in a hun-

---

[4]See Angus Campbell, Philip E. Converse, Warren E. Miller, and Donald E. Stokes, *The American Voter* (New York: John Wiley & Sons, 1960), p. 124.

dred years has foundered on the reef of traditional Republican and Democratic loyalties. But there is also little question that this voting is largely nonprogrammatic in nature. A growing body of evidence indicates that party loyalties are typically learned early in life, free of ideological or issue content, with the family as the main socializing agency. Certainly the findings of adult interview studies show that such loyalties are extremely long-lived and, summed across the population, give rise to extraordinarily stable distributions.[5] The very persistence of party identification raises suspicion as to whether the country is responding to the parties' current legislative actions when it votes its party loyalties.

That this suspicion is fully warranted in the mid-term election is indicated by several kinds of evidence from this research. To begin with, the electorate's perceptions of the parties betray very little information about current policy issues. For the past ten years the Survey Research Center has opened its electoral interviews with a series of free-answer questions designed to gather in the positive and negative ideas that the public has about the parties. The answers, requiring on the average nearly ten minutes of conversation, are only very secondarily couched in terms of policy issues. In 1958, for example, more than six thousand distinct positive or negative comments about the parties were made by a sample of 1,700 persons. Of these, less than 12 per cent by the most generous count had to do with contemporary legislative issues. As this sample of Americans pictured the reasons it liked and disliked the parties, the modern battlefields of the legislative wars—aid-to-education, farm policy, foreign aid, housing, aid to the unemployed, tariff and trade policy, social security,

medical care, labor laws, civil rights, and other issues—rarely came to mind. The main themes in the public's image of the parties are not totally cut off from current legislative events; the political activist could take the group-benefit and prosperity-depression ideas that saturate the party images and connect them fairly easily with issues before Congress. The point is that the public itself rarely does so.

How little awareness of current issues is embodied in the congressional vote also is attested by the reasons people give for voting Republican or Democratic for the House. In view of the capacity of survey respondents to rationalize their acts, direct explanations of behavior should be treated with some reserve. However, rationalization is likely to increase, rather than decrease, the policy content of reasons for voting. It is therefore especially noteworthy how few of the reasons our respondents gave for their House votes in 1958 had any discernible issue content. The proportion that had—about 7 per cent— was less even than the proportion of party-image references touching current issues.

Perhaps the most compelling demonstration of how hazardous it is to interpret party voting as a judgment of the parties' legislative records is furnished by the evidence about the public's knowledge of party control of Congress. When our 1958 sample was asked whether the Democrats or the Republicans had had more Congressmen in Washington during the two preceding years, a third confessed they had no idea, and an additional fifth gave control of the eighty-fifth Congress to the Republicans. Only 47 per cent correctly attributed control to the Democrats. These figures improve somewhat when nonvoters are excluded. Of those who voted in 1958, a fifth did not know which party had controlled Congress, another fifth thought the Republicans had, and the remainder (61 per cent) correctly gave control to the Democrats. However, when a

---

[5] For evidence on this point, see *ibid.*, pp. 120–67.

discount is made for guessing, the proportion of voters who really *knew* which party had controlled the eighty-fifth Congress probably is still not more than half.[6]

It would be difficult to overstate the significance of these figures for the problem of party government. The information at issue here is not a sophisticated judgment as to what short of coalition had *effective* control of Congress. It is simply the question of whether the country had a Democratic or a Republican Congress from 1956 to 1958. This elementary fact of political life, which any pundit would take completely for granted as he interpreted the popular vote in terms of party accountability, was unknown to something like half the people who went to the polls in 1958.

It is of equal significance to note that the parties' legislative record was no more salient to those who *deviated* from party than it was to those who voted their traditional party loyalty. It might be plausible to suppose that a floating portion of the electorate gives the parties programmatic support, even though most voters follow their traditional allegiances. If true, this difference would give the responsible-

party model some factual basis, whether or not the greater part of the electorate lived in darkness. But such a theory finds very little support in these data. In 1958 neither the issue reasons given for the congressional vote nor the awareness of party control of the eighty-fifth Congress was any higher among those who voted *against* their party identification than it was among those who voted *for* their party, as the entries of Table 2 demonstrate. If anything, correcting perceived party control for guessing suggests that voters who deviated from their party in 1958 had poorer information about the course of political events over the preceding two years.

Nor do the perceptions of party control of Congress that *are* found supply a key to understanding the congressional vote. Whatever awareness of control the electorate had in 1958 was remarkably unrelated to its support of candidates for the House. To make this point, Table 3 analyzes deviations from party according to three perceptions held by party identifiers voting in 1958: *first*, whether they thought the country's recent domestic affairs had gone well or badly; *second* (to allow for the complication of divided government), whether they thought Congress or President had the greater influence over what the government did; and, *third*, whether they thought the Democrats or Republicans had controlled Congress. To recreate the basis on which the voter might assign credit or blame to the parties, the second and third of these perceptions may be combined; that is, partisans may be classified according to whether they thought their own party or the opposite party had controlled the more effective branch of government. Crossing this classification with perceptions of whether domestic affairs had gone well yields four groups for analysis, two of which (I and IV) might be expected to show little deviation from party, the other two (II and III) substantially more. In fact, however, the differ-

---

[6]Plainly, some deduction has to be made for guessing. One model of the situation would be to think of the sample as composed of three types of people: those who knew, those who didn't know and said so, and those who didn't know but guessed. Assuming that for those who guessed $p = q = \frac{1}{2}$, where p is the probability of guessing Republican, we would deduct from the Democratic answers a percentage equal to the 18 per cent who guessed Republican incorrectly, hence reducing the proportion of voters who really knew which party controlled Congress to 43 per cent. This model may be too severe, however, in view of the presence of the Republican President. It may be more reasonable to admit a fourth type of person, those who did not guess but were misled by Republican control of the White House. Or we might think of the guessers as following a probability law in which $p > \frac{1}{2} > q$. In either of these cases something less than 18 per cent would be deducted from the Democratic answers; hence, the proportion of voters who *knew* which party controlled Congress would lie somewhere between 43 and 61 per cent.

TABLE 2

Issue Responses and Awareness of Which Party Controlled
85th Congress among Party Supporters and Voters Who
Deviated from Party

	Of Party Identifiers Who	
	Voted for Own Party	Voted for Other Party
Per cent aware of party control:		
Uncorrected	61	60
Corrected for guessing*	44	35
Per cent giving issue reasons		
for House vote	6	7

*This correction deducts from the proportion attributing control to the Democrats a percentage equal to the proportion attributing control to the Republicans. See footnote 6.

TABLE 3

Percentage of Party Identifiers Voting against Party in 1958,
by Perception of Party Control of Government
and Course of Domestic Affairs

Thought That Domestic Affairs	Thought That More Effective Branch of Government Was Controlled by	
	Own Party	Other Party
	I	II
Had gone well	16 (N = 43)	22 (N = 46)
	III	IV
Had gone badly	14 (N = 152)	22 (N = 122)

ences between these groups are almost trifling. According to the familiar lore, the groups that thought affairs had gone badly (III and IV) are the ones that should provide the clearest test of whether perceptions of party control are relevant to voting for the House. Moreover, with a recession in the immediate background, most people who could be classified into this table in 1958 fell into one of these two groups, as the frequencies indicate. But when the two groups that felt there had been domestic difficulties are compared, it seems not to make a particle of difference whether the Democrats or Republicans were thought to have controlled the ac-

tions of government. And when the two groups (I and II) that felt things had gone well are compared, only a slight (and statistically insignificant) difference appears. Interestingly, even this small rise in the rate of deviation from party (in cell II) is contributed mainly by Democratic identifiers who wrongly supposed that the Congress had been in Republican hands.

The conclusion to be drawn from all this certainly is not that national political forces are without *any* influence on deviations from party in the mid-term year. Clearly these forces do have an influence. Although the fluctuations of the mid-term party vote, charted over half a century or more, are very much smaller than fluctuations in the presidential vote or of the congressional vote in presidential years, there is *some* variation, and these moderate swings must be attributed to forces that have their focus at the national level.[7] Even in 1958 one party received a larger share of deviating votes than the other. Our main point is rather that the deviations that *do* result from national forces are not in the main produced by the parties' legislative records and that, in any case, the proportion of deviating votes that can be attributed to national politics is likely to be a small part of the total votes cast by persons deviating from party in a mid-term year. This was specifically true in 1958.

If the motives for deviations from party are not to be found primarily at the national level, the search moves naturally to the local congressional campaign. A third possibility—that deviations are by-products of state-wide races—can be discounted with some confidence. Despite the popular lore on the subject, evidence both from interview studies and from aggregate election statistics can be used to show that the influence of contests for Governor and Senator on the outcome of House races is slight in mid-term elections, although these contests can have an immense influence on turnout for the House.[8] In our 1958 sample, a majority of those who deviated from party in voting for the House *failed* to deviate also at the state level; more often than not, what had moved them into the other party's column at the House level was dissociated from the contests for Governor or Senator in which they voted. Moreover, the fact that an elector deviates from his party in voting both for the House and some office contested on a state-wide basis is not conclusive evidence that the state race has influenced his choice for the House, rather than the other way round. When the possibility of *reverse* coat-tail effects is allowed for, the reasons for believing that the state-wide race is a potent force on the House vote seem faint indeed.[9] As we search for the motives for deviation from party, analysis of the local congressional race pays greater dividends.

[7] A simple but persuasive comparison is this: from 1892 to 1960 the standard deviation of the two-party division of the mid-term congressional vote was 3.9 per cent; of the presidential-year congressional vote, 5.5 per cent; of the presidential vote, 8.2 per cent. Moreover, if the realignment of party loyalties that occurred in the early 1930's is taken into account by computing deviations from pre- and post-1932 means, rather than from a grand mean for the whole period, the standard deviation of the mid-term congressional vote is found to have been 2.4 per cent, compared with a standard deviation of 7.5 per cent for the presidential vote. Some of the remaining variability of the mid-term vote may be due to fluctuations of turnout that do not involve deviations from party. Yet, even ignoring this possibility, the bounds within which national political forces can have influenced the off-year vote by inducing deviations from party appear narrow indeed.

[8] A remarkable fact is that while the total vote for the House increased by 3 million between 1954 and 1958, more than 2 million of this increase was contributed by New York, where Rockefeller sought the governorship; by Ohio, where a fierce referendum battle was fought over the issue of "right-to-work"; and by California, where the fantastic Knight-Knowland-Brown free-for-all was held.

[9] This conclusion is fully supported by an analysis of the variance of turnout and party vote in the mid-term congressional elections of the 1950's. If state-wide races have a major influence on local House races, the election results for the several congressional districts of a state should vary together; similar changes of turnout and party division should be seen in the districts that are influenced by the same state-wide contests. An analysis of the variance of the differences between the 1954 and 1958 turnout level and partisan division for all congressional districts in states having at least two districts indicates that state races have a large effect on turnout; the intraclass correlation expressing the ratio of the between-state variance to the total variance of turnout was more than .45. But this analysis shows, too, that statewide races have almost no effect whatever on the party division of the House vote; the intraclass correlation expressing the ratio of the between-state variance to the total variance of the party division was not more than .02.

THE SALIENCY OF CONGRESSIONAL CANDIDATES

By the standards of the civics text, what the public knows about the candidates for Congress is as meager as what it knows about the parties' legislative records. Of the people who lived in districts where the House seat was contested in 1958, 59 per cent—well over half—said that they had neither read nor heard anything about either candidate for Congress, and less than 1 in 5 felt that they knew something about both candidates. What is more, these remarkable proportions are only marginally improved by excluding nonvoters from the calculations. Of people who went to the polls and cast a vote between rival House candidates in 1958, fully 46 per cent conceded that they did so without having read or heard anything about either man. What the other half *had* read or heard is illuminating; we will deal with its policy content presently. Many of our respondents said they knew something about the people contesting the House seat on the basis of very slender information indeed.

The incumbent candidate is by far the better known. In districts where an incumbent was opposed for re-election in 1958, 39 per cent of our respondents knew something about the Congressman, whereas only 20 per cent said they knew anything

at all about his nonincumbent opponent. The incumbent's advantage of repeated exposure to the electorate is plain enough. In fact, owing to the greater seniority and longer exposure of Congressmen from safe districts, the public's awareness of incumbents who were unopposed for re-election in 1958 was as great as its awareness of incumbents who had had to conduct an election campaign that year.

The saliency of a candidate is of critical importance if he is to attract support from the opposite party. However little the public may know of those seeking office, any information at all about the rival party's candidate creates the possibility of a choice deviating from party. That such a choice occurs with some frequency is shown by the entries of Table 4, whose columns separate party identifiers in contested districts in 1958 according to whether they were aware of both candidates, the candidate of their own party or the other party only, or neither candidate. The condition of no information leads to fairly unrelieved party-line voting, and so to an even greater degree does the condition of information only about the candidate of the voter's own party. But if partisan voters know something about the opposition's man, substantial deviations from party appear. In fact, if such voters know *only* the opposition candidate, almost half can be induced to cast a vote contrary to their

TABLE 4

Percentage Voting for Own Party Candidate and Other Party Candidate
for House in 1958, by Saliency of Candidates in
Contested Districts

Voted for Candidate	Both Candidates ($N = 196$)	Own Party Candidate Only ($N = 166$)	Other Party Candidate Only ($N = 68$)	Neither Candidate ($N = 368$)
	Voter Was Aware of			
Of own party	83	98	60	92
Of other party	17	2	40	8
Total	100	100	100	100

party identification. In the main, recognition carries a positive valence; to be perceived at all is to be perceived favorably. However, some *negative* perceptions are found in our interviews, and when these are taken into account the explanation of deviation from party becomes surer still. For example, if we return to Table 4 and select from the third column only the voters who perceived the candidate of the other party *favorably*, a clear majority is found to have deviated from party allegiance in casting their votes. And if we select from the first column only the handful of voters who perceived the candidate of their own party *negatively* and of the opposite party *positively*, almost three-quarters are found to have deviated from their party loyalty in voting for the House.

What our constituent interviews show about the increment of support that accrues to the salient candidate is closely aligned to what the candidates themselves see as the roots of their electoral strength. Our interviews with incumbent and non-incumbent candidates seeking election to the House explored at length their understanding of factors aiding—or damaging—their electoral appeal. In particular, these interviews probed the candidates' assessment of four possible influences on the result: traditional party loyalties, national issues, state and local contests, and the candidates' own record and personal standing in the district. Caution is in order in

dealing with answers to questions that touch the respondent's self-image as closely as these. Specifically, we may expect some overstatement of the candidate's own importance, particularly from the victors, and we may expect, too, that too large a discount will be applied to party allegiance, since this "inert" factor, having little to do with increments of strength, is so easily taken for granted.

After these allowances are made, it is still impressive how heavy a weight the incumbent assigns his personal record and standing. The Congressman's ranking of this and the other factors in the election is shown in Table 5. As the entries of the table indicate, more than four-fifths of the incumbents re-elected in 1958 felt that the niche they had carved out in the awareness of their constituents had substantial impact on the race, a proportion that exceeds by half the percentage who gave as much weight to any of the three other factors. This difference is more than sheer puffing in the interview situation, and the perceptual facts it reveals deserve close attention. Among the forces the Representative feels may enhance his strength at the polls, he gives his personal standing with the district front rank.

In view of the way the saliency of candidates can move the electorate across party lines, great stress should be laid on the fact that the public sees individual candidates for Congress in terms of party

TABLE 5
Relative Importance of Factors in Re-election
as Seen by Incumbent Candidates in 1958
(in per cent)

Perceived As	Personal Record and Standing	National Issues	Traditional Party Loyalties	State and Local Races
Very important	57	26	25	14
Quite important	28	20	21	19
Somewhat important	9	20	24	27
Not very important	3	27	18	19
Not important at all	3	7	12	21
	100	100	100	100

programs scarcely at all. Our constituent interviews indicate that the popular image of the Congressman is almost barren of policy content. A long series of open-ended questions asked of those who said they had any information about the Representative produced mainly a collection of diffuse evaluative judgments: he is a good man, he is experienced, he knows the problems, he has done a good job, and the like. Beyond this, the Congressman's image consisted of a mixed bag of impressions, some of them wildly improbable, about ethnicity, the attractiveness of family, specific services to the district, and other facts in the candidate's background. By the most reasonable count, references to current legislative issues comprised not more than a thirtieth part of what the constituents had to say about their Congressmen.

The irrelevance of legislative issues to the public's knowledge of Representatives is underscored by the nature of some primary *determinants* of saliency. A full analysis of the causes of constitutional awareness of candidates goes beyond the scope of this paper. Although our investigation has given a good deal of attention to communication factors and to characteristics of Congressmen and constituents themselves that determine the probability a given Congressman will be known to a given constituent, this interplay of causes cannot be explored very deeply here. However, it *is* noteworthy in the present discussion that many factors increasing the saliency of candidates are unlikely to enhance what the public knows about their stands on issues. An excellent example is sex. Both for incumbents and non-incumbents, a candidate property that is related to saliency is gender; one of the best ways for a Representative to be known is to be a Congress*woman*. How irrelevant to policy issues this property is depends on what we make of the causal relation between sex and salience. The fact of being a woman may make a candi-

date more visible, but a woman may have to be unusually visible (like a Congressman's widow, say) before she can be elected to the House, or even become a serious candidate. If the first of these inferences is even partially right, the salience of the candidate is not likely to be in terms of positions taken on legislative issues.

Given the number of women who run for Congress, the role of sex may seem a trivial example to demonstrate the irrelevance of issue stands to saliency. However, the same point can be made for a much wider set of districts by the greater saliency of candidates who live in the constituent's home community. Just as there is enormous variety in the communities that make up the American nation, so there is the widest possible variation in how well a congressional district coincides with a natural community, and the goodness of this fit is a fundamental way of typing districts. At one extreme is the constituency whose area is lost within one of the country's great metropolitan centers, comprising at best a small fraction of the whole community. At the middle of the range is the district that is itself a natural community, consisting of a single medium-sized city and its environs. At the other extreme is the district whose territory includes a great number of small communities, as well as surrounding open country that goes on, in some cases, for hundreds of miles. In all but the metropolitan districts the salience of the candidate for the voter differs markedly according to whether candidate and voter live in the same community. The fact of common residence—of being "friends and neighbors"—stands for important facts of communication and community identification. Candidates will be joined by formal and informal communication networks to many of the voters living in the same community, and they may also be objects of considerable community pride.

The reality of this local effect is dem-

TABLE 6

Influence of "Friends and Neighbors" Factor
on Saliency of Candidates for Voters*
(in per cent)

	Incumbent Candidate Lives in		Non-incumbent Candidate Lives in	
	Same Community as Voter	*Other Community than Voter*	*Same Community as Voter*	*Other Community than Voter*
Voter Is	($N = 269$)	($N = 414$)	($N = 304$)	($N = 447$)
Aware of candidate	67	45	47	22
Not aware of candidate ..	33	55	53	78
Total	100	100	100	100

*Metropolitan and large urban districts, for which the notion of the candidate living outside the voter's community has no clear meaning, are excluded from the analysis.

onstrated by Table 6. As the entries of the table show, dividing a nationwide sample of constituents according to whether they live in the same community as their Congressman or his opponent produces marked differences of saliency. The "friends and neighbors" effect made familiar by studies of primary voting in one-party areas has a counterpart in voting for Representatives throughout the country, apart from the large metropolitan areas.[10] And despite the fact that localism is found here in the context of as tightly party-determined an election as any in American politics, the irrelevance of local appeal to legislative issues is probably as great as it is in the wide-open, one-party primary.

CONCLUSION

What the public knows about the legislative records of the parties and of individual congressional candidates is a principal reason for the departure of American practice from an idealized conception of

party government. On the surface the legislative elections occurring in the middle of the President's term appear to be dominated by two national parties asking public support for their alternative programs. Certainly the electorate whose votes they seek responds to individual legislative candidates overwhelmingly on the basis of their party labels. Despite our kaleidoscopic electoral laws, the candidate's party is the one piece of information every voter is guaranteed. For many, it is the only information they ever get.

However, the legislative events that follow these elections diverge widely from the responsible-party model. The candidates who have presented themselves to the country under two party symbols immediately break ranks. The legislative parties speak not as two voices but as a cacophony of blocs and individuals fulfilling their own definitions of the public good. Party cohesion by no means vanishes, but it is deeply eroded by the pressures external to party to which the Congressman is subject.

The public's information about the legislative record of the parties and of Members of Congress goes far toward reconciling these seemingly contradictory facts. In the congressional election, to be sure, the country votes overwhelmingly for party symbols, but the symbols have limited

[10]See V. O. Key, Jr., *Southern Politics*, New York, Knopf, 1949, pp. 37ff. We have demonstrated the "friends and neighbors" effect in terms of candidate salience because of our interest in the policy content of candidate perceptions. However, owing to the impact of salience on the vote, living in the same community with the candidate has a clear effect on voting as well.

meaning in terms of legislative policy. The eddies and cross-currents in Congress do not interrupt a flow of legislation that the public expects but fails to see. The electorate sees very little altogether of what goes on in the national legislature. Few judgments of legislative performance are associated with the parties, and much of the public is unaware even of which party has control of Congress. As a result, the absence of party discipline or legislative results is unlikely to bring down electoral sanctions on the ineffective party or the errant Congressman.

What the public's response to the parties lacks in programmatic support is not made up by its response to local congressional candidates. Although perceptions of individual candidates account for most of the votes cast by partisans against their parties, these perceptions are almost untouched by information about the policy stands of the men contesting the House seat. The increment of strength that some candidates, especially incumbents, acquire by being known to their constituents is almost entirely free of policy content. Were such content present, the Congressman's solidarity with his legislative party would by no means be assured. If the local constituency possessed far greater resources of information than it has, it might use the ballot to pry the Congressman away from his party quite as well as to unite him with it. Yet the fact is that, by plying his campaigning and servicing arts over the years, the Congressman is able to develop electoral strength that is almost totally dissociated from what his party wants in Congress and what he himself has done about it. The relevance of all this to the problem of cohesion and responsibility in the legislative party can scarcely be doubted.

The description of party irresponsibility in America should not be overdrawn. The American system *has* elements of party accountability to the public, although the issues on which an accounting is given are relatively few and the accounting is more often rendered by those who hold or seek the Presidency than by the parties' congressional delegations. Especially on the broad problem of government action to secure social and economic welfare it can be argued that the parties have real differences and that these have penetrated the party images to which the electorate responds at the polls.

Nevertheless, American practice does not diverge widely from the model of party government, and the factors underlying the departure deserve close analysis. An implication of the analysis reported here is that the public's contribution to party irregularity in Congress is not so much a matter of encouraging or requiring its Representatives to deviate from their parties as it is of the public having so little information that the irregularity of Congressmen and the ineffectiveness of the congressional parties have scant impact at the polls. Many of those who have commented on the lack of party discipline in Congress have assumed that the Congressman votes against his party because he is forced to by the demands of one of several hundred constituencies of a superlatively heterogeneous nation. In some cases, the Representative may subvert the proposals of his party because his constituency demands it. But a more reasonable interpretation over a broader range of issues is that the Congressman fails to see these proposals as part of a program on which the party—and he himself—will be judged at the polls, because he knows the constituency isn't looking.

THE RELATION BETWEEN PUBLIC POLICY AND SOME STRUCTURAL AND ENVIRONMENTAL VARIABLES IN THE AMERICAN STATES*

Richard I. Hofferbert

What is the relationship between certain major structural aspects of state governments and the content of policies adopted in the states? Do the socio-economic environments of the states relate significantly to political structures or the type of policies enacted?

The thesis advanced here is that differences in policy, at least in certain substantive areas, are more readily explained in terms of differences in the socio-economic environments of the states than by an examination of structural variables. It will also be maintained that, as policy is independent of structure, so structure is also largely independent of some major aspects of the environment. The specific structural variables to be examined are apportionment, party competitiveness, and divided party control between governors and their legislatures.

Six specific propositions will be examined:

Proposition 1. The more imbalance in a state's apportionment, the less likely the legislature is to pass "liberal" or welfare-oriented policies beneficial to urban groups.

Proposition 2. The more imbalance in a state's apportionment, the less financial aid large cities will receive directly from the state.

Proposition 3. The more imbalance in a state's apportionment, the less competitive will be its major parties.

    3a. The less competitive a state's two major parties, the less welfare-oriented will be the policies adopted by its legislature.

Proposition 4. The more imbalance in a state's apportionment, the more likely it is that control of the executive and legislative branches will be divided between parties.

    4a. The more frequently control of the legislature and executive are divided, the less likely a state will be to adopt welfare-oriented policies.

Proposition 5. The more industrialized a state, the more imbalance there will be in its apportionment system.

Proposition 6. The more industrialized a state, the higher will be its welfare-orientation.

The derivation of each of these propositions and the means used to test them will be discussed individually in the sections which follow.

I. APPORTIONMENT AND PUBLIC POLICY

The first two propositions suggest an inverse relationship between numerical equality of apportionment systems and the willingness of states to pass policies beneficial to urban groups and governmental units. Although this thesis is a common one,[1] it is increasingly under at-

---

*Reprinted from the *American Political Science Review*, Vol. LX (March 1966) pp. 73–82. Copyright 1966, The American Political Science Association.

I am grateful to the Roper Center for Public Opinion Research for the use of their equipment and facilities while conducting this study.

---

[1]See, for example, William C. Havard and Loren P. Beth, *The Politics of Mis-Representation* (Baton Rouge: Louisiana State University Press, 1962), p. 77; Charles W. Shull, "Political and

tack in reports of recent research.[2] Nevertheless, the propositions have sufficient acceptance to warrant their further investigation.

Apportionment and Welfare Orientation

The argument for Proposition 1 assumes that the claims and attitudes which inform the predominantly rural legislators and which define their conception of the public interest are substantially different from those of many urban groups. The need for an active role by the state demanded by urban-industrial groups is not recognized by malapportioned legislatures. And it is assumed that there are no alternative courses for the expression of urban influence which might neutralize this obstacle, such as gubernatorial influence or direct legislation in one form or another.

In order to test this proposition, two measures or indices must be constructed: a measure of malapportionment and one of "liberalism" of policies. The latter is best achieved by a composite measure which accurately reflects the phenomenon or set of phenomena being studied and which allows for ordinal ranking of the states.

In a recent article in this *Review*, Glendon Schubert and Charles Press carefully examine the various measures of malapportionment which have been used. Their objections and suggestions do not require

restatement here.[3] Their proposal has also been examined and compared to available alternatives by Thomas R. Dye, in another recent publication.[4] It is enough here to note that, inasmuch as the Schubert-Press measure takes account of most of the major relevant variables. I have employed the apportionment ranking they propose.

For a measure of "liberalism" or what I will label "welfare orientation," guidance is taken from a study of inter-party competitiveness and welfare policies by Richard E. Dawson and James A. Robinson.[5] They employ a nine-policy test to measure a state's welfare orientation, including four revenue items and five expenditure items.[6]

Partisan Implications of State Legislative Apportionment," *Law and Contemporary Problems*, 17 (Spring, 1952), 417–39; Gordon E. Baker, *Rural versus Urban Political Power* (Garden City, N.J.: Doubleday, 1955), p. 23; Malcolm Jewell, *The State Legislature: Politics and Practice* (New York: Random House, 1962), p. 24; William J. Keefe and Morris S. Ogul, *The American Legislative Process* (Englewood Cliffs, N.J.: Prentice-Hall, 1964), p. 86; Duane Lockard, *New England State Politics* (Princeton, N.J.: Princeton University Press, 1959), p. 275; Frank J. Sorauf, *Party and Representation* (New York: Atherton, 1962), pp. 22f.

[2]See, for example, Thomas R. Dye, "Malapportionment and Public Policy in the States," *Journal of Politics*, Vol. XXVII (August, 1965), 586–601; Herbert Jacob, "The Consequences of Malapportionment: A Note of Caution," *Social Forces*, Vol. XLIII (December, 1964), 256–61.

[3]Glendon Schubert and Charles Press, "Measuring Malapportionment," *American Political Science Review*, Vol. VIII (June, 1964), 302–27; see also "Communications," *ibid.*, pp. 966–70, for corrections to calculations in the original article. The measure they propose suffers somewhat from the shortcomings of any composite quantitative device, with the possible exception of unidimensional scale categories. For example, by combining house and senate scores, they derive a score which does not necessarily reflect any real situation but acts as an average and has all the potential pitfalls of an average. Also, it is unable to take account of the gerrymander (a point consciously noted by the authors). But, as a recent article by Thomas R. Dye indicates, when employed as an explanatory device, the Schubert-Press measure seems to be no less useful than other measures that have been proposed. (See Thomas R. Dye, *op. cit.*) And the disadvantages of the other measures, discussed by Schubert and Press as well as by Dye, would seem to tip the scales in favor of the Schubert-Press technique.

[4]Dye, *op. cit.*

[5]Richard E. Dawson and James A. Robinson, "Inter-party Competition, Economic Variables, and Welfare Policies in the American States," *Journal of Politics*, Vol. XXV (May, 1963), 265–89.

[6]The nine items are:

1. Per cent of revenue from death and gift taxes
2. Per cent of revenue from the federal government
3. Per capita amount of all revenue
4. State and local revenue according to personal income
5. Per pupil expenditure for elementary and secondary education
6. Per recipient monthly aid to the blind
7. Per family monthly aid to dependent children
8. Per recipient monthly old age assistance
9. Per recipient weekly unemployment compensation.

The specific policies were chosen largely on the basis of availability of data and interstate comparability as well as to include policies both independent of federal programs and those encouraged by federal aid.

Dawson and Robinson utilize each item independently in their study of the impact of inter-party competitiveness on welfare orientation. However, for the sake of convenience, clarity of exposition, and reliability of the measures employed, I shall select from their list those items which demonstrate, by a high degree of covariation, a common policy orientation within the various states. These will then be combined into a single rank ordering. Where Dawson and Robinson select policies from a single year to test their propositions, I shall utilize ten-year means, calculated on the basis of biennial figures.[7]

Each particular policy yields a high average intercorrelation of ranks ($\bar{p}$ = around .90 in each case) from year to year, indicating that there is stability in the states' commitment to particular lines of policy. However, when the means for each item of expenditure and revenue were ranked and average inter-correlations of ranks calculated between items, only the five expenditure ranks correlated closely ($\bar{p}$ = .67). This figure was the highest of any combination of five items on the scale. The assumption here is that anything less than five items would not be measuring a general policy orientation, but would be merely a reflection of particular issue-responses by the legislatures.

The final figure employed, therefore, to rank the states by welfare orientation is the sum of the individual ranks of mean expenditures for ten years on the following items: per-pupil expenditure for ele-

mentary and secondary education, per-recipient aid to the blind, per-family aid to dependent children, per-recipient old age assistance, and per-recipient weekly unemployment compensation. This ranking is the dependent variable related to the independent structural variable of Proposition 1, malapportionment. The results of this procedure are readily seen in Table 1.

TABLE 1

Rank Order Correlation between Apportionment and Welfare Orientation in 48 States*

State	Apportionment Rank†	Welfare Orientation Rank†
Alabama	44	47
Arizona	34	18
Arkansas	12	45
California	40	3
Colorado	21	11
Connecticut	37	2
Delaware	22	27
Florida	41	37
Georgia	48	38
Idaho	27	23
Illinois	23	10
Indiana	10	28
Iowa	42	16
Kansas	46	15
Kentucky	43	39
Louisiana	32	31
Maine	7	36
Maryland	36	29
Massachusetts	5	6
Michigan	28	13
Minnesota	47	8
Mississippi	30	48
Missouri	26	35
Montana	25	20
Nebraska	4	26
Nevada	38	12
New Hampshire	3	19
New Jersey	17	4
New Mexico	39	30
New York	11	1
North Carolina	19	44
North Dakota	35	17
Ohio	1	22
Oklahoma	45	25
Oregon	2	7
Pennsylvania	9	24

---

[7]Thus, I have 45 rankings for 48 states. Hawaii and Alaska are excluded as they have not been states throughout the period encompassed by the data. All of the data in the welfare-orientation index may be found in various volumes of the *Book of the States*, Council of State Governments, Chicago.

TABLE 1—Continued

State	Apportionment Rank†	Welfare Orientation Rank‡
Rhode Island	31	14
South Carolina	20	46
South Dakota	14	33
Tennessee	8	43
Texas	33	32
Utah	6	21
Vermont	24	34
Virginia	29	41
Washington	15	42
West Virginia	13	40
Wisconsin	18	5
Wyoming	16	9

$\rho = .03$.

*Alaska and Hawaii excluded because they have not been states throughout the period covered by the data.

†See Schubert and Press, "Communications," *op. cit.*

‡Based on mean per-recipient expenditure, 1952–1961, for aid to the blind, old age assistance, unemployment compensation, expenditure for elementary and secondary education, and aid to dependent children.

Even without the aid of sophisticated measures of covariation, it is clear from Table 1 that there is no obvious relationship between the numerical equality of a state's apportionment system and the legislative response to the type of proposals reflected in the welfare orientation measure. When $\rho = .03$, which is very nearly no relation at all, it does not provide any justification for accepting Proposition 1.[8]

[8]The strength of this assertion would be substantially enhanced if it were possible to view the patterns of reapportionment and their impact upon policy developmentally within each state. This has been done in one state: see Gilbert Y. Steiner and Samuel R. Gove, *Legislative Politics in Illinois* (Urbana: University of Illinois Press, 1960), p. 132. But it is difficult to make comparative statements due to the absence of any uniformity in the various reapportionment acts. I have examined one aspect of this by checking the rate of increase in spending for public welfare before and after reapportionment in every state which reapportioned between 1955 and 1962 (N = 22). No change could be detected; in fact, there was a slight drop in the mean rate of increase following reapportionment. The possibility of such investigation will be improved once the present stream of reapportionment suits is settled, assuming that the courts will be able to impose some standards of uniformity.

A conclusion similar to mine has been reached

Apportionment and Aid to Large Cities

The data employed to calculate welfare orientation yield only crude outlines of the patterns of policy-making followed by the various states. It may be argued that gross figures on expenditure fail to reveal the manner in which funds are distributed within the states. Equally relevant, in other words, is the manner in which funds collected by state governments are distributed among the various governmental jurisdictions.

To test Proposition 2, which suggests a relationship between malapportionment and the amount of aid received by large cities from the states, a rank order correlation has been calculated between the apportionment rank and what may be called the "state aid index." The latter has been derived from the Census Bureau's *Compendium of City Government Fi-*

by Dye respecting the relationship between apportionment and policy. He employs a much larger number of policy variables individually and uses somewhat different statistical tests. He does not, however, employ an extended period of time to demonstrate policy orientations. This is probably a minor refinement, as my data show little overall change from year to year in the relative positions of the states on any of the items included in the welfare orientation index. See Dye, *op. cit.*, pp. 595ff.

The findings on Proposition 1 and Dye's conclusions also relate to David R. Derge's study of roll-call voting in the Missouri and Illinois legislatures. Derge examines more than 19,000 roll call votes over a decade of legislative activity. He concludes that, at the voting stage in these two states, there is no evidence of urban-rural antagonism—that the urban legislators are able to obtain passage of their legislation whenever they can maintain internal unity. David R. Derge, "Metropolitan and Outstate Alignments in Illinois and Missouri Legislative Delegations," *American Political Science Review*, Vol. LII (December, 1958), p. 1065; see also a critique by Richard T. Frost, "On Derge's Metropolitan and Outstate Legislative Delegations," *ibid.*, Vol. LIII (September, 1959), 792–95, and Derge's reply, *ibid.*, 1097–99. Derge's conclusions are supported in a survey of Ohio politics conducted by Thomas A. Flinn. One of Flinn's conclusions is that, "Urban-rural factionalism is unimportant in the Ohio General Assembly." "The Outline of Ohio Politics," *Western Political Quarterly*, Vol. XIII (September, 1960), 702–21.

nances by calculating the percentage of "general revenue" in 1962 of each state's two largest cities which was supplied directly from the state government to these cities.[9]

The aim here has been to obtain a measure of state legislative receptiveness to the claims of the states' urban subdivisions. Given the wide variation in the pattern of state financial assistance to a host of intrastate political and functional entities, it is very difficult to obtain a measure that includes data from state to state on a truly comparable basis. For example, some states' welfare programs are largely or entirely administered by county governments, irrespective of the presence of a large city within the county. School aid is usually distributed on some basis of equalization, taking account of the ability of the school districts to support their own institutions. Also, peculiar historical factors sometimes affect the propensity of the state to monopolize revenue sources and thereby provide, via the legislature, seemingly larger amounts of aid to the cities.

The Census Bureau's definitions, however, would indicate that the measure here

being employed comes about as close to a device having high interstate comparative value as anything else that could be achieved without a monumental research effort seeking a variety of other data directly from state and city officials. And I suspect that even such an effort would still leave considerable room for doubt as to the comparability of data from city to city and state to state.

Bearing in mind the possible shortcomings of the state-aid index, therefore, one still must come to the tentative conclusion that there is no significant relationship between apportionment, the structural variable, and the policy outcome. In this case ρ is only .22.

The Impact of Southern States

With both Propositions 1 and 2, it might be contended that the presence of several southern states has distorted the outcome. It is widely recognized (and readily demonstrated by Table 1) that the states south of the Mason-Dixon line are less disposed to pursue the type of welfare-oriented policies more characteristic of their northern counterparts. The eleven states of the Confederacy have a mean rank of 41 on the welfare orientation scale. This may be attributed to a variety of factors. Chiefly, the exploitation of race as a major political concern, it might be contended, has set the politics of southern states apart from the rest of the country.[10] And, although not under the same sort of pressures which conceivably lead to resistance to reapportionment elsewhere (particularly partisan pressures and rapid urbanization), these states may still pursue the same conservative policies of poorly apportioned, non-southern states but for different reasons. Thus, their presence in the foregoing calculations may cloud the relationship between welfare orientation or state aid and apportionment.

---

[9]U.S. Bureau of the Census, *Compendium of City Government Finances in 1962* (Washington, D.C.: U.S. Government Printing Office, 1963). This document lists only cities over 50,000 in population. In a few states, there is only one such city. In these cases, only the percentage of the one city's general revenue from the state was used to calculate the state aid index.

This particular source of city funds is listed in the *Compendium* under "General Revenue" and classified as "Intergovernmental Revenue, from state government only." The relevant definitions are:

General Revenue: "All city revenue except utility revenue, liquor stores revenue, and employees retirement or other insurance trust revenue. The basis for distinction is not the fund or administrative unit receiving particular amounts, but rather the nature of the revenue source concerned."

Intergovernmental Revenue: "Amounts received from other governments as fiscal aid or as reimbursement for performance of general governmental services for the paying government. Excludes any amounts received from other governments for sale of property, commodities, or utility services. All intergovernmental revenue is classified as general revenue."

---

[10]See V. O. Key, *Southern Politics* (New York: Alfred A. Knopf, 1949), Ch. 1.

When these eleven states are removed from the calculations, however, the relationship is not strengthened. In fact, it is slightly weakened, as is demonstrated by a ρ of $-$ .005 between welfare orientation and apportionment and $-$ .04 between state aid to cities and apportionment in non-southern states.

II. APPORTIONMENT AND PARTY COMPETITION

The presumed direct effect upon public policy is but one class of results attributed to the lack of equity in the apportionment systems found in many states. This aspect of political structure is also presumed to affect—laterally, as it were—another variable which may be classified "structural" (if a little conceptual generosity is allowed), namely inter-party competition.

Malapportionment has been accused of being a major hindrance to responsible party government. It is maintained that this legislative inequity weakens the two-party system in a variety of ways. One most frequently suggested is that malapportionment denies legislative control to an occasionally successful aspirant for the governorship from a state's normal minority party. V. O. Key has stated, "By far the most important element producing [divided control] is the malapportionment of representation. . . ."[11]

A further obstacle to strong, responsible two-party competition is presumably created by malapportionment in that it encourages lassitude on the part of secure legislators, notably Republicans. Their personal success in retaining legislative positions makes them reluctant to approve programs that might encourage their parties' strength and growth, particularly in capturing and holding the governorship in highly industrial states.[12]

It may further be argued that, as party competition is weakened, the likelihood of governmental units responding to the needs of industrializing, urbanizing society is lessened. The problems of urban man are too complex for the governmental structures of an agrarian era. They require intelligent, resourceful leadership exercised through institutional channels which encourage rather than inhibit its development.

One would expect, from this reasoning, that any evidence of less than optimum operation of a responsible two-party system would be clearly reflected in the type of policies produced—or not produced, as maintained in Proposition 3a.

In order to test Propositions 3 and 3a, it is necessary to obtain a measure of inter-party competitiveness. There are a number of problems involved in this apparently simple concept. These have been reviewed by various writers and they have proposed several alternative methods. The technique to be employed here is one which I have proposed elsewhere.[13] By utilizing contests for President, governor, and United States senator in each state and taking account of the percentage of the popular vote obtained by the majority party as well as the frequency of party turnover, a scale of inter-party competitiveness (IPC) has been obtained which ranks all the states but Alaska and Hawaii.

The results of a rank ordering of apportionment (again using the Schubert-Press schema) and competitiveness are seen in Table 2. Again, the near absence of a relationship ($\rho = .17$) allows no basis for accepting the proposition.

---

[11]V. O. Key, *American State Politics: An Introduction* (New York: Alfred A. Knopf, 1956), p. 64; see also, Malcolm Jewell, *op. cit.*, p. 24; Keefe and Ogul, *op. cit.*, p. 92.

[12]See Jewell, *op. cit.*, p. 31.

[13]Richard I. Hofferbert, "Classification of American State Party Systems," *Journal of Politics*, Vol. XXVI (August, 1964), 550–67; see also, Austin Ranney and Wilmoore Kendall, "The American Party Systems," *American Political Science Review*, Vol. XLVII (June, 1954), 477–85; Joseph A. Schlesinger, "A Two-Dimensional Scheme for Classifying the States According to Degree of Inter-Party Competition," *American Political Science Review*, Vol. XLIX (December, 1955), 1120–28.

TABLE 2

Rank Order Correlation between Apportionment
and Inter-Party Competitiveness in 48 States

State	Apportionment Rank	IPC Rank
Alabama	44	45
Arizona	34	31
Arkansas	12	44
California	40	17
Colorado	21	4
Connecticut	37	6
Delaware	22	1
Florida	41	40
Georgia	48	47
Idaho	27	12
Illinois	23	5
Indiana	10	11
Iowa	42	14
Kansas	46	36
Kentucky	43	24
Louisiana	32	43
Maine	7	35
Maryland	36	13
Massachusetts	5	9
Michigan	28	10
Minnesota	47	16
Mississippi	30	48
Missouri	26	26
Montana	25	23
Nebraska	4	30
Nevada	38	25
New Hampshire	3	32
New Jersey	17	8
New Mexico	39	22
New York	11	15
North Carolina	19	42
North Dakota	35	29
Ohio	1	7
Oklahoma	45	34
Oregon	2	21
Pennsylvania	9	3
Rhode Island	31	33
South Carolina	20	46
South Dakota	14	28
Tennessee	8	37
Texas	33	38
Utah	6	20
Vermont	24	41
Virginia	29	39
Washington	15	19
West Virginia	13	27
Wisconsin	18	18
Wyoming	16	2

$\rho = .17$.

Party Competition and Welfare Orientation

As for the minor proposition, 3a, assuming its continued relevance once the major proposition from which it derives has been challenged—this has been extensively examined by Dawson and Robinson using techniques similar to those being employed here.[14] A ρ of .67 between welfare orientation and inter-party competitiveness corroborates Dawson and Robinson's findings. However, they find that the relationship proves spurious when certain socio-economic variables are held constant. They conclude that *both* inter-party competitiveness and welfare orientation are likely to be products of particular basic social processes and characteristics, i.e., aspects of the political environment. The implications of this relationship will be explored further below.

III. APPORTIONMENT AND DIVIDED CONTROL

The fourth proposition suggests a relationship between divided control and apportionment. Presumably a party whose strength stems from a distribution of population and resources no longer predominant in a given state can, by refusal to reapportion, maintain itself in the legislature despite popular acceptance of the opposition. This transferal of popular allegiance is manifested in the election of governors who face either one or both legislative houses containing a majority of their partisan opponents. It is on these grounds that the late V. O. Key was the most outspoken critic of the separation of powers at the state level.[15] The possibility and frequency of divided control is the main stimulus of his criticisms. And his argument credits malapportionment with causing the greatest number of partisan divisions between governors and their legislatures.

[14]Dawson and Robinson, *op. cit., passim.*
[15]Key, *American State Politics,* Ch. 3.

In order to test this proposition, each situation in which a governor confronted a newly constituted legislature was examined for the six bienniums included between 1952 and 1962. As all but three states elect at least some of their legislators every two years, by examining party control in these years, it is possible to calculate fairly accurately the total number of individual executive-legislative situations in all the states.

Table 3 divides these executive-legislative situations into those which saw a governor facing at least one house controlled by the opposition and those which saw both houses and the governorship controlled by the same party. As the table reveals, American governors, collectively, face at least one opposition controlled house about 35 per cent of the time.

In Table 3, it is also seen, as with the previous propositions, that there is no particular relationship between the presumed dependent variable—divided control—and apportionment, the independent variable, the actual difference between the most and least equally apportioned groups being less than 2 per cent.

The Impact of Southern States

The question may be raised in this context, as it was regarding the presumed connection between welfare-orientation and apportionment, whether the presence of the southern states may not be suppressing an otherwise significant relationship. However, the fact that the non-southern states have no monopoly on malapportionment removes this as a relevant consideration. The percentages of divided control outside the eleven southern states are 41.7, 43.9, and 41.7 for the three apportionment groups shown in Table 3 (most to least equal apportionment, respectively). The larger figures for non-southern states compared to those for all states merely reflect the fact that division of control never occurred in the South

TABLE 3

Apportionment and Divided Control
in 46 States,* 1952–1962

	Apportionment Rank		
	1–16 (Most nearly equal) $N = 90$	*17–31* $N = 90$	*32–48* (Most unequal) $N = 96$
Unified Control ...	64.4%	66.7%	62.5%
Divided Control† ..	35.6	33.3	37.5
Total	100.0	100.0	100.0

*Nebraska and Minnesota are eliminated due to the non-partisan election of their legislators. N, in each case, represents the total number of biennial legislatures. A total of 276 executive-legislative situations are, therefore, included in the calculations.

†The majority of the members of at least one legislative house are of the party opposite that of the governor.

during the period chosen for examination. But there is still no evident relationship between divided control and malapportionment.

Divided Control and Welfare Orientation

With respect to Proposition 4a, we are again in the anomalous position of considering a minor proposition which has been derived from a major proposition of dubious validity. However, although divided control cannot be related to malapportionment in any manner revealed by the data employed here, the impact on policy of party division between the branches of government is still interesting in its own right.

It is interesting precisely because the

TABLE 4

Welfare Orientation and Divided Control
in 35 Non-Southern States,
1952–1962

	Welfare Orientation		
	High $N = 66$	*Medium* $N = 72$	*Low* $N = 72$
Unified Control ...	56.1%	48.5%	68.1%
Divided Control ..	43.9	51.5	31.9
Total	100.0	100.0	100.0

TABLE 5
Expenditure and Party Control: Non-Southern States, 1952–1962

Per Recipient Expenditure For Year Following Legislative Session	Democratic Governors N = 70		Republican Governors N = 105		All Governors N = 175	
	At Least 1 House Rep.	Both Houses Dem.	At Least 1 House Dem.	Both Houses Rep.	Divided Control	Unified Control
Education:	%	%	%	%	%	%
High	25.7	7.1	14.3	21.9	18.9	16.0
Medium	20.0	15.8	11.4	21.9	14.9	19.4
Low	10.0	21.4	7.6	22.9	8.6	22.3
Total	55.7	44.3	33.3	66.7	42.4	57.7
ADC:						
High	20.0	8.6	8.6	33.3	13.1	23.4
Medium	21.4	12.8	10.5	19.1	14.9	16.6
Low	15.8	21.4	13.3	15.2	14.3	17.7
Total	57.2	42.8	34.7	65.6	42.8	57.2
Old Age Relief:						
High	21.4	11.4	7.1	26.6	12.0	21.2
Medium	22.9	7.1	10.5	23.8	15.4	17.1
Low	12.9	24.3	17.1	15.2	15.4	18.9
Total	57.2	42.8	34.7	65.6	42.8	57.2
Unemp. Comp.:						
High	28.6	7.1	12.4	20.0	18.9	14.9
Medium	17.1	12.9	13.3	26.7	14.9	21.1
Low	11.4	22.9	7.6	20.0	9.1	21.1
Total	57.1	42.9	33.3	66.7	42.9	57.1
Aid to Blind:						
High	20.0	12.9	6.7	23.8	12.0	19.5
Medium	22.8	7.1	14.3	21.0	17.7	15.4
Low	15.8	21.4	15.2	19.0	15.4	20.0
Total	58.6	41.4	36.2	63.8	45.1	54.8

major concern here is not a particular variable, such as apportionment, but a mode of analysis. The separation of powers and the factors leading to party division between branches of government have come in for their own share of scorn on the basis of theoretical presuppositions which give high prominence to structure, including party, as a core determinant of the operation of democratic systems (or subsystems, as we may be wont to classify the American states).

Table 4, however, arranging welfare orientation against unity-division of control (in the same manner as Table 3, but including only non-southern states), re-

veals no relationship between this type of policy and party control. This is demonstrated in more detail in Table 5, which arrays each of the items in the welfare orientation measure against party control in the previous year, with respect to both the specific parties and the coincidence or differences of the partisan complexion of the legislatures and governors. Table 5 does bear out the frequently encountered contention that Democratic governors face opposition controlled legislatures with greater frequency than their Republican counterparts.[16] However, the table fails to

16See *ibid.*, p. 57.

TABLE 6
Index of Industrialization: Rank Order Correlation
(ρ) of Components

	Mean Per Capita Income (1952–1961)*	% Urban (1960)†	% Non-Agricultural Employment (1963)‡
Mean Per Capita Income (1952–1961)	X	.76	.87
% Urban (1960)	.76	X	.74
% Non-Agricultural Employment(1963) ..	.87	.74	X

*U.S. Bureau of the Census, *Stastical Abstract of the United States,* (1953 to 1963 editions) Washington, D.C.
†U.S. Bureau of the Census, *U.S. Census of Population,* 1960, Vol. I.
‡U.S. Bureau of the Census, *Statistical Abstract of the United States,* 1964, p. 224.

show a relationship either between unity of control and higher expenditure for individual citizens' benefit or between control by one party or the other and such policies. Those seeking state assistance, as reflected by the few policies examined here, may neither blame their misfortune on one or the other party nor upon any particular constellation of partisan control of the branches of government.

IV. INDUSTRIALIZATION AND APPORTIONMENT

Thus far, the limited evidence presented indicates there is no significant relationship between apportionment and public policy, apportionment and partisan competition, apportionment and divided control, divided control and public policy, or between the party in power and public policy. It may be, however, that, as studies by both Golembiewski[17] and by Dawson and Robinson indicate, there is some relationship between certain structural and environmental characteristics. These two studies find a strong relationship between

inter-party competitiveness and such environmental factors as urbanism, per capita income, non-agricultural employment, and per cent white population. Although inter-party competitiveness is, admittedly, "structural" only by a very broad usage of the term, these studies might lead one to expect a covariance between similar environmental factors and a structural variable such as apportionment. This is the implication of Proposition 5.

Although several complex demographic factors are involved, one of the most commonly encountered explanations of the unequal conditions of apportionment in many states is that, as the states have industrialized, their populations have shifted to the urban areas. In the absence of a re-drawing of district lines, the relative population of districts not sharing in this increase, i.e., those in rural areas, declines, thereby leading to urban–rural imbalance.

Following the suggestions of Dawson and Robinson, an index of industrialization may be constructed. This index is based upon the items in Table 6, which also shows the rank order correlations of the individual components. The individual ranks of each state for mean per capita income (1952–1961), per cent urban, and

[17]Robert T. Golembiewski, "A Taxonomic Approach to State Political Party Strength," *Western Political Quarterly,* Vol. XI (September 1958), 494–513.

per cent in non-agricultural employment were summed and the rank of these totals comprise the industrialization rank. That these items may justifiably be combined, from a statistical point of view, is demonstrated by a ρ of .79. Furthermore, they each measure a facet of the process commonly called "industrialization." Styles of life and occupational pursuits are reflected in the urbanization and employment figures. In addition, the expected fruits of industrialization (at least as conceived in western society) are measured by the income figures.

Apparently, apportionment systems and the willingness or reluctance of legislators to restructure their own electoral bases are largely idiosyncratic. Or, at least, they are independent of the type of environmental factors examined here, as is demonstrated by the fact that $\rho = .20$ between apportionment and industrialization.

V. INDUSTRIALIZATION AND WELFARE ORIENTATION

Proposition 6 posts a direct relationship between the level of economic development in a state and the proclivity of its policy-makers to enact welfare-oriented or "liberal" policies.

The reasoning behind this assertion might suggest that, as a state becomes industrialized, the life styles of its inhabitants no longer rest upon an agrarian, modified kinship basis stressing the values of individual self-sufficiency and the mutual obligations of members of small communities.[18] Rather, the complexities of ex-

istence, the massiveness of mutual needs, and the difficulties of communicating these needs through small, private organizations creates a set of claims which are reflected in governmental activity. Whereas in a less industrialized society there may be other systems (themselves only a remote part of the *political* environment) which meet the individual needs of the society's members, as the style of life of the members reaches a certain level of interdependence (reflected in industrialization) there are claims for action (and the mechanisms for the statement of these claims) which are reflected in what has here been labelled the "welfare orientation" of governmental organs.

Insofar as this line of reasoning is the basis for Proposition 6, it finds fairly strong support in the data, as $\rho = .70$ between industrialization and welfare orientation.

VI. CONCLUSION

The line of investigation suggested here seems to justify the recent concentration of scholarly efforts seeking to discover the impact of environmental factors on the shape and operation of state politics. Structural characteristics and, if one prefers to give partisan variables a separate berth, the nature of the party system and its operation do not seem to go very far toward explaining the kind of policies produced in the states.

Environment probably affects structure indirectly. And, in studies comparing national systems, such might be a fruitful avenue of inquiry. But in the American states, environmental forces do not seem to be differentiated enough to account for major differences in structure, with the possible exception of party competition. We might conclude that there is a nationwide "structural tradition" in the United States, seen in the impact of pre-independence and British experience on the federal Constitution, and in turn inherited by the states.

We see by the data presented here and

---

18 An appreciation of this contrast may be gained from Arthur Vidich and Joseph Bensman's *Small Town in Mass Society* (Princeton, N.J.: Princeton University Press, 1958). They describe in considerable detail the variations of life style contained within a small, rural community and the manner in which these modes of existence are affected by and respond to the changing external world. One of the striking implications, often not recognized by the authors themselves, is that politics are not relevant to many aspects of life in "Springdale"—aspects long ago made political by urban man.

elsewhere, however, clear indication that there is a relationship between environment and policy. Remaining to be studied is the specific manner in which environmental forces are translated into policy. To investigate this will require a more intensive examination than has so far been conducted into political interest formulation (or evolution) and aggregation. It will also be necessary to conduct careful studies of political communication and leadership processes.

In summary, the chief challenge for inquiry is to specify the factors which link environment and public policy in the American states.

DISCERNING A CAUSAL PATTERN AMONG DATA ON VOTING BEHAVIOR*

Arthur S. Goldberg

I. CAUSAL EXPLANATIONS: SIMON'S MODEL

The present analysis is devoted to making an empirically based choice among alternate causal explanations. This entails making causal inferences from statistical correlations. While this might, at one time, have constituted a heresy, I believe that the procedure to be followed here will soon be a part of statistical orthodoxy.[1]

This is not the place for an extended philosophical discussion of the problem of causality. Yet I would like to make my position on the problem as clear as concise presentation will permit. My basic sympathies are with that school which argues that scientifically relevant causal explanation inheres only in our theories, i.e., that the explained event takes the shape which it does because our postulates and logic preclude any other shape on pain of being themselves incorrect.[2] However, the development of such theory, containing such postulates, is usually the product of an inspired insight on the part of one thoroughly immersed in the manifestations of the empirical phenomenon under consideration. The production and verification of such insight in a systematic and reproducible way is the goal of inductive research. Where controlled experimentation is possible, Mill's canons may apply. Where such experiments are either impossible or impracticable, statistical inference becomes necessary. It is in this situation

*Reprinted from the *American Political Science Review*, Vol. LX (December 1966), pp. 913–22. Copyright, 1966, The American Political Science Association.

While I have incurred a great many intellectual debts in the conduct of this inquiry, I am most particularly indebted to Hayward R. Alker, Jr., at Yale University, for so generously making available to me his understanding of causal inference strategies. I also wish to thank the University of Rochester for the research fellowship which enabled me to devote the summer of 1964 to the study of causality and causal inference techniques. Of course, neither mentor nor patron is responsible for such errors as may have been perpetrated herein. For these I alone am culpable.

[1]Cf. Warren E. Miller and Donald E. Stokes, "Constituency Influence in Congress," *American Political Science Review*, Vol. LVII (March, 1963), 45–56; Donald C. Pelz and Frank M. Andrews, "Causal Priorities in Panel Study Data," *American Sociological Review*, Vol. XXIV (December, 1964), 836–47; Hayward R. Alker, Jr., *Mathematics and Politics* (New York: The Macmillan Company, 1965), chap. VI.

[2]Cf. Robert Brown, *Explanation in Social Science* (Chicago: Aldine Publishing Company, 1963), chap. XI. See also Norwood Russell Hanson, *Patterns of Discovery* (Cambridge: Cambridge University Press, 1958), chap. III; and William H. Riker, "Causes of Events," *Journal of Philosophy*, Vol. LV (1958), 281–91.

that the present approach, based upon a model developed by Herbert Simon and others, seems justified.[3]

Simon's model is designed to capture the asymmetry in our notions of causality. When one speaks of A as a cause of B, one usually has in mind a unidirectional forcing, and not merely a covariation, or phased covariation. Thus, if one speaks of rains as a cause of floods, one expects that a variation in rainfall will be accompanied by a variation in flooding, *but* one does *not* expect that variations in flooding deriving from other causes, e.g., faulty dam construction, will be accompanied by variations in rainfall. Again, it should be noted that the concept of alternate causes is alien to deductive theory, which seeks to postulate the most inclusive principles. However, inductive inference is concerned with perceiving an ever-increasing proportion of the total set of alternate causes in order to facilitate formulation of a principle of commonality.

Simon suggests that a patterned causal ordering can and should be described as a recursive set of simultaneous equations dealing sequentially with each of the variables in the causal ordering and describing each in terms of the regression of its causal antecedents upon it. Thus if one had four variables, $x_1 \cdots x_4$, in which x_1 was considered causally independent of all of the rest, and x_4 was considered causally dependent upon all of the rest, and in which x_2 and x_3 were causally intervening, this could be described as follows:[4]

$$x_1 = e_1$$
$$x_2 = b_{21}x_1 + e_2$$
$$x_3 = b_{31.2}x_1 + b_{32.1}x_2 + e_3$$
$$x_4 = b_{41.23}x_1 + b_{42.13}x_2 + b_{43.12}x_3 + e_4$$

The non-zero regression coefficients describe the impact of each of the causal antecedents upon a given variable; the pattern of impacts is inferable from the zero regression coefficients, and asymmetry is accomplished in that manipulation of the value of a given variable leaves unaltered the relationships among its causal antecedents, and can affect only causally subsequent variables.[5]

Since it is the case that causal impacts should appear as non-zero value regression coefficients, causal models in which any of the variables contribute directly to less than the full set of subsequent variables have implied zero value regression coefficients. Hubert Blalock points out that such regression coefficients imply zero value correlation coefficients. It thus becomes possible with the aid of partial correlation coefficients to make an empirically based decision among alternate causal models purporting to describe the causal relationships within the same set of variables. This is the technique which will be used in the present analysis.

It should be noted that there are several assumptions being made which bear substantially upon the logic of the analysis. These are: that the effects on the dependent variable of variables excluded from the model are not related to effects produced by any of the independent variables in the model; that all variables which have a substantial impact on the dependent variable and are correlated with independent variables in the model are also included in the model (i.e., the error terms are uncorrelated); that the phenomena to be explained entail no reciprocal causation.[6]

It should also be noted that there is a

---

[3]See Herbert A. Simon, *Models of Man* (New York: John Wiley & Sons, Inc., 1957), chaps. I–III; and Hubert M. Blalock, Jr., *Causal Inferences in Nonexperimental Research* (Chapel Hill: The University of North Carolina Press, 1964), chaps. I–III. These authors, in turn, have drawn heavily upon the work of econometricians. Among basic sources are, for example, Ragnar Frisch, *Statistical Confluence Analysis by Means of Complete Regression Systems* (Oslo: Universitets Økonomiske Institutt, 1934) and T. C. Koopmans (ed.), *Statistical Inference in Dynamic Economic Models* (New York: John Wiley & Sons, 1950).

[4]Simon, *op. cit.*, chap. I.

---

[5]Blalock, *op. cit.*, pp. 52–60.
[6]See *ibid.*, pp. 46–54.

serious controversy among econometricians with regard to the uncorrelated error term assumption.[7] Although I do not wish to indulge in an extended discussion of the subject, it is perhaps only fair that I make my own position explicit. In general, I believe that this assumption is almost always invalid, and that science proceeds not only in spite of this invalidity, but to a large extent through efforts to cope with it. When the limit of a theory is encountered, in the form of the occurrence of a theoretically precluded phenomenon, the search is begun for some component of the error term which is correlated in the relevant sense, and in conjunction with its discovery, the substance of the theory is revised. This is but one form of the retroductive process.[8]

II. CAUSAL RELATIONS AMONG SIX VARIABLES

The present analysis is concerned with making inferences about the pattern of causal relationships among six variables: father's sociological characteristics (FSC); father's party identification (FPI); respondent's sociological characteristics (RSC); respondent's party identification (RPI); respondent's partisan attitudes (RPA); and respondent's vote for President in 1956 (RV). The assumed causal ordering is the sequence in which the variables are listed above, except when otherwise noted. In each case to be examined, the model will be presented schematically, and the variables will be numbered in accordance with their assumed causal sequence.

Variables were selected for inclusion in the analysis on the bases of their repeated occurrence in the voting literature and their availability in a reliable body of data.[9] The sociological characteristics of

the respondent's father and the father's party identification were taken as indicators of the context in which the respondent underwent his early political socialization. The literature is replete with the importance of this early socialization for political behavior in general and for voting behavior in particular.[10] The respondent's sociological characteristics were taken as an indicator of the constraints placed upon him by his current social environs. This variable represents the approach taken by Berelson et al. in Voting, and thus the general sociological explanation of voting behavior.[11] The respondent's party identification was included because of its well established and substantial correlation with direction of vote in a number of major studies.[12] Finally, the respondent's partisan attitudes were included as an indicator of his perceptions of the po-

Survey Research Center at The University of Michigan, and made available to me through the Inter-University Consortium for Political Research. The exact operationalization of the variables is described in the Technical Note at the end of the article. The number of respondents in the present analysis is 645 out of the 1762 provided in the SRC survey. The 645 are those who had full information on the full set of variables. There is thus a slight overrepresentation of Republicans and upper SES respondents. This bias is slight and there appears to be no other systematic bias in the sub-sample. For more detailed discussion, see Arthur S. Goldberg, *The Intergenerational Transmission of Party Identification* (unpublished doctoral dissertation, Yale University, 1966), Appendix B.

[10]Surveys of the literature on this point are available in Herbert H. Hyman, *Political Socialization* (Glencoe, Illinois: The Free Press, 1959); and Robert E. Lane and David O. Sears, *Public Opinion* (Englewood Cliffs: Prentice-Hall, Inc., 1964).

[11]See, for example, Bernard R. Berelson, Paul F. Lazarsfeld, and William N. McPhee, *Voting* (*Chicago*: The University of Chicago Press, 1954), chaps. IV–VII. See also Seymour Martin Lipset, *Political Man* (Garden City, New York: Doubleday & Company, Inc., 1960, Part II.

[12]See, for example, Angus Campbell, Gerald Gurin, and Warren E. Miller, *The Voter Decides*, (Evanston, Illinois: Row, Peterson and Company, 1954), chap. VII. See also Angus Campbell, Philip E. Converse, Warren E. Miller, and Donald E. Stokes, *The American Voter* (New York: John Wiley & Sons, Inc., 1960), chap. VI.

[7]See, for example, Fritz C. Holte, *Economic Shock-Models* (Oslo: Norwegian Universities Press, 1962), pp. 14–17.

[8]See Hanson, *op. cit.,* chap. IV.

[9]The body of data used consisted of that generated in the 1956 election study (#417) by the

litical arena, on the basis of the argument made in *The American Voter,* and because of the high correlation of these attitudes with voting behavior in that study.[13]

III. MODEL I

As a point of departure, let us consider one version of an attitude-field theory model, that presented in *The American Voter*.[14] The authors have told us very little about what to expect in such a model, except that in pure Gestalt thoery, the attitude field is the final mediator of all causes of the behavior in question. Based upon this requirement, let us consider one plausible model. In this model the attitude field is taken to be the result of two causal streams, one consisting in the sociological conditioning of childhood and adult life,[15] and the other consisting in affective conditioning to the party label.[16] This model is presented in Figure 1. Let us call this Model I, Attitude as Final Mediator. Figure 1 contains a schematic of the model, the theoretical prediction equations implied by the model, and the empirical values which those equations yielded from the data in the analysis.[17]

---

[13]*The American Voter,* chap. IV. See also Donald E. Stokes, Angus Campbell, and Warren E. Miller, "Components of Electoral Decision," *American Political Science Review,* Vol. LII (June, 1958), 367–87.

[14]Cf. *The American Voter,* pp. 24–37.

[15]Cf. Berelson, Lazarsfeld, and McPhee, *loc. cit.*

[16]Cf. Lane and Sears, *op. cit.,* pp. 18–19.

[17]Although the aid of a computer was enlisted for the statistical computations in the present article, the lower order partials could be calculated with a slide rule or desk calculator. The appropriate formulae are available in Hubert M. Blalock, *Social Statistics* (New York: McGraw-Hill Book Co., Inc., 1960), pp. 333–36. For those who wish to check the computation of some of the lower order partials, the matrix of simple correlations is provided below:

	FSC	FPI	RSC	RPI	RPA	RV
FSC	1.000					
FPI	0.454	1.000				
RSC	0.808	0.420	1.000			
RPI	0.400	0.603	0.411	1.000		
RPA	0.318	0.453	0.289	0.710	1.000	
RV	0.282	0.466	0.271	0.722	0.742	1.000

FIGURE 1

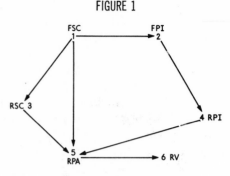

MODEL I
Attitude as Final Mediator

Prediction Equations	*Actual Values*
$r_{41.23} = 0$	0.017
$r_{61.2345} = 0$	−0.019
$r_{32.1} = 0$	0.101
$r_{52.134} = 0$	0.032
$r_{62.1345} = 0$	0.053
$r_{43.12} = 0$	0.130
$r_{63.1245} = 0$	−0.022
$r_{64.1235} = 0$	0.365

Given the assumption of a unidirectional causal ordering, there are fifteen possible causal arrows in a six variable model.[18] In Model I there are seven arrows present. The eight missing arrows mean that the model posits no causal impact in eight of the possible fifteen causal connections. One therefore expects the regression coefficients, and therefore the correlation coefficients associated with the missing arrows to be zero. This yields the set of prediction equations consisting in the list of partial "r's" predicted to be equal to zero in Figure 1.

While Model I may seem plausible, there are some substantial incongruities between the prediction equations and the actual values. Most notably, these incongruities derive from the omission of causal links between RPI and RV, between RSC and RPI, and between FPI and RSC. Of greatest theoretical importance is the size of $r_{64.1235}$, i.e., 0.365. While this amounts to only 13.3% of the variance, it is sufficient

---

[18]Assuming that reciprocal causation is not involved, there are always $n!/2(n-2)!$ possible arrows among n variables.

to give one qualms about regarding attitudes, as operationalized by *The American Voter*, as the final mediator. Clearly party identification has an impact not caught in the screen which those researchers drew across their funnel of causality.[19] The need for a link between RSC and RPI, based upon the actual value of $r_{43.12}$ being equal to 0.130 instead of zero, reflects the idea that adult sociological characteristics play a role in party identification. The fact that this role accounts for a miniscule proportion of the variance (1.7%) suggests that the adult sociological environs are supportive of earlier learned behavior, rather than the primary source of this behavior. The need for a link between FPI and RSC is suggested by the value of $r_{32.1} = 0.101$. The size of this value suggests that the link is quite weak, and a more parsimonious model might well do without it. A possible explanation may be in upwardly aspirational parents adopting a party identification normally associated with higher status groups and transmitting their status aspirations to their offspring with sufficient impact to have them realized to some extent. This is, to be sure, a most tentative explanation, but then this particular linkage is also rather tentative.

IV. MODEL II

On the basis of the experience provided by Model I, a second model is proposed. In Model II party identification is taken as the final arbiter. Three arrows have been dropped: those linking FSC and RPA, RSC and RPA, and RPA and RV. The first two were dropped in a search for parsimony, and the third was dropped to implement the central idea of this particular model. Finally the lessons of Model I have been incorporated in Model II presented in Figure 2. Note that in Model II the time sequence between RPI and RPA

---

[19]*The American Voter*, p. 35. The relative size of this impact is a function of factors which will be dealt with later in the present analysis. See pp. 113–14, below.

FIGURE 2

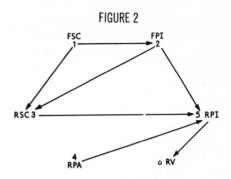

MODEL II
Party Identification as Final Mediator

Prediction Equations		Actual Values
$r_{41.23} = 0$	....	−0.017
$r_{51.234} = 0$	....	0.037
$r_{61.2345} = 0$	....	−0.019
$r_{42.13} = 0$	....	0.357
$r_{62.1345} = 0$	....	0.053
$r_{43.12} = 0$	....	0.031
$r_{63.1245} = 0$	....	−0.022
$r_{64.1235} = 0$	....	0.470

is the reverse of what it was in Model I. Thus the subscripts do not necessarily refer to those variables which carried the same subscripts in Model I. Comparisons between models require translation of subscript numbers, which indicate causal ordering, into variable symbols through the use of the schematic diagrams. Each set of subscripts should be used only within its own diagram.

Examination of Figure 2 indicates two rather gross discrepancies between predicted and actual values. One of these, $r_{64.1235} = 0.470$, simply invalidates the notion of party identification as final arbiter. It suggests the need for a direct causal link between RPA and RV. The other major discrepancy, $r_{42.13} = 0.357$, requires a more complex interpretation. Given the causal ordering in this model, what is implied is the need for a causal link between FPI and RPA. However, if one glances back at Model I, it can be seen that the omission of the causal link between FPI and RPA produced no serious discrepancy (predicted value = 0, actual value = 0.032). It is this pair of findings which enables a choice to be made between the two causal orderings. On the basis of Simon's asymmetric model of causality, the causal link between two variables may be affected by all of the variables antecedent to the dependent variable, but *cannot* be affected by any of the variables subsequent to the dependent variable.[20] Thus, in Model I the antecedents to RPA are FSC, FPI, RSC, and RPI. In describing the impact of FPI upon RPA, it was therefore necessary to control for FSC, RSC, and RPI. However, in Model II, RPA is assumed to be antecedent to RPI. Therefore, in describing the impact of FPI upon RPA in this model, one is prohibited from including RPI as a control. Clearly, the omission of the control yields a poor fit with the data and suggests that to the extent that unidirectionality is assumed and parsimony desired, the RPI ought to be regarded as prior to RPA. Support is thus lent to the positions of Lane and Sears, Greenstein, and others who have urged the importance of the early socialization of political symbols.[21]

V. MODEL III

Reverting, then, to the causal ordering in Model I, and incorporating the lessons taught by Models I and II, a third model is proposed, that of dual mediation. The schematic, prediction equations, and findings are presented in Figure 3. Here, in Model III, one has a model which fits the data relatively well. Its distinctive features are: it hypothesizes *both* party identification and partisan attitudes as direct causes of vote direction; it assigns a pivotal position to party identification in denying that any of the antecedents to party identification have a direct bearing on partisan

20Blalock, *Causal Inference* . . . , p. 59.

21Lane and Sears, *loc. cit.* Fred I. Greenstein, "The Benevolent Leader: Children's Images of Political Authority," *American Political Science Review*, Vol. LIV (1960), 934–43.

FIGURE 3

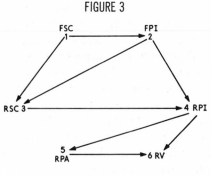

MODEL III
Dual Mediation

Prediction Equations	Actual Values
$r_{41.23} = 0$	−0.017
$r_{51.234} = 0$	0.083
$r_{61.2345} = 0$	−0.019
$r_{52.134} = 0$	0.032
$r_{62.1345} = 0$	0.053
$r_{53.124} = 0$	−0.073
$r_{63.1245} = 0$	−0.022

attitudes or vote direction; within the framework of the model, no causes are hypothesized for partisan attitudes other than party identification. The last point, of course, suggests that the framework of the model is too restricted, since party identification in its total impact accounts for only about 50% of the variance in partisan attitudes ($r = .710$, see n. 17, above). This point will be elaborated upon. However, before launching into a serious critique of Model III, one ought to consider that while the model fits the data rather well, it is not a perfect fit. Since it is possible to make perfectly valid direct inferences from correlation coefficients to regression coefficients only where the former are actually zero, and since the inferences here have been based upon correlation coefficients slightly different from zero, a further analytic step seems warranted, i.e., calculation of standardized regression coefficients (beta weights). Based upon the causal ordering of Model III, such coefficients were generated for all of the linkages possible within that ordering. In general, the inferences made from the correlation coefficients are supported. That is, the implied zero impacts prove to be very small and statistically insignificant at the .05 level.[22] However, there is one exception: the FSC to RPA linkage, while relatively small, proved to be significant at the .05 level. Thus there is occasioned the revision presented in Model IV, in Figure 4. Within the assumptions made with regard to unidirectional causality and causal ordering, this is the model which best fits the data, and which requires critical assessment.

VI. MODEL IV

From the viewpoint of theory, Model IV has both desirable and undesirable features. Let us first look at the happier side of this situation. Certainly the model achieves a certain amount of parsimony. Of fifteen possible causal arrows, six have been eliminated and of the remaining nine, two are clearly of secondary importance, leaving a dominant seven-arrow model. Moreover, the model is theoretically informative, both in terms of what it omits and in terms of its dominant patterns. The omission of direct causal links between sociological characteristics, both childhood (FSC) and adult (RSC), and voting behavior, as well as the omission of such a link between childhood sociological

---

[22]The decision to accept or reject linkages on the basis of significance tests poses some problems. The significance test is designed to deal with the type I error (rejection of the null hypothesis when it is true). That is to say, it provides a statement of the probability that a strength of association as great as that found in the sample could have been drawn from a population in which there was in fact no relationship between the variables in question. However, in deciding to omit a link, one is concerned with the risk of a type II error (acceptance of the null hypothesis when it is false). The information desired in this case is the probability that a strength of association as weak as that in the sample could have been drawn from a population in which there was a stronger association. Unless one has an a priori expectation of the strength of association in the population, it is not possible to calculate this probability.

FIGURE 4

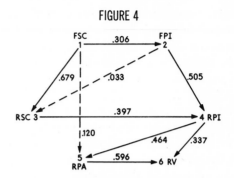

MODEL IV
Dual Mediation, Revised

Key: The beta weights of the implied linkages appear either immediately above or immediately to the right of their representational arrows. The beta weights of the linkages represented by solid arrows prove significant at the .001 level. Those represented by broken arrows prove significant at the .05 level but not at the .01 level. None of the possible linkages which have been omitted have beta weights which are significant even at the .05 level.

characteristics and adult party identification certainly justify the qualms of the authors of *The American Voter* about the sociological explanations of voting behavior.[23] However, it can also be seen, in this empirically supported model, that sociological characteristics do have a substantial *indirect* impact on voting behavior, exerted primarily through party identification. The mediating role of party identification as described in Model IV suggests that father's sociological characteristics, father's party identification, and respondent's sociological characteristics have almost no impact upon voting behavior save as they act through respondent's party identification. Therefore one expects $r_{65.4} = r_{65.1234}$. The actual values are: $r_{65.4} = 0.472$, $r_{65.1234} = 0.470$.

The fact that party identification rather than partisan attitudes proves to be the pivotal encapsulator of political socialization, substantiates the position that such socialization entails an affective relationship to symbols rather than a conscious evaluative relating of political means to

---

[23]*The Amercan Voter*, pp. 32–37.

ends. This position is given still further support by the absence of a direct link between childhood sociological characteristics and adult party identification; there is a relationship, but it is dependent upon mediation by paternal party identification. However, this is not to say that there is no rational calculus involved in voting. The fact that partisan attitudes have a substantial impact beyond that of party identification, suggests that such a calculus is operative, but operative against a set of predispositions dominated by party identification.[24] Thus, the model suggested by this study comports well with the data of other studies and imposes a certain order upon their findings.

Yet certain caveats are in order. One should bear in mind that the present study has dealt, to this point, only with respondents who claimed a Republican or a Democratic party identification for themselves. Those who were classified as Independents or as apolitical have been excluded. This has an important bearing upon the partial correlation between party identification and vote, controlling for partisan attitudes. In the present study, this partial correlation is 0.415, amounting to 17.2% of the variance. It has been pointed out to me by Professor Donald Stokes of the Michigan Survey Research Center that in the full sample, which, of course, includes Independents and those classed as apolitical (together amounting to 12.6% of the sample), this partial correlation drops to 0.238, thus accounting for less than 5.7% of the variance.

To one interested primarily in mapping a particular population, the figures based upon the full sample ought to be more salient. However, for one interested in the logic of the explanatory theory, both sets of figures are of interest. Taken together they suggest that the impact of party

identification on voting behavior in a given population will depend upon the ratio of partisans to non-partisans in that society. In those instances in which, for whatever reasons, individuals have not developed a party identification, the impact of partisan attitudes would be substantially increased, if the logic of Model IV is correct. As the proportion of such instances in a population increased, the net impact of party identification on vote would be expected to diminish.[25] Essentially this is the obverse of the argument made in *The American Voter* about the efficacy of partisan attitudes as a guide to voting behavior.[26]

At this point attention is directed to certain unsatisfactory features of the model itself. While it leaves room for a rational calculus prior to the voting act, it does not permit party identification to benefit from this calculus. This prohibition derives from the requirements of the mathematical model of causality used in the analysis. A major requirement of that model, it will be recalled, was unidirectionality. Yet this is a limitation which, in the long run, must be circumvented, if theory is to be relevant to events. As this model stands, party identification is nearly immutable. There is very little if any variation over time in its antecedents, nor is there any provision for what V. O. Key calls a critical election.[27] This derives from two factors. First the model does not permit partisan attitudes to have an impact upon party identification. Second, the model does not include among its components the political events in the environment in which it is assumed to operate. The failure of partisan attitudes

---

[24]Cf. Berelson, Lazarsfeld, and McPhee, *op. cit.*, pp. 227–33. See also *The American Voter*, pp. 128–31; and Lane and Sears, *op. cit.*, pp. 81–82.

[25]Note that this "net impact" refers to a population parameter, or statistic thereof, rather than to the impact of party identification on the vote of any single individual in the population. While the latter would doubtless be of interest, it would be extremely difficult to come by in non-experimental data.

[26]See *The American Voter*, pp. 139–42.

[27]V. O. Key, Jr., "A Theory of Critical Elections," *Journal of Politics*, 18 (1955), 3–18.

to feed back upon party identification would mean that even if the correlation between partisan attitudes and party identification were substantially reduced, voting behavior would be influenced, but party identification would be unaffected. Clearly the model needs revision on this point. Moreover, unless one includes an additional variable there is no source within the model for variation of partisan attitudes. Thus, the model is itself a partial description of the impact of the past upon the present, but its connection with the future rests almost entirely in the error factors of the recursive equations which define the model—a situation both undesirable and unnecessary.

Let us first consider amending the model to permit partisan attitudes to have an impact upon party identification. This could be done within a recursive set of equations by "lagging" some of the variables, as Blalock suggests.[28] This entails treating a single variable through time as a set of discrete variables, and treating two interacting variables as two sets of discrete variables. Thus in the time interval $t_0 \cdots t_n$, an interaction between X and Y could be schematized as follows: $X_{t0} \rightarrow Y_{t1} \rightarrow X_{t2} \rightarrow Y_{t3} \rightarrow X_{t4} \cdots$. This technique, of course, requires data through time, and will not be utilized with the data of the present study, but is presented for future research purposes.

Introjection of political events into the model presents rather more difficult problems. All of the variables in the model are, in some sense, attributes or activities of the actors. Political events, on the other hand, are external to the actors and cannot be brought into the model directly. They can, however, be brought in through his perceptions. Now to some extent these perceptions are measured in partisan attitudes. These attitudes are, however, assessed only immediately prior to the election itself. What would have to be done

_____
[28]Blalock, *Causal Inferences* . . . , pp. 53–57.

in a more dynamic and adaptive model would be to sample perceptions of political events as they arise in the political arena, probing in each case for evaluation of the party's handling of the event. The adequacy of the series of events selected would depend upon the astuteness of the analyst and could be tested by the amount of variance in partisan attitudes immediately prior to the election which is accounted for by the attitudes on the full set of events. Moreover, selected probing techniques, such as factor analysis, could be applied to draw inferences about the factors underlying shifts in partisanship over time.

A model incorporating these modifications is presented in Figure 5 below. The

FIGURE 5

MODEL V
A Proposed Dynamic

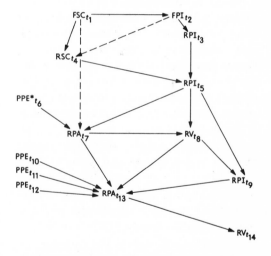

*PPE = perception of political events.

model exploits the mediating roles of partisan attitudes and party identification in order to avoid reincorporation of political socialization characteristics over time. This is not to say that these are not operative. On the contrary, they form the background, encapsulated largely in party identification, against which partisan attitudes are formed and operate. The model represents a continual reality-testing and adjustment process. To the extent that party identification exceeds the impact of partisan attitudes, little learning is taking place. To the extent that partisan attitudes exceed and have the same directional impact as party identification, reinforcement is taking place. Finally, to the extent partisan attitudes operate in a direction opposite to party identification, that identification is being eroded. There are several other points in the proposed model that bear discussion, e.g., the requirement that partisan attitudes operate on party identification through vote (or vote intention). However, this and other excluded arrows had best wait upon the systematic analysis of data in future studies.

VII. CONCLUSION

In concluding the present analysis, it is important to bear in mind that we are as yet very far from concluding the inquiry into causality in voting behavior. First, it should be noted that the full set of independent variables accounts for only 50% of the variance in voting. This suggests, of course, that one or more important variables have been excluded from the model. In itself, this is only an indication of the need for a broader searching effort. However, there is a distinct possibility that the omitted variable(s) may be correlated with both the dependent variable and one or more of the independent variables in the present model. In such a case the regression coefficients in the model might be substantially affected, even to the extent of reducing to zero some of the now nonzero coefficients, and of reasserting causal linkages estimated as zero in the present model.[29] The present model is thus tentative, an initial approximation to be

continually retested not only with the same variables in different populations at different times, but against the impact of the inclusion of new variables.

TECHNICAL NOTE

The variables were operationalized from the source decks of the 1956 election study (Project 417) of the Survey Research Center at the University of Michigan in the following manner:

1. Father's Sociological Characteristics (FSC)

This variable consists in an index generated by running five sociological characteristics of the father against the father's party identification in order to generate an expected value of his being Republican.[30] This value constituted the index. The variables utilized, their sources, and their categorizations are presented below:

Variable (Source Deck: Column)	Categories	(Rows)
Religion (5: 27)	Protestant	(1)
	Catholic	(2)
	Jewish	(3)
Class (8: 11)	Working	(1, 2, 3)
	Middle	(4, 5, 6)
Size of community (6: 34)	Farm	(1)
	Town	(2, 3, 4, 5, 6, 8)
	Metropolis	(7, 9)
Region (6: 31–32)	South	(1 in col. 31, 4 or 5 in col. 32)
	Non-South	(all others)
Race (6: 10)	White	(1)
	Negro	(2)

2. Father's Party Identification (FPI)

This was established on the basis of data gathered in a later wave with the

---

[29]*Ibid.*, pp. 46–47. See also Herman Wold and Lars Jureen, *Demand Analysis* (New York: John Wiley & Sons, 1953), pp. 37–38, and Fritz C. Holte, *loc. cit.*

[30]Since the variables were comprised of nominal data, the categories of the variables were appropriately as "1–0" dummy variables. See Daniel B. Suits, "Use of Dummy Variables in Regression Equations," *Journal of the American Statistical Association*, Vol. LII, No. 280 (December, 1957), 548–51.

Variable (Source Deck: Column)	Categories	(Rows)
Religion (5: 27)	Protestant	(1)
	Catholic	(2)
	Jewish	(3)
Class (8: 10)	Working	(1, 2, 3)
	Middle	(4, 5, 6)
Size of community (1: 17)	Farm	(6, –, &)
	Town	(3, 4, 5, 8, 9, 0)
	Metrópolis	(1, 2, 7)
Region (1: 15)	South	(8, 9, 0)
	Non-South	(1–7)
Race (6: 10)	White	(1)
	Negro	(2)

same panel, i.e., the 1958 election study, project 431. Within that study, the information was taken from Deck C04: column 23, and the only categories used were Democrat (Row 1) and Republican (Row 2).

3. Respondent's Sociological Characteristics (RSC)

The procedure here was the same as that entailed in building the index of father's sociological characteristics, except that the variables used in the regression were characteristics of the respondent rather than of the father.

4. Respondent's Party Identification (RPI)

This information was taken from Deck 4, column 9. It was dichotomized as follows: Democrat (rows 1–3), Republican (rows 5–7).

5. Respondent's Partisan Attitudes (RPA)

This variable was received directly from the Survey Research Center at the University of Michigan as an index, drawn from their analysis deck number 86, columns 3–9, and based upon their regression of six dimensions of partisan attitudes against reported vote in 1956.

6. Respondent's Vote

Deck 7: Column 26 Democrat (row 1), Republican (row 2).

SECTION III

The Pressure Groups Model

The brunt of criticism and support for group theory in politics focuses on David Truman's *The Governmental Process.* This concentration undoubtedly denotes the seminal nature of his effort and the daring in which he presents the theory's structure. The elements of the pressure group model are all here. Because man is a social animal, he cannot be viewed apart from the groups to which he belongs; and these groups shape his perspectives and opinion while giving them voice in the making of public policy. Other than the fact that groups have members, the individual is unimportant—in that groups, as the teachers of opinions, give expression to all opinions. The governmental process may be viewed as the interaction among groups, Truman argues. But in the second selection of this section, Rothman notes that Truman also conceives of an additional theory of the mobilization of previously unorganized groups who share opinions—potential interest groups. Thus on one hand, opinion is solely the result of group educational efforts, and on the other, groups can originate from shared opinions. In either case, however, public opinion is carried to government by way of groups.

But why should governmental officials heed the opinions of groups? They may do so because they feel these groups give legitimate expression to public opinion, which should be considered in making policy; but this is more the argument of the role-playing model, and we are getting ahead of ourselves. The coercive element of the pressure groups model would cause us to look for ways a group might punish a legislator for failing to heed their opinion. Such a technique would be their ability to deliver the votes of their membership to the legislator's opponent in the next election. But can groups control their memberships' vote? Angus Campbell *et al.* seek to to assess this. They find groups can align their members' votes with a party over a period of years if the members identify with the group and are not merely forced into membership by birth or circumstance. But the process is such that they cannot readily have them vote for the other party for one election. Labor can get involved members to vote Democratic after some effort, but it cannot affect a quick change to the Republican party should the Democrats prove unresponsive to Labor's opinions.

If groups are to serve as aggregate expressions of opinions within the public, a group's leadership should be able to accurately express their group's opinions. Luttbeg and Zeigler consider whether leaders accurately perceive membership opinions or share the opinions of their members. Within a professional teachers' organization both methods for leaders to express group opinion prove somewhat biased.

To affect public policy a group must work with elected officials, but can a group's lobbying efforts affect legislator's voting? Harmon Zeigler explored legislator–lobbyist relations, finding substantial variations between states. Massachusetts lobbyists face frustrating unresponsiveness from Massachusetts legislators; thus the pressure group model seems less effective in Massachusetts than in Oregon, with its excellent legislator–lobbyist relations.

GROUPS AND SOCIETY*

David E. Truman

Man is a social animal. Among other meanings involved in this Aristotlelian statement is the observation that with rare exceptions man is always found in association with other men. John Dewey has observed: "Associated activity needs no explanation; things are made that way."[1] This association includes varying degrees of organization; that is, certain of the relationships among a collection of men regularly occur in certain consistent patterns and sequences. But there is another meaning in this classic proposition, closer to the one that Aristotle probably intended, namely, that men must exist in society in order to manifest those capacities and accomplishments that distinguish them from the other animals. These human accomplishments embrace not only the wondrous array of skills and creations that are thought of as civilization but also humbler and more fundamental developments such as primary intellectual growth and language.

We do not have to rely solely on Aristotle's confidence concerning the virtues of life in the city-state for support of the proposition that man is essentially social. The Robinson Crusoe hypothesis that men are best conceived of as isolated units is inadequate psychology as well as unfashionable economics. Accounts, at least partially authenticated, of children who by some chance of fate have been raised among animals, isolated from all contact with human beings, indicate not only that speech is not acquired under such circumstances but also that it is developed only very slowly after the child has been returned to human society. Cases of children who have been kept in solitary confinement during their early years illustrate the same point. An essentially human and social characteristic, speech, is not acquired, and, in fact, the very capacity to learn is apparently stunted or atrophied.[2] Man becomes characteristically human only in association with other men.

A more obvious sort of interdependence also requires man to live in society—purely physical dependence on others of his species. The family, the most primitive social unit, the only one that man shares generally with other mammals, exists in part

---

*David E. Truman, The Governmental Process (New York: Alfred A. Knopf, Inc., 1951), pp. 14–17, 33–44, 506–19. Copyright 1951 by Alfred A. Knopf, Inc. Reprinted by permission.

[1] John Dewey: The Public and Its Problems (New York: Henry Holt & Company, Inc., 1927), p. 151. Copyright by and used with the permission of Henry Holt & Company, Inc.

[2] See Arnold Gesell: Wolf Child and Human Child (New York: Harper and Brothers, 1939) and Kingsley Davis: "Extreme Social Isolation of a Child," American Journal of Sociology, Vol. XLV, no. 4 (January, 1940), pp. 554–65.

to provide protection and training for the offspring during their long period of helplessness. Furthermore, the division of labor or specialization, which appears even in the simple family unit on the basis of age and sex differences and on which a high degree of skill and large productivity fundamentally depend, almost by definition involves the mutual dependence of men. A modern urban dweller who has experienced the consequences of an interruption in the milk supply, in the public transportation system, or in the distribution of electric power needs no introduction to the implications of specialization.

In this chapter, as the remarks above suggest, we shall not focus our attention primarily upon "political" behavior. We shall rather examine groups of all kinds and their significance in the social process generally. The point to bear in mind is that the dynamics of groups are not essentially different because the groups are labeled "political." Basically they show the same regularities as do other continuing social patterns. In this connection we shall discuss the meaning of the terms "group" and "interest group" and shall examine some of the characteristics of a peculiarly important type of group, the association.

GROUP AFFILIATIONS AND INDIVIDUAL BEHAVIOR

In all societies of any degree of complexity the individual is less affected directly by the society as a whole than differentially through various of its subdivisions, or groups. In the first place, even in the simplest society, it is literally impossible for any one individual to function in all the groups of which the society is made. Just as he can become highly skilled in only one or a few techniques, so he can participate in only a limited number of the groups that are formed about such specializations. In a society in which locality groupings are important, an individual never "belongs" to more than a few and rarely to more than one. In the

second place, the positions occupied by the individual in his society limit the effects upon him of society as a whole. The technical term usually applied to these positions is *statuses*.[3] He may not participate in those groups confined to persons of the opposite sex or of a differing age level. Ordinarily he belongs to only one "extended" family, one church, one economic institution, and one political unit at a given level, such as the nation. At any point in time and frequently over his entire life span he cannot belong to more than one class or caste grouping.

To the extent that the range and type of behavior in these groupings vary from one to another—and even in the simplest societies they inevitably vary to some degree—the patterns of action and attitude among individuals will differ from one another in large measure according to the clusters of group affiliations that the individuals have. In John Dewey's words: "The underlying and generative conditions of concrete behavior are social as well as organic: much more social than organic as far as the manifestation of *differential* wants, purposes and methods of operation is concerned."[4] Because such groups may come into conflict from time to time, various theorists have attempted to account for both the groups and the conflict in terms of "instincts." Gaetano Mosca, for example, asserts that men have an "instinct of herding together and fighting with other herds" that accounts not only for the conflicts between societies but also for "the formation of all the divisions and subdivisions . . . that arise within a given society and occasion moral and, sometimes, physical conflicts."[5] It is

[3]Ralph Linton: *The Cultural Background of Personality* (New York: Appleton-Century-Crofts, Inc., 1945), pp. 75–82.

[4]Dewey: *The Public and Its Problems*, p. 103. Copyright 1927 by and used with the permission of Henry Holt & Company, Inc.

[5]From *The Ruling Class* by Gaetano Mosca, translated from the Italian by Hannah D. Kahn, edited by Arthur Livingston, p. 163. Copyright 1939. Courtesy of McGraw-Hill Book Company, Inc.

quite unnecessary to resort to any such crude *deus ex machina,* for, like the similar devices employed by the social contract philosophers of the seventeenth century to account for the origin of government and society, it implies the temporal priority of the individual over the group. That is, it implicitly assumes that individuals exist first in some degree of isolation and then form into societies or groups, a notion impossible to document.

It is simpler and more realistic to say with James Madison that the tendencies toward such groupings are "sown in the nature of man," meaning by that statement, as he apparently meant, that such tendencies are "sown" by the differing group experiences of individuals. When such groups become active, whether in conflict or not, that stage of development can be accounted for, again in Madison's words, in terms of "the different circumstances of civil society."[6] In slightly different terms: "The human being whom we fasten upon as individual *par excellence* is moved and regulated by his association with others; what he does and what the consequences of his behavior are, what his experience consists of, cannot even be described, much less accounted for, in isolation."[7]

.   .   .   .

INTEREST GROUPS

Various of these established designations will be useful from time to time, but one identifying term, which was used without definition in the previous chapter, may be discussed at some length, since it involves the central concern of these pages, the term "interest group." Like so many terms associated with the processes of government, it has been used for the purposes of polemics so freely that it has

acquired certain emotional connotations which may render it ambiguous when used in analysis. *Political, partisan,* and even the word *politics* itself share with *interest, vested interest, special interest,* and *interest group,* among others, a connotation of impropriety and selfishness that almost denies them the neutral precision requisite to careful discussion.

As used here "interest group" refers to any group that, on the basis of one or more shared attitudes, makes certain claims upon other groups in the society for the establishment, maintenance, or enhancement of forms of behavior that are implied by the shared attitudes. In earlier paragraphs of this chapter it was indicated that from interaction in groups arise certain common habits of response, which may be called norms, or shared attitudes. These afford the participants frames of reference for interpreting and evaluating events and behaviors. In this respect all groups are interest groups because they are shared-attitude groups. In some groups at various points in time, however, a second kind of common response emerges, in addition to the frames of reference. These are shared attitudes toward what is needed or wanted in a given situation, observable as demands or claims upon other groups in the society. The term "interest group" will be reserved here for those groups that exhibit both aspects of the shared attitudes.

The shared attitudes, moreover, constitute the interests. It has been suggested that a distinction be made between the two terms, reserving the latter to designate "the objects toward which these . . . [attitudes] are directed."[8] Such a distinction may be highly misleading. If, for example, reference were made to oil interests, one would presumably be referring,

---

[6]*The Federalist,* No. 10.

[7]Dewey: *The Public and Its Problems,* p. 188. Copyright 1927 by, and used with the permission of Henry Holt & Company, Inc.

[8]Robert M. MacIver: "Interests," *Encyclopaedia of the Social Sciences.* Cf. Avery Leiserson: *Administrative Regulation: A Study in Representation of Interests* (Chicago: University of Chicago Press, 1942), pp. 1–10.

among other things, to certain elements in the physical environment, petroleum and its by-products. These features, however, have no significance in society apart from the activities of men. There were no oil attitudes prior to the time when the productive behaviors of men led them to do something with petroleum.[9] As a consequence of the use of oil, an array of attitudes with respect to that use has developed—that it should not be wasted, that it should be marketed in a particular way, that it should be produced by many small groups or enterprises, that it should be controlled by an international organization, and so on. Some of these attitudes are represented by interest groups asserting that the behaviors implied by the attitudes should be encouraged, discouraged, or altered. The physical features of oil production have no significance for the student of society apart from the attitudes, or interests, and the behaviors that they suggest.

Definition of the interest group in this fashion has a number of distinct advantages in the task of political analysis. In the first place, it permits the identification of various potential as well as existing interest groups. That is, it invites examination of an interest whether or not it is found at the moment as one of the characteristics of a particular organized group. Although no group that makes claims upon other groups in the society will be found without an interest or interests, it is possible to examine interests that are not at a particular point in time the basis of interactions among individuals, but that may become such. Without the modern techniques for the measurement of attitude and opinion, this position would indeed be risky, since it would invite the error of ascribing an interest to individuals quite apart from any overt behavior that they might display.[10] In the scientific

study of society only frustration and defeat are likely to follow an attempt to deal with data that are not directly observable. Even the most insistent defenders of the scientific position, however, admit that, although activity is the basic datum of social science, a "becoming" stage of activity must be recognized as a phase of activity if any segment of a moving social situation is to be understood. There are, in other words, potential activities, or "tendencies of activity."[11] These tendencies are the central feature of the most widely accepted social psychological definition of attitude. Gordon W. Allport, after examining a series of definitions, arrived at his own generally used statement: "An attitude is a mental and neural *state of readiness,* organized through experience, exerting a directive or dynamic influence upon the individual's response to all objects and situations with which it is related.[12] On the basis of widely held attitudes that are not expressed in interaction, therefore, it is possible to talk of potential interest groups.

In the second place, as these statements suggest, this concept of interest group permits attention to what Lundberg calls the "degree of integrative interaction."[13] The frequency, or rate, of interaction will in part determine the primacy of a particular group affiliation in the behavior of an individual and, as will be indicated in more detail later, it will be of major importance in determining the relative effectiveness with which a group asserts its claims upon other groups.[14] This approach affords all the advantages and none of the disadvantages that once accrued to the sociologists' concepts of "primary groups" and "secondary groups," meaning by the

---

[9]Cf. Bentley: *The Process of Government,* pp. 193-94.

[10]*Ibid.,* p. 213.

[11]*Ibid.,* pp. 184 ff.

[12]Gordon W. Allport: "Attitudes," in Carl Murchison (ed.): *A Handbook of Social Psychology* (Worcester, Mass.: Clark University Press, 1935), chap. 17.

[13]Lundberg: *Foundations of Sociology,* p. 310.

[14]See below, chaps. 6 and 7 [not reproduced here].

former face-to-face interaction as opposed to indirect contacts such as those made through the media of mass communication. Before the enormous expansion and development of the latter techniques, and still in societies where they have not penetrated, it was a verifiable fact that solidarity of group behavior depended largely upon physical proximity. Frequent face-to-face contact in no small measure accounted for the influence of such primary groups as the family, the neighborhood, and the like. As the social functions performed by the family institution in our society have declined, some of these secondary groups, such as labor unions, have achieved a rate of interaction that equals or surpasses that of certain of the primary groups. This shift in importance has been facilitated largely by the development of means of communication that permit frequent interaction among individuals not in face-to-face contact or not continuously so.

In this connection note the confidence that James Madison, in seeking restraints upon the "mischiefs of faction" (interest groups), placed in "the greater obstacles opposed to the concert" of such groups by the "extent of the Union."[15] Such faith in physical dispersion had some basis in a period when it took a week to travel a distance of three hundred miles. It would not be true to say that primary groups no longer achieve the integration once ascribed to them. A recent study has indicated, for example, that the prolonged resistance of the German army in the face of repeated defeats in 1944 and 1945 was a result largely of the solidarity and continued structural integrity of such primary groups as the squad.[16] It is primarily from the degree of interaction that the face-to-face group fosters, however, that its in-

fluence is derived. A high degree may also be achieved through secondary means.

In the third place, this concept of the interest group permits us to evaluate the significance of formal organization. The existence of neither the group nor the interest is dependent upon formal organization, although that feature has significance, particularly in the context of politics. Organization indicates merely a stage or degree of interaction.[17] The fact that one interest group is highly organized whereas another is not or is merely a potential group—whether the interest involved is that of affording more protection to consumers, greater privileges for brunettes, or more vigorous enforcement of civil rights—is a matter of great significance at any particular moment. It does not mean, however, that the momentarily weaker group, or interest, will inevitably remain so. Events may easily produce an increased rate of interaction among the affected individuals to the point where formal organization or a significant interest group will emerge and greater influence will ensue. The point may be illustrated by noting that this increased rate of interaction is usually what is meant when the journalists speak of "an aroused public opinion."

Finally, this use of the concept also gives a proper perspective to the political activities of many interest groups that are the principal concern of this book. Although a characteristic feature of these groups is that they make claims upon other groups in the society, these claims may be asserted or enforced by means of a variety of techniques and through any of the institutions of the society, not merely the government. An interest group con-

---

15 *The Federalist, op. cit.,* No. 10; see also No. 51 for similar arguments.

16 Edward A. Shils and Morris Janowitz: "Cohesion and Disintegration in the Wehrmacht in World War II," *Public Opinion Quarterly,* Vol. XII, no. 2 (Summer, 1948), pp. 280–315.

---

17 For an influential characterization along similar lines of the phenomenon of organization, see John M. Gaus: "A Theory of Organization in Public Administration" in John M. Gaus, Leonard D. White, and Marshall E. Dimock: *The Frontiers of Public Administration* (Chicago: University of Chicago Press, 1936), pp. 66–91.

centrating upon replacing the valuable shade trees in a village adjacent to a large gentleman's farm may achieve its objective by prevailing upon the baronial family to purchase the trees and pay for their planting. A group interested in the protection of certain moralities among the younger generation may secure the behaviors they desire in part through inducing motion picture producers to permit its officers to censor films before they are released.[18] Whether a group operates in such fashions as these or attempts to work through governmental institutions, thereby becoming a political interest group, may be a function of circumstances; the government may have primary or exclusive responsibility in the area involved, as in the war-time allocation of scarce materials. Or the choice between political and other modes of operation may be a function of technique; it may be easier or more effective to achieve temperance objectives through the government than by prevailing upon people to sign pledges. The process is essentially the same whether the interest group operates through other institutions or becomes political.

To summarize briefly, an interest group is a shared-attitude group that makes certain claims upon other groups in the society. If and when it makes its claims through or upon any of the institutions of government, it becomes a political interest group. These are the meanings that we shall attach to these terms throughout this book. At times it will be convenient to omit the modifying term "political" in discussing interest group activity in the government. In such instances it will be clear from the context whether we are dealing with political interest groups or with groups that are making claims otherwise than through or upon the institutions of government.

It follows that any group in the society may function as an interest group and that any of them may function as political interest groups, that is, those that make their claims through or upon governmental institutions. An economic group, such as a corporation, that seeks a special tax ruling is in that respect functioning as a political interest group. Trade associations, labor unions, philatelic societies, world government societies, political parties, professional organizations, and a host of others can and do seek to achieve all or a portion of their objectives by operating through or upon the institutions of government. Even a family group, whose prestige or financial interests approach imperial proportions, may make such claims. It will be useful and significant to identify or classify such groups according to the regularity or the success with which such claims are advanced through these channels. Even the casual observer will give somewhat different places to the philatelic society that prevails upon the Postmaster General to provide special handling for letters bearing a new stamp issue and a trade association that seeks legislation to protect it against its competitors. These may sensibly be placed in separate subcategories, but they both display the fundamental characteristics of such groups.

Seen in these terms, is an interest group inherently "selfish"? In the first place, such judgments have no value for a scientific understanding of government or the operation of society. Schematically, they represent nothing more than the existence of a conflicting interest, possibly, but not necessarily, involving another group or groups.[19] Judgments of this kind are and must be made by all citizens in their everyday life, but they are not properly a

[18]Ruth A. Inglis: *Freedom of the Movies* (Chicago: University of Chicago Press, 1947), chaps. 3–5.

[19]See, for example, the transparent interest preferences involved in the interesting popular treatment by Kenneth G. Crawford: *The Pressure Boys: The Inside Story of Lobbying in America* (New York: Julius Messner, Inc., 1939).

part of the systematic analysis of the social process. Secondly, many such political interest groups are from almost any point of view highly altruistic. One need only recall those groups that have consistently risen to defend the basic guarantees of the American constitution, to improve the lot of the underprivileged, or to diffuse the advantages stemming from scientific advance. Evaluations such as these may be made of particular groups, depending on the observer's own attitudes, but, as was indicated in the preceding chapter, they will not facilitate one's understanding of the social system of which the groups are a part.

Where does the term "pressure group" fit into this scheme? This expression, perhaps more than any other, has been absorbed into the language of political abuse. It carries a load of emotional connotations indicating selfish, irresponsible insistence upon special privileges. Any group that regards itself as disinterested and altruistic will usually repudiate with vigor any attempt to attach this label to it, a fact that suggests that the term has little use except to indicate a value judgment concerning those groups of which one disapproves. Some writers, however, in a courageous effort to reclaim for the term a core of neutral meaning, use it as a synonym for "political interest group."[20] This usage has certain disadvantages aside from the obvious possibility that many readers will be unable to accept the suggestion that "the objectives of the pressure group may be good or bad; the group may be animated by the highest moral purpose or it may be driving for the narrowest kind of class gain."[21] If the word "pressure" has

more than a simply figurative meaning, it suggests a method or a category of methods that may be used by an interest group to achieve its objectives.[22] Even if the methods implied can be described precisely, unless we can demonstrate that all political interest groups use them, the term "pressure group" will indicate merely a stage or phase of group activity and will not serve as a satisfactory equivalent for "interest group" or "political interest group," as these have been defined.[23] In view of the improbability of satisfying the conditions specified, it will be avoided in these pages in favor of the more inclusive and more nearly neutral term.

ASSOCIATIONS AS INTEREST GROUPS

Any group, as we have already seen, may function from time to time as an interest group. There is one type of group, which almost invariably operates as an interest group, that has become of such importance in our culture that it deserves special treatment. This type may be called the association. We are using this familiar term in a technical sense. The justification for doing so is that we are here making use of a recent and highly significant body of research in the measurement of human relations in which this concept has been developed to designate a type of group whose genesis and functions are unique.[24]

The association is a type of group that grows out of what have been called tan-

---

[20]See, for example, V. O. Key, Jr.: *Politics, Parties, and Pressure Groups* (2d edition, New York: Thomas Y. Crowell Company, 1947). Key, however, uses the terms somewhat more narrowly, confining them to "private associations formed to influence public policy" (p. 15). A similar use of the term will be found in Ogburn and Nimkoff: *Sociology*, p. 287.

[21]*Ibid.*, pp. 16–17.

[22]Robert M. MacIver: "Pressures, Social," *Encyclopaedia of the Social Sciences.*

[23]Mary E. Dillon specifies the method of propaganda as the distinguishing characteristic of the pressure group, a usage that does not make it the equivalent of the political interest group. "Pressure Groups," *American Political Science Review*, Vol. XXXVI, no. 3 (June, 1942), pp. 471–81. The best case for a specific meaning of the term "pressure" can be made in connection with the effect of a group on its own membership rather than on those outside its boundaries.

[24]See Chapple and Coon: *Principles of Anthropology*, chap. 17, from which this section is adapted.

gent relations.[25] In a society of any appreciable complexity we find many institutionalized groups and well-defined subdivisions within them. We also find in these cases that there are individuals who participate in or are common to more than one such group, or subdivision. Such groups or subdivisions are said to be tangent to one another through the individuals who participate in both. Thus, to use a simple example, a family and a school are tangent to one another through a child who interacts in both. The workers in the motor assembly department and those in the body stamping department of the Ford Motor Company are tangent to one another through the managers who direct both. The General Motors Corporation is tangent to the International Harvester Company through the officers of the United Automobile Workers of America, who lead labor unions in both companies. This tangency between groups may exist not only through an individual, but through a third group by which the tangent groups are similarly affected or through a common technique.

When a disturbance occurs within two or more of these tangent groups, or subdivisions, the affected individuals are likely to seek an adjustment through interaction with others in the tangent group, with whom they have "something in common." Thus in a family that is disturbed by a child's poor performance in school, the mother is likely to visit (interact with) the teacher or principal to discuss the problem. This interaction is called a tangent relation. Similar tangent relations may occur between workers in the departments of the Ford Motor Company in consequence of an unusual "speed-up" in the assembly lines. They may occur also between officials of General Motors and International Harvester as a result of extreme demands by the U.A.W. leaders.

An association is said to emerge when

a considerable number of people have established tangent relations of the same sort and when they interact with one another regularly on that basis. It is a group, a continuing pattern of interactions, that functions as a "bridge" between persons in two or more institutionalized groups or subdivisions thereof. The word "tangent" is appropriate because it suggests a set of relationships that are in a sense peripheral to those that define the central functions of the institutionalized group. Thus, if, out of the family-school tangency mentioned above, a number of mothers and teachers interact fairly regularly with one another in consequence of their tangent relations, an association may be said to exist. Such is the nature of the Parent-Teachers Association that is a familiar feature of a great many American communities. The P.T.A. has its origins in disturbances in the equilibriums of individuals in two or more institutionalized groups. Mothers and teachers may interact in casual tangent relations for an indefinite period of time without an association (group) emerging. At some point a disturbance occurs in these casual relations—owing to a sudden increase in their frequency or to a crisis resulting from the failure of a number of students to be accepted by a university (if the school is a high school) or from an increase in juvenile delinquency, playground accidents or any number of such things—and it is felt that "something must be done." If that "something" involves establishing the teachers and mothers as an habitually interacting group, an association has been formed.

As the above example suggests, the function of an association is to stabilize the relations of individuals in tangent groups. This stability it may create at the expense of disturbing the accustomed behavior of those through whom the participant individuals are tangent. Thus the formation of the P.T.A. may result in restraining some of the disapproved behaviors of the school children, such as study-

[25]*Ibid.*, pp. 337 ff.

ing with the radio on, loafing at a pool room, or engaging in dangerous play. The formation of a labor union may similarly disturb the habitual actions of managers by preventing their paying whatever wages they wish to and by equivalent actions. The processes of the association—which may involve a formal constitution, officers, and meetings governed by Robert's *Rules of Order,* or which may depend upon certain largely informal techniques—facilitate among the participant individuals an adjustment of the equilibriums within the institutions disturbed by the events that gave rise to the association. If the association persists, that is, if it meets satisfactorily the needs of the participants that grow out of their tangent relations, similar and related disturbances in the institutional groups will also be adjusted by the association.

The simple example of the Parent-Teachers Association can be supplemented by hundreds and thousands in our society whose origins and functions are of the same type. A few additional cases will suffice here, since the development of these groups will be discussed in more detail in the following two chapters. The labor union organizes tangent relations among workers that are created by workers' contacts with management (or perhaps an employers' association). Thus, when the character or frequency of the customary interactions between workers and management is disturbed, the workers may increase the frequency of their tangent interactions. This increase may result in the formation of an association (labor union). Its function is that of a "compensatory mechanism" that stabilizes the relations among workers and tends to order those between management and workers through the union hierarchy. It is a "bridge" between workers in different plants or different departments of the same plant. Similarly, the merchants of a community are tangent to one another through their customers and through the

town government. Consequently a disturbance in these relations, such as is reflected in a slogan like "patronize home enterprise" or such as might follow upon a drastic increase in taxes on business property, may result in the formation of a merchants association, chamber of commerce, or board of trade. This association would act as a bridge between the mercantile establishments, would stabilize their relationships, and would tend to order their relations with their customers or with the city government. Again, businessmen in a particular line have tangent relations through their customers (or "the market"), the government, the labor unions, and their specialty. Disturbances in the accustomed interactions in these areas are likely to produce a trade association or employers association. College students, also, have tangent relations through the officers of the school. In the 1830's these relations were disturbed by the resistance of college faculties to the introduction of "modern" secular literature and similar materials into the curricula. In part for this reason student associations—fraternities—developed as literary societies. They still constitute a means of stabilizing relations between their members and college authorities, though along somewhat different lines. Other fraternal societies, professional associations, political parties, philanthropic organizations, and a host of others are of the same type.

In all societies the association operates to relate and stabilize the interactions among persons in basic institutionalized groups.[26] The association also has the attitude-forming, behavior-influencing group functions that we discussed earlier in the chapter.

Because of their functions, moreover, associations are peculiarly likely to oper-

[26]*Ibid.,* pp. 424–25 and 426–29. See also Eliot D. Chapple: "The Theory of Associations as Applied to Primitive and Civilized Communities with Special Emphasis Upon the Functional Approach" (unpublished Ph.D. dissertation, Harvard University, 1933).

ate both as interest groups and as political interest groups. The political role constitutes their importance in the present context. In the process of affording a means of adjustment for the members of various institutionalized groups, they are likely to make claims upon other groups not part of the institutions of government—as the labor union upon management. They are equally likely to assert claims upon or through the government. So common is this tendency that some students choose to limit the concept of the political interest group to groups that qualify as associations.[27] Although a large proportion of the familiar political interest groups are of this type, it is not strictly accurate, for the reasons indicated in an earlier paragraph, to omit from the category other types of groups whose relations with governmental institutions are of the same general character. The Standard Oil Company of New Jersey is not an association. Nevertheless, it may operate as a significant political interest group. In addition, its officers may function through an association, such as the National Association of Manufacturers, that is also a political interest group. Any group in the society may at one time or another operate as a political interest group. The considerable political importance of associations, that is, the groups formed around tangent relations, lies not only in their strong tendency to operate through or upon the institutions of government but in their stabilizing functions, in the larger resources of various kinds that they can command as compared with any of the participant elements, and in their great numbers in our society. These points we shall examine more fully in the following two chapters.

CONCLUSION

Stating the argument of this chapter in general terms, we find that any society is composed of groups, the habitual inter-

actions of men. Any society, even one employing the simplest and most primitive techniques, is a mosaic of overlapping groups of various specialized sorts. Through these formations a society is experienced by its members, and in this way it must be observed and understood by its students. These group affiliations, with varying degrees of completeness and finality, form and guide the attitudes and therefore the behavior of their participants. How completely and finally a particular group controls the attitudes and behavior of its members is a matter to be determined through observation of the degree to which habitual patterns of interaction persist. The frequency and persistence of interactions within a group will determine its strength. The groups that form this mosaic emerge from the particular techniques of the society. Some, especially associations, which constitute a major concern of these pages, develop more immediately out of crises and disturbances within those groups in which the basic techniques of the society are institutionalized. The moving pattern of a complex society such as the one in which we live is one of changes and disturbances in the habitual subpatterns of interaction, followed by a return to the previous state of equilibrium or, if the disturbances are intense or prolonged, by the emergence of new groups whose specialized function it is to facilitate the establishment of a new balance, a new adjustment in the habitual interactions of individuals.

.   .   .   .

INTEREST GROUPS AND THE NATURE OF THE STATE

The institutions of government are centers of interest-based power; their connections with interest groups may be latent or overt and their activities range in political character from the routinized and widely accepted to the unstable and highly controversial. In order to make claims,

[27]See Key, *op. cit.*

political interest groups will seek access to the key points of decision within these institutions. Such points are scattered throughout the structure, including not only the formally established branches of government but also the political parties in their various forms and the relationships between governmental units and other interest groups.

The extent to which a group achieves effective access to the institutions of government is the resultant of a complex of interdependent factors. For the sake of simplicity these may be classified in three somewhat overlapping categories: (1) factors relating to a group's strategic position in the society; (2) factors associated with the internal characteristics of the group; and (3) factors peculiar to the governmental institutions themselves. In the first category are: the group's status or prestige in the society, affecting the ease with which it commands deference from those outside its bounds; the standing it and its activities have when measured against the widely held but largely unorganized interests or "rules of the game;" the extent to which government officials are formally or informally "members" of the group; and the usefulness of the group as a source of technical and political knowledge. The second category includes: the degree and appropriateness of the group's organization; the degree of cohesion it can achieve in a given situation, especially in the light of competing group demands upon its membership; the skills of the leadership; and the group's resources in numbers and money. In the third category, are: the operating structure of the government institutions, since such established features involve relatively fixed advantages and handicaps; and the effects of the group life of particular units or branches of the government.

The product of effective access, of the claims of organized and unorganized interests that achieve access with varying degrees of effectiveness, is a governmental decision. Note that these interests that achieve effective access and guide decisions need not be "selfish," are not necessarily solidly unified, and may not be represented by organized groups. Governmental decisions are the resultant of effective access by various interests, of which organized groups may be only a segment. These decisions may be more or less stable depending on the strength of supporting interests and on the severity of disturbances in the society which affect that strength.

A characteristic feature of the governmental system in the United States is that it contains a multiplicity of points of access. The federal system establishes decentralized and more or less independent centers of power, vantage points from which to secure privileged access to the national government. Both a sign and a cause of the strength of the constituent units in the federal scheme is the peculiar character of our party system, which has strengthened parochial relationships, especially those of national legislators. National parties, and to a lesser degree those in the States, tend to be poorly cohesive leagues of locally based organizations rather than unified and inclusive structures. Staggered terms for executive officials and various types of legislators accentuate differences in the effective electorates that participate in choosing these officers. Each of these different, often opposite, localized patterns (constituencies) is a channel of independent access to the larger party aggregation and to the formal government. Thus, especially at the national level, the party is an electing-device and only in limited measure an integrated means of policy determination. Within the Congress, furthermore, controls are diffused among committee chairmen and other leaders in both chambers. The variety of these points of access is further supported by relationships stemming from the constitutional doctrine of the separation of powers, from related checks and balances, and at the State and local level from the common practice of choosing an array of executive officials by popular election. At the Federal level the formal simplicity of the executive branch has been complicated by a Supreme Court decision that has placed a number of administrative agencies beyond the removal power of the president. The position of these units, however, differs only in degree from that of many that are constitutionally within the executive branch. In consequence of alternative lines of access available through the legislature and the executive and of divided channels for the control of administrative policy, many nominally executive agencies are at various times virtually independent of the chief executive.

Although some of these lines of access may operate in series, they are not arranged in a stable and integrated hierarchy. Depending upon the whole political context in a given period and upon the relative strength of contending interests, one or another of the centers of power in the formal government or in the parties may become the apex of a hierarchy of controls. Only the highly routinized governmental activities show any stability in this respect, and these may as easily be subordinated to elements in the legislature as to the chief executive. Within limits, therefore, organized interest groups, gravitating toward responsive points of decision, may play one segment of the structure against another as circumstances and strategic considerations permit. The total pattern of government over a period of time thus presents a protean complex of crisscrossing relationships that change in strength and direction with alterations in the power and standing of interests, organized and unorganized.

There are two elements in this conception of the political process in the United States that are of crucial significance and that require special emphasis. These are, first, the notion of multiple or overlapping

membership and, second, the function of unorganized interests, or potential interest groups.

The idea of overlapping membership stems from the conception of a group as a standardized pattern of interactions rather than as a collection of human units. Although the former may appear to be a rather misty abstraction, it is actually far closer to complex reality than the latter notion. The view of a group as an aggregation of individuals abstracts from the observable fact that in any society, and especially a complex one, no single group affiliation accounts for all of the attitudes or interests of any individual except a fanatic or a compulsive neurotic. No tolerably normal person is totally absorbed in any group in which he participates. The diversity of an individual's activities and his attendant interests involve him in a variety of actual and potential groups. Moreover, the fact that the genetic experiences of no two individuals are identical and the consequent fact that the spectra of their attitudes are in varying degrees dissimilar means that the members of a single group will perceive the group's claims in terms of a diversity of frames of reference. Such heterogeneity may be of little significance until such time as these multiple memberships conflict. Then the cohesion and influence of the affected group depend upon the incorporation or accommodation of the conflicting loyalties of any significant segment of the group, an accommodation that may result in altering the original claims. Thus the leaders of a Parent-Teacher Association must take some account of the fact that their proposals must be acceptable to members who also belong to the local taxpayers' league, to the local chamber of commerce, and to the Catholic Church.

The notion of overlapping membership bears directly upon the problems allegedly created by the appearance of a multiplicity of interest groups. Yet the fact of such overlapping is frequently overlooked or neglected in discussions of the political role of groups. James Madison, whose brilliant analysis in the tenth essay in *The Federalist* we have frequently quoted, relied primarily upon diversity of groups and difficulty of communication to protect the new government from the tyranny of a factious majority. He barely touched on the notion of multiple membership when he observed, almost parenthetically: "Besides other impediments, it may be remarked that, where there is a consciousness of unjust or dishonorable purposes, communication is always checked by distrust in proportion to the number whose concurrence is necessary." John C. Calhoun's idea of the concurrent majority, developed in his posthumously published work, *A Disquisition on Government* (1851), assumed the unified, monolithic character of the groups whose liberties he was so anxious to protect. When his present-day followers unearth his doctrines, moreover, they usually make the same assumption, although implicitly.[28] Others, seeking a satisfactory means of accounting for the continued existence of the political system, sometimes assume that it is the nonparticipant citizens, aroused to unwonted activity, who act as a kind of counterbalance to the solid masses that constitute organized interest groups.[29] Although this phenomenon may occur in times of crisis, reliance upon it reckons insufficiently with the established observation that citizens who are nonparticipant in one aspect of the governmental process, such as voting, rarely show much concern for any phase of political activity. Multiple membership is more important as a restraint upon the activities of organized groups than the rarely aroused protests of chronic nonparticipants.

Organized interest groups are never

solid and monolithic, though the consequences of their overlapping memberships may be handled with sufficient skill to give the organizations a maximum of cohesion. It is the competing claims of other groups *within* a given interest group that threaten its cohesion and force it to reconcile its claims with those of other groups active on the political scene. The claims within the American Medical Association of specialists and teaching doctors who support group practice, compulsory health insurance, and preventive medicine offer an illustration. The presence within the American Legion of public-housing enthusiasts and labor unionists as well as private homebuilders and labor opponents provides another example. Potential conflicts within the Farm Bureau between farmers who must buy supplementary feed and those who produce excess feed grains for the market, between soybean growers and dairymen, even between traditional Republicans and loyal Democrats, create serious political problems for the interest group. Instances of the way in which such cleavages impose restraints upon an organized group's activities are infinitely numerous, almost as numerous as cases of multiple membership. Given the problems of cohesion and internal group politics that result from overlapping membership, the emergence of a multiplicity of interest groups in itself contains no dangers for the political system, especially since such overlapping affects not only private but also governmental "members" of the organized group.

But multiple membership in organized groups is not sufficiently extensive to obviate the possibility of irreconcilable conflict. There is little overlapping in the memberships of the National Association of Manufacturers and the United Steelworkers of America, or of the American Farm Bureau Federation and the United Automobile Workers. Overlapping membership among relatively cohesive organized interest groups provides an insuffi-

---

[28]Cf. John Fischer: "Unwritten Rules of American Politics," *Harper's Magazine* (November, 1948), pp. 27–36.

[29]Cf. Herring: *The Politics of Democracy*, p. 32.

cient basis upon which to account for the relative stability of an operating political system. That system is a fact. An adequate conception of the group process must reckon with it. To paraphrase the famous words of John Marshall, we must never forget that it is a going polity we are explaining.

We cannot account for an established American political system without the second crucial element in our conception of the political process, the concept of the unorganized interest, or potential interest group. Despite the tremendous number of interest groups existing in the United States, not all interests are organized. If we recall the definition of an interest as a shared attitude, it becomes obvious that continuing interaction resulting in claims upon other groups does not take place on the basis of all such attitudes. One of the commonest interest group forms, the association, emerges out of severe or prolonged disturbances in the expected relationships of individuals in similar institutionalized groups. An association continues to function as long as it succeeds in ordering these disturbed relationships, as a labor union orders the relationships between management and workers. Not all such expected relationships are simultaneously or in a given short period sufficiently disturbed to produce organization. Therefore only a portion of the interests or attitudes involved in such expectations are represented by organized groups. Similarly, many organized groups—families, businesses, or churches, for example—do not operate continuously as interest groups or as political interest groups.

Any mutual interest, however, any shared attitude, is a potential group. A disturbance in established relationships and expectations anywhere in the society may produce new patterns of interaction aimed at restricting or eliminating the disturbance. Sometimes it may be this possibility of organization that alone gives the potential group a minimum of influence

in the political process. Thus Key notes that the Delta planters in Mississippi "must speak for their Negroes in such programs as health and education," although the latter are virtually unorganized and are denied the means of active political participation.[30] It is in this sense that Bentley speaks of a difference in degree between the politics of despotism and that of other "forms" of government. He notes that there is "a process of representation in despotisms which is inevitable in all democracies, and which may be distinguished by quantities and by elaboration of technique, but not in any deeper 'qualitative' way." He speaks of the despot as "representative of his own class, and to a smaller, but none the less real, extent of the ruled class as well."[31] Obstacles to the development of organized groups from potential ones may be presented by inertia or by the activities of opposed groups, but the possibility that severe disturbances will be created if these submerged, potential interests should organize necessitates some recognition of the existence of these interests and gives them at least a minimum of influence.

More important for present purposes than the potential groups representing separate minority elements are those interests or expectations that are so widely held in the society and are so reflected in the behavior of almost all citizens that they are, so to speak, taken for granted. Such "majority" interests are significant not only because they may become the basis for organized interest groups but also because the "membership" of such potential groups overlaps extensively the memberships of the various organized interest groups.[32] The resolution of conflicts

---

[30]Key: *Southern Politics*, pp. 235 and *passim*.
[31]Bentley, *op. cit.*, pp. 314-15. Copyright 1908 by and used with the permission of Arthur F. Bentley.
[32]See the suggestive discussion of this general subject in Robert Bierstedt: "The Sociology of Majorities," *American Sociological Review*, Vol. XIII, no. 6 (December, 1948), pp. 700-10.

between the claims of such unorganized interests and those of organized interest groups must grant recognition to the former not only because affected individuals may feel strongly attached to them but even more certainly because these interests are widely shared and are a part of many established patterns of behavior the disturbance of which would be difficult and painful. They are likely to be highly valued.

These widely held but unorganized interests are what we have previously called the "rules of the game." Others have described these attitudes in such terms as "systems of belief," as a "general ideological consensus," and as "a broad body of attitudes and understandings regarding the nature and limits of authority."[33] Each of these interests (attitudes) may be wide or narrow, general or detailed. For the mass of the population they may be loose and ambiguous, though more precise and articulated at the leadership level. In any case the "rules of the game" are interests the serious disturbance of which will result in organized interaction and the assertion of fairly explicit claims for conformity. In the American system the "rules" would include the value generally attached to the dignity of the individual human being, loosely expressed in terms of "fair dealing" or more explicitly verbalized in formulations such as the Bill of Rights. They would embrace what in Chapter 5 we called "the democratic mold," that is, the approval of forms for broad mass participation in the designation of leaders and in the selection of policies in all social groups and institutions. They would also comprehend certain semi-egalitarian notions of material

welfare. This is an illustrative, not an exhaustive, list of such interests.

The widely held, unorganized interests are reflected in the major institutions of the society, including the political. The political structure of the United States, as we have seen, has adopted characteristic legislative, executive, and judicial forms through the efforts of organized interest groups. Once these forms have been accepted and have been largely routinized, the supporting organized interest groups cease to operate as such and revert to the potential stage. As embodied in these institutional forms and in accepted verbal formulations, such as those of legal and constitutional theory, the interests of these potential groups are established expectations concerning not only *what* the governmental institutions shall do, but more particularly *how* they shall operate. To the extent that these established processes remain noncontroversial, they may appear to have no foundation in interests. Nevertheless, the widespread expectations will receive tacit or explicit deference from most organized interest groups in consequence of the overlapping of their memberships with these potential groups.[34] Violation of the "rules of the game" normally will weaken a group's cohesion, reduce its status in the community, and expose it to the claims of other groups. The latter may be competing organized groups that more adequately incorporate the "rules," or they may be groups organized on the basis of these broad interests and in response to the violations.

The pervasive and generally accepted character of these unorganized interests, or "rules," is such that they are acquired by most individuals in their early experiences in the family, in the public schools (probably less effectively in the private and parochial schools), and in similar institutionalized groups that are also ex-

---

[33]Kluckhohn: *Mirror for Man*, pp. 248 and *passim;* Sebastian de Grazia: *The Political Community: A Study of Anomie* (Chicago: University of Chicago Press, 1948), pp. ix, 80, and *passim;* Almond: *The American People and Foreign Policy*, p. 158; Charles E. Merriam: *Systematic Politics* (Chicago: University of Chicago Press, 1945), p. 213.

[34]Cf. Bentley: *The Process of Government, op. cit.*, p. 397, and MacIver: *The Web of Government*, p. 79.

pected to conform in some measure to the "democratic mold." The "rules" are likely to be reinforced by later events. Persons who aspire to, or occupy, public office of whatever sort are particularly likely to identify with these expected behaviors as part of their desired or existing roles. With varying degrees of effectiveness the group life of government agencies—legislative, executive, and judicial—reinforces the claims of these unorganized interests, which overlap those of the official group itself and those of "outside" political interest groups. Marked and prolonged deviation from these expected behaviors by public officials, who are expected to represent what Bentley calls the "'absent' or quiescent group interests," will normally produce restrictive action by other governmental functionaries, by existing organized interest groups, by ones newly organized in consequence of the deviations, or by all three.

It is thus multiple memberships in potential groups based on widely held and accepted interests that serve as a balance wheel in a going political system like that of the United States. To some people this observation may appear to be a truism and to others a somewhat mystical notion. It is neither. In the first place, neglect of this function of multiple memberships in most discussions of organized interest groups indicates that the observation is not altogether commonplace. Secondly, the statement has no mystical quality; the effective operation of these widely held interests is to be inferred directly from verbal and other behavior in the political sphere. Without the notion of multiple memberships in potential groups it is literally impossible to account for the existence of a viable polity such as that in the United States or to develop a coherent conception of the political process. The strength of these widely held but largely unorganized interests explains the vigor with which propagandists for organized groups attempt to change other attitudes

by invoking such interests.[35] Their importance is further evidenced in the recognized function of the means of mass communication, notably the press, in reinforcing widely accepted norms of "public morality."[36]

The role of the widespread unorganized interests and potential groups does not imply that such interests are always and everywhere dominant. Nor does it mean that the slightest action in violation of any of them inevitably and instantly produces a restrictive response from another source. These interests are not unambiguous, as the long history of litigation concerning freedom of speech will demonstrate. Subjectively they are not all equally fundamental. Thus since the "rules" are interests competing with those of various organized groups, they are in any given set of circumstances more or less subject to attenuation through such psychological mechanisms as rationalization. Moreover, the means of communication, whether by word of mouth or through the mass media, may not adequately make known particular deviations from the behavior indicated by these broad interests.

In a relatively vigorous political system, however, these unorganized interests are dominant with sufficient frequency in the behavior of enough important segments of the society so that, despite ambiguity and other restrictions, both the activity and the methods of organized interest groups are kept within broad limits. This interpretation is not far from Lasswell's view of the state as a relational system defined by a certain frequency of subjective events.[37] According to his definition, "the state . . . is a time-space manifold

---

[35]Cf. Lazarsfeld *et al.*: *The People's Choice*, preface to 2d edition, pp. xxi-xxii.

[36]Cf. Paul F. Lazarsfeld and Robert K. Merton: "Mass Communication, Popular Taste and Organized Social Act," in Lyman Bryson (ed.): *The Communication of Ideas* (New York: Harper and Brothers, 1948), pp. 102 ff.

[37]Lasswell: *Psychopathology and Politics*, pp. 240-61.

of similar subjective events. . . . That subjective event which is the unique mark of the state is the recognition that one belongs to a community with a system of paramount claims and expectations."[38] All citizens of the state as thus conceived need not experience this "event" continuously or with equal intensity. Nor need the attitudes of all citizens be favorable toward these "claims and expectations." But the existence of the state, of the polity, depends on widespread, frequent recognition of and conformity to the claims of these unorganized interests and on activity condemning marked deviations from them. "All this," says Lasswell, "is frequently expressed as the 'sense of justice'. . . ."[39]

Thus it is only as the effects of overlapping memberships and the functions of unorganized interests and potential groups are included in the equation that it is accurate to speak of governmental activity as the product or resultant of interest group activity. As Bentley has put it:

There are limits to the technique of the struggle, this involving also limits to the group demands, all of which is solely a matter of empirical observation. . . . Or, in other words, when the struggle proceeds too harshly at any point there will become insistent in the society a group more powerful than either of those involved which tends to suppress the extreme and annoying methods of the groups in the primary struggle. It is within the embrace of these great lines of activity that the smaller struggles proceed, and the very word struggle has meaning only with reference to its limitations.[40]

To assert that the organization and activity of powerful interest groups constitutes a threat to representative government without measuring their relation to and effects upon the widespread potential groups is to generalize from insufficient data and upon an incomplete conception of the political process. Such an analysis would be as faulty as one that, ignoring differences in national systems, predicted identical responses to a given technological change in the United States, Japan, and the Soviet Union.

INTEREST GROUPS AND MORBIFIC POLITICS

No conception of the political process is adequate that does not take into account the possibilities of revolution and decay. There is some danger that recognition of the censoring and restraining functions of the widespread but unorganized interests in a viable polity will lead to the comforting but unwarranted assumption of some immanent harmony in the body politic. The existence of a going polity testifies to the present effectiveness of these functions, but it does not justify the projection of a present equilibrium into the indefinite future. Predictions concerning future stability, if they can be made at all, must be based upon an accumulation of research and measurement, even the barest outlines of which we cannot undertake in these pages. We can indicate, however, some of the factors that might contribute to the growth of a morbific politics and that might justify the predictions of those who view with alarm the development of organized political interest groups.

Because the unorganized interests may not be a central concern of most individuals and because those interests may have to be activated in the face of insistent violations, there is no guarantee that they will become operative in time to avoid profound disturbance or collapse. In a domestic crisis the continued latency of these unorganized interests may prevent the development of a viable compromise and encourage resort to less orderly means of adjustment.[41] In an international crisis

[38]Ibid., p. 245.
[39]Ibid., p. 246.
[40]Bentley, op. cit., p. 372. Copyright 1908 by and used with the permission of Arthur F. Bentley.

[41]Cf. Williams: The Reduction of Intergroup Tensions, p. 75.

the ineffectiveness of these interests may permit diplomatic or military decisions to be so warped and may allow shifts in prevailing policy to be so delayed that the governmental system will not survive the supreme test of war. These are typical possibilities. The conflict between more restricted organized interests may at any time be carried beyond safe limits before the struggle is seen as one affecting the interests of extensive potential groups.

Group conflict and a certain inconsistency of governmental policy are not in themselves signs of the weakening of the widespread potential groups. A measure of conflict is an unavoidable consequence of the multiplication of groups and of specialized individual activities.[42] The process of accommodating group claims, moreover, does not necessarily produce a nice symmetry of public policy. As in the feverish activity of the early New Deal, the adoption of superficially contradictory policies may in a larger view be a means of assuring the strength of the system rather than a sign of its decomposition.[43] Nor is dollar economy an indication of the health of the process. Fiscal neatness may or may not be a system of political stability. There is evidence, moreover, that the American political system is inherently productive of fiscal confusion and is "not highly suited to a straightforward business-like management of finance." As Herring has further observed: "Government has matters other than finances to manage. Our present form of government is not to be judged simply in terms of its ineptness for fiscal control."[44] Except as fiscal confusion may frustrate the expressed objectives of political policy, matters of financial efficiency are not close to

the foundations of the governmental system.

The effective activation of widespread unorganized interests depends upon the character of the society's means of communication, broadly conceived. We have previously seen that one of the elements in a president's ability to lead these interests is the ease with which he can gain for his statements ample space in the media of mass communication. Research evidence indicates that individuals who hold a broad interest of the type we are here concerned with may or may not see a given set of events as bearing upon that interest. How they will perceive such occurrences depends not only upon the importance they attach to the interest but also upon the adequacy of the information available to them concerning the events.[45] The quality and character of the mass media, therefore, and of the various means of interpersonal communication—rumors, letters, and conversations—are of fundamental importance in assuring the influence of unorganized interests. Not only censorship and distortion in the channels of communication but inadequate coverage may prevent the assertion of claims based upon the interests of potential groups. There are indications, for example, that one reason for the improvements in recent years in the treatment of Negroes in the United States is that most of them are likely to know when one of their number is dealt with in a manner seriously violating the "rules of the game" and that many will act on the basis of such information.[46] Successive claims of this sort in defense of the "rules of the game" not only may check the specific violations but also may strengthen the affected interests throughout the society.

[42]See *ibid.*, p. 56 and *passim.*

[43]See O. H. Taylor: "Economics Versus Politics," in Douglas Brown *et al.: The Economics of the Recovery Program* (New York: McGraw-Hill Book Company, 1934), pp. 160–88.

[44]Pendleton Herring: "The Politics of Fiscal Policy," *Yale Law Journal*, Vol. 47, no. 5 (March, 1938), pp. 737–8.

[45]M. Brewster Smith: "Personal Values as Determinants of a Political Attitude," *Journal of Psychology*, Vol. XXVIII (1949), pp. 477–86.

[46]See Arnold and Caroline Rose: *America Divided: Minority Group Relations in the United States* (New York: Alfred A. Knopf, Inc, 1948), p. 192.

In the absence of adequate communication, restraints upon governmental acts that violate widespread unorganized interests must rely upon officials' "memberships" in the potential groups. While these "memberships" are not to be discounted, without the likelihood of additional support they may be too weak to effect significant restraints.

Broadly speaking, the communications channels include not only the media but also group organizations to facilitate the expression of claims. Not only freedom of speech and of the press, but also the third in the classic triumvirate, freedom of assembly, is essential to the activation of unorganized interests. These freedoms are parts of the "rules of the game" in a representative democracy and at the same time are essential elements in the continued vitality of the unorganized interests. Obstacles to organization not only may obstruct communication but, by frustrating expectations based on the "rules of the game," may even weaken attachment to segments of the governmental institution. One of the most serious consequences of the courts' restrictive interpretations of the law in cases dealing with the organization of labor, especially between the 1890's and the 1930's, was workers' loss of confidence in the judiciary, reflected in a very general and not wholly unwarranted assumption that judges would not deal "fairly" with workers' attempts to organize.[47]

Since the major target for the claims of extensive potential groups is the institution of government, the established governmental patterns may operate to weaken the effect of widespread interests. Peculiarities of structure may so restrict and dam up the channels of adjustment that the "justice" interests may conflict with the claim for nonviolent change. Such a

situation in the society as a whole is not materially different from those we have discussed in connection with particular organized interest groups. Just as the structure of the American Federation of Labor in the 1920's and early 1930's was poorly representative of the dynamic elements within the group and among workers generally, so conventional patterns within the institution of government may be so rigid that they undermine the acceptance of representative methods of peaceful change. Established patterns of access, defended and rationalized in terms of the ambiguous "rules of the game," may block the assertion of claims based on alternative interpretations of widely held interests.

Adequate research has never been done on the incidence of widespread unorganized interests and on the extent to which they are central in the attitude hierarchies of various segments of the population. Such research needs to be carried on not only in terms of demographic aggregates, but also on the basis of classifications that reflect the relative power of individuals and organized groups.[48] The methods for such research are not fully developed, but existing techniques could provide far more information than is presently available. Though adequate evidence of this sort is not at hand, however, it seems probable that the widespread unorganized interests are adequately strong within power centers in and outside the government in the United States. If this assumption is valid, dangers to the continuance of representative government derive less from lack of basic support for these interests than from other features of the political system.

---

[47]Millis and Montgomery: *Organized Labor*, pp. 669–70.

[48]See Almond: *The American People and Foreign Policy*, chap. 6; Avery Leiserson: "Opinion Research and the Political Process," *Public Opinion Quarterly*, Vol. 13, no. 1 (Spring, 1949), pp. 31–8; Truman: "Political Behavior and Voting."

SYSTEMATIC POLITICAL THEORY:

OBSERVATIONS ON THE GROUP APPROACH*

Stanley Rothman

The great task in the study of any form of social life is the analysis of these groups. When the groups are adequately stated, everything is stated. When I say everything I mean everything. The complete description will mean the complete science, in the study of social phenomena, as in any other field.—Arthur Bentley[1]

Of the spate of articles on interest group behavior and interest group theory which have appeared since the "rediscovery" of Bentley, only a few have been mildly critical. Two American commentators have criticized the vagueness of certain terms and a British observer has noted that, somehow, empirical research on group behavior rarely makes use of the theoretical schemes which have been devised.[2]

But surely if we are to accept the claim of the group theorists that this is indeed the key to a science of politics, it is legitimate to ask that they submit their propositions to the tests imposed by science as a method. Perhaps the gap between research and theory stems less from a lack of data than from some limitations inherent in the group approach itself? This, in fact, is the argument of the present essay. The failure of group theory to serve as an adequate guide to research is the result both of the logical inconsistencies of its propositions and of its inability to explain what it purports to explain. The two weaknesses are related, for in their empirical work group theorists are constantly forced into inconsistencies as a result of the inability of the theory to deal with certain dimensions of experience. The ability of those who use the approach to ignore these consequences stems both from a certain looseness of vocabulary and a tendency, not limited to American scholars, to universalize their own political experience.

This will sound like a rather harsh indictment, but it is not meant to deny the

*Reprinted from *The American Political Science Review*, Vol. XLIV, No. 1 (March 1960), pp. 15–33. Copyright 1960, The American Political Science Association.

[1] *The Process of Government* (Bloomington, 1908), pp. 208–9.

[2] The critics are H. W. Ehrmann in his (ed.), *Interest Groups on Four Continents* (Pittsburgh, 1958); Peter H. Odegard, "A Group Basis of Politics: A New Name for an Old Myth," *Western Political Quarterly*, Vol. II (September, 1958), pp. 689–701; and W. J. M. MacKenzie, "Pressure Groups: The Conceptual Framework," *Political Studies*, Vol. 3 (October, 1955), pp. 247–55. Among the more notable "group" studies are: Pendleton Herring, *Group Representation Before Congress* (Baltimore, 1920); E. E. Schattschneider, *Politics, Pressures and the Tariff* (New York: 1935); Peter Odegard, *Pressure Politics* (New York, 1928); Donald C. Blaisdell, *American Democracy Under Pressure* (New York, 1957); Bertram D. Gross, *The Legislative Struggle* (New York, 1953); E. Latham, *The Group*

Basis of Politics (Ithaca, 1952); S. Finer, *Anonymous Empire* (London, 1958); "Unofficial Government: Pressure Groups and Lobbies," *The Annals of the American Academy of Political and Social Science*, No. 319 (September, 1958); Jean Meynaud, *Les Groupes de pression en France* (Paris, 1958); Charles B. Hagan, "The Group in Political Science," in Roland Young (ed.), *Approaches to the Study of Politics* (Evanston, 1958).

value of studying interest groups and attempting to develop propositions concerning regularities in their behavior. My argument, rather, is that if group theory is to be useful, group theorists must give up their claim to have developed a comprehensive system and limit their scope to a more narrow, though still important, range of phenomena.

Since David Truman's *The Governmental Process*[3] remains the most comprehensive and sophisticated contemporary statement of group theory, the essay will concentrate its fire on his analysis, although the criticisms are, as will be seen, more generally applicable. Following an exposition and critique some attempt will be made to indicate more fruitful lines of approach and the proper role of group theory within the discipline.

I

To Truman, as to many others, the scientific study of politics is the study of power relationships.[4] It is the study of who gets what, when, how. Since government is that institution in any community through which are made the most authoritative allocations of resources, those who seek these resources seek access to this key focus of decisions. An understanding of the power relationships within any community, however, requires adequate conceptual tools. The human actors behave in a wide variety of ways to gain their ends. Scientific analysis requires an apparatus which will enable us to reduce this chaos to some kind of order so that we may be in a position to handle it intelligently. The relationships between men, ideas and institutions must be structured in such a way as to permit predictions of the outcome of interactions and hence permit us to exercise some control over events.[5]

Group theory, as Truman presents it, is basically a theoretical system consisting of three theoretical concepts and three highest level, or "supernumerary," propositions.[6] The concepts are "group," "potential group," and "equilibrium." The propositions will be stated after these concepts are examined.

The Concepts

A *group* is a plurality of individuals interacting with some frequency.[7] Truman is careful to distinguish this technical definition of a group from mere aggregations of individuals and, more importantly, from statistical compilations of individuals who simply share any of a wide variety of common characteristics, *e.g.*, soldiers, men, blondes, alcoholics, Jews, *et cetera*. These statistical compilations he calls categoric groups.[8] Interaction is the key word in the definition of group, for without interaction one has merely aggregations of individuals.

Truman offers none of the traditional analytic distinctions between primary and secondary groups,[9] (face-to-face groups, such as the family versus large formal groups) or between what might be called involuntary and voluntary groups. He does differentiate between groups and what he calls associations, but the distinction appears to be relatively unimportant

---

[6]The term supernumerary is from R. B. Braithwaite, *Scientific Explanation* (Cambridge, 1953). It is only fair to note that Truman would probably deny that he ever meant to establish as closely defined a system as I am attributing to him. However, one test of the utility of any theoretical approach is to see what happens when one does attempt to systematize it, and to make implicit assumptions explicit. Again, the argument is that the seeming explanatory power of group theory is based on the *sub rosa* introduction of propositions which stand in contradiction to the major assumptions of the theory itself, and that any attempt to systematize these major assumptions reveals serious weaknesses in the approach.

[7]Truman, *op. cit.*, p. 24.

[8]*Ibid.*, p. 23.

[9]The distinction has its origins in Charles H. Cooley's *Social Organization* (New York, 1909).

---

[3]David Truman, *The Governmental Process* (New York, 1951).

[4]*Ibid.*, pp. 13, 507 ff.

[5]*Ibid.*, p. 12.

for purposes of analysis, and the words will be used interchangeably.[10] Somewhat more significant is his distinction between groups and a sub-class called "interest groups." Each group has an interest which is nothing more nor less than the shared attitudes of its members. An interest group, however, is a group which on the basis of one or more of these attitudes "makes certain claims upon other groups in the society for the establishment, maintenance, or enhancement of forms of behavior that are implied by the shared attitudes."[11]

A *potential group* is essentially a conglomeration of individuals with certain shared attitudes, who are not yet interacting, but who will form an actual group if other groups already organized act in ways which they regard as detrimental to their common interest.

We know of these factors (interests) only from the behavior and the habitual interactions of men. If they exist in this fashion, they are interests. We can account for their operation . . . by recognizing such interests as representing "potential" interest groups in the "becoming" state of activity. It makes no difference that we cannot find the home office and the executive secretary of such a group. Organization in this formal sense . . . represents merely a stage or degree of interaction.[12]

Potential groups are of many different kinds. On one level they may represent quite narrow interests which would "become" if they were violated, and, as such, existing groups must take them into account in their actions. Truman mentions the example of white planters on the Mississippi Delta who must take into account the "interests" of their Negro workers to a certain extent if these workers are not to organize.[13] Of more significance to the

analyst of group theory are certain broader kinds of potential groups. These consist of the very widely held attitudes (interests) of the society which represent the "moral code of a people."[14] In the United States these interests include beliefs in democracy, civil liberties,[15] and a host of other moral imperatives. These potential groups set the rules of the game within which the various existing groups must act, as well as the type of organization which these groups must develop, for they insist that internal organization must be democratic:[16]

These widely held but unorganized interests are what we have previously called the "rules of the game." Others have described these attitudes in such terms as "systems of belief," as a general ideological consensus. . . . In any case the "rules of the game" are interests, the serious disturbance of which will result in organized interaction and the assertion of fairly explicit claims for conformity.[17]

Equilibrium is a state which is reached when patterns of interaction are characterized by a relatively high degree of stability.[18] The concept may be applied to three levels of social analysis. An individual's interactions may be said to be in equilibrium when both its internal and external interactions exhibit stability, and finally a society may be said to have reached a state of equilibrium when the interactions among the various groups which compose it are relatively stable.[19]

The Propositions

Of the three supernumerary propositions one is "socio-political," one is "psychological" and the third applies equally to both dimensions. While the three are

---

[10]Truman does distinguish between them on p. 43, but fails to do so throughout most of the remainder of his book.

[11]Truman, *op. cit.*, p. 33.

[12]*Ibid.*, p. 51.

[13]*Ibid.*, p. 511.

[14]*Ibid.*, pp. 512, 513, 159 and *passim*.

[15]*Ibid.*, p. 51.

[16]*Ibid.*, p. 138.

[17]*Ibid.*, p. 512.

[18]*Ibid.*, p. 27. Truman never defines the term. This definition and the later propositions have been constructed from his use of it.

[19]*Ibid.*, pp. 27–31, 58–60.

logically independent they are interrelated in that all are equally basic to the system.

A. The "socio-political" proposition states that society should be conceived of simply as a plurality of groups interacting with each other, and that the political process is essentially a process of group competition for power over the allocation of resources.[20] While these groups operate through political institutions, the institutional patterns of any society are the reflection of group competition and, hence, are dependent variables.[21]

B. The "psychological" proposition states that group interaction is the primary source of individual attitudes. That is, while *some* people may derive *some* of their attitudes from other sources, we can, *for purposes of analysis,* ignore this fact. Thus, with one exception to be dealt with below, the argument is that the political scientist has effectively located the sources of individual political attitudes when he has uncovered the group affiliations of the individual.[22]

Basically, the group can impose its norms upon the individual because the very categories in which he thinks, including his language, are determined by his interaction with other individuals. More particularly, however, his adaptation to group norms stems from a conscious or even unconscious desire to belong.[23] To give illustrations of the impact of group norms upon the individual, Truman cites,

among others, the Western Electric Company, the Erie County, and the Bennington studies.[24]

The exception is the use of the dual concept "status-role."[25] In one sentence on page 16 of *The Governmental Process* Truman mentions the word "status." Later, on page 346, in trying to explain the behavior of American Congressmen, he notes that their status or role may play a significant part in molding their attitudes, and he continues:

Looking more closely at statuses, we can conceive of a whole society as a system of inter-related positions that people occupy. . . . For each recognized status in a society there are norms that prescribe more or less definitely how the occupant is to behave toward persons in related statuses.[26]

Elsewhere he uses the concept again, primarily to account for the influence of office.[27] The dual concepts of role and status, of course, have become an integral part of modern sociology and social psychology since their formulation by Linton.[28] In these fields the concept is of basic importance not only in explaining the

---

20*Ibid.,* pp. 14–65 and *passim.*

21*E.g.:* "The Constitution . . . was not only a compromise product of the efforts of a collection of able men; it was . . . more significantly the reflection of many demands and expectations concerning government. . . . That many of the stipulations in that document are fully operative nearly two centuries later speaks for the skill with which they reflected certain of the strong and lasting interests in the society." *Ibid.,* p. 448.

22*Ibid.,* p. 165; see also p. 505. Truman is careful to note that present affiliations will not give a complete picture of the individual's norms. Rather they are the result of a genetic process "that includes the whole of [his] life experiences." *Ibid.,* p. 22.

23*Ibid.,* pp. 19–20.

24The studies are to be found in: F. J. Roethlisberger, *Management and Morale* (Cambridge, 1941); P. F. Lazarsfeld, *et al., The People's Choice* (2d ed., New York, 1948); and Theodore M. Newcomb and Eugene L. Hartley, *Readings in Social Psychology* (New York, 1947). For recent summaries of the literature see: Robert K. Merton and Alice S. Rossi, "Contributions to the Theory of Reference Groups and Social Structure," pp. 225–80; R. K. Merton, *Social Theory and Social Structure* (rev. ed., Glencoe, 1957), pp. 281–386; M. and C. Sherif, *An Outline of Social Psychology* (rev. ed., New York, 1956); and E. Katz and P. E. Lazarsfeld, *Personal Influence* (Glencoe, 1955).

25In his theoretical analysis Truman also introduces the variable of biological make-up. Some behavioral differences result, he argues, from the fact that no two human organisms are identical in biological functioning and endowment. *Op. cit.,* p. 22. However, he never uses the concept for explanatory purposes. I think it safe to assume, therefore, that he feels it can be ignored for purposes of macro-societal analysis.

26*Ibid.,* pp. 21, 23, and 505.

27*Ibid.,* pp. 346–50, and *passim.*

28R. Linton, *The Study of Man* (New York, 1936).

structure of individual attitudes within any society but also in explaining the patterns of values characteristic of any society. It is, first of all, on a different analytic level than the concept of group, for it represents an abstraction from action rather than a type of actor; and, secondly, its traditional definition calls for (1) its application throughout any social system, and (2) its use as a variable which is at least as important if not more important than group membership for explaining individual attitudes.

Truman can, if he wishes, use the term, as defined by the sources he cites, as part of a general theory; in that case, of course, he would not be developing a "group" theory of politics. Or, he can redefine the term to suit his purposes. What he cannot logically do, however, and what he does attempt to do, is to bring it in *ad hoc* to explain a dimension of experience which cannot be handled by his own analysis.

The scientific reasons for a prohibition on this type of endeavor are obvious. Theories are tested by testing the explanatory power of their supernumerary propositions through propositions of lesser generality which are deduced from them. One may criticize a system because it cannot explain an important dimension of experience which it purports to explain; because, in fact, other propositions, not an integral part of its theoretical scheme, are required to explain these phenomena. However, if an author can introduce new propositions where he will, it becomes impossible to test the system, for then the author can prove anything he wishes to prove.[29] The fact that Truman is forced to rely upon the *ad hoc* use of the concept of role to explain an important dimension of political action is evidence of a serious weakness in his system.

C. The final supernumerary proposition states that interaction tends toward equilibrium, *i.e.*, toward stability. This ap-

plies on the individual, the group, and the societal level. The process is as follows. Some disturbance occurs which disrupts previous patterns of interaction. The reaction of the group may be random or disorganized. More likely, however, the members of the group will engage in increased activity designed either to restore the old equilibrium (their primary desire), or to create a new one.[30] This activity will disrupt the patterns of other individuals and groups in a wave-like effect until a new balance on all three levels develops. For illustration:

Perhaps the most instructive examples of the growth of associations . . . are to be seen in the labor movement. Labor organizations . . . embody one of a variety of responses to the innovations (disturbances) that for more than a century have been at the vortex of a rapidly changing society, namely the disturbances in economic institutions. [He then speaks of the shift from a preindustrial to an industrial society and the differentiation between capitalist and employee.] . . . varying disturbances inevitably increased interaction among workers, and the emergence of associations to stabilize these relationships followed. These disturbances, it should be noted . . . [are] not narrowly economic. Wage demands have usually been symptoms of an unacknowledged need for achieving equilibrium in the lives of workers both within and outside of the factory.[31]

But trade unions, as Truman himself admits, are uniquely the product of an industrial society and the patterns produced by it. In other words, propositions formed by using the concepts of group and equilibrium alone cannot explain the rise of trade unions. Implicit in this paragraph are assumptions about the relationship between changes in economic structure, the pattern of group activity, and the formation of attitudes, which are not logically consistent with the basic concepts of the theory.

---

[29]Braithwaite, *op. cit.*, p. 19.

[30]Truman, *op. cit.*, pp. 27–31, 59, and *passim.*
[31]*Ibid.*, pp. 66–67.

Just as significant is the assumption, repeated elsewhere in the book, that the normal reaction of workers to "disturbances" of this kind is the formation of "business" unions. But, of course, one of the problems social scientists have wrestled with for some time has to do with why trade unionism takes such different forms in different countries. The concepts of the theory cannot handle this problem, as we shall see in more detail later on.

For another illustration, Truman deals with the position of the Negro in the United States:

Similar disturbances of equal or greater intensity are part of the continuing experience of racial minorities, especially the Negro . . . it is worth noting that largely in compensation for the disturbances consequent upon discrimination, there are relatively more "voluntary" associations among Negroes than among whites . . . political activity for the Negro is primarily a means of securing legal justice—justice in the courts . . . police protection, and protection against the persecution of the police; ability to get administrative jobs through civil service; and a fair share in . . . public facilities.[32]

Actually at least some existing evidence indicates less participation in associations among Negroes than among whites, though according to Truman's definition of equilibrium, there should be more.[33] But this is a minor point. According to the quoted passage the Negro engages in associational activity because his equilibrium has been shattered. Theoretically he should want to restore it or create a new one. But what was the equilibrium that he might wish to restore? Certainly not a return to increased discrimination, slavery, or African tribal life. These, however, were his previous conditions. In fact, of course, the aim of the Negro is, as Truman actually states, to achieve the same treatment which is accorded to Americans of white skin. His aim could be different. He could wish to form a separate social group with particular privileges, such as has been the wish, in the past, of so many European ethnic groups. Neither the concept of equilibrium nor any of the other concepts of Truman's scheme enable us to explain why he should not so desire.[34] This is not to deny the value of equilibrium as a concept, for, as we shall see, it can be useful if integrated with a more adequate theoretical system.

II

Truman's system contains one middle range proposition which is worth examining because of the light it throws upon the inherent explanatory weaknesses and logical inconsistencies of the system. The relative stability of American democracy, he argues, is the result of two factors: multiple membership, and certain kinds of potential groups.

1. Americans are joiners.[35] All of them belong to many groups. The result is that group membership is overlapping, and no group can command the total loyalty of any individual.[36] Individual opinions are moderated by this fact, and the leadership of an organization, usually somewhat more committed to its goals than the rank and file, is limited in how far it can go. Should group leadership attempt to push too far, members will feel conflicts, will balk, will refuse to support the leaders, and may even drop out of the group. Leaders, then, anxious to remain in power and to preserve the group, will retrench. The conflict which members feel

. . . may be clear and recognized, as when a man who belongs to a local improvement

---

[32]*Ibid.*, p. 103.

[33]See C. R. Wright and H. H. Hyman, "Voluntary Association Memberships of American Adults," *American Sociological Review*, Vol. 23 (June, 1958), p. 287. There is every reason, furthermore, to conclude that the amount of associational activity has increased as discrimination has decreased.

[34]For an interesting discussion of this issue see Joseph Margolis, "The American Negro and the Issue of Segregation," *The American Scholar*, Vol. 28 (Winter, 1958–59), pp. 73–80.

[35]Truman, *op. cit.*, pp. 7, 157, 508–10.

[36]*Ibid.*, pp. 156–67.

association that is demanding the repavement of a neighborhood street is also a member of a taxpayers' group that is opposing an appropriation for this purpose. At the other extreme it may be a scarcely conscious feeling of incongruity between the moral standards of a family or church and the drive of a trade association for preferred treatment at the hands of public officials.[37]

But, in fact, Americans are not notably joiners of voluntary associations. Very few join more than one or two associations and their attendance is sporadic. There is very little evidence that these associations have an appreciable effect upon the attitudes of their membership.[38] But even assuming that Americans were joiners and that membership did overlap we should still have to explain why it did. In France a left wing trade unionist will join a left wing veterans' group, and a militant anti-clerical organization of some kind.[39] Why should it be different in the United States? There is some truth in Truman's statement for, with the exception of the Negro and of immigrant groups when they first arrived, there does seem to be overlapping among *primary* groups in this country.[40] Children of various religious backgrounds go to the same schools, and friendship groups tend to cross class lines. Whether this overlapping is more significant than that in France is a question for empirical research. There has certainly been more overlap here than in England, where, until very recently, workers and middle-class Englishmen engaged in different sports,

went to different schools, and even spoke different languages. But English politics has been amazingly peaceful. How does group theory explain this?

Furthermore, a good deal of what limited evidence we have indicates that often it is not the rank and file which moderates demands, but rather a prudent leadership which seems to have a better conception of what political and social realities permit.[41] In sum, the concept of overlapping membership would seem of very little help as part of an explanation of the relatively peaceful character of American politics.

2. It is the membership of Americans in potential groups setting the rules of the game which produces consensus and stability. And even more importantly:

It is multiple memberships in potential groups based on widely held and accepted interests that serve as a balance wheel in a going political system like that of the United States.[42]

But what exactly does this statement mean? In our discussion of Truman's second supernumerary proposition we noted that, to him, interacting groups were the source of all attitudes, in other words, that attitudes emerged from groups.[43] But potential groups are essentially attitudes which may crystallize into groups.[44] Now

---

[37]*Ibid.*, p. 157.

[38]See Wright and Hyman, *op. cit.*, pp. 284–94; J. C. Scott, Jr., "Membership and Participation in Voluntary Associations," *American Sociological Review*, Vol. 22 (June, 1957), pp. 315–26; Scott Greer, "Individual Participation in Mass Society," Young (ed.), *op. cit.*, pp. 329–43; Lazarsfeld and Katz, *op. cit.*, and the extensive literature cited by them.

[39]See, for example, Rene Remond, "Les anciens combattants et la politique," *Revue Française de Science Politique*, Vol. 5 (April–June, 1944), pp. 267–90.

[40]And, again, it is these which seem to have the really important influence upon attitude developments. See Lazarsfeld and Katz, *op. cit.*, and the literature cited therein.

---

[41]And this means more than merely what is politically possible. For example, in England, trade union leaders have sometimes been more willing than the rank and file to accept a policy of wage restraints, because of an awareness of objective economic problems. For some evidence of this from England, see John D. Stewart, *British Pressure Groups* (Oxford, 1958), pp. 35, 176; and G. B. Baldwin, "Nationalization in Great Britain: A Sobering Decade," in *Annals of the American Academy of Political and Social Science*, No. 310 (March, 1957), pp. 39–54; and from France, P. Williams, *Politics in Post-War France* (London, 1954), p. 340.

[42]Truman, *op. cit.*, p. 514.

[43]See above, p. 142.

[44]See above, p. 141. Note also the striking contradiction in these two quotations taken from succeeding pages of Truman's essay:

". . . From interaction in groups arise certain common habits of response, which may be called norms or shared attitudes. . . . In this respect all
(*Footnote continued on next page*)

the formation of attitudes precedes the formation of groups. Truman cannot have it both ways. The concept and the proposition both stand in fundamental contradiction to everything else Truman has said, despite his notion of "becoming." In fact the whole concept of potential groups acts as a sort of *deus ex machina* which can be brought in for any purpose. Why are British trade unions Socialist? Strong Socialist potential group. Why did the Germans prefer a strong authoritarian regime? Strong authoritarian potential group. It can explain everything, but fundamentally it explains nothing. What Truman is saying here is that we have consensus and believe in civil liberties because we have consensus and believe in civil liberties. By all the canons of logical coherence the proposition has no place in his system.[45]

And in the end the system completely breaks down, for Truman is forced to use the concept over and over again to deal

with crucial aspects of American life. Its use is the strongest evidence of the weakness of the system as it stands.

In his effort to cram all of social reality into a relatively narrow framework Truman has committed an error of fact and an error of method. Taking a truth which is as old as Plato (*i.e.*, that one cannot speak of men in isolation from other men), he makes the unwarranted deduction that all attitudes stem from group membership. He then compounds this error by refusing to distinguish between the more important primary (from the point of view of attitude formation) and much less important secondary groups. Little of the work being done in social psychology[46] or sociology lends credence to either of these positions. At one time, reference group theory might have been cited in support of the first, but, as Merton has pointed out, reference group theory is not group theory, for a reference group can be an individual or a social stratum or any of a wide variety of what Truman has called categoric groups.[47]

The refusal to distinguish between primary and secondary groups, incidentally, is what gives group theory its superficial appearance of utility as an approach, and, at the same time, enables its partisans to protect themselves from criticism. The whole thrust of the analysis is that political action can be examined in terms of conflicts among interest groups. The acceptance of this proposition entails the proposition that attitudes are primarily derived from group sources (see footnote 51 below), and the utility of this tool for research purposes requires that the significant groups be the major institutionalized groups of a society, *i.e.*, medical associations, business organizations, trade unions, etc. If, however, one points out to group theorists that one cannot fully analyze the

---

groups are interest groups because they are shared-attitude groups." (p. 33).

". . . It is possible to examine interests that are not at a particular point in time the basis of interactions, but that may become such," (p. 34).

[45]We find here an interesting paradox. Truman has firmly denied that one can speak of a national interest. After all, the nation is not a group and only groups have interests. (Truman, *op. cit.*, pp. 51–52) But if interests and groups and attitudes are different ways of speaking about the same things, as he often asserts, and the nation as a whole shares the widespread attitudes that he lists as a potential group, then these attitudes would constitute the national interest. Part of his confusion here, aside from the whole problem of the potential group, is the identification of interests with attitudes or values. One can, of course, define interests in any way one wishes. But if they are attitudes it becomes difficult to discuss changes in the attitudes of group members as to what constitute their interests, and one cannot distinguish between the group's attitudes on the relative merits of Bach and Beethoven as against their attitudes on the effect of a new tax law on the state of the country or on the group. All in all, it would seem wiser to retain the traditional distinction and regard interests as ends or goals about which people have attitudes. See R. M. MacIver and Charles H. Page, *Society* (New York, 1949), pp. 23–40.

[46]See Lazarsfeld and Katz, *op. cit.*

[47]See Merton, "Continuities in the Theory of Reference Groups and Social Structure," *op. cit.*

behavior of Congressmen, say, in these terms, their response is, "Oh, this doesn't really destroy the group hypothesis, for what we mean is that individual attitudes are really the result of the whole life pattern of an individual's group membership, starting with childhood."[48] If this is so, however, then to understand a Congressional decision one would be forced to examine at least the history of the group membership of *each* Congressman from infancy on, including all the various friendship groups of childhood. Thus even if the propositions of the theory were adequate it would be at best a very blunt tool of analysis.

The methodological error is equally significant. Taking the psychological proposition that most attitudes derive from groups, Truman has attempted to build a socio-political theory on it. But psychology and sociology, while dealing ultimately with the same phenomena, must be kept analytically separate. Pointing out that the individual derives a goodly portion of his attitudes from the society of which he is a part tells us nothing about the structure of attitudes which will characterize that society.[49] We have known for a very long time that the family and other childhood groups are specially important as determiners of individual attitudes. What we want to know, and where Truman does not help us at all, is why the content of the political culture that these groups transmit assumes certain forms at certain times and not others. This is not to say that one cannot attempt to build a system which relates the psychological and sociological dimensions. Indeed, such a system is necessary if one is to understand society.[50] The building, however, must follow an awareness of the analytic differences.

III

A close examination of *The Governmental Process* quickly reveals a difference between what the author says he is going to do and what he actually does in the empirical sections of his book. For in these latter sections he actually relies implicitly upon a quasi-group theory of politics which is somewhat removed from the one he had announced. This is by no means an accident, for Truman's explicit theory really has no explanatory power whatsoever. If group purposes are determined by the interaction of the members of groups, then these purposes can only be random; *i.e.*, not capable of being analyzed scientifically. The fact that a businessman joins with other businessmen becomes purely fortuitous, as does the fact that group interaction leads to the development of one set of shared attitudes rather than another. To take just one example: Truman can not really explain why southern planters take the possible actions of Negro workers into account on the basis of group action, since, by definition, the attitudes of the group are formed not by the perception of an external threat, but rather by the process of interaction itself. Nor does that "brooding omnipresence," the potential group, satisfactorily handle the problem, for even if the concept could be used Truman still could not explain why different groups have different attitudes on issues not covered by the national potential group.[51]

In his empirical analysis, then, Truman implicitly recognizes, as he must, that groups are made up of purposively acting individuals, and the essay contains a whole variety of implicit non-group explanations

---

[48]Truman, *op. cit.,* p. 22 and *passim.*

[49]The point is made by M. S. Olmsted in *The Small Group* (New York, 1959).

[50]See T. Parsons and E. Shils (eds.), *Toward a General Theory of Action* (Cambridge, 1951).

---

[51]Truman could conceivably retort by pointing to his remark (pp. 23-4) that individuals generally begin to interact on the basis of some characteristic, and hence common interest, which they share. But this proposition stands in direct contradiction to the rest of his system. What con-
(Footnote continued on next page)

of both individual attitudes and the pattern of group attitudes within any society. The implicit theory (or theories) is worth examining on its own, for the assumptions which underlie it serve to give group theory its superficial plausibility, especially when it is applied to the American scene. Examining it and evaluating it will lead us to some tentative attempts to define the proper role of the study of groups within the discipline.

Quite early in *The Governmental Process* Truman asks why group patterns vary from society to society and over time. He answers his question as follows:

Why this variation occurs has been only incompletely ascertained, since comparative analyses of complex cultures are virtually non-existent. The most satisfactory hypothesis, however, indicates that the relative complexity of such interactions depends upon the degree of diversity in everyday life.[52]

This ends his systematic effort to deal with this problem, and, indeed, he cannot deal with it systematically within his own explicit framework. However, scattered through the book are statements which indicate that he actually believes much more can be said. On page 53, to take just one, he tells us that as

stitutes a common characteristic is defined by attitudes. Thus, in our own society, blondes do not form groups while businessmen do.

To admit that individuals join together on the basis of perceived interests (attitudes) is to admit that groups are not the only or even necessarily the primary determiners of attitudes and hence of actions. Such an admission completely destroys the scientific status of group theory as *the* theory of politics. For if groups are not the determiners of attitudes there is no obvious reason to concentrate on their behavior as against the behavior of individuals. Groups become just one of two possible kinds of political actors. And if groups do not structure all attitudes then the question of the sources of attitudes and hence action is once again open. The ideas which men accept as guides to action may stem from the writings of a political philosopher, from the internalization of certain conceptions of what is right, from the socio-economic structure of the society, from the universality of the oedipus complex, etc. Most so-called group theorists (see Latham, *op. cit.*) usually make just such an admission.

[52]Truman, *op. cit.*, p. 25.

... the Tanala of Madagascar shifted from a dry-land method of rice growing to a method based on irrigation, a series of consequent changes in the culture gradually took place.

And when discussing the rise of modern trade unionism he notes that the industrial revolution and consequent shift in the productive process led to the growth of a capitalist class and a working class, and that the ". . . functional differentiation of employer and employee permitted the development of attitudes (interest) peculiar to each."[53]

Both statements represent a quasi-Marxist interpretation of shifts in attitudes and interests, and an abandonment of his supernumerary socio-political proposition. Changes in the mode of production yield different attitudes, and position in the system of productive relationships does the same. A similar abandonment of his supernumerary psychological proposition occurs when he gives an actual example of group determination of norms and other attitudes:

A young person's aspirations and values, even his skills, will be quite different depending on the character of his early group experience. If he has spent the early years of his life on a family farm in the Middle West, some distance from any urban community, in a large family, the demands of whose daily existence limit the household's recreational facilities to the radio and the Bible, he will be quite unlike his contemporary whose parents move from one section of the country to another with changes in the social season.[54]

Without analyzing the statement in full or judging its explanatory adequacy, we can see that Truman is arguing for an explanation of the genesis of individual attitudes in terms of total life experience. Middle western farmers, Bible reading families, *et cetera*, are if anything "categoric" groups,[55] and "the demands of daily

[53]*Ibid.*, p. 67.
[54]*Ibid.*, p. 18.
[55]While individual families are groups, any similarities one finds among Bible-reading families of the type described, are likely to be the

existence" are a feature of the objective (non-social) environment.

Similar examples are characteristic of the entire book. As we go through the text we find that only in a very few instances does Truman actually use the concept of group interaction by itself to explain behavior. When he does, it is primarily in terms of a sort of vested stake which the group has in survival or which leaders have in power for its own sake. Thus, in describing the difficulties faced by federated structures (such as the former American Federation of Labor), he argues that when local units are established first and the federated national organization has been granted only limited powers, the latter will find it difficult to subject local units to national policy. This fact stems in large measure from the vested interest of the local unit in maintaining its own power.[56] What, then, are the underlying assumptions of Truman's analysis? The following is, I think, a fair summary.

Individuals, Truman seems to assume, develop certain attitudes as to their needs and desires as the result of their interaction with reality.[57] It is the nature of this contact which determines what kinds of attitudes will develop. In dealing with this problem Truman emphasizes primar-

ily position in the mode of production, the technological level of society, and, in general, the material conditions of the environment. The framework within which individuals form their evaluations is determined partially by the groups of which they are members, especially the primary groups, although, again, the norms of the groups to which they belong are a complex resultant of the experience of their members.

By and large, individuals are striving to maximize their economic position as they see it, and the way they see their economic position is dependent upon their experience. Their goals and aspirations, as they define them, constitute their interests. People with similar interests may combine into interest groups to pursue these interests. Membership in these secondary groups will further crystallize, and even slightly shift the direction of, conceptions of interest or other attitudes held by members.

Superficially *The Governmental Process* would seem to rest on a combination of sociological relativism (with a strong Marxist or Mannheimian tinge), and logical positivism. However, we must be cautious, for the author's positivism is not quite so free of value judgments as it might seem. His own commitments emerge in his discussion of trade union history as well as in other places. In describing the failure of the old Knights of Labor, for example, he notes:

> The American Federation of Labor, before which the Knights of Labor declined, was in tune with reality in that it was based on a firmer foundation of common interest. Individualism was de-emphasized by being harnessed firmly to the objective of controlling skilled jobs.[58]

Why was the Knights of Labor less in tune with reality? Instead of concentrating on wage increases, the Knights, Truman tells us, wished to bring about a new society in which the artificial disharmonies

---

function of similar experience rather than interaction.

[56] *Ibid.*, p. 69. The explanation, incidentally, is not sufficient to clarify the reasons for the A.F. of L.'s difficulty in securing agreement on national policies. In England local trade unions were established before the T.U.C., which has always had very limited formal power, and, in Germany, a federal system like that of the United States, the same development occurred. Yet in both countries the sense of national trade union discipline has been much higher than that of American trade unions. The literature is extensive, but see: Francis Williams, *Magnificent Journey* (London, 1954); B. C. Roberts, *Trade Union Government and Administration in Great Britain* (Cambridge, 1956); G. D. H. Cole, *An Introduction to Trade Unionism;* P. Taft, "Germany," in Walter Galenson (ed.), *Comparative Labor Movements* (New York, 1952); and Evelyn Anderson, *Hammer or Anvil: The Story of the German Working Class Movement* (London, 1954).

[57] Both social and non-social objects, to use Parsons' terminology.

[58] Truman, *op. cit.*, p. 69.

between workers and employers would disappear. They hoped to change the kind of capitalism which was inevitably developing. Thus, the organization was utopian.[59] The author seems to be arguing that the clash of interests in society is permanent. A group's "real" interest therefore lies in striving rationally to attain limited ends within the confines of the system.[60] Thus, underlying Truman's positivism and sociological relativism, we find the world he has so explicitly disowned: the world of Hobbes, Bentham and James Mill and, in general, of classical Liberal Utilitarianism. While Truman talks of groups rather than individuals, the norm is still rational groups pursuing rational self-interest. And Truman is not alone in this orientation. It stands out even more clearly in the writings of other American "group" analysts of the American scene.[61] These assumptions are not limited to group analysis; rather, they stem from a general parochialism on the part of American scholars.[62] However, group theorists have contributed to this parochialism, for insofar as they attempt to explain the patterns of a social system in terms of the concrete units of which it is composed, they can easily blind themselves to many of the most basic problems of social analysis. The observation is not a new one; Durkheim, Weber, and Pareto, to cite just three European analysts, were aware of the dilemma of this "utilitarian" analysis at the turn of the century, and the whole problem was the subject of a lengthy essay by Talcott Parsons in 1937.[63]

The basic reason for the continued

blindness of American political scientists to the issues involved lies, I think, in the fact that on the surface American politics seems to fit the model nicely. When we examine Truman's analysis of operative groups we discover an interesting fact, characteristic of other group studies. Despite his call for the study of all types of groups, almost all his efforts are expended in dealing with economic interest groups as they pursue their rational self-interest within certain well defined parameters. And, in fact, the analysis seems quite capable of handling the behavior of these groups until we ask why, indeed, they limit themselves to these parameters. For example, why do American workers accept the system? Why don't they vote for a Communist Party or join Communist trade unions, as French workers have done? And why is American business generally committed to democracy? Business groups in other countries have not always revealed the same attachment.[64] Examples could be multiplied. In many European countries an officer corps constituted a group with attitudes relatively hostile to bourgeois democracy when bourgeois democratic states were finally established.[65] The Catholic Church, too, was hostile to democratic capitalism and for a long time represented a cohesive group which actively fought it.[66] Further, various ethnic groups in many European countries saw ethnic survival and power as more important than economic self-interest, and so forth.

Groups of these types are almost never dealt with in any detail by American writers on interest groups. The reason is plain. Despite some tensions, the individuals

---

[59]*Ibid.*, p. 68.

[60]Thus interests are not merely attitudes, nor even attitudes about interests. (See above, p. 141).

[61]For example Bertram M. Gross, *op. cit.*, and Earl Latham, *op. cit.* Latham goes back to the beginning of the tradition and sounds almost like a Hobbist.

[62]See Louis Hartz, *The Liberal Tradition in America* (New York, 1955).

[63]*The Structure of Social Action* (New York, 1937).

---

[64]See, for example, H. W. Ehrmann, *Organized Business in France* (Princeton, 1957), and Robert Scalapino, *Democracy and the Party Movement in Prewar Japan* (Berkeley, 1953).

[65]For Germany, see Gordon A. Craig, *The Politics of the Prussian Army, 1640–1945* (London, 1955).

[66]For France, see Adrien Dansetts, *Histoire religieuse de la contemporaine*, 3 vol. (Paris, 1948, 1951, 1957).

who compose them have been integrated into a common way of life and the groups do not reflect a substantially different basic outlook than other groups. Most Americans accept the utilitarian parameter. But to generalize from this fact to a theory of society is to confuse Americans with man in general.[67]

IV

The pattern of interest group politics, not to speak of the general pattern of social life, in any country, cannot be understood either in terms of the explicit propositions of group theorists or in terms of the assumptions which underlie their political analysis. Actually, it is these assumptions (a dash of Marx, mixed with a good deal of Locke) which, as Louis Hartz points out,[68] have helped to create the particular kind of polity in which we live and which give group theory a superficial plausibility. For providing the framework of social action in this country they seem so natural that they can be ignored or assumed when one begins to structure a theory which is in reality based upon them.

If, then, we are to increase our understanding, we must recognize that these assumptions represent just one set of normative guides to action. But implicit in this recognition is the further awareness that the comprehension of any society, whatever the terms used, will always require an examination of its culture and the structure of values and beliefs which are held by the individuals who compose it.

The most fruitful contemporary approach, stemming from the work of Durkheim, Pareto and Weber, would seem to be an analysis which approaches social systems in terms of patterns of action and attempts to relate these to each other.

As developed by Parsons and others, such an approach recognizes that action is goal-oriented and that values must be treated as one among many analytic variables.[69]

What is the place of group theory within the framework of a theoretical system of this kind? First, groups are systems of action and, thus, one may legitimately attempt to develop propositions dealing with regularities in the behavior of interest groups which are part of the logic of group action in a wide variety of socio-political systems. This is an area which is analytically independent of, although related to, a study of the impact of groups on the formation of political attitudes. Second, a social system must be examined in the last analysis in terms of patterns of action, but it consists of both individuals and groups as actors. It is thus perfectly legitimate for certain purposes to describe the behavior of these actors (*i.e.*, both groups and individuals) in analyzing political decisions, and to relate behavior to the patterns of action of a given system.[70]

But the study of groups is only one part of the study of politics and not the whole of it. And such studies can only yield intelligible results when related to other variables. The pattern of French interest group behavior, to take just one example, is characterized by the violent hostility

---

[67]To paraphrase Marx's criticism of Bentham. It also, incidentally, distorts our analysis of American politics, although not quite so seriously.

[68]Hartz, *op. cit.*

[69]In addition to the works of Parsons previously cited, see D. Easton, "An Approach to the Analysis of Political Systems," *World Politics*, Vol. III (April, 1957), pp. 383–401; S. H. Beer and A. Ulam (eds.) *Patterns of Government* (New York, 1958), pp. 3–15; G. Almond, "Comparative Political Systems," *Journal of Politics*, Vol. XVIII (August, 1956), pp. 391–410; and W. C. Mitchell, "The Polity and Society," *Midwest Journal of Political Science*, Vol. II (November, 1958), pp. 403–20. All of them rely on the action frame of reference, and all would appear to agree with my statement on the role of values.

[70]See the Report of the First Research Planning Session of the Committee on Comparative Politics of the Social Science Research Council, "A Comparative Study of Interest Groups and the Political Process," *American Political Science Review*, Vol. LII (March, 1958), pp. 270–83.

(and willingness to resort to violence) of most of the groups involved. As one political scientist has noted:

The difficulties of France, the rancour left by the war, the bitterness caused by the indecision of the political teams which have succeeded one another in power, and the more apparent defects of our political system have made the political struggles very bitter. People quickly accuse one another of the worst offenses, they customarily resort to exaggerations.

The result is a frenzy which soon reaches its climax in the declarations and positions of the different interest groups and even of the most harmless ones. . . . All confidence in discussion and the impartiality of the state seems lost. Everyone seems to think that only a demonstration of strength will attract attention to his claims and to his point of view.[71]

But this is not the only feature which strikes our interest. Many others are significant and they all seem related to each other. Historically, the continued bitterness of the political struggle has been related to the "economic Malthusianism" of French business, which has, in turn, contributed to the bitterness. And the emphasis on the virtues of peasant life and of the "little man" has abetted both the continued existence of marginal enterprises and also economic Malthusianism.[72] Historically, too, both the fear of Caesarism and French "individualism" have contributed to the weakness of political institutions. These attitudes are also related to the fragmentation of interest group life itself, as is the political system.[73]

Contrast this with England where interest groups, by and large, behave with a peculiar kind of British reasonableness and responsibility.[74] Or, contrast this pattern with both England and Germany where interest groups are reasonably well organized and disciplined and where bigness and combination are not nearly so suspect.[75] And finally contrast this with the United States and the relative optimism and dynamism of American businessmen.[76]

To understand the differences in the pattern of interest group behavior in France, in contrast with other countries, one must examine them, then, in their relationships to other patterns in an ongoing social system, including patterns of values and beliefs. In this task one can make fruitful use of a concept like equilibrium. A state of equilibrium is one in which the patterns of social relationships of any system are integrated; that is, when they are compatible with each other. The system is in a state of disequilibrium when patterns of action develop which are incompatible with other patterns in the system. Again, these patterns of action cannot be understood without a consideration of ideas and values, and the incompatibility must ultimately be related to psychological variables.[77] However, Truman's attempt to reduce human behavior to patterns of group interaction and their disturbance blinds him to all sorts of dimensions of human experience. His discussion of the American Negro, for example, would certainly be more convincing if he dealt with the problem in terms of

[71]G. E. Lavau, "Political Pressures in France," in Ehrmann (ed.), op. cit., pp. 89–90.

[72]See Ehrmann, op. cit.; J. H. Clapham, The Economic Development of France and Germany, 4th ed. (Cambridge, 1951; and D. Landes, "Observations on France: Economy, Society, and Polity," World Politics, Vol. IX (April, 1957), pp. 329–51; and the essays by Landes and Sawyer in E. M. Earle (ed.), Modern France (Princeton, 1951).

[73]Jean Meynaud, op. cit., pp. 227–28, and passim.

[74]S. E. Finer, op. cit.; J. D. Stewart, op. cit.; and S. H. Beer, "Pressure Groups and Political Parties in Britain," American Political Science Review (March, 1956), pp. 1–24.

[75]Wolfgang Hirsch-Weber, "Some Remarks on Interest Groups in the German Federal Republic," in Ehrmann (ed.), op. cit., pp. 96–117; S. E. Finer, "The Federation of British Industries," Political Studies, Vol. IV (February, 1956), p. 71; and Beer, op. cit., p. 19 .

[76]Frances X. Sutton et al., The American Business Creed (Cambridge, 1956), pp. 326–46 and passim.

[77]Parsons and Shils, op. cit., pp. 107–9 and passim. The authors also use the term "equilibrium" to refer to the tendency of the system to maintain itself within certain boundaries relative

an incompatibility between the actual position of the Negro in American society and certain patterns of beliefs and values regarding equality in the society.[78]

V

Certain concluding remarks are in order. As has been shown, the basic weakness of Truman's system lies not in the propositions of the system but in the conceptual framework itself. An analysis of political behavior in terms of groups gives little information as to the pattern of group politics in a given society. Thus it cannot tell us why and how individuals will do or behave politically. The superficial plausibility of the group approach rests upon a certain partial reading of American politics which enables group theorists to ignore the real premises from which they operate. If this is so, there is no warrant to assume that the study of politics is the study of groups. Rather groups are reduced to the status of one kind of political actor.

Given this, the study of politics must not only involve the study of groups and individuals; it must also involve (and more importantly) the study of the patterns of normatively oriented political action which characterize a given social system. However, to recognize this is to recognize, too, that the sources of these patterns are once again an open question. Changing conceptions of reality, the ideas of political theorists, changes in socioeconomic structure may all be found to play a role in determining these patterns if one examines a society historically. And, without citing the evidence, there is every reason to believe that insofar as political institutional patterns become internalized

these two structure action and play an important role in determining the future orientation of action.[79] Actually, Truman sometimes admits all of this in the course of his empirical analysis; and Madison, whom the group theorists often cite as among their founding fathers, explicitly affirms it.[80]

For all these reasons, then, there is much to be said for the continued study, with, we hope, ever-increasing sophistication, of those areas which political scientists have traditionally studied. And there is certainly room for studies of the kind which rely upon the mature judgment of their authors, rather than being bound by conceptual schemes which appear to be simple keys to reality, but which only serve to blind students to obvious facts of politics.

---

to an environment. I am not prepared to deal with this second definition. For a discussion of some of the issues see Walter Buckley, "Structural-Functional Analysis in Modern Sociology," pp. 236–59, in Howard Becker and Alvin Boskoff (eds.), *Modern Sociological Theory* (New York, 1957).

[78]This is essentially G. Myrdal's analysis in *An American Dilemma* (New York, 1944).

[79]At least, the burden of proof is upon those who would eliminate any or all of these factors from consideration.

[80]On p. 530, *op. cit.*, Truman states: "For better or for worse . . . the Constitution has acquired the quality of a sacred writ that renders it immune to examination *de novo*." But compare this statement with footnote 21. And he goes even further. At a later point he implies that a proper understanding of "reality" can result in a change in values:

"Since such advantages derive from the structure and values of the society, elite groups change with changes in the society. The values that give such groups their power provide a frame of reference by which most members of the society interpret experience. . . . When experience can no longer be understood in such a frame of reference . . . the values change . . ." (p. 250).

Madison explicitly stated that both leadership and ideas played an autonomous role in the political process, in addition to arguing explicitly that a knowledge of reality could influence the making of public policy under certain circumstances. Two quotations from *The Federalist*, No. 10, should suffice:

"A zeal for different opinions concerning religion, concerning government, and many other points, as well of speculation as of practice; an attachment to different leaders ambitiously contending for pre-eminence and power . . . have, in turn, divided mankind into parties, inflamed them with mutual animosity."

"The effect of the first difference is . . . to refine and enlarge the public views by passing them through the medium of a chosen body of citizens, whose wisdom may best discern the true interest of their country. . . ."

MEMBERSHIP IN SOCIAL GROUPINGS*

Angus Campbell, Philip E. Converse, Warren E. Miller, and Donald E. Stokes

During each political campaign we hear comment about the "Catholic vote," the "Negro vote," the "labor vote," and so on. Unlike the political parties, these groups stand at one remove from the political order. Their reason for existence is not expressly political. The labor union exists to force management to provide more liberally for the worker; the Catholic church exists for religious worship. But members of these groups appear to think and behave politically in distinctive ways. We assume that these distinctive patterns are produced, in one fashion or another, by influence from the group.

THE PROBLEM OF GROUP INFLUENCE

Groups have influence because we tend to think of them as wholes, and come to respond positively or negatively to them in that form. In this sense, even people who are not members of a group may be influenced by the position that a group takes in politics. Groups can become reference points for the formation of attitudes and decisions about behavior; we speak then of *positive* and *negative reference groups*. People who are actually members of the group are likely to have a more differentiated image of it. But there remains a sense of norms and values attributed to a generalized "group": these are the expectations concerning appropriate behavior for the "loyal" Catholic or union member. It is the group standards that are psychologically real and are responsible for influence when it occurs.

In this chapter we are concerned with the apparent political influence exerted among major, nationwide groupings such as the labor unions, Negroes, Catholics, and Jews. This is not the only level at which political influence dependent on social contact may be examined. Much influence is exerted in smaller, face-to-face "primary" groups such as families, circles of friends, and the like. In fact, there is some evidence that when primary-group influences run counter to secondary-group political standards, the more intimate contacts may more often than not carry the day.[1] Nonetheless, although many of the mechanisms of influence may be the same in both cases, the study of secondary-group effects has its own unique fruits. It is probably accurate to assume that influence ramifies through primary groups at the grass roots of the nation in a manner fairly constant for both parties. The success or failure of influence at a face-to-face level is not likely to account for the gross trends of the sort constituted by secondary-group voting. If every man managed to influence his wife to vote as he does, we would have no more than a "multiplier" effect on both sides of the political fence. In contrast, successful influence by secondary groups can cause a large-scale, unidirectional shift in the partisan division of the national vote. We are interested in understanding the conditions under which

---

*Reprinted from Campbell, *et al.*, *The American Voter: An Abridgement* (New York: John Wiley & Sons, 1964), chap. 11.

[1]Norman Kaplan, "Reference Group Theory and Voting Behavior" (unpublished doctoral dissertation, Columbia University, 1955).

these group pressures are more or less successful.

When we discussed the political parties, it seemed reasonable to speak in terms of a "psychological group," in part because the boundaries of the parties are so poorly delimited by the fact of official membership. In secondary membership groups like labor unions, these formal group boundaries are quite clear. We do not have to ask our informants whether they "consider" they belong to one or another groups; membership is a factual matter. But as we examine these groups more closely, it turns out that the concept of group identification and psychological membership remains extremely valuable. Individuals, all of whom are nominal group members, vary in *degree* of membership, in a psychological sense; and this variation provides us with an excellent tool for breaking apart a voting "bloc," like the American Negro community, in order to understand the workings of influence within the secondary group.

The significance of group identification in all social groupings provides us with a foundation for a more general model of group influence in politics. The scheme would tell us what dimensions of the situation were important for measurement, and how these measures should be combined once they were taken. Appropriate measurements based on such a scheme would allow us to anticipate the direction and degree of the influence that the grouping would wield in the specific situation.

In this chapter we treat membership in social groupings by sketching the outlines for a general model of this sort. The specific currents observed in the Negro vote in the 1956 election become, in this light, substance of a case study to lay against the more abstract elements called for by the scheme. Likewise, the distinctive behavior of union members toward the objects of politics becomes a special case of the broad phenomenon of group influence.

THE ELEMENTS OF THE MODEL

A model for group influence should perform two distinct services:

1. Increase our understanding of deviation from group political standards by individual members. If the group exerts influence on its membership, and these individuals are members, how and why do they resist?

2. Increase our understanding of the waxing and waning of distinctive political behavior on the part of certain social groupings in the population. What specific conditions govern this variation in group political "strength"?

The same system of variables can handle both problems, for the problems are closely related. If we can specify the conditions under which an individual fails to be influenced by his group, then it is likely that the decline of group potency in politics will result from the extension of these conditions to an increasing proportion of the membership.

At the simplest level, there is a triangle of elements involved in the situation: (1) the individual, (2) the group, and (3) the world of political objects. This triangle suggests three different relationships among these elements: (a) the relationship of the individual to the group; (b) the relationship of the group to the political world; and (c) the relationship of the individual to the political world. These three relationships determine the types of variables that we take into account. A full model will call for measurements that adequately capture the important dimensions of each relationship, if we are to understand the way in which the individual will respond to politics *given the presence of a group that is real in the sense that it can exert a greater or lesser influence on his behavior.*

The relationship of the individual to the world of politics represents a combination of group and nongroup forces. The group forces in the field are predictable as a function of two "background" terms; the relationship of the individual to the group and the relationship of the group to the world of politics. The nongroup forces are, of course, independent of either of these terms. An analysis of the social origins of political motives therefore involves (1) the manner in which the two background terms interact to produce group forces; and (2) the manner in which group forces interact with other forces in the immediate field of political attitudes.

Two important implications are suggested by a logical exercise of this sort. On one hand, we must arrive at some means of sorting the group forces in which we are interested from nongroup forces, within the total field that characterizes the relationship of the individual to the world of politics. But if we pay little systematic attention to the total relationship of the individual to the political world in elaborating this portion of the model, we must not forget that these nongroup forces exist. In fact, this is a first-level answer to the problem of member deviation from group political standards. Group members do not make political decisions in a psychological field limited to group forces, any more than nonmembers make decisions in a vacuum. The current objects of orientation in the political world are available to everybody and, if perceived, have characteristics that can be distorted only within limits.

Our immediate concern lies with the strength of group-generated forces. We wish to understand the conditions under which that strength varies, over time, from individual to individual and from group to group. For this task we can conceptually ignore other forces in the field, which derive from the relation of the individual to politics, *group considerations aside*. But we must remember that these forces exist and contribute to the final attitudes and behavior.

ESTABLISHING THE FACT OF GROUP INFLUENCE

The immediate problem is to find ways to estimate the strength of group forces on the individual. With other forces present in the field, it is easy to mistake their effects for the effects of group influence.

First, it is important to think in terms of the *distinctiveness* of group behavior, rather than its absolute nature. For example, a majority of Catholics in our 1956 sample voted Republican. Traditionally, there has been a Democratic norm among Catholics. Does this finding mean that the norm has died away, or that the group now has new, pro-Republican standards? It means neither. The Catholic Republican vote moved only slightly above the 50 per cent mark, when the nation as a whole was voting 57 per cent Republican. The group force was weak and nongroup forces pushing toward a Republican vote were strong; the nongroup forces were dominant enough to pull a majority of Catholics into the Republican camp, but the presence of group forces in a Democratic direction remains detectable, *relative to the behavior of nongroup members.*

With vote distinctiveness as a criterion, Table 1 summarizes the behavior of several key secondary membership groups with traditional Democratic voting norms over a period of three presidential elections. Several aspects of the table are striking. First we find that there is considerable variation in *degree* of distinctiveness, from election to election and from group to group. We also find that each group seems to vary within a characteristic range. Catholics tend to be least distinctive throughout; the labor unions fall in a middle range. Negroes, despite a sharp drop in distinctiveness between 1952 and 1956, remain on the high side along with Jewish voters.

Nevertheless, there is room for dissatisfaction with distinctiveness, cast in this

TABLE 1

The Distinctiveness of Voting Behavior among Several Social Groupings
with Democratic Norms, 1948–1956*

	1948	1952	1956
Members of union households†	+35.8	+19.8	+18.1
Union members	...‡	+24.9	+21.4
Catholics	+16.2	+12.8	+7.1
Negroes	...§	+41.2	+24.7
Non-South	...§	+50.8	+33.1
South	...§	+17.6	−1.1
Jews	...§	+31.9	+40.8

*The entry in each cell represents the deviation in per cent Democratic of the two-party vote division from the comparable per cent among the residual, nonmember portion of the total sample. A positive deviation indicates that the group vote was more Democratic; a negative deviation indicates that the group was more Republican than the residual nongroup.

†"Members of union households" includes both union members, where interviews were conducted with the member himself, and other nonunion individuals living in a household that contained a union member. In most cases, the nonmember is the wife of a member.

‡Members and nonmembers were not separated within our sample of union households in 1948.

§Due to the reduced size of the 1948 sample and the small proportion of Negroes and Jews in the parent population, insufficient cases are available for presentation.

form, as a working measure of influence. The fact of membership in secondary groupings of the type we are considering locates the person in a peculiar position in social structure, which *in itself* ensures a distinctive pattern of life experience. For example, Negroes have been kept in the lower levels of the nation's status structure; they tend to predominate in the least desirable occupations, receive the lowest pay, are least well educated, and so on. Their high birth rate means that young people are more numerous among Negroes than among other elements in the population. In the North, they tend to reside in metropolitan areas; in the South, in small towns and rural areas. All of these distinctive characteristics have a potential effect on their reactions to politics; and this would be true *even if the group did not exist as an entity cognized by its members*. Northern Negroes as a group made a massive shift of allegiance from the Republican to the Democratic Party during the 1930's. Was this group cohesiveness in response to an Administration interested in the welfare of the Negro community, or was it simply the independent reaction

of a set of individuals to economic pressures, part and parcel of the nationwide establishment of Democratic dominance at the lower status levels? In the one case, we would speak of group influence; in the other, we would turn to considerations of social class and economic deprivation.

Of course, we cannot ignore the fact that group influence is in part contingent upon the life situations of the membership. But the important point remains that group influence *is* an additional element in the picture; shared membership provides a focus and direction for behavior that is lacking among nongroup members who happen to be placed in the same life situation. Therefore, it is important to distinguish between the patterns of behavior that develop from the life situations of group members, without reference to the group *qua* group, and the residual distinctiveness that may be traced directly to the fact of group membership.

Hence we must contrast behaviors of group members not simply with those of the remainder of the population, but with the restricted part of that population that shares the peculiar life situations of group

TABLE 2

Distinctiveness of Presidential Vote among Certain Groups, with Life Situation Controlled, 1956*

	1956 Presidential Vote
Members of union households	+17.1
Union members	+20.4
Catholics	+2.9
Negroes	
Non-South	+11.6
South	+15.4
Jews	+45.4

*The entry in each cell represents a deviation in per cent Democratic of the two-party vote within the test group from a comparable per cent computed for control groups matched with the test groups for a variety of conditions of life situation.

members. We want to isolate a "control" group of nonmembers that matches the "test" group of members on all important aspects of life situation save the fact of membership.

With life situation controlled, our estimate of group distinctiveness should be materially improved. Table 2 summarizes this new estimate for our groups in the context of the 1956 election. If we compare the figures for vote distinctiveness with those in Table 1, we find that much of the picture has remained the same. Catholic distinctiveness has almost disappeared, and the estimate of Jewish distinctiveness has risen slightly. But the major change has been a substantial reduction in the estimate of distinctiveness of the non-Southern Negro vote. This group remains significantly Democratic; but taking into account its extremely low status, its relative youth, and its Southern origins leaves it less Democratic than might appear at first glance.[2]

With such controls, we have more nearly reduced the relationship between the individual and the world of politics to its group-relevant aspects. In effect, we have

[2]The application of the Southern-origin factor to Negroes represents one point at which we lack information to exercise controls prudently. As the matter stands, the distinctiveness of the Negro group may be underestimated in Table 2.

arrived at an improved estimate of the strength of group forces in the total field at the time of the voting act. The estimate is not perfect and depends on an aggregation of cases; we cannot say that any specific group member is more swayed by the group than any other, although we get the clear impression that some groups exert more effective influence than others. We must now turn to other elements in the model for this variation in influence.

THE RELATIONSHIP OF THE INDIVIDUAL TO THE GROUP

The first variables to be considered must define the way in which the individual relates himself to the group. We would like to measure aspects of the individual-group relationship that are meaningful for the relationship of *any* individual to *any* group, whether or not that group ever expends effort in political affairs.

Let us think of the group as a psychological reality that exerts greater or lesser attractive force upon its members. Whatever the nominal membership status of the individual, there is room for a great deal of variation in the degree of psychological membership that characterizes the relationship. Just as party identification measures the sense of personal attachment to a political party, so a measure of group identification will indicate the closeness or "*we* feeling" that an individual senses with regard to his membership group.

We have measured group identification by asking members of various politically significant groups the following questions:

Would you say that you feel pretty close to (e.g.) Negroes in general or that you don't feel much closer to them than you do to other kinds of people?

How much interest would you say you have in how (e.g.) Negroes as a whole are getting along in this country? Do you have a good deal of interest in it, some interest, or not much interest at all?

From responses to these items an index of group identification was prepared. The first hypothesis that the model suggests is as follows: *the higher the identification of the individual with the group, the higher the probability that he will think and behave in ways which distinguish members of his group from nonmembers.*

Actually hypotheses much like this have found supporting evidence in other empirical work on voting behavior. Therefore, we are not surprised to find that if we take all members of groups that vote distinctively Democratic, the people who are highly identified with these groups vote even more distinctively Democratic than members who are less highly identified. The least identified third voted 43 per cent Democratic, a figure not very different from the vote proportion in the population as a whole. Medium identifiers, however, voted 56 per cent Democratic; and those most highly identified with these groups voted 69 per cent Democratic. In general, then, the hypothesis receives clear support, and strength of group identification deserves a place as a variable in our model.

Secondary groups that are not primarily political take little interest in some issues, and in these cases group members do not hold attitudes that differ significantly from those of nonmember control groups nor do high identifiers differ from more pe-

ripheral members. But as a general rule, whenever a group holds distinctive beliefs about some issue, then within the group a differentiation appears between members according to the strength of their group identification.

This combination of facts argues most conclusively that we are dealing here with a true group-influence phenomenon. To ascertain that influence exists is but a first step, however. We are also interested in assessing the relative strength of influence exerted by various groups and the conditions under which this strength increases or decreases. We find considerable variation in the degree of disparity in presidential vote between strong and weak identifiers within various groups. Table 3 summarizes this variation. If we compare these figures with those in Table 2, we find some interesting similarities in the rank ordering of the groups. Vote distinctiveness *within the group* bears some relation to distinctiveness between the group and a control group matched for life situation, as we would expect if both were taken to reflect strength of group political influence. But there are differences, also: high identifiers are more distinct in the union case and less distinct in the Negro case than Table 2 would lead us to expect. Most Negroes are highly identified with their group; therefore the total group is more clearly Democratic than it might appear if the proportion of high and low identifiers within the Negro group was closer to that found within the union group. But part of the discrepancy results from other factors to be added to the model shortly.

Group identifications help to answer the two primary questions with which a theory of group influence must deal. At the individual level, we may sort out a set of nominal members who are most likely to deviate from the group position under nongroup forces. They are the people who do not strongly identify with the group, who are psychologically peripheral to it.

TABLE 3

Vote Division within Four Test Groups, According to
Strength of Group Identification, 1956*

	Highly Identified	Weakly Identified	Discrepancy
Members of union households	64	36	+28
Catholics	51	39	+11
Negroes			
Non-South	72	63	+9
South	...†	...†	...†
Jews	83	55	+28

*The entries in the first two columns represent the per cent Democratic of the two-party vote division. The final column summarizes the differences between percentages in the first two, a plus indicating the high identifiers in the group voted more strongly Democratic.

†Southern Negro voters in the sample are too few for further subdivision.

TABLE 4

Relation of Group Cohesiveness to Group Identification, 1956

Cohesiveness	Mean Identification Score*	Group
High	⎰ 2.5	Southern Negro
	{ 2.2	Non-Southern Negro
	⎱ 2.2	Jewish
Low	⎰ 1.8	Union member
	{ 1.6	Catholic
	⎱ 1.6	Member, union household

*The responses to the two identification questions (see p. 159) are scored such that a maximum value on the index is 3.0, when the most positive response is made to both items. The corresponding minimum value is 0.0, when the most negative response is made to both items. About 61 per cent of Southern Negroes responded positively toward the group on both items; the corresponding proportion among Catholics was 28 per cent.

A similar proposition can be formulated at the group level. Some groups boast memberships intensely loyal to group purposes and interests. Others have trouble maintaining member identifications. We shall call a group enjoying high member identification a *cohesive group*.[3] Group cohesiveness is one determinant of the influence which a group can wield over its membership.

If a group has generated distinctive political attitudes and behavior among its members, this distinctiveness will fade if group cohesiveness is destroyed. Cohesiveness itself must depend on a number

[3]Dorwin P. Cartwright and Alvin Zander, *Group Dynamics: Research and Theory* (Row, Peterson and Co., Evanston, Ill., 1953), Part II, pp. 71–134.

of factors according to the type of group and the setting involved. Within the large and far-flung social groupings under discussion in this chapter, a prime determinant may simply be the degree to which group members feel set apart from other people by virtue of social barriers. If we set up a mean identification score as a simple index of cohesiveness for each group, the resulting array (see Table 4) seems to support this hypothesis.

THE RELATIONSHIP OF THE GROUP TO THE WORLD OF POLITICS

If the relationship between individual and group is summarized by the concept of identification, attempts to deal with the relationship of the group to the world of politics focus upon a vaguer concept of *proximity*. All of our secondary membership groups except the political party have their basic existence outside of the political order. At this point it becomes important to specify this distance from the world of politics more precisely.

If we analyze our intuitions concerning proximity, we find that they depend upon the frequency with which we have seen the group *qua* group associated intimately with objects that are clearly political—issues, candidates, and parties. We would think, for example, of lobbying activity, political pronouncements, and candidates who publicize the fact of membership in that group. We would consider what we know of the primary goals of the group, and their apparent relevance to politics. The perceived relationship between the group and the world of politics has substantial grounding in objective events, constituted largely by the actions of group leaders. But we could not expect that all individuals, or even all group members, would perceive the relationship of the group to politics in precisely the same manner. Thus we shall think of proximity as a subjective dimension, a tendency to associate group and politics at a psychological level.

Where proximity has partisan significance we would hypothesize that: *as proximity between the group and the world of politics increases, the political distinctiveness of the group will increase.*

Or, at the individual level: *as perception of proximity between the group and the world of politics becomes clearer, the susceptibility of the individual member to group influence in political affairs increases.*

The concept of proximity will have to undergo further refinement before these hypotheses have full meaning. We must specify a good deal more precisely the dimensions that are involved in our general sense of proximity, and attempt to measure them more objectively.

We have suggested that perceptions of proximity between one's group and the world of politics rest upon associations that have been built up between the group and the political objects. How do these links become established? In some cases, the associations are directly given, as when the political candidate is a highly visible member of the group. The link is, so to speak, "built into" the object of orientation itself. We shall discuss phenomena of this sort under the general heading of *group salience* in politics. More often, however, the establishment of associations between the group and politics depends on conscious effort by elements within the group to propagate certain standards of member behavior. This *transmission of standards* is a communication process, and its effectiveness depends on the clarity with which the standard is transmitted and the insistence that accompanies it.

But the perceived proximity of the group to the world of politics depends on more than the perception of a group standard at a point in time. While the successful transmission of a group standard in a particular situation may increase the member's sense of proximity, we would propose that the effect of any particular standard, once received, will vary according to the individual's generalized, preexisting sense of proximity between group and politics. In part, then, proximity is dependent upon reception of past standards; in part, too, it is dependent on the individual's sense of the *fitness* of group activity in politics. Underlying values that deny the group a legitimate role in the world act as barriers to reduce the sense of proximity, however clearly standards may be received.

What we have roughly labeled proximity, then, has a number of dimensions that demand independent treatment, and we shall discuss several of these. Throughout, we encounter evidence that the perceived relationship of the group to politics, like the relationship of the individual to the group, bears directly upon the strength of group forces in the field at the time of political decision.

The Transmission of Group Political Standards

Whatever the process of communication that alerts the member to a partisan group standard, we can think of group norms as forces, having a given direction and varying degrees of strength. The standard prescribes support of one party, candidate, or issue position, and forbids support of the other. And these prescriptions are propagated with varying amounts of urgency or intensity.

There are two conditions in which group standards may lack sufficient clarity to permit influence. The end result of each is the same—a lack of distinctiveness in the aggregate group vote—but the differences are of considerable theoretical interest. In one case, the usual channel for communication of such norms is silent as to a particular standard, or emits it very weakly. For example, within international unions where standards were most clear according to the content analysis of pre-election editions of official journals, the vote division among members in our sample was 67 per cent Democratic. This fell to 55 per cent, then to 51 per cent, and finally to 44 per cent where standards were least clear. These differences occurred even though the proportion of high identifiers from category to category varied over a range of only 3 per cent, so that we cannot explain the variation in vote by differences in group cohesiveness.

In the other case, conflicting standards are conveyed to the membership. When standards conflict, there are several possible outcomes. At one extreme, we might find that no single member became aware of the conflict in standards, but that various sets of members felt pressures in opposing directions. Here is the point at which analysis of influence at the individual level becomes more accurate than that at a group level. For in such a situation, even if every member responded to

influence, the aggregate outcome might lead the observer to believe that no influence had occurred at all.

At the other extreme, all members may be aware of a conflict in standards. To some degree, the group force is cancelled out: even if the member is concerned with respectability in the eyes of the group, he can pick the standard that would best suit his desires independent of group considerations and act accordingly without feeling guilt. If, however, the situation is ripe for influence—if the individual is motivated to conform to the group—it is unlikely that events will work out in just this way. A conflict in group standards usually occurs as a result of decentralization of leadership. Few large and far-flung groups can long maintain a leadership with monolithic control over group standards. Among the secondary membership groups this is especially true. But if an unwieldy group tends to develop its subgroups with their conflicting standards, the general model still applies. Although awareness of different standards among other elements of the total group may relax group pressures to some degree, the individual is likely to feel most strongly the forces from the subgroup with which he is most strongly identified.

Conflicting Standards: A Case Study

We have found the Negro community to be the most cohesive of the groups we have surveyed. Furthermore, Negroes, as we shall see, are almost unanimous in their belief that the group has a right to further its ends by political activity. Several of the necessary conditions for influence are fulfilled. In 1952, there was a good deal of solidarity among Negro leaders in their endorsement of the Democratic presidential ticket. And the Negro vote itself in 1952 was very distinctively Democratic.

In 1956, however, Negro leaders were much less enthusiastic about the Democratic Party, owing in part to the role of

Southern Democratic legislators in blocking civil rights legislation and in part to Republican sympathy with Negro aspirations. The National Association for Advancement of Colored People adopted a posture of watchful waiting, with occasional executive threats of a Republican endorsement. The two senior United States Congressmen from the Negro community gave clear public support to opposing candidates for the presidency: Adam Clayton Powell in New York City endorsed Eisenhower, whereas William L. Dawson of Chicago supported Stevenson.

This conflict in standards was reflected in the perceptions of Negroes in our sample. When asked how they thought Negroes around the country would vote in the 1956 election, responses had shifted sharply away from the near Democratic unanimity that the same question elicited in 1952. Furthermore, the conflict was most clearly perceived at the level of the leadership. Almost as many Negroes saw the leadership voting Republican as Democratic in 1956. The distinctiveness of the Negro vote fell off sharply.

We hypothesized that when a secondary group fragments into subgroups propagating standards that conflict, much the same influence process goes on, with identification focused on the appropriate subgroup rather than the total group. In Chicago, where Dawson had stood firm for the Democrats, there was an overall decline of 5 per cent in the Democratic presidential vote, by comparison with 1952. Within the city, three of the most clearly Negro wards declined 4 per cent, 4 per cent, and 9 per cent—close to the city average. In New York City, the picture was different. In the heavily colored New New York Assembly Districts 11 and 12, which included much of Powell's constituency, the Democratic presidential vote fell about 15 per cent. And this occurred despite a fraction of a per cent increase in the Stevenson vote in New York County as a whole. The effect of conflicting standards is to reduce the distinctiveness of the total group vote; but where we can isolate subgroups, we find evidence of influence.

The Political Salience of the Group

In some situations, the need for active propagation of group standards is at a minimum, because the standard is self-evident. This is the case when important political objects of orientation embody group cues, so that the course of behavior characteristic of a "good" group member cannot be held in doubt. Fundamentally, this situation is no more than a special case of the transmission of clear and strong standards. But it deserves separate treatment because it implies a simpler and less fallible communication process and because it involves a stratagem dear to the hearts of political tacticians. This dimension is one component of the model that is especially subject to short-term variation, since salience usually depends on the most transient objects of political orientation: the candidates and the issues.

Political salience of the group is high, for example, when a candidate for the election is recognized as a member of the group. Attracting the votes of members of a particular group by nominating a candidate who is a group member is, of course, a time-worn strategy in the art of political maneuver. Frequent executive appointment of group members to high posts is of the same order, although perhaps less potent in creating salience. It is our thesis that the success of the maneuver among group members depends upon the values of other variables in the total model. High salience alone does not create a unanimous group response.

The political salience of the group can also be increased by a coincidence between group goals and current political issues. The degree of salience that accrues with regard to issues in any particular situation is some joint function of the importance of the issue in the campaign and the importance of the goal to the group.

TABLE 5

Political Salience: The Vote of Catholics for Catholic Congressional
Candidates in Races Involving Non-Catholics, 1956*

	Catholic Identification		
	High	Low	Total Group
Catholic voters	63%	59%	61%
	(43)	(51)	(94)
Catholic	...	...	49%
			(76)

*The per cent entry refers to the proportion of the indicated group voting for the Catholic candidate in the split-religion congressional race. The figure in parentheses indicates the number of cases involved in each proportion.

One of the central issues of the 1948 campaign was the Taft-Hartley Act, which union leadership felt threatened vital aspects of the movement. To the degree that these elements communicated to the rank and file, the labor union ought to have been particularly salient for members voting in the election. Since that time, civil rights controversies have tended to increase the political salience of Negro membership.

Salience: A Case Study

The behavior of Catholic voters toward Catholic candidates for the United States Congress allows us to examine the salience phenomenon. We recall that in Table 2 the presidential vote among Catholics in 1956 was barely more Democratic than that among a Catholic control group (a margin of 3 per cent). We find a much more distinctive vote if we shift the scene to those congressional races in which a Catholic candidate was pitted against a non-Catholic (Table 5). Furthermore, Catholic voters are quite willing to cross party lines to support a candidate of the same creed. Thus if we decompose Table 5 we find that where the Catholic candidate is a Democrat, Catholics vote over 10 per cent more Democratic than their control group; but where the Catholic candidate is Republican, Catholics vote over 10 per cent more *Republican* than their controls.

By sacrificing a large proportion of our cases, we can refine the data in a manner that sharpens these relationships further. Obviously, the theory underlying the salience hypotheses demands that the voter recognize the candidate as a group member if salience effects are to emerge. If we restrict attention to those voters (one-third of the total) who can refer to their congressional choices by name after the election, we should clear away some individuals for whom we could little expect salience to be operative.

Although the cases for analysis are few, Table 6 shows a group vote much more distinctive yet than that in Table 5. And the inadequate number of cases is offset somewhat by the fact that similar results are to be found when we look for the same patterns within the 1956 U.S. senatorial races in which Catholics were involved. These similarities emerge even though the Catholic voters appearing in both segments of the table are few indeed.

There is, therefore, substantial evidence that the salience of a group membership, created by group cues in the political object, intensifies group forces in the member's psychological field at the time of the vote decision. On the other hand, we should note that the sharpening of findings from Table 5 to Table 6 indicates that lack of attention to candidates for House and Senate may make severe inroads upon the vote increment which the aspirant can reap from salience effects.

TABLE 6

Group Salience: The Vote of Catholics for Catholic Candidates
Whose Names Can Be Recalled, in Races Involving
Non-Catholics, 1956*

	Catholic Identification		
	High	*Low*	*Total Group*
U.S. House of Representatives:			
Catholic voters	85%	69%	77%
	(13)	(13)	(26)
Catholic control	...	...	51%
			(25)
U.S. Senate:			
Catholic voters	86%	57%	70%
	(22)	(28)	(50)
Catholic control	...	...	49%
			(47)

*The per cent entry refers to the proportion of the indicated group who voted for the Catholic candidate in the split-religion congressional or senatorial race. The figure in each parenthesis indicates the number of cases involved in each proportion.

The Legitimacy of Group Political Activity

However strong the group identification, and however firm the association between group and political objects, the member may resist the intrusion of "nonpolitical" groups upon the political scene. There are cultural values bound up with beliefs about democracy and the individual that inveigh against such activity. The sophisticated view of democracy as a competition between interest groups does not have great popular currency. Voting, whether at the mass or the legislative level, is morally a matter of individual judgment and conscience; recognition of group obligation and interests is thoroughly taboo to some Americans.

We asked members of various groups whether they felt it was "all right" for organizations representing the group to support legislative proposals and candidates for office. The responses to these questions showed a fairly strong relationship with the group identification variable. The more highly identified a group member, the more likely he was to grant the group a right to engage in political activity. Within each level of group identi-

fication, however, members of the two religious groups—Catholics and Jews—show much greater reluctance to accept the legitimacy statements than either of the two more secular groupings—Negroes and union members. Also, with identification controlled, there is somewhat less readiness to grant legitimacy among older people. This fact would conform with the impressions that popular values opposing frank interest-group politics represent an older America.

The Backgrounds of Group Identifications

We have indicated some of the sources of feelings about legitimacy. It is natural to inquire as well concerning the roots of group identification. Why do some group members identify with the group, whereas others fail to?

This is a difficult problem, and our evidence to date is fragmentary. But we can draw a few general conclusions about major determinants of identification. There are numerous groups, of course, that are created for the purpose of political and ideological persuasion, such as the National Economic Council or the American Civil Liberties Union. Members are recruited and come to identify with the group on the basis of pre-existing beliefs and sympathies. Here the case for influence is much less clear, except as group activity serves to reinforce and guide member efforts. But in most groups formed along occupational, ethnic, or religious lines membership is more likely to determine attitudes than are attitudes to determine membership.

There is little doubt of this fact in the groups we have watched most closely. Except in some semiorganized areas of the South, even membership in the labor union is effectively involuntary. If labor union members vote distinctively, we cannot say that only workers with certain attitudes join the union; rather, we must concede that influence exists. But if membership is involuntary, identification is not. How can we be sure that high union identification plays a formative role in the development of political attitudes?

There is a clear and substantial relationship between strength of union identification and length of membership in the union. The longer an individual has belonged to the union, the more likely he is to identify strongly with it, and we can find no other causative factors that begin to approach this relationship in strength. A relationship between age and union identification has been observed before, but it was never clear whether the relationship existed because of simple contact with the union over time, or because the unusual "barricades" generation of the 1930's would currently constitute the bulk of older union members. Our data show clearly that older men who have recently joined the union have weak identification with it, whereas younger men aged 25 and 30 who have belonged to the union for longer periods show stronger identifications with it. In fact, if we control length of union membership, we find that the relationship between age and union identification is somewhat negative. The later in life a person joins a union, the less

completely he will be identified with it given any particular length of membership. His identification will still increase with length of membership, but the level will not be quite as strong at it would be for a person who had joined when younger.

This cluster of findings is of considerable theoretical significance. In the first place, it makes it difficult to maintain that identification with the union results as a rule from existing political attitudes similar to those represented by the union. Instead, we get a sense of an acculturation process—slow and cumulative influence over a period of time, with identification as the key intervening factor. It appears that a potent force in the growth of group identifications is simple contact and familiarity, just as an immigrant comes to identify with the new country and accept its customs as time passes. Furthermore, like the immigrant, identifications never become as strongly rooted if the initiate is no longer young.

These findings are important from another point of view as well. For the pattern of relationships between age, length of membership, and strength of identification is precisely the same as we found where the group involved is the political party. That is, party identification appears to grow stronger with age; but the critical variable, instead of being age, is length of psychological membership in the party. With length of membership controlled, age is negatively related to party identification, just as it is in the union case.

Those few persons who have been union members for long periods of time yet who have remained unidentified are less likely to vote Democratic than any of the other union subgroups isolated. Not only are they much more Republican in their vote than union members generally; they are even more Republican than the control group matched with union members on aspects of life situation (33 per cent Democratic vote among those who have been members 15 years or more, as opposed to 36 per cent for the control group). Thus lack of identification among long-standing members of the union may have actively negative implications not present among new members who are not yet strongly identified.

We find no such clear relation between age and group identification among Catholics, Negroes, or Jews. Age, in these groups, logically coincides with "length of membership." There is some faint increase in identification among older Catholics, and an equally faint decrease in identification among older Negroes. We would expect these differences to appear if Catholic cohesiveness is waning and if the current civil rights ferment is beginning to sharpen cohesiveness among Negroes. But these tendencies are very weak, and there is no trend visible at all in the Jewish situation. We must conclude that no reliable relationship is present.

The contrast in the development of identification between these groups and the union or party is sharp. We are led to consider differences in the characteristics of the several groups that might account for such variation. It is obvious that the individual takes on serious membership in a union or in the psychological group represented by a political party later in life than is the case with the other groups. The individual grows up within the atmosphere of a religious or ethnic group in a much more inclusive sense than with either the party or the union.

Thus, different patterns of identification may be traced to basic differences in types of groups. But it is possible to suggest a more general proposition to cover all cases: instead of considering age or even the absolute length of time of group membership as the proper independent variable, let us employ the *proportion of the individual's life* spent as a member. Recast in this fashion, the presence of the strong positive relationship between length of membership and identification,

the negative relationship between age and identification with length of membership constant, and the fact that certain ascribed groups show no variation with age would all be predicted by a single independent variable. If there is no relationship between "length of membership" and identification among Catholics, Jews, and Negroes, it is because members of these groups have held membership for 100 per cent of their lives, and variation in their identification must be explained with other factors. We arrive at the general proposition that one fundamental determinant of group identifications is the proportion of one's life spent in close (psychological) contact with the group.

SECONDARY GROUPS, THE POLITICAL PARTY, AND THE INFLUENCE PROCESS

If the political party, and psychological membership in it, fit a more general model for social memberships and political influence, it is equally clear that the party has a peculiar location in the space that the model encompasses. We have laid out with some care what seem to be the components of the relationship between any group and the world of politics. This effort was necessary because the secondary groups with which we dealt were not at base political, and this fact turns out to be a crucial limitation in the political influence they can wield. Now if we were to fill in the values that the scheme requires for prediction, we would find that in the case of the party, proximity is at an upper limit, for the party has a central position in the world of politics. In all major elections, its salience is absolutely high: one candidate is always a group member, the prime group goal is political victory, and all controversial issues represent subordinate goals that the group has assumed. The legitimacy of its activity in politics goes without question, for the major parties at least, and the communication of their standards is perfect. Therefore, we would expect that the political influence of psychological membership in a party would be extremely potent, relative to other secondary memberships. If we take distinctiveness of political attitudes and behavior as a criterion, this proposition cannot be questioned.

We are most directly interested, at this point, in suggesting the processes by which nonpolitical membership groups come to have a certain amount of political influence. Thus far we have paid little attention to the fact that these processes have duration over time. The political influence of secondary memberships, as witnessed in the distinctiveness of a group vote, is not necessarily a product of the immediate situation. The labor union need not indoctrinate its membership anew at each election. If the labor vote was distinctive in 1956, there is no need to presume that this distinctiveness represents only the political action of the union during the 1956 campaign. Influence, when successful, has enduring effects, and in this sense the distinctiveness of a group vote at any point in time represents cumulative influence. We hypothesize that the political party plays a crucial role in the durability of this influence.

When a political candidate is a member of one's group, or when the issues of politics bear directly upon goals important to the group, membership in that group becomes salient in the individual's orientation to politics. In these instances, the need for political translation, for communication of specific standards regarding proper group behavior, is slight. But under normal circumstances, when salience is not high, the group, if it is to have influence, must lend the observed world political meaning in terms relevant to the group.

Now issues and candidates are transient political objects; the entity that endures is the party. If group influence leads the identified member to take on identification with the party, then little renewal of in-

fluence is needed. The individual has, as it were, acceded to a self-steering mechanism, that will keep him politically "safe" from the point of view of group standards. He will respond to new stimuli as a party member and code them properly. As time passes, his identification with the party will increase of its own accord, because the individual will find that event after event demonstrates—in nongroup matters as well as group matters now—the rectitude of his own party and the obnoxiousness of its opponent.

If there were no parties, but only a flux of candidates and issues, it does not follow that there would be no political influence exerted by other membership groups. The psychological economy of the individual demands parties as an organizing principle, and if bereft of this, there might be much more straightforward dependence on other groups for guidance. In situations of this sort, secondary groups with quite apolitical origins have in fact come to function as political parties.[4] But where parties exist, influence from nonpolitical secondary groups is likely to have a good deal of continuity.

Given the flux of objects like candidates and issues, group influence is likely to be most effective when meaningful contact is established between the group and the party, for parties subsume candidates and issues and, more important, endure over time. However, this proposition very particular way, that is, as cumulative over time. An individual led to a Democratic orientation by a group membership in 1930 may still be registering a manifesis true only if we define influence in a tation of that influence in 1956.

But for the practical politician who wants to know how many votes a group

---

[4]As an example, see Key's treatment of factionalism in the South. Secondary groups constitute one type of nucleus for the factions that compete for political power in a one-party system. V. O. Key, *Southern Politics in State and Nation* (Alfred Knopf, New York, 1950), pp. 52–57.

leader can "deliver" to one party or the other in a specific election, influence may have a rather different meaning. Here we encounter a paradox. If party identification is a trustworthy bridge from group identification to "proper" political behavior, it is also a structure which, once laid down, is not readily moved. Thus the mechanisms that are best calculated to build a reliably distinctive group vote are at the same time mechanisms that tend to undermine the maneuverability of the group in politics.

When political events cause a group leadership to switch official support to the opposing party, the strong party loyalties that it has helped to create and reinforce may be reversed only with great difficulty.[5] We can imagine that these loyalties, even when direct creations of group

[5] It is interesting to note that for large-scale, secondary groups at the national level, these switches are rare and tend to be limited to rebellious factions. Many aspects of political process seem to converge toward maintenance of these continuities. Factors such as the dependence of the party on group support and the loyalties and interpersonal commitments built up between group leaders and the party enhance the temptation to work for reform within the chosen party when things go awry. These facts make treatment of influence in its cumulative sense the more meaningful.

influence, gain some functional autonomy as they grow stronger. They come to have a force of their own, rather than remaining dependent on forces from the nonpolitical secondary group. And, since the political party can exert unusually intense influence on political motives, this force may turn out to be stronger than any counter-force that the nonpolitical group can bring to bear *in politics* at a later date. It would follow from the general outlines of our theory that when such reversals of group standards occur, the new influence will have most effect among the youngest group members.

The political party may be treated, then, as a special case of a more general group-influence phenomenon. The party may be located within our model, and values on appropriate dimensions may be calculated for the party member at any point in time. The nature of the group, so located, ensures the power of its influence within the world of politics. But of great significance also is the role of the party as a bridge between other social groupings and that political world. The influence of other secondary groups in politics comes to have more enduring effects as loyalties directed toward them may be transferred to abiding political loyalties.

ATTITUDE CONSENSUS AND CONFLICT IN AN INTEREST GROUP:
AN ASSESSMENT OF COHESION*

Norman R. Luttbeg and Harmon Zeigler

In America, interest groups operate within the democratic frame of reference. Like all political organizations, they are accorded more legitimacy when they can show that they are representative of the attitudes and values of a particular segment of the population. Consequently, the leaders of interest groups frequently spend a great deal of time explaining just how democratic their organizations are. If one examines the testimony of interest group leaders at state and national legislative hearings, he is likely to find that much of it is begun with an introductory statement explaining that the leadership of the testifying group is merely the voice of the membership. The personal values of the interest group leader are played down, and his function as representative (as distinguished from delegate) is exaggerated.

On the other hand, relatively few political interest groups have systematic and formalized means of ascertaining the desires of members. We know that most of the devices used to solicit member opinion are not very effective. Truman has shown that the affairs of most interest groups are run on a day-to-day basis by a fraction of the total membership. The mass of the membership takes a relatively passive role with regard to the formation of public policies by the organization.[1]

Communication between leaders and followers is spasmodic and cannot provide efficient guidelines for the actions of leaders. Whether or not leadership of an organization seeks to become a manifestation of Michel's iron law of obligarchy, the realities of communication within an organization suggest that most of the communication undertaken by leaders will be with other members of the leadership clique rather than with the larger body of followers in the group.

This situation is not necessarily dysfunctional for the organization. By many criteria the leader's decision is superior to that of the average member. Leaders have more time to give to matters of special concern to the organization. The information on which they make their decisions is likely to be more extensive than that of the average member, and they are likely to be more cognizant of the long-term impact of a particular decision. Unlike the average member, however, the leader's decision is complicated by his need to consider the extra-group and intra-group impact of his various alternative decisions and actions.

In the area of extra-group considerations, he must estimate the probable responses of other actors in the political pro-

*From *The American Political Science Review*, Vol. LX (September 1966), pp. 655–65. Copyright 1966, The American Political Science Association.

The research reported here was made possible by a grant from the Center for the Advanced Study of Educational Administration, University of Oregon.

[1]David B. Truman, *The Governmental Process* (New York: Alfred A. Knopf, Inc., 1951), pp. 129–39.

cess and the effect of these responses upon the chances of achieving a desired goal, assuming that he does not possess all capabilities of realizing this goal himself. Concerning intra-group considerations he must consider how the followers will respond to a decision. Will they be aware of it? Do they care about the alternatives, and if so, how will they respond to a decision which is contrary to their desires?

Even in the absence of efficient consultative mechanisms, leaders and followers exist in a functional relationship.[2] That is to say, leaders are limited by the followers' expressed or latent values and expectations. Regardless of the efficiency of corrective mechanisms and apart from how extensive the violation of the followers' values must be before the corrective mechanism comes into play, the leader's position is less secure if he fails to satisfy the followers. If another leader is vying with him for the followers' support, the implications of failing to satisfy the followers are even more threatening. In a political interest group, the functional relationship of leaders to followers is keyed to the necessity for cohesion as a weapon in extra-group competition. The actuality or at least the appearance of unity is essential.[3]

Assuming that the leader desires to maintain an extra-group competitive position, he will therefore undertake efforts toward the fostering of intra-group cohesion. In a voluntary organization, one of the prime requisites for this cohesion is the extent to which the membership is satisfied with the performance of leaders.[4] There are three ways in which a leader may satisfy the desires of an organiza-

tion's membership. First, he may unconsciously act consistently with their desires. For example, he may decide to act on the basis of his evaluation of extra-group factors in such a way that the membership will be entirely satisfied. Second, he may respond entirely in terms of his personal attitudes and beliefs and, because he so accurately reflects the attitudes of his membership, again satisfy their desires. Third, a leader may consciously seek to do what he believes the membership of the organization desires. His success in satisfying the membership by this effort is dependent upon the accuracy of his perceptions of their attitudes and expectations.

RESEARCH DESIGN

In this paper we examine the latter two dynamics by which leaders can satisfy members. Our data were gathered from the membership of the Oregon Education Association. Three sets of information were collected: the beliefs and attitudes of the members of the Association, the beliefs and attitudes of the leaders of the Association, and the perception of the attitudes of the members as held by the leaders. The analysis consists of comparing these three sets of information and noting changes in their interrelationships on different attitudes. The nature of the analysis is illustrated by Figure 1.

FIGURE 1

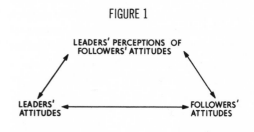

The sample of group members used in this study is a clustered stratified random sample of 803 high school teachers. This

[2]William Haythorn, *et al.*, "The Effects of Varying Combinations of Authoritarian and Equalitarian Leaders and Followers," *Journal of Abnormal and Social Psychology*, Vol. LIII (September, 1956), 210–19.

[3]Truman, *op. cit.*, pp. 167–87.

[4]Herbert Simon, *Administrative Behavior* (New York: The Macmillan Co., 1957), pp. 110–22.

represents 14% of the high school teachers in Oregon.[5]

The sample of leaders includes all nine of the OEA's top administrative officials. These are the members of the executive staff, which is employed by the organization's Board of Trustees. Its official responsibility is to implement the policies of the Representative Council, which consists of 200 representatives elected by local teachers' organizations. The Representative Council is the official policy-making body of the Association. However, both the Representative Council, which meets only once a year, and the Board of Trustees, which is supposed to deal with the specifics of the council's directives, are part-time functions. Thus, the permanent administrative staff is often forced to act in areas in which directives are vague or nonexistent. As is frequently the case in formal organizations, therefore, the permanent administrative staff has great flexibility and is a major delineator of policy.

In interviewing the leaders, we used a majority of the questions included in the teachers' interview schedule. Certain modifications in wording were made to allow for differences in organizational position. Leaders were first asked to answer the questions in terms of their own attitudes. They were then asked to take the point of view of the "average teacher" answering the same questions as they thought the "average teacher" would answer them. Only one of the leaders displayed any difficulty in assuming this attitude perspective; he had difficulty in keeping from answering questions in terms of what the teachers *should* believe rather than what he thought they actually *did* believe. The little difficulty the leaders experienced in answering these questions is evidence that the distinction between personal attitudes and the attitudes

of the membership is a meaningful one for them.

These three sets of attitudes (teachers' attitudes, leaders' attitudes, and leaders' perceptions of teachers' attitudes) are studied in four attitudinal contexts. They are:

1. Mandates for organizational action,
2. Expectations and satisfaction with the direction of leadership behavior,
3. Abstract political values, and
4. Norms of teachers' political participation.

The mandates for organizational action consist of two parts: expectations of behavior on the part of leaders themselves and expectations of action undertaken by teachers' organizations. In both cases, the satisfaction of the members with a particular action is dependent upon a congruence of the attitudes of the leaders with the actual attitudes of the followers.

Attitudes related to satisfaction with the direction of leadership are concerned with three of the Oregon Education Association's most strenuous activities; efforts toward salary improvement, efforts to raise teacher standards and accreditation, and efforts toward the establishment of a state sales tax with the revenues going to the public schools.

Abstract political values describe a set of attitudes, many of which are clichés often used by persons to persuade others to accept their position. They represent the basic "truths" of both the conservative and liberal points of view. A leader perceiving the membership as adhering to conservative values is ascribing conservatism to the membership and at the same time indicating that he believes an argument for action based upon these values would draw support from the membership.

The attitudes dealing with teachers' political participation concerned a broad set of politically related activities which might be undertaken by teachers in the classroom or during leisure time. The

---

[5]Attitudes were assessed by personal interviews. There were 91 teachers in the original sample with whom interviews were not completed.

leadership's ability to satisfy members in this regard will be reflected in their efforts or lack of efforts to support teachers in trouble in their local communities for various political activities and in the formal or informal articulation of a professional ethic with respect to these activities.

Although it would be possible to analyze these data using contingency tables, the existence of 50 attitude items and three comparisons for each item would tax the reader's ability to follow the analysis. A single measure which characterizes the relationship on each comparison of attitudes is therefore required. Although numerous measures of association and correlation were considered for this purpose, we settled upon Kendall's tau chi (τ_c).[6] This measure has its faults, the principal one being that its maximum value is dependent upon the marginals of the table. Our tables frequently have marginals of 803 and 9 (the N's of our two samples). Such great differences will yield a correlation of only .044 for a perfect relationship on a 2×2 table. Since we are more interested in finding a measure to characterize the comparison of attitude distributions of leaders and followers than in

using the measure as a test of statistical significance, it was decided to rely upon a new measure, τ_c over τ_c maximum.

As we are using this measure in comparing the distributions of attitudes of leaders and followers, a high correlation would indicate a strong relationship between attitudes and the person holding them. That is to say, a high correlation would indicate that leaders hold attitudes different from those of the followers. The sign of the measure will indicate the direction of this difference. Notice that a correlation of .000 indicates that leaders share the attitudes of the followers or that the two sets of attitudes compared have the same distribution.

Some may inquire of the statistical significance of the findings. There are two problems with the application of statistical significance tests to these data. First, one of the samples is not a sample at all but the universe of the administrative leaders of the Oregon Education Association. Thus, with no sampling error contributed by the leadership sample the comparing of leaders' and followers' attitudes does not necessitate as strong a relationship to achieve statistical significance as would be normally required. In the data comparing leaders' attitudes and their perceptions of followers' attitudes, clearly no statistical significance tests are applicable because the differences are real differences for the universe of leaders. Even if the leaders did constitute a sample, their small number places an unnecessarily strict requirement on the strength of the relationship necessary to achieve statistical significance.[7] In general, therefore, greater reliance is placed upon the consistency of a relationship within an attitude area rather than on the statistical significance of any one item. However, those single-item relationships which are significant are indicated by a small "s" in the tables (the

---

[6]Our data justify the use of ordinal measures of association, but there are several characteristics of our data and properties of various measures of association which complicate the choice of such a measure. First, on some of the items only two responses are possible while others are seven-point Likert scales. Thus any measure which is sensitive to the shape of the contingency table from which it is computed will decrease the comparability of the data across items. A measure which reached unity when only one cell is zero is also undesirable, as instances in which the leaders are in perfect agreement while the followers differ are common in our data. Such measures would be insensitive to the degree of followers' disagreement with the leaders. The final difficulty is that some measures are sensitive to the marginals of the contingency table. No measure was discovered which did not have at least one of the characteristics. See Hubert Blalock, *Social Statistics* (New York: McGraw-Hill Book Co., 1960), p. 323; and Leo A. Goodman and William H. Kruskal, "Measures of Association for Cross Classifications," *Journal of the American Statistical Association*, Vol. XLIX (December, 1954), p. 750.

---

[7]David Gold, "Some Problems in Generalizing Aggregate Associations," *American Behavioral Scientist*, Vol. VIII (December, 1964), p. 18.

Kruskal-Wallis h test is used to test statistical significance).

FINDINGS

Leaders' Perceptions of Their Roles

Before comparing the three sets of attitudes contained in this study, some discussion should be made of the leaders' perceptions of their roles within the organization. We refer here to the extent to which leaders believe they should act primarily in accordance with their own personal values rather than trying to reflect the desires of those whom they lead. We are asking whether leaders believe they should be delegates or representatives.[8]

Two questions were included in the leaders' interview schedule dealing with the problem of whose attitudes should be acted upon, those of the leaders or those of the followers. In one question the leaders were offered a brief dialogue between two persons, one arguing that a leader must do as the members wish and the other arguing that the leader must do what he personally believes to be correct. The leader was given the opportunity of selecting the argument which he found most satisfactory. Only one leader answered that the membership's desires should rule. Five answered that the leader should do what he personally believes to be right, although they added the comment that they thought the problem would occur very infrequently. Three of the lead-

---

[8] The terms "delegate" and "representative" are borrowed from the literature on the legislative process, whereby they are applied to the role perceptions of legislators. Heinz Eulau presents three legislative role orientations in John C. Wahlke, Heinz Eulau, William Buchanan, and LeRoy C. Ferguson, *The Legislative System* (New York: John Wiley and Sons, Inc., 1962), pp. 267–86. The "trustee" of Eulau's scheme has traditionally been described as a "delegate" while the "delegate" corresponds to "representative." These roles are the extremes, with "politico" falling somewhere between them.

ers said that if this problem could not be resolved the leader should resign.

The second question approached the problem from a slightly different angle and achieved very dissimilar results. The leaders were asked if they felt the organization should do pretty much what the average teacher wants, what the more influential teachers want, what the school administrators want, or what they themselves want. The "pretty much" phrase in the first alternative apparently was easier to accept than the wording in the other question, as five leaders chose this alternative. Two altered the second response to indicate that they believed they should do what the "more informed" teachers wanted while two indicated that they would prefer to do what they themselves thought best.

It would seem, therefore, that the leaders accept the maxim that they should do what the followers want, but they are also jealous of their autonomy to do what they think best. There appears to be a clear internalized conflict between the representative and delegate roles. Obviously the best of all possible worlds for the leaders would be perfect consensus between them and the members. In the absence of this consensus, they appear unable to reach a clear resolution of the conflict and to find a stable definition of their roles.

The leaders' acute awareness of the problem of communication with followers is indicated by a final question. Leaders were asked what policies of the Oregon Education Association they were most dissatisfied with. Seven volunteered the answer that the greatest problem was the OEA's failure to be true to the desires of its membership. Two of the leaders who gave this response explicitly criticized the administrative structure for not administering impartially the policy decisions of the Representative Council. It appears, therefore, that the representative nature of the organization is not only meaningful

TABLE 1
Comparison of the Three Attitude Sets in the Area of Mandate for Actions by
Leaders, Teachers' Organizations, and the OEA

	Sets of Attitudes Compared		
Questions	Followers' Attitudes vs. Leaders' Attitudes	Followers' Attitudes vs. Leaders' Perception of Followers' Attitudes	Leaders' Attitudes vs. Followers' Perception of Followers' Attitudes
Leaders should:			
1. Fight attacks on educational principles and methods.	−.134	−.134	.000
2. Fight against dismissal of teachers.	−.073	−.073	.000
3. Defend teachers from public attacks from getting involved in controversial issues.	−.059	−.059	.000
4. Eliminate political liberals from staff	+.284	+.061	−.222
5. Give helping hand to school board members coming up for election.	−.317(s)	+.211	+.528
Teachers' organizations should:			
6. Endorse political candidates.	−.419(s)	+.184	+.603
7. Take sides on public issues.	−.404(s)	+.221	+.625
OEA should:			
8. Endorse candidates in school elections.	−.387(s)	+.058	+.444
9. Try to influence legislation.	.000	.000	.000

to leaders but is also potentially divisive of the leadership.

Expectations Concerning Organizational Activity

The exact nature of this potential conflict within the organization will become clearer as we proceed to the analysis of the four attitude areas. We will first consider the mandates for organizational activity.

Table 1 presents the correlations for each of the attitude comparisons for each of the questions. In this, as in the tables which follow, the first column presents the objective attitudes, the "real world," and thus measures the extent of actual conflict. The second column shows the degree to which leaders are accurate in their perceptions of followers' attitudes, while the third column measures the extent of conflict as seen by the leaders. The negative sign of the correlation means that the bottom set of attitudes is more heavily

weighted in the direction of believing that leaders of the organization *should* undertake a particular action. For example, in the first column a negative sign means that leaders believe more than the followers that they or the organization should undertake a given activity. In the second column the negative sign means that the leaders perceive the followers as being more in favor of undertaking a particular action than they actually are. The positive sign in the second column means that the followers are more in favor of undertaking a particular activity than the leaders believe them to be. A negative sign in the third column means that the leaders perceive the followers as more supportive of a particular activity than the leaders are. A positive sign in the third column indicates the reverse.

The table indicates that, with the single exception of eliminating from the OEA staff people believed to be politically extreme, the leaders are more inclined to favor the involvement of the organization in each of the actions presented. This is shown by the fact that in seven of the nine cases the signs of the first column are negative. The first three of these items are the more clearly "professional" of the set. They involve the traditional academic values of freedom of expression and the protection of teachers against hostile forces in the community. These are at best *quasi* political activities. Yet even here the followers are more restrained than the leaders. Note that on the question of eliminating political liberals from the OEA staff, the followers are more in favor of such action than are the leaders. However, it is true that the greatest discrepancy between followers' and leaders' attitudes occur on those questions involving the more purely political aspects of the organization, such as endorsing political candidates, taking sides on public issues, and taking part in the electoral activities of school board members.

With regard to these political activities, the followers are much more restrained than they are concerning more purely educational activities. Granted that the distinction between quasi-political and political is arbitrary at best, the followers do appear to make it. Thus, they are much more inclined to support the activities of the OEA if it defends teachers against public attacks than they would be if the teachers' organization endorsed political candidates.

The glaring exception to the general reluctance of the teachers to support the OEA's political activities is on the question of lobbying. Here there is nearly perfect agreement between leaders and followers. Lobbying is perceived by teachers to be an absolutely legitimate function of the organization. Teachers, therefore, are making a distinction between legislative politics and electoral politics.[9] The Asso-

ciation is currently engaged in a vigorous lobbying program at the state legislative level. With regard to lobbying, it is interesting to notice that not only do the attitudes of the leaders and followers converge, but also the leaders perceive that the followers support the lobbying activities. This is indicated by the zero correlation in the second and third columns.

Notice also that with regard to the first three activities (fighting attacks on educational principles and methods, fighting against the dismissal of teachers, and defending teachers from public attacks) the leaders see *more* support among the teachers than actually exists. Since the leaders overestimate the enthusiasm of followers, they see a consensus which does not hold true in the "real world." Hence the perfect correlation in the third column between the leaders' attitudes and their perceptions of teachers' attitudes is based upon faulty perceptions. This is not true with regard to the consensus about lobbying.

It is in the more purely electoral activities of the organization that discrepancies occur. Notice that on questions five, six, seven, and eight, the negative signs of the first column become positive signs in the second column. This means that, whereas leaders are more likely to want to engage in the electoral activities than are followers, the leaders perceive the followers as far more hesitant than the followers actually are. Consequently, these electoral activities can be contrasted with the professional and lobbying activities. In these professional and lobbying activities, the third column indicates that the leaders see little or no discrepancy between their point of view and the point of view of the followers, whereas the correlations on items five, six, seven, and eight in the third column indicate that the leaders see a considerable conflict between their values and those of the followers. With regard to these political activities, the leaders are correct in perceiving conflict although conflict also exists in educational

---

[9] Cf. Gabriel Almond and Sidney Verba, *The Civic Culture* (Boston: Little, Brown, and Co., 1965), pp. 250–51.

TABLE 2

Comparison of the Three Attitude Sets in the Areas of Expectations
and Satisfaction with Leaderships' Actions

| | | Sets of Attitudes Compared | |
Questions	Followers' Attitudes vs. Leaders' Attitudes	Followers' Attitudes vs. Leaders' Perception of Followers' Attitudes	Leaders' Attitudes vs. Leaders' Perception of Followers' Attitudes
1. How important do you think has been the role played by the OEA in getting improved salaries and benefits?	+.556(s)	+.026	−.667
2. How about the Teachers' Union; how important do you think its role was in getting improved salaries and benefits?	−.297	−.098	+.185
3. Do you think the OEA is doing enough to improve teachers' salaries and benefits?	−.332	−.444	−.111
4. How about the Teachers' Union; is it doing enough in improving teachers' salaries and benefits?	−.396	−.396	.000
5. Do you think the OEA is doing enough in its support for higher teacher standards and accreditation to improve professional status?	−.016	−.016	.000
6. Do you think there should be a state sales tax with the revenue going to the schools?	+.253	+.364	+.111

activities but is missed by the leaders.

At this point in its organizational history, the OEA is in fact more likely to engage in professional and lobbying activities than it is in electoral activities. It is these activities in which the leaders see the followers as being entirely supportive of the organization, although they are correct only with regard to lobbying. If the OEA were to increase its electoral activities, therefore, it would be engaging in practices which are less favored by the followers. However, the fact that the teachers are perceived as being more reluctant to support these activities than they actually are might result in the leaders engaging in these activities to a lesser extent than would be tolerated by the followers.

Evaluations of Organizational Performance

Turning from the extent to which leaders and followers are in agreement as to what the organization should do, we consider now the relationships between sets of attitudes concerning the extent of satisfaction with the actual behavior of the leaders of the organization. In Table 2 a negative sign indicates that the bottom set of attitudes is less satisfied with the performance of the teachers' organization. A positive sign indicates that the bottom set is more satisfied.

In the first analysis, we found that the leaders consistently underestimate the followers' activism. In Table 2 we find a similar tendency with several notable exceptions. On the question of the importance of the OEA's role in getting improved salaries and benefits in the past, we find a great discrepancy between leaders' and followers' attitudes: the followers are inclined to give the OEA less credit than are the leaders. However, the second column shows that the leaders' perception is accurate. Hence, they perceive followers as exhibiting more dissatisfaction with past performance than the leaders do. Leaders, intimately involved in the successes and failures of the organization, see their role as more significant than do the more passive followers. Only about one-third of the followers think that the OEA was "very important" in securing past benefits, whereas all the leaders are of this opinion.

With regard to current performance a different situation exists. The leaders are more dissatisfied with the performance of the organization and its constant fight for better salaries. Once again, however, they perceive more dissatisfaction among the followers than actually exists. Although accurate in their perceptions of teacher satisfaction with past performance, leaders fail in their evaluation of current satisfaction. In fact, 56% of the followers indicated that they think the OEA is doing enough about salaries. This is not exactly an overwhelming vote of confidence, but it is apparent that more satisfaction exists in reality than is perceived by the OEA leadership.

In view of the current conflict between teachers' unions and professional organizations for the loyalties of teachers, it is interesting to note that the OEA leaders are more likely to denigrate the efforts of the teachers' union than are the teachers themselves. This is indicated by the negative sign of the correlations in column one considering the role of the union in past and present efforts toward salary increases. Again column two tells us that in both of these cases leaders perceive that followers are more dissatisfied with the union than they actually are. This distinction between past and present produces some curious results in the third column, showing the extent of conflict perceived by leaders. While they exaggerate the extent of dissatisfaction on the part of followers, perhaps projecting their own desires more than an objective evaluation would indicate, they recognize that the followers are more impressed with past union performance than they (the leaders) are. Yet they persist in seeing perfect

agreement between themselves and teachers concerning current union performance, an agreement which does not exist. These distortions lead the leadership to assume a "what-have-you-done-for-me-lately" attitude somewhat along the lines of old fashioned bread and butter unionism. It seems likely that these perceptions will cause them to channel more of their resources into salary increase efforts at the risk of providing less satisfactory efforts in other areas. On the other hand this risk does not appear to be very great. For example, the leaders are extremely accurate in their perceptions of teacher satisfaction with regard to support for higher professional standards and accreditation. A consensus only slightly weaker than that regarding lobbying exists here.

The final item in the table dealing with the question of state sales tax enables us to return once again to lobbying. We may well ask "Lobbying for what?" The OEA has been strongly lobbying for a state sales tax with revenues going to the public schools, but only a slight majority (53%) of the teachers agree that a state sales tax should be enacted, while more than two-thirds of the leadership favor the tax. This is apparently an elite-derived effort enjoying only weak support from the followers. In this case, however, the leaders perceive far more support than actually exists. They actually believe that followers support this effort more than the leaders do, whereas the opposite is the case. Thus, although high consensus is achieved on the legitimacy of lobbying, leaders do not show a great capability of deciding how much effort should be devoted to the pursuit of certain policies by means of lobbying. The leaders want a sales tax, perceive the followers as wanting a sales tax, and pursue this effort vigorously. It is possible that if the efforts to achieve a sales tax are continued with increased intensity, membership support might be reduced beyond the bare majority it enjoys now, and intragroup conflict may result. If this happens the perceptual errors of the leaders could prove costly.

Abstract Political Values

Up to this point we have been considering the explicit programs of the Oregon Education Association, and the extent to which there is a congruence between leaders' and followers' values with regard to these programs. Members of organizations, however, may have values which are not directly translatable into explicit programs but which nevertheless color the relationship between leaders and followers. The overall ideological pattern of leaders and followers is, therefore, a component in determining the extent to which leaders represent the followers' values. It is this assumption which leads us to inquire about abstract political values. The items in Table 3 are offered as important in the leaders' evaluations as to what programs might appeal to the followers and also what the nature of appeals to the membership for support on a given issue

TABLE 3

Comparison of the Attitude Sets in the Area of Orthodox Values

Questions	Sets of Attitudes Compared		
	Followers' Attitudes vs. Leaders' Attitudes	Followers' Attitudes vs. Leaders' Perceptions of Followers' Attitudes	Leaders' Attitudes vs. Leaders' Perceptions of Followers' Attitudes
Conservative			
1. The American form of government may not be perfect, but it's the best type of government yet devised by man.	$-.137$	$+.078$	$+.222$
2. Democracy is considered the ideal form of government by most of the world.	$-.160$	$-.658$	$-.407$
3. Private enterprise could do better most of the things the government is now doing.	$+.365$	$-.171$	$-.568$
4. The participation of the federal government in local affairs leads to undesirable federal controls.	$+.564(s)$	$-.389$	$-.926$
5. Communism is a total evil.	$+.142$	$-.466$	$-.630$
6. People of most underdeveloped countries are by nature incapable of self-government.	$+.303$	$-.226$	$-.506$
7. Private enterprise is the only really workable system in the modern world capable of satisfying our economic needs.	$+.257$	$-.182$	$-.469$
Liberal			
8. Economic and social planning by government does not necessarily lead to dictatorship.	$-.326$	$+.125$	$+.444$
9. Man is the maker of his own society, such events as wars and depressions could be controlled by man.	$-.122$	$+.161$	$+.259$
10. The growth of large corporations makes government regulation of business necessary.	$-.190$	$+.088$	$+.309$
11. We could increase spending for many government services without harming the nation's economy.	$-.402$	$+.035$	$+.432$
12. The federal government represents the needs of most people better than local government.	$-.030$	$+.284$	$+.259$
13. The government should increase its activities in matters of health, retirement, wages, and old-age benefits.	$-.205$	$-.034$	$+.185$

might be. On the basis of their content, the items are separated into those indicating conservatism and those indicating liberalism. The first seven questions are the conservative questions, and the last six are the liberal questions. For each group, a negative sign indicates that the bottom set of attitudes shows greater acceptance of the item.

Looking at the first column, it can readily be seen that the leaders are more likely to disagree with the conservative items and more likely to agree with the liberal items than are the followers. Furthermore, the high correlations in the third column show that the leaders believe that the followers differ greatly from them with regard to these items. Once again, however, the leaders' perceptions of teachers' attitudes tends to exaggerate the differences. In eleven of the thirteen cases, leaders perceive followers to be more conservative and less liberal than they actually are. Thus, although the OEA leaders are a biased section of the teachers with respect to their political and economic values, they tend to perceive their atypical posture as more extreme than it actually is. This discrepancy in perception is likely to influence the leaders to use more conservative appeals to the followers in the urging support of particular programs than would be called for by an accurate inventory of their values.

Combined with the bread and butter perception described previously, this perceived conservatism of teachers leads the leaders into the path of heavy emphasis on salaries and other basic issues while at the same time forcing them to restrict their activities in the realm of expansion of organizational activities. If the leadership seeks to venture into untried areas which are not specifically related to educational problems, it may be hesitant to begin for fear that the programs are too liberal for the membership.

Of course, as Krech and Crutchfield point out, the degree of association be-

tween cognitive attitudes and action-orientated attitudes is not necessarily great.[10] Thus, a person holding conservative beliefs does not automatically favor conservative actions by government. To ascertain the extent to which abstract values are translatable into immediate preferences for governmental action, we administered the items from the Survey Research Center's domestic attitude scale.[11] As in the abstract value index, the leaders proved to be much more liberal than the followers. Also, the leaders saw the followers as not being as liberal as they actually are. In this case, however, the leaders are not so greatly more liberal and they do not see the followers as so greatly more conservative than they actually are. The main thrust of the conservative scale is identical to that of the abstract political value index, but the discrepancies are not as great. It may be, therefore, that the leaders are less in danger of undercutting the cohesion of the organization should they lend its support to an explicit governmental program outside the realm of education related issues. The danger to cohesion may be not so much in the undertaking of new programs but in the appeal to followers on the basis of their perceived conservatism.

The Political Role of the Teacher

Teachers, like the holders of any social position, have perceptions of what is permissible behavior by holders of their social position. Others who do not hold this position also have expectations. The interaction of these two expectations constitutes a role. Table 4 presents the compari-

---

[10]David Krech and Richard Crutchfield, *Theory and Problems of Social Psychology* (New York: McGraw-Hill Book Co., 1948), p. 251.

[11]See Angus Campbell, *et al.*, *The American Voter* (New York: John Wiley and Sons, 1960), pp. 194–98. V. O. Key gives the items used in this scale. See V. O. Key, Jr., *Public Opinion and American Democracy* (New York: Alfred A. Knopf, 1961), p. 561.

TABLE 4

Comparison of the Attitude Sets in the Area of the Norms of Teachers' Political Participation

Questions	Followers' Attitudes vs. Leaders' Attitudes	Followers' Attitudes vs. Leaders' Perceptions of Followers' Attitudes	Leaders' Attitudes vs. Leaders' Perceptions of Followers' Attitudes
Teachers should if they want to:			
1. Join a teachers' union.	−.135	+.532(s)	+.667
2. Go on strike to secure higher salaries and other benefits.	+.067	+.317(s)	+.250
3. Join a political party organization.	−.036	+.186	+.222
4. Serve as party precinct worker in pre-election activities.	−.064	+.269	+.333
5. Publicly criticize local government officials.	−.268	+.510(s)	+.778
6. In a presidential election, outside school time, make speeches or give other services on the behalf of a candidate.	−.110	+.335(s)	+.444
7. Run for political office.	−.104	+.451(s)	+.556
8. In a presidential election, explain to class reasons for preferring one candidate.	−.055	+.279	+.333
9. Belong to the NAACP or CORE.	−.129	+.316(s)	+.444
10. Take part in a CORE or NAACP demonstration, such as public picketing.	−.112	+.460(s)	+.571
11. Allow an atheist to address the class.	−.126	+.430(s)	+.556
12. Argue in class against the censoring of literature by people who feel it is pornographic.	−.226	+.039	+.306
13. Speak out in class against the John Birch Society and groups like it.	−.153	+.180	+.333
14. Speak in favor of nationalizing the steel industry and the railroads.	−.249	+.307	+.556
15. Speak in class in favor of the Medicare program.	−.169	+.276	+.444
16. Speak in class in favor of the United Nations.	−.043	+.291	+.333
17. Allow the distribution of anticommunist literature put out by the National Association of Manufacturers.	−.254	+.191	+.444
18. Speak in class favorably about socialism.	−.105	+.229	+.333
19. Argue in class that labor unions should be more regulated or controlled by the government.	−.158	+.176	+.333
20. Allow the distribution of anticommunist literature put out by the John Birch Society.	−.443(s)	+.123	+.556

sons between the three sets of attitudes with regard to norms of teachers' political participation. A negative sign indicates that the bottom set of attitudes in the comparison favors teacher participation more than does the top set of attitudes.

Here we see a remarkably consistent pattern. Leaders are, in every case save one, more supportive of actions by teachers in these areas than are the teachers. This is even true of joining a teachers'

union, but it is not true of striking to secure higher salaries and other benefits. In this latter case, the teachers are slightly more likely than leaders to be willing to undertake this activity and are much more likely to be willing to strike than leaders perceive them to be. This is the single example of followers being more "activist" than leaders to achieve liberal goals. In every other case, no matter what type of action is involved, leaders are more willing to take a risk, more willing to engage in controversial activity than are followers. When we examine the leaders' perception of followers' attitudes, we find once again the consistent pattern of underevaluation of the experimental nature of teachers. Leaders perceive teachers as being unlikely to engage in these activities whereas teachers themselves, although less anxious than leaders to take part in these activities, are more willing to do so than leaders believe them to be. Thus, the teachers are more willing to join teachers' unions, political party organizations, or racial organizations than leaders believe them to be.

CONCLUSIONS

To summarize the findings of this analysis, the following points may be offered. As is true of most organizations, the leaders of the Oregon Education Association are more active than the followers. They are more liberal than the followers and they are more willing than the followers to expand the activities of the organization, but they consistently exaggerate the atypical nature of their position. They see the followers as being more conservative and restrained than they actually are. These discrepancies, both in perception and in actual attitudes, lead us to speculate as to how they came about. Is the relative activism of leaders a function of their social role, their organizational position, or their personality? It is certainly not feasible to argue that leadership positions somehow recruit more daring people. It is more feasible to seek explanations within the nature of the organization and the teaching profession. Consider, for example, the items dealing with political participation by teachers. Leaders would be subject to none of the pressures that teachers would feel from their community. Also, while teachers can recall relatively few cases in which the community made demands upon the school system for the

dismissal of a teacher for engaging in controversial activity, those who can recall such incidents are of the opinion that the teachers' organization was ineffective in the defense of teachers. It is also true that the teachers look upon the local affiliates of the Oregon Education Association much more favorably than they look upon the statewide organization which employs the leaders considered in this study. In arguing for organizational position as a fundamental contributor to differential perception, we draw added support from the reaction of the leaders to the competition of the union. Leaders behave in much the same fashion as political party leaders.[12] They are more emotionally committed to the organization than are the rank and file. Hence, they find it difficult to comprehend the problems of teaching and the restrictions traditionally imposed upon teachers by the community.

It might be useful to know something about the leaders' backgrounds. All have at one time been teachers and all have passed through some lower administrative position before achieving their present status. Most have taken graduate work, usually in educational administration. All earn in excess of ten thousand dollars per year. Thus, although they do have a teaching background, they are much more upwardly mobile than the average teacher and make more money. They are also substantially better educated. The upward mobility of the leaders of the OEA can be gleaned from the backgrounds of their fathers. Most of their fathers had less than a high school education and held low status occupations. Thus holding a position in the OEA marks more of a step up than does teaching. Perhaps, therefore, the leaders consider themselves as more

---

[12]Herbert McClosky, "Consensus and Ideology in American Politics," *American Political Science Review*, Vol. LVIII (June, 1964), 361–82.

sophisticated and advanced than teachers.

When we consider the fact that serving as an OEA administrator is in a sense moving beyond a teaching position, the explanation offered above becomes more plausible. Combine this with the fact that leaders have interaction with a more heterogeneous environment and their perception of teachers becomes even more understandable. Unlike the teachers, who interact mostly with teachers, students, principals, and parents, the OEA administrative staff interacts with lobbyists, legislators, state officials, and national educational officials.

As a final alternative to the explanation offered above, we considered the possibility that, whereas the leaders incorrectly perceive the political values and political role perceptions of teachers, they may base their reactions upon communication with a biased sample. There are, of course, many different shades of opinion among teachers just as there are among the general public. Is it true that the OEA leaders interact with a segment of the teaching population which is more conservative and more restrained? If this is true, then their perceptions of followers' attitudes might not be a function of their social position but might be the result of an unrepresentative sample of opinion being communicated to them. However, our evidence indicates quite clearly that there is no relationship between political conservatism and participation in organizational affairs. There is no evidence that the conservative teachers have any more interaction with OEA leaders than do the liberal teachers. Also, those teachers who take a restrained view of the political role of the teacher are no more likely to communicate with OEA leaders than are those teachers who take a more expansionist

view.[13] Thus, we can say that there is no weighting of communication which comes to the attention of OEA leaders in favor of conservatism and restraint.

Assuming, therefore, that being a leader in an organization contributes to a discrepancy between leaders' and followers' attitudes, we may inquire finally into the possibility of having a democratic interest group without frequent and carefully supervised consultative mechanisms. Can leaders be representative simply because they intuitively comprehend what is required of them? In considering this question, let us note that, with the exception of the last table, the discrepancy between leaders' attitudes and followers' attitudes is generally *greater* than the errors made by leaders in perceiving these attitudes. Thus, OEA leaders operating entirely upon their personal values would not be representative of the values of their followers. On the other hand, if they adopted a purely representative role, they would become more conservative and restrained than the teachers would prefer. Yet, with exception of the last set of attitudes, the error would be less than would be true if followers' wishes were ignored. That is to say, if they followed their understanding of followers' values, the resulting conservatism and restraint would be closer to the actual desires of teachers than would be true if leaders used their personal values as the sole criteria of judgment. "Virtual" representation in an interest group cannot serve as a substitute for actual representation, because the position of group leader contributes to the development of attitudes which differ from those of the followers.

---

[13]It is true, however, that there is more interaction between leaders and small-town teachers; these teachers are considerably more conservative and restrained than their big-city counterparts.

THE EFFECTS OF LOBBYING: A COMPARATIVE ASSESSMENT*

Harmon Zeigler

Heinz Eulau once asked a question which might appear to "realistic" students of American politics as absurd. He asked: "What would politics in America be like without lobbies and lobbyists?"[1] To a generation of political scientists raised on the writings of Bentley and Truman, the question seems, at first glance, not only absurd, but *reactionary*. When the "behavioral revolution" reached a fever pitch in the 1950's, political scientists turned first to those writers who rejected the legalism of the past in an effort to describe the interaction of individuals rather than the structure of institutions. Arthur Bentley clearly stood out as a potential source of inspiration. Anybody who, in 1908, could write that "formal study of the most external characteristics of governing institutions" is worthless and must be replaced by the enterprise of getting hold of "political institutions, legislatures, courts, executive officers, and get them stated as groups, in terms of groups. . . ."[2] appeared

as a logical Marx for the behavioral revolution.

Although most political scientists did not pay much attention to Bentley, various case studies of "pressure groups in action" began to appear, culminating in the summary statement of Truman.[3] While there are enough ambiguities in Bentley to make a direct application of his theories virtually impossible, interest groups approached the status of a "first cause" of public policy. Of course, Truman (who replaced Bentley) never really said that in order to study legislation one need only to account for the activities of formal groups, but such an inference was made by readers of *The Governmental Process*, if only because the data to support his theories were not easily obtained from formal organizations.

TWO CONSTRASTING MODELS OF THE GROUP BASIS OF POLITICS

The belief that interest groups are, by definition, powerful has been described as a "mechanistic" theory. In some extreme cases perhaps it was. Yet the better writers on the subject did not argue that all groups were powerful, nor did they believe that legislators made decisions solely as a result of their interactions with lobbyists. However, the "group theorists" did, if all their writings are summed up, outline a model of the political process roughly along the following lines. Individuals

---

*The author wishes to acknowledge the support of the Center for the Advanced Study of Educational Administration during a portion of the time he devoted to the preparation of this paper. CASEA is a national research and development center which was established at the University of Oregon under the provisions of the Cooperative Research Program of the U.S. Office of Education. I wish to acknowledge the assistance of Heinz Eulau, who carefully evaluated an earlier draft and made numerous suggestions for improvement.

[1] Heinz Eulau, "Lobbyists: The Wasted Profession," *Public Opinion Quarterly*, Vol. XXVIII (Spring 1964), p. 27.

[2] Arthur Bentley, *The Process of Government* (San Antonio, Texas: Principia Press of Trinity University, 1949), p. 210.

---

[3] David Truman, *The Governmental Process* (New York: Alfred A. Knopf, Inc., 1951).

within a society have a variety of needs, some of which can be achieved only, or at least more efficiently, through governmental activity. Most of the values and beliefs of individuals are derived from the groups that they belong to or that they have contact with. Some of these groups are determined *for* an individual; others are joined voluntarily. Yet even the voluntary joining of an association has its roots in the deeper group affiliations of the individual. Since most of the needs of the individual derive from his group affiliations, the logical method of translating needs into demands is through formal groups. Of course, groups do not automatically become formal organizations. The formalization of group relationships occurs when, through intense and sustained interaction, individuals systematize their relationships. Hence farmers, druggists, doctors, or automobile workers find that their shared attitudes make it efficient to be represented by an interest group. The interest group, by means of its lobbyists, relates to the decision makers the needs of its members.

Viewed from this angle, group theorists were suggesting that interest groups are *transmission belts* between individual needs and governmental institutions. Other possible channels of communication, especially political parties, were not considered to be as effective primarily because they were too heterogeneous to be capable of presenting a cohesive point of view.

Crucial to the theory is the notion that, as societies become more complex, secondary associations replace primary associations as the essential group-referents of individuals. Consequently, in a complex industrial society such as America, formal associations are the essential means of communication. Froman has provided a useful summary of the function of interest groups, as defined by the group theorists. Interest groups channel communications to decision makers, help structure alterna-

tive policy choices, act as buffers between the government and the people, help check demands made by others, provide functional representation, compartmentalize access to decision makers, lead to a system of minorities rule, and provide people with an emotional outlet.[4]

Of course, such a brief outline of traditional group theory hardly does justice to many of its complexities and modifications. The essence of their theories is that interest groups are powerful because they monopolize access to governmental decision makers. The difficulty with this body of knowledge is that most of the empirical justifications assumed the validity of the theory, and many of them were case studies of a single legislative episode or a single interest group. Although in some cases this research involved interviewing legislators and lobbyists, the assumption that lobbyists were (naturally) influential lead to some distortions of the findings to fit the mechanistic model.

The writer can provide personal evidence of the confusion which results from an unquestioning acceptance of the mechanistic model. In writing *The Politics of Small Business,* it was discovered that the lobbyists for small business organizations described themselves as intimately involved in the affairs of the House and Senate Small Business Committees and of the Small Business Administration. However, members of these committees, their staffs, and the administrators of the Small Business Administration not only did not share this evaluation, but in many cases did not know the names of the lobbyists! It seemed as if the decision makers regarded the interest groups as without either power or legitimacy.[5] This was, of course, only a single case study of one

[4]Lewis A. Froman, Jr., "Some Effects of Interest Group Strength in State Politics," *American Political Science Review,* Vol. LX (December 1966), p. 954.

[5]Harmon Zeigler, *The Politics of Small Business* (Washington: The Public Affairs Press, 1961).

area of public policy. However, it seemed to fit with what Donald R. Matthews was finding out at about the same time. His interviews with legislators led him to conclude that the effects of lobbying were greatly exaggerated.[6] Actually, the research of those not committed to group-theoretical notions gave support to Matthews' assessment. Studies of Congressional decision making did not emphasize groups unless such an emphasis was the a priori purpose of the investigation. Zeigler concluded in 1964 that "Since interest groups do not monopolize the communication of demands to the legislature, it is not likely that the effects of lobbying are as great as lobbyists themselves or journalistic writers seem to believe."[7] Empirical evidence was inadequate, however.

Evidence was soon forthcoming; in fact, some already existed. Wahlke, Eulau, Buchanan, and Ferguson, in a comparative study of four state legislatures, assessed the attitudes of state legislators toward interest groups. Categorizing legislators into "facilitators," "neutrals," and "resistors," they found that while a minority of legislators were overtly hostile to lobbyists, there was substantial state-by-state variation.[8] In other words, in some political systems interest groups were dominant while in others they were not. There are some problems in interpreting these data which relate primarily to the fact that the sole measure of legislators' relationships with lobbyists is their attitude rather than their actual interaction. These problems will be taken up again. For the moment, it is important to observe that, in the Wahlke, Eulau, Buchanan, Ferguson study, the role of the legislator vis à vis lobbyists was an open question.

Shortly after the publication of *The Legislative System*, two studies of lobbying in Washington took direct issue with traditional group theory. Bauer, Pool, and Dexter, echoing an earlier protest by Cohen that the legend of "pressure group potency . . . appears to be accepted and passed on without evidence. . . . ,"[9] discovered that, with regard to reciprocal trade legislation, lobbyists and the organizations they represented were a relatively minor factor in the ultimate decision: ". . . the groups did not appear to have the raw material of great power. We noted shortages of money, men, information, and time."[10] Although the authors are careful to disclaim any intention to suggest that their particular case is typical, their conclusions certainly strike at the heart of the stereotype of the powerful, active interest group. Bauer, Pool, and Dexter speculated about the extent to which lobbyists aided in the perpetuation of the myth. However, Milbrath, interviewing a random sample of Washington lobbyists, generally supported the conclusions of Bauer, Pool, and Dexter.[11] He discovered that legislators did not feel very dependent upon the information supplied by lobbyists; consequently, only a small portion of lobbyists (9 percent) are consulted frequently. Milbrath uses the responses of lobbyists, suggesting that legislators and their staffs do not need them, to argue that the net result of lobbying is minimal.

THE NATURE OF THIS EXPLORATION

Thus we have come full circle. The mechanistic model has been buried, and we are now in the position of arguing that interest groups (or at least the lobbyists

---

[6]Donald R. Matthews, *U.S. Senators and Their World* (Chapel Hill: University of North Carolina Press, 1960), pp. 195–96.

[7]Harmon Zeigler, *Interest Groups in American Society* (Englewood Cliffs: Prentice-Hall, Inc., 1964), p. 276.

[8]John C. Wahlke *et al.*, *The Legislative System* (New York: John Wiley & Sons, Inc., 1962), pp. 311–42.

[9]Bernard C. Cohen, *The Influence of Non-Governmental Groups on Foreign Policy-Making* (Boston: World Peace Federation, 1959), p. 2.

[10]Raymond A. Bauer *et al.*, *American Business and Public Policy* (New York: Atherton Press, 1963), p. 398.

[11]Lester Milbrath, *The Washington Lobbyists* (Chicago: Rand McNally and Co., 1963).

who represent them) could very easily be eliminated from the decision-making process without any appreciable change in public policy. This strikes me as a curious situation. Do we have to decide that the "truth" lies in either one direction or the other? Clearly, we do not. The research problem is to try to measure the effects of interest groups in different decision-making arenas and to offer some explanations as to the variations that can be expected to exist. This seems to be the thrust of the recent arguments by Eulau. In evaluating Milbrath's book, he agrees that the concept of "pressure" is too "strong" to be useful as an explanatory device. There is probably substantial consensus that "pressure group" is a misnomer. However, Eulau maintains that Milbrath's alternative explanatory model, "communications," is too "weak." By this he means that attempting to define the lobbying act as a communications process cannot provide a guide to reliable explanations because the concept is too inclusive. Obviously, lobbying is communications because *every* social interaction is an example of the communications process. Correct in his assessment of the nature of communications, Eulau seems to deny Milbrath's communications model its real virtue; it indicates that the interactions between legislators and lobbyists (albeit slight) takes a variety of forms, with "pressure" being a very minor one. That is to say, the concept of communications includes the notion of pressure, along with the transmission of information.

The real virtue of Eulau's criticism is his plea that we should address ourselves to "the critical problems of the impact of lobbying on governmental decisions."[12] I gather that Eulau believes this problem is best approached by means of a model which depends heavily upon a description of the *total* role definition system of legislators. In order to understand the attitude of legislators toward interest groups (and,

by inference, the behavior of legislators with regard to lobbyists), we have to understand their self-perceptions in relation to their colleagues, constituents, parties, and any other source from which legislators derive cues.

One can hardly quarrel with Eulau's plea, as far as it goes. However, there are alternative ways of approaching the problem. A conspicuous gap in *The Legislative System* is the failure of the authors to pay more than cursory attention to the total environment in which the legislators perform their functions. This gap is made even more troublesome because of recent research on outputs. Recent efforts by Dye, Hofferbert, Grumm, and others to explain the outputs of state legislatures has led to the conclusion that knowing the characteristics of the political system (such as extent of malapportionment, strength of parties, and party cohesion) does not enable one to predict what kinds of decisions a given state will make.[13] Knowing something about the economic and social environment, on the contrary, enables us to make relatively strong predictions about state outputs. Thus, one can ask the same question of party organizations that Eulau asked about interest groups: what would happen if they were to disappear? Clearly, the time has not yet come to make the statement that nothing would happen, but this kind of research has made compelling the need to look at total environment. This is not to assert, however, that environmental conditions *necessarily* influence the behavior of interest groups; rather it is to suggest the desirability of *asking* whether or not they do. It may be true that behavioral patterns, unlike outputs, are not related.

The interaction of legislators and lobbyists, and the relative effect of interest

---

[12]Eulau, *op. cit.*, p. 35.

[13]This literature is evaluated in John G. Grumm, "Structure and Policy in the Legislature" (manuscript presented at the Conference on the Comparative Study of State Politics, University of Michigan, August 1–12, 1966).

groups which flows from this interaction, must be placed within the context of total environment in order to ascertain the existence of a relationship between environment and behavior. Some of the more obvious aspects of environment can be derived from aggregate statistics. For instance, I used percentage of the population residing in urban areas, per capita income, and industrialization to hypothesize that interest groups are strongest in less urban, less wealthy, less industrial states.[14] Consequently, more group-oriented activity can be expected in these areas. Although urban, industrial societies generate more membership in voluntary associations, a more open and competitive group system reduces the chances of any one interest becoming dominant. Therefore, interest groups would be more likely to achieve a monopoly of communications in low-participant states with a low potential for group politics. Since the nonurban, nonindustrial, less wealthy states are those with the *least* participation and the *strongest* interest groups, the theory "fits." However, this argument is based upon a very unreliable measure of interest group strength. Indeed, due to the questionable nature of the measure, it remains an open question as to whether there is a relationship between the socioeconomic environment and the strength of the interest group system. To anticipate a later argument, this article will suggest that there is *not*.

Whereas cross-national research is an obvious testing ground for theories concerned with environmental variables, so are the American states. The states, because of their relative accessibility to researchers, are more useful than cross-national studies. Further, there appears to be as much variety among the states

as there is between various national political cultures. Finally, while there are large varieties in the socioeconomic nature of the states, there are enough institutional similarities to make the task of comparative research less trying. The data for this research is interviews conducted with legislators and lobbyists in Oregon, North Carolina, Utah, and Massachusetts.[15] The states were selected to provide a maximum dispersion of socioeconomic conditions. Table 1 outlines some of the dimensions of these differences. There is, of course, no way of causally linking these variables to the behavior of lobbyists and legislators. However, one could infer that empirically observed differences in behavior are related to differences in environment. Conversely, if it appears that environmental differences are randomly distributed in regard to the behavior of legislators and lobbyists, one can assume that no relationship exists.

Attention to environment is not intended to submerge the importance of individual role perceptions, but rather to provide them with a setting. Indeed, most of the empirical portions of this paper are based directly upon perceptions of self and perceptions of others. The basic assumption, derived directly from Eulau rather than in opposition to him, is that ". . . one should conduct empirical work . . . at both ends of the legislator–lobbyist

<hr>

[14]Harmon Zeigler, "Interest Groups in the States," in Herbert Jacob and Kenneth Vines, eds., *Politics in the American States* (Boston: Little, Brown and Co., 1965), pp. 101–46.

[15]Interviews were conducted during February and March 1966. Efforts were made to interview each legislator and lobbyist. For the legislators, the percentage of completed interviews is: Massachusetts, 87%, North Carolina, 97%, Oregon, 94%, and Utah, 94%. For lobbyists, the percentage interviewed is more difficult to assess. In Utah, there is no list of registered lobbyists and in the other states it was found that some lobbyists do not register. In Massachusetts and North Carolina, the number of completed interviews exceeds the number of registered lobbyists. In Oregon, 94% of the registered lobbyists were interviewed. In Utah, since we first had to construct a list based upon preliminary interviews with experienced legislators, newspaper reporters, and more visible lobbyists, no percentage calculation can be given.

TABLE 1
Cultural Variations in Four States

	Massachusetts	North Carolina	Oregon	Utah
Total population	5,296,000	4,787,000	1,999,000	971,000
Percent increase: 1960–63	2.9	5.1	4.7	9.0
Percent urban	83.6	39.5	62.2	74.9
Percent Negro	2.2	24.5	1.0	0.5
Percent foreign parentage	28.8	1.0	13.0	12.0
Population mobility: percent of 1960 population residing in different county than 1955 residence	13.5	15.6	25.7	21.2
Percent living in largest SMSA	49.7	6.7	39.9	45.6
Per capita income	2,853	1,807	2,502	2,119
Percent failure, Draft Board Mental Tests, 1963	14.1	43.8	6.9	5.5
Median school years completed	11.6	8.9	11.8	12.2
Industrialization index*	98.7	86.7	92.1	94.0
Voter turnout in gubernatorial and senatorial elections in non-Presidential years	58.8	25.1	55.9	64.3
Ranney index of party competition (adjusted)†	.0227	.3793	−.1455	−.0395
Percent Democratic, 1964 Presidential election	76.5	56.2	63.9	54.7
Number of days in legislative session, 1963–64	505	145	163	63
Bills considered per day	18.9	14.2	9.8	17.0
Percent bills passed	18.3	66.0	45.5	20.3

*Percentage of population not employed in agriculture, forestry, or fishing.
†.5000 equals perfect competition.

relationship."[16] This points to another criticism of *The Legislative System* (derived, as noted, from one of the authors of the book). It is difficult to draw inferences about the actual nature of the lobbying process without talking to both lobbyists and legislators. When this is not done, the assumption that legislators are the best judge of what is actually happening is tacitly made. Garceau and Silverman, and Lockard indicate that in some cases legislators are actually *not* aware of the "real" world.[17] On the other hand, lobbyists are

not necessarily any more reliable. The inability of either set of participants to provide an "accurate" assessment of the situation is not a function of dishonesty but is simply an obvious illustration of the fact that two actors participating in the same act might have entirely different perceptions of the situation. This is true because ". . . the essential features of the interpersonal behavior event . . . may be thought of as a process . . . in which the action of one person is a response to the second person . . . the actions of each are in reference to the other."[18] Hence, the role definitions of lobbyists and leg-

[16]Heinz Eulau and Katherine Hincley, "Legislative Institutions and Processes," in James A. Robinson, ed., *Political Science Annual* (Indianapolis and New York: The Bobbs-Merrill Co., Inc., 1966), p. 147.

[17]Oliver Garceau and Corinne Silverman, "A Pressure Group and the Pressured: A Case Report," *American Political Science Review*, 43

(September 1954), pp. 672–91; Duane Lockard, *New England State Politics* (Princeton: Princeton University Press, 1959), p. 42.

[18]David Krech *et al.*, *Individual in Society* (New York: McGraw-Hill, 1962), p. 4.

islators are derived as a consequence of their interaction, although neither lobbyist nor legislator need have shared assumptions about the purpose of the encounter. Indeed, certain behavior might be a consequence of misperceptions. Note that this model does not necessarily imply that the only way to understand the legislator–lobbyist relationship is to account for the *total* network of interactions and expectations that each actor has. Rather the idea is that the best approach is to understand expectations with *regard to each other*.[19]

Thus the research is simply the analysis of encounter between legislators and lobbyists within the context of political culture. The purpose of the research is an assessment rather than a theory. Eulau is right in saying that neither the mechanistic nor the communications theory is adequate. He is also correct in wondering, if lobbyists do not perform the functions normally ascribed to them, who does? However, the generalizations about the lack of impact of lobbyists is not comparative, but rather is drawn from various studies of Washington. The only comparative study of lobbying is *The Legislative System,* which does not describe the perceptions of lobbyists. Consequently, the time is right for a comparative assessment. We need to know: (1) how much interaction between legislators and lobbyists actually takes place, (2) what is the nature of this interaction, and (3) what is the effect of this interaction.

How Much Communication Takes Place?

To be effective, lobbyists have to interact with legislators on a regularized and frequent basis. State legislators are busy, and the sources competing for their time

are many. Therefore, the beginning of an assessment of interest group strength must be frequency of interaction. Legislators and lobbyists were asked how many contacts (of any kind) occurred per week during the legislative session.[20] The following table indicates, first, that there are substantial interstate differences and, second, with regard to interstate differences, that the perceptions of legislators and lobbyists differ (Table 2). It seems quite

TABLE 2
Mean Interactions Per Week as Reported
by Legislators and Lobbyists

	Mean	N
Massachusetts		
Legislators	7.8	244
Lobbyists	10.7	185
North Carolina		
Legislators	8.5	164
Lobbyists	25.9	132
Oregon		
Legislators	34.0	84
Lobbyists	31.0	193
Utah		
Legislators	16.0	90
Lobbyists	18.5	134

clear that both legislators and lobbyists report more contact in Oregon. More interaction takes place in Oregon than in any other state, regardless of who is making the judgment. It also is clear that legislators and lobbyists have the fewest number of interactions in Massachusetts. Utah falls between the two extremes, and again there is substantial consensus. The real problem is North Carolina. In each of the other states legislators and lobbyists are relatively close in their assessment of the extent of interactions, but in North Carolina legislators think little interaction takes place, while lobbyists would "rank"

---

[19]On this point, see Edward E. Jones and John W. Thibaut, "Interaction Goals as Bases of Inference in Interpersonal Perception," in Renato Tagiuri and Luigi Petrullo, *Person Perception and Interpersonal Behavior* (Stanford: Stanford University Press, 1958).

[20]It is obviously better to *observe* the number of interactions than to ask the participants to recall them, but to do so would have been impossible both in terms of comparative research and in terms of time involved. The table should be interpreted as an estimate.

their state second only to Oregon. Here we encounter a basic problem in Eulau's suggestion that both actors in the interaction should be examined. Who is right? One possibility is, of course, that lobbyists are exaggerating their importance, as McAdams has suggested in another context, while legislators, conforming to their perception of the good legislator, believe they are acting "independently."[21] This explanation has the obvious flaw of failing to account for the tendency of legislators in other states to approximate the estimates of lobbyists. In Oregon, legislators see *more* interaction than do lobbyists.

Still, there might be some truth in the explanation. North Carolina is less urban, less industrialized, and less wealthy than the other states. It also has the lowest rate of political participation. These conditions generally contribute to the strength of the interest group system, but at the same time might contribute to the reluctance of legislators to discuss interest groups, or to the failure of legislators to be able to offer accurate assessments. North Carolina has, according to Elazar, a *traditionalistic political culture*. The essential attributes of such a culture are "a paternalistic and elitist concept of the commonwealth." Consequently, such a culture confines "real political power to a relatively small and self-perpetuating group drawn from an established elite" who have a "right" to govern.[22] If legislators reflect these kinds of attitudes, they would admit very little "outside" influence, whether from party, interest group, or constituents. Eulau's evaluation of Tennessee—a state with essentially the same political culture as North Carolina—is suggestive of this conclusion. There are more "trustees" in Tennessee than in any of the other states

examined.[23] Trustees define their legislative role as that of free agent, relying on their own conscience and principles rather than the advice of any external forces. Therefore, they would be reluctant either to place much reliance on lobbyists or, perhaps, to *admit* that they do so.

The fact that interest groups seem to be such a minor part of the Massachusetts legislative system might be a function of the strong party cohesion in that legislature. Further, Massachusetts is a populous, ethnically diverse state which might, on the one hand, produce more demands for legislative action, but at the same time increase the number of competitors for rewards (still, there are fewer registered lobbyists in Massachusetts than in Oregon).

In addition to the strength of party, Massachusetts has nearly three times as many legislators as does either Oregon or Utah, making the task of interaction difficult purely on the basis of the ratio of legislators to lobbyists.[24] Boston is a large city in which one can easily submerge oneself in anonymity; Salem, Oregon, is a small town with the legislature as the main focal point of activity. Salt Lake City, between Boston and Salem in population, yields an interaction rate also between these two extremes. Of course, one can hardly maintain that the size of the capital city per se is a basic contributor to the rate of interaction, but coupled with the limited visibility of interest groups in comparison to the strong political parties of Massachusetts, it might be a reinforcement. The weakness of groups in North Carolina and Massachusetts appears easier

---

[21]Alan K. McAdams, *Power and Politics in Labor Legislation* (New York: Columbia University Press, 1964), p. 193.

[22]David Elazar, *American Federalism: A View from the States* (New York: Thomas Y. Crowell Co., 1966), p. 93.

[23]Wahlke *et al., op. cit.,* p. 281.

[24]The idea of the difficulty of the lobbyists' job being related to the size of the audience can be explored by examining the interaction rates of the state senates, which have fewer members. In Massachusetts and Utah there is substantially more interaction in the Senate than in the House. However, in North Carolina, there is substantially less contact in the Senate, while in Oregon the interaction rates are virtually the same.

to explain than the strength of groups in Oregon and Utah. As the explanation develops, attempts will be made to correct this deficiency.

The fact that legislators and lobbyists have different perceptions of the extent of communication might be indicative of actual *patterns* of interaction. Both sets of judges might be correct. Assuming this is true, we might conclude that in the states in which legislators perceive more communication than do lobbyists, the bulk of the contact comes from a *few* lobbyists trying to communicate with a large body of legislators. The target of communications might be large. The best examples of this possibility are Oregon and Utah. The larger targets of lobbyists might reflect the relatively open decision-making structure of these legislatures. Neither strong parties nor traditionalistic cultures would restrict the number of legislators who might be viewed as useful targets for communication. The strategy would thus be to contact as many legislators as possible, whether or not they hold important party or legislative positions. Yet, since a relatively small proportion of lobbyists are full-time "professionals" who make lobbying a business, this relatively large body of legislators would interact with a smaller proportion of lobbyists. In Oregon, in contrast to Utah, more lobbyists are "professionals" and put in longer hours on the job. In this state, therefore, there is both the necessity of contacting a larger body of legislators and a larger number of lobbyists trying to interact.

Two contrasting patterns are presented by North Carolina and Massachusetts, neither of which have broad target areas. In Masachusetts, few legislators interact with few lobbyists. In North Carolina, many lobbyists interact with few legislators. Thus, the rigidity of party control in Massachusetts might eliminate the rank-and-file from the communication process, while the traditionalism and value placed upon experience might do so in North Carolina. In North Carolina, however, the case for a restricted target zone appears strengthened because of the greater activity of lobbyists. North Carolina brings to mind the research of Garceau and Silverman, which suggested that many Vermont legislators are unaware of intense lobbying activity, and of Wahlke, Eulau, Buchanan, and Ferguson, who find Tennessee legislators uninformed, but draw a different sort of conclusion: that there not much lobbying takes place. It is clear, in North Carolina, that most legislators are not involved in the lobbying process, but this does not necessarily mean that little lobbying takes place.

The problem would not have existed had only legislators been interviewed, but the description emerging from a single set of interviews would have been less valid. One approach to the problem is to find out what *kinds* of lobbyists and legislators are most likely to interact. For instance, it may be that interaction increases with the experience of both or either sides. In the case of lobbyists, it may take time to locate key decision makers, become familiar with the rules of the game, learn the technicalities of legislation, establish a reputation, and get on friendly terms with legislators. Legislators might have increased contact with lobbyists if they have had considerable legislative experience and if their position in the legislature is sufficiently important to attract the attention of lobbyists. Since turnover in the ranks of both groups is fairly high, perhaps a minority really get involved. To some extent these speculations are supported by the data, but not in a clear fashion. In all states except Utah, the experienced lobbyists do interact more with legislators than do the novices. However, the Oregon novice lobbyists interact with legislators as much as do the experienced lobbyists in North Carolina. Thus, intense interaction is limited in North Carolina but is more "open" in Oregon. In Utah, the novice lobbyists actually have more contacts with legislators than do the experienced ones. Assuming that the experienced lobbyists know more about their jobs, this suggests that a better strategy is to limit contact. Both North Carolina (52 percent) and Utah (44 percent) have a higher proportion of experienced lobbyists than Oregon (30 percent) and Massachusetts (29 percent).[25] However, in spite of the relative experience of their lobbyists, the two states differ markedly with respect to intensity of interaction.

A similar pattern emerges for legislators; those with the most experience have the greatest contact with lobbyists, except for North Carolina, which is a puzzling development. We have described North Carolina as a relatively "closed" state in which only the more experienced lobbyists actually get into the act of contacting a few legislators. But the experienced legislators do not absorb the bulk of the efforts of lobbyists, as they do in other states. Nor do committee chairmen or party leaders receive more communications from lobbyists than nonleaders, as is generally true.[26] The structure of power in North Carolina's legislature—insofar as it can be ascertained from the efforts of lobbyists—is totally unrelated to the formal structure of the institution.

On the basis of interaction—without concern for the *effects* of interaction—Oregon and Massachusetts stand at opposite ends of a continuum with North Carolina (depending upon the judges) and Utah falling in between. Of course, interaction need not be an indicator of effect. Perhaps one contact by a good lobbyist is worth 100 contacts by an amateur. Also, perhaps the greater the contact—indicating a more intense set of demands—the less effective any one contact is likely to be. Further, intensity of interaction might simply be a function of how busy legislators are. The more bills there are to consider, the more

frequent will be the interaction (assuming that interest groups are the basic communicator of demands). Such an assumption clearly does not work because Massachusetts, with its low rate of interaction, considers almost twice as many bills per day (19) as does Oregon (10).

Although the explanation of the reasons for varied rates of interaction is parted at this point, let us proceed to the next step in the argument. The question is: to what extent does frequency of interaction provide clues both about the nature and effects of the interaction?

What Is the Nature of the Interaction?

Although a communications model may be too weak, communicating with legislators is what lobbyists are supposed to do. It is certainly true that the purpose of *any* communication is to change behavior, yet the communications and mechanistic models offer markedly different interpretations of the nature of communications. The supporters of the communications model believe that lobbyists transmit *information* to legislators. The consequences of this assumption are: (1) most interaction occurs between two partisans: "Its [the interest group's] role became that of an auxiliary service bureau for a senator with whom it was in complete agreement,"[27] and (2) successful lobbyists are those upon whom legislators know they can rely for accurate information, preferably information which is available most conveniently (or exclusively) from lobbyists. One lobbyist phrased the job of the informant in these words: "I will try to establish a reputation for having certain . . . technical information which is otherwise unavailable to them [legislators]."

The assumptions of the mechanistic model are fundamentally different. Lobbyists have as their fundamental goal the *persuasion* of legislators. Subscribers to the mechanistic theory believe: (1) lob-

[25]The cut-point for experience is eleven years (the mean).

[26]From data to be reported in the future.

[27]Bauer *et al., op. cit.,* p. 357.

TABLE 3

Percentage of Legislators and Lobbyists Classifying Their Roles as:

	Persuader	Informant	Both	N
Massachusetts				
Legislators	30	42	28	244
Lobbyists	54	18	28	185
North Carolina				
Legislators	20	53	27	164
Lobbyists	45	29	27	132
Oregon				
Legislators	26	55	19	84
Lobbyists	48	34	19	193
Utah				
Legislators	29	57	14	90
Lobbyists	38	36	25	134

byists communicate with opponents or undecided legislators, and (2) successful lobbyists are those able to convert opponents into supporters and firm up waverers. According to one such lobbyist: "Well, I may as well be honest about it. We are trying to influence votes on certain measures. We spend most of our time trying to influence votes on legislative measures."

Just as Eulau argues that neither the mechanistic nor the communications models are entirely correct, it is reasonable to assume that there is a bit of truth in the behavioral consequences which flow from either model. Certainly the data suggest that this is the case (Table 3).

Legislators and lobbyists are categorized according to whether they spend more of their time sending or receiving messages with a content either primarily informational or persuasive.[28] Obviously, such a categorization of the nature of communication is ideal. Information is certainly an instrument of persuasion, and most messages are probably a "mix." Nev-

ertheless, respondents were able to decide what the perceived essential purpose of a message was. The table is illustrative of some fundamental concepts in the examination of the interaction process. The evaluation of an encounter will be based upon self-perceptions and perceptions of the other person, as is illustrated by Figure 1. To apply the figure to the table, it

FIGURE 1

A Model Interaction

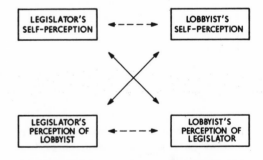

will be noticed that the nature of the interaction is seen quite differently by the two participants. The pattern is quite consistent from state to state. In every case, a higher proportion of lobbyists are classified as persuaders and a higher proportion of legislators define their role as receivers of information. These contrasting perceptions of the encounter can be expected to have an impact upon the behavior of the

---

[28]The categorization is derived from the "purposive" and "non-purposive" distinction found in the literature of communications. See Bruce H. Westley and Malcolm S. MacLean, Jr., "A Conceptual Model for Communications Research," in James H. Campbell and Hal W. Helper, eds., *Dimensions in Communication* (Belmont, Calif.: Wadsworth Publishing Co., Inc., 1965), pp. 61–62.

actors. As we have argued, the nature of the encounter is defined by the perceptions of the participants. It stands to reason that the more congruent the perceptions of the participants, the less ambiguous will be the encounter. In this case, the effectiveness of the lobbyist should be related to the extent of harmony between his perceptions and that of the legislator. In other words, the clearer the mutual expectations, the more effective will be the lobbyist.)

Table 3 provides categories based solely upon whether or not one type of communication outweighs another. To get an idea of the extent of congruence, let us examine the rate of interaction spent in either informational or persuasive communication (Table 4). We can now see

TABLE 4

Interaction Rates of Legislators and Lobbyists
Devoted to Persuasion or Information

	Persuasion	Information
Massachusetts		
Legislators	.25	.33
Lobbyists	.46	.22
North Carolina		
Legislators	.09	.17
Lobbyists	.33	.22
Oregon		
Legislators	.21	.30
Lobbyists	.37	.25
Utah		
Legislators	.23	.38
Lobbyists	.33	.32

that the greatest congruence concerning perception of persuasion occurs in Oregon, followed by Utah, North Carolina, and Massachusetts. Thus, the two states with the highest interaction have the greatest congruence. It will be argued shortly that Oregon and Utah are the states with the strongest groups, thus supporting the idea of the relationship between congruence and effectiveness. Further, the fact that there is greater congruence in states with high interaction indi-

cates that stereotypic perceptions probably dictate the terms of an *initial* encounter, but that more accurate images develop as the interactions become more frequent. Hence, Massachusetts and North Carolina, with the lowest rates of interaction, also have the least congruence and the least effective lobbyists. Notice also that there is uniformly greater congruence concerning informational communication. This may indicate a greater acceptance of the legitimacy of this type of communication and, incidentally, suggest an introductory chapter to a textbook for beginning lobbyists.

The Effects of Lobbying

Measuring the effects of lobbying is especially difficult in view of contrasting perceptions, and because of the existence of at least two functions of lobbying. If lobbying is persuasion, we need to know how often this goal is achieved. If lobbying is information, we need to know how much confidence is placed in this information. The point to be made is that a single measure of influence is not able to account for the *ends* attached to various lobbying *means*. Mention was made earlier of the report by Zeller.[29] Political scientists were asked to describe the influence of interest groups in their states as "strong," "moderate," or "weak." The defects of this method are apparent. The panel of judges is, at best, questionable. Asking people to evaluate the effects of interest groups in terms of such an ambiguous concept as "power" compounds the felony. A better method was devised by Wahlke, Eulau, Buchanan, and Ferguson. Their measure was based on questions dealing with both the legislators' awareness of interest groups and their acceptance of the legitimacy of lobbying. By combining legislators' attitudes (as measured by a series of scales)

[29]Belle Zeller, ed., *American State Legislatures* (New York: Thomas Y. Crowell Co., 1954), pp. 190–91.

and awareness (as measured by ability to identify certain organizations), legislators were classified into three role-orientations: facilitators, neutrals, and resistors. Thus, in no case is anybody simply asked about the power of interest groups. However, as I noted earlier, there are some problems with this scheme. The classifications are only minimally behavioral. They do not deal with the effects of actual interaction but only with attitudes. Wahlke reasons that legislators can be expected to behave according to their role definitions and that the behavioral consequences follow naturally from role definitions.

Whereas this assumption may be correct, no actual behavior is described.[30] Our data does indicate, in support of Wahlke, that the extent of contact, effect of contact, and attitudes toward lobbyists are clearly interrelated. However, one of the conclusions of *The Legitimate System,* that percentage of resistors declines as legislative experience increases, is challenged. It was found that, whereas the *attitudes* of legislators toward lobbyists become more favorable as experience increases, legislators *do not* become more persuadable. The lack of connection between behavior and attitude is illustrated by Wahlke's discussion of the potential for interest group politics in the various states, avoiding a discussion of what happens in favor of an estimate of what might happen. Finally, the potential and the actuality are gradually merged until the distinction is lost.

There is no clear way out of these dilemmas. The approach offered here is to consider lobbying as both a persuasive and informational process and to assess the effects of both attempts, relying upon

[30]Since this analysis is based upon reports of behavior rather than independent observations of behavior, the point of the objection is questionable. Nevertheless, in using reports as a surrogate for behavior, the effort to describe behavior is made clear.

reports of behavior more than upon assessment of attitudes.

Initially, we might observe some apparent differences between lobbying in the states and lobbying in Washington. In Washington, where informational lobbying seems typical, lobbyists talk to sympathetic legislators. In the states, where there is more persuasion, opponents seem to have considerable contact with each other. It is true that more contact takes place among like-minded lobbyists and legislators than among those who do not see things in the same way, but in all states at least a third of the legislators and lobbyists indicate substantial contact with opponents. In Oregon, to use a slightly atypical case, about the same number of contacts take place among those with conflicting points of view as between those in agreement. In fact, lobbyists tend to lean toward contacts with legislators whose position is unclear. In short, lobbyists appear to "lobby" in the traditional stereotype more in the states than in Washington. Concerning stereotypes, the younger lobbyists are more likely to talk to opponents and to define their role as persuader than are the older lobbyists; hence, they fit the stereotype more easily. There is a sort of professionalization process which reduces the stereotypic behavior of lobbyists as they begin to learn the rules of the game. Such a process of professionalization is certainly related to the number of interactions. The greater the number of interactions, the more realistic become the actors' images of each other. Hence, younger lobbyists who do not get "into the game" very much have not had the opportunity to correct their stereotypes.

Another aspect of stereotypic behavior which is probably related to extent of interaction concerns the notion of "pressure." According to popular and some scholarly characterizations, pressure groups do just what the name implies. No one is really sure what pressure tactics are available to lobbyists, and the research in the Washington setting of Milbrath and Bauer, Pool, and Dexter suggests that "information groups" is a more appropriate appellation. Nevertheless, the image persists. To legislators and lobbyists, pressure is an undesirable connotation. When a legislator says that he is being pressured, he means that he perceives the lobbyist to be trying vigorously to overcome his resistance by any available means.

The perceived incidence of pressure varies from state to state and between legislators and lobbyists. Massachusetts lobbyists, who report very little contact with legislators, believe that they engage in pressure tactics far more so than do the lobbyists of the other states. In Massachusetts, as is true for the other states, legislators tend to see less pressure than lobbyists, but the discrepancy between the perceptions of the two judges is substantially greater.[31]

By contrast, Oregon, which appears to have the greatest interaction, also appears to have the lowest perception of pressure tactics on the part of both legislators and lobbyists. The general rule seems to be that interaction and perceptions of pressure exist in a functional relationship. The greater the interaction between legislators and lobbyists, the more favorable become the evaluations of the encounter. The exception is Utah, which is a high interaction state with high perceptions of pressure. Indeed, Utah legislators believe themselves to be more pressured than the legislators of any other state. As will become evident shortly, although Utah and Oregon seem to be the two states in which interest groups are most active, the attitudes of legislative participants in these states is quite different. There is a general reluctance on the part of legislators in Utah to accept interest groups as legitimate, even though they come into fre-

quent contact with them. It can be demonstrated that, whereas the interaction frequency in Utah is either the same or slightly less than that in Oregon, the effects of interaction are somewhat less in Utah.

Effectiveness of lobbying is measured by three questions based upon the assumptions of Guttman scaling. Legislators were asked, first, whether they could recall being influenced by a lobbyist to the point of questioning their position about any given issue. Next, they were asked if they could recall being influenced by a lobbyist to the extent of changing their opinion on an issue so that the positions of legislator and lobbyist were not as far apart as they were initially. Finally, legislators were asked if they could recall being influenced to the extent of reaching total agreement with the position of the lobbyist. Thus, the first question represents minimum effect and the last question represents maximum effect. Lobbyists were also asked these questions with appropriate modification in wording so that the legislators became the object rather than the subject of persuasion. The assumptions require that the frequency of success would decrease with the difficulty of the task. The assumptions held true for lobbyists. In terms of what they think they are doing, the more difficult the task, the fewer the favorable responses. According to lobbyists, they are able to produce "questioning" and "leaning" responses more often than they are able to produce a "conversion" (Table 5).

With legislators, the assumptions are not so neatly fulfilled. In both Oregon and Utah, more legislators indicate that they have changed positions more often than they have undergone more moderate forms of persuasion. The table confirms pretty well what we have learned so far about the four states under examination. Massachusetts lobbyists are far more skeptical about their ability to achieve successful results than are the lobbyists

---

[31]From data to be reported in the future.

TABLE 5

Percentage* of Legislators and Lobbyists Believing that They Have
(Have Been) Influenced to the Extent of:

	Questioning a Previously Held Opinion	Leaning More Toward the Views of the Lobbyist	Changing from One Position to Another	N
Massachusetts				
Legislators	34	31	20	244
Lobbyists	51	39	26	185
North Carolina				
Legislators	22	20	18	164
Lobbyists	76	70	39	132
Oregon				
Legislators	45	42	51	84
Lobbyists	79	52	41	193
Utah				
Legislators	32	38	42	90
Lobbyists	77	66	48	134

*Percentages are of those who indicate that a particular event has occurred "frequently" or "occasionally."

in any other states. This pessimism is shared to some extent by legislators, although the gap between perceptions is far less severe than it is in North Carolina. North Carolina lobbyists see their influence as far greater than do legislators. Indeed, the difference between the North Carolina lobbyists (whose legislators consider them impotent) and the Oregon lobbyists (whose legislators consider them powerful), is minimal and in one case the North Carolina lobbyists appear to be more optimistic. The table also firms up the argument that Oregon and Utah appear to be strong lobbying states, whereas Massachusetts and North Carolina appear to be weak lobbyist states, especially if we consider the attitudes of legislators.

Naturally, lobbyists exaggerate the impact of their efforts. However, there is one exception to the rule of lobbyists' overestimation which deserves mention. In Oregon, more legislators than lobbyists believe that conversion has occurred. The difference in Oregon is especially striking. In this particular case, lobbyists are underestimating substantially the im-

pact of their communications. The differences in the perceptions between legislators and lobbyists is least in Oregon and in Massachusetts, with both judges in Oregon agreeing that lobbyists are powerful and both in Massachusetts agreeing that lobbyists are ineffective (Table 6). These sorts of realistic appraisals are, of course, not found in North Carolina or in Utah. The optimism of the Oregon lobbyists is earned, as is the pessimism of the Massachusetts lobbyists. To a lesser extent, the optimism of the Utah lobbyists is realistic, but the optimism of the North Carolina lobbyists is apparently without foundation.

Finally, conversion does occur more frequently than the research on national legislation has suggested. We would expect legislators to underestimate the extent of conversion; but even taking this into account, a slight majority of Oregon lawmakers and a large minority of Utah legislators indicated that they have been switched from one position to another by lobbyists. Even in Massachusetts, 34 percent of the legislators have been influenced by lobbyists, albeit to the limited

TABLE 6

Differences in the Effects of Communication as Reported by Legislators and Lobbyists

	Questioning a Previously Held Position	Leaning More Toward the Views of the Lobbyist	Changing from One Position to Another	Average
Massachusetts	−17*	− 8	− 6	−10
North Carolina	−54	−50	−21	−42
Oregon	−34	−10	+10	−15
Utah	−44	−28	− 6	−26

*Entries are differences between the percentages reported in Table 5. Negative signs indicate a higher percentage of lobbyists reporting on effects; positive signs indicate the reverse.

extent of questioning a previously held opinion. These data assume, of course, that the job of the lobbyist is that of changing minds. In fact, we have seen that there are two role definitions of the job of the lobbyist: that of persuader and that of informant. Needless to say, these role definitions are not mutually exclusive, making it possible for lobbyists to perform different roles at separate points in time or even simultaneously. Further, the data should not be interpreted to mean that more subtle, less explicit modes of communication cannot have a persuasive consequence.

This paper is not concerned with lobbying strategies, but rather with an assessment of lobbying strengths. Nevertheless, one source of strength, and indeed perhaps a crucial source, is the extent to which legislators accept the lobbyist as a legitimate source of information. Our data indicate that, whereas there is no relationship between the amount of contact between legislators and lobbyists and the persuasability of legislators, there is a clear and strong relationship between the extent of communication *initiated* by legislators and this degree of persuasability (Table 7). Legislators who seek out lobbyists are more likely to be persuaded by them in comparison to legislators who do not initiate as much interaction. Consequently, one source of the strength of interest groups in Oregon and Utah might

be found in the fact that two thirds of the legislators in these states indicate that they solicit the opinions of lobbyists when an issue arises about which they have legitimate concern. In contrast, only slightly more than one third of the legislators in Massachusetts and North Carolina do so.

We would assume that the seeking out of lobbyists indicates an acceptance on the part of the legislators of the legitimacy of interest groups in the legislative process. However, by a variety of measures it appears that the attitude of Utah legislators toward lobbyists is far more hostile than their behavior would indicate. Consider, for example, a question approaching legitimacy from a slightly different angle. Legislators were asked if they believed it was proper to be seen socially with a lobbyist. Whereas 83 percent of the Oregon legislators indicated that it was proper to be seen with a lobbyist, 68 percent of those in Utah indicated that it was proper. Although more Utah legislators are uneasy in the presence of lobbyists than Massachusetts legislators (75 percent), they are exceeded only by North Carolina legislators (58 percent). Thus, legislators in one of the "strong lobby states" indicate more circumspection in the presence of lobbyists than legislators in a "weak lobby state."

This pattern can be amplified further by the return to the problem of the relationship between attitudes and behavior.

TABLE 7

Percentage* of Legislators Reporting Influence Related to the
Extent of Interaction Initiated by the Legislator

	Questioning a Previously Held Opinion	Leaning more Toward the Views of the Lobbyist	Changing from One Position to Another	N‖
Massachusetts				
Low† 28		26	24	156
Medium‡ 51		42	44	41
High§ 47		53	60	15
North Carolina				
Low 19		18	15	130
Medium 32		32	23	22
High 38		13	38	8
Oregon				
Low 29		33	42	24
Medium 63		53	57	30
High 46		50	63	24
Utah				
Low 24		32	44	50
Medium 39		46	39	26
High 60		50	50	10

*Percentage indicating that an event had occurred "frequently" or "occasionally."
†Less than five contacts per week.
‡Six to twenty-five contacts per week.
§Twenty-six or more contacts per week.
‖"Don't know's" are excluded.

We noted that there was a relationship between the two, but the caveat should be added that this relationship does not emerge very clearly in Utah. For instance, there is no relationship in Utah between the attitudes of legislators toward interest groups and the extent of interaction.[32] Those who have an unfavorable attitude are just about as likely to interact as those who do not. Also, more legislators in Massachusetts than in Utah believe that lobbyists are "absolutely necessary" in the legislative process. A good illustration of the suspicion of the lobbying process in Utah can be seen in Table 8, which presents the attitudes legislators have toward the information they receive from lobbyists.

It can be seen that Utah legislators depend upon lobbyists for information almost as much as they do in Oregon, but

that the confidence they have in this information is substantially less. Also, only a minority of Utah legislators in contrast to Oregon find this information especially helpful. Indeed, they appear almost as unimpressed with such information as the Massachusetts legislators. Thus, it is clear that the dependence of Utah legislators upon the services of lobbyists is not based solely upon a facilitating attitude. It appears that the interaction of Utah lobbyists and legislators is not entered into in a purely voluntary way. The interaction seemed forced upon each actor, somewhat in the nature of the exception Homans cites to his principle that interaction and attraction are related.[33]

In political systems there are compelling reasons for the continual functioning of a system in spite of private attitude

[32]From data not reported in this article.

[33]See George C. Homans, *The Human Group* (New York: Harcourt, Brace and World, 1950), pp. 116–17.

TABLE 8

Attitudes of Legislators Toward Information Received
from Lobbyists: Percent Indicating They:

	Depend upon* Information from Lobbyists	Have Confidence† in Information from Lobbyists	Find Informa-‡ tion from Lobbyists Helpful	N
Massachusetts	50	55	41	244
North Carolina	41	56	28	164
Oregon	83	88	61	84
Utah	80	70	43	90

*Percentage reporting they depend upon information from lobbyists "a good deal" or "some" of the time.
†Percentage indicating they have "a lot" and "quite a bit" of confidence in information.
‡Percentage indicating "all" or "most" of the information is helpful.

systems; the interaction system is more compelling than the attitude system. Certain things have to be done; laws have to be passed, information must be gathered. There are very few staff services in Utah, and the legislators are very inexperienced in comparison to the other states. Thus, attitudes alone do not explain the nature of the Utah legislative system. The Utah legislators' attitudes are perhaps traceable to the fact that two thirds of them are Mormons (in contrast to less than half the population of the state). Utah is the only state in which a religio-economic group controls a majority of the seats. Since the Mormon church has such total access it is naturally not seen as an interest group. The dominance of the Mormon church probably diminishes the favorable attitude of legislators toward other "outside" groups. In addition, there is a stern moralism associated with the Utah legislature. Perhaps one source of these hostile attitudes is an orientation booklet which tells the beginning legislator:

Perhaps the most overwhelming experience for any new legislator is his first contact with the lobbyist—the person representing a special interest. Since each lobbyist is committed to advancing the cause of his own group, the legislator can expect to encounter considerable pressure to vote a narrowly seen "right way." There is nothing wrong with listening to the case presented by a lobbyist. He may

provide valuable information. But the legislator should always remember that the lobbyist will volunteer only information which is helpful to his cause; that which is contrary must be learned elsewhere.[34]

In spite of these pressures against lobbyists, Utah still has a strong interest group system.

Services Provided by Lobbyists

Since we know that a favorable persuasive situation is created when the legislator asks the lobbyist to perform a service for him, we now need to know the nature of the services performed by lobbyists. We have previously discussed the nature of the interaction between lobbyists and legislators in terms of either persuasion or information. A slight modification needs to be made with respect to the kinds of services performed. Here we are dichotomizing services into those involving a display of power or influence and those involving the provision of information. Three kinds of services are selected as being typical of the use of lobbyists as sources of influence by legislators. They are, first, calling upon lobbyists to have them influence other legislators; second, calling upon lobbyists to have them help

---

[34]*The Utah Legislator's Orientation Manual* (1966), p. 6.

TABLE 9

Percentage* of Legislators and Lobbyists Interacting for "Influence" Services

	Influencing Other Legislators	Mobilizing Public Support	Participating in Planning Strategy	N
Massachusetts				
Legislators	11	17	17	244
Lobbyists	22	38	36	185
North Carolina				
Legislators	25	27	39	164
Lobbyists	51	65	73	132
Oregon				
Legislators	53	32	65	84
Lobbyists	55	46	64	193
Utah				
Legislators	46	45	42	70
Lobbyists	68	65	73	134

*Percentages indicate those who "frequently" and "occasionally" request (or are requested to) perform a service.

amass public opinion in favor of a legislator's position; third, including lobbyists in planning strategy in an effort to negotiate a bill through the legislature. The extent to which lobbyists are called upon to perform these services are given in Table 9.

Considering only the relative importance of lobbying in the various states, nothing new is learned by this table. Oregon still appears as the most lobbying-oriented state; Utah runs a close second, with North Carolina and Massachusetts bringing up the rear. However, there are some variations both in the kinds of services likely to be performed within a given state and in the extent to which the perceptions of legislators and lobbyists differ. For instance, participation in the planning strategy preceding the introduction of a bill seems relatively more important in Oregon and North Carolina than it does in Utah and Massachusetts. At the same time, helping to amass public opinion does not seem as prominent in Oregon as it should be in comparison to the relative utilization of other services. It appears that a greater amount of the services performed by Oregon lobbyists are kept within the internal politics of the legislature.

This type of service is not found to the same extent in any other state. Indeed, the amassing of public opinion is the single item on which both sets of judges in Utah "rank" their state higher than Oregon.

The other type of service which lobbyists can perform consists of the provision of information. We consider here two types of such services: the communication to the legislator of the opinions of other legislators or lobbyists, and the actual conducting of research for the legislators for use in the presentation of arguments for or against legislation. The first kind of service is, essentially, the utilization of lobbyists for the "nose-counting" which usually precedes any decision by the legislator concerning strategy. The second kind of service, the actual production of information based upon technical research, is usually performed in Washington by staffs. Since state legislators typically do not have staff assistants, legislators come to rely upon lobbyists more than any other service, as Table 10 indicates.

The tables, considered together, suggest that even though informational services are more frequently provided than are influence-type services, lobbyists ap-

TABLE 10

Percentage* of Legislators and Lobbyists Interacting
for "Informational" Services

	Communicating with Other Lobbyists	Researching a Bill	N
Massachusetts			
Legislators 25		46	244
Lobbyists 22		43	185
North Carolina			
Legislators 19		47	164
Lobbyists 51		71	132
Oregon			
Legislators 40		89	84
Lobbyists 53		73	193
Utah			
Legislators 49		78	90
Lobbyists 63		63	134

*Percentages indicate those who "frequently" or "occasionally" request (or are requested to) perform a service.

parently do not consider them as glamorous. With the exception of North Carolina, the general tendency is for legislators to agree with lobbyists that informational services are typical of the legislator–lobbyist relationship. Thus, an examination of the differences between the percentages indicates that there is a mean difference of about 21 percent between the perceptions of legislators and lobbyists with regard to influence services as compared to a difference of 7 percent with respect to informational services (Table 11).

Indeed, only in North Carolina do the differences between the perceptions of legislators and lobbyists with respect to informational services approach the magnitude of the difference on influence services. When evaluating influence services, lobbyists exaggerate (or legislators minimize). When evaluating informational services, both legislators and lobbyists see lobbyists' performance in a similar manner. In Oregon and Utah, for example, legislators indicate they call upon lobbyists for research quite a bit more than do lobbyists. It should also be noted, however, that the differences in perception in Oregon are relatively small no matter whether influence or informational services are being evaluated, indicating a high congruence in perception in comparison to the other states. Nevertheless, it does appear that these answers are

TABLE 11

Differences in Legislators' and Lobbyists' Perception of
the Services Performed by Lobbyists

	Influence	Information
Massachusetts	−17%	+ 3%
North Carolina	−37%	−28%
Oregon	− 5%	+ 2%
Utah	−25%	+ 1%

*Entries are the average differences in the answer of legislators and lobbyists reported in Tables 9 and 10. Negative signs indicate that more lobbyists than legislators believe the service is performed.

somewhat indicative of idealized roles. It appears that legislators look upon lobbyists as providers of information, but lobbyists like to think of themselves as agents of influence.

These findings support the earlier conclusions with respect to how lobbyists spend their time. At any rate, pedestrian though it may be, it is clear that even in weak lobbying states, such as Massachusetts, lobbyists are frequently called upon to provide legislators with facts. In strong lobbying states there is a considerable amount of influence-trading, but even here research is the basic task.

To lobbyists, the prominence of research means that persuasion has to be accomplished by indirect means. We noted earlier that experienced lobbyists are inclined to define their role as that of informant. Concurrently, legislators indicate a substantial preference for the services of experienced lobbyists, especially if they have had previous governmental experience. In all states, these kinds of lobbyists are sought out for services far more than are the inexperienced lobbyists. The experienced lobbyists frequently engage in an explicit attempt to define their role to the legislators. Consider, for example, the following statement: "Last session there were eleven people on the House Financial Affairs Committee. Five of them were freshmen. My first job was to introduce myself to them and let them know that I would be around, be at the Committee meetings, and that I am the fount of all information with respect to the insurance industry and if they have questions they should call on me. Certainly I try to persuade them, but I try to persuade them with information." In this case the lobbyist is seeking to establish a relationship based solely upon his role as informant. The purpose is to produce perceptions on the part of the legislators congruent with the lobbyists' self-perceptions. If successful, this lobbyist would have built a substantial influence base, resting upon the willingness of legislators to seek him out.

SUMMARY AND CONCLUSIONS

This comparative analysis has probably raised more questions than it has provided answers to existing questions. In the first place, it is obvious that neither the mechanistic nor the communications model are universally applicable, suggesting that less inclusive theories are more useful. There seems to be little question that interest groups are very powerful in Oregon and very weak in Massachusetts. To phrase the conclusions in terms of Eulau's rhetorical question, very little would happen in Massachusetts if there were no lobbies, but the legislature would function in an entirely different fashion in Oregon were this situation to come to pass. On the other hand, in the case of North Carolina and Utah it would be very difficult to say what the consequences would be because the perceptions, especially in North Carolina, are so incongruent. Also, in Utah the high activity and moderate impact of lobbyists is not matched by a favorable set of attitudes on the part of Utah legislators. Attitudinally, Utah is as similar to Massachusetts as it is to Oregon.

To return to the initial question about the effect of environmental variables, it appears that they are randomly distributed. The "weak lobby states"—Massachusetts and North Carolina—have little in common. Massachusetts is urban, heterogeneous, industrialized, with a relatively wealthy, well-educated population. North Carolina is the reverse. Massachusetts is competitive, North Carolina is not. Indeed, Massachusetts is more similar to the "strong lobby states"—Utah and Oregon—in its degree of party competition, than it is to North Carolina.

On the other hand, Utah and Oregon seem somewhat more similar. Yet, on a variety of measures they are approximations of Massachusetts. The population of Utah and Oregon is quite a bit more mobile than that of the weak lobby states.

TABLE 12
Expenditure and Revenue of Strong and Weak Lobby States

	Strong			Weak		
	Oregon	California	Utah	Massachusetts	Tennessee	North Carolina
Revenue: per capita	$257	$251	$251	$185	$171	$183
Expenditure: per capita ...	$260	$254	$255	$190	$164	$171

Indeed, this is the only characteristic which is consistent.

The socioeconomic environment does not appear to effect interaction of legislators or lobbyists and consequences of the lobbying effect, with the exception of mobility. Mobility, however, is in reality an artifact of a more fundamental distinction between weak and strong lobby states which is more *developmental* than environmental. To illustrate this point, let us add to our sample of four states two states examined by Wahlke, Eulau, Ferguson, and Buchanan: California, which is clearly a strong lobby state, and Tennessee, which is clearly a weak lobby state.[35] We can now see that a basic distinction is between the newer, late developing states, and the older, now established political systems. California, Oregon, and Utah did not develop viable *stakes* for the political game until the twentieth century. By the time that Massachusetts, Tennessee, and North Carolina had developed enough complexity to support an interest group system, the rules of the game of politics had been established and, in a sense, closed to interest groups. In the South, legislators are likely to view *all* "outsiders" (interest groups, parties, constituents) as having doubtful legitimacy. In Massachusetts, interest groups have a difficult time competing with established parties. In both areas, therefore, there is an oligarchical type of politics which do not include interest groups.

In contrast to the old New England or southern states stands the new west. Political systems and interest groups developed simultaneously in a much more open fashion. Interest groups did not have to fight existing political institutions; they shared in the developing of the political system; also, political development coincided with economic development. Lobbyists and politicians "grew up" together. Finally, the western political tradition—nonpartisanship, open primaries, a high rate of participation—invites interest groups, along with everybody else, to compete for the stakes of politics.

A further possibility is raised by this notion of the stakes of politics. We have explained high interaction and the effects so far without reference to the obvious possibility that interest groups will be attracted to the arenas where important decisions are being made—where the stakes are the biggest. Do the stakes vary from state to state? Do some states do a "bigger business" than others? If so, how does this relate to patterns of group politics? To answer this question, consider Table 12, which compares the per capita revenues and expenditures of the strong and weak lobby states. Clearly the strong lobby states have a greater output than the weak lobby states. In the research of Dye, Hofferbert, and others mentioned earlier, the environment influences the output. In this case, a sort of reverse of this suggestion is developed. The magnitude of the outputs influences the pattern of activity accompanying the output.

[35]Ohio and New Jersey are excluded because their classification is less certain.

SECTION IV

More Complex Statements of Linkage

Both Robert Dahl and V. O. Key, Jr. emphasize our need to understand the functioning of the American political system and other ongoing democratic systems, and stability and endurance are the most unusual characteristics of such systems. But if the three preceding models prove ineffective, is stable democracy a lie in the sense that our present political systems are democracies in name only; is stability a characteristic of a society run by a minority able to convince the majority that they are running the system? Both Dahl and Key think not. They offer rather complex theories as to how American communities avoid domination by economic interests and how public opinion finds expression in public policy, even given great apathy. As I argued in the introduction to this reader, these theories do not afford ready testing; but two of the concepts they find important—shared opinions and leaders' desires to behave democratically—lead to the models discussed and evaluated in Sections V and VI.

THE POLYARCHY MODEL*

Robert A. Dahl

THE AMBIGUITY OF LEADERSHIP

One of the difficulties that confronts anyone who attempts to answer the question, "Who rules in a pluralist democracy?" is the ambiguous relationship of leaders to citizens.

Viewed from one position, leaders are enormously influential—so influential that if they are seen only in this perspective they might well be considered a kind of

ruling elite. Viewed from another position, however, many influential leaders seem to be captives of their constituents. Like the blind men with the elephant, different analysts have meticulously examined different aspects of the body politic and arrived at radically different conclusions. To some, a pluralistic democracy with dispersed inequalities is all head and no body; to others it is all body and no head.

Ambiguity in the relations of leaders and constituents is generated by several closely connected obstacles both to observation and to clear conceptualization.

*From *Who Governs?* by Robert A. Dahl, New Haven: Yale University Press, 1961, pp. 89–94, 305–12, 315–25. Copyright © 1961 by Yale University.

To begin with, the American creed of democracy and equality prescribes many forms and procedures from which the actual practices of leaders diverge. Consequently, to gain legitimacy for their actions leaders frequently surround their covert behavior with democratic rituals. These rituals not only serve to disguise reality and thus to complicate the task of observation and analysis, but—more important—in complex ways the very existence of democratic rituals, norms, and requirements of legitimacy based on a widely shared creed actually influences the behavior of both leaders and constituents even when democratic norms are violated. Thus the distinction between the rituals of power and the realities of power is frequently obscure.

Two additional factors help to account for this obscurity: First, among all the persons who influence a decision, some do so more directly than others in the sense that they are closer to the stage where concrete alternatives are initiated or vetoed in an explicit and immediate way. Indirect influence might be very great but comparatively difficult to observe and weigh. Yet to ignore indirect influence in analysis of the distribution of influence would be to exclude what might well prove to be a highly significant process of control in a pluralistic democracy.

Second, the relationship between leaders and citizens in a pluralistic democracy is frequently reciprocal: leaders influence the decisions of constituents, but the decisions of leaders are also determined in part by what they think are, will be, or have been the preferences of their constituents. Ordinarily it is much easier to observe and describe the distribution of influence in a political system where the flow of influence is strongly in one direction (an asymmetrical or unilateral system, as it is sometimes called) than in a system marked by strong reciprocal relations. In a political system with competi-

tive elections, such as New Haven's, it is not unreasonable to expect that relationships between leaders and constituents would normally be reciprocal.

One who sets out to observe, analyze, and describe the distribution of influence in a pluralistic democracy will therefore encounter formidable problems. It will, I believe, simplify the task of understanding New Haven if I now spell out some of the theory and assumptions that guided our story of the distribution of influence.

The Political Stratum

In New Haven, as in other political systems, a small stratum of individuals is much more highly involved in political thought, discussion, and action than the rest of the population. These citizens constitute the political stratum.

Members of this stratum live in a political subculture that is partly but not wholly shared by the great majority of citizens. Just as artists and intellectuals are the principal bearers of the artistic, literary, and scientific skills of a society, so the members of the political stratum are the main bearers of political skills. If intellectuals were to vanish overnight, a society would be reduced to artistic, literary, and scientific poverty. If the political stratum were destroyed, the previous political institutions of the society would temporarily stop functioning. In both cases, the speed with which the loss could be overcome would depend on the extent to which the elementary knowledge and basic attitudes of the elite had been diffused. In an open society with widespread education and training in civic attitudes, many citizens hitherto in the apolitical strata could doubtless step into roles that had been filled by members of the political stratum. However, sharp discontinuities and important changes in the operation of the political system almost certainly would occur.

In New Haven, as in the United States, and indeed perhaps in all pluralistic democracies, differences in the subcultures of the political and the apolitical strata are marked, particularly at the extremes. In the political stratum, politics is highly salient; among the apolitical strata, it is remote. In the political stratum, individuals tend to be rather calculating in their choice of strategies; members of the political stratum are, in a sense, relatively rational political beings. In the apolitical strata, people are notably less calculating; their political choices are more strongly influenced by inertia, habit, unexamined loyalties, personal attachments, emotions, transient impulses. In the political stratum, an individual's political beliefs tend to fall into patterns that have a relatively high degree of coherence and internal consistency; in the apolitical strata, political orientations are disorganized, disconnected, and unideological. In the political stratum, information about politics and the issues of the day is extensive; the apolitical strata are poorly informed. Individuals in the political stratum tend to participate rather actively in politics; in the apolitical strata citizens rarely go beyond voting and many do not even vote. Individuals in the political stratum exert a good deal of steady, direct, and active influence on government policy; in fact some individuals have a quite extraordinary amount of influence. Individuals in the apolitical strata, on the other hand, have much less direct or active influence on policies.

Communication within the political stratum tends to be rapid and extensive. Members of the stratum read many of the same newspapers and magazines; in New Haven, for example, they are likely to read the *New York Times* or the *Herald Tribune,* and *Time* or *Newsweek.* Much information also passes by word of mouth. The political strata of different communities and regions are linked in a national network of communications. Even in small towns, one or two members of the local political stratum usually are in touch with members of a state organization, and certain members of the political stratum of a state or any large city maintain relations with members of organizations in other states and cities, or with national figures. Moreover, many channels of communication not designed specifically for political purposes—trade associations, professional associations, and labor organizations, for example, serve as a part of the network of the political stratum.

In many pluralistic systems, however, the political stratum is far from being a closed or static group. In the United States the political stratum does not constitute a homogeneous class with well-defined class interests. In New Haven, in fact, the political stratum is easily penetrated by anyone whose interests and concerns attract him to the distinctive political culture of the stratum. It is easily pentrated because (among other reasons) elections and competitive parties give politicians a powerful motive for expanding their coalitions and increasing their electoral followings.

In an open pluralistic system, where movement into the political stratum is easy, the stratum embodies many of the most widely shared values and goals in the society. If popular values are strongly pragmatic, then the political stratum is likely to be pragmatic; if popular values prescribe reverence toward the past, then the political stratum probably shares that reverence; if popular values are oriented toward material gain and personal advancement, then the political stratum probably reflects these values; if popular values are particularly favorable to political, social, or economic equality, then the political stratum is likely to emphasize equality. The apolitical strata can be said to "govern" as much through the sharing of common values and goals with members of the political stratum as by other means. However, if it were not for elections and competitive parties, this sharing would—other things remaining the same—rapidly decline.

Not only is the political stratum in New Haven not a closed group, but its "members" are far from united in their orientations and strategies. There are many lines of cleavage. The most apparent and probably the most durable are symbolized by affiliations with different political parties. Political parties are rival coalitions of leaders and subleaders drawn from the members of the political stratum. Leaders in a party coalition seek to win elections, capture the chief elective offices of government, and insure that government officials will legalize and enforce policies on which the coalition leaders can agree.

In any given period of time, various issues are salient within the political stratum. Indeed, a political issue can hadly be said to exist unless and until it commands the attention of a significant segment of the political stratum. Out of all the manifold possibilities, members of the political stratum seize upon some issues as important or profitable; these then become the subject of attention within the political stratum. To be sure, all the members of the political stratum may not initially agree that a particular issue is worthy of attention. But whenever a sizable minority of the legitimate elements in the political stratum is determined to bring some question to the fore, the chances are high that the rest of the political stratum will soon begin to pay attention.

Although political issues are sometimes generated by individuals in the apolitical strata who begin to articulate demands for government action, this occurs only rarely. Citizens in the apolitical strata are usually aware of problems or difficulties in their own circle; through word of mouth or the mass media they may become aware of problems faced by people in other circles. But to be aware of a problem is by no means equivalent to perceiving a political solution or even formulating a political demand. These acts are ordinarily performed only by members of the political stratum. Within the political stratum, issues and alternatives are often formulated by intellectuals, experts, and reformers, whose views then attract the support of professionals. This is how questions as abstract and difficult as the proper rate of growth in the Gross National Product are injected into national politics; and, as we shall see, this is roughly the route by which urban redevelopment came into the politics of New Haven.

However, in gaining attention for issues, members of the political stratum operate under constraints set by party politicians with an eye on the next election. Despite the stereotype, party politicians are not necessarily concerned *only* with winning elections, for the man who is a party politician in one role may, in another, be a member of a particular interest group, social stratum, neighborhood, race, ethnic group, occupation, or profession. In this role he may himself help to generate issues. However, simply qua party politician, he not only has a powerful incentive to search for politically profitable issues, but he has an equally strong motive for staying clear of issues he thinks will not produce a net gain in his votes in the next election.

Because of the ease with which the political stratum can be penetrated, whenever dissatisfaction builds up in some segment of the electorate party politicians will probably learn of the discontent and calculate whether it might be converted into a political issue with an electoral payoff. If a party politician sees no payoff, his interest is likely to be small; if he foresees an adverse effect, he will avoid the issue if he can. As a result, there is usually some conflict in the political stratum between intellectuals, experts, and others who formulate issues, and the party politicians themselves, for the first group often demands attention to issues in which the politicians see no profit and possibly even electoral damage.

The independence, penetrability, and heterogeneity of the various segments of the political stratum all but guarantee that any dissatisfied group will find spokesmen in the political stratum, but to have a spokesman does not insure that the group's problems will be solved by political action. Politicians may not see how they can gain by taking a position on an issue; action by government may seem to be wholly inappropriate; policies intended to cope with dissatisfaction may be blocked; solutions may be improperly designed; indeed, politicians may even find it politically profitable to maintain a shaky coalition by keeping tension and discontent alive and deflecting attention to irrelevant "solutions" or alternative issues.

In his search for profitable issues, the party politician needs to estimate the probable effects various actions he might take will have on the future votes of his constituents. Although he is generally unaware of it, he necessarily operates with a theory, a set of hypotheses as to the factors that influence the decisions of various categories of voters and the rough weights to assign to these factors.

The subculture of the political stratum provides him with the relevant categories —businessmen, Italians, wage earners, and the like. It also furnishes him with information as to the voting tendencies of these groups, e.g., their predisposition to vote Democratic or Republican. Given a category and its voting tendency, the party politician typically operates on the simple but sound assumption that human responses can be influenced by rewards and deprivations, both past and prospective. His task then is to choose a course of action that will either reinforce the voting tendency of categories predisposed in fa-

vor of him or his party, or weaken the voting tendency of categories predisposed to vote against him or his party. This he does by actions that provide individuals in these categories with rewards or the expectation of rewards.

Some Political Axioms

Most of the people in the political stratum at any given moment take for granted a number of assumptions so commonplace in the political culture of the time and so little subject to dispute that they function as "self-evident" axioms. The axioms include both factual and normative postulates. In New Haven, the most relevant current axioms among the political stratum would appear to be the following:

1. To build an effective political coalition, rewards must be conferred on (or at least promised to) individuals, groups, and various categories of citizens.

2. In devising strategies for building coalitions and allocating rewards, one must take into account a large number of different categories of citizens. It would be dangerous to formulate strategies on the assumption that most or all citizens can be divided into two or three categories, for a successful political coalition necessarily rests upon a multiplicity of groups and categories. (In the early decades of the century a minority in the political stratum, leaders of the Social Democratic and Socialist Labor parties, pursued a strategy that reflected a confident belief in the existence of a bipolar socioeconomic structure in which political beliefs and actions were almost wholly determined by working-class or white-collar ways of making a living. But because this strategy failed to win elections, it has never been widely approved, least of all among the party politicians in the two major parties.)

3. Although a variety of attributes are relevant to political strategy, many different attributes can either be subsumed un-

der or are sometimes overridden by ethnic, racial, and religious affiliations.

4. In allocating rewards to individuals and groups, the existing socioeconomic structure must be taken as given, except for minor details. (The local political stratum has not been strongly reformist, certainly not on social and economic matters. Except perhaps for socialists, local reform movements have concentrated on defects in the political system, not the socioeconomic structure of the society. And except for a few men who dreamed and spoke of changing the face of the city, until recently the political stratum has assumed that the physical and economic features of the city are determined by forces beyond their control.)

5. Although a certain amount of legal chicanery is tolerable, legality and constitutionality are highly prized. The pursuit of illegal practices on a sizable scale is difficult to conceal; illegal actions by public officials ordinarily lead, when known, to loss of public office; unconstitutional action is almost certain to become entangled in a complex network of judicial processes. The use of violence as a political weapon must be avoided; if it were used it would probably arouse widespread alarm and hostility.

6. The American creed of democracy and equality must always be given vigorous and vociferous support. No one who denies the validity of this creed has much chance of winning political office or otherwise gaining influence on the local scene. Among other things, the creed assumes that democracy is the best form of government, public officials must be chosen by majority vote, and people in the minority must have the right to seek majority support for their beliefs.[1]

7. In practice, of course, universalistic propositions in the American creed need to be qualified. Adherence to the creed as a general goal and a set of criteria for a good government and a good society does not mean that the creed is, or as a practical matter can be, fully applied in practice. (Some elements in the political stratum are deeply disturbed by the gap between ideal and reality. Most people in the political stratum, however, are probably either unaware of any sharp conflict between ideal and reality, or are indifferent to it, or take the gap for granted in much the same spirit that they accept the fact that religious behavior falls short of religious belief.)

STABILITY, CHANGE, AND THE PROFESSIONALS

New Haven, like most pluralistic democracies, has three characteristics of great importance to the operation of its political system: there are normally "slack" resources; a small core of professional politicians exert great influence over decisions; and the system has a built-in, self-operating limitation on the influence of all participants, including the professionals.

Slack in the System

Most of the time, as we have already seen, most citizens use their resources for purposes other than gaining influence over government decisions. There is a great gap between their actual influence and their potential influence. Their political resources are, so to speak, slack in the system. In some circumstances these resources might be converted from nonpolitical to political purposes; if so, the gap between the actual influence of the average citizen and his potential influence would narrow.

The existence of a great deal of political slack seems to be a characteristic of pluralistic political systems and the liberal societies in which these systems operate.

In liberal societies, politics is a sideshow in the great circus of life. Even when citizens use their resources to gain influence, ordinarily they do not seek to influence officials or politicians but family members, friends, associates, employees, customers, business firms, and other persons engaged in nongovernmental activities. A complete study of the ways in which people use their resources to influence others would require a total examination of social life. Government, in the sense used here, is only a fragment of social life.

The Professionals

The political system of New Haven is characterized by the presence of two sharply contrasting groups of citizens. The great body of citizens use their political resources at a low level; a tiny body of professionals within the political stratum use their political resources at a high level. Most citizens acquire little skill in politics; professionals acquire a great deal. Most citizens exert little direct and immediate influence on the decisions of public officials; professionals exert much more. Most citizens have political resources they do not employ in order to gain influence over the decisions of public officials; consequently there is a great gap between their actual and potential influence. The professionals alone narrow the gap; they do so by using their political resources to the full, and by using them with a high degree of efficiency.

The existence of a small band of professionals within the political stratum is a characteristic of virtually all pluralistic systems and liberal societies. The professionals may enjoy much prestige or little; they may be rigidly honest or corrupt; they may come from aristocracies, the middle strata, or working classes. But in every liberal society they are easily distinguished by the rate and skill with which they use their resources and the resulting degree of direct influence they exert on government decisions.

Probably the most important resource of the professional is his available *labor time*. Other citizens usually have occupations that demand a large part of their labor time; they also feel a need for recreation. Measured by the alternatives he has to forego, the average citizen finds it too costly to sacrifice at most more than a few hours a week to political activities.

The professional, by contrast, organizes his life around his political activities. He usually has an occupation that leaves him freer than most citizens to engage in politics; if he does not, he is likely to change jobs until he finds one that fits easily into political routines. Celentano was an undertaker, Lee a public relations man for Yale, DiCenzo a lawyer, Golden an insurance broker—all occupations that permit innumerable opportunities for political work. As a public official, of course, the politician can work virtually full-time at the tasks of politics.

Most citizens treat politics as an avocation. To the professional, politics is a vocation, a calling. Just as the artist remains an artist even as he walks down a city street, and the scientist often consciously or unconsciously remains in his laboratory when he rides home in the evening, or the businessman on the golf course may be working out solutions to his business problems, so the successful politician is a full-time politician. The dedicated artist does not regard it as a sacrifice of precious time and leisure to paint, the dedicated scientist to work in his laboratory, nor the dedicated businesman to work at his business. On the contrary, each is likely to look for ways of avoiding all other heavy claims on his time. So, too, the dedicated politician does not consider it a sacrifice to work at politics. He is at it, awake and asleep, talking, negotiating, planning, considering strategies, building alliances, making friends, creating contacts—and increasing his influence.

It is hardly to be wondered at that the professional has much more influence on decisions than the average citizen. The professional not only has more resources at the outset than the average citizen, but he also tends to use his resources more efficiently. That is to say, he is more *skillful*.

Skill

Skill in politics is the ability to gain more influence than others, using the same resources. Why some people are more skillful than others in politics is a matter of great speculation and little knowledge. Because skill in politics is hard to measure, I shall simply assume here that professionals are in fact more skillful. However, two hypotheses help to account for the superior skill of the politician.

First, the stronger one's motivation to learn, the more one is likely to learn. Just why the professional is motivated to succeed in politics is as obscure as the motives of the artist, the scientist, or the businessman. But the whole pattern of his calling hardly leaves it open to doubt that the professional *is* more strongly motivated to acquire political skills than is the average citizen.

Second, the more time one spends in learning, the more one is likely to learn. Here the professional has an obvious advantage, as we have just seen: he organizes his life, in effect, to give him time to learn the art of politics.

I have just said the *art* of politics. Although politicians make use of information about the world around them, and hence depend on "scientific" or empirical elements, the actual practice of politics by a skilled professional is scarcely equivalent to the activities of an experimental physicist or biologist in a laboratory.

Even the professional cannot escape a high degree of uncertainty in his calculations. If the professional had perfect knowledge of his own goals, the objective situation, and the consequences of alternative strategies, then his choice of strategy would be a relatively simple and in-

deed a "scientific" matter. But in fact his knowledge is highly imperfect. He cannot be sure at what point rival professionals will begin to mobilize new resources against his policies. When new opposition flares up, he cannot be sure how much further the battle may spread or what forces lie in reserve. He cannot even be certain what will happen to his own resources if he pursues his policies. He may lose some of his popularity; campaign contributions may fall off in the future; the opposition may come up with a legal block, an ethnic angle, a scandal.

Because of the uncertainty surrounding his decisions, the politician, like the military leader, rarely confronts a situation in which his choice of strategies follows clearly and logically from all the information at his disposal, even when he happens to be well-informed as to his own goals. Surrounded by uncertainty, the politician himself necessarily *imputes* a structure and meaning to the situation that goes beyond empirical evidence and scientific modes of analysis. What the politician imputes to the situation depends, in sum, not only on the information at his disposal but also on his own inner predispositions. His strategy therefore reflects his predispositions for caution or boldness, impulsiveness or calculation, negotiation or toughness, stubbornness or resilience, optimism or pessimism, cynicism or faith in others. The strategies of professionals may vary depending on the forces that generate needs for approval, popularity, domination, manipulation, deception, candor, and so on. The effect of inner dispositions on a professional's strategies is by no means clear or direct. But as one works back from a given situation with all its uncertainties to the professional's interpretation of the situation and his choice of strategies, usually some element in the interpretation or the choice is difficult to account for except as a product of his own special dispositions imposing themselves on his selection of strategies.

Differences in predispositions that result in differences in strategies often reveal themselves in dramatic differences in the style of a chief executive: the differences between a Roosevelt and Eisenhower, for example, or a Wilson and a Coolidge, or the early Truman doubtful of his inherent fitness for the presidency and the later, cocky, self-confident President. Differences also show up at the local level—for example, the contrast between the cautious demeanor of Mayor Celentano and the aggressive, programmatic behavior of Mayor Lee.

Just as individuals vary, so professionals vary in the extent to which they use all the resources at their disposal. Some professionals seem driven not only to use all the resources they have but to create new resources and thus to pyramid their influence. They are a kind of political entrepreneur. In an authoritarian milieu perhaps the political entrepreneur might even be driven to dictatorship. But in a pluralistic political system, powerful self-limiting tendencies help to maintain the stability of the system.

The Art of Pyramiding

We have seen that in the pluralistic political system of New Haven, the political order that existed before 1953—the pattern of petty sovereignties—was gradually transformed into an executive-centered order. How could this change take place? There were few formal changes in the structure of government and politics. The city charter not only remained unaltered, but as we have seen a proposed charter that in effect would have conferred full legality and legitimacy on the executive-centered order was turned down decisively in the same election in which the chief of the new order was re-elected by one of the greatest popular majorities on record.

The transformation of petty sovereignties into an executive-centered order was possible only because there were slack resources available to the mayor which,

used skillfully and to the full, were sufficient to shift the initiative on most questions to the chief executive. Initially the new mayor had access to no greater resources than his predecessor, but with superb skill he exploited them to the limit. In this way, he managed to accumulate new resources; he rose to new heights of popularity, for example, and found it increasingly easy to tap the business community for campaign contributions. His new resources in turn made it easier for him to secure the compliance of officials in city agencies, enlarge his staff, appoint to office the kinds of people he wanted, obtain the cooperation of the Boards of Finance and Aldermen, and gain widespread support for his policies. Thus the resources available to the mayor grew by comparison with those available to other officials. He could now increase his influence over the various officials of local government by using these new resources fully and skillfully. An executive-centered order gradually emerged.

This transformation had two necessary conditions. First, when the new mayor came into office he had to have access either to resources not available to his predecessor or to slack resources his predecessor had not used. In this instance, the new mayor initially relied on a fuller and more efficient use of substantially the same resources available to his predecessor. By using slack resources with higher efficiency the new mayor moved his actual influence closer to his potential influence. Then because of his greater influence he was able to improve his access to resources. In this fashion he pyramided both his resources and his influence. He was, in short, a highly successful political entrepreneur.

There is, however, a second necessary condition for success. The policies of the political entrepreneur must not provoke so strong a countermobilization that he exhausts his resources with no substantial increase in his influence.

What then stops the political entrepreneur short of dictatorship? Why doesn't the political entrepreneur in a pluralistic system go on pyramiding his resources until he overturns the system itself? The answer lies in the very same conditions that are necessary to his success. If slack resources provide the political entrepreneur with his dazzling opportunity, they are also the source of his greatest danger. For nearly every citizen in the community has access to unused political resources; it is precisely because of this that even a minor blunder can be fatal to the political entrepreneur if it provokes a sizable minority in the community into using its political resources at a markedly higher rate in opposition to his policies, for then, as with the White Queen, it takes all the running he can do just to stay in the same place. Yet almost every policy involves losses for some citizens and gains for others. Whenever the prospect of loss becomes high enough, threatened citizens begin to take up some of the slack in order to remove the threat. The more a favorable decision increases in importance to the opposition, the more resources they can withdraw from other uses and pour into the political struggle; the more resources the opposition employs, the greater the cost to the political entrepreneur if he insists on his policy. At some point, the cost becomes so high that the policy is no longer worth it. This point is almost certain to be reached whenever the opposition includes a majority of the electorate, even if no election takes place. Normally, however, far before this extreme situation is approached the expected costs will already have become so excessive that an experienced politician will capitulate or, more likely, search for a compromise that gives him some of what he wants at lower cost.

Three aspects of Mayor Lee's situation made it possible for him to avoid costly opposition. These were: the wide degree of latent support for redevelopment that already existed in New Haven and needed

only to be awakened; the evident need for a high degree of coordination among city agencies if redevelopment were to be carried out; and the Mayor's unusual skill at negotiating agreement and damping down potential disagreements before they flared into opposition. These aspects of Lee's situation are not prevalent in New Haven all the time, nor, certainly, do they necessarily exist in other cities. In the absence of any one of them, opposition might have developed, and the attempt to transform the independent sovereignties into an executive-centered order might have become altogether too costly.

Thus the distribution of resources and the ways in which they are or are not used in a pluralistic political system like New Haven's constitute an important source of both political change and political stability. If the distribution and use of resources gives aspiring leaders great opportunities for gaining influence, these very features also provide a built-in throttle that makes it difficult for any leader, no matter how skillful, to run away with the system.

These features are not, however, the only source of stability. Widespread consensus on the American creed of democracy and equality, referred to many times in the previous pages, is also a stabilizing factor. The analysis in the preceding pages surely points, however, to the conclusion that the effectiveness of the creed as a constraint on political leaders depends not only on the nature of the political consensus as it exists among ordinary citizens but also as it exists among members of the political stratum, particularly the professionals themselves. This is the subject of the following pages.

STABILITY, CHANGE, AND THE DEMOCRATIC CREED

Leaving to one side as a doubtful case the elected oligarchy that governed New Haven during its first century and a half, public officials in New Haven have been selected for the last century and a half through democratic institutions of a rather advanced sort. For more than a century, indeed, New Haven's political system has been characterized by well-nigh universal suffrage, a moderately high participation in elections, a highly competitive two-party system, opportunity to criticize the conduct and policies of officials, freedom to seek support for one's views, among officials and citizens, and surprisingly frequent alternations in office from one party to the other as electoral majorities have shifted. (Hereafter, when I speak of the political system of New Haven, I will assume what I have just enumerated to be the defining characteristics of that system: "stability" will mean the persistence of these characteristics.)

During this period New Haven has not, so far as I can discover, fallen at any time into the kind of semi-dictatorship occasionally found in other American communities. Violence is not and seems never to have been a weapon of importance to New Haven's rulers. Party bosses have existed and exist today; the parties tend to be highly disciplined, and nominations are centrally controlled. But despite occasional loose talk to the contrary, today the parties are too competitive and the community too fragmented for a party boss to be a community boss as well.

Like every other political system, of course, the political system of New Haven falls far short of the usual conceptions of an ideal democracy; by almost any standard, it is obviously full of defects. But to the extent that the term is ever fairly applied to existing realities, the political system of New Haven is an example of a democratic system, warts and all. For the past century it seems to have been a highly stable system.

Theorists have usually assumed that so much stability would be unlikely and even impossible without widespread agreement among citizens on the key ideas of democracy, including the basic rights, duties,

and procedures that serve to distinguish democratic from nondemocratic systems. Tocqueville, you will recall, concluded that among the three causes that maintained democracy among the people of the United States—their physical, social, and economic conditions, their laws, and their customs—it was the customs that constituted "the peculiar cause which renders that people the only one of the American nations that is able to support a democratic government." By "customs," he explained, he meant "the whole moral and intellectual condition of a people." Considering his remarkable eye for relevant detail, Tocqueville was uncharacteristically vague as to the specific nature of these customs. But the general import of his argument is perfectly clear. "Republican notions insinuate themselves," as he says at one place, "into all the ideas, opinions, and habits of the Americans and are formally recognized by the laws; and before the laws could be altered, the whole community must be revolutionized."[2]

Before the days of the sample survey it was difficult to say with confidence how widely shared various ideas of democracy actually were in the United States, or even in New Haven. The data are still inadequate. However, some recent findings[3] cast doubt on the validity of the hypothesis that the stability of the American democratic system depends, as Tocqueville and others seem to argue, on an almost universal belief in the basic rules of the democratic game. These studies offer support for some alternative hypotheses. First, although Americans almost unanimously agree on a number of general propositions about democracy, they disagree about specific applications to crucial cases. Second, a majority of voters fre-

---

[2]Tocqueville, *Democracy in America*, pp. 310, 334, 436.

[3]Especially Samuel Stouffer, *Communism, Conformity and Civil Liberties* (New York: Doubleday, 1955) and James W. Prothro and Charles M. Grigg, *op. cit.*

quently hold views contrary to rules of the game actually followed in the political system. Third, a much higher degree of agreement on democratic norms exists among the political stratum than among voters in general. Fourth, even among the political stratum the amount of agreement is hardly high enough to account by itself for the stability of the system.

I propose, therefore, to examine some alternative explanations. Because my data on New Haven are not wholly adequate for the task at hand, the theory I shall sketch out might properly be regarded more as reflections on the process of creating consensus than as a testing of theory by a hard examination of the facts in New Haven. But New Haven will provide a convenient reference point.

Some Alternative Explanations

There are at least five alternative ways (aside from denying the validity or generality of recent findings) to account for the stability of the political system in New Haven.

First, one may deny that New Haven is "democratic" and argue that it is in fact run by a covert oligarchy of some sort. Thus the problem, it might be said, is illusory. Yet even in the absence of comparable studies our findings argue strongly that New Haven is not markedly *less* democratic than other supposedly democratic political systems. Some of these, we know, have proved to be unstable; hence the problem does not vanish after all.

Second, one might argue that things were different in the good old days. Yet it is hardly plausible to suppose that in 1910, when slightly less than half the population of New Haven consisted of first- and second-generation immigrants (many of them from countries with few democratic traditions), democratic beliefs were more widespread than they are now. In any case, the main characteristics of the

political system—majority rule, the legitimacy of opposition, and so on—do not show any signs of disappearing.

Third, it might be said that the political system of New Haven is scarcely autonomous enough to furnish us with adequate explanations of its own stability, for stability may depend much less on the beliefs of citizens locally than on state and national institutions. There is much truth in this objection, but it does not altogether explain why some American towns, cities, and counties have at various times moved a good deal farther from democratic norms than New Haven has.

Fourth, one might argue that the system has not been entirely stable, that in fact most seemingly stable democratic systems are constantly in transition. Surely this is a valid point, but it is one that cuts both ways. In New Haven, as elsewhere, the rules of the game have altered in quite important, one is tempted to say fundamental, ways over the past century and a half. For example, organized, overt political competition, which was anathema to the patrician oligarchy, seems to have been fully legitimate since about 1840. Consider the electorate—the active voters. Partly as a result of the abolition of property qualifications in 1845, but probably more as a result of party organization and competition, the proportion of voting adults shot up and then stabilized at a moderate level. In most elections from 1800–33 the voters comprised less than a quarter of the adult males and sometimes less than 10 per cent; since 1834, however, they have made up from a half to three-quarters of the adult male (and since 1920, female) population. A final example: throughout the nineteenth century, an implicit norm excluded persons of foreign birth or non-Yankee origins from nomination or election to the mayoralty; since the mayoralty election of 1899, the norm has very nearly come to operate in reverse.

Because of, or in spite of, these

changes, however, the essential characteristics of the political system as I described them have remained substantially intact for the past century. With appropriate techniques, probably one could detect and describe significant fluctuations in the "intensity," "degree," or "magnitude" of the various characteristics, but this line of inquiry would not help much in the present problem.

Fifth, one might argue that the stability of New Haven's political system does not depend on a widespread belief that certain democratic norms, rules, or procedures are highly desirable or intrinsically preferable to other rules; in some circumstances a democratic system could be highly stable if a substantial part of the electorate merely *accepted* them. A majority of voters who do not really believe in extending freedom of speech to individuals and groups beyond the pale of popular morality—and who would readily say so during an interview—might nonetheless acquiesce in such extensions on a variety of pragmatic grounds.

There is, I think, a good deal more truth in this view than many enthusiastic democrats care to admit. Let me suggest some circumstances in which this explanation might be valid.

Whenever the costs of disagreement are believed to be very high, there are innumerable conditions under which a collection of people might knowingly agree on a choice that no one preferred, simply because this was the only choice on which they could agree. Stable systems of international politics, such as the balance of power system in the nineteenth century, surely have been of this kind. Or suppose that 80 per cent of the voters are in favor of a more restricted suffrage than

actually exists. Suppose that 40 per cent would like to restrict the suffrage to taxpayers, another 40 per cent would like to restrict it to college graduates, and only 20 per cent would like to retain the present suffrage. Suppose further that their other choices were as shown in the table below. One does not need to assume a great amount of rationality to conclude that they would retain the existing broad suffrage requirements, even though this would be the preferred choice of only a minority.

Moreover, this example hints at the fact that the stability of a political system, even a democratic one, is not merely a matter of the *numbers* of persons who adhere to it but also of the *amount of political resources* they use—or are expected to use—in acting on their beliefs. The amount of political resources an individual is likely to use is a function, among other things, of the amount of resources he has access to, the strength or intensity of his belief, and the relevance he sees in political action as a way of acting on his beliefs. Other things being equal, rules supported only by a wealthy, educated minority (money and knowledge being important political resources) and opposed by the rest of the voters are surely likely to endure longer than rules supported only by a poor, uneducated minority and opposed by the rest of the voters. Likewise, rules that are *strongly* believed in by a minority and weakly opposed by the rest are more likely to endure than rules *weakly* believed in by a majority and strongly opposed by a minority.

In addition to numbers and resources, however, skill is obviously a critical factor. Rules supported by a politically skill-

	40% prefer:	40% prefer:	20% prefer:
First choice:	Taxpayers	College graduates	Present requirements
Second choice:	Present requirements	Present requirements	College graduates
Third choice:	College graduates	Taxpayers	Taxpayers

ful minority may withstand the opposition of a less skilled majority, and in any case are likely to endure longer than if they are supported only by an unskilled minority.

Let us now imagine a society with a political system approximately like that in New Haven. Suppose the rules, procedures, and essential characteristics of this system are strongly supported by a minority which, in comparison with the rest of the population, possesses a high degree of political skill. Suppose further that a majority of voters would prefer rules different from those prevailing, though they might not all prefer the same alternatives. Suppose finally that the majority of voters have access to fewer resources of influence; that their preferences for other rules are not salient or strong; that because of their relative indifference they do not employ what potential influence they have; and that they are not very skillful in using their political resources anyway. Such a political system, its seems to me, might be highly stable.

On the other hand, if any of the characteristics of this hypothetical minority were to shift to the majority, then the system would surely become less stable. Instability would increase, then, if the minority favoring the system no longer had superior resources, or if it became less skillful, or if the question of rules became salient and urgent to a majority of voters.

I should like to advance the hypothesis that the political system we have just been supposing corresponds closely to the facts of New Haven, and in all probability to the United States. If it errs, it is in supposing that *even among the political stratum* the level of agreement on the rules of the game is, at any given moment, high enough to explain the persistence of the rules.

Consensus as a Process

Most of us, I suppose, are ready to recognize long-run changes in the beliefs ex-

pressed by the more articulate segments of the political stratum and the intelligentsia, and we can infer from various kinds of evidence—all of it, alas, highly debatable—that changes of some sort take place over long periods of time in the attitudes about democracy held in the general population. We tend to assume, however, that except for these long-run shifts beliefs about democracy are more or less static. I want to propose an alternative explanation, namely that democratic beliefs, like other political beliefs, are influenced by a recurring *process* of interchange among political professionals, the political stratum, and the great bulk of the population. The process generates enough agreement on rules and norms so as to permit the system to operate, but agreement tends to be incomplete, and typically it decays. So the process is frequently repeated. "Consensus," then, is not at all a static and unchanging attribute of citizens. It is a variable element in a complex and more or less continuous process.

This process seems to me to have the following characteristics:

1. Over long periods of time the great bulk of the citizens possess a fairly stable set of democratic beliefs at a high level of abstraction. Let me call these beliefs the democratic creed. In Ann Arbor and Tallahassee, Prothro and Grigg found that very nearly everyone they interviewed agreed with five abstract democratic propositions.[4] We can, I think, confidently conclude that most Americans believe in democracy as the best form of government, in the desirability of rights and procedures insuring a goodly measure of majority rule and minority freedom, and in a wide but not necessarily comprehensive electorate. At a somewhat lower level of

---

[4]"Democracy is the best form of government." "Public officials should be chosen by majority vote." "Every citizen should have an equal chance to influence government policy." "The minority should be free to criticize majority decisions." "People in the minority should be free to try to win majority support for their opinions." Prothro and Grigg, *op. cit.*, pp. 282, 284.

agreement, probably the great majority of citizens also believe in the essential legitimacy of certain specific American political institutions: the presidency, Congress, the Supreme Court, the states, the local governments, etc.

2. Most citizens assume that the American political system is consistent with the democratic creed. Indeed, the common view seems to be that our system is not only democratic but is perhaps the most perfect expression of democracy that exists anywhere; if deficiencies exist, either they can, and ultimately will, be remedied, or else they reflect the usual gap between ideal and reality that men of common sense take for granted. Moreover, because leading officials with key roles in the legitimate political institutions automatically acquire authority for their views on the proper functioning of the political institutions, as long as these various officials seem to agree, the ordinary citizen is inclined to assume that existing ways of carrying on the public business do not violate, at least in an important way, the democratic creed to which he is committed.

3. Widespread adherence to the democratic creed is produced and maintained by a variety of powerful social processes. Of these, probably formal schooling is the most important. The more formal education an American has, the more democratic formulas he knows, expresses, and presumably believes. But almost the entire adult population has been subjected to *some* degree of indoctrination through the schools. Beliefs acquired in school are reinforced in adult life through normal exposure to the democratic creed, particularly as the creed is articulated by leading political figures and transmitted through the mass media.

These social processes have an enormous impact on the citizen, partly because they begin early in life and partly because the very unanimity with which the creed is espoused makes rejection of it almost impossible. To reject the creed is infinitely more than a simple matter of disagreement. To reject the creed is to reject one's society and one's chances of full acceptance in it—in short, to be an outcast. (As a mental experiment, try to imagine the psychic and social burdens an American child in an American school would incur if he steadfastly denied to himself and others that democracy is the best form of government.)

To reject the democratic creed is in effect to refuse to be an American. As a nation we have taken great pains to insure that few citizens will ever want to do anything so rash, so preposterous—in fact, so wholly un-American. In New Haven, as in many other parts of the United States, vast social energies have been poured into the process of "Americanization," teaching citizens what is expected in the way of words, beliefs, and behavior if they are to earn acceptance as Americans, for it was obvious to the political stratum that unless the immigrants and their children quickly accepted American political norms, the flood of aliens, particularly from countries with few traditions of self-government, would disrupt the political system. In a characteristic response, the Board of Education of the city of New Haven created a supervisor for Americanization (a post, incidentally, that still exists). Something of the feeling of urgency and accomplishment that must have prevailed in many segments of the political stratum shines through these enthusiastic words in the annual report of the New Haven superintendent of schools in 1919:

The public school is the greatest and most effective of all Americanization agencies. This is the one place where all children in a community or district, regardless of nationality, religion, politics, or social status, meet and work together in a cooperative and harmonious spirit. . . . The children work and play together, they catch the school spirit, they live the democratic life, American heroes become their own, American history wins their loyalty, the Stars and Stripes, always before their eyes in the school room, receives their daily salute. Not only are these immigrant children Americanized through the public school, but they, in turn, Americanize their parents carrying into the home many lessons of democracy learned at school.[5]

For their part, the immigrants and their children were highly motivated to learn how to be Americans, for they were desperately, sometimes pathetically, eager to win acceptance as true Americans.

In one form or another the process of Americanization has absorbed enormous social energies all over the United States. As a factor in shaping American behavior and attitudes, the process of Americanization must surely have been as important as the frontier, or industrialization, or urbanization. That regional, ethnic, racial, religious, or economic differences might disrupt the American political system has been a recurring fear among the political stratum of the United States from the very beginning of the republic. Doubtless this anxiety was painfully stimulated by the Civil War. It was aroused again by the influx of immigrants. Throughout the country then the political stratum has seen to it that new citizens, young and old, have been properly trained in "American" principles and beliefs. Everywhere, too, the pupils have been highly motivated to talk, look and believe as American should. The result was as astounding an act of voluntary political and cultural assimilation and speedy elimination of regional, ethnic, and cultural dissimilarities as history can provide. The extent to which Americans agree today on the key propositions about democracy is a measure of the almost unbelievable success of this deliberate attempt to create a seemingly uncoerced nation-wide consensus.

4. Despite wide agreement on a general democratic creed, however, citizens frequently disagree on specific applications. Many citizens oppose what some political philosophers would regard as necesary implications of the creed. Many citizens also disagree with the way the creed is actually applied—or perhaps it would be more accurate to say, with the existing rules of the game, the prevailing political norms. Again and again, for example, surveys indicate that a large number of Americans, sometimes even a majority, do not approve of the extension of important rights, liberties, and privileges to individuals and groups that do in fact enjoy them.

A citizen is able to adhere to these seemingly inconsistent beliefs for a great variety of reasons. For one thing, he himself need not see any inconsistency in his beliefs. The creed is so vague (and incomplete) that strict deductions are difficult or impossible even for sophisticated logicians. Moreover, propositions stated in universal terms are rarely assumed by men of common sense to imply universality in practice; to the frequent dismay of logicians, a common tendency of mankind—and not least of Americans—is to qualify universals in application while leaving them intact in rhetoric. Then, too, the capacity for (or interest in) working out a set of consistent political attitudes is rather limited. As the authors of *The American Voter* have recently shown, most voters seem to operate at a low level of ideological sophistication; even among intelligent (though not necessarily highly educated) citizens, conceptions of politics are often of a simplicity that the political philosopher might find it hard to comprehend.[6] In addition, most citizens operate with a very small fund of political information; often they lack the elementary information required even to be aware of inconsistencies between their views and what is actually happening in the political

---

[5] "Report of the Superintendent of Schools," *Annual Report of the Board of Education of the New Haven City School District*, 1919.

[6] A. Campbell, P. E. Converse, W. E. Miller, D. D. Stokes, *The American Voter* (New York, Wiley, 1960), chs. 9 and 10.

system, particularly if the subject is (as most questions of rights and procedures are) arcane and complex. Again, questions that bother theorists are often not interesting or salient to most voters; their attention and energies are diverted elsewhere, usually to activities that lie entirely outside the political arena. As long as a citizen believes that democracy is the best political system, that the United States is a democracy, and that the people in office can be trusted, by and large, to apply the abstract creed to specific cases, issues of democratic theory and practice hotly discussed by political philosophers, or even by publicists and columnists, are likely never to penetrate through the manifold barriers to abstract political thinking that are erected by the essentially apolitical culture in which he lives. Finally, even if the issues do manage to get through, many citizens feel themselves incompetent to decide them; this, after all, is what Supreme Court judges, presidents, and members of Congress are supposed to do. Worse yet, many citizens feel that no one in public office will care much about their opinions anyway.

5. Members of the political stratum (who live in a much more politicized culture) are more familiar with the "democratic" norms, more consistent, more ideological, more detailed and explicit in their political attitudes, and more completely in agreement on the norms. They are more in agreement not only on what norms are implied by the abstract democratic creed but also in supporting the norms currently operating. This relatively higher degree of support for the prevailing norms in the existing political system is generated and maintained by a variety of processes. Because members of the political stratum have on the average considerably more formal education than the population as a whole, they have been more thoroughly exposed to the creed and its implications. Because they are more involved in, concerned with, and articulate about politics,

they invest more time and effort in elaborating a consistent ideology. Because they participate more extensively in politics, they more frequently express and defend their views, encounter criticism, and face the charge of inconsistency. They know more about politics, read more, experience more, see more.

Within the political stratum, the professionals tend to agree even more on what the norms should be, what they are, and the desirability of maintaining them substantially as they are. Agreement among the professionals is generated by all the factors that account for it among the rest of the political stratum and even among the apolitical strata. Mastery over the existing norms of the political system represents the particular stockpile of skills peculiar to the professional's vocation. Norms also tend to legitimate his power and position in the political system, furnish an agreed-on method of getting on with the immediate tasks at hand, carry the authority of tradition, and help to reduce the baffling uncertainty that surrounds the professional's every choice. Finally, the professional is likely to support the existing norms because his own endorsement of existing norms was initially a criterion in his own recruitment and advancement; complex processes of political selection and rejection tend to exclude the deviant who challenges the prevailing norms of the existing political system. Most of the professionals might properly be called democratic "legitimists."

6. The professionals, of course, have access to extensive political resources which they employ at a high rate with superior efficiency. Consequently, a challenge to the existing norms is bound to be costly to the challenger, for legitimist professionals can quickly shift their skills and resources into the urgent task of doing in the dissenter. As long as the professionals remain substantially legitimist in outlook, therefore, the critic is likely to

make little headway. Indeed, the chances are that anyone who advocates extensive changes in the prevailing democratic norms is likely to be treated by the professionals, and even by a fair share of the political stratum, as an outsider, possibly even as a crackpot whose views need not be seriously debated. No worse fate can befall the dissenter, for unless he can gain the attention of the political stratum, it is difficult for him to gain space in the mass media; if he cannot win space in the mass media, it is difficult for him to win a large following; if he cannot win a large following, it is difficult for him to gain the attention of the political stratum.

7. Sometimes, of course, disagreements over the prevailing norms occur within the political stratum and among the professionals themselves. But these disagreements need not, and perhaps ordinarily do not, produce much effort to involve the general public in the dispute. The disagreements are not, to be sure, secret; the electorate is not *legally* barred from finding out about the conflict and becoming involved. It does not need to be. Given the low salience of politics in the life of the average citizen, most conflicts over the prevailing norms might attract more attention if they were held behind locked doors. Unless a professional is willing to invest very great resources in whipping up public interest, he is not likely to get much effective support. In any case, public involvement may seem undesirable to the legitimist, for alterations in the prevailing norms are often subtle matters, better obtained by negotiation than by the crudities and oversimplifications of public debate.

8. Among the rules and procedures supported strongly by the legitimists in the political stratum, and particularly by the professionals, are some that prescribe ways of settling disagreements as to rules and procedures. These involve appeals to authorities who give decisions widely accepted as binding, authoritative, and le-

gitimate—though not necessarily as "good" or "correct." Typically these include appeals to courts or quasi-judicial institutions that ostensibly arrive at their decisions by appeals to norms, codes, formulas, and beliefs that appear to transcend partisan and policy differences in the political stratum.

9. Ordinarily, then, it is not difficult for a stable system of rights and privileges to exist that, at least in important details, does not have widespread public support and occasionally even lacks majority approval. As long as the matter is not a salient public issue—and whether it is or not depends partly on how the political stratum handles it—the question is substantially determined within the political stratum itself. When disagreements arise, these are adjudicated by officials who share the beliefs of the political stratum rather than those of the populace; and even when these officials adopt positions that do not command the undivided support of the political stratum, members of the political stratum, and particularly the professionals, tend to accept a decision as binding until and unless it can be changed through the accepted procedures. This is the essence of their code of democratic legitimism.

10. Occasionally, however, a sizable segment of the political stratum develops doubts that it can ever achieve the changes it seeks through accepted procedures that are, in a sense, internal to the political stratum and the professionals. One or more of these dissenters may push his way into the professional group, or the dissenters may be numerous and vocal enough to acquire a spokesman or two among the professionals. The strategy of the dissenters may now begin to shift. Instead of adjudicating the matter according to the accepted procedures, the dissenters attempt to arouse public support for their proposals, hoping that when a sufficient number of voters are won over to their cause, other professionals—legiti-

mists or not—will have to come around.

The professionals, as I have said, live in a world of uncertainty. They search for omens and portents. If the auguries indicate that the appeal to the populace has failed, then the legitimists may confidently close ranks against the dissenter. But if the auguries are uncertain or unfavorable, then the legitimists, too, are forced to make a counter-appeal to the populace. Since public opinion is often as difficult to interpret as the flights of birds or the entrails of a sheep, political professionals may and frequently do misread the auspices. In October 1954, the Survey Research Center discovered that only 12 per cent of their sample said they would be more likely to vote for a candidate who had the support of Senator McCarthy; 37 per cent said they would be less likely, and 43 per cent said it would make no difference.[7] In retrospect, these proportions do not look wildly off, but in 1954 belief in McCarthy's mass following was widespread throughout the whole political stratum and not least among the professionals. The legitimists could probably have ignored the late Senator with impunity—as they later did—but he followed a classic strategy—(required, I am suggesting, by the tendency of the legitimists to monopolize the internal devices for adjudicating disputes over norms)—by taking the issue out of the hands of the professionals, where the rules of the game were bound to run against him, and appealing instead to the populace.

If the dissenters succeed in forcing the issue out beyond the political stratum, and dissenters and legitimists begin making appeals to the populace, then the nature of the debate begins to change. Technical questions, subtle distinctions, fine matters of degree are shed. The appeal is now shaped to the simple democratic creed which nearly every citizen believes in. Because the creed does not constitute a tightly logical system, it is possible for the legitimists to demonstrate that existing norms are necessary consequences of the creed, and for the dissenters to show that existing norms run counter to the creed. Because the creed is deeply laden with tradition and sentiment, emotion rises and reasoned discussion declines.

11. Ordinary citizens who normally remain outside these debates now find their attention—and their votes—solicited by both sides. They become aware that the very officials who ordinarily decide these matters, to whom the citizen himself turns for his cues as to what is legitimate and consistent with the creed, are locked in deadly, heated battle. These citizens must now find ways of applying the creed to the issue. One way is to withdraw even more deeply into the political shadows; a citizen can simply refuse to choose. Many do. In March 1937, at the height of the debate over President Roosevelt's proposal to enlarge the Supreme Court, 50 per cent of the people interviewed in a Gallup poll had listened to neither of the President's two recent radio speeches defending his plan. A month later, one out of seven persons who were asked whether Congress should pass the President's bill expressed no opinion.[8] In New Haven, after several years of public discussion and debate over charter reform, when a sample of registered voters was asked in 1959 whether they personally would do anything if a revision of the charter was proposed that would make the mayor stronger, over 40 per cent of those who disapproved of such an idea said they would do nothing to oppose it, and nearly three-quarters of those who approved said they would do nothing to support it. (These seemed to be tolerably honest re-

---

[7]Angus Campbell and Homer C. Cooper, *Group Differences in Attitudes and Votes, A Study of the 1954 Congressional Election* (Ann Arbor, Mich.: University of Michigan Survey Research Center, 1954), p. 145.

[8]Hadley Cantril, ed., *Public Opinion, 1935–1946* (Princeton: Princeton University Press, 1951), p. 150.

sponses; in the preceding election, after wide discussion among the political stratum and hot debate among the professionals over a new charter, less than half the voters who went to the polls even bothered to vote on the charter.) Thus when dissenters and legitimists appeal to the populace to settle questions they ordinarily decide among themselves, they cannot be at all sure that they will actually produce much of a response no matter how much they try to stir up the public.

However, citizens who *do* make up their minds must find some ways for arriving at a choice. For many citizens the decision is eased by their existing loyalties to parties or political leaders. In April 1937, 68 per cent of the Democrats in a Gallup poll said that Congress should pass Roosevelt's court plan; 93 per cent of the Republicans said Congress should not. Those who had no strong party identifications were, as one might expect, split—42 per cent in favor and 58 per cent against.[9] In 1954, attitudes toward McCarthy were closely related to party identifications. Among strong Democrats, those who said that McCarthy's support would make them *less* likely to vote for a candidate were six times as great as those who said his support would make them *more* likely; strong Republicans, by contrast, split about evenly. Among Catholics who were strong Democrats, the ratio was two to one against McCarthy; among Catholics who were strong Republicans it was nearly two to one in his favor.[10]

If the parties give no clear guidance, citizens may look to particular leaders or institutions. They may turn to spokesmen in their churches, for example, or trade unions, or regions. They often turn, of course, to attitudes prevalent in their own circle of intimates, friends, associates, ac-

quaintances. If their search yields no consistent cues, they may give up. In the struggle over charter reform in New Haven in 1958, when Democratic leaders were split from the top down, judging from a sample of registered voters interviewed shortly after the election the proportion of people who went to the polls and voted on the general election but did not vote either for or against the charter was higher among Democrats than among either Republicans or independents.

12. An appeal to the populace may terminate in several ways. The appeal may simply fail to create a stir. Interest in political matters wanes rather quickly; since complex issues of democratic norms nearly always lack a direct relation to the ongoing life of an individual, they have even less capacity for holding attention than many other issues. However passionately the dissenters feel about their case, life does move on, old questions become tiresome, and the newspapers begin to shove the conflict to the inside pages. Perhaps the legitimists, buoyed by their reading of the electorate, defeat the dissenters in a clear-cut trial of strength and, having done so, close ranks and go on to the next business. Perhaps the dissenters win, or a compromise is worked out; if so the dissenters, like as not, turn into the next generation of legitimists.

The Role of Democratic Beliefs

The specific beliefs of the average citizen thus have a rather limited though important function. Ordinarily, conflicts over democratic norms are resolved among the professionals, with perhaps some involvement by parts of the political stratum but little or no involvement by most citizens. Thus the fact that a large number of citizens do not believe in the political norms actually applied, particularly extending political liberties to unpopular individuals and groups, has slight effect on the outcome.

The beliefs of the ordinary citizen be-

---

[9] *Ibid.*

[10] Campbell and Cooper, *Group Differences in Attitudes*, Tables VI–VIII (p. 92) and B–81 (p. 149). See also Nelson W. Polsby, "Towards an Explanation of McCarthyism," *Political Studies*, 8, No. 3 (1960), 250-71.

come relevant only when professionals engage in an intensive appeal to the populace. Even then, the actual outcome of the appeal does not necessarily reflect majority attitudes at all accurately. These are not always known; they are guessed at in a variety of inaccurate ways, and they have to be filtered through the tighter mesh of the political stratum and the professionals before they can become public policy.

Nonetheless, wide consensus on the democratic creed does have two important kinds of consequences. On the one hand, this very consensus makes occasional appeal all but inevitable, for the creed itself gives legitimacy to an appeal to the populace. On the other hand, widespread adherence to the creed limits the character and the course of an appeal. It insures that no appeal is likely to succeed unless it is framed in terms consistent with the creed—which is perhaps not so small a constraint. Some solutions pretty evidently are *not* consistent. Because an appeal must take place in the face of criticism from legitimists and extensive appraisal by members of the political stratum, blatant inconsistencies are likely to be exposed. Moreover, because the appeal is legitimized by the creed, it provides an orderly way to conduct a dispute that exceeds the capacities of the professionals to resolve among themselves.

No one, I imagine, has ever supposed that the existence of the creed entails no risks. People can be deceived by appeals intended to destroy democracy in the name of democracy. Dissenters who believe in the democratic creed may unwittingly advocate or legitimists may insist on preserving rules of the game destined to have unforeseen and unintended consequences disastrous to the stability and perhaps the survival of the democracy. Nonetheless, we can be reasonably sure

of this: even if universal belief in a democratic creed does not guarantee the stability of a democratic system, a substantial decline in the popular consensus would greatly increase the chance of serious instability. How the professionals act, what they advocate, what they are likely to believe, are all constrained by the wide adherence to the creed that exists throughout the community. If a substantial segment of the electorate begins to doubt the creed, professionals will quickly come forth to fan that doubt. The nature and course of an appeal to the populace will change. What today is a question of applying the fundamental norms of democracy will become tomorrow an inquiry into the validity of these norms. If a substantial number of citizens begin to deny not merely to *some* minorities but to minorities *as such* the rights and powers prescribed in the creed, an appeal to the populace is likely to end sooner or later in a call to arms.

Thus consensus on political beliefs and practices has much in common with other aspects of a democratic system. Here, too, leaders lead—and often are led. Citizens are very far indeed from exerting equal influence over the content, application, and development of the political consensus. Yet widely held beliefs by Americans in a creed of democracy and political equality serve as a critical limit on the ways in which leaders can shape the consensus.

Neither the prevailing consensus, the creed, nor even the political system itself are immutable products of democratic ideas, beliefs, and institutions inherited from the past. For better or worse, they are always open, in some measure, to alteration through those complex processes of symbiosis and change that constitute the relations of leaders and citizens in a pluralistic democracy.

PUBLIC OPINION AND DEMOCRATIC POLITICS*

V. O. Key, Jr.

The exploration of public attitudes is a pursuit of endless fascination—and frustration. Depiction of the distribution of opinions within the public, identification of the qualities of opinion, isolation of the odd and of the obvious correlates of opinion, and ascertainment of the modes of opinion formation are pursuits that excite human curiosity. Yet these endeavors are bootless unless the findings about the preferences, aspirations, and prejudices of the public can be connected with the workings of the governmental system. The nature of that connection has been suggested by the examination of the channels by which governments become aware of public sentiment and the institutions through which opinion finds more or less formal expression.

When all these linkages are treated, the place of public opinion in government has still not been adequately portrayed. The problem of opinion and government needs to be viewed in an even broader context. Consideration of the role of public opinion drives the observer to the more fundamental question of how it is that democratic governments manage to operate at all. Despite endless speculation on that problem, perplexities still exist about what critical circumstances, beliefs, outlooks, faiths, and conditions are conducive to the maintenance of regimes under which public opinion is controlling, at least in principle, and is, in fact, highly influential.

*From *Public Opinion and American Democracy* by V. O. Key, Jr. Copyright © 1961 by V. O. Key, Jr. Reprinted by permission of Alfred A. Knopf, Inc.

1 · A MISSING PIECE OF THE PUZZLE

Though the preceding analyses did not uncover the secret of the conditions precedent to the practice of democratic politics, they pointed to a major piece of the puzzle that was missing as we sought to assemble the elements that go into the construction of a democratic regime. The significance of that missing piece may be made apparent in an indirect manner. In an earlier day public opinion seemed to be pictured as a mysterious vapor that emanated from the undifferentiated citizenry and in some way or another enveloped the apparatus of government to bring it into conformity with the public will. These weird conceptions, some of which were mentioned in our introductory chapter, passed out of style as the technique of the sample survey permitted the determination, with some accuracy, of the distribution of opinions within the population. Vast areas of ignorance remain in our information about people's opinions and aspirations; nevertheless, a far more revealing map of the gross topography of public opinion can now be drawn than could have been a quarter of a century ago.

Despite their power as instruments for the observation of mass opinion, sampling procedures do not bring within their range elements of the political system basic for the understanding of the role of mass opinion within the system. Repeatedly, as we have sought to explain particular distributions, movements, and qualities of mass opinion, we have had to go beyond the survey data and make assumptions and estimates about the role and behavior of that thin stratum of persons referred to variously as the political elite, the political activists, the leadership echelons, or the influentials. In the normal operation of surveys designed to obtain tests of mass sentiment, so few persons from this activist stratum fall into the sample that they cannot well be differentiated, even in a static description, from those persons less involved politically. The data tell us almost nothing about the dynamic relations between the upper layer of activists and mass opinion. The missing piece of our puzzle is this elite element of the opinion system. That these political influentials both affect mass opinion and are conditioned in their behavior by it is obvious. Yet systematic knowledge of the composition, distribution in the social structure, and patterns of behavior of this sector of the political system remains far from satisfactory.

The longer one frets with the puzzle of how democratic regimes manage to function, the more plausible it appears that a substantial part of the explanation is to be found in the motives that actuate the leadership echelon, the values that it holds, in the rules of the political game to which it adheres, in the expectations which it entertains about its own status in society, and perhaps in some of the objective circumstances, both material and institutional, in which it functions. Focus of attention on this sector of the opinion system contrasts with the more usual quest for the qualities of the people that may be thought to make democratic practices feasible. That focus does not deny the importance of mass attitudes. It rather emphasizes that the pieces of the puzzle are different in form and function, and that for the existence of a democratic opinion-oriented system each piece must possess the characteristics necessary for it to fit together with the others in a

working whole. The superimposition over a people habituated to tyranny of a leadership imbued with democratic ideals probably would not create a viable democratic order.

Values and Motives of the Activist Subculture

The traits and characteristics of political activists assume importance in the light of a theory about why the leadership and governing levels in any society behave as they do. That theory amounts to the proposition that these political actors constitute in effect a subculture with its own peculiar set of norms of behavior, motives, and approved standards. Processes of indoctrination internalize such norms among those who are born to or climb to positions of power and leadership; they serve as standards of action, which are reinforced by a social discipline among the political activists. In some regimes the standards of the ruling groups prescribe practices of firmness toward the governed who are regarded as menials with no rights; they deserve no more than the rough and arbitrary treatment they receive. The rules of the game may prescribe that the proper practice for rulers is to maximize their own advantage as well as the correlative deprivations of the ruled. The ignorant, the poor, and the incompetent may be seen as entitled to what they get, which is very little. Or the rules of the game of a regime may mitigate the harshness of these outlooks by a compassionate attitude toward the wretched masses who cannot help themselves. Hence, we may have little fathers of the people. The point is that the politically active classes may develop characteristic norms and practices that tend to guide their behavior. In a loose sense these may be the norms of a subculture, that of the specialists in politics and government. Beliefs generally accepted among these persons tend to establish habits and patterns of behavior with considerable power of self-maintenance or persistence through time.

While the ruling classes of a democratic order are in a way invisible because of the vagueness of the lines defining the influentials and the relative ease of entry to their ranks, it is plain that the modal norms and standards of a democratic elite have their peculiarities. Not all persons in leadership echelons have precisely the same basic beliefs; some may even regard the people as a beast. Yet a fairly high concentration prevails around the modal beliefs, even though the definition of those beliefs must be imprecise. Fundamental is a regard for public opinion, a belief that in some way or another it should prevail. Even those who cynically humbug the people make a great show of deference to the populace. The basic doctrine goes further to include a sense of trusteeship for the people generally and an adherence to the basic doctrine that collective efforts should be dedicated to the promotion of mass gains rather than of narrow class advantage; elite elements tethered to narrow group interest have no slack for maneuver to accommodate themselves to mass aspirations. Ultimate expression of these faiths comes in the willingness to abide by the outcome of popular elections. The growth of leadership structures with beliefs including these broad articles of faith is probably accomplished only over a considerable period of time, and then only under auspicious circumstances.

If an elite is not to monopolize power and thereby to bring an end to democratic practices, its rules of the game must include restraints in the exploitation of public opinion. Dimly perceptible are rules of etiquette that limit the kinds of appeals to public opinion that may be properly made. If it is assumed that the public is manipulable at the hands of unscrupulous leadership (as it is under some conditions), the maintenance of a democratic order requires the inculcation in leadership elements of a taboo against appeals

that would endanger the existence of democratic practices. Inflammation of the sentiments of a sector of the public disposed to exert the tyranny of an intolerant majority (or minority) would be a means of destruction of a democratic order. Or by the exploitation of latent differences and conflicts within the citizenry it may at times be possible to paralyze a regime as intense hatreds among classes of people come to dominate public affairs. Or by encouraging unrealistic expectations among the people a clique of politicians may rise to power, a position to be kept by repression as disillusionment sets in.[1] In an experienced democracy such tactics may be "unfair" competition among members of the politically active class. In short, certain restraints on political competition help keep competition within tolerable limits. The observation of a few American political campaigns might lead one to the conclusion that there are no restraints on politicians as they attempt to humbug the people. Even so, admonitions ever recur against arousing class against class, against stirring the animosities of religious groups, and against demagoguery in its more extreme forms. American politicians manifest considerable restraint in this regard when they are tested against the standards of behavior of politicians of most of those regimes that have failed in the attempt to establish or maintain democratic practices.

The norms of the practice of politics in an order that has regard for public opinion include broad rules of etiquette governing relations among the activists, as well as rules governing the relations of activists with the public. Those rules, in their fundamental effect, assure the existence of a minority among the political activists; if those who control government can suppress opposition activists, an instrument essential for the formation and

---

[1] The politicians of some of the new democracies have installed new regimes as they took the unfortunate step of arousing popular expectations beyond hope of early fulfillment.

expression of public opinion is destroyed. A body of customs that amounts to a policy of "live and let live" must prevail. In constitutional democracies some of these rules are crystallized into fundamental law in guarantees such as those of freedom of speech, freedom of press, and the right to appeal to the electorate for power. Relevant also are procedures for the protection of property rights; a political opposition may be destroyed by expropriation as well as by execution.[2] While such rules extend in their application to the entire population, one of their major functions is to prevent politicians from putting each other into jail or from destroying each other in the ordinary course of their competitive endeavors. All these elements of the rules of the game gain strength, not from their statement in the statutes and codes, but from their incorporation into the norms that guide the behavior of the political activists.[3]

Form and Structure

Certain broad structural or organizational characteristics may need to be maintained among the activists of a democratic order if they are to perform their functions in the system. Fundamental is the absence of sufficient cohesion among the activists to unite them into a single group dedicated to the management of public affairs and public opinion. Solidification of the elite by definition forecloses opportunity for public choice among alternative governing groups and also destroys the mechanism for the unfettered expression of public opinion or of the

opinions of the many subpublics. Maintenance of division and competition among political activists requires the kinds of etiquette that have been mentioned to govern their relations among themselves. Those rules, though, do not create the cleavages among the activists. Competitive segments of the leadership echelons normally have their roots in interests or opinion blocs within society. A degree of social diversity thus may be, if not a prerequisite, at least helpful in the construction of a leadership appropriate for a democratic regime. A series of independent social bases provide the foundations for a political elite difficult to bring to the state of unification that either prevents the rise of democratic processes or converts them into sham rituals.

At a more earthy level, maintenance of a multiplicity of centers of leadership and political activism requires arrangements by which men may gain a livelihood despite the fact that they are out of power. Consider the consequences for the structure of opinion leadership of a socioeconomic system in which those skilled in the arts of governance have open to them no way of obtaining a livelihood save by the exercise of those skills. In the United States the high incidence of lawyers among the politically influential provides a base of economic independence; the defeated politician can always find a few clients. Extensive reliance on part-time, amateur politicians in representative bodies and in many governing commissions has assured an economic cushion for many political activists. The custom of making many such offices economically unattractive has, in effect, required that they be filled by persons with an economic base independent of the public treasury. Opinion leaders and managers often find economic independence in posts with business associations and other voluntary societies. Communications enterprises, important in the operation of democracies, gain independence from government by their commercial position. The structure

---

[2]Rules against the use of public authority for the private advantage of officials also have their political bearing. Officials who build huge fortunes or enterprises by the abuse of official position can yield power only at enormous cost.

[3]Probably a critical stage in the evolution toward democracy occurs at the moment when those in authority conclude that their acceptance of the unfavorable outcome of an election would not result in grievous harm to them. Genetic analyses of democracies with a focus of attention on this point would be instructive.

of government itself, through its many independent units and agencies, assures havens of some security for spokesmen for a variety of viewpoints. All this may boil down to the contention that development and maintenance of the type of leadership essential for the operation of a democratic political order is facilitated by the existence of a social system of some complexity with many centers that have some autonomy and economic independence. Perhaps a safer formulation would be that societies that do not meet these requisites may encounter difficult problems in the support of a fractionalized stratum of political activists; they need to construct functional equivalents of the means we have been describing to assure the maintenance of competing centers of leadership.[4]

When viewed from another angle, these comments about the utility of independent foundations for competing sectors of the political elite relate to the more general proposition that regimes deferential to public opinion may best flourish when the deprivations contingent upon the loss of an election are limited. The structure of government itself may also contribute to that loss limitation. In federal regimes and in regimes with extensive devolution to elective local governmental authorities the prospect of loss of a national election may be faced with some equanimity, for the national minority may retain its position in many subordinate units of the nation and remain in a measure undisturbed by the alternations of control within the nation as a whole. The same function of loss limitation may be served by constitutional and customary expectations that limit the permissible range of governmental action.

Another characteristic may be mentioned as one that, if not a prerequisite to government by public opinion, may profoundly affect the nature of a democratic order. This is the distribution through

the social structure of those persons highly active in politics. By various analyses, none founded on completely satisfactory data, we have shown that in the United States the political activists— if we define the term broadly—are scattered through the socio-economic hierarchy. The upper-income and occupational groups, to be sure, contribute disproportionately; nevertheless, individuals of high political participation are sprinkled throughout the lesser occupational strata. Contrast the circumstances when the highly active political stratum coincides with the high socio-economic stratum. Conceivably the winning of consent and the creation of a sense of political participation and of sharing in public affairs may be far simpler when political activists of some degree are spread through all social strata. The alternative circumstance may induce an insensitivity to mass opinion, a special reliance on mass communications, and a sharpened sense of cleavage and separatism within the political order. The contention made here amounts to more than the axiom that democracies can exist only in societies that possess a well-developed middle class. In a modern industrial society with universal suffrage the chances are that a considerable sprinkling of political activists needs to exist in groups below the "middle class," however that term of vague referent may be defined. The correct general proposition may be that the operation of democratic processes may be facilitated by the distribution of persons participating in the order through all strata of the electorate. When the belief that democracy depended upon the middle class flourished, a comparatively narrow suffrage prevailed.

Allied with these questions is the matter of access to the wider circles of political leadership and of the recruitment and indoctrination of these political activists. Relative ease of access to the arena of active politics may be a preventive of the rise of intransigent blocs of opinion managed by those denied participation in

---

[4]Consider the problem of a regime that seeks to carry out economic development in large measure through governmental enterprise.

the regularized processes of politics. In a sense, ease of access is a necessary consequence of the existence of a somewhat fragmented stratum of political activists. Systems built on rigid class lines or on the dominance of clusters of families may be especially prone to the exclusion of those not to the proper status born—or married. Yet ease of access does not alone suffice. It must be accompanied by means, either deliberate or informal, for the indoctrination of those admitted in the special mores and customs of the activist elements of the polity. Otherwise, ease of access may only facilitate the depredations of those alienated from the values of the political order. By their nature democratic political systems have large opportunity—if there is the necessary will—to extend widely opportunities for political participation in lesser capacities and thereby to sift out those capable of achieving access to the more restricted circles of influentials. Whether the builders of political orders ever set about deliberately and systematically to tackle such problems of recruitment and indoctrination may be doubtful. Those problems may be solved, when they are solved, by the unconscious and unwilled processes of evolutionary adaptation of social systems.

This discussion in terms of leadership echelons, political activists, or elites falls painfully on the ears of democratic romantics. The mystique of democracy has in it no place for ruling classes. As perhaps with all powerful systems of faith, it is vague on the operating details. Yet by their nature governing systems, be they democratic or not, involve a division of social labor. Once that axiom is accepted, the comprehension of democratic practices requires a search for the peculiar characteristics of the political influentials in such an order, for the special conditions under which they work, and for the means by which the people keep them in check. The vagueness of the mystique of democracy is matched by the intricacy of its operating practices. If it is true that those

who rule tend sooner or later to prove themselves enemies of the rights of man—and there is something to be said for the validity of this proposition—then any system that restrains that tendency however slightly can excite only awe.

2 · MASS OPINION: VARIATIONS IN NATURE AND FUNCTION

The demarcation between the political activists and the "mass" must be regarded as a zone of gray rather than as a sharp line, but we may make a distinction between the two types of people with respect to their roles in a system in which public opinion conditions governmental action. The assumption of the preceding paragraphs has been that political activists must possess certain modal characteristics if a political system is to be a viable democracy. Without an imposing foundation of empirical data, an attempt was made to specify some of these characteristics of the activist stratum. Presumably the mass of the people must also possess attitudes and behavioral tendencies congenial to the necessities of a democratic order. That assumption involves us in a process of some circularity, for it has been repeatedly noted that the political activists may shape the opinions of the rest of the people. If the activists control, there is no need to consider mass opinion. Yet the remolding of popular attitudes is not the work of a day; they have a considerable viscosity. Hence, it is permissible to speak of the mass of the people as independent in their characteristics of the activist stratum and as one of the elements that combine with appropriate types of leadership behavior to create a functioning system. Specification of what modal qualities or attitudes should characterize the mass of the people if a society is to have a working democracy presents its difficulties. Although the survey data tell us a great deal about mass opinion, the available materials still leave wide gaps in the information relevant to the broad question that concerns us at the moment. Nevertheless, from what is known and surmised about mass opinion, we may grope toward an identification of those characteristics that may make it compatible with the practice of democracy.

Differentiations within the Public: Clues to Democratic Capabilities

Students of public opinion quickly learn that it is not illuminating to speak of "the public." In their biological characteristics men are animals of endless diversity; in their political behavior they may be equally varied. To bring that diversity within our comprehension, students of public opinion often attempt broad classifications of the citizenry. Thus, we have differentiations according to kinds of participation in political matters, ranging from the sector of the public with a continuing interest in public affairs and an inclination to write their congressman at the drop of a hat to those persons who pay virtually no attention to politics and rarely bother even to vote. The relevance of such categories at this point lies in the possibility that they may provide clues as we search for those qualities of outlook and behavior of the mass of the people or of large sectors of the public that are congenial to the workings of a democratic order—that help make possible the existence of a regime in which public opinion plays a role.

A recurring classification is that of the attentive public (or publics) and the inattentive public. So crude a statement conceals a variety in the objects as well as in the degrees of attention. Our data have identified, for example, variations in attention to presidential campaigns. Some people—nearly 10 per cent—do not follow even presidential campaigns through any of the media, while at the opposite end of the scale are others who follow the campaigns through all the media and entertain a deep concern about their outcome. Doubtless those who manifest high in-

terest in campaigns also maintain a continuing interest in the flow of action between campaigns. Their focus of attention on the stream of events certainly has its consequences at the next election, not only in their votes but in their influence on the less attentive to whom they communicate their views. Beyond this audience with its focus of attention on a range of political events generally, there exists a complex population of special publics whose attentions center more or less continuously on specific governmental agencies or fields of policy. We lack surveys to define the dimensions of these publics, the objects of their attention, or the extent to which they overlap. Nevertheless, some types of such publics can be indicated. The most obvious attentive publics consist of those with a direct concern in particular policies or actions. That concern may rest, though not necessarily, on an economic self-interest. In any case, these special publics extend considerably beyond the leaders and spokesmen of formalized organizations. For example, farmers make up an attentive public; to be sure, not all farmers earn a place in that public, but the better-informed and more alert of them center attention on farm policy and its administrators, and have their views both solicited and taken into account by officialdom. Or consider the old folks. With both the leisure and the motivation of interest, many of them have a familiarity with policies and practices with respect to benefits for the aged as well as an eager eye for helpful new proposals. Congressmen are likely to hear from them.

Veterans constitute another attentive public whose attention seems to be especially capable of producing a feedback into the halls of government. Another attentive public keeps a continuing watch over policy toward education; teachers' associations and PTA's are the more prominent spokesmen for this public, but many (sometimes, one suspects, too many) people consider themselves to be experts on education and do not hestitate to give confident vent to their assured views. One could identify for almost every governmental function comparable attentive publics varying both in size and in the intensity of their concern. Not all such publics are motivated by a direct self-interest. Consider the public attentive to foreign policy. Sprinkled over the land are societies, associations, circles, and study groups whose members give attention to international affairs, entertain visiting ambassadors, advise both the government and their fellow citizens on recondite issues of foreign policy, and look down generally on those clods among their fellow men who do not pay heed to the really important questions of this world.

Another type of attentive public, probably of special influence, consists of professional groups. Professions develop their own codes of ethics as well as their standards of practice. Members of the professions who deviate from the norms of their group may be cold-shouldered by their brethren and under some circumstances even deprived of the right to earn a livelihood by the practice of their trade. Members of the professions who occupy official positions carry on their functions under the scrutiny of the nongovernmental members of the profession and are thus subjected to the gaze of an attentive public equipped with standards of appraisal of some precision. Consider the relations between the bench and the bar. Judges may have the last word with attorneys who practice before them, but they are not unmindful of the expectations of the bar generally. Their work is open to the criticism of their professional peers. Engineers are equipped with greater technical precision than lawyers but with a less compelling system of professional ethics. Nevertheless, engineers in public posts, when they botch a job, incur the disapproval of the attentive public of engineers. Medical men in public posts are not beyond the pull of their professional norms even as they develop public policy on medical care. Among persons engaged in general

administration professional norms seem to be in the process of development, and these group standards emerge from an attentive public which is largely, but not entirely, intragovernmental.[5]

This kind of differentiation between the attentive and nonattentive public is a commonplace of speculation about the place of the citizen in a democracy. It is often accompanied by attempts to estimate the proportions of the public that share varying degrees and kinds of attentiveness, estimates often unsupported by the data of observation. But surely the highly attentive and active public of which we have been speaking constitutes normally no more than 10 to 15 per cent of the adult population, although at times of crisis far higher proportions may focus their attention on particular actions of government.

The reason, though, for the introduction here of the question of political differentiations among people was the hope that it might suggest popular characteristics conducive to, if not essential for, the existence of democratic practices. Obviously the highly attentive publics, as they monitor the actions of government and let their judgments be known, play a critical role in assuring a degree of responsiveness of government to nongovernmental opinion. For these publics to perform that function, though, an understanding and acceptance of their role must prevail among many people. The belief must exist that it is the public's business to engage in such activities of surveillance and criticism of government. Societies have existed and do exist in which there is a radically different role system; it may

<hr />

[5] An interesting question relevant to the relation of attentive publics and government is the effect of the competition of different areas of public activity for attention. For example, some of the troubles of urban government may come from the fact that the more dramatic activities of the federal government divert to it the attention of those persons who might, under other conditions, constitute the watchful audience for the conductors of municipal affairs.

be improper for private persons to concern themselves with the business of officials. For lack of adequate comparative data, it is difficult to make vivid the significance of behaviors we regard as commonplace.[6] It is sufficient to note that there is nothing in human nature to assure that the attentive publics will act as they do. Development of understandings of roles and of appropriate behaviors among large numbers of people requires considerable time and a good deal of trial and error; this is one reason why democracies are not created by decree but, rather, evolve.[7]

Attentiveness with its correlative behaviors will wane unless it is associated with a belief that watchfulness and articulateness ultimately have some bearing on what government does or does not do. That belief can be engendered only if it has some foundation in reality. In turn, that reality depends upon the outlooks of those persons who constitute the highly activist element—the officials, the occupants of points of nongovernmental power, the persons who may next occupy points of private and public power. That is, each of the elements of the political system must have characteristics that make it possible for them to fit together. Thus, democratic politicians defer to expressions of opinion. They listen with patience to the crackpot and even maintain their composure in the face of unfair and uninformed criticism—especially when it comes from an influential constituent. In all this there is a core of genuine concern about public opinion even though imprac-

ticable and intemperate expressions of opinion may be greeted with a ceremonial courtesy devoid of substantive deference. All these observations may amount to is the contention that if a democracy is to exist, the belief must be widespread that public opinion, at least in the long run, affects the course of public action. In a technical sense that belief may be a myth, an article of faith, yet its maintenance requires that it possess a degree of validity. It seems even that those critics who most successfully perpetuate their myths are those who can turn up a miracle for their communicants now and then.

Political involvement is another type of differentiation among the citizenry that may provide clues to those characteristics of people which are congenial to the workings of a democracy. Variations in the degree of psychological "care" and "interest" in campaigns have served as a crude but useful index for many of our analyses. Almost by definition there must exist a fairly widespread psychological involvement in political affairs if a society is to operate by democratic procedures. Involvement probably carries with it at least a degree of attention to political affairs. Yet as we move from the most highly attentive and most highly involved sector of society, involvement may take on rather special dimensions. A substantial proportion of the citizenry may not belong to the highly attentive sector of the public of which we have spoken but may pay a routine heed to politics, may "care" about how elections come out, and may have an "interest" in campaigns. This involvement tends to carry with it some sense of sharing in the political process, some belief that participation makes a difference, some faith in the reality of the dogmas of democracy. Yet the activities associated with this sense of involvement are of a different order from those of the highly attentive publics whose members may be especially well informed and fairly closely in touch with political processes.

---

[6]Probably what all this boils down to is that in a democratic order the indignant private citizen regards it as proper to raise a popular commotion. When he does so, he acts with the expectation that he will not be jailed, but that he will be heard with courtesy and that his views may have some effect.

[7]One way in which the understandings and behaviors appropriate for national democracies may develop is through widespread participation in the relatively simple affairs of local government.

The psychological involvement of a substantial sector of the populace represents, of course, an acquired cultural characteristic. It takes some learning and habituation for a people to acquire a sense of participation, a sense of sharing in a political order.[8] Yet this sense of involvement may be of prime significance. It is basic for any popular participation in governmental processes. Beyond this, the sense of involvement may be a fundamental means by which discontents and ambitions and desires are steered into constitutional channels. Earlier we identified even in the American system blocs of opinion of high intensity that were associated with low involvement, with a low sense of political efficacy, and with low levels of political participation. Groups of persons not involved in democratic processes but possessed of intense discontents may occur in any order. The practical question is how large such blocs of sentiment need to be and what circumstances need to exist for them to become destructive of the normal democratic processes.[9]

Loyalties, Orientations, Expectations

In the division of labor in a democratic order the highly attentive publics, a comparatively small sector of the whole, need to develop an understanding of their special role in the workings of the system. Other kinds of understandings and outlooks, which may be associated with con-

siderably less in the way of overt participation, must permeate most of the population. To specify those understandings and outlooks requires that we grope beyond data that can be neatly set forth in demonstrative tables.

A basic prerequisite is that the population be pervaded by a national loyalty. Or, perhaps more accurately, that the population not consist of segments each with its own sense of separateness. The condition is best illustrated by synthetic nations consisting of blocs with their own history, language, culture, and memories of, if not aspirations for, a separate national identity. Students of public opinion long ago noted the incompatibility of these circumstances with democratic processes. That incompatibility comes not so much from the psychological characteristics of the mass of the people as from the fact that those characteristics invite exploitation by elements of leadership. Reckless leaders can disrupt the processes of government by diversionary appeals that weaken or destroy the foundations of national unity. Regimes with tight discipline in the ranks of political leadership—dictatorships, semidictatorships, monarchies—can restrain those who would activate the latent or not so latent divisive animosities of the mass of people. Democratic elites ordinarily have less capacity to restrain their irresponsible elements. Hence, mass attitudes that yield readily to divisive appeals create special difficulties for democratic orders.[10]

Closely related to this acceptance of the regime is what might be called a sense of the collectivity or of the community. Probably for the existence of an order

---

[8]Hence, one may express pessimism about the outcome when a society that is attempting to move almost from the Stone Age to the Atomic Age overnight immediately franchises all its people. None of the more mature democracies acquired the habit patterns of democratic governance at so rapid a rate.

[9]For a sense of political involvement to be widespread within the population, the conditions of life must be such that the struggle for subsistence does not monopolize the efforts of most men. In a random sample of the American population a few respondents are found whose struggle for the bare necessities of life so occupy their time and energy that their political involvement is at a zero level.

[10]Federal regimes may, to some extent, overcome the difficulties of cultural diversity but even so a price must be paid. Thus, the Canadian system, as it took form under the protection of the British Crown, developed a political elite with norms appropriate to the mixed culture of the Commonwealth. Yet the cost of unity includes both constitutional and customary restraints on governmental action.

deferential to public opinion the mass of people must share some sense of the legitimacy of the collectivity, in contrast with a situation in which large sectors of the population have no sense of a community of interest but center their attachments upon group, class, or even upon some smaller subnational entity. Perhaps a shadow of this sentiment of commonality was captured by the survey questions analyzed earlier about the influence on government of big business and trade unions. People of all occupational and income levels tended to think that both these interests should be kept in their place, that each should have its say but neither should have too much power. The view among the articulate seemed to be that some greater common interest should prevail. The same sense of the collectivity may manifest itself when people say that they have "something in common" with their fellow citizens of other social classes. It appears again on policy question after policy question as people of all sorts share attitudes on issues that might be expected, on a simple calculus of self-interest, to draw sharp class cleavages.

The bearing of this sense of community or of commonality upon democratic processes can best be surmised by estimates of what occurs when it is absent. If mass attachments are to subdivisions of the nation and if elements of the leadership both exploit those attachments and become anchored to them, the basis exists for national paralysis, since there is no freedom for a quest for common interest.[11] Sooner or later people, or some of them, may weary of the democratic game and resort

to nondemocratic steps to attain their ends.

How people acquire this sense of political community is not clear. Doubtless, as with all basic social outlooks, the development of these attitudes is the product of a prolonged process. While all the apparatus of civic education plays a part, the sense of community must also be in part a product of public policy; that is, without appropriate practices in leadership echelons to give it a basis in reality the sense of community may languish.

These observations resemble the proposition that a consensus needs to prevail for democracy to exist; yet they should not be taken as the equivalent of that proposition. Perhaps among the upper-activist stratum a consensus does need to prevail on the technical rules of the game by which the system operates. What kind of consensus, if any, extends throughout the population beyond a general acceptance of the regime remains problematic. In the main, the notion of consensus has sprung from the inventive minds of theorists untainted by acquaintance with mass attitudes. Knowledge of the relevant mass attitudes is slight, but such as it is it does not give much comfort to those who suppose that most people carry around in their heads the elements of democratic theory even in the most attenuated form. Nevertheless, the mass may possess outlooks that permit the regime to function as if a consensus prevailed, though precisely what those outlooks are is another question.

Another psychological characteristic of the mass of people that probably bears upon the workability of democratic processes relates to popular expectations. We may differentiate level and focus of expectations. Some optimum level of expectation may render a populace susceptible to the wiles of the high bidder whose unrealistic promises may sweep him to power and bring only disillusionment to the people. Governmental instability may develop as the bids are raised and one set

---

[11] In the preceding chapters demonstrations recur of the incohesiveness of subnational interests on the American scene. Social researchers give great emphasis to manifestations of solidarity of subsectors of the nation, but the fact of greater import for the nature of the political system is the relative weakness of such solidarity. Group cohesiveness, always something less than complete, waxes and wanes as considerations transcending group concerns assume greater or lesser salience.

of rulers replaces another. At the other pole, an extremely low level of expectation may be a reflection of mass cynicism and alienation from democratic processes. Doubtless, a good deal of experience and political indoctrination must go into the formation of mass attitudes characterized by the appropriate mixture of realism and optimism, of patience and eagerness. Good faith on the part of the leadership echelons is essential for this state of mind to exist in the mass of people; there also must be sprinkled through the population a substantial number of persons with sufficient understanding of the limitations and possibilities of politically induced social change to generate an optimum level of expectation in the mass.[12]

The question of the focus of mass expectations raises a problem different from that of their level. People's expectations may center on political or nonpolitical sources of fulfillment. Since one set of expectations tends to be fulfilled (except in a rapidly expanding economy) at the expense of others, it might plausibly be expected that a sustained high level of expectation associated with a focus upon government for fulfillment would tend to generate high stresses within a society.[13] On the contrary, with the focus of expec-

tations diffused—upon the self, upon the family, upon business corporations, upon trade unions, and upon other nonpolitical institutions—the stakes of the political game might be expected to be more readily kept within those limits that make defeat tolerable. This is, in effect, a translation of the hackneyed question of whether democracy is feasible only under some variant of capitalism. When government decree controls almost completely the allocation of the social product as well as the assignment of resources, human and material, to productive tasks, the stakes of politics become enormous indeed. The easy answer to the problem is that mass tensions that could be stirred over such questions by competing factions of the political elite make it impossible for the struggle to be contained within the bounds of the easy give-and-take of democratic processes. The correct answer, though, may be that under the conditions described the development of democratic practices requires the creation of rules of the game among the political activists together with expectations among the masses of the people appropriate to the special requirements of a socialist economy. Though such an evolution of behavioral patterns would have to surmount formidable obstacles, the possibility of its occurrence should not be excluded, for political man is a malleable creature.[14]

3 · INTERACTION AND DISCRETION

Analytically it is useful to conceive of the structure of a democratic order as consisting of the political activists and the mass of people. Yet this differentiation

---

[12]The reader has doubtless observed that in these characterizations of mass prerequisites for democratic processes we have moved far away from hard data. The kinds of problems of which we speak have not been explored by the use of sample surveys which have centered mostly on more manageable problems such as the explanation of voting behavior. Yet it seems clear that appropriate use of survey procedures could bring far more understanding of mass political attitudes than we have.

[13]Democratic politicians, though, are skilled in the contrivance of formal actions that fulfill expectations at a verbal level but are cushioned in the reality of their application. Thus, though the American progressive income tax in form heavily taxes the rich, in fact the statutes are such that most men of wealth, with the advice of a competent tax lawyer, can greatly mitigate the impact of the high rates in the upper brackets. See Murray Edelman, "Symbols and Political Quiescence," *American Political Science Review*, LIV (1960), 695–704.

[14]The problem mentioned in the text is not hypothetical but a pressing reality in young and underdeveloped countries with democratic aspirations. If our broad analysis of the conditions requisite for the rise of democratic practice has validity, these nations, as they attempt to install such practices, work under the most unfavorable circumstances. Whatever evolves will probably diverge markedly from the patterns of the mature Western democracies.

becomes deceptive unless it is kept in mind that the democratic activists consist of people arranged along a spectrum of political participation and involvement, ranging from those in the highest posts of official leadership to the amateurs who become sufficiently interested to try to round up a few votes for their favorite in the presidential campaign. In the preceding discussion we sought to isolate some of the characteristics of both activists and mass that appear to be compatible with, if not essential for, the operation of a democratic order, thus setting up a static picture of two broad political strata. It is in the dynamics of the system, the interactions between these strata, that the import of public opinion in democratic orders becomes manifest. Between the activists and the mass there exists a system of communication and interplay so complex as to defy simple description; yet identification of a few major features of that system may aid in our construction of a general conception of democratic processes.

Opinion Dikes

In the interactions between democratic leadership echelons and the mass of people some insight comes from the conception of public opinion as a system of dikes which channel public action or which fix a range of discretion within which government may act or within which debate at official levels may proceed. This conception avoids the error by personifying "public opinion" as an entity that exercises initiative and in some way functions as an operating organism to translate its purposes into governmental action.

In one of their aspects the dikes of opinion have a substantive nature in that they define areas within which day-to-day debate about the course of specific action may occur. Some types of legislative proposals, given the content of general opinion, can scarcely expect to attract serious attention. They depart too far from the

general understandings of what is proper. A scheme for public ownership of the automobile industry, for example, would probably be regarded as so far outside the area of legitimate public action that not even the industry would become greatly concerned. On the other hand, other types of questions arise within areas of what we have called permissive consensus. A widespread, if not a unanimous, sentiment prevails that supports action toward some general objective, such as the care of the ill or the mitigation of the economic hazards of the individual. Probably quite commonly mass opinion of a permissive character tends to develop in advance of governmental action in many areas of domestic policy. That opinion grows out of public discussion against the background of the modal aspirations and values of people generally. As it takes shape, the time becomes ripe for action that will be generally acceptable or may even arouse popular acclaim for its authors.

The qualities of this substantive opinion doubtless differ widely from issue to issue and from person to person. On some issues opinion may be oriented favorably toward broadly defined objectives; on others, perhaps extremely few, opinion may become focused on sharply defined proposals. On any issue the more alert and informed persons may have fairly well-formed opinions about sharply defined issues; others may have broad preferences —for example, something ought to be done for the farmers but not too much.

Opinion dikes may bear on the manner as well as on the substance of action. And it may be that in a democratic order those opinions that control or guide the mode of action may be of special importance as substantive action moves into areas where it encounters formidable opposition. Action taken in a seemingly fair and equitable manner may be acceptable, but arbitrary action to the same effect may be regarded as intolerable. The procedural content of American public opinion has been little explored. The division of opinion and the spontaneous comment on the proposition that government employees accused of communism ought to be fired even though the charge is not proved suggest that notions of fair play may be widely held within the population. Doubtless other procedural notions have wide popular acceptance that could be demonstrated by survey methods.

The idea of public opinion as forming a system of dikes which channel action yields a different conception of the place of public opinion than does the notion of a government by public opinion as one in which by some mysterious means a referendum occurs on every major issue. In the former conception the articulation between government and opinion is relatively loose. Parallelism between action and opinion tends not to be precise in matters of detail; it prevails rather with respect to broad purpose. And in the correlation of purpose and action time lags may occur between the crystallization of a sense of mass purpose and its fulfillment in public action. Yet in the long run majority purpose and public action tend to be brought into harmony.

Modifications of the Opinion Context

The content of mass opinion changes through time; it is perhaps in such alterations that the power of mass opinion is made manifest. Though changes in opinion content occur continuously, at some moments combinations of events, imaginative leadership, and action induce relatively rapid and marked changes in popular preferences and expectations. These episodes may bring new opinion orientations, which in turn become rather rigid elements of the pattern of popular attitudes.

The movement of opinions and the expectations that accompanied the fulfillment of the program of the New Deal illustrate well the process of change and its consequences for governmental action.

A spirited leadership with programs of action deviating markedly from past practice won approval and generated a new set of popular expectations about governmental action. The "power" of public opinion manifested itself in a negative way. Those candidates and leaders tainted with the suspicion that they wanted to turn the clock back had hard sledding for years. Until they could make a show of acceptance of changes they could not capture control of the government. Thus, through elections opinion ratified past reforms by its rejection of those who appeared to be at odds with the new balance of public sentiment.

Similarly, in the area of foreign policy World War II brought with it a reorientation of the context of public opinion, which became more supportive of involvement in international politics. Probably the body of popular opinion in this area has a less solid base and a less constricting effect upon public action than does opinion on domestic welfare policy. The radically changed position of the United States in world affairs creates new problems not only for a government that rests on public opinion, but also for those who seek to inform and to lead that opinion. The conduct of domestic debates over foreign policy carries hazards for external policy. On the other hand, repression of debate results in a failure to inform the people of incompetence in the conduct of foreign affairs.[15]

Mass opinions, aspirations, and expecta-

---

[15]The dilemma which the circumstances of a garrison state creates for democracies leads some American scholars to advocate fundamental reconstruction of the structure of government. The fixed term of the president makes it impossible for a bumbling administration to be thrown out of power until the date for the next presidential election rolls around. The limitations on debate and discussion imposed by the necessities of external unity and by diplomatic secrecy make it difficult adequately to inform the electorate. The remedy urged by some scholars is some variant of the cabinet system by which Congress, a body better informed than the electorate, could cast out an incompetent administration.

tions change as the political system moves through time. It is in this moving situation that the power of mass opinion makes itself manifest in its interactions with democratic leadership, chiefly in its rejection of leadership factions whose outlook lags notably behind or strikes out markedly ahead of the moving average of opinion. Those who wish to turn the clock back, to reverse decisions already rooted in popular acceptance, gradually learn their lesson as they meet rebuff after rebuff. Those too far ahead of opinion, though they may contribute to the forces impelling alteration of the opinion context, likewise find themselves rejected. Deviants from dominant opinion, though, play a critical role in the preservation of the vitality of a democratic order as they urge alterations and modifications better to achieve the aspirations of men. Hence the fundamental significance of freedom of speech and agitation. Those activists closest to the core of power may hesitate to assume the risks of political entrepreneurship, but others, with less to lose, may by their efforts gradually make the endeavor that is not "practical politics" today feasible tomorrow.

Opinion Context and Governmental Discretion

This discussion of the anchorage of leadership to public opinion should not be taken to mean that wide ranges of discretion do not exist within which a creative role may be played by popular leadership. Glum political philosophers meditate in their melancholy fashion about how the pursuit of the good of the Republic is frustrated as the mass pulls superior men down to its own mean and grasping material level. The long-run good of the polity, the argument goes, must be neglected as leadership is compelled to cater to the greed and to the ignorance of the masses. Measures that obviously promote the greater public good cannot be undertaken because of mass opposition and misunderstanding.

That at times mass opinion may handicap desirable action cannot be denied. Yet as one puzzles over the nature of interactions between government and mass opinion and ponders such empirical data as can be assembled on the matter, he can arrive only at the conclusion that a wide range of discretion exists for whatever wisdom leadership echelons can muster in the public service. The generality of public preferences, the low intensity of the opinions of many people, the low level of political animosities of substantial sectors of the public, the tortuousness of the process of translation of disapproval of specific policies into electoral reprisal, and many other factors point to the existence of a wide latitude for the exercise of creative leadership. While the winning of consent for innovation may require skill in popular exposition and in political technique, those political leaders who shirk the task of popular education are misfits who do not understand the responsibilities of their jobs. And those leaders who act as if they thought the people to be fools responsive only to the meanest appeals deserve only scorn.

The Basic Weapon of Public Opinion

These concluding observations about the interaction of the activists and the mass take on an ethereal tenor, and they should be tied to their referent in institutional reality, which is the party system. In the give-and-take between the leadership echelons, with their intense policy drives and attachments, and the mass of people, the ultimate weapon of public opinion is the minority party. The effect of opinion on the grand course of public opinion depends on the existence of a crowd of outs who can be elevated to power—and the capacity to boot the ins from office. The mechanism is cumbersome and produces no minute fit of public preference and public policy. At times the remedy to the public becomes effective only over the long run, for the outs may offer no alternative congruent with the dissatisfactions against the ins. Yet the party system introduces the possibility of a fluidity in the political order to offset the policy myopia of governments long secure in their position. Parodoxically the party system may also introduce a saving degree of stability into orders dependent upon public opinion. It creates among many people loyalties that transcend and neutralize the vagaries of the opinion of the moment. It introduces traditional and stable policy outlooks with strength but susceptible of modification as they are abraded by their moving contact with the future. It provides ways and means of recruitment of leadership and for its indoctrination with the basic values and working habits of the political order.

Inevitability of the Decay of Democracies?

Our exposition of the interactions between leadership and mass opinion enables us better to understand the argument that democracies, by their inner logic, tend toward decay. That in the long sweep of time all regimes tend toward decay is a proposition at least not negated by the annals of recorded history. Yet the contention, advanced by respectable authorities, is that democracies possess within themselves defects that inevitably lead to their decay in a manner peculiar to democracies.

The fatal weakness of modern mass democracies, so the argument goes, rests in the subjection of government to a public opinion whose mandates are certain to be destructive of the order. Implicit in that proposition is the assumption that mass opinion in the long run tends toward positions incompatible with the demands of the health of the order and that mass opinion tends to pull governments into harmony with those positions. Thus, we have the picture of a mass opinion animated by greed and by a disregard for

the rights of man. Politicians must, the conclusion is, sooner or later adopt that view and in the process ultimately create a dictatorship of a majority dedicated to the reduction of all men to a drab equality, an action to be maintained only by a destruction of freedom. Or the argument is that governments accountable to democratic masses invariably tend to take the easy route, to dodge the hard decisions, to avoid at moments of crisis demands for the sacrifices by the populace necessary for the maintenance of the system. Governments, by their subjection to mass opinion, lose decisiveness and are bereft of the will to act, a condition creative of special dangers for the democracy that exists in a hostile international environment. All these consequences flow inevitably from the interaction between leadership and mass opinion as cliques of leaders seek power and, in so doing, are compelled to appeal to mass opinions that contain within themselves the seeds of national destruction. By a kind of Gresham's law, those leadership cliques with a wisdom greater than that of mass opinion either perish or embrace the follies of the mass.[16]

What can we say about this melancholy hypothesis? For a certainty, there are democracies and democracies. Perhaps in some situations the hypothesis fits the facts, but our analyses of the American scene caution us against easy acceptance of so glib a theory of the dynamics of democratic self-destruction. We have pictured public opinion as the product of an interaction between political influentials and the mass of the people, an interaction that may produce alterations in mass opinion. In the course of time that interaction

---

[16]An argument to the effect of this paragraph but in a far more sophisticated form is put in Walter Lippmann, *The Public Philosophy* (Boston: Little, Brown, 1955), especially chs. 3–5. See the perceptive comment on Lippmann's analysis in David B. Truman, "The American System in Crisis," *Political Science Quarterly*, LXXIV (1959), 481–97.

may also alter the modal position of the influentials as a novel doctrine asserted by one sector of the influentials gains acceptance among the masses. Mass opinion is not self-generating; in the main, it is a response to the cues, the proposals, and the visions propogated by the political activists.

If this conception of the formation of opinion has validity, democracies decay, if they do, not because of the cupidity of the masses, but because of the stupidity and self-seeking of leadership echelons. Politicians often make of the public a scapegoat for their own shortcomings; their actions, they say, are a necessity for survival given the state of public opinion. Yet that opinion itself results from the preachings of the influentials, of this generation and of several past generations.

Moreover, even if mass opinion assumes forms incompatible with the national interest, the articulation between government and mass opinion is so loose that politicians enjoy a considerable range of discretion within which to exercise prudence and good sense. Our explorations into the nature and form of mass opinion leave no doubt that its directives tend toward generality rather than specificity. Even on broad issues on which opinion becomes fairly well crystallized room may remain for choice among a variety of specific actions. Furthermore, translation of opinion into actions of electoral punishment or reward is a tortuous and uncertain procedure. The predictability of electoral response to a particular action remains so uncertain that the avoidance of a sensible decision because it will lose votes is usually the work of a man whose anxieties outweigh his capacities of prediction.

The argument amounts essentially to the position that the masses do not corrupt themselves; if they are corrupt, they have been corrupted. If this hypothesis has a substantial strain of validity, the critical element for the health of a democratic order consists in the beliefs, standards, and competence of those who constitute the influentials, the opinion-leaders, the political activists in the order. That group, as has been made plain, refuses to define itself with great clarity in the American system; yet analysis after analysis points to its existence. If a democracy tends toward indecision, decay, and disaster, the responsibility rests here, not in the mass of the people.[17]

_____

[17]This analysis and its implications should be pondered well by those young gentlemen in whose education the Republic has invested considerable sums.

SECTION V

The Belief-Sharing or Consensus Model

So long as leaders are not treated from their early childhood as a class apart, they will share life experiences and be exposed to a culture similar to that of other men. To the degree that experiences are common and values and beliefs are taught to all, leaders will share with their fellowmen the goals, values, and beliefs of the society; an unbiased selection of leaders will result in their being not unlike the society they lead. Neither process operates perfectly in the American society, since consensus is absent on many issues, such as the war in Vietnam, and a disproportionate number of leaders are born with "a silver spoon in their mouths." But how correctly do leaders' personal opinions reflect the opinions of the public? The selections in this section present the first attempts to assess the sharing of beliefs between the leaders and those they lead.

Americans vary greatly in their interest in politics and in the extensiveness of their information about governmental decisions. As I have commented earlier, most have only a marginal interest in politics and little information; but there is an activist minority. Philip Converse finds that while it is useful to speak of this activist minority as having liberal or conservative beliefs, the general public's beliefs lack any such underlying consistency; in fact he finds that on many issues their opinions seem chosen at random. This undoubtedly reflects the average man's disinterest in politics; perhaps a disturbing finding, but it should not be taken to mean that the public has no opinions important to themselves or their leaders. However, it does serve as a warning to not expect from the public those characteristics that are common among activists.

Samuel Patterson reviews the research literature on the concept of political culture. One important element of this culture is shared beliefs, and contrary to what might be expected from Converse's analysis, Patterson finds much to suggest that individuals within different regions of the United States share opinions and attitudes. But do the leaders reflect such subcultures?

The three selections by Herbert McClosky et al., Edmond Constantini, and Samuel Eldersveld might well have been included among the selections for the political parties model because they deal with attitude differences between activists in American political parties and the rank-and-file voters. But the findings are at least suggestive of what might be discovered in studying governmental leaders and their constituencies. While McClosky and his associates find both parties' leaders to be more ideological than their public supporters, a conclusion quite consistent with Converse's theory, Constantini shows that it is the party's young firebrands who are fervently ideological, not the responsible higher level leaders. Eldersveld explores other factors that affect differences of opinion among leaders and followers. But do the actual decision makers of a society share opinions with the masses?

In a study of two communities, Luttbeg finds public leaders consistently more favorable than the publics on pertinent issues in those communities. But these biases are not necessarily the result of leaders who are from a more affluent, better educated class of people. He states that it is inadequate to conclude that leaders do not reflect public opinion because they are better educated and have higher incomes.

Finally Herbert McClosky assesses the presence of an American consensus. Although he is dealing with acceptance of basic democratic and constitutional values that the democracy's stability supposedly depends on, he supports Converse's theory in that only leaders show consistent beliefs.

Certainly these few assessments deny the complete congruency between leaders' and the public's beliefs, but it is also obvious that there is substantial sharing. Futhermore the nature of leaders' bias is unclear. Do they reflect greater thought and consistency, greater intensity, or the opinions of the wealthy? This model needs a great deal more research.

THE NATURE OF BELIEF SYSTEMS IN MASS PUBLICS*

Philip E. Converse

Belief systems have never surrendered easily to empirical study or quantification. Indeed, they have often served as primary exhibits for the doctrine that what is important to study cannot be measured and that what can be measured is not important to study. In an earlier period, the behaviorist decree that subjective states lie beyond the realm of proper measurement gave Mannheim a justification for turning his back on measurement, for he had an unqualified interest in discussing belief systems.[1] Even as Mannheim was writing,

however, behaviorism was undergoing stiff challenges, and early studies of attitudes were attaining a degree of measurement reliability that had been deemed impossible. This fragment of history, along with many others, serves to remind us that no intellectual position is likely to become obsolete quite so rapidly as one that takes current empirical capability as the limit of the possible in a more absolute sense. Nevertheless, while rapid strides in the measurement of "subjective states" have been achieved in recent decades, few would claim that the millennium has arrived or that Mannheim could now find all of the tools that were lacking to him forty years ago.

This article makes no pretense of surpassing such limitations. At the same time,

*This abridged selection is reprinted with permission of The Macmillan Company from *Ideology and Discontent* by David Apter. Copyright © The Free Press of Glencoe, a division of The Macmillan Company, 1964.

[1] Karl Mannheim, *Ideology and Utopia* (New York, 1946), especially pp. 39ff.

our substantive concern forces upon us an unusual concern with measurement strategies, not simply because we propose to deal with belief systems or ideologies, but also because of the specific questions that we shall raise about them. Our focus in this article is upon differences in the nature of belief systems held on the one hand by elite political actors and, on the other, by the masses that appear to be "numbered" within the spheres of influence of these belief systems. It is our thesis that there are important and predictable differences in ideational worlds as we progress downward through such "belief strata" and that these differences, while obvious at one level, are easily overlooked and not infrequently miscalculated. The fact that these ideational worlds differ in character poses problems of adequate representation and measurement.

The vertical ordering of actors and beliefs that we wish to plumb bears some loose resemblance to the vertical line that might be pursued downward through an organization or political movement from the narrow cone of top leadership, through increasing numbers of subordinate officials, and on through untitled activists to the large base formally represented in membership rolls. It is this large base that Michels noted, from observations of political gatherings, was rarely "there," and analogues to its physical absence do not arise accidentally in dealing with belief systems. On the other hand, there is no perfect or necessary "fit" between the two orderings, and this fact in itself has some interest.

That we intend to consider the total mass of people "numbered" within the spheres of influence of belief systems suggests both a democratic bias and a possible confusion between numbers and power or between numbers and the outcomes of events that power determines. We are aware that attention to numbers, more or less customary in democratic thought, is very nearly irrelevant in many

political settings. Generally, the logic of numbers collides head on with the logic of power, as the traditional power pyramid, expressing an inverse relation between power and numbers, communicates so well. "Power" and "numbers" intersect at only one notable point, and that point is represented by the familiar axiom that numbers are one resource of power. The weight of this resource varies in a systematic and obvious way according to the political context. In a frankly designed and stable obligarchy, it is assumed to have no weight at all. In such a setting, the numbers of people associated with particular belief systems, if known at all, becomes important only in periods of crisis or challenge to the existing power structure. Democratic theory greatly increases the weight accorded to numbers in the daily power calculus. This increase still does not mean that numbers are of overriding importance; in the normal course of events it is the *perception* of numbers by democratic elites, so far as they differ from "actual" numbers, that is the more important factor. However this may be, claims to numbers are of some modest continuing importance in democratic systems for the legitimacy they confer upon demands; and, much more sporadically, claims to numbers become important in nondemocratic systems as threats of potential coercion.

I. SOME CLARIFICATION OF TERMS

A term like "ideology" has been thoroughly muddied by diverse uses.[2] We shall depend instead upon the term "belief system," although there is an obvious overlap between the two. We define a *belief system* as a configuration of ideas and attitudes in which the elements are bound together by some form of con-

[2]Minar has compiled a useful if discouraging survey of this diversity. See David W. Minar, "Ideology and Political Behavior," *Midwest Journal of Political Science*, 5 (November 1961), No. 4, 317–31.

straint or functional interdependence.[3] In the static case, "constraint" may be taken to mean the success we would have in predicting, given initial knowledge that an individual holds a specified attitude, that he holds certain further ideas and attitudes. We depend implicitly upon such notions of constraint in judging, for example, that, if a person is opposed to the expansion of social security, he is probably a conservative and is probably opposed as well to any nationalization of private industries, federal aid to education, sharply progressive income taxation, and so forth. Most discussions of ideologies make relatively elaborate assumptions about such constraints. Constraint must be treated, of course, as a matter of degree, and this degree can be measured quite readily, at least as an average among individuals.[4]

In the dynamic case, "constraint" or "interdependence" refers to the probability that a change in the perceived status (truth, desirability, and so forth) of one idea-element would *psychologically* require, from the point of view of the actor, some compensating change(s) in the status of idea-elements elsewhere in the configuration. The most obvious form of such constraint (although in some ways the most trivial) is exemplified by a structure of propositions in logic, in which a change in the truth-value of one proposition necessitates changes in truth-value elsewhere within the set of related propositions. Psychologically, of course, there may be equally strong constraint among idea-elements that would be apparent to

logical analysis at all, as we shall see.

We might characterize either the idea-elements themselves or entire belief systems in terms of many other dimensions. Only two will interest us here. First, the idea-elements within a belief system vary in a property we shall call *centrality*, according to the role that they play in the belief system as a whole. That is, when new information changes the status of one idea-element in a belief system, by postulate some other change must occur as well. There are usually, however, several possible changes in status elsewhere in the system, any one of which would compensate for the initial change. Let us imagine, for example, that a person strongly favors a particular policy; is very favorably inclined toward a given political party; and recognizes with gratification that the party's stand and his own are congruent. (If he were unaware of the party's stand on the issue, these elements could not in any direct sense be constrained within the same belief system.) Let us further imagine that the party then changes its position to the opposing side of the issue. Once the information about the change reaching the actor has become so unequivocal that he can no longer deny that the change has occurred, he has several further choices. Two of the more important ones involve either a change in attitude toward the party or a change in position on the issue. In such an instance, the element more likely to change is defined as less central to the belief system than the element that, so to speak, has its stability ensured by the change in the first element.[5]

---

[3]Garner uses the term "constraint" to mean "the amount of interrelatedness of structure of a system of variables" when measured by degree of uncertainty reduction. Wendell R. Garner, *Uncertainty and Structure as Psychological Concepts* (New York, 1962), pp. 142ff. We use the term a bit more broadly as relief from such polysyllables as "interrelatedness" and "interdependence."

[4]Measures of correlation and indices of the goodness of fit of a cumulative scale model to a body of data are measures of two types of constraint.

---

[5]Definitions of belief systems frequently require that configurations of ideas be stable for individuals over long periods of time. The notion of centrality fulfills this requirement in a more flexible way. That is, once it is granted that changes in the perceived status of idea-elements are not frequent in any event and that, when change does occur, the central elements (particularly in large belief systems) are amply cushioned by more peripheral elements that can be adjusted, it follows that central elements are indeed likely to be highly stable.

In informal discussions of belief systems, frequent assumptions are made about the relative centrality of various idea-elements. For example, idea-elements that are logically "ends" are supposed to be more central to the system than are "means." It is important to remain aware, however, that idea-elements can change their relative centrality in an individual's belief-system over time. Perhaps the most hackneyed illustration of this point is that of the miser, to whom money has become an end rather than a means.

Whole belief systems may also be compared in a rough way with respect to the *range* of objects that are referents for the ideas and attitudes in the system. Some belief systems, while they may be internally quite complex and may involve large numbers of cognitive elements, are rather narrow in range: Belief systems concerning "proper" baptism rituals or the effects of changes in weather on health may serve as cases in point. Such other belief systems as, for example, one that links control of the means of production with the social functions of religion and a doctrine of aesthetics all in one more or less neat package have extreme ranges.

By and large, our attention will be focused upon belief systems that have relatively wide ranges, and that allow some centrality to political objects, for they can be presumed to have some relevance to political behavior. This focus brings us close to what are broadly called *ideologies*, and we shall use the term for aesthetic relief where it seems most appropriate. The term originated in a narrower context, however, and is still often reserved for subsets of belief systems or parts of such systems that the user suspects are insincere; that he wishes to claim have certain functions for social groupings; or that have some special social source or some notable breadth of social diffusion.[6] Since we are concerned

here about only one of these limitations—the question of social diffusion—and since we wish to deal with it by hypothesis rather than by definition, a narrow construction of the term is never intended.

II. SOURCES OF CONSTRAINT ON IDEA-ELEMENTS

It seems clear that, however logically coherent a belief system may seem to the holder, the sources of constraint are much less logical in the classical sense than they are psychological—and less psychological than social. This point is of sufficient importance to dwell upon.

Logical Sources of Constraint

Within very narrow portions of belief systems, certain constraints may be purely logical. For example, government revenues, government expenditures, and budget balance are three idea-elements that suggest some purely logical constraints. One cannot believe that government expenditures should be increased, that government revenues should be decreased, and that a more favorable balance of the budget should be achieved all at the same time. Of course, the presence of such objectively logical constraints does not ensure that subjective constraints will be felt by the actor. They will be felt only if these idea-elements are brought together in the same belief system, and there is no guarantee that they need be. Indeed, it is true that, among adult American citizens, those who favor the expansion of government welfare services tend to be those who are more insistent upon reducing taxes "even if it means putting off some important things that need to be done."[7]

Where such purely logical constraint is concerned, McGuire has reported a fascinating experiment in which propositions from a few syllogisms of the Barbara type

---

[6]Minar, *loc. cit.*

[7]See A. Campbell, P. E. Converse, W. Miller, and D. Stokes, *The American Voter* (New York, 1960), pp. 204–9.

were scattered thinly across a long questionnaire applied to a student population. The fact that logical contingencies bound certain questions together was never brought to the attention of the students by the investigator. Yet one week later the questionnaire was applied again, and changes of response to the syllogistic propositions reduced significantly the measurable level of logical inconsistency. The conclusion was that merely "activating" these objectively related ideas in some rough temporal contiguity was sufficient to sensitize the holders to inconsistency and therefore to occasion readjustment of their beliefs.[8]

On a broader canvas, such findings suggest that simple "thinking about" a domain of idea-elements serves both to weld a broader range of such elements into a functioning belief system and to eliminate strictly logical inconsistencies defined from an objective point of view. Since there can be no doubt that educated elites in general, and political elites in particular, "think about" elements involved in political belief systems with a frequency far greater than that characteristic of mass publics, we could conservatively expect that strict logical inconsistencies (objectively definable) would be far more prevalent in a broad public.

Furthermore, if a legislator is noted for his insistence upon budget-balancing and tax-cutting, we can predict with a fair degree of success that he will also tend to oppose expansion of government welfare activities. If, however, a voter becomes numbered within his sphere of influence by virtue of having cast a vote for him directly out of enthusiasm for his tax-cutting policies, we cannot predict that

the voter is opposed as well to expansion of government welfare services. Indeed, if an empirical prediction is possible, it may run in an opposing direction, although the level of constraint is so feeble that any comment is trivial. Yet we know that many historical observations rest directly upon the assumption that constraint among idea-elements visible at an elite level is mirrored by the same lines of constraint in the belief systems of their less visible "supporters." It is our argument that this assumption not only can be, but is very likely to be, fallacious.

Psychological Sources of Constraint

Whatever may be learned through the use of strict logic as a type of constraint, it seems obvious that few belief systems of any range at all depend for their constraint upon logic in this classical sense. Perhaps, with a great deal of labor, parts of a relatively tight belief system like that fashioned by Karl Marx could be made to resemble a structure of logical propositions. It goes without saying, however, that many sophisticated people have been swept away by the "iron logic" of Marxism without any such recasting. There is a broad gulf between such logic and the quasi-logic of cogent argument. And where the elements in the belief system of a population represent looser cultural accumulations, the question of logical consistency is even less appropriate. If one visits a Shaker community, for example, one finds a group of people with a clear-cut and distinctive belief system that requires among other things plain dress, centrality of religious concerns, celibacy for all members, communal assumptions about work and property, antagonism to political participation in the broader state, and a general aura of retirement from the secular world. The visitor whose sense of constraint has been drawn from belief configurations of such other retiring sects

---

[8]William J. McGuire, "A Syllogistic Analysis of Cognitive Relationships," in Milton J. Rosenberg, Carl I. Hovland, William J. McGuire, Robert P. Abelson, and Jack W. Brehm, *Attitude Organization and Change*, Yale Studies in Attitude and Communication, Vol. 3 (New Haven, 1960), pp. 65–111.

as the Amish is entirely surprised to discover that the Shakers have no abhorrence of technological progress but indeed greatly prize it. In their heyday, a remarkable amount of group energy appears to have been reserved for "research and development" of labor-saving devices, and among the inventions they produced was a prototype of the washing machine. Similar surprise has been registered at idea-elements brought together by such movements as Perónism and Italian Fascism by observers schooled to expect other combinations. Indeed, were one to survey a limited set of ideas on which many belief systems have registered opposite postures, it would be interesting to see how many permutations of positions have been held at one time or another by someone somewhere.

Such diversity is testimony to an absence of any strict logical constraints among such idea-elements, if any be needed. What is important is that the elites familiar with the total shapes of these belief systems have *experienced* them as logically constrained clusters of ideas, within which one part necessarily follows from another. Often such constraint is quasi-logically argued on the basis of an appeal to some superordinate value or posture toward man and society, involving premises about the nature of social justice, social change, "natural law," and the like. Thus a few crowning postures—like premises about survival of the fittest in the spirit of social Darwinism—serve as a sort of glue to bind together many more specific attitudes and beliefs, and these postures are of prime centrality in the belief system as a whole.

Social Sources of Constraint

The social sources of constraint are twofold and are familiar from an extensive literature in the past century. In the first place, were we to survey the combinations of idea-elements that have occurred historically (in the fashion suggested above), we should undoubtedly find that certain postures tend to co-occur and that this co-occurrence has obvious roots in the configuration of interests and information that characterize particular niches in the social structure. For example, if we were informed that dissension was rising within the Roman Catholic Church over innovations designed to bring the priest more intimately into the *milieu* of the modern worker, we could predict with a high degree of success that such a movement would have the bulk of its support among the *bas-clergé* and would encounter indifference or hostility at the higher status levels of the hierarchy.

Of course, such predictions are in no sense free from error, and surprises are numerous. The middle-class temperance movement in America, for example, which now seems "logically" allied with the small-town Republican right, had important alliances some eighty years ago with the urban social left, on grounds equally well argued from temperance doctrines.[9] Nonetheless, there are some highly reliable correlations of this sort, and these correlations can be linked with social structure in the most direct way. Developmentally, they have status similar to the classic example of the spurious correlation —two terms that are correlated because of a common link to some third and prior variable. In the case of the belief system, arguments are developed to lend some more positive rationale to the fact of constraint: The idea-elements go together not simply because both are in the interest of the person holding a particular status but for more abstract and quasi-logical reasons developed from a coherent world view as well. It is this type of constraint

---

[9]Joseph R. Gusfield, "Status Conflicts and the Changing Ideologies of the American Temperance Movement," in Pittman and Snyder, eds., *Society, Culture and Drinking Patterns* (New York, 1962).

that is closest to the classic meaning of the term "ideology."

The second source of social constraint lies in two simple facts about the creation and diffusion of belief systems. First, the shaping of belief systems of any range into apparently logical wholes that are credible to large numbers of people is an act of creative synthesis characteristic of only a miniscule proportion of any population. Second, to the extent that multiple idea-elements of a belief system are socially diffused from such creative sources, they tend to be diffused in "packages," which consumers come to see as "natural" wholes, for they are presented in such terms ("If you believe this, then you will also believe that, for it follows in such-and-such ways"). Not that the more avid consumer never supplies personal innovations on the fringes—he is very likely to suppress an idea-element here, to elaborate one there, or even to demur at an occasional point. But any set of relatively intelligent consumers who are initially sympathetic to the crowning posture turns out to show more consensus on specific implications of the posture as a result of social diffusion of "what goes with what" than it would if each member were required to work out the implications individually without socially provided cues.

Such constraint through diffusion is important, for it implies a dependence upon the transmission of information. If information is not successfully transmitted, there will be little constraint save that arising from the first social source. Where transmission of information is at stake, it becomes important to distinguish between two classes of information. Simply put, these two levels are what goes with what and why. Such levels of information logically stand in a scalar relationship to one another, in the sense that one can hardly arrive at an understanding of why two ideas go together without being aware that they are supposed to go together. On

the other hand, it is easy to know that two ideas go together without knowing why. For example, we can expect that a very large majority of the American public would somehow have absorbed the notion that "Communists are atheists." What is important is that this perceived correlation would for most people represent nothing more than a fact of existence, with the same status as the fact that oranges are orange and most apples are red. If we were to go and explore with these people their grasp of the "why" of the relationship, we would be surprised if more than a quarter of the population even attempted responses (setting aside such inevitable replies as "those Communists are for everything wicked"), and, among the responses received, we could be sure that the majority would be incoherent or irrelevant.

The first level of information, then, is simple and straightforward. The second involves much more complex and abstract information, very close to what Downs has called the "contextual knowledge" relevant to a body of information.[10] A well informed person who has received sufficient information about a system of beliefs to understand the "whys" involved in several of the constraints between idea-elements is in a better position to make good guesses about the nature of other constraints; he can deduce with fair success, for example, how a true believer will respond to certain situations. Our first interest in distinguishing between these types of information, however, flows from our interest in the relative success of information transmission. The general premise is that the first type of information will be diffused much more readily than the second because it is less complex.

It is well established that differences in information held in a cross-section pop-

---

[10]Anthony Downs, *An Economic Theory of Democracy* (New York, 1957), p. 79.

ulation are simply staggering, running from vast treasuries of well organized information among elites interested in the particular subject to fragments that could virtually be measured as a few "bits" in the technical sense. These differences are a static tribute to the extreme imperfections in the transmission of information "downward" through the system: Very little information "trickles down" very far. Of course, the ordering of individuals on this vertical information scale is largely due to differences in education, but it is strongly modified as well by different specialized interests and tastes that individuals have acquired over time (one for politics, another for religious activity, another for fishing, and so forth).

Consequences of Declining Information for Belief Systems

It is our primary thesis that, as one moves from elite sources of belief systems downward on such an information scale, several important things occur. First, the contextual grasp of "standard" political belief systems fades out very rapidly, almost before one has passed beyond the 10% of the American population that in the 1950s had completed standard college training.[11] Increasingly, simpler forms of information about "what goes with what" (or even information about the simple identity of objects) turn up missing. The net result, as one moves downward, is that constraint declines across the universe of

idea-elements, and that the range of relevant belief systems becomes narrower and narrower. Instead of a few wide-ranging belief systems that organize large amounts of specific information, one would expect to find a proliferation of clusters of ideas among which little constraint is felt, even, quite often, in instances of sheer logical constraint.[12]

At the same time, moving from top to bottom of this information dimension, the character of the objects that are central in a belief system undergoes systematic change. These objects shift from the remote, generic, and abstract to the increasingly simple, concrete, or "close to home." Where potential political objects are concerned, this progression tends to be from abstract, "ideological" principles to the more obviously recognizable social groupings or charismatic leaders and finally to such objects of immediate experience as family, job, and immediate associates.

Most of these changes have been hinted at in one form or another in a variety of sources. For example, "limited horizons," "foreshortened time perspectives," and "concrete thinking" have been singled out as notable characteristics of the ideational world of the poorly educated. Such observations have impressed even those investigators who are dealing with subject matter rather close to the individual's immediate world: his family budgeting, what he thinks of people more wealthy than he, his attitudes toward leisure time, work regulations, and the like. But most of the stuff of politics—particularly that played on a national or international stage —is, in the nature of things, remote and abstract. Where politics is concerned, therefore, such ideational changes begin to occur rapidly below the extremely thin stratum of the electorate that ever has

---

[11]It should be understood that our information dimension is not so perfectly correlated with formal education as this statement implies. Since educational strata have a more ready intuitive meaning, however, we shall use them occasionally as convenient ways of measuring off levels in the population. In such cases, the reader may keep in mind that there are always some people of lesser education but higher political involvement who are numbered in the stratum and some people with education befitting the stratum who are not numbered there because their interests lie elsewhere and their information about politics is less than could be expected.

---

[12]There is a difference, of course, between this statement and a suggestion that poorly educated people have no systems of belief about politics.

occasion to make public pronouncements on political affairs. In other words, the changes in belief systems of which we speak are not a pathology limited to a thin and disoriented bottom layer of the *lumpenproletariat;* they are immediately relevant in understanding the bulk of mass political behavior.

It is this latter fact which seems to be consistently misunderstood by the sophisticated analysts who comment in one vein or another on the meaning of mass politics. There are some rather obvious "optical illusions" that are bound to operate here. A member of that tiny elite that comments publicly about political currents (probably some fraction of 1% of a population) spends most of his time in informal communication about politics with others in the same select group. He rarely encounters a conversation in which his assumptions of shared contextual grasp of political ideas are challenged. Intellectually, he has learned that the level of information in the mass public is low, but he may dismiss this knowledge as true of only 10 to 20% of the voters, who affect the course of mass political events in insignificant ways if at all.[13] It is largely from his informal communications that he learns how "public opinion" is changing and what the change signifies, and he generalizes facilely from these observations to the bulk of the broader public.[14]

[13]This observation is valid despite the fact that surveys showing ignorance of crucial political facts are much more likely to run in a range from 40–80% "unaware." At the height of the 1958 Berlin crisis, 63% of the American public did not know that the city was encircled by hostile troops. A figure closer to 70% is a good estimate of the proportion of the public that does not know which party controls Congress.

[14]In this regard, it was enlightening to read the stunned reactions of the political columnist Joseph Alsop when, during the 1960 presidential primaries, he left the elite circuits of the East Coast and ventured from door to door talking politics with "normal" people in West Virginia. He was frank to admit that the change in perceived political worlds was far greater than anything he had ever anticipated, despite his prior recognition that there would be some difference.

III. ACTIVE USE OF IDEOLOGICAL DIMENSIONS OF JUDGMENT

Economy and constraint are companion concepts, for the more highly constrained a system of multiple elements, the more economically it may be described and understood. From the point of view of the actor, the idea organization that leads to constraint permits him to locate and make sense of a wider range of information from a particular domain than he would find possible without such organization. One judgmental dimension or "yardstick" that has been highly serviceable for simplifying and organizing events in most Western politics for the past century has been the liberal-conservative continuum, on which parties, political leaders, legislation, court decisions, and a number of other primary objects of politics could be more—or less—adequately located.[15]

[15]The phrase "less adequately" is used to show recognition of the frequent complaint that the liberal-conservative dimension has different meanings in different politics at different times. More importantly, it takes into account the fact that in most politics new issues are constantly arising that are difficult before the fact to relate to such a yardstick. Some of these intrinsically "orthogonal" issues may remain unrelated to the dimension, and, if they become of intense importance, they can split existing parties and redefine alignments. More typically, however, elites that are known on some other grounds to be "liberal" or "conservative" ferret out some limited aspect of an issue for which they can argue some liberal-conservative relevance and begin to drift to one of the alternative positions in disproportionate numbers. Then, either because of the aspect highlighted or because of simple pressures toward party competition, their adversaries drift toward the opposing position. Thus positions come to be perceived as "liberal" or "conservative," even though such alignments would have been scarcely predictable on logical grounds. After the fact, of course, the alignments come to seem "logical," by mechanisms discussed earlier in this paper. Controversy over British entry into the European Common Market is an excellent example of such a process. Currently the conservatives are officially pro-entry, and Labour leadership has finally declared against it, but the reverse of this alignment had frequently been predicted when the issue was embryonic.

The efficiency of such a yardstick in the evaluation of events is quite obvious. Under certain appropriate circumstances, the single word "conservative" used to describe a piece of proposed legislation can convey a tremendous amount of more specific information about the bill—who probably proposed it and toward what ends, who is likely to resist it, its chances of passage, its long-term social consequences, and, most important, how the actor himself should expect to evaluate it if he were to expend further energy to look into its details. The circumstances under which such tremendous amounts of information are conveyed by the single word are, however, twofold. First, the actor must bring a good deal of meaning to the term, which is to say that he must understand the constraints surrounding it. The more impoverished his understanding of the term, the less information it conveys. In the limiting case—if he does not know at all what the term means—it conveys no information at all. Second, the system of beliefs and actors referred to must in fact be relatively constrained: To the degree that constraint is lacking, uncertainty is less reduced by the label, and less information is conveyed.

The psychological economies provided by such yardsticks for actors are paralleled by economies for analysts and theoreticians who wish to describe events in the system parsimoniously. Indeed, the search for adequate overarching dimensions on which large arrays of events may be simply understood is a critical part of synthetic description. Such syntheses are more or less satisfactory, once again, according to the degree of constraint operative among terms in the system being described.

The economies inherent in the liberal-conservative continuum were exploited in traditional fashion in the early 1950s to describe political changes in the United States as a swing toward conservatism or a "revolt of the moderates." At one level,

this description was unquestionably apt. That is, a man whose belief system was relatively conservative (Dwight D. Eisenhower) had supplanted in the White House a man whose belief system was relatively liberal (Harry Truman). Furthermore, for a brief period at least, the composition of Congress was more heavily Republican as well, and this shift meant on balance a greater proportion of relatively conservative legislators. Since the administration and Congress were the elites responsible for the development and execution of policies, the flavor of governmental action did indeed take a turn in a conservative direction. These observations are proper description.

The causes underlying these changes in leadership, however, obviously lay with the mass public, which had changed its voting patterns sufficiently to bring the Republican elites into power. And this change in mass voting was frequently interpreted as a shift in public mood from liberal to conservative, a mass desire for a period of respite and consolidation after the rapid liberal innovations of the 1930s and 1940s. Such an account presumes, once again, that constraints visible at an elite level are mirrored in the mass public and that a person choosing to vote Republican after a decade or two of Democratic voting saw himself *in some sense or other* as giving up a more liberal choice in favor of a more conservative one.

On the basis of some familiarity with attitudinal materials drawn from cross-section samples of the electorate,[16] this assumption seems thoroughly implausible. It suggests in the first instance a neatness of organization in perceived political worlds, which, while accurate enough for elites, is a poor fit for the perceptions of

_____

16 All American data reported in this paper, unless otherwise noted, have been collected by the Survey Research Center of The University of Michigan under grants from the Carnegie Corporation, the Rockfeller Foundation, and the Social Science Research Council.

the common public. Second, the yardstick that such an account takes for granted—the liberal-conservative continuum—is a rather elegant high-order abstraction, and such abstractions are not typical conceptual tools for the "man in the street." Fortunately, our interview protocols collected from this period permitted us to examine this hypothesis more closely, for they include not only "structured" attitude materials (which merely require the respondent to choose between prefabricated alternatives) but also lengthy "open-ended" materials which provided us with the respondent's current evaluations of the political scene in his own words. They therefore provide some indication of the evaluative dimensions that tend to be spontaneously applied to politics by such a national sample. We knew that respondents who were highly educated or strongly involved in politics would fall naturally into the verbal shorthand of "too conservative," "more radical," and the like in these evaluations. Our initial analytic question had to do with the prevalence of such usage.

It soon became apparent, however, that such respondents were in a very small minority, as their unusual education or involvement would suggest. At this point, we broadened the inquiry to an assessment of the evaluative dimensions of policy significance (relating to political issues, rather than to the way a candidate dresses, smiles, or behaves in his private life) that seemed to be employed *in lieu of* such efficient yardsticks as the liberal-conservative continuum. The interviews themselves suggested several strata of classification, which were hierarchically ordered as "levels of conceptualization" on the basis of *a priori* judgments about the breadth of contextual grasp of the political system that each seemed to represent.

In the first or top level were placed those respondents who did indeed rely in some active way on a relatively abstract and far-reaching conceptual dimension as a yardstick against which political objects and their shifting policy significance over time were evaluated. We did not require that this dimension be the liberal-conservative continuum itself, but it was almost the only dimension of the sort that occurred empirically. In a second stratum were placed those respondents who mentioned such a dimension in a peripheral way but did not appear to place much evaluative dependence upon it or who used such concepts in a fashion that raised doubt about the breadth of their understanding of the meaning of the term. The first stratum was loosely labeled "ideologue" and the second "near-ideologue."

In the third level were placed respondents who failed to rely upon any such over-arching dimensions yet evaluated parties and candidates in terms of their expected favorable or unfavorable treatment of different social groupings in the population. The Democratic Party might be disliked because "it's trying to help the Negroes too much," or the Republican Party might be endorsed because farm prices would be better with the Republicans in office. The more sophisticated of these group-interest responses reflected an awareness of conflict in interest between "big business" or "rich people," on the one hand, and "labor" or the "working man," on the other, and parties and candidates were located accordingly.

It is often asked why these latter respondents are not considered full "ideologues," for their perceptions run to the more tangible core of what has traditionally been viewed as ideological conflict. It is quite true that such a syndrome is closer to the upper levels of conceptualization than are any of the other types to be described. As we originally foresaw, however, there turn out to be rather marked differences, not only in social origin and flavor of judgmental processes but in overt political reactions as well, between people of this type and those in the upper levels. These people have a clear image of politics as an arena of group interests and, provided that they have been properly advised on where their own group interests lie, they are relatively likely to follow such advice. Unless an issue directly concerns their grouping in an obviously rewarding or punishing way, however, they lack the contextual grasp of the system to recognize how they should respond to it without being told by elites who hold their confidence. Furthermore, their interest in politics is not sufficiently strong that they pay much attention to such communications. If a communication gets through and they absorb it, they are most willing to behave "ideologically" in ways that will further the interests of their group. If they fail to receive such communication, which is most unusual, knowledge of their group memberships may be of little help in predicting their responses. This syndrome we came to call "ideology by proxy."

The difference between such narrow group interest and the broader perceptions of the ideologue may be clarified by an extreme case. One respondent whom we encountered classified himself as a strong Socialist. He was a Socialist because he knew that Socialists stood foursquare for the working man against the rich, and he was a working man. When asked, however, whether or not the federal government in Washington "should leave things like electric power and housing for private businessmen to handle," he felt strongly that private enterprise should have its way, and responses to other structured issue questions were simply uncorrelated with standard socialist doctrine. It seems quite clear that, if our question had pointed out explicitly to this man that "good Socialists" would demand government intervention over private enterprise or that such a posture had traditionally been viewed as benefiting the working man, his answer would have been different. But since he had something less than a college education and was not generally interested enough in politics to

struggle through such niceties, he simply lacked the contextual grasp of the political system or of his chosen "ideology" to know what the appropriate response might be. This case illustrates well what we mean by constraint between idea-elements and how such constraint depends upon a store of relevant information. For this man, "Socialists," "the working man," "non-Socialists" and "the rich" with their appropriate valences formed a tightly constrained belief system. But, for lack of information, the belief system more or less began and ended there. It strikes us as valid to distinguish such a belief system from that of the doctrinaire socialist. We, as sophisticated observers, could only class this man as a full "ideologue" by assuming that he shares with us the complex undergirding of information that his concrete group perceptions call up in our own minds. In this instance, a very little probing makes clear that this assumption of shared information is once again false.

The fourth level was, to some degree, a residual category, intended to include those respondents who invoked some policy considerations in their evaluations yet employed none of the references meriting location in any of the first three levels. Two main modes of policy evaluation were characteristic of this level. The first we came to think of as a "nature of the times" response, since parties or candidates were praised or blamed primarily because of their temporal association in the past with broad societal states of war or peace, prosperity or depression. There was no hint in these responses that any groupings in the society suffered differentially from disaster or profited excessively in more pleasant times: These fortunes or misfortunes were those that one party or the other had decided (in some cases, apparently, on whim) to visit upon the nation as a whole. The second type included those respondents whose only approach to an issue reference involved some single narrow policy for which they felt personal

TABLE 1

Distribution of a Total Cross-Section Sample of the American Electorate
and of 1956 Voters, by Levels of Conceptualization

	Proportion of Total Sample	Proportion of Voters
I. Ideologues	2½%	3½%
II. Near-Ideologues	9	12
III. Group interest	42	45
IV. Nature of the times	24	22
V. No issue content	22½	17½
	100%	100%

gratitude or indignation toward a party or candidate (like social security or a conservation program). In these responses, there was no indication that the speakers saw programs as representative of the broader policy postures of the parties.

The fifth level included those respondents whose evaluations of the political scene had no shred of policy significance whatever. Some of these responses were from people who felt loyal to one party or the other but confessed that they had no idea what the party stood for. Others devoted their attention to personal qualities of the candidates, indicating disinterest in parties more generally. Still others confessed that they paid too little attention to either the parties or the current candidates to be able to say anything about them.[17]

The ranking of the levels performed on *a priori* grounds was corroborated by further analyses, which demonstrated that independent measures of political information, education, and political involvement all showed sharp and monotonic declines as one passed downward through the levels in the order suggested. Furthermore, these correlations were strong

[17]This account of the "levels of conceptualization" is highly abbreviated. For a much more detailed discussion and rationale, along with numerous illustrations drawn at random from interviews in each stratum, see Campbell *et al., op. cit.*, Chapter 10.

enough so that each maintained some recontrolled, despite the strong underlying relationship between education, information, and involvement.

The distribution of the American electorate within these levels of conceptualization is summarized in Table 1. The array is instructive as a portrait of a mass electorate, to be laid against the common elite assumption that all or a significant majority of the public conceptualizes the main lines of politics after the manner of the most highly educated. Where the specific hypothesis of the "revolt of the moderates" in the early 1950s is concerned, the distribution does not seem on the face of it to lend much support to the key assumption. This disconfirmation may be examined further, however.

Since the resurgence of the Republicans in the Eisenhower period depended primarily upon crossing of party lines by people who normally considered themselves Democrats, we were able to isolate these people to see from what levels of conceptualization they had been recruited. We found that such key defections had occurred among Democrats in the two bottom levels at a rate very significantly greater than the comparable rate in the group-interest or more ideological levels. In other words, the stirrings in the mass electorate that had led to a change in administration and in "ruling ideology" were primarily the handiwork of the very people for whom assumptions of any liberal-conservative dimensions of judgment were most farfetched.

Furthermore, within those strata where the characteristics of conceptualization even permitted the hypothesis to be evaluated in its own terms, it was directly disproved. For example, the more sophisticated of the group-interest Democrats were quite aware that Eisenhower would be a more pro-business president than Stevenson. Those of this group who did defect to Eisenhower did not, however, do so because they were tired of a labor-oriented administration and wanted a business-oriented one for a change. Quite to the contrary, in the degree that they defected they did so *in spite of* rather than *because of* such quasi-ideological perceptions. That is, their attitudes toward the respective interests of these groups remained essentially constant, and they expected misgivings about an Eisenhower vote on precisely these grounds. But any such worries were, under the circumstances, outweighed by admiration for Eisenhower's war record, his honesty, his good family life, and (in 1952) his potential for resolving the nagging problem of the Korean War. Among respondents at higher levels (ideologues and near-ideologues), there was comparable attraction to Eisenhower at a personal level, but these people seemed more careful to hew to ideological considerations, and rates of Democratic defection in these levels were lower still. In short, then, the supposition of changing ideological moods in the mass public as a means of understanding the exchange of partisan elites in 1952 seems to have had little relevance to what was actually going on at the mass level. And once again, the sources of the optical illusion are self-evident. While it may be taken for granted among well educated and politically involved people that a shift from a Democratic preference to a Repub-

lican one probably represents a change in option from liberal to conservative, the assumption cannot be extended very far into the electorate as a whole.

IV. RECOGNITION OF IDEOLOGICAL DIMENSIONS OF JUDGMENT

Dimensions like the liberal-conservative continuum, as we have observed, are extremely efficient frames for the organization of many political observations. Furthermore, they are used a great deal in the more ambitious treatments of politics in the mass media, so that a person with a limited understanding of their meaning must find such discussions more obscure than enlightening. Aside from active cognitive use, therefore, the simple status of public comprehension of these terms is a matter of some interest.

It is a commonplace in psychology that recognition, recall, and habitual use of cognized objects or concepts are rather different. We are capable of *recognizing* many more objects (or concepts) if they are directly presented to us than we could readily *recall* on the basis of more indirect cues; and we are capable of recalling on the basis of such hints many more objects (or concepts) than might be *active* or *salient* for us in a given context without special prompting. In coding the levels of conceptualization from free-answer material, our interest had been entirely focused upon concepts with the last status (activation or salience). It had been our assumption that such activation would be apparent in the responses of any person with a belief system in which these organizing dimensions had high centrality. Nevertheless, we could be sure at the same time that if we presented the terms "liberal" and "conservative" directly to our respondents, a much larger number would recognize them and be able to attribute to them some kind of meaning. We are interested both in the proportions of a normal sample who would show some recognition and also in the meaning that might be supplied for the terms.

In a 1960 reinterview of the original sample whose 1956 responses had been assigned to our levels of conceptualization, we therefore asked in the context of the differences in "what the parties stand for," "Would you say that either one of the parties is more *conservative* or more *liberal* than the other?" (It was the first time we had ever introduced these terms in our interviewing of this sample.) If the answer was affirmative, we asked which party seemed the more conservative and then, "What do you have in mind when you say that the Republicans (Democrats) are more conservative than the Democrats (Republicans)?" When the respondent said that he did not see differences of this kind between the two parties, we were anxious to distinguish between those who were actually cynical about meaningful party differences and those who took this route to avoid admitting that they did not know what the terms signified. We therefore went on to ask this group, "Do you think that people generally consider the Democrats or the Republicans more conservative, or wouldn't you want to guess about that?" At this point, we were willing to assume that if a person had no idea of the rather standard assumptions, he probably had no idea of what the terms meant; and indeed, those who did try to guess which party other people thought more conservative made a very poor showing when we went on to ask them (paralleling our "meaning" question for the first group), "What do people have in mind when they say that the Republicans (Democrats) are more conservative than the Democrats (Republicans)?" In responding to the "meaning" questions, both groups were urged to answer as fully and clearly as possible, and their comments were transcribed.

The responses were classified in a code inspired by the original work on levels of conceptualization, although it was considerably more detailed. Within this code, top priority was given to explanations that called upon broad philosophical differences. These explanations included mentions of such things as *posture toward change* (acceptance of or resistance to new ideas, speed or caution in responding to new problems, protection of or challenge to the *status quo*, aggressive posture toward problems *vs.* a *laissez-faire* approach, orientation toward the future or lack of it, and so forth); *posture toward the welfare state, socialism, free enterprise, or capitalism* (including mention of differential sensitivity to social problems, approaches to social-welfare programs, governmental interference with private enterprise, and so forth); *posture toward the expanding power of federal government* (issues of centralization, states' rights, local autonomy, and paternalism); and *relationship of the government to the individual* (questions of individual dignity, initiative, needs, rights, and so forth). While any mention of comparably broad philosophical differences associated with the liberal-conservative distinction was categorized in this top level, these four were the most frequent types of reference, as they had been for the full "ideologues" in the earlier open-ended materials.

Then, in turn, references to differences in attitude toward various interest groupings in the population; toward spending or saving and fiscal policy more generally, as well as to economic prosperity; toward various highly specific issues like unemployment compensation, highway-building, and tariffs; and toward postures in the sphere of foreign policy were arrayed in a descending order of priority, much as they had been for the classification into levels of conceptualization. Since respondents had been given the opportunity to mention as many conservative-liberal distinctions as they wished, coding priority was given to the more "elevated" responses, and all the data that we shall subsequently cite rests on the "best answer" given by each respondent.[18]

The simple distributional results were as follows. Roughly three respondents in eight (37%) could supply no meaning for the liberal-conservative distinction, including 8% who attempted to say which party was the more conservative but who gave up on the part of the sequence dealing with meaning. (The weakest 29% will, in later tables, form our bottom stratum "V," while the 8% compose stratum "IV.") Between those who could supply no meaning for the terms and those who clearly did, there was naturally an intermediate group that answered all the questions but showed varying degrees of uncertainty or confusion. The situation required that one of two polar labels (conservative or liberal) be properly associated with one of two polar clusters of connotations and with one of two parties. Once the respondent had decided to explain what "more conservative" or "more liberal" signified, there were four possible patterns by which the other two dichotomies might be associated with the first. Of course, all four were represented in at least some interviews. For example, a respondent might indicate that the Demo-

crats were the more conservative because they stood up for the working man against big business. In such a case, there seemed to be a simple error consisting in reversal of the ideological labels. Or a respondent might say that the Republicans were more liberal because they were pushing new and progressive social legislation. Here the match between label and meaning seems proper, but the party perception is, by normal standards, erroneous.

The distribution of these error types within the portion of the sample that attempted to give "meaning" answers (slightly more than 60%) is shown in Table 2. The 83% entered for the "proper" patterns is artificially increased to an unknown degree by the inclusion of all respondents whose connotations for liberalism-conservatism were sufficiently impoverished so that little judgment could be made about whether or not they were making proper associations (for example, those respondents whose best explanations of the distinction involved orientations toward defense spending). The error types thus represent only those that could be unequivocally considered "errors." While Table 2 does not in itself constitute proof that the error types resulted from pure guesswork, the configuration does resemble the probable results if 20–25% of the respondents had been making random guesses about how the two labels, the two polar meanings, and the two parties should be sorted out. People making these confused responses might or might not *feel* confused in making their assessments. Even if they knew that they were confused, it is unlikely that they would be less confused in encountering such terms in reading or listening to political communications, which is the important point where transmission of information is concerned. If, on the other hand, they were wrong without realizing it, then they would be capable of hearing that Senator Goldwater, for example, was an

---

[18]Some modest internal support for the validity of the distinction between those who spoke in terms of broad philosophy and those who offered narrower explanations may be seen in the fact that only 5% of the former category had previously judged the Democrats to be more conservative than the Republicans. Among those giving less elevated "best answers," 14% deemed the Democrats the more conservative party. And, to give some sense of the "continental shelf" being explored here, among those who had responded that a certain party was more conservative than the other but who subsequently confessed that they did not know what the distinction implied, 35% had chosen the Democrats as the more conservative, a figure that is beginning to approach the 50–50 assignment of sheer guesswork.

TABLE 2

Association of Ideological Label with Party and Meaning

Ideological Label	Meaning	Party	Proportion of Those Giving Some Answer
Conservative	Conservative	Republican	83%
Liberal	Liberal	Democrat	
Conservative	Liberal	Republican	
Liberal	Conservative	Democrat	5
Conservative	Conservative	Democrat*	
Liberal	Liberal	Republican	6
Conservative	Liberal	Democrat	
Liberal	Conservative	Republican	6
			100%

*While this pattern may appear entirely legitimate for the southern respondent reacting to the southern wing of the Democratic Party rather than to the national party, it showed almost no tendency to occur with greater frequency in the South than elsewhere (and errors as well as lacunae occurred more frequently in general in the less well educated South). Data from a very different context indicate that southerners who discriminate between the southern wing and the national Democratic Party take the national party as the assumed object in our interviews, if the precise object is not specified.

extreme conservative and believing that it meant that he was for increased federal spending (or whatever other more specific meaning they might bring to the term). In either case, it seems reasonable to distinguish between the people who belong in this confused group at the border of understanding and those who demonstrate greater clarity about the terms. And after the confused group is set aside (stratum III in Tables 3-4), we are left with a proportion of the sample that is slightly more than 50%. This figure can be taken as a maximum estimate of reasonable recognition.

We say "maximum" because, once within this "sophisticated" half of the electorate, it is reasonable to consider the quality of the meanings put forth to explain the liberal-conservative distinction. These meanings varied greatly in adequacy, from those "best answers" that did indeed qualify for coding under the "broad philosophy" heading (the most accurate responses, as defined above) to those that explained the distinction in narrow or nearly irrelevant terms (like

Prohibition or foreign-policy measures). In all, 17% of the total sample gave "best answers" that we considered to qualify as "broad philosophy."[19] This group was defined as stratum I, and the remainder, who gave narrower definitions, became stratum II.

Perhaps the most striking aspect of the liberal-conservative definitions supplied was the extreme frequency of those hinging on a simple "spend-save" dimension *vis-à-vis* government finances. Very close to a majority of all "best" responses (and two-thirds to three-quarters of all such responses in stratum II) indicated in essence that the Democratic Party was liberal because it spent public money freely and that the Republican Party was more conservative because it stood for economy in government or pinched pennies. In our earlier coding of the levels of conceptuali-

[19]In all candor, it should probably be mentioned that a teacher grading papers would be unlikely to give passing marks to more than 20% of the attempted definitions (or to 10% of the total sample). We made an effort, however, to be as generous as possible in our assignments.

zation, we had already noted that this simple dimension seemed often to be what was at stake when "ideological" terms were used. Frequently there was reason to believe that the term "conservative" drew its primary meaning from the cognate "conservation." In one rather clear example, a respondent indicated that he considered the Republicans to be more conservative in the sense that they were ". . . more saving with money and our *natural resources.* Less apt to slap on a tax for some non-essential. More conservative in promises that can't be kept." (Italics ours.)

Of course, the question of the proportion of national wealth that is to be spent privately or channeled through government for public spending has been one of the key disputes between conservatives and liberal "ideologies" for several decades. From this point of view, the great multitude of "spend-save" references can be considered essentially as accurate matching of terms. On the other hand, it goes without saying that the conservative-liberal dialogue does not exhaust itself on this narrow question alone, and our view of these responses as an understanding of the differences depends in no small measure on whether the individual sees this point as a self-contained distinction or understands the link between it and a number of other broad questions. On rare occasions, one encounters a respondent for whom the "spend-save" dimension is intimately bound up with other problem areas. For example, one respondent feels that the Republicans are more conservative because ". . . they are too interested in getting the budget balanced—they should spend more to get more jobs for our people." More frequently when further links are suggested, they are connected with policy but go no further:

[Republicans more conservative because] "Well, they don't spend as much money." [What do you have in mind?] "Well, a lot

of them holler when they try to establish a higher interest rate but that's to get back a little when they do loan out and make it so people are not so free with it."

Generally, however, the belief system involved when "liberal-conservative" is equated with "spend-save" seems to be an entirely narrow one. There follow a number of examples of comments, which taken with the preceding citations, form a random drawing from the large group of "spend-save" comments:

[Democrats more conservative because] "they will do more for the people at home before they go out to help foreign countries. They are truthful and not liars."
[Republicans more liberal judging] "by the money they have spent in this last administration. They spent more than ever before in a peace time. And got less for it as far as I can see."
[Republicans more conservative because] "Well, they vote against the wild spending spree the Democrats get on."
[Republicans more conservative because] "they pay as you go."
[Democrats more conservative because] "I don't believe the Democrats will spend as much money as the Republicans."
[Republicans more conservative because] "it seems as if the Republicans try to hold down the spending of government money." [Do you remember how?] "Yes," [by having] "no wars."

From this representation of the "spend-save" references, the reader may see quite clearly why we consider them to be rather "narrow" readings of the liberal-conservative distinction as applied to the current partisan scene. In short, our portrait of the population, where recognition of a key ideological dimension is concerned, suggests that about 17% of the public (stratum I) have an understanding of the distinction that captures much of its breadth. About 37% (strata IV and V) are entirely vague as to its meaning. For the 46% between, there are two strata, one of

TABLE 3

Levels of Conceptualization (1956) by Recognition and Understanding of Terms
"Conservatism" and "Liberalism" (1960)

		Levels of Conceptualization				
	Stratum	*Ideologue*	*Near Ideologue*	*Group Interest*	*Nature of the Times*	*No Issue Content*
Recognition and understanding*	I	51%	29%	13%	16%	10%
	II	43	46	42	40	22
	III	2	10	14	7	7
	IV	2	5	6	7	12
	V	2	10	25	30	49
		100%	100%	100%	100%	100%
Number of cases		(45)	(122)	(580)	(288)	(290)

*The definitions of the strata are: I. recognition and proper matching of label, meaning, and party and a broad understanding of the terms "conservative" and "liberal"; II. recognition and proper matching but a narrow definition of terms (like "spend-save"); III. recognition but some error in matching; IV. recognition and an attempt at matching but inability to give any meaning for terms: V. no apparent recognition of terms (does not know if parties differ in liberal-conservative terms and does not know if anybody else sees them as differing).

which demonstrates considerable uncertainty and guesswork in assigning meaning to the terms (stratum III) and the other of which has the terms rather well under control but appears to have a fairly limited set of connotations for them (stratum II). The great majority of the latter groups equate liberalism-conservatism rather directly with a "spend-save" dimension. In such cases, when the sensed connotations are limited, it is not surprising that there is little active use of the continuum as an organizing dimension. Why should one bother to say that a party is conservative if one can convey the same information by saying that it is against spending?

Since the 1960 materials on liberal-conservative meanings were drawn from the same sample as the coding of the active use of such frames of reference in 1956, it is possible to consider how well the two codings match. For a variety of reasons, we would not expect a perfect fit, even aside from coding error. The earlier coding had not been limited to the liberal-conservative dimension, and, although empirical instances were rare, a person could qualify as an "ideologue" if he assessed politics with the aid of some other highly abstract organizing dimension. Similarly, among those who did em-

ploy the liberal-conservative distinction, there were no requirements that the terms be defined. It was necessary therefore to depend upon appearances, and the classification was intentionally lenient. Furthermore, since a larger portion of the population would show recognition than showed active use, we could expect substantial numbers of people in the lower levels of conceptualization to show reasonable recognition of the terms. At any rate, we assumed that the two measures would show a high correlation, as they in fact did (Table 3).

Of course, very strong differences in education underlie the data shown in Table 3. The 2% of the sample that occupy the upper left-hand cell have a mean education close to seven years greater than that of the 11% that occupy the lower right-hand cell. Sixty-two per cent of this lower cell have had less formal education than the least educated person in the upper corner. The differences in education show a fairly regular progression across the intervening surface of the table (see Table 4). Although women have a higher mean education than men, there is some sex bias to the table, for women are disproportionately represented in the lower right-hand quadrant of the table. Furthermore, although age is negatively corre-

TABLE 4

Levels of Conceptualization (1956) and Term Recognition (1960) by Mean Years of Formal Education

		Levels of Conceptualization				
	Stratum	Ideologue	Near Ideologue	Group Interest	Nature of the Times	No Issue Content
Recognition and understanding‡	I	14.9†	14.2	12.3	11.1	11.9
	II	13.9	11.9	10.7	10.7	11.5
	III	*	11.1	10.6	9.8	9.6
	IV	*	*	10.4	9.9	10.3
	V	*	10.0	9.5	8.5	8.2

*Inadequate number of cases.

†The cell entry is mean number of years of formal education. Partial college was arbitrarily assumed to represent an average of 14 years, and work toward an advanced degree an average of 18 years.

‡See Table 3 for definitions of the five strata.

lated with education, there is also rather clear evidence that the sort of political sophistication represented by the measures can accumulate with age. Undoubtedly even sporadic observation of politics over long enough periods of time serves to nurture some broader view of basic liberal-conservative differences, although of course the same sophistication is achieved much more rapidly and in a more striking way by those who progress greater distances through the educational system.

It is not surprising that political sophistication goes hand in hand with political activism at the "grass roots" (Table 5). The relationship is certainly not perfect:

About 20% of those in the most sophisticated cell engaged in none of the forms of participation beyond voting that were surveyed (see †footnote, Table 5) in either the 1956 or 1960 election campaigns, and there is more "stray" participation than has sometimes been suspected among those who express little interest in politics or comprehension of party differences yet who may, for example, happen on a political rally. Furthermore, even the active hard core is not necessarily sophisticated in this sense: Two of the thirteen most active people fall in the lower right half of the table, and their activism is probably to be understood more in terms of mundane social gratifications

TABLE 5

Amount of 1956–1960 Political Activity by Level of Conceptualization (1956) and Term Recognition (1960)

		Levels of Conceptualization				
	Stratum	Ideologue	Near Ideologue	Group Interest	Nature of the Times	No Issue Content
Recognition and understanding‡	I	3.8†	2.6	2.5	2.6	2.2
	II	3.4	3.0	1.7	1.8	1.3
	III	*	2.5	2.2	1.5	1.1
	IV	*	*	1.9	1.5	.8
	V	*	1.7	1.0	.8	.4

*Inadequate number of cases.

†The cell entry represents a mean of the number of acts of political participation exclusive of voting reported for the two presidential campaigns of 1956 and 1960. For 1956, a point was awarded to each respondent for party membership, campaign contributions, attendance at political rallies, other party work, attempts to convince others through informal communication, and displaying campaign buttons or stickers. In 1960, essentially the same scoring applied, except that on two items more differentiated information was available. A point was awarded for attending one or two political rallies, two points for three to six rallies, and three points for seven or more. Similarly, a second point was awarded for people who reported having attempted in 1960 to convince others in more than one class (friends, family, or coworkers). A total score of 15 was possible, although empirically the highest score was 14. Only about 1% of the sample had scores greater than 9.

‡See Table 3 for definitions of the five strata.

TABLE 6

The Sophistication Composition of a "Typical" Political Rally, Compared to the
Composition of the Total Electorate*

	A Rally					The Electorate				
	High				Low	High				Low
High	5%	5%	11%	11%	2%	2%	3%	6%	3%	2%
	6	8	11	11	4	1	4	18	9	5
	0	5	9	0	†	†	1	6	1	2
	†	0	1	†	†	†	*	3	2	3
Low	†	2	7	1	0	†	1	11	7	11

†Less than half of 1%.
*Both five-by-five matrices are those employed in Tables 3, 4, and 5. Aside from rounding error, the proportions entered in each matrix total 100%. The table should be read by observing differences between proportions in the same regions of the two tables. For example, the three least sophisticated cells in the lower right-hand corner constitute 21% of the electorate and 1% of a typical rally audience.

than through any concern over the policy competition of politics.

Nonetheless, persistent and varied participation is most heavily concentrated among the most sophisticated people. This fact is important, for much of what is perceived as "public reaction" to political events depends upon public visibility, and visibility depends largely upon forms of political participation beyond the vote itself. Anyone familiar with practical politics has encountered the concern of the local politician that ideas communicated in political campaigns be kept simple and concrete. He knows his audience and is constantly fighting the battle against the overestimation of sophistication to which the purveyor of political ideas inevitably falls prey. Yet, even the grass-roots audience that forms a reference point for the local politician is, we suspect, a highly self-selected one and quite sophisticated relative to the electorate as a whole.

Since we have 1960 information on the number of political rallies attended by each of our respondents, we may simulate the "sophistication composition" of the typical political gathering. "Typical" is loosely used here, for real gatherings are various in character: A dinner for the party faithful at $15 a plate obviously attracts a different audience from the one that comes to the parade and street rally.

Nonetheless, the contrast between the electorate and an hypothetical average rally is instructive (Table 6). People located in the three upper left-hand corner cells of the matrix (6% of the electorate) form more than 15% of the composition of such rallies, and probably, in terms of further rally participation (vocal and otherwise), seem to form a still higher proportion. Yet on election day their vote (even with a 100% turnout) is numerically outweighed by those votes mustered by people in the single cell at the opposite corner of the table who do not attend at all.

One of the most intriguing findings on the surface of the matrix is that strength of party loyalty falls to one of its weakest points in the upper left-hand corner cell of the matrix. In other words, among the most highly sophisticated, those who consider themselves "independents" outnumber those who consider themselves "strong" partisans, despite the fact that the most vigorous political activity, much of it partisan, is carried on by people falling in this cell. If one moves diagonally toward the center of the matrix, this balance is immediately redressed and redressed very sharply, with strong partisans far outnumbering independents. In general, there is a slight tendency (the most sophisticated cell excepted) for strength of party loyalty to decline as one moves diagonally across the table, and the most "independent" cell is that in the lower right-hand corner.[20]

This irregularity has two implications. First, we take it to be one small and special case of our earlier hypothesis that group-objects (here, the party as group) are likely to have less centrality in the belief system of the most sophisticated and that the centrality of groups as referents increases "lower down" in the sophistication ordering. We shall see more handsome evidence of the same phenomenon later. Second, we see in this reversal at least a partial explanation for the persistence of the old assumption that the "independent voter" is relatively informed and involved. The early cross-section studies by Lazarsfeld and his colleagues turned up evidence to reverse this equation, suggesting that the "independent voter" tends instead to be relatively uninformed and uninvolved. Other studies have added massively to this evidence. Indeed, in many situations, the evidence seems so strong that it is hard to imagine how any opposing perceptions could have developed. The perception is somewhat easier to understand, however, if one can assume that the discernment of the informed observer takes in only 5, 10, or 15% of the most sophisticated people in the public as constituting "the public." This "visible" or "operative" public is largely made up of people from the upper left-hand corner of our preceding tables. The

[20]This cell is laden, of course, with people who are apathetic and apolitical, although more than half of them vote in major elections. Flanigan, working with the total sample, set aside those who never vote as politically inconsequential and then set about comparing the remainder of self-styled independents with strong partisans. Some of the customary findings relating political independence with low involvement and low information then became blurred or in some cases reversed themselves altogether. Our highly sophisticated independents contribute to this phenomenon. See William H. Flanigan, "Partisanship and Campaign Participation" (Unpublished doctoral dissertation, Yale University, 1961).

illusion that such people are the full public is one that the democratic sample survey, for better or for worse, has destroyed.

V. CONSTRAINTS AMONG IDEA-ELEMENTS

In our estimation, the use of such basic dimensions of judgment as the liberal-conservative continuum betokens a contexual grasp of politics that permits a wide range of more specific idea-elements to be organized into more tightly constrained wholes. We feel, furthermore, that there are many crucial consequences of such organization: With it, for example, new political events have more meaning, retention of political information from the past is far more adequate, and political behavior increasingly approximates that of sophisticated "rational" models, which assume relatively full information.

It is often argued, however, that abstract dimensions like the liberal-conservative continuum are superficial if not meaningless indicators: All that they show is that poorly educated people are inarticulate and have difficulty expressing verbally the more abstract lines along which their specific political beliefs are organized. To expect these people to be able to express what they know and feel, the critic goes on, is comparable to the fallacy of assuming that people can say in an accurate way why they behave as they do. When it comes down to specific attitudes and behaviors, the organization is there nonetheless, and it is this organization that matters, not the capacity for discourse in sophisticated language.

If it were true that such organization does exist for most people, apart from their capacities to be articulate about it, we would agree out of hand that the question of articulation is quite trivial. As a cold empirical matter, however, this claim does not seem to be valid. Indeed, it is for this reason that we have cast the argument in terms of constraint, for constraint and organization are very nearly the

TABLE 7

Constraint between Specific Issue Beliefs for an Elite Sample and a Cross-Section Sample, 1958*

	Domestic					Foreign		
	Employment	Education	Housing	F.E.P.C.	Economic	Military†	Isolationism	Party Preference
Congressional candidates								
Employment	.62	.59	.35	.26	.06	.17	.68
Aid to education	. . .	.61	.53	.50	.06	.35	.55
Federal housing		. . .	.47	.41	−.03	.30	.68
F.E.P.C.			. . .	.47	.11	.23	.34
Economic aid					. . .	.19	.59	.25
Military aid						. . .	.32	−.18
Isolationism							. . .	.05
Party preference								. . .
Cross-Section Sample								
Employment	.45	.08	.34	−.04	.10	−.22	.20
Aid to education	. . .	.12	.29	.06	.14	−.17	.16
Federal housing		. . .	.08	−.06	.02	.07	.18
F.E.P.C.			. . .	.24	.13	.01	−.04
Economic aid					. . .	.16	.33	−.07
Soldiers abroad†						. . .	.21	.12
Isolationism							. . .	−.03
Party preference								. . .

*Entries are tau-gamma coefficients, a statistic proposed by Leo A. Goodman and William H. Kruskal in "Measures of Association for Cross Classification," *Journal of the American Statistical Association*, 49 (Dec. 1954), No. 268, 749. The coefficient was chosen because of its sensitivity to constraint of the scalar as well as the correlational type.

†For this category, the cross-section sample was asked a question about keeping American soldiers abroad, rather than about military aid in general.

same thing. Therefore when we hypothesize that constraint among political idea-elements begins to lose its range very rapidly once we move from the most sophisticated few toward the "grass roots," we are contending that the organization of more specific attitudes into wide-ranging belief systems is absent as well.

Table 7 gives us an opportunity to see the differences in levels of constraint among beliefs on a range of specific issues in an elite population and in a mass population. The elite population happens to be candidates for the United States Congress in the off-year elections of 1958, and the cross-section sample represents the national electorate in the same year. The assortment of issues represented is simply a purposive sampling of some of the more salient political controversies at the time of the study, covering both domestic and foreign policy. The questions posed to the two samples were quite comparable, apart

from adjustments necessary in view of the backgrounds of the two populations involved.[21]

For our purposes, however, the specific elite sampled and the specific beliefs tested are rather beside the point. We would

---

[21]As a general rule, questions broad enough for the mass public to understand tend to be too simple for highly sophisticated people to feel comfortable answering without elaborate qualification. The pairings of questions, with those for the mass public given first, are as follows:

Employment. "The government in Washington ought to see to it that everybody who wants to work can find a job." "Do you think the federal government ought to sponsor programs such as large public works in order to maintain full employment, or do you think that problems of economic readjustment ought to be left more to private industry or state and local government?"

Aid to Education. "If cities and towns around the country need help to build more schools, the government in Washington ought to give them the money they need." "Do you think the government should provide grants to the states for the construction and operation of public schools, or do you think the support of public education

TABLE 8
Summary of Differences in Level of Constraint within and between Domains,
Public and Elite (based on Table 7)

| | Average Coefficients | | | |
	Within Domestic Issues	*Between Domestic and Foreign*	*Within Foreign Issues*	*Between Issues and Party*
Elite	.53	.25	.37	.39
Mass	.23	.11	.23	.11

expect the same general contrast to appear if the elite had been a set of newspaper editors, political writers, or any other group that takes an interest in politics. Similarly, we would expect the same results from any other broad sampling of political issues or, for that matter, any sampling of beliefs from other domains: A set of questions on matters of religious controversy should show the same pattern between an elite population like the clergy and the church members who form

should be left entirely to the state and local government?"

Federal Housing. "The government should leave things like electric power and housing for private businessmen to handle." "Do you approve the use of federal funds for public housing, or do you generally feel that housing can be taken care of better by private effort?"

F.E.P.C. "If Negroes are not getting fair treatment in jobs and housing, the government should see to it that they do." "Do you think the federal government should establish a fair employment practices commission to prevent discrimination in employment?"

Economic Aid. "The United States should give economic help to the poorer countries of the world even if those countries can't pay for it." "First, on the foreign economic aid program, would you generally favor expanding the program, reducing it, or maintaining it about the way it is?"

Military Aid. "The United States should keep soldiers overseas where they can help countries that are against Communism." "How about the foreign military aid program? Should this be expanded, reduced, or maintained about as it is?"

Isolationism. "This country would be better off if we just stayed home and did not concern ourselves with problems in other parts of the world." "Speaking very generally, do you think that in the years ahead the United States should maintain or reduce its commitments around the world?"

their mass "public." What is generically important in comparing the two types of population is the difference in levels of constraint among belief-elements.

Where constraint is concerned, the absolute value of the coefficients in Table 7 (rather than their algebraic value) is the significant datum. The first thing the table conveys is the fact that, for both populations, there is some falling off of constraint *between* the domains of domestic and foreign policy, relative to the high level of constraint *within* each domain. This result is to be expected: Such lowered values signify boundaries between belief systems that are relatively independent. If we take averages of appropriate sets of coefficients entered in Table 7 however, we see that the strongest constraint *within* a domain for the mass public is less than that *between* domestic and foreign domains for the elite sample. Furthermore, for the public, in sharp contrast to the elite, party preference seems by and large to be set off in a belief system of its own, relatively unconnected to issue positions (Table 8).[22]

It should be remembered throughout, of course, that the *mass* sample of Tables

[22]We are aware that drawing an average of these coefficients has little intepretation from a statistical point of view. The averages are presented merely as a crude way of capturing the flavor of the larger table in summary form. More generally, it could be argued that the coefficients might be squared in any event, an operation that would do no more than heighten the intuitive sense of contrast between the two publics. In this format, for example, the elite-mass difference in the domestic-issue column of Table 8 would shift from .53 *vs.* .23 to .28 *vs* .05. Similarly, that in the party column would become .15 *vs.* .01.

7 and 8 does not exclude college-educated people, ideologues, or the politically sophisticated. These people, with their higher levels of constraint, are represented in appropriate numbers, and certainly contribute to such vestige of organization as the mass matrix evinces. But they are grossly outnumbered, as they are in the active electorate. The general point is that the matrix of correlations for the elite sample is of the sort that would be appropriate for factor analysis, the statistical technique designed to reduce a number of correlated variables to a more limited set of organizing dimensions. The matrix representing the mass public, however, despite its realistic complement of ideologues, is exactly the type that textbooks advise against using for factor analysis on the simple grounds that through inspection it is clear that there is virtually nothing in the way of organization to be discovered. Of course, it is the type of broad organizing dimension to be suggested by factor analysis of specific items that is usually presumed when observers discuss "ideological postures" of one sort or another.

Although the beliefs registered in Table 7 are related to topics of controversy or political cleavage, McClosky has described comparable differences in levels of constraint among beliefs for an elite sample (delegates to national party conventions) and a cross-section sample when the items deal with propositions about democracy and freedom—topics on which fundamental consensus among Americans is presumed.[23] Similarly, Prothro and Grigg, among others, have shown that, while there is widespread support for statements of culturally familiar principles of freedom, democracy, and tolerance in a cross-section sample, this support becomes rapidly obscured when questions turn to specific cases that elites would see as the most direct applications of these

principles.[24] In our estimation, such findings are less a demonstration of cynical lip service than of the fact that, while both of two inconsistent opinions are honestly held, the individual lacks the contextual grasp to understand that the specific case and the general principle belong in the same belief system: In the absence of such understanding, he maintains psychologically independent beliefs about both. This is another important instance of the decline in constraint among beliefs with declining information.

While an assessment of relative constraint between the matrices rests only on comparisons of absolute values, the comparative algebraic values have some interest as well. This interest arises from the sophisticated observer's almost automatic assumption that whatever beliefs "go together" in the visible political world (as judged from the attitudes of elites and the more articulate spectators) must naturally go together in the same way among mass public. Table 7 makes clear that this assumption is a very dangerous one, aside from the question of degree of constraint. For example, the politician who favors federal aid to education could be predicted to be more, rather than less, favorable to an internationalist posture in foreign affairs, for these two positions in the 1950s were generally associated with "liberalism" in American politics. As we see from Table 7, we would be accurate in this judgment considerably more often than chance alone would permit. On the other hand, were we to apply the same assumption of constraint to the American public in the same era, not only would we have been wrong, but we would actually have come closer to reality by assuming no connection at all.

All the correlations in the elite sample except those that do not depart significantly from zero exhibit signs that any-

[23]Herbert McClosky, "Consensus and Ideology in American Politics," *American Political Science Review*, 58 (June 1964), No. 2, pp. 361-82.

[24]James W. Prothro and C. W. Grigg, "Fundamental Principles of Democracy: Bases of Agreement and Disagreement," *Journal of Politics*, 22 (May 1960), No. 2, 276-94.

body following politics in the newspapers during this period could have predicted without hesitation. That is, one need only have known that Democrats tended to favor expansion of government welfare activities and tended to be internationalists in foreign affairs, to have anticipated all the signs except one. This exception, the − .18 that links advocacy of military aid abroad with the Republican Party, would hold no surprises either, for the one kind of international involvement that Republicans came to accept in this period limited foreign aid to the military variety, a view that stood in opposition to "soft" liberal interests in international economic welfare. If these algebraic signs in the elite matrix are taken as the culturally defined "proper" signs—the sophisticated observer's assumption of what beliefs go with what other beliefs—then the algebraic differences between comparable entries in the two matrices provide an estimate of how inaccurate we would be in generalizing our elite-based assumptions about "natural" belief combinations to the mass public as a whole. A scanning of the two matrices with these differences in mind enhances our sense of high discrepancy between the two populations.

To recapitulate, then, we have argued that the unfamiliarity of broader and more abstract ideological frames of reference among the less sophisticated is more than a problem in mere articulation. Parallel to ignorance and confusion over these ideological dimensions among the less informed is a general decline in constraint among specific belief elements that such dimensions help to organize. It cannot therefore be claimed that the mass public shares ideological patterns of belief with relevant elites at a specific level any more than it shares the abstract conceptual frames of reference.

Constraints and Overt Behavior

There is still another counter-hypothesis that deserves examination. This view would grant that the political belief systems of the less well educated may be more fragmented and chaotic. It would maintain at the same time, however, that this fact is inconsequential in the determination of behavior. The presence, absence, or incoherence of these "intervening" psychological states is thus epiphenomenal: Social structure commits behavior to certain channels quite independent of specific cognitions and perceptions of the actors themselves.[25] In other versions, researchable intervening mechanisms are suggested. The "opinion leader" model is one of them. If it is true that the mass of less knowledgeable people rely upon informal communication from a few more informed people for cues about desirable or appropriate behavior, then the lines of behavior choices followed in politics might indeed show strong sociostructural patterns, even though many uninformed actors have little of the opinion leaders' coherent and organized understanding of why one behavior is more appropriate than another. What these points of view have in common is the insistence that strong constraints can be expected to operate between sociostructural terms and conscious behavior choices quite apart from the presence or absence of appropriate intervening psychological "definitions of the situation."

---

[25]There is unquestionably a class of social behaviors for which this description is more rather than less apt, although one need not have recourse to mystical or unexplained terms to understand the processes involved. In any social system, some beliefs and behavior patterns are learned by the young in such a way that there is no awareness of the possibility of alternatives. Where beliefs are concerned, a phrase like "unspoken cultural assumptions" provides an appropriate description, and there are analogues in socially learned behaviors. Most of politics, however, involves competition between explicit alternatives, which means that conscious belief systems and conscious behavior choices have an important influence—which is *not* to say that these belief systems are not often better understood if one takes account of the sociostructural position of the actor who holds them. It *is* to say

(*Footnote continued on next page*)

FIGURE 1

The Correlation of Occupation and Vote Preference within Levels of Conceptualization

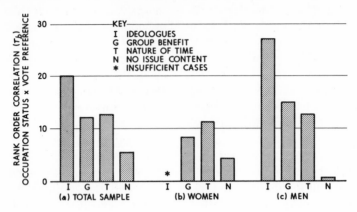

Figure 1 is addressed to such arguments. The graphs indicate the varying degrees of association between objective class position and partisan preference in the 1956 presidential election, as a function of differences in the nature of political belief systems captured by our "levels of conceptualization." If objective locations in the social structure served to produce behavioral consequences regardless of the presence or absence of relevant intervening organizations of conscious beliefs, then we would not expect any particular slope to the progression of bars within each graph. As Figure 1(a) shows for a sample of the adult electorate as a whole, however, the differences in intervening belief organization produce very marked and orderly differences in the degree to which partisanship reflects sociostructural position. Of course, from one point of view, this observation seems only common sense, yet the doctrinaire position that the intervening psychological terms are unimportant or epiphenomenal continues to be argued with more vehemence than empirical evidence.

Since it can be seen that a perfectly functioning opinion-leader model would also produce something approaching a rectangular distribution of bars in Figure

1, the slope depicted in Figure 1(a) can also be taken as a commentary on the practical imperfections with which opinion leader processes operate in this domain. That is, the "ideologues" and "near-ideologues" represented by the first bar of each graph are opinion leaders *par excellence*. While they tend to be disproportionately well educated, they nevertheless include representatives from all broad social *milieux*. Empirically they differ sharply from the less sophisticated in their attention to new political events and in the size of their store of information about past events. They get news firsthand and, presumably, form opinions directly from it. By their own report, they are much more likely than the less sophisticated to attempt to persuade others to their own political opinions in informal communications. Finally, much social data leads us to assume that the bulk of these informal communications is addressed to others within their own social *milieu*. Since social-class questions are important for these opinion leaders and since their own partisan preferences are rather clearly geared to their own class, we would suppose that "opinion leading" should serve to diffuse this connection between status and behavior through less knowledgeable members of their *milieu*, whether or not the more complicated rationales were diffused. In other words, most of what goes on in

that, whether or not they are present is not a matter of indifference for the course of behavior, as we shall see.

the heads of the less informed of our respondents would indeed be irrelevant for study if the respondents could at least be counted upon to follow the lead of more informed people of their own *milieu* in their ultimate partisanship. And to the extent that they can be counted on to behave in this way, we should expect Figure 1 to show a rectangular distribution of bars. The departure from such a pattern is very substantial.

Now there is one type of relationship in which there is overwhelming evidence for vigorous opinion-leading where politics is concerned in our society. It is the relationship within the family: The wife is very likely to follow her husband's opinions, however imperfectly she may have absorbed their justifications at a more complex level. We can do a fair job of splitting this relationship into its leader-follower components simply by subdividing our total sample by sex. As Figure 1(b) suggests, our expectation that the presence or absence of intervening belief systems is of reduced importance among sets of people who are predominantly opinion followers is well borne out by the relatively flat and disordered progression of bars among women. Correspondingly, of course, the same slope among men becomes steeper still in Figure 1(c).[26]

The fact that wives tend to double their husbands' votes is, from a broader "system" point of view, a relatively trivial one. If we are willing to consider the family as the basic voting unit, then Figure 1(c) suggests that diffusion of the sociostructurally "proper" behavior without diffusion of understanding of that behavior through simple opinion-leading processes is a very feeble mechanism indeed across

the society as a whole, at least where political decisions of this sort are concerned.[27] The organization of partisanship among those who give no evidence of intervening issue content shows no trace whatever of those residual effects that should be left by any systematic opinion-following (and that are visible among comparable women). Thus, while we are in no way questioning the existence of some opinion-leading, it seems doubtful that it represents the dominant, effective phenomenon sometimes supposed, a phenomenon that succeeds in lending shape to mass politics despite the absence of more detailed individual comprehension of the political context.[28]

Much more broadly, we have become convinced that this class of finding—the declining degree of constraint between a term representing social structure and one representing an important political choice as one moves from the more to the less politically sophisticated in the society—is a powerful and general one. It is powerful (for readers not accustomed to the statistics employed) in the simple sense that

---

[26]The reader is cautioned, in comparing Figures 1(b) and 1(c), that women classed (for example) as "no issue content" are not necessarily the wives of husbands who are also "no issue content." Indeed, the point of the comparison is that wives tend themselves to be qualified at less elevated levels than their husbands but organize their behavior in terms of their husband's "opinion leadership."

[27]It should be remembered in assessing Figure 1(c) that the complete absence of this kind of opinion-leading would not produce a graph with a single tall bar at the left and an absence of height for the three other bars. That is, opinion-leading quite aside, we should expect some kind of slope, albeit a steep one, since people represented by the second and (to a fainter degree) the third bars have cruder versions of the intervening images of politics that we are arguing have key behavioral importance. It is only the people represented by the fourth bar who give no evidence of this type of intervening organization at all.

[28]The empirical base for this argument becomes even more dramatic than is shown by Figure 1 if we consider all the psychological terms that a class orientation in voting presupposes. That is, Figure 1 treats the relationship between objective status and vote. To the degree that there are ideologues whose class identifications are not what their objective statuses would lead us to expect, they lower the degree of the association. Figure 13–3 of Campbell *et al., op. cit.,* p. 352, which is conceptually parallel to Figure 1 of this paper, shows that ideologues with reported awareness of their social classes have a towering monopoly on the association of *subjective status* and vote partisanship.

the variation in constraint as a function of sophistication or involvement is extremely large: There are no other discriminating variables that begin to separate populations so cleanly and sharply as these measures. It is a general finding in at least two senses. First, it replicates itself handsomely across time: In every instance within the span of time for which appropriate data are available, the finding is present where class and partisanship are concerned. Secondly, it has some incipient claim to generality where sociostructural terms other than "social class" are concerned: The same sharp finding emerges, for example, when the relationship between religion and partisanship (Protestant *vs.* Catholic) is examined.

And, of course, if class or religious membership is considered to constitute one set of idea-elements and the predispositions that lead to particular partisan preferences and final choice to form another, then the whole phenomenon takes its place as another large class of special cases of the decline of constraints and the narrowing of belief systems to which this paper is devoted.*

X. CONCLUSION

We have long been intrigued, in dealing with attitudinal and behavioral materials drawn from cross-section publics, at the frequency with which the following sequence of events occurs. An hypothesis is formed that seems reasonable to the

---

*Editor's note: The reader is cautioned that substantial portions of this work have been deleted because of space limitations. The deleted sections are:

VI.   Social Groupings as Central Objects in Belief Systems
VII. The Stability of Belief Elements over Time
VIII. Issue Publics
IX.   Summary

The deleted sections do not alter the overall conclusions of the chapter but consider other aspects of constraint and its sources. The student is urged to read the total selection.

analyst, having to do with one or another set of systematic differences in perceptions, attitudes, or behavior patterns. The hypothesis is tested on materials from the general population but shows at best some rather uninteresting trace findings. Then the sample is further subdivided by formal education, which isolates among other groups the 10% of the American population with college degrees or the 20% with some college education. It frequently turns out that the hypothesis is then very clearly confirmed for the most educated, with results rapidly shading off to zero within the less educated majority of the population.

We do not claim that such an analytic approach always produces findings of this sort. From time to time, of course, the hypothesis in question can be more broadly rejected for all groups, and, on rare occasions, a relationship turns out to be sharper among the less educated than among the well educated. Nevertheless, there is a strikingly large class of cases in which confirmation occurs only, or most sharply, among the well educated. Usually it is easy to see, after the fact if not before, the degree to which the dynamics of the processes assumed by the hypothesis rest upon the kinds of broad or abstract contextual information about currents of ideas, people, or society that educated people come to take for granted as initial ingredients of thought but that the most cursory studies will demonstrate are not widely shared. As experiences of this sort accumulate, we become increasingly sensitive to these basic problems of information and begin to predict their results in advance.

This awareness means that we come to expect hypotheses about wide-ranging yet highly integrated belief systems and their behavioral consequences to show results among relative elites but to be largely disconfirmed below them. It is our impression, for example, that even some of the more elaborate "ideological" patterns associated with the authoritarian personality syndrome follow this rule. Some recent results that have accumulated in connection with the Protestant-ethic hypothesis of Weber seem to hint at something of the same pattern as well.

In this paper, we have attempted to make some systematic comments on this kind of phenomenon that seem crucial to any understanding of elite and mass belief systems. We have tried to show the character of this "continental shelf" between elites and masses and to locate the sources of differences in their belief systems in some simple characteristics of information and its social transmission.

The broad contours of elite decisions over time can depend in a vital way upon currents in what is loosely called "the history of ideas." These decisions in turn have effects upon the mass of more common citizens. But, of any direct participa-

tion in this history of ideas and the behavior it shapes, the mass is remarkably innocent. We do not disclaim the existence of entities that might best be called "folk ideologies," nor do we deny for a moment that strong differentiations in a variety of narrower values may be found within subcultures of less educated people. Yet for the familiar belief systems that, in view of their historical importance, tend most to attract the sophisticated observer, it is likely that an adequate mapping of a society (or, for that matter, the world) would provide a jumbled cluster of pyramids or a mountain range, with sharp delineation and differentiation in beliefs from elite apex to elite apex but with the mass bases of the pyramids overlapping in such profusion that it would be impossible to decide where one pyramid ended and another began.

THE POLITICAL CULTURES OF THE AMERICAN STATES*

Samuel C. Patterson

The term "political culture" is not one of unambiguous content. For many social scientists *culture* remains in the exclusive and esoteric province of anthropology, where internecine warfare continues over

its definition.[1] For others, *political culture* cues reminiscences of the more unfortunate qualities of national character analyses.[2] Happily, we can extract what is use-

---

*Prepared for the Conference on the Comparative Study of American Political Behavior Related to State Government and Politics of the Inter-University Consortium for Political Research, Ann Arbor, Michigan, August 1–12, 1966.

Author's note: Professor Vernon Van Dyke gave an earlier version of this manuscript a critical reading with results that can be fully appreciated only by those who have profited by having their manuscripts read by Vernon Van Dyke. I also wish to thank my other colleagues, George Robert Boynton and George Platt, and my students, Ronald Hedlund, Phillip Althoff, and Garrison Nelson, for enlightening and helpful comments and suggestions on the manuscript. Finally, I appreciate the help of David Brady and the Laboratory for Political Research, Department of Political Science, University of Iowa.

[1] I can by no means claim exhaustive familiarity with the varied and venerable literature of cultural anthropology. Some of the major considerations involved in the culture concept can be found in A. L. Kroeber and Clyde Kluckhohn, *Culture: A Critical Review of Concepts and Definitions* (New York, 1963); Clyde Kluckhohn, *Culture and Behavior* (New York, 1962); and, Philip Bagby, *Culture and History: Prolegomena to the Comparative Study of Civilizations* (Berkeley and Los Angeles, 1963).

[2] I have found the most useful summary and critique of the "national character" literature to be that of Walter P. Metzger, "Generalizations about National Character: An Analytical Essay," in Louis Gottschalk (ed.), *Generalization in the Writing of History* (Chicago, 1963), pp. 77–102. Also, see Margaret Mead, "The Study of Na-
(*Footnote continued on next page*)

ful for political analysis from both traditions, without resolving the well-known definitional and analytical difficulties they present. In somewhat the same vein, certain dangers attend entry into comparative analysis of state politics beyond the standard, even though relatively recent, emphasis upon state party politics and elections.[3] It is possible, nonetheless, to make the case that our research in state politics ought to be comparative, and that it can in important ways fruitfully be guided by the organizing notion of political culture.

I. THE CONCEPT OF POLITICAL CULTURE

Political culture is a somewhat open-ended, multifaceted, sensitizing concept. It is open-ended in the sense that a rather wide variety of cognitions, values, and emotional commitments might be included in an analysis. It is multifaceted, or multidimensional, in the sense that it consists of several analytically distinct though presumably interrelated factors. Finally, it is a sensitizing concept in the sense that it directs attention to potential,

or largely unexploited, political data for the purpose of enhancing knowledge about subjective orientations to politics. The concept is not a theory about politics, nor does it invoke new political phenomena. It does focus attention on the symbolic, evaluative, and cognitive responses people have to the political system, and on the relationships of these orientations to other aspects of politics.

The concept had its genesis in the seminal formulation of Almond a decade ago, and has been applied mainly in the cross-national research nurtured by the Committee on Comparative Politics of the Social Science Research Council.[4] Verba gives the most lucid and thorough treatment of the concept in his essay on "Comparative Political Culture."[5] He defines it as "the system of empirical beliefs, expressive symbols, and values which defines the situation in which political action takes place."[6] By *empirical beliefs* he means the ways people perceive and interpret the nature of political relationships. By *expressive symbols* he means the ways people feel toward political institutions and leaders; patterns of political loyalty, identification, and commitment in the political system. By *values* he means the

tional Character," in Daniel Lerner and Harold D. Lasswell (eds.), *The Policy Sciences* (Stanford, 1951), pp. 70–85. The most provocative work on American national character has been done by Riesman. See David Riesman, with Nathan Glazer and Reuel Denney, *The Lonely Crowd: A Study of the Changing American Character* (New York, 1955); and, several of the essays in Seymour Martin Lipset and Leo Lowenthal (eds.), *Culture and Social Character* (New York, 1961).

[3]The "wide-openness" of state political research is indicated by the trail-blazing papers edited by Herbert Jacob and Kenneth N. Vines, *Politics in the American States: A Comparative Analysis* (Boston, 1965). Of course, V. O. Key, Jr. opened the territory; see *American State Politics: An Introduction* (New York, 1956). And Doug Price has tried to keep the subject of comparative state political analysis alive in papers prepared for the Annual Meeting of the American Political Science Association; see "Comparative Analysis in State and Local Politics: Potential and Problems" (1963), and "Southern Politics in the Sixties: Notes on Economic Development and Political Modernization" (1964).

[4]Gabriel A. Almond, "Comparative Political Systems," *Journal of Politics*, 18 (1956), 391–409; Gabriel A. Almond and James Coleman (eds.), *The Politics of the Developing Areas* (Princeton, 1960); Gabriel A. Almond and Sidney Verba, *The Civic Culture* (Princeton, 1963); and Lucian W. Pye and Sidney Verba (eds.), *Political Culture and Political Development* (Princeton, 1965).

[5]Pye and Verba, *op. cit.*, pp. 512–60.

[6]*Ibid.*, p. 513. Easton uses the term "basic political orientations" to characterize these elements. See David Easton and Robert D. Hess, "Youth and the Political System," in Lipset and Lowenthal, *op. cit.*, pp. 226–51, and "The Child's Political World," *Midwest Journal of Political Science*, VI (1962), pp. 229–46. Verba's basic framework is undoubtedly adapted from Parsons and Shils. See Talcott Parsons, Edward A. Shils, and James Olds, "Systems of Value Orientation," in Parsons and Shils (eds.), *Toward a General Theory of Action* (Cambridge, Mass., 1954), pp. 159–89.

FIGURE 1
Paradigm of Political Culture

Levels of a Political System	Elements of Political Culture		
	Empirical Beliefs	Expressive Symbols	Values
Government			
Regime			
Community			

standards used to set the general goals of the political system; standards used to evaluate political demands, processes, and products. A political culture can be characterized by relative, empirically determinable, levels of *consensus* in the sharing among people of these elements.

Political Culture and Political System

Following Easton, we suggest that subjective political orientations may be directed toward three distinctive levels of the political system: the government, the regime, and the political community. The government refers to those who occupy official positions, the authorities who make the binding decisions for the society. The *regime* means the constitutional order, the norms and basic form of the system. *Political community* refers to the group of persons who are bound or drawn together to solve common problems, participating in a common division of labor.[7] These levels of the political system are closely interlaced, but it is possible for changes to occur at one level without corresponding changes at others.

Each level of the political system may be regarded as an object of orientation for elements of the political culture. Borrowing from Easton's familiar diagram, it is useful to draw a simple paradigm (Fig-

ure 1) of political culture in terms of its major objects of orientation. Evaluations, commitments, interpretations, identifications, and loyalties may vary in a political system between government, regime, and community. These analytical distinctions have utility if for no other reason than to avoid neglect. Research on political orientations in the United States has, for instance, much more frequently focused on responses to government than on support for the regime. Even now our knowledge about empirical beliefs supportive of the regime is fragmentary.[8]

Dimensions of Political Culture

The integration and maintenance of political systems is heavily dependent upon adequate resolution of the problem of conflict and consensus over "basic political orientations."[9] Political culture may be said to regulate—provide limits and opportunities for—*the want conversion process* in a political system, and thus affect the frequency, intensity, and quality of demand input. As Easton suggests, "the values and biases of a political culture will prevent many demands from ever aris-

---

[7]See David Easton, *A Systems Analysis of Political Life* (New York, 1965), pp. 171–219. The concept of regime is used in a somewhat different sense in Robert E. Agger, Daniel Goldrich, and Bert E. Swanson, *The Rulers and the Ruled* (New York, 1964), pp. 82–93.

[8]James W. Prothro and Charles M. Grigg, "Fundamental Principles of Democracy: Bases of Agreement and Disagreement," *Journal of Politics*, XXII (1960), pp. 276–94; Herbert McClosky, "Consensus and Ideology in American Politics," *American Political Science Review*, LVIII (1964), pp. 361–82; Robert A. Dahl, *Who Governs?* (New Haven, 1961), pp. 311–25.

[9]Easton speaks of cultural "inhibitors" and "releasers" in *A Systems Analysis of Political Life*, pp. 100–116.

ing."[10] By inhibiting demand input, political culture may reduce elapsed time in demand processing, and thus contribute to the effectiveness or capability of the political system in managing demand overload.

Since the demand input load of a political system is directly related to the degree of political participation, and the political culture regulates the extent to which, and in what ways, individuals become politically involved, the importance of political culture is manifest. If the political culture facilitates wide political participation, demands for want conversion are relatively numerous, and the pressures on the political leaders are great to respond to, anticipate, and represent the demands of followers. On the other hand, where participation is constricted, demands on the political elite for want conversion may be minimal, and followers may be willing to leave wide areas of otherwise public concern to the authorities.

In addition to affecting the demand input of political systems, the political culture lies across the feedback channels of the system, responding to system outputs. Orientations to system outputs—to decisions, services, events, and images—may have important effects on political cohesion and stability, and on future demand inputs. Thus, the consequences of political culture are dynamic, regulating not only input demands and the system of political interactions but also influencing the conversion of system outputs into new or modified inputs.

Political integration and performance capability are dependent upon the supportive dimension of political identification. As Verba points out, "It is the sense of identity with the nation that legitimizes the activities of national elites and makes it possible for them to mobilize the commitment and support of their followers."[11]

System identification, pride, commitment, and loyalty may be associated with political subsystems as well as with the national entity, and a sequence or matrix of identifications may be either cleavage-tending or consensus-building. A high degree of pride, loyalty, and identification with Indiana may contribute to national unity in the particular circumstances of the United States, but identification with Quebec contributes to cleavage and system-periling disunity in Canada. Uncertainties about political identity are related to individual attributes of self-confidence and self-esteem, as well as to conflicts between parochial and national loyalties. Again, a political culture can be characterized "by the extent to which individuals identify with each other as members of the same system."[12] Ego identity and self-other attachments probably work together with system identification to constitute a cluster of intertwined dimensions of political identity. Faith in self, faith in people, and faith in the system are qualities of a political culture that enhance stability and, in all probability, provide the best support for democratic polity.

Political Style and Learning

Political style is an important aspect of political culture. The term refers to the ways in which political beliefs are held and applied.[13] Verba makes an important distinction between ideological and pragmatic political styles. The ideological style "involves a deeply affective commitment to a comprehensive and explicit set of political values which covers not merely political affairs but all of life, a set of values which is hierarchical in form and often deduced from a more general set of 'first principles'."[14] The pragmatic political style "consists of an evaluation of problems in terms of their individual merits rather than in terms of some pre-existing

[10]*Ibid.*, p. 103.

[11]Pye and Verba, *op. cit.*, p. 529. See also Gabriel A. Almond, "A Developmental Approach to Political Systems," *World Politics*, XVII (1964), pp. 204–5.

[12]Pye and Verba, *op. cit.*, p. 535.

[13]*Ibid.*, pp. 544–50.

[14]*Ibid.*, p. 545.

FIGURE 2
Paradigm of Political Style

Types of Political Style	Dimensions of Political Beliefs					
	Receptivity		Specificity		Symbolic Formulation	
	Open	Closed	Implicit	Explicit	Instrumental	Expressive
Ideological						
Pragmatic						

comprehensive view of reality."[15] Verba then identifies three distinctive dimensions of political belief, which can be summarized in a simple diagram (see Figure 2). Both ideological and pragmatic political styles can be analyzed in terms of the degree of receptivity, specificity, and symbolic formulation of beliefs. Thus, political beliefs may be held or expressed tentatively or rigidly, explicitly or implicitly, instrumentally or expressively. Edelman has explored political language and ritual along the expressive-instrumental dimension of political acts, identifying four distinctive styles of language: hortatory, legal, administrative, and bargaining.[16]

Political values, beliefs, and commitments are learned from experiences with the political process or from a host of nonpolitical experiences. Political socialization is continuous over the lifespan, although the available research indicates the great importance of childhood experiences and the impact of the political values of primary groups.[17] Where the socialization process results in disparities between what is learned in childhood and the experiences of adult contact with the political process, the political system suffers some strain. In a society, variations in politi-

cal socialization may occur in terms of the content—the politico-cultural values—learned, and in terms of the relative gaps between preadult and adult experiences when, for example, the nature of political processes varies.

II. AMERICAN POLITICAL CULTURE

The American political culture has been characterized as allegiant, participant, and civic.[18] Americans are relatively highly exposed to and involved in politics, have a relatively potent sense of civic competence, and tend to have a high degree of pride in and attachment to the political system. Substantial proportions of the population exhibit positive orientations to the national government, and attitudes toward the national government show little change across ethnic, racial, or other group boundaries.[19]

Basic American political beliefs are homogeneous, and can be characterized in a general way as liberal in the Lockean

---

[15]*Ibid.*

[16]Murray Edelman, *The Symbolic Uses of Politics* (Urbana, 1964), pp. 130-51.

[17]See Herbert Hyman, *Political Socialization* (Glencoe, Ill., 1959); Almond and Verba, *The Civic Culture*, pp. 323-74; Roberta Sigel (ed.), "Political Socialization: Its Role in the Political Process," *Annals of the American Academy of Political and Social Science*, CCCLXI (1965), pp. 1-129; and Fred I. Greenstein, *Children and Politics* (New Haven, 1965).

[18]Almond and Verba, *op. cit.*, pp. 440-55. Value orientations in American society have been treated by Robin Williams, *American Society* (New York, 1951); Seymour Martin Lipset, *The First New Nation* (New York, 1963); Gabriel A. Almond, *The American People and Foreign Policy* (New York, 1950), pp. 29-68; David M. Potter, *People of Plenty* (Chicago, 1954); John Gillin, "National and Regional Cultural Values in the United States," *Social Forces*, XXXIV (1955), pp. 107-13; Lee Coleman, "What Is American? A Study of Alleged American Traits," *Social Forces*, XIX (1941), pp. 492-99; Geoffrey Gorer, *The American People* (New York, 1964).

[19]Donald E. Stokes, "Popular Evaluations of Government: An Empirical Assessment," in Harlan Cleveland and Harold D. Lasswell (eds.), *Ethics and Bigness* (New York, 1962), pp. 61-72.

sense.[20] Following Mitchell, we can summarize the major themes associated with the American political belief system:[21]

—Political action should be minimized, and allocations of values should be dependent chiefly on private action.

—Political power is tangible and limited in quantity, and tends to be evil.

—Legitimate political power has rational-legal authority as its only adequate basis.

—Citizenship is a duty distinct from social life generally.

—Americans exhibit ambivalent attitudes toward compromise.

—Public office is a public trust, and political action should be taken only in the public interest.

—Politics tends to be thought of as a game.

—Political interpretations and assessments tend to be moralistic.

—Political problems can be resolved by intelligence, good will, and hard work.

If these attributes roughly characterize the basic American belief system, it must be noted that they are not universally accepted. Civic obligation has, under the stress of national crisis, often in America been converted into extreme insecurity about the political loyalty of others, as can best be illustrated by McCarthyism.[22] When ambivalence about compromise and distrust of politics get converted into conspiratorial interpretations of the most extreme sort, we observe the "paranoid style" in American politics.[23] As Hofstadter and others have pointed out, these elements of the American belief system are not new, extending from the domestic panic over the allegedly subversive activities of Weishaupt's Illuminati in the late eighteenth century to the contemporary political style of Robert Welsh and his followers. Finally, particularistic intolerance with respect to racial political equality, most notable in the southern states, has for over a hundred years constituted an important source of stress in the political system.[24]

III. INTERSTATE VARIATIONS IN POLITICAL CULTURE

The notion of interstate variations in political culture within the American political system certainly is intuitively attractive. The states are political subsystems which, in all probability, crucially affect the persistence of the national political system. Obviously, the states are highly influenced by national policy, and politics in the United States has become increasingly nationalized. Yet, the states can be treated for analytical purposes as relatively independent political systems with political cultures at least somewhat distinctive to themselves.

We clearly have very little empirical data on the characteristics of political culture within American states. That there are differences seems obvious, and these have been noted by a number of observers of American politics. A variety of differences were noted by John Gunther from his rich impressionistic experience with the practice of politics across the country. He thought "Oregon and Washington are twins except as to character," but "nowhere else in the country can the extraordinary tenacity of state characteristics be better observed, the deep-rooted instinct of a state to grow its own way without regard to its neighbors."[25] Key

[20]Louis Hartz, *The Liberal Tradition in America* (New York, 1955).

[21]William C. Mitchell, *The American Polity* (New York, 1962), pp. 104–21.

[22]Edward A. Shils, *The Torment of Secrecy* (Glencoe, Ill., 1956).

[23]Richard Hofstadter, *The Paranoid Style in American Politics* (New York, 1965).

[24]For instance, see James W. Vander Zanden, "The Klan Revival," *American Journal of Sociology*, 65 (1960), 456–62; Avery Leiserson (ed.), *The American South in the 1960's* (New York, 1964); and Allan P. Sindler (ed.), *Change in the Contemporary South* (Durham, N.C., 1963).

[25]John Gunther, *Inside U.S.A.* (rev. ed.; New York, 1951), pp. 89 and 93.

found significant differences between two southern states:[26]

The political distance from Virginia to Alabama must be measured in light years. Virginian deference to the upper orders and the Byrd machine's restraint of popular aberrations give Virginia politics a tone and a reality radically different from the tumult of Alabama. There a wholesome contempt for authority and a spirit of rebellion akin to that of the Populist days resist the efforts of the big farmers and "big mules"—the local term for Birmingham industrialists and financiers —to control the state. Alabamians retain a sort of frontier independence, with an inclination to defend liberty and to bait the interests.

The generality of these kinds of differences is unknown. No one would expect the American political culture to be uniformly distributed spatially; our evidence is adequate enough to show that the political culture of Mississippi is not the same as that of Iowa. Some states may stand out more distinctly than others, and some group themselves in sections or regions that are distinctive.[27] Barring these potential complications, at least for the moment, it may be useful to set forth some of the kinds of interstate variability in political culture and refer to the fragmentary data.

Basic Attitudes Vary

Attitudes of tolerance of nonconformity vary on an areal basis; North–South differ-

ences have been shown to be independent of differences in urbanism or education. After a very shrewd analysis of his survey data, Stouffer concluded:[28]

Southerners are more rural than Northerners. Southerners also tend to have less education. But neither of these facts alone will explain the North–South differences in tolerance of nonconformists. There is something in Southern culture that tends to differentiate Southerners, in cities as well as rural areas, at all educational levels, from all other regional groups.

Stouffer's research dealt mainly with the threat of Communism and intolerance of nonconformity. Prothro and Grigg drew samples from two states—Michigan (Ann Arbor) and Florida (Tallahassee)—and interviewed respondents about their basic attitudes toward majority rule and minority rights.[29] While the authors considered education to have the greatest effect on intercommunity differences over democratic values, interregional differences presumably remained intact, and could not, of course, have been influenced by rural–urban differences since the respondents were drawn from urban areas in both states. As Table 1 shows, the Michigan sample exhibited considerably more democratic beliefs than the Florida sample; especially in the area of minority rights. A Harris Survey in late 1965 underscored the difference in tolerance of nonconformity levels between the South and the rest of the country: 68 percent of southerners were scored as intolerant of nonconformist political or professional behavior, while the East was at 56 percent, the Midwest at 58 percent, and the

[26]V. O. Key, Jr., *Southern Politics* (New York, 1950), p. 36. Key's monumental comparative analysis of southern party politics has been followed by volumes on other regions: see Duane Lockard, *New England State Politics* (Princeton, N.J., 1959); John H. Fenton, *Politics in the Border States* (New Orleans, 1957); the less useful collection edited by Frank H. Jonas, *Western Politics* (Salt Lake City, 1961); and John H. Fenton, *Midwest Politics* (New York, 1966).

[27]V. O. Key stressed intersectional similarities in attitudes in *Public Opinion and American Democracy* (New York, 1961), pp. 100–10. For a discussion of interregional cultural differences, see Gillin, "National and Regional Values," *loc. cit.*

[28]Samuel A. Stouffer, *Communism, Conformity, and Civil Liberties* (Garden City, N.Y., 1955), pp. 109–30. For an extensive analysis of the foreign policy attitudes of southerners, and voluminous material on the southern subculture, see Alfred O. Hero, Jr., *The Southerner and World Affairs* (Baton Rouge, La., 1965).

[29]Prothro and Grigg, "Fundamental Principles of Democracy: Bases of Agreement and Disagreement," *loc. cit.*

TABLE 1

Percentage of "Democratic" Responses to Basic Principles of Democracy
Among Selected Population Groups (1960)

	Democratic Response*	Michigan (Ann Arbor)	Florida (Tallahassee)
Majority Rule			
Only informed vote	—	56	38
Only taxpayers vote	—	21	21
Bar Negro from office	—	89	67
Bar Communist from office	—	41	46
AMA right to bloc voting	+	45	46
Minority Rights			
Allow antireligious speech	+	67	57
Allow socialist speech	+	81	77
Allow Communist speech	+	51	33
Bar Negro from candidacy	—	86	58
Bar Communist from candidacy	—	44	38

*Agreement $= +$; disagreement $= -$.
Source: James W. Prothro and Charles M. Grigg, "Fundamental Principles of Democracy;
Bases of Agreement and Disagreement," *Journal of Politics*, XXII (1960), 285.

West at 56 percent. The Harris Survey included questions about toleration of American Communists, people who do not believe in God, anti-Vietnam war pickets and other demonstrators, members of the Birch Society, lawyers who defend notorious criminals, and so forth, and the relatively high intolerance levels are the result of the rather wide sweep of the questions asked.[30]

A Harris Survey in 1964 makes it possible to view one aspect of the political culture of Mississippi, perhaps the most traditional, ascriptive, particularistic, and underdeveloped state in the country.[31] Senator Goldwater received 87 percent of the 1964 Presidential election vote in Mississippi. After the election, the Harris Survey asked Mississippians to rate the performance of Lyndon Johnson on a variety of criteria, and these were compared with the South and the nation as a whole. The

data are so striking they are worth reproducing here, in Table 2. They indicate sharp differences between Mississippi and other states in images of Presidential performance. In addition, the same survey found that more than three times as many Mississippians as Americans generally saw Communist infiltration of the government as the major problem in the nation faced, and 96 percent of those in the Mississippi sample opposed the Civil Rights Acts (compared to 54 percent of southerners). Further, while most Americans viewed Lyndon Johnson as a conservative or middle-of-the-roader, more than half of the Mississippians viewed him as a liberal and an additional quarter classified him as a "radical." While most Americans saw Barry Goldwater as a "radical," nearly three fourths of the Mississippians saw him as a conservative. Finally, while 64 percent of the national sample and 58 percent of the southern sample classified themselves as liberal or middle-of-the-road, 88 percent of the Mississippians classed themselves as conservative.

V. O. Key described the substantial interstate variations in the South of political

---

[30]Harris Survey, September 27, 1965; see also, Allen W. Moger, "Virginia's Conservative Political Heritage," *South Atlantic Quarterly*, L (1951), pp. 318–29.

[31]See James W. Silver, *Mississippi: The Closed Society* (New York, 1963).

TABLE 2

Images of the President: Ratings of Lyndon Johnson's Performance by Mississippians, Southerners, and the Nation (1964)

	Percentage Who Rated Johnson Positively*		
	Mississippi	South	Nation
Overall performance	19	58	74
Getting Congress to act	70	76	86
Keeping U.S. defenses strong	44	70	86
Working for peace	20	79	82
Firm stand on Berlin	27	67	79
Keeping economy healthy	23	59	69
Antipoverty program	18	55	64
Reducing taxes	27	56	60
Keeping Communists out of government	13	52	58
Handling Vietnam	25	43	57
Handling Castro	21	45	56
Keeping spending under control	17	43	56
Handling farm problems	17	44	56
Handling civil rights and race	4	41	53
Handling corruption in government	18	38	51
Handling safety on the streets	15	37	50
Handling foreign aid	25	41	50
Handling racial outbreaks	2	30	50
Handling Bobby Baker case	2	15	30

*Data for the South include Mississippi; data for the nation include the South. There may be reason to suspect oversampling of whites in the Mississippi sample.
Source: Harris Survey, November 23, 1964.

structure and practice, which suggest differences of political culture in the region. Mississippi certainly differs in important ways from the rest of the South. The South has, for obvious reasons, attracted the most attention in terms of its cultural peculiarities. To what extent the scope and content of basic political orientations vary between states generally we do not know.

Political Identification Varies

Almond and Verba found pride in governmental and political institutions more prevalent in the United States than in the United Kingdom, Germany, Italy, or Mexico; 85 percent of the Americans interviewed said they were proud of their government.[32] Van Dyke has underscored the importance of national pride in the

policy-making process, with special reference to the space program.[33] We can assume that Americans feel identified with, and proud of, their nation *and their states*. In a federal structure, the states are likely to constitute important focuses for identification, loyalty, and pride. National integration will be influenced by some mix of national and state loyalties.

Unfortunately, political scientists have not given the integrating factor of national identification much attention, perhaps especially in research on the American political system. The importance of this factor is suggested by the speculation of Almond and Verba:[34]

The attitude most relevant to long-term political stability may not be the individual's level of satisfaction with governmental out-

[32]Almond and Verba, *op. cit.*, p. 102.

[33]Vernon Van Dyke, *Pride and Power* (Urbana, Ill., 1964), pp. 136–62.
[34]Almond and Verba, *op. cit.*, p. 246.

put or with his role as participant. Rather, long-run political stability may be more dependent on a more diffuse sense of attachment or loyalty to the political system—a loyalty not based specifically on system performance.

But, if we really know very little about the effects of national identification for the United States, we know almost nothing about the effects of state identifications on the stability of state political systems, nor do we know much from empirical data about the unifying–divisive functions of the intermingling of national and state loyalties. The example of the American Civil War is temporally distant, and not likely to recur, though it undoubtedly provides instructive lessons on this point. In all, de Tocqueville may have been right that "every citizen of the United States transfuses his attachment to his little republic in the common store of American patriotism."[35]

We are all, presumably, aware of the phenomenon of state pride. We suspect Americans are generally proud to be Iowans, Texans, Wisconsinites, or Michiganders. Gunther found the phenomenon of state pride ("Maine has great pride. Almost all its people are proud, from the marmoreally entrenched aristocracy of Bar Harbor to the lonely professor living in a shack on a deserted beach."),[36] and believed it to be stronger in some states than others. He identifies Maine, Texas, Kansas, and Indiana as the states where pride

and loyalty were most notable. The pride of Texans is notorious, and it surely seems to have had political consequences there. Pappy O'Daniel, politician and poet laureate of the Texas flour industry, once wrote a local hit song called "Beautiful Texas."[37]

Yet, pride in a state may sometimes be largely an artifact of history, tradition, or sentiment. It may not always be converted into pride in the state political system, especially where state political institutions and issues have low cognitive salience. Intervening identifications may wash out state identification; those who live in New York City are likely to identify with the city, and only much less to the state. Finally, state pride may under some circumstances be manifested by its counterpart, humiliation or mortification. It may be that many in the South accept racial integration not so much because they believe that integration is desirable, but because they want to avoid stigma in the eyes of those who live elsewhere in the country. They want to be proud, but cannot when they know that most people in the United States (and in other parts of the world) look at their states with reproof. Interstate comparisons as referents for pride are probably fairly generally made, and the rank of a state on one criterion or another may have a bearing on the extent to which citizens are proud or mortified.

The data from the Almond-Verba Five Nations Study reveal some interregional variations in national pride (see Table 3). Pride in governmental and political institutions is highest in New England, the South Atlantic states, and the Mountain states, and lowest in the East South Central part of the country. Explanations for these interregional differences are not fully apparent, and controlling the regional comparisons for differences in educational levels does not entirely eliminate

---

[35]Alexis de Tocqueville, *Democracy in America* (London, 1946), pp. 107–8. Converse comments that "even in the modern United States, there are scattered pockets of the population that are rather vague about national identity. We encounter respondents, for example, who when asked if they were born in the United States, answer "No, I was born in Georgia." See Philip E. Converse, "The Nature of Belief Systems in Mass Publics," in David E. Apter (ed.), *Ideology and Discontent* (New York, 1964), p. 258.

[36]Gunther, *op. cit.*, p. 498. For an interesting treatment of the distinctiveness of Indiana Hoosiers, see John R. Seeley *et al.*, *Community Chest* (Toronto, 1957), pp. 48–55.

---

[37]W. Eugene Hollon, *The Southwest: Old and New* (New York, 1961), p. 372.

TABLE 3

Regional Variations in Aspects of Nation in Which Respondents Report Pride

(in percentages)

Percentage Who Say They Are Proud of:	New England*	Middle Atlantic	South Atlantic	East South Central	West South Central	East North Central	West North Central	Mountain	Pacific	U.S. Total
Governmental, political institutions	92	84	89	70	86	82	84	94	86	85
Social legislation	20	12	11	21	12	10	13	13	10	12
Position in international affairs	12	13	11	5	7	8	8	16	7	9
Economic system	33	27	21	14	23	24	11	13	31	24
Characteristics of people	2	7	7	11	4	4	6	10	13	7
Spiritual values and religion	4	†	5	4	4	4	2	...	4	3
Contributions to the arts	2	2	†	2	†	3	†	...	2	2
Contributions to science	4	1	4	4	2	1	7	3	7	3
Physical attributes of country	4	6	2	4	4	6	4	6	7	5
Nothing or don't know	...	4	†	4	†	1	...	...	†	1
Other	12	7	3	7	8	4	8	16	3	6
Total % of Responses‡	185	163	154	146	151	147	143	171	170	1522
Total % of Respondents	100	100	100	100	100	100	100	100	100	100
Total Number of Cases	51	198	147	56	109	170	102	31	106	970

*The regional breakdown conforms to the standard U.S. Census classification, as follows: *New England*: Maine, New Hampshire, Vermont, Massachusetts, Connecticut, Rhode Island; *Middle Atlantic*: New York, New Jersey, Pennsylvania; *South Atlantic*: West Virginia, Maryland, Delaware, Virginia, North Carolina, South Carolina, Georgia, Florida; *East South Central*: Kentucky, Tennessee, Alabama, Mississippi; *West South Central*: Oklahoma, Texas, Arkansas, Louisiana; *East North Central*: Wisconsin, Illinois, Indiana, Michigan, Ohio; *West North Central*: North Dakota, South Dakota, Nebraska, Kansas, Minnesota, Iowa, Missouri; *Mountain*: Montana, Idaho, Wyoming, Nevada, Utah, Colorado, Arizona, New Mexico; *Pacific*: Washington, Oregon, California, Alaska, Hawaii.

†Less than 1%.

‡Percentages exceed 100 because of multiple responses.

Source: Almond-Verba Five Nations Study. The data are from the Inter-University Consortium for Political Research, Ann Arbor, Michigan, and were processed by the Laboratory for Political Research, Department of Political Science, University of Iowa.

TABLE 4

Percent Who Say They are Proud of the Governmental and
Political System by Region and Education

	Educational Level		
Region*	Primary or Less	Secondary or More	Total
New England	100	86	92
Middle Atlantic	72	93	84
South Atlantic	89	90	89
East South Central	70	70	70
West South Central	83	91	86
East North Central	75	90	82
West North Central	76	92	84
Mountain	85	100	94
Pacific	85	86	86
All states	80	90	85

*The regional breakdowns by state are found in Table 3.
Source: Almond-Verba Five Nations Study. The data are from the Inter-University Consortium for Political Research, Ann Arbor, Michigan, and were processed by the Laboratory for Political Research, Department of Political Science, University of Iowa.

the interregional variations in national pride. Table 4 shows the proportions of those in the Almond-Verba United States sample who, within each region, said they were proud of the governmental and political system. Differences in educational levels apparently have no effect on the tendency of respondents to express national pride in the South Atlantic, East South Central, and Pacific states. In New England the expected direction of the effect of education on national pride is reversed, and in the other regions better educated people are generally more prideful than less well-educated people. While these interregional comparisons are interesting, and suggest numerous possibilities for further investigation, they do not in themselves allow us to make firm generalizations about regional variations in national pride. We cannot know from the Almond-Verba data to what extent interstate differences in national pride are contributing to the interregional variations.

Participation–Subject Orientations Vary

The extent of political participation varies from state to state, and so does the extent to which individuals submit

apathetically to decisions participated in by others. As Milbrath puts it, "the political cultures of some states such as Idaho and Utah facilitate the involvement of citizens in political activity," while "the political cultures of other states, especially those in the deep South, place barriers to participation in politics."[38] Milbrath deals with a variety of correlates of participation. The illustrations here will be confined to fragments of data at the level of basic political attitudes.

Since levels of educational attainment vary among the states, and political participation is highly related to education, interstate differences in participation (other than merely in voting) may be expected. Americans are characterized by relatively high degrees of subjective civic competence.[39] Are attitudes supportive of political participation variable among states? That is a plausible expectation. Interregional variations in the degree of political efficacy and citizen duty are suggestive, though again the South is the main villain. In Table 5 are reproduced the

[38]Lester W. Milbrath, "Political Participation in the States," in Jacob and Vines, op. cit., pp. 25-60.

[39]Almond and Verba, op. cit., p. 186.

TABLE 5

Regional Differences in Political Efficacy and Citizen Duty (1952)

(in percentages)

Region	Political Efficacy		Citizen Duty	
	High	Low	High	Low
Northeast	30	15	50	7
Midwest	30	19	49	6
South	18	32	28	20
Far West	30	12	45	2

Source: Angus Campbell, Gerald Gurin, and Warren E. Miller, *The Voter Decides* (Evanston, Ill., 1954), pp. 192 and 197.

regional comparisons for the 1952 Survey Research Center (Michigan) study, showing the high and low political efficacy and civic duty scores. South–Non-South differences in sense of political efficacy and sense of citizen duty are sustained after control for differences in education, though of course highly educated individuals tend to feel much more politically potent and civically competent than those with limited educations.[40]

It ought to be possible to array the states on a continuum from highly participant to highly subject (nonparticipant). This is easy to do simply in terms of voter turnout in state elections, but it would also be desirable to include other indicators of participation (subjective competence, civic obligation, working in campaigns, contributing money, letter writing, etc.).[41] For example, Idaho, Connecticut, and Indiana might be considered highly participant political cultures, while South Carolina, Georgia, and Mississippi might be considered highly subject political cultures. This kind of an analysis might seem quite conventional; it is commonplace, for instance, to talk of the effects of party systems and partisan conflict on voter

turnout. What is being suggested is that we now also ask what are the differential bases of support for political systems in political cultures that vary in participant–subject orientations. To put it another way, does the more participant culture of Idaho contribute to the stability and performance of the Idaho political system in ways different from the support the political culture of South Carolina provides for its political system?

Political Styles Vary

If there are interstate variations in basic political orientations, we would expect political styles to vary.[42] Even where political cultures are quite similar, ways of holding and applying beliefs may differ. Some state political cultures are manifestly more homogeneous than those in other states, and a relatively diverse state political culture may lead to distinctively different political styles within a state.

Where states have highly homogeneous political cultures (perhaps most of the states of the South, the Midwest, the Great Plains, and the Rocky Mountains), it may be possible to characterize them in terms of dominant political styles. The dominant Iowa political style can be described as highly pragmatic, nonprogrammatic, cautious, and moderate. The Virginia political style may be distinctive in

[40]Angus Campbell, Philip E. Converse, Warren E. Miller, and Donald E. Stokes, *The American Voter* (New York, 1960), pp. 479–80.

[41]Data might be gathered for the states along the lines of Julian L. Woodward and Elmo Roper, "The Political Activity of American Citizens," *American Political Science Review*, XLIV (1950), pp. 872–85.

[42]See Frank J. Sorauf, *Political Parties in the American System* (Boston, 1964), p. 149.

its sense of honor and gentility.[43] Though the demagogic-hortatory political style is by no means limited to them, Louisiana and Mississippi political cultures seem to be dominated by this style.[44] In states with mixed political cultures, differential styles arise. The ethnically and religiously diverse, relatively cynical, alien and hostile political environment of Massachusetts produces a variety of response styles.[45] Pennsylvania provides an example of the consequences of sharply different rural and urban political subcultures, and the styles associated with them.[46] The ethnic bifurcation of New Mexico (and of Texas) produces stylistic differences, where the distinctive political style of the Spanish-American sector is that of "patronism" or "bossism."[47] California's political culture is divided geographically, separated by the Tehachapi mountains. The distinctive political style of Southern California is extremist, paranoid, and hortatory.[48] Though surveys have indicated that Californians support the geographical integrity of the state, numerous attempts have been made to divide the state in two, the most recent by Senator Richard J. Dolwig of San Francisco. The distinctiveness of Southern California arises mainly from the torrential inflow of population (Gunther said, "Los Angeles is Iowa with palms").[49] Lipset has tried to account for the strength of the Birchite

style of politics in Southern California in terms of tensions in population growth and community integration.[50] The political styles of Massachusetts, Pennsylvania, and California appear to be relatively more ideological in character than those of other states for which we have explicit evidence.

Political Socialization Varies

We have no systematic evidence of the interstate variability in political socialization, and the subject itself is only beginning to be studied. Children do learn to become Iowans, Hoosiers, Oregonians, or South Carolinians, even though images of the national government and its authority figures are more prominent in their socialization.[51] Strength of identity with the state political systems probably varies, as may comparative positive or negative affect toward the political system and participation in it.[52] Evidence for substantial differences in most basic democratic values children learn in different states or regions does not exist, although of course southern children learn different attitudes toward racial equality than children in other regions of the country.[53]

In terms of adult political socialization, variability is to be expected as a

---

[43]Key, Southern Politics, op. cit., p. 19.

[44]See Allan P. Sindler, Huey Long's Louisiana (Baltimore, 1956); and A. J. Liebling, The Earl of Louisiana (New York, 1961).

[45]Edgar Litt, The Political Cultures of Massachusetts (Cambridge, Mass., 1965); Murray B. Levin with George Blackwood, The Complete Politician (Indianapolis, 1962); and Lawrence H. Fuchs, The Political Behavior of American Jews (Glencoe, Ill., 1956).

[46]Frank J. Sorauf, Party and Representation (New York, 1963), p. 149.

[47]John C. Russell, "State Regionalism in New Mexico," Social Forces, XVI (1937), pp. 268–71; and Key, Southern Politics, op. cit., pp. 271–76.

[48]Paul Seabury, "The Antic Politics of California," Harper's Magazine (June, 1965), 82–93.

[49]Gunther, op. cit., p. 50.

[50]Seymour Martin Lipset, "Three Decades of the Radical Right: Coughlinites, McCarthyites, and Birchers," in Daniel Bell (ed.), The Radical Right (Garden City, N.Y., 1963), pp. 436–37.

[51]At least in Chicago, Ill., and New Haven, Conn. See David Easton and Jack Dennis, "The Child's Image of Government," Annals of the American Academy of Political and Social Science, CCCLXI (1965), p. 51; and Fred I. Greenstein, "The Benevolent Leader: Children's Images of Political Authority," American Political Science Review, LIV (1960), 937–39.

[52]A comparative analysis of socialization effects is Edgar Litt, "Civic Education, Community Norms, and Political Indoctrination," American Sociological Review, XXVIII (1963), 69–75.

[53]For interregional comparisons of the attitudes of teenagers toward political involvement and the Bill of Rights, see H. H. Remmers and D. H. Radler, The American Teenager (Indianapolis, 1957), pp. 178–221.

function both of politico-cultural support for participation and of political institutions available and operating as socializing agents. The data now available are limited to state legislators in California, New Jersey, Ohio, and Tennessee, but it does indicate variations in socializing agents among these states.[54] For instance, Eulau argues that, since more than half the legislators in New Jersey and a fifth in Ohio referred to party work as initiating their interest in politics, "this is likely to be due to the more solid institutionalization of party politics in these two states, and in New Jersey to the highly politicized atmosphere characteristic of that state's metropolitan areas. In other words, party politics seems to operate as its own socializing agent."[55] Furthermore, adults generally seem to be differently socialized to partisan loyalties and attachments when northern states are grouped according to those where election laws maximize, and those where the laws minimize, partisanship.[56]

IV. CORRELATES OF POLITICO-CULTURAL VARIABILITY

If there are significant variations in the elements of political cultures among American states, and the foregoing section should not be taken to suggest that this is not still an open question, then why do these variations occur? What seem to be some of the correlates of interstate variance in political culture?

One obvious set of variables is that of *group differences* in education, ethnicity, race, religion, sex, and social class. Almond and Verba found from cross-national comparisons that education had the greatest impact on political culture.[57]

That higher education tends to reduce national differences suggests that the nature of political culture is greatly determined by the distribution of education . . . the more highly educated segments of all five nations show a cross-national uniformity in political orientation. . . . To say that education replaces national differences is of course an exaggeration; national differences persist . . . even among the highly educated; moreover, the generalization being made here applies only to specific political orientations. Nevertheless, the highly educated participate in politics, no matter what their nation; participation by the less educated depends more heavily upon nation.

Since education is unevenly distributed across the American states, we would expect variants in political culture to be, in part, a function of variation in educational attainments. Variations in the ethnic mix of state populations and "ethnic salience" make a contribution to differences in political cultures; thus, "it appears that concern with national origins is much greater in the Northeast than in some other parts of the country."[58] Ethnicity and religious differences work closely together, though religious differences seem to have independent consequences on politicocultural variations.[59] Differences in racial composition have a substantial impact on state political cultures, suggested by North–South and Negro–White differences in political socialization.[60] Sex differences in acculturation are plainly of importance, especially between the regions of the North

---

[54]John C. Wahlke, Heinz Eulau, William Buchanan, and LeRoy C. Ferguson, *The Legislative System* (New York, 1962), pp. 77–94.

[55]*Ibid.*, p. 86.

[56]Campbell, Converse, Miller, and Stokes, *op. cit.*, pp. 270–71.

[57]Almond and Verba, *op. cit.*, p. 383.

[58]Raymond E. Wolfinger, "The Development and Persistence of Ethnic Voting," *American Political Science Review*, LIX (1965), pp. 896–908; Litt, *The Political Cultures of Massachusetts*, *op. cit.*, pp. 64–67, 159-62; Lockard, *op. cit.*, pp. 305–19.

[59]See Gerhard Lenski, *The Religious Factor* (Garden City, N.Y., 1961), pp. 134–211; Arnold M. Rose, "The Mormon Church and Utah Politics; An Abstract of a Statistical Study," *American Sociological Review*, VII (1942), pp. 853–54.

[60]Dwaine Marvick, "The Political Socialization of the American Negro," *Annals of the American Academy of Political and Social Science*, CCCLXI (1965), pp. 112–27.

and South.[61] Difference in social class composition, and especially differences in status polarization and mobility, have significant political effects which vary among states and regions.[62]

Another set of correlates of variations in political cultures among American states is that of *social and economic forces.* Urbanization, industrialization, population movement, affluence and economic growth probably have substantial consequences in terms of interstate politicocultural differences. The metropolitan-industrial milieu fosters technocratic political styles and expectations which Litt has aptly characterized as "managerial progressivism."[63] Population in-migration and out-migration not only provide a source of demand stress for political systems, but affect basic political orientations as well. Differential economic development can affect political cultures in the sense that abundance and economic growth are more likely to support a civic culture than poverty and immiserization. As affluence increases, interpersonal trust increases, political partisanship takes on a different meaning, class awareness relaxes and class voting diminishes in importance, the openness of the political system of participation by racial minorities is facilitated, and political alienation declines.[64]

Interstate variations in political culture have fairly often been explained in terms of *historical patterns of settlement.* In-migrants are shown to bring to a state particular political beliefs and attachments which persist over time. Munger and Key argued that "the long persistence of county patterns of party affiliation despite changes in 'interest' and the disappear-

ance of issues that created the pattern, and the existence of contrasting partisan patterns in essentially similar counties, point toward a 'political' grouping at least to some extent independent of other social groupings," and "their persistence suggests that they may represent, no mere derivatives from other social groupings, but political groups with a life of their own."[65]

A final set of variables which seem to be related to variations in state political cultures is that of *institutional impact.* The authors of *The American Voter* have suggested, for example, that "quite apart from differences in the level of partisanship from state to state we find that identifiers in some communities behave differently from their counterparts elsewhere."[66] Differences in meanings given to electoral institutions are indicated as having a causal linkage to variations in political responses. Again, where political parties are highly organized they not only are available as socializing agents but they are also, Eldersveld's study of Detroit politics suggests, important contributors to public confidence in the political system.[67] Further, the structure and beliefs of the elite in the political system have an impact on the political culture. In this regard, Virginia has been a comparatively closed system. "Of all the American states," Key said, "Virginia can lay claim to the most thorough control by an oligarchy." There "political power has been closely held by

[61]Campbell, Converse, Miller, and Stokes, *op. cit.,* pp. 483–93.

[62]*Ibid.,* pp. 367–68.

[63]Litt, *The Political Cultures of Massachusetts, op. cit.,* pp. 87–90.

[64]Robert E. Lane, "The Politics of Consensus in an Age of Affluence," *American Political Science Review,* LIX (1965), pp. 874–95.

[65]V. O. Key, Jr. and Frank Munger, "Social Determinism and Electoral Decision: the Case of Indiana," in Eugene Burdick and Arthur J. Brodbeck (eds.), *American Voting Behavior* (Glencoe, Ill., 1959), p. 287. On the pattern of settlement hypothesis, see also Gunther, *op. cit.,* p. 79; Key, *American State Politics, op. cit.,* pp. 218–27; Fenton, *op. cit.,* pp. 205–6; and Thomas A. Flinn, "The Outline of Ohio Politics," *Western Political Quarterly,* XIII (1960), pp. 702–21.

[66]Campbell, Converse, Miller, and Stokes, *op. cit.,* p. 272.

[67]Samuel J. Eldersveld, *Political Parties: A Behavioral Analysis* (Chicago, 1964), pp. 492–501.

a small group of leaders who, themselves and their predecessors, have subverted democratic institutions and deprived most Virginians of a voice in their government."[68] The contrast is marked between Virginia and, to take one illustration, Washington, where cultural traditions and political institutions support a high degree of political independence and participation.[69]

Another kind of institutional impact that is felt on state political cultures comes from the federal structure and the federal government. States affect each other, and some of these manifest institutional effects are obvious. For instance, interstate comparisons are often made by citizens and political leaders as referents for political behavior (goals) or as sources for the articulation of state pride. The federal impact is also obvious, though its more subtle forms have scarcely been examined. For example, Key pointed out that:[70]

In the organization and spirit of their politics the states vary markedly. Their oddities and variations may be accounted for in part by the fact that they are members of a federal system. The impact of national policies and parties powerfully influences the form and behavior of state political systems. The manner in which that impact strikes different states, differently constituted and situated, contributes to the variations in organization and conduct of state politics.

The national welfare state, with economic policies reaching into every state and almost every life, seems to have a rather fundamental impact on state politi-cal cultures. Litt points out, for instance, that in Massachusetts political corruption, rather than issues of substantive policy, provides the focus of major public attention. He argues that attention to political corruption is a characteristic of a political system in a state of flux, especially "when the causes of transition are largely outside the state political system and seriously threaten values within the system." He contends further that "the national political economy has altered the power position of many local interests in industrial states such as Massachusetts," and "that corruption itself is an attempt to compensate for values that are dysfunctional to the official norms of the system."[71]

V. CONCLUSION

This essay has attempted to suggest and illustrate some focuses for research in comparative state politics which, while not novel in principle, are presently severely limited in application. Such research will greatly improve our understanding of the maintenance of state political systems, and contribute to knowledge about national integration. In the past political scientists have tended to view the states as sources of national diversity and political conflict. That is important, but now we probably need to give more attention to the states in terms of their contribution to national cohesion and stability, where conflicts can be managed without disintegration.

To those whose principal focus is on the formulation and administration of public policy, one can say that components of state political cultures are often considered as determinants of policy processes and output, or they are simply assumed to be in the field. For an enlightening illustration of the explanation of a

---

[68]Key, *Southern Politics, op. cit,* p. 19. Little is known systematically about interestate variations in the basic political orientations of leaders compared to rank-and-file citizens. See Herbert McClosky, "Consensus and Ideology in American Politics," *loc. cit.*

[69]Morris Showel, "Political Independence in Washington State," *Public Opinion Quarterly,* XVI (1952), pp. 399–409.

[70]Key, *American State Politics, op. cit.,* pp. 19–20.

---

[71]Both quotations above are from Litt, *The Political Cultures of Massachusetts, op. cit.,* p. 87.

particular policy issue in terms of politico-cultural factors, read Rogow's description of the outcome of the loyalty oath issue in Iowa:[72]

The Senate's refusal to support Doud (major proponent of the loyalty oath bill) also owes much to the general character of Iowa political and social life. Thus far, Iowa has experienced few of the tensions that elsewhere have generated major controversies about loyalty and subversion. Political, economic, and social homogeneity have been more characteristic of Iowa than of a large number of other states. The agricultural section of the population, which is heavily represented in the legislature, enjoys a substantial measure of economic security, social influence, and political dominance. The urban–rural division, while it is increasing, has not yet become a major factor in Iowa poli-

tics. The AFL-CIO is relatively insignificant compared with the Iowa Farm Bureau Federation, or even the Iowa Manufacturers Association. Even the usual rich man–poor man distinctions are more difficult to make; the extremes of wealth and poverty are not as visible in Iowa as elsewhere in the nation. There are no large numbers of recent immigrants to assimilate, and the state's non-white population has remained small. Political differences exist, but they exist less between the parties than within the parties, and within the parties they tend more to be personal or factional than ideological. At any given moment, therefore, the political mood of the state is likely to be conservative, cautious, and "standpat."

The political cultures of American states ought to be a major focus of study, in terms of systemic analysis, in terms of inhibitions or restrictions on the scope and substance of policy issues, and in terms of policy processes and application. Such research will open a significant area for comparative study.

[72]Arnold A. Rogow, "The Loyalty Oath Issue in Iowa, 1951," *American Political Science Review*, LV (1961), pp. 861–69. Quote is at p. 869.

ISSUE CONFLICT AND CONSENSUS AMONG PARTY LEADERS AND FOLLOWERS*

Herbert McClosky, Paul J. Hoffmann, and Rosemary O'Hara

American political parties are often regarded as "brokerage" organizations, weak in principle, devoid of ideology, and inclined to differ chiefly over unimportant questions. In contrast to the "ideological"

parties of Europe—which supposedly appeal to their followers through sharply defined, coherent, and logically related doctrines—the American parties are thought to fit their convictions to the changing demands of the political con-

*Reprinted from *The American Political Science Review*, Vol. LIV (June, 1960), pp. 406–27. Copyright 1960, The American Political Science Association.

This article was the first in a series reporting the findings of a national field study of political belief and affiliation among American party leaders and followers. The study was carried out through the Laboratory for Research in Social Relations at the University of Minnesota

under grants made to the senior author by the Committee on Political Behavior of the Social Science Research Council, and supplementary grants from the Graduate School Research Fund. The manuscript was prepared at the Survey Research Center, University of California, Berkeley, under a Fellowship in Legal and Political Philosophy awarded to the senior author by the Rockefeller Foundation.

test.[1] According to this view, each set of American party leaders is satisfied to play Tweedledee to the other's Tweedledum.

I. PRESSURES TOWARD UNIFORMITY AND CLEAVAGE

Although these "conclusions" are mainly derived from *a priori* analysis or from casual observations of "anecdotal" data (little systematic effort having been made so far to verify or refute them), they are often taken as confirmed—largely, one imagines, because they are compatible with certain conspicuous features of American politics. Among these features is the entrenchment of a two-party system which, by affording both parties a genuine opportunity to win elections, tempts them to appeal to as many diverse elements in the electorate as are needed to put together a majority.[2] Since both parties want to attract support from the centrist and moderate segments of the electorate, their views on basic issues will, it is thought, tend to converge. Like giant business enterprises competing for the same market, they will be led to offer commodities that are in many respects identical.[3] It is one thing for a small party in a multi-party system to preserve its ideological purity, quite another for a mass party in a two-party system to do so. The one has little hope of becoming a majority, and can most easily survive by remaining identified with the narrow audience from which

it draws its chief supporters; the other can succeed only by accommodating the conflicting claims of many diverse groups —only, in short, by blunting ideological distinctions.[4]

Constraints against enlarging intellectual differences also spring from the loosely confederated nature of the American party system, and from each national party's need to adjust its policies to the competing interests of the locality, the state, and the nation.[5] Many party units are more concerned with local than with national elections, and prefer not to be handicapped by clear-cut national programs. Every ambitious politician, moreover, hopes to achieve a *modus vivendi* tailored to the particular and often idiosyncratic complex of forces prevailing in his constituency, an objective rarely compatible with doctrinal purity.[6] Often, too, local politics are largely nonpartisan or are partisan in ways that scarcely affect the great national issues around which ideologies might be expected to form.[7] The development and enforcement of a sharply delineated ideology is also hindered by the absence in either party of a firmly established, authoritative, and continuing organizational center empowered to decide questions of doctrine and discipline.[8] Party affiliation is loosely defined, responsibility is weak or non-existent, and organs for indoctrinating or communicating with party members are at best rudimentary.

Cultural and historical differences may also contribute to the weaker ideological emphasis among American, as compared

[1]Maurice Duverger, *Political Parties, their Organization and Activity in the Modern State* (New York, 1955), p. 102.

[2]The analysis of these and related tendencies associated with the American party system is ably set forth in Pendleton Herring, *The Politics of Democracy* (New York, 1940), p. 102 and *passim*. Also, James M. Burns, *Congress on Trial: The Legislative Process and the Administrative State* (New York, 1949), p. 34.

[3]See especially E. E. Schattschneider, *Party Government* (New York, 1942), p. 92 and *passim*; and V. O. Key, *Politics, Parties, and Pressure Groups*, 4th ed. (New York, 1958), ch. 8; Howard R. Penniman, *Sait's American Parties and Elections*, 5th ed. (New York, 1952), p. 162.

[4]William Goodman, *The Two-Party System in the United States* (New Jersey, 1956), p. 43.

[5]Duverger, *op. cit.*, pp. 187, 418.

[6]Pendleton Herring, *op. cit.*, p. 133.

[7]*American State Legislatures*, ed. Belle Zeller (New York, 1954); but see also Malcolm E. Jewell, "Party Voting in American State Legislatures," *American Political Science Review*, Vol. XLIX (Sept. 1955), pp. 773–91.

[8]Report of the Committee on Political Parties, American Political Science Association, *Toward a More Responsible Two-Party System* (New York, 1950), *passim*.

with European, parties. Many of the great historical cleavages that have divided European nations for centuries—monarchism *vs.* republicanism; clericalism *vs.* anticlericalism; democracy *vs.* autocracy, etc.—have never taken root in this country. Apart from the slavery (and subsequently the race) issue, the United States has not experienced the intense class or caste conflict often found abroad, and contests of the capitalism *vs.* socialism variety have never achieved an important role in American politics. In addition, never having known a titled nobility, we have largely been freed from the conflicts found elsewhere between the classes of inherited and acquired privilege.

Consider, too, the progress made in the United States toward neutralizing the forces which ordinarily lead to sharp social, and hence intellectual and political, differentiation. The class and status structure of American society has attained a rate of mobility equalling or exceeding that of any other long established society. Popular education, and other facilities for the creation of common attitudes, have been developed on a scale unequalled elsewhere. Improvements in transportation and communication, and rapid shifts in population and industry have weakened even sectionalism as a source of political cleavage. Rural–urban differences continue to exist, of course, but they too have been diminishing in force and have become less salient for American politics than the differences prevailing, for example, between a French peasant proprietor and a Parisian *boulevardier.*[9] In short, a great many Americans have been subjected in their public lives to identical stimuli—a condition unlikely to generate strong, competing ideologies.

The research reported here was designed not to refute these observations but to test the accuracy of the claim that

they are sufficient to prevent differences in outlook from taking root in the American party system. We believed that the homogenizing tendencies referred to are strongly offset by contrary influences, and that voters are preponderantly led to support the party whose opinions they share. We further thought that the competition for office, though giving rise to similarities between the parties, also impels them to diverge from each other in order to sharpen their respective appeals. For this and other reasons, we expected to find that the leaders of the two parties, instead of ignoring differences alleged to exist within the electorate, would differ on issues more sharply than their followers would. We believed further that even in a brokerage system the parties would serve as independent reference groups, developing norms, values, and self-images to which their supporters could readily respond.[10] Their influence, we felt, would frequently exceed that of ethnic, occupational, residential and other reference groups. In sum, we proceeded on the belief that the parties are not simply spokesmen for other interest groups, but are in their own right agencies for formulating, transmitting, and anchoring political opinions, that they attract adherents who in general share those opinions, and that through a feedback process of mutual reinforcement between the organization and its typical supporters, the parties develop integrated and stable political tendencies. Other hypotheses will be specified as we present and analyze our findings.

II. PROCEDURES

The questions considered in this paper were part of a large field study made in

---

[9]Data bearing on these generalizations will be presented in companion articles which specifically deal with sectional and rural–urban influences on issue outlook.

[10]*Cf.* James W. Prothro, Ernest Q. Campbell, and Charles M. Grigg, "Two Party Voting in the South: Class vs. Party Identification," *American Political Science Review,* Vol. LII (March 1958), pp. 131–39. Also, Peter H. Odegard and E. Allen Helms, *American Politics: A Study in Political Dynamics* (New York, 1947 ed.), pp. 200–221.

1957–1958 on the nature, sources, and correlates of political affiliation, activity, and belief in the American party system (hereafter referred to as the PAB study). Pilot studies on Minnesota samples had led us to suspect that many "settled" notions about party affiliation and belief in America would not stand up under careful empirical scrutiny; further, we felt that little progress would be made in the exploration of this subject until a comprehensive portrait of party membership in America had been drawn. Accordingly, a nationwide study was launched to acquire a detailed description of party leaders and supporters, gathering data on their backgrounds, political experiences, personality characteristics, values, motivations, social and political attitudes, outlooks on key issues, and related matters.

For our samples of party "leaders" we turned to the Democratic and Republican national conventions, largely because they are the leading and most representative of the party organs, their delegates coming from every part of the United States and from every level of party and government activity. Our samples ranged from governors, senators, and national committeemen at the one end to precinct workers and local officials at the other. In the absence of comprehensive information about the characteristics of the party elites in America, no one can say how closely the convention delegates mirror the total party leadership. We felt it fair to assume, nevertheless, that the delegates represented as faithful a cross section of American party leadership as could be had without an extraordinary expenditure of money and labor. Using convention delegates as our universe of leaders also held some obvious advantages for research, since the composition of this universe (by name, address, party, state, sex, place of residence, and party or public office) can usually be ascertained from the convention calls. Of the 6,848 delegates and alternates available to be sampled, 3,193 actually participated; 3,020 (1,788 Dem-

ocrats and 1,232 Republicans) completed and returned questionnaires that were usable in all respects.[11] The proportion of returns was roughly equivalent for both sets of party leaders.

The rank-and-file sample, which we wanted both for its intrinsic value and for its utility as a control group, was obtained by special arrangement with the American Institute of Public Opinion. In January 1958, Gallup interviewers personally distributed our questionnaire to 2,917 adult voters in two successive national cross-section surveys. Some 1,610 questionnaires were filled out and returned, of which 1,484 were completely usable. This sample closely matched the national population on such characteristics as sex, age, region, size of city, and party affiliation, and, though it somewhat oversampled the upper educational levels, we considered it sufficiently large and representative for most of our purposes. Of the 1,484 respondents, 821 were Democratic supporters (629 "pure" Democrats, plus 192 whom we classified as "independent" Democrats) and 623 were Republican supporters (479 "pure" Republicans, plus 144 "independent" Republicans). Forty respondents could not be identified as adherents of either party.

The lengthy questionnaire developed for the study was designed to be self-administered. It contained, in addition to questions on the respondents' personal backgrounds, a number of queries on their political history and experience, their attitudes toward the party system and toward such related matters as party organization, discipline and responsibility, their self-images with regard to social class and

---

[11] This gratifyingly large number of returns of so lengthy and detailed a questionnaire was attained through a number of follow-up mailings and special letters. These and other procedures designed to check the adequacy of the sample will be fully described in the volume containing the report of the overall study. The difference in the number of returns from the two parties was largely a result of the greater number of Democratic delegates to begin with.

liberalism-conservatism, their reference group identifications, and their views on party leadership and ideology. The largest part of the questionnaire consisted of 390 scale items, randomly arranged, which when sorted and scored fell into 47 scales for measuring the personality, attitude, and value characteristics of each of the respondents. We had validated and used all but three of these scales in earlier studies.

The questions most relevant for the present article were those which asked each respondent to express his attitudes toward twenty-four important national issues, and to state whether he believed support for each issue should be "increased," "decreased," or "remain as is." The list of issues and the responses of each sample will be found in Tables H2A through H2E, where for convenience of analysis, the issues have been grouped under five broad headings: Public Ownership, Government Regulation of the Economy, Equalitarianism and Human Welfare, Tax Policy and Foreign Policy.

In tabulating the results, we first scored each individual on each issue and then computed aggregate scores for all the members of a given sample. To begin with, percentages were used to show the proportion who favored increasing, decreasing, or retaining the existing level of support on each issue. But as it was clumsy to handle three figures for each issue, we constructed a single index or "ratio of support" which would simultaneously take account of all three scores. The index was built by assigning a weight of 1.0 to each "increase" response in the sample, of 0 to each "decrease" response, and of .50 to each "remain as is" (or "same") response. Thus the ratio-of-support score shown for any given sample is in effect a mean score with a possible range of 0 to 1.0, in which support for an issue increases as the scores approach 1.0 and decreases as they approach 0. In general, the scores can be taken to approximate the following overall positions: .0

to .25—strongly wish to reduce support; .26 to .45—wish to reduce support; .46 to .55—satisfied with the *status quo;* .56 to .75—wish to increase support; and .76 to 1.00—strongly wish to increase support. Note that the differences in degree suggested by these categories refer not to the *strength of feeling* exhibited by individuals toward an issue but rather to the *numbers of people* in a sample who hold points of view favoring or opposing that issue.

Because they include the "same" and "no code" as well as "increase" and "decrease" responses, our ratios of support sometimes flatten the differences between groups. Had we employed only the percentage scores for the "increase" or "decrease" responses, the differences between samples would in many instances have seemed larger. Nevertheless, the ratio of support offers so many advantages that we have employed it as our principal measure. For one thing, as the equivalent of a mean score, it takes into account all scores, omitting no respondent from the tabulation. For the same reason it enables us to assess the amount of dispersion or homogeneity exhibited by any sample and makes it easy to calculate significances of difference.[12] Reliance upon a single, uniform statistic also allows us to make ready comparisons not only *between* but *within* samples, and to determine quickly how large the differences actually are. By observing whether a ratio of support is above or below .50 we can see at once whether a particular group predominant-

---

[12]The measure of dispersion used for this purpose was the standard deviation, which was computed by using the scores of 0, .50 and 1.00 as intervals in the calculations. To avoid having to calculate separate significances of difference for each of the comparisons we wanted to observe, we simply made the assumption—erring on the side of caution—that the maximum variance of .50 had occurred in each instance. The magnitude of the significance of difference is, in other words, often greater than we have reported. The significance test used in this procedure was the critical ratio. Unless otherwise indicated, all the differences reported are statistically significant at or beyond the .01 level.

TABLE 1

Average Differences in the Ratio-of-Support Scores among Party Leaders
and Followers for Five Categories of Issues

Category of Issues	Democratic Leaders vs. Republican Leaders	Democratic Followers vs. Republican Followers	Democratic Leaders vs. Democratic Followers	Republican Leaders vs. Republican Followers	Democratic Leaders vs. Republican Followers	Republican Leaders vs. Democratic Followers
a. Public ownership of resources ...	.28	.04	.06	.18	.10	.22
b. Government regulation of the economy	.22	.06	.08	.10	.12	.16
c. Equalitarianism, human welfare ..	.22	.05	.08	.21	.06	.25
d. Tax policy	.20	.06	.06	.20	.04	.26
e. Foreign policy	.16	.02	.05	.08	.07	.10
Average differences in ratio scores for all categories	.21	.04	.07	.15	.08	.20

Sample Sizes: Democratic Leaders, 1,788; Republican Leaders, 1,232; Democratic Followers, 821; Republican Followers, 623.

ly favors or opposes the issue in question, and how strongly it does so. The use of ratio scores also makes it possible to compare issues as well as groups, *e.g.*, to see whether one issue is more preferred than another.

For further information on the meaning of the issue responses, we also compared samples on a number of related scales and items. Tabulating and statistical operations were carried out to control for demographic influences like education, occupation, age, and sectionalism; to ascertain homogeneity of opinion within the several samples; to rank the issues according to the magnitude of the differences between samples; to compare members' positions on issues against official platform statements; and to determine whether leaders and followers are able to name the issues which actually divide the parties. Some of the findings yielded by these operations will be considered here, while others, for reasons of space, will have to be reserved for future publications.

A word of caution before we turn to the findings. The respondents were offered only the twenty-four issues that impressed us in February, 1957, as most significant and enduring. However, they may

not all be as salient today as they seemed at that time. Nor, within the limitations of a single questionnaire, could we explore every issue that informed observers might have considered important. Some presumably vital issues such as states rights, political centralization, and expansion of government functions could not be stated explicitly enough within our format to be tested properly. These are issues that are so generalized as to encompass many other specific issues, and so highly charged as to awaken a profusion of symbolic and emotive associations.

The *form* of our issue questions may also be open for criticism, for space limitations prevented our subjects from indicating how strongly they felt and how much they knew about each of the issues. This deficiency, however, may be less important than it appears, since for the groups we most wanted to compare (*e.g.*, Democratic *vs.* Republican leaders), the degree of political knowledge and intensity is likely to be rather similar. The difficulty is greater when comparing leaders with followers, but is somewhat offset by controlling for education and socio-economic status. Although some subtleties of interpretation are bound to be lost because these variables have been omitted, we are satisfied that our issue questions in their present form furnish a useful measure for assessing *group* (as distinguished from *individual*) opinion.

Finally, one may wonder about the value of opinions stated on a questionnaire compared with the worth of views formally expressed by an organization or implicit in the actions of its leaders. Advantages can be cited on both sides. The beliefs expressed in official party statements or in legislative roll calls, it might be claimed, represent the *operating* beliefs of the organization by virtue of having been tested in the marketplace or in the competition of legislative struggle. Positions taken on issues on which a party stakes its future may be more valid evidence of what the party truly believes than are the opinions expressed by individual members under conditions of maximum safety. On the other hand, the responses to the issue and attitude questions in the PAB study represent the anonymous, private opinions of party leaders and followers, uncomplicated by any need to make political capital, to proselytize, to conciliate critics, or to find grounds for embarrassing the opposition at the next election. Hence they may for some purposes represent the most accurate possible reflection of the "actual" state of party opinion. The controversy over the value of the two approaches is to some extent spurious, however, for they offer different perspectives on the same thing. In addition, considerable correspondence exists between the party positions evident in congressional roll calls and the privately expressed opinions of the party leaders in our study.[13]

III. FINDINGS: COMPARISONS BETWEEN LEADERS

No more conclusive findings emerge from our study of party issues than those growing out of the comparisons between the two sets of party leaders. Despite the brokerage tendency of the American parties, their active members are obviously separated by large and important differences. The differences, moreover, conform with the popular image in which the Democratic party is seen as the more "progressive" or "radical," the Republican as the more "moderate" or "conservative" of the two.[14] In addition, the disagreements are remarkably consistent, a function not of chance but of systematic points of view, whereby the responses to any one of the issues could reasonably have been predicted from knowledge of the responses to the other issues.

Examination of Tables 2A–2E and 3 shows that the leaders differ significantly on 23 of the 24 issues listed and that they are separated on 15 of these issues by .18 or more ratio points—in short, by differences that are in absolute magnitude very large. The two samples are furthest apart in their attitudes toward public ownership and are especially divided on the question of government ownership of natural resources, the Democrats strongly favoring it, the Republicans just as strongly wanting it cut back. The difference of .39 in the ratio scores is the largest for any of the issues tested. In percentages, the differences are 58 per cent (D) vs. 13 per cent (R) in favor of increasing support, and 19 per cent (D) vs. 52 per cent (R) in favor of decreasing support. Both parties preponderantly support pub-

[13]See, for example, the congressional roll-call results reported by Julius Turner, *Party and Constituency: Pressures on Congress,* The Johns Hopkins University Studies in Historical and Political Science Series, Vol. LXIX, No. 1 (1951). The complexities affecting the determination of party votes in Congress are thoroughly explored in David B. Truman, *The Congressional Party: A Case Study* (New York, 1959).

[14]Conservatism is here used not in the classical but in the more popular sense, in which it refers to negative attitudes toward government ownership, intervention, and regulation of the economy; resistance to measures for promoting equalitarianism and social welfare through government action; identification with property, wealth, and business enterprise; etc.

TABLE 2A

Comparison of Party Leaders and Followers on "Public Ownership" Issues,
by Percentages and Ratios of Support

	Leaders		Followers	
	Dem.	Repub.	Dem.	Repub.
	$N = 1,788$	$N = 1,232$	$N = 821$	$N = 623$
Issues		(%s down)		
Public ownership of natural resources				
% favoring: Increase	57.5	12.9	35.3	31.1
Decrease	18.6	51.9	15.0	19.9
Same, n.c.*	23.8	35.2	49.7	49.0
Support ratio	.69	.30	.60	.56
Public control of atomic energy				
% favoring: Increase	73.2	45.0	64.2	59.4
Decrease	7.2	15.3	7.1	10.0
Same, n.c.	19.6	39.7	28.7	30.6
Support ratio	.83	.65	.79	.75
Mean support ratios for the public ownership category	.76	.48	.70	.66

*n.c. = no code.

lic control and development of atomic energy, but the Democrats do so more uniformly.

V. O. Key, among others, has observed that the Republican party is especially responsive to the "financial and manufacturing community,"[15] reflecting the view that government should intervene as little as possible to burden or restrain prevailing business interests. The validity of this observation is evident throughout all our data, and is most clearly seen in the responses to the issues listed under Government Regulation of the Economy, Equalitarianism and Human Welfare, Tax Policy. Democratic leaders are far more eager than Republican leaders to strengthen enforcement of anti-monopoly laws and to increase regulation of public utilities and business. Indeed, the solidarity of Republican opposition to the regulation of business is rather overwhelming: 84 per cent want to decrease such regulation and fewer than .01 per cent say they want to increase it. Although the Democrats, on balance, also feel that government controls on business should not be expanded further, the differences between the two

[15] Key, op. cit., p. 239.

samples on this issue are nevertheless substantial.

The two sets of leaders are also far apart on the farm issue, the Democrats preferring slightly to increase farm supports, the Republicans wanting strongly to reduce them. The Republican ratio score of .20 on this issue is among the lowest in the entire set of scores. The magnitude of these scores somewhat surprised us, for while opposition to agricultural subsidies is consistent with Republican dislike for state intervention, we had expected the leaders to conform more closely to the familiar image of the Republican as the more "rural" of the two parties.[16] It appears, however, that the party's connection with business is far more compelling than its association with agriculture. The Republican desire to reduce government expenditures and to pro-

[16] The friendlier attitude toward farmers among Democratic leaders than Republican leaders is borne out in the responses to several other questions used in the study. For example, the Republican leaders list farmers as having "too much power" far more frequently than do the Democratic leaders. Equally, the Democrats are significantly more inclined to regard farmers as having "too little power."

TABLE 2B

Comparison of Party Leaders and Followers on "Government Regulation
of the Economy" Issues, by Percentages and Ratios of Support

	Leaders		Followers	
	Dem. $N = 1,788$	*Repub.* $N = 1,232$	*Dem.* $N = 821$	*Repub.* $N = 623$
Issues		(*%s down*)		
Level of farm price supports				
% favoring: Increase 43.4		6.7	39.0	23.0
Decrease 28.1		67.4	27.6	40.3
Same, n.c. 28.5		25.8	33.4	36.7
Support ratio .... .58		.20	.56	.41
Government regulation of business				
% favoring: Increase 20.2		0.6	18.6	7.4
Decrease 38.5		84.1	33.4	46.2
Same, n.c. 41.3		15.3	48.0	46.4
Support ratio .... .41		.08	.43	.31
Regulation of public utilities				
% favoring: Increase 59.0		17.9	39.3	26.0
Decrease 6.4		17.6	11.1	12.0
Same, n.c. 34.6		64.5	49.6	62.0
Support ratio .... .76		.50	.64	.57
Enforcement of anti-monopoly laws				
% favoring: Increase 78.0		44.9	53.2	51.0
Decrease 2.9		9.0	7.9	6.6
Same, n.c. 19.1		46.1	38.9	42.4
Support ratio .... .88		.68	.73	.72
Regulation of trade unions				
% favoring: Increase 59.3		86.4	46.6	57.8
Decrease 12.4		4.5	8.9	10.6
Same, n.c. 28.3		9.2	44.5	31.6
Support ratio .... .73		.91	.69	.74
Level of tariffs				
% favoring: Increase 13.0		19.2	16.6	15.2
Decrease 43.0		26.3	25.3	21.3
Same, n.c. 43.9		54.5	58.1	63.4
Support ratio .... .35		.46	.46	.47
Restrictions on credit				
% favoring: Increase 24.8		20.6	26.1	25.7
Decrease 39.3		20.6	22.2	23.8
Same, n.c. 35.9		58.8	51.8	50.5
Support ratio .... .43		.50	.52	.51
Mean support ratios for "government regulation of the economy" category .... .59		.48	.58	.53

mote independence from "government
handouts" prevails on the farm question
as it does on other issues, while the Democratic preference for a more regulated
economy in which government intervenes

to reduce economic risk and to stabilize
prosperity is equally evident on the other
side. Party attitudes on this issue appear
to be determined as much by ideological
tendencies as by deliberate calculation of

the political advantages to be gained by favoring or opposing subsidies to farmers. Comparison of our findings with Turner's earlier data on farm votes in Congress[17] suggests, in addition, that the sharp party difference on the farm issue is neither a recent development nor a mere product of the personal philosophy of the present Secretary of Agriculture.

Having implied that agricultural policies partly result from principle, we must note that on three other issues in this category (trade unions, credit, and tariffs), principle seems to be overweighed by old-fashioned economic considerations. In spite of their distaste for government interference in economic affairs, the Republicans almost unanimously favor greater regulation of trade unions and they are more strongly disposed than the Democrats toward government intervention to restrict credit and to raise tariffs. Of course, party cleavages over the credit and tariff issues have a long history,[18] which may by now have endowed them with ideological force beyond immediate economic considerations.[19] The preponderant Democratic preference for greater regulation of trade unions is doubtless a response to recent "exposures" of corrupt labor practices, though it may also signify that the party's perspective toward the trade unions is shifting somewhat.

The closer Republican identification with business, free enterprise, and economic conservatism in general, and the friendlier Democratic attitude toward labor and toward government regulation of the economy, are easily observed in the

data from other parts of our questionnaire. Republican leaders score very much higher than Democratic leaders on, for example, such scales as economic conservatism, independence of government, and business attitudes. On a question asking respondents to indicate the groups from which they would be most and least likely to take advice, 41 per cent of the Democratic leaders but only 3.8 per cent of the Republican leaders list trade unions as groups from which they would seek advice. Trade unions are scored in the "least likely" category by 25 per cent of the Democrats and 63 per cent of the Republicans. Similarly, more than 94 per cent of the Republican leaders, but 56 per cent of the Democratic leaders, name trade unions as groups that have "too much power." These differences, it should be noted, cannot be accounted for by reference to the greater number of trade union members among the Democratic party leadership, for in the 1956 conventions only 14 per cent of the Democrats belonged to trade unions, and while an even smaller percentage (4 per cent) of the Republicans were trade unionists, this disparity is hardly great enough to explain the large differences in outlook. The key to the explanation has to be sought in the symbolic and reference group identifications of the two parties, and in their underlying values.

Nowhere do we see this more clearly than in the responses to the Equalitarian and Human Welfare issues. The mean difference in the ratio scores for the category as a whole is .22, a very large difference and one that results from differences in the expected direction on all six issues that make up the category. On four of these issues—federal aid to education, slum clearance and public housing, social security, and minimum wages—the leaders of the two parties are widely separated, the differences in their ratio scores ranging from .36 to .21. The percentages showing the proportions who favor increased

---

[17]Turner, op. cit., p. 64.

[18]See John B. Johnson, Jr., The Extent and Consistency of Party Voting in the United States Senate, Ph.D. thesis, University of Chicago, 1943. By applying the Rice Index-of-Likeness to Senate votes, Johnson finds the tariff to have been the most partisan issue before the Congress in the years 1880–1940.

[19]Corinne Silverman, "The Legislator's View of the Legislative Process," Public Opinion Quarterly, Vol. 18 (1954–55), p. 180.

TABLE 2C

Comparison of Party Leaders and Followers on "Equalitarian and Human Welfare" Issues,
by Percentages and Ratios of Support

	Leaders		Followers	
	Dem. $N = 1,788$	Repub. $N = 1,232$	Dem. $N = 821$	Repub. $N = 623$
Issues		(%s down)		
Federal aid to education				
% favoring: Increase	66.2	22.3	74.9	64.8
Decrease	13.4	43.2	5.6	8.3
Same, n.c.	20.4	34.5	19.5	26.8
Support ratio	.76	.40	.85	.78
Slum clearance and public housing				
% favoring: Increase	78.4	40.1	79.5	72.5
Decrease	5.6	21.6	5.8	7.9
Same, n.c.	16.0	38.3	14.6	19.6
Support ratio	.86	.59	.87	.82
Social security benefits				
% favoring: Increase	60.0	22.5	69.4	57.0
Decrease	3.9	13.1	3.0	3.8
Same, n.c.	36.1	64.4	27.5	39.2
Support ratio	.78	.55	.83	.77
Minimum wages				
% favoring: Increase	50.0	15.5	59.0	43.5
Decrease	4.7	12.5	2.9	5.0
Same, n.c.	45.2	72.0	38.1	51.5
Support ratio	.73	.52	.78	.69
Enforcement of integration				
% favoring: Increase	43.8	25.5	41.9	40.8
Decrease	26.6	31.7	27.4	23.6
Same, n.c.	29.5	42.8	30.7	35.6
Support ratio	.59	.47	.57	.59
Immigration into United States				
% favoring: Increase	36.1	18.4	10.4	8.0
Decrease	27.0	29.9	52.0	44.6
Same, n.c.	36.9	51.7	37.6	47.4
Support ratio	.54	.44	.29	.32
Mean support ratios for "equalitarian and human welfare" category	.71	.50	.70	.66

support for these issues are even more striking. In every instance the Democratic percentages are considerably higher: 66 vs. 22 per cent (education); 78 vs. 40 per cent (slum clearance and housing); 60 vs. 23 per cent (social security); and 50 vs. 16 per cent (minimum wages). The Democratic leaders also are better disposed than the Republican leaders toward immigration: twice as many of them (36 per cent vs. 18 per cent) favor a change in policy to permit more immigrants to enter. The overall inclination of both party elites, however, is to accept the present levels of immigration, the Democratic ratio score falling slightly above, and the Republican slightly below, the midpoint.

More surprising are the differences on the segregation issue, for, despite strong southern influence, the Democratic leaders express significantly more support for enforcing integration than the Republicans do. Moreover, the difference between the two parties rises from .12 for the national samples as a whole to a difference of .18 when the southern leaders are excluded. In his study of Congress, Turner found that the Republicans gave more support to Negro rights than the Democrats did.[20] The reversal of this finding in our data does not necessarily mean that a change has occurred since Turner made his study, but only that the votes of the congressional parties do not always reflect the private feelings of the national party leadership. Then, too, southern influence is disproportionately stronger in the Democratic congressional party than in the national Democratic organization as a whole, and disproportionately weaker in the Republican congressional party than in the Republican organization as a whole.

Examination of the actual magnitude of the ratio scores in this category reveals that the Republicans want not so much to abrogate existing social welfare or equalitarian measures as to keep them from being broadened. The Democrats, by comparison, are shown to be the party of social equality and reform, more willing than their opponents to employ legislation for the benefit of the underprivileged. Support for these inferences and for the greater liberalism of the Democrats can be found elsewhere in our data as well. Analysis of the scale results show Republican leaders scoring higher than Democratic leaders on such measures as chauvinism, elitism, conservatism, and right-wing values, and lower on tolerance, procedural rights, and faith in democracy. No differences worth noting, however, were found for ethnocentrism, faith in freedom, or the California F scale. The Democrats had a slightly higher average score on the left-wing scale, but the num-

ber of leaders in either party who scored high on this measure was fairly small.

The self-images and reference group identifications of the two parties also should be noted in this connection. For example, many more Democratic than Republican leaders call themselves liberal and state that they would be most likely to take advice from liberal reform organizations, the Farmers' Union, and (as we have seen) from the trade unions; only a small number consider themselves conservative or would seek advice from conservative reform organizations, the National Association of Manufacturers, or the Farm Bureau Federation. The Republicans have in almost all instances the reverse identifications: only a handful regard themselves as liberal or would seek counsel from liberal organizations, while more than 42 per cent call themselves conservative and would look to the NAM or to conservative reform organizations for advice. Almost two-thirds of the Republicans (compared with 29 per cent of the Democrats) regard the Chamber of Commerce as an important source of advice. Businessmen are listed as having "too much power" by 42 per cent of the Democrats but by only 9 per cent of the Republicans. The Democrats are also significantly more inclined than the Republicans to consider Catholics, Jews, and the foreign born as having "too little power." While self-descriptions and reference group identifications often correspond poorly with actual beliefs—among the general population they scarcely correspond at all, in fact—we are dealing, in the case of the leaders, with a politically informed and highly articulate set of people who have little difficulty connecting the beliefs they hold and the groups that promote or obstruct those beliefs.

Our fourth category, Tax Policy, divides the parties almost as severely as do the other categories. The mean difference for the category as a whole is .20, and it would doubtless have been larger but for

TABLE 2D

Comparison of Party Leaders and Followers on "Tax Policy" Issues,
by Percentages and Ratios of Support

	Leaders		Followers	
	Dem.	*Repub.*	*Dem.*	*Repub.*
	$N = 1,788$	$N = 1,232$	$N = 821$	$N = 623$
Issues		*(%s down)*		
Corporate income tax				
% favoring: Increase	32.3	4.0	32.0	23.3
Decrease	23.3	61.5	20.5	25.7
Same, n.c.	44.4	34.5	47.5	51.0
Support ratio	.54	.21	.56	.49
Tax on large incomes				
% favoring: Increase	27.0	5.4	46.6	34.7
Decrease	23.1	56.9	13.8	21.7
Same, n.c.	49.9	37.7	39.6	43.6
Support ratio	.52	.24	.66	.56
Tax on business				
% favoring: Increase	12.6	1.0	24.6	15.9
Decrease	38.3	71.1	24.1	32.6
Same, n.c.	49.1	27.8	51.3	51.5
Support ratio	.37	.15	.50	.42
Tax on middle incomes				
% favoring: Increase	2.7	0.8	4.5	3.0
Decrease	50.2	63.9	49.3	44.3
Same, n.c.	47.1	35.3	46.2	52.6
Support ratio	.26	.18	.28	.29
Tax on small incomes				
% favoring: Increase	1.4	2.9	1.6	2.1
Decrease	79.2	65.0	77.5	69.6
Same, n.c.	19.4	32.1	20.9	28.3
Support ratio	.11	.19	.12	.16
Mean support ratios for "tax policy" category	.36	.19	.42	.38

the universal unpopularity of proposals to increase taxes on small and middle income groups. Table 2D shows that the differences between the parties on the tax issues follow the patterns previously observed and that tax policy is for the Democrats a device for redistributing income and promoting social equality. Neither party, however, is keen about raising taxes for *any* group: even the Democrats have little enthusiasm for new taxes on upper income groups or on business and corporate enterprises. The Republican leaders are overwhelmingly opposed to

increased taxes for *any* group, rich *or* poor. This can be seen in their low ratio scores on the tax issues, which range from only .15 to .24. But while they are far more eager than the Democratic leaders to cut taxes on corporate and private wealth, they are less willing to reduce taxes on the lower income groups. These differences, it should be remarked, are not primarily a function of differences in the income of the two samples. Although there are more people with high incomes among the Republican leaders, the disproportion between the two samples is not

TABLE 2E

Comparison of Party Leaders and Followers on "Foreign Policy" Issues,
by Percentages and Ratios of Support

	Leaders		Followers	
	Dem. $N = 1,788$	Repub. $N = 1,232$	Dem. $N = 821$	Repub. $N = 623$
Issues		(%s down)		
Reliance on the United Nations				
% favoring: Increase	48.9	24.4	34.7	33.4
Decrease	17.6	34.8	17.3	19.3
Same, n.c.	33.5	40.7	48.0	47.3
Support ratio	.66	.45	.59	.57
American participation in military alliances				
% favoring: Increase	41.5	22.7	39.1	32.3
Decrease	17.6	25.7	14.0	15.4
Same, n.c.	40.9	51.6	46.9	52.3
Support ratio	.62	.48	.62	.58
Foreign aid				
% favoring: Increase	17.8	7.6	10.1	10.1
Decrease	51.0	61.7	58.6	57.3
Same, n.c.	31.1	30.7	31.3	32.6
Support ratio	.33	.23	.26	.26
Defense spending*				
% favoring: Increase	20.7	13.6	50.5	45.7
Decrease	34.4	33.6	16.4	15.4
Same, n.c.	44.8	52.8	33.0	38.8
Support ratio	.43	.40	.67	.65
Mean support ratios for "foreign policy" category (excl. defense spending)	.54	.39	.49	.47

*See footnote 22.

nearly great enough to account for the dissimilarities in their tax views.

Of the five categories considered, Foreign Policy shows the smallest average difference, but even on these issues the divergence between Democratic and Republican leader attitudes is significant. Except for defense spending the Democrats turn out to be more internationalist than the Republicans, as evidenced in their greater commitment to the United Nations and to American participation in international military alliances like NATO. Twice as many Democrats as Republicans want the United States to rely more heavily upon such organizations, while many more Republicans want to reduce our international involvements. Both parties are

predominantly in favor of cutting back foreign aid—a somewhat surprising finding in light of Democratic public pronouncements on this subject—but more Republicans feel strongly on the subject. Our data thus furnish little support for the claim that the parties hold the same views on foreign policy or that their seeming differences are merely a response to the demands of political competition.[21]

Nevertheless, it would be incorrect to

[21]Cf. Turner, op. cit., p. 56, in which he found differences on foreign policy difficult to assess in Congress, partly because of its tie with the executive branch; see also, George Belknap and Angus Campbell, "Political Party Identification and Attitudes toward Foreign Policy," Public Opinion Quarterly, Vol. XV (Winter 1951–52), pp. 608–19.

conclude that one party believes in internationalism and the other in isolationism. The differences are far too small to warrant any such inference. Traces of isolationism, to be sure, remain stronger in the Republican party than in the Democratic party—an observation buttressed by the finding that twice as many Republicans as Democrats score high on the isolationism scale. The pattern of Republican responses on both the issue and scale items signifies, however, that the leaders of that party generally accept the degree of "internationalism" now in effect, but shrink from extending it further. Consider too, the similarities in the leaders' scores on defense spending, for despite their greater leaning toward isolationism, the Republicans are no more inclined than the Democrats to leave the country defenseless.[22]

In treating issues in the Elmira election study of 1948, Berelson, Lazarsfeld, and McPhee[23] found it helpful to distinguish between "style" and "position" issues. "Style" issues principally yield symbolic, psychological, or subjective gratifications, and have relatively intangible consequences; "position" issues reflect direct, personal and material interests, and

have more objective consequences. According to the Elmira report, "position" issues (or what politicians might call "bread and butter" issues) divide voters more sharply than style issues. Most of the issues tested in the present study would have to be classified as "position" issues, but five of them—United Nations, international alliances, foreign aid, immigration, and segregation—could be classified as style issues. Four others—natural resources, atomic energy, education, and slum clearance—contain both symbolic and material elements and can best be described as "mixed."

Although the classification is crude, the findings it yields are generally consistent with the claims of the Elmira study. On the fourteen position issues—taxes, trade unions, tariffs, minimum wages, farm prices, social security, credit restrictions, and the regulation of business, public utilities and monopolies—Democratic and Republican leaders show an average ratio score difference of .21. On the style issues the two parties differ by .13—a significantly smaller difference. Largest of all, however, are the differences for the "mixed" issues, which average more than .30. This result should occasion little surprise, for when ideology and interest are *both* at work, partisanship is likely to be intensified. Several considerations could account for the superiority of position over style issues as causes of political cleavage: they are "bread and butter" issues, and are thus more often subject to pressure by organized interest groups; they have immediate and tangible consequences, which may lead politicians to pay greater attention to them than they do to issues whose payoff is more uncertain; and, finally, they are not so likely to be part of the common core of values upon which the community structure rests.

Comparison of the magnitude of the differences between groups can be seen in Table 3, p. 312, where we have ranked the issues, high to low, according to the size of the difference between the groups

---

[22]The issue of defense spending has been kept separate from the other foreign policy issues because the magnitude of the scores for some of the leaders and all of the followers were obviously inflated by the launching of Sputnik I in November, 1957. The Sputnik incident occurred between the first and second wave of the leader survey and produced an increase in the number favoring defense spending of 40 per cent for the Democrats and 33 per cent for the Republicans. While this is a fascinating testimonial to the influence sometimes exercised by events on public opinion, its effect in this case was to distort scores in such a way as to make the leader and follower samples non-comparable. With proper caution, however, comparisons can be made between the Democratic and Republican leaders since both samples were affected in roughly the same way by Sputnik. For a similar reason we can also compare the Democratic followers with the Republican followers. Comparisons between leaders and followers on this issue cannot, however, be justified from our data.

[23]Bernard R. Berelson, Paul F. Lazarsfeld, and William N. McPhee, *Voting* (Chicago, 1954), ch. 9.

being compared. By presenting a rank-order of differences for the two leader groups, for the two follower groups, and for the leaders and followers of each party, this table makes it possible to observe not only which issues most and least divide the several party groups, but whether they divide the leaders and followers in the same way.

Notice that the issues commonly thought to be most divisive do not always evoke the greatest cleavage between the parties. Immigration, tariffs, civil rights, monopoly control, and credit regulation fall toward the lower end of the rank order, while farm supports, federal aid to education, slum clearance, social security, minimum wages, public housing, and issues dealing with the regulation and taxation of business fall toward the upper end. Though by no means uniformly, the older, more traditional issues appear to have been superseded as sources of controversy by issues that have come into prominence chiefly during the New Deal and Fair Deal.

IV. COMPARISONS BETWEEN FOLLOWERS

So far we have addressed ourselves to the differences between Democratic and Republican *leaders*. In each of the tables presented, however, data are included from which the two sets of party *followers* may also be compared.

The observation most clearly warranted from these data is that the rank-and-file members of the two parties are far less divided than their leaders. Not only do they diverge significantly on fewer issues—seven as compared with 23 for the leader samples—but the magnitudes of the differences in their ratio scores are substantially smaller for every one of the 24 issues. No difference is larger than .14, and on the majority of the issues the disparity is smaller than .05. Insofar as they differ at all, however, the followers tend to divide in a pattern similar to that shown by the leaders, the correlation be-

tween their rank orders being .72. All the issues on which the followers significantly disagree are of the "bread and butter" variety, the more symbolic issues being so remotely experienced and so vaguely grasped that rank-and-file voters are often unable to identify them with either party. Policies affecting farm prices, business regulation, taxes, or minimum wages, by contrast, are quickly felt by the groups to whom they are addressed and are therefore more capable of arousing partisan identifications. It should also be noted that while the average differences are small for all five categories, they are smallest of all for foreign policy—the most removed and least well understood group of issues in the entire array.[24]

Democratic and Republican followers were also compared on a number of scales and reference group questions. The results, while generally consistent with the differences between the leaders, show the followers to be far more united than their leaders on these measures as well. Even on business attitudes, independence of government, and economic conservatism, the differences are small and barely significant. No differences were found on such scales as tolerance, faith in democracy, procedural rights, conservatism–liberalism (classical), the California F scale and isolationism. The average Democrat is slightly more willing than the average Republican to label himself a liberal or to seek advice from liberal organizations; the contrary is true when it comes to adopting conservative identifications.

---

[24]For comparative data on party affiliation and issue outlooks among rank-and-file voters, see Angus Campbell, Phillip E. Converse, Warren E. Miller, and Donald E. Stokes, *The American Voter* (New York, 1960), especially chs. 8 and 9 dealing with issues and ideology. The text of this important report on the 1956 election study carried out by the Michigan Survey Research Center unfortunately reached us too late to be used to full advantage in the present analysis. The findings of the Michigan and the PAB studies, relative to the role of issues and ideology among the general population, corroborate and supplement each other to a very great degree.

Only in the differential trust they express toward business and labor are the two sets of followers widely separated.

These findings give little support to the claim that the "natural divisions" of the electorate are being smothered by party leaders.[25] Not only do the leaders disagree more sharply than their respective followers, but the level of consensus among the electorate (with or without regard to party) is fairly high. Inspection of the "increase" and "decrease" percentage scores (Tables 2A–2E) shows that substantial differences of opinion exist among the electorate on only five of the 24 issues (credit restrictions, farm supports, segregation, and corporate and business taxes). Of course, voters may divide more sharply on issues at election time, since campaigns intensify party feeling and may also intensify opinions on issues. Available data from election studies allow no unequivocal conclusion on this point,[26] but even the party-linked differences found among voters during elections may largely be echoes of the opinions announced by the candidates—transient sentiments developed for the occasion and quickly forgotten.

V. LEADER CONFLICT AND FOLLOWER CONSENSUS: EXPLANATIONS

Considering the nature of the differences between the leader and follower

samples, the interesting question is not why the parties fail to represent the "natural division" in the electorate (for that question rests on an unwarranted assumption) but why the party elites disagree at all, and why they divide so much more sharply than their followers.

Despite the great pressures toward uniformity we have noted in American society, many forces also divide the population culturally, economically, and politically. The United States is, after all, a miscellany of ethnic and religious strains set down in a geographically large and diverse country. Many of these groups brought old conflicts and ideologies with them, and some have tried to act out in the new world the hopes and frustrations nurtured in the old. Then, too, despite rapid social mobility, social classes have by no means been eliminated. No special political insight is needed to perceive that the two parties characteristically draw from different strata of the society, the Republicans from the managerial, proprietary, and to some extent professional classes, the Democrats from labor, minorities, low income groups, and a large proportion of the intellectuals.[27] Partly because the leaders of the two parties tend to overrespond to the modal values of the groups with which they are principally identified, they gradually grow further apart on the key questions which separate their respective supporters.[28] The Republican emphasis on business ideology is both a cause and a consequence of its managerial and proprietary support; the greater Democratic emphasis on social justice, and on economic and social levelling, is both the occasion and the product

---

[25]Cf. Stephen K. Bailey, *The Condition of Our National Parties* (monograph), Fund for the Republic, 1959.

[26]The data reported by the Elmira study of 1948 show the supporters of the two parties to be largely in agreement on issues. See *ibid.*, pp. 186, 190, 194, 211. The findings of the 1956 Michigan Survey suggest strongly that most voters, even at election time, do not know much about issues and are unable to link the parties with particular issues. Campbell and his associates conclude, for example, that "many people fail to appreciate that an issue exists; others are insufficiently involved to pay attention to recognized issues; and still others fail to make connections between issue positions and party policy." *The American Voter, op. cit.*, ch. 8.

[27]For an analysis of the connection between intellectuals and liberal politics, see Seymour M. Lipset, *Political Man* (New York, 1960), ch. 10; also Paul F. Lazarsfeld and Wagner Thielens, Jr., *The Academic Mind* (Glencoe, 1958), chs. 1 and 2.

[28]Samuel P. Huntington, "A Revised Theory of American Party Politics," *American Political Science Review*, Vol. XLIV (1950), p. 676.

of the support the party enjoys among intellectuals and the lower strata. These interrelationships are strengthened, moreover, by the tendency for a party's dominant supporters to gain a disproportionate number of positions in its leadership ranks.[29]

The differences which typically separate Democratic from Republican leaders seem also to reflect a deep-seated ideological cleavage often found among Western parties. One side of this cleavage is marked by a strong belief in the power of collective action to promote social justice, equality, humanitarianism, and economic planning, while preserving freedom; the other is distinguished by faith in the wisdom of the natural competitive process and in the supreme virtue of individualism, "character," self-reliance, frugality, and independence from government. To this cleavage is added another frequent source of political division, namely, a difference in attitude toward change between "radicals" and "moderates," between those who prefer to move quickly or slowly, to reform or to conserve. These differences in social philosophy and posture do not always coincide with the divisions in the social structure, and their elements do not, in all contexts, combine in the same way. But, however crudely, the American parties do tend to embody these competing points of view and to serve as reference groups for those who hold them.

Party cleavage in America was no doubt intensified by the advent of the New Deal, and by its immense electoral and intellectual success. Not only did it weld into a firm alliance the diverse forces that were to be crucial to all subsequent Democratic majorities, but it also made explicit the doctrines of the "welfare state" with which the party was henceforth to be inseparably identified.

Because of the novelty of its program and its apparently radical threat to the familiar patterns of American political and economic life, it probably deepened the fervor of its Republican adversaries and drove into the opposition the staunchest defenders of business ideology. The conflict was further sharpened by the decline of left-wing politics after the war, and by the transfer of loyalties of former and potential radicals to the Democratic party. Once launched, the cleavage has been sustained by the tendency for each party to attract into its active ranks a disproportionate number of voters who recognize and share its point of view.

Why, however, are the leaders so much more sharply divided than their followers? The reasons are not hard to understand and are consistent with several of the hypotheses that underlay the present study.

(1) Consider, to begin with, that the leaders come from the more articulate segments of society and, on the average, are politically more aware than their followers and far better informed about issues.[30] For them, political issues and opinions are the everyday currency of party competition, not esoteric matters that surpass understanding. With their greater awareness and responsibility, and their greater need to defend their party's stands, they have more interest in developing a consistent set of attitudes—perhaps even an ideology. The followers of each party, often ignorant of the issues and their consequences, find it difficult to distinguish their beliefs from those of the opposition and have little reason to be concerned with the consistency of their attitudes. Furthermore, the American parties make only a feeble effort to educate the rank-and-file politically, and since no central source exists for the authoritative pronouncement of party policy,[31] the

---

[29]PAB data supporting this generalization will be presented in a future publication.

[30]For the effects of education on issue familiarity, see Campbell *et al., op. cit.,* ch. 8.

[31]Schattschneider, *op. cit.; Toward a More Responsible Two-Party System, op. cit., passim.*

followers often do not know what their leaders believe or on what issues the parties chiefly divide. In short, if we mean by ideology a coherent body of informed social doctrine, it is possessed mainly by the articulate leadership, rarely by the masses.

(2) Differences in the degree of partisan involvement parallel the differences in knowledge and have similar consequences. The leaders, of course, have more party spirit than the followers, and, as the election studies make plain, the stronger the partisanship, the larger the differences on issues. The leaders are more highly motivated not only to belong to a party appropriate to their beliefs, but to accept its doctrines and to learn how it differs from the opposition party. Since politics is more salient for leaders than for followers, they develop a greater stake in the outcome of the political contest and are more eager to discover the intellectual grounds by which they hope to make victory possible. Through a process of circular reinforcement, those for whom politics is most important are likely to become the most zealous participants, succeeding to the posts that deal in the formation of opinion. Ideology serves the instrumental purpose, in addition, of justifying the heavy investment that party leaders make in political activity. While politics offers many rewards, it also makes great demands on the time, money, and energies of its practitioners—sacrifices which they can more easily justify if they believe they are serving worthwhile social goals. The followers, in contrast, are intellectually far less involved, have less personal stake in the outcome of the competition, have little need to be concerned with the "correctness" of their views on public questions, and have even less reason to learn in precisely what ways their opinions differ from their opponents'. Hence, the party elites recruit members from a population stratified in some measure by ideology, while the rank-and-file

renews itself by more random recruitment and is thus more likely to mirror the opinions of a cross section of the population.

(3) Part of the explanation for the greater consensus among followers than leaders resides in the nature and size of the two types of groups. Whereas the leader groups are comparatively small and selective, each of the follower groups number in the millions and, by their very size and unwieldiness, are predisposed to duplicate the characteristics of the population as a whole. Even if the Republicans draws disproportionately from the business-managerial classes and the Democrats from the trade union movement, neither interest group has enough influence to shape distinctively the aggregate opinions of so large a mass of supporters. Size also affects the nature and frequency of interaction within the two types of groups. Because they comprise a smaller, more selectively chosen, organized, and articulate elite, the leaders are apt to associate with people of their own political persuasion more frequently and consistently than the followers do. They are not only less cross-pressured than the rank-and-file but they are also subjected to strong party group efforts to induce them to conform. Because their political values are continually renewed through frequent communication with people of like opinions, and because they acquire intense reference group identifications, they develop an extraordinary ability to resist the force of the opposition's arguments. While the followers, too, are thrown together and shielded to some extent, they are likely to mingle more freely with people of hostile political persuasions, to receive fewer partisan communications, and to hold views that are only intermittently and inconsistently reinforced. Since, by comparison with the leaders, they possess little interest in or information about politics, they can more easily embrace "deviant" attitudes without

discomfort and without challenge from their associates. Nor are they likely to be strongly rewarded for troubling to have "correct" opinions. The followers, in short, are less often and less effectively indoctrinated than their leaders. The group processes described here would function even more powerfully in small, sectarian, tightly organized parties of the European type, but they are also present in the American party system, where they yield similar though less potent consequences.

(4) Political competition itself operates to divide the leaders more than the followers. If the parties are impelled to present a common face to the electorate, they are also strongly influenced to distinguish themselves from each other.[32] For one thing, they have a more heightened sense of the "national interest" than the followers do, even if they do not all conceive it in the same way. For another, they hope to improve their chances at the polls by offering the electorate a recognizable and attractive commodity. In addition, they seek emotional gratification in the heightened sense of brotherhood brought on by the struggle against an "outgroup" whose claim to office seems always, somehow, to border upon usurpation. As with many ingroup–outgroup distinctions, the participants search for moral grounds to justify their antagonisms toward each other, and ideologies help to furnish such grounds. Among the followers, on the other hand, these needs exist, if at all, in much weaker form.

VI. LEADERS VERSUS FOLLOWERS

In comparing each party elite with its own followers we were mainly interested in seeing how closely each body of supporters shared the point of view of its leaders, in order to test the hypothesis that party affiliation, even for the rank-and-file, is a function of ideological agree-

ment. In predicting that the parties would tend to attract supporters who share their beliefs, we expected, of course, to find exceptions. We knew that many voters pay little attention to the ideological aspects of politics and that, in Gabriel Almond's phrase, a party's more "esoteric doctrines" are not always known to its followers.[33] Nevertheless we were not prepared for the findings turned up by this phase of the inquiry, for the differences between leaders and followers—among the Republicans at least—are beyond anything we had expected. Indeed, the conclusion is inescapable that the views of the Republican rank-and-file are, on the whole, much closer to those of the Democratic leaders than to those of the Republican leaders. Although conflicts in outlook also exist between Democratic leaders and followers, they are less frequent or severe.

If we turn once again to the table of rank-order differences, we see that the Democratic followers differ significantly from their leaders on twelve of the 23 issues, and that the average difference in the ratio scores of the two samples is .07. Democratic leaders and Republican followers differ significantly on only eleven of the 23 issues, with an average difference between them of only .08. Notice, by contrast, that Republican leaders and followers diverge significantly on 18 of the 23 issues, and show an average difference of .16. To complete the comparison, the Republican leaders and Democratic followers were in disagreement on 19 of the 23 issues, their average difference being .20. As these comparisons make plain, there is substantial consensus on national issues between Democratic leaders and Democratic and Republican followers, while the Republican leaders are separated not only from the Democrats but from their own rank-and-file members as well.

---

[32]See E. E. Schattschneider, *Party Government, op. cit.,* p. 192.

[33]Gabriel Almond, *The Appeals of Communism* (Princeton, 1954), pp. 5–6, and ch. 3.

TABLE 3

Rank Order of Differences in the Support-Ratio Scores of Party Leaders and Followers*

Democratic vs. Republican Leaders		Democratic vs. Republican Followers		Democratic Leaders vs. Followers		Republican Leaders vs. Followers	
Issues	Diff. between ratio scores†	Issues	Diff. between ratio scores	Issues	Diff. between ratio scores	Issues	Diff. between ratio scores
1. Natural resources	+.39	Farm supports	+.14	Immigration	+.25	Fed. aid to edu.	−.39
2. Farm supports	+.38	Gov't. reg. of business	+.12	Anti-monopoly	+.15	Taxes–large income	−.32
3. Fed. aid. to edu.	+.37	Taxes–large income	+.10	Taxes–large income	−.15	Taxes–corp.	−.28
4. Taxes–corp.	+.33	Minimum wages	+.09	Taxes–business	−.13	Taxes–business	−.27
5. Reg.–business	+.33	Taxes–business	+.09	Reg. pub. util.	+.12	Natural resources	−.23
6. Taxes–large inc.	+.28	Reg. pub. util.	+.07	Tariffs	−.11	Pub. housing	−.23
7. Pub. housing	+.27	Taxes–corp.	+.07	Restrict. credit	−.09	Reg. business	−.22
8. Reg. pub. util.	+.26	Social security	+.07	Natural resources	+.09	Social security	−.22
9. Social security	+.23	Fed. aid to edu.	+.06	Fed. aid to edu.	−.08	Farm supports	−.22
10. Taxes–business	+.22	Reg. trade unions	−.05	Foreign aid	+.08	Minimum wages	−.18
11. Minimum wages	+.21	Natural resources	+.05	Reliance on U.N.	−.05	Reg. trade unions	+.17
12. Reliance on U.N.	+.21	Public housing	+.05	Minimum wages	−.05	Immigration	+.13
13. Anti-monopoly	+.20	Taxes–small income	−.04	Social security	−.05	Reliance on U.N.	−.12
14. Atomic energy control	+.18	American participation, NATO	+.04	Reg. trade unions	+.05	Enforce integration	−.12
15. Reg. trade unions	−.18	Atomic energy control	+.04	Atomic energy control	+.04	Taxes–middle income	−.11
16. American participation, NATO	+.13	Immigration	−.03	Farm supports	+.02	Atomic energy control	−.10
17. Enforce integration	+.12	Defense spending	+.02	Reg. business	−.02	American participation, NATO	−.10
18. Tariffs	−.11	Taxes–middle income	−.02	Enforce integration	+.01	Reg. public utilities	−.07
19. Foreign aid	+.10	Reliance on U.N.	+.02	Taxes–middle income	−.01	Anti-monopoly	−.04
20. Increase immigration	+.10	Tariffs	−.01	Taxes–corporation	−.01	Foreign aid	−.03
21. Taxes–small income	−.08	Enforce integration	−.01	Taxes–small income	−.01	Taxes–small income	+.03
22. Taxes–middle income	+.08	Restriction credit	+.01	American participation, NATO	−.01	Restriction credit	−.01
23. Restriction credit	−.07	Foreign aid	−.01	Public housing	.00	Tariffs	−.01
24. Defense spending	+.03	Anti-monopoly	.00	Defense spending	‡	Defense spending	‡

N's. Democratic Leaders: 1,788; Rebublican Leaders: 1,232; Democratic Followers: 821; Republican Followers: 623.

*The plus sign means that the first group listed in the heading is more favorable to the issue named than the second group; the minus sign means that the second group is the more favorable.

†Leaders and Followers cannot be compared on defense spending, for reasons given in footnote to Table 2E.

‡Size of difference required for differences to be significant at .01 level: Democratic Leaders vs. Republican–.048; Democratic Leaders vs. Democratic Followers–.068; Democratic Leaders vs. Democratic Followers–.054; Republican Leaders vs. Republican Followers–.063.

Examination of the Democratic scores shows the leaders to be slightly more "progressive" than their followers on most of the issues on which differences appear. The leaders are, for example, more favorable to public ownership of natural resources, to regulation of monopolies and public utilities, to a reduction of tariffs, and to a liberalized credit policy. They are more internationalist on the foreign aid and United Nations issues and substantially more sympathetic to the maintenance and expansion of immigration. The results showing the relative radicalism of the two samples are not unequivocal, however, for on several issues—federal aid to education, minimum wages, and taxes on business enterprise and large incomes—the followers take the more radical view. Nor are the differences significant on such issues as atomic energy, slum clearance, segregation, farm price supports, government control of business and trade unions, and taxes on middle and small income groups. In general, the followers turn out more radical chiefly on a few of the "bread and butter issues"—a reflection, no doubt, of their lower socioeconomic status. When we control for occupation, the differences between Democratic leaders and followers on these issues largely disappear.

Consideration of the scores of Republican leaders and followers shows not only that they are widely separated in their outlooks but also that the leaders are uniformly more conservative than their followers. Only on the immigration issue is this trend reversed. The followers hold the more "radical" ideas on the two public ownership issues, on five of the six equalitarian and human welfare issues, on four of the seven regulation-of-the-economy issues, and on four of the five tax policy issues. They are also more willing to place greater reliance upon the U.N. and upon international military alliances. Observe that the largest differences occur on those issues which have most sharply separated

New Deal-Fair Deal spokesmen from the hard core of the Republican opposition—federal aid to education, redistribution of wealth through taxes on business, corporations and the wealthy, public ownership of natural resources, public housing, regulation of business, social security, farm price supports, minimum wages, and trade union regulations.

In short, whereas Republican leaders hold to the tenets of business ideology and remain faithful to the spirit and intellectual mood of leaders like Robert A. Taft, the rank-and-file Republican supporters have embraced, along with their Democratic brethren, the regulatory and social reform measures of the Roosevelt and Truman administrations. This inference receives further support from the scores on our Party Ideology scale where, on a variety of attitudes and values which characteristically distinguish the leaders of the two parties, the Republican followers fall closer to the Democratic than to the Republican side of the continuum. Thus, in addition to being the preferred party of the more numerous classes, the Democrats also enjoy the advantages over their opponents of holding views that are more widely shared throughout the country.

Assuming the findings are valid, we were obviously wrong to expect that party differentiation among followers would depend heavily upon ideological considerations.[34] Evidently, party attachment is so much a function of other factors (e.g. class and primary group memberships, religious affiliation, place of residence, mass media, etc.) that many voters can maintain their party loyalties comfortably even while holding views that contradict the beliefs of their own leaders.

Still, we are not entitled to conclude

---

[34]See the discussion bearing on this conclusion in Campbell et al., op. cit., chs. 8 and 9. Also, Avery Leiserson, Parties and Politics, An Institutional and Behavioral Approach (New York, 1958), pp. 162–66.

that issue outlook has no effect on the party affiliation of ordinary members. It is conceivable, for example, that the Republican party has come to be the minority party partly because the opinions of its spokesmen are uncongenial to a majority of the voters. We have no way of knowing from our data—collected at only a single point in time—how many "normally" Republican voters, if any, have defected to the Democrats or fled into independency because they disapprove of Republican beliefs. At the present stage of the analysis, we have no grounds for going beyond the proposition that political affiliation without conformity on issues is possible on a wide scale. In future analyses we shall attempt to learn more about the nature of the relationship between belief and party affiliation by stratifying voters according to the frequency with which they conform to the beliefs of their party leaders. We hope, in this way, to discover whether those who conform least are also less firm in their party loyalties.

VII. THE HOMOGENEITY OF SUPPORT FOR LEADERS AND FOLLOWERS

So far we have only considered conflict and agreement *between* groups. We should now turn to the question of consensus *within* groups. To what extent is each of our samples united on fundamental issues?

In order to assess homogeneity of opinion within party groups, standard deviation scores were computed on each issue for each of the four samples. The higher the standard deviation, of course, the greater the disagreement. The range of possible sigma scores is from 0 (signifying that every member of the sample has selected the same response) to .500 (signifying that all responses are equally divided between the "increase" and "decrease" alternatives). If we assume that the three alternative responses had been randomly (and therefore equally) select-

ed, the standard deviations for the four samples would fall by chance alone around .410. Scores at or above this level may be taken to denote extreme dispersion among the members of a sample while scores in the neighborhood of .300 or below suggest that unanimity within the sample is fairly high. By these somewhat arbitrary criteria we can observe immediately (Table 4) that consensus within groups is greater on most issues than we would expect by chance alone, but that it is extremely high in only a few instances. Although the Republican leaders appear on the average to be the most united and the Democratic leaders the least united of the four groups, the difference between their homogeneity scores (.340 vs. .310) is too small to be taken as conclusive. The grounds are somewhat better for rejecting the belief that leaders are more homogeneous in their outlooks than their followers, since the hypothesis holds only for one party and not for the other.

While generalizations about the relative unity of the four samples seem risky, we can speak more confidently about the rank order of agreement *within* samples. In Table 4 we have ranked the issues according to the degree of consensus exhibited toward them by the members of each of the four party groups. There we see that the leaders of the Republican party are most united on the issues that stem from its connections with business— government regulation of business, taxes (especially on business), regulation of trade unions, and minimum wages. The Democratic leaders are most united on those issues which bear upon the support the party receives from the lower and middle income groups—taxes on small and middle incomes, anti-monopoly, slum clearance, social security, and minimum wages. The Republican leaders divide most severely on federal aid to education, slum clearance, U.N. support, segregation, and public control of atomic energy and

TABLE 4
Consensus within Party Groups: Rank Order of Homogeneity of Support on Twenty-Four Issues

Average Rank Order*	Issue	Democratic Leaders		Republican Leaders		Democratic Followers		Republican Followers	
		Rank Order	Sigma	Rank Order	Sigma	Rank Order	Sigma	Rank Order	Sigma
1	Tax on small incomes	1	.220	6	.270	1	.224	1	.250
2	Tax on middle incomes	3	.276	4	.248	6	.292	2	.278
3	Social security benefits	5	.282	8	.296	2	.266	3	.286
4	Minimum wages	6	.292	5	.268	4	.276	4	.294
5	Enforcement of anti-monopoly	2	.246	13	.321	8	.324	7	.314
6	Regulation of public utilities	8	.307	10	.300	10	.336	5.5	.310
7	Slum clearance	4	.276	23	.386	3	.274	5.5	.310
8	Regulation of trade unions	12	.356	3	.240	9	.331	15	.345
9	Government regulation of business	17	.376	1	.192	20	.363	8	.315
10	Tax on business	9	.338	2	.236	19	.362	16	.348
11	Level of tariffs	10	.350	16	.344	11	.338	9	.316
12	Public control of atomic energy	7	.302	20	.362	7	.312	13	.340
13	Federal aid to education	13	.360	24	.394	5	.283	11	.322
14	Foreign aid	19	.383	12	.317	12.5	.340	12	.340
15	Tax on large incomes	11	.356	9	.298	17	.358	22	.379
16	American participation in military alliances, NATO	14	.370	18	.351	14	.350	14	.344
17	Immigration into U.S.	21	.399	17	.345	12.5	.340	10	.318
18	Corporate income tax	16	.375	7	.284	21	.371	17	.361
19	Restrictions on credit	22	.400	14	.324	16	.358	18	.362
20	Defense spending	15	.371	15	.334	22	.380	21	.366
21	Public ownership of natural resources	20	.393	19	.354	15	.352	19	.362
22	Reliance on U.N.	18	.380	22	.384	18	.359	20	.365
23	Level of farm supports	24	.421	11	.306	23	.414	23	.397
24	Enforce integration	23	.416	21	.382	24	.418	24	.399

*The range of sigma scores is from .192 to .421, out of a possible range of .000 (most united) to .500 (least united). Hence, the lower the rank order the greater the unity on the issue named.

natural resources; the Democratic leaders are most divided on farm prices, segregation, credit restrictions, immigration, and the natural resources issue. Among the followers the patterns of unity and division are very similar, as attested by the high correlation of .83 between the rank orders of their homogeneity scores. Both Republican and Democratic followers exhibit great cohesion, for example, on taxes on small and middle incomes, social security, slum clearance, and minimum wages. Both divide rather sharply on segregation, farm price support, defense spending, U.N. support, and taxes on large incomes. The two sets of followers, in short, are alike not only in their opinions on issues but in the degree of unanimity they exhibit toward them.

Inspection of the homogeneity data furnishes additional evidence on the between-group comparisons made earlier. Whereas Democratic and Republican followers divide on issues in approximately the same way, the two sets of leaders differ from each other in this respect also (the correlation between their rank orders on homogeneity is only .28). Democratic leaders and followers tend to unite or divide on the same issues for the most part (r equals .77), but Republican leaders and followers are not parallel in this respect either (r equals .30). The pattern of homogeneity and dispersion among Republican followers is, in fact, much closer to that of the Democratic leaders (r equals .75).

In computing scores for homogeneity we were in part concerned to test the belief that political parties develop greatest internal solidarity on those questions which most separate them from their opponents. According to this hypothesis, external controversy has the effect of uniting the members further by confronting them with a common danger. Whether or not this hypothesis would be borne out in a study of small, sectarian parties we cannot say, but it receives no support from the present study of the American mass parties. Comparisons of the rank-order data in Tables 3 and 4 show that there is no consistent connection between interparty conflict and intraparty cohesion. The correlations between the rank orders of difference and the rank orders of homogeneity are in every case insignificant.[35]

SUMMARY AND CONCLUSIONS

The research described in this paper—an outgrowth of a nationwide inquiry into the nature and sources of political affiliation, activity, and belief—was principally designed to test a number of hypotheses about the relation of ideology to party membership. Responses from large samples of Democratic and Republican leaders and followers were compared on twenty-four key issues and on a number of attitude questions and scales. Statistical operations were carried out to assess conflict and consensus among party groups and to estimate the size and significance of differences. From the data yielded by this inquiry, the following inferences seem warranted.

---

[35]For an interesting set of comparative data on the relation of internal party cohesion to issue outlook, see Morris Davis and Sidney Verba, "Party Affiliation and International Opinions in Britain and France, 1947–1956," *Public Opinion Quarterly*, Winter 1960–61.

1. Although it has received wide currency, especially among Europeans, the belief that the two American parties are identical in principle and doctrine has little foundation in fact. Examination of the opinions of Democratic and Republican leaders shows them to be distinct communities of co-believers who diverge sharply on many important issues. Their disagreements, furthermore, conform to an image familiar to many observers and are generally consistent with differences turned up by studies of Congressional roll calls. The unpopularity of many of the positions held by Republican leaders suggests also that the parties submit to the demands of their constituents less slavishly than is commonly supposed.

2. Republican and Democratic leaders stand furthest apart on the issues that grow out of their group identification and support—out of the managerial, proprietary, and high-status connections of the one, and the labor, minority, low-status, and intellectual connections of the other. The opinions of each party elite are linked less by chance than by membership in a common ideological domain. Democratic leaders typically display the stronger urge to elevate the lowborn, the uneducated, the deprived minorities, and the poor in general; they are also more disposed to employ the nation's collective power to advance humanitarian and social welfare goals (*e.g.*, social security, immigration, racial integration, a higher minimum wage, and public education). They are more critical of wealth and big business and more eager to bring them under regulation. Theirs is the greater faith in the wisdom of using legislation for redistributing the national product and for furnishing social services on a wide scale. Of the two groups of leaders, the Democrats are the more "progressively" oriented toward social reform and experimentation. The Republican leaders, while not uniformly differentiated from their opponents, subscribe in greater measure to the

symbols and practices of individualism, *laissez-faire,* and national independence. They prefer to overcome humanity's misfortunes by relying upon personal effort, private incentives, frugality, hard work, responsibility, self-denial (for both men and government), and the strengthening rather than the diminution of the economic and status distinctions that are the "natural" rewards of the differences in human character and fortunes. Were it not for the hackneyed nature of the designation and the danger of forcing traits into a mold they fit only imperfectly, we might be tempted to describe the Republicans as the chief upholders of what Max Weber has called the "Protestant Ethic."[36] Not that the Democrats are insensible to the "virtues" of the Protestant-capitalistic ethos, but they embrace them less firmly or uniformly. The differences between the two elites have probably been intensified by the rise of the New Deal and by the shift of former radicals into the Democratic party following the decline of socialist and other left-wing movements during and after the war.

3. Whereas the leaders of the two parties diverge strongly, their followers differ only moderately in their attitudes toward issues. The hypothesis that party beliefs unite adherents and bring them into the party ranks may hold for the more active members of a mass party but not for its rank-and-file supporters. Republican followers, in fact, disagree far more with their own leaders than with the leaders of the Democratic party. Little support was found for the belief that deep cleavages exist among the electorate but are ignored by the leaders. One might, indeed, more accurately assert the contrary, to wit: that the natural cleavages between the leaders are largely ignored by the voters. However, we cannot presently conclude that ideology exerts no in-

fluence over the habits of party support, for the followers do differ significantly and in the predicted directions on some issues. Furthermore, we do not know how many followers may previously have been led by doctrinal considerations to shift their party allegiances.

4. Except for their desire to ingratiate themselves with as many voters as possible, the leaders of the two parties have more reason than their followers to hold sharply opposing views on the important political questions of the day. Compared with the great mass of supporters, they are articulate, informed, highly partisan, and involved; they comprise a smaller and more tightly knit group which is closer to the wellsprings of party opinion, more accessible for indoctrination, more easily rewarded or punished for conformity or deviation, and far more affected, politically and psychologically, by engagement in the party struggle for office. If the leaders of the two parties are not always candid about their disagreements, the reason may well be that they sense the great measure of consensus to be found among the electorate.

5. Finding that party leaders hold contrary beliefs does not prove that they *act* upon these beliefs or that the two parties are, in practice, governed by different outlooks. In a subsequent paper we shall consider these questions more directly by comparing platform and other official party pronouncements with the private opinions revealed in this study. Until further inquiries are conducted, however, it seems reasonable to assume that the views held privately by party leaders can never be entirely suppressed but are bound to crop out in hundreds of large and small ways—in campaign speeches, discussions at party meetings, private communications to friends and sympathizers, statements to the press by party officials and candidates, legislative debates, and public discussions on innumerable national, state, and local questions. If, in other words,

[36]Max Weber, *Protestant Ethic and the Spirit of Capitalism* (London, 1948), ch. V.

the opinions of party leaders are as we have described them, there is every chance that they are expressed and acted upon to some extent. Whether this makes our parties "ideological" depends, of course, on how narrow we define that term. Some may prefer to reserve that designation for parties that are more obviously preoccupied with doctrine, more intent upon the achievement of a systematic political program, and more willing to enforce a common set of beliefs upon their members and spokesmen.

6. The parties are internally united on some issues, divided on others. In general, Republican leaders achieve greatest homogeneity on issues that grow out of their party's identification with business, Democratic leaders on issues that reflect their connection with liberal and lower-income groups. We find no support for the hypothesis that the parties achieve greatest internal consensus on the issues which principally divide them from their opponents.

In a sequel to this paper we shall offer data on the demographic correlates of issue support, which show that most of the differences presented here exist independently of factors like education, occupation, age, religion, and sectionalism. Controlling for these influences furnishes much additional information and many new insights but does not upset our present conclusions in any important respect. Thus, the parties must be considered not merely as spokesmen for other interest groups but as reference groups in their own right, helping to formulate, to sustain, and to speak for a recognizable point of view.

INTRAPARTY ATTITUDE CONFLICT: DEMOCRATIC PARTY LEADERSHIP IN CALIFORNIA*

Edmond Costantini

Attitude conflict is a phenomenon occurring within as well as between political parties. And if party members are differentiated in terms of their political dispositions, so too are they differentiated in terms of the status they have within their party. The relationship between these two forms of differentiation—between

*From *The Western Political Quarterly,* Vol. 25 (1963) pp. 956–72. Reprinted by permission of the University of Utah, copyright owners.

Author's note: I would like to express my appreciation to the Falk Foundation, to Professor Eugene C. Lee and the Institute of Governmental Studies, University of California at Berkeley, and to James Earle Sandmire for their generous assistance in this study and in the larger study of California party leadership of which it is a part.

membership stratification and attitude conflict—is the central concern of this study. It is a relationship which has recently been the subject of some interest to students of political behavior.

David Butler, for example, has suggested that a principal dilemma of party leaders is that they are caught between the disparate demands of their followership: "Their most loyal and devoted followers tend to have more extreme views than they have themselves, and to be still farther removed from the mass of those who actually provide the vote." The leaders therefore have "to conciliate those who support them with money or with voluntary work, without alienating that large body of moderate voters whose attitudes make them most likely to swing to the other party and thus to decide the next election."[1]

Professor Butler's definition of "party leader" is limited to the elected government official, and the elaboration of his hypothesis is limited to diagrammatic representations which, he concludes, "are no more than pedagogic devices." And yet his suggestion seems to bear significantly on another recent study, more comprehensive and more empirical in nature, conducted by Herbert McClosky, Paul J. Hoffmann, and Rosemary O'Hara. [This study is reproduced in the preceding reading.] They have demonstrated that "whereas the leaders of the two [American] parties diverge strongly, their followers differ only moderately in their attitudes toward issues," one conclusion among several drawn from the results of questionnaire studies of delegates to the 1956 national party conventions and of a nationwide sample of adult voters.[2]

The Butler hypothesis is not incompatible with the findings of McClosky and his colleagues. It does suggest, however, that the relationship between party status and attitudes may be significantly more complex than the leadership–followership dichotomy would indicate.

The research reported here seeks to put a slightly revised version of Butler's hypothesis to a limited empirical test: it seeks to compare the political perspectives of differentiated groups of party leaders which, taken together, are somewhat more inclusive than Butler's elected government officials. The hypothesis is simply that the substructure of party leadership deviates in attitudes more radically from the actual political center than does the superstructure; that the top party

leaders are, indeed, faced with the dilemma not only of a voting public holding more centrist, or moderate, views—amply demonstrated by McClosky and his colleagues—but also of a more extremist group of party militants standing below them in the hierarchy of party leadership.[3]

FOCUS

The data used to test this hypothesis are focused on the California delegation to the 1960 Democratic national convention.[4] As would be true of any other delegation, such a focus allows us to compare different levels of party leadership by differentiating delegates from alternates.[5] But there are characteristics of this particular delegation which are advantageous for the purposes of this paper while not being of such universal incidence. Of prime significance in this respect is the exceptional degree to which the delegation constituted a generous cross section of the state's Democratic leadership. Replete with party notables of all sorts, it was characterized by a representativeness which is not always found among convention delegations.

---

[1]David Butler, "The Paradox of Party Difference," American Behavioral Scientist, IV (November 1960), pp. 3–5.

[2]Herbert McClosky, et al., Issue Conflict and Consensus among Party Leaders and Followers," American Political Science Review, LIV (June 1960), pp. 406–27.

[3]The fact that Butler considers the party militant to be a part of the party followership rather than leadership arises from his more limited definition of party leadership and poses a terminological difficulty which does not seem to affect materially the efficacy of the conclusions herein drawn. Indeed, what will be identified as one of the groups composing the substructure of party leadership—the "caucus nominees"—is quite similar to what Butler calls the "party militant" group.

[4]The story of this delegation is lucidly told by John H. Bunzel and Eugene C. Lee, The California Democratic Delegation of 1960, Inter-University Case Study No. 67 (University, Ala.: University of Alabama Press, 1962). See also Eugene C. Lee, "Organization and Administration of a Large Delegation: California Democrats," in Paul Tillett (ed.), The National Conventions (Dobbs Ferry, N.Y.: Oceana Publications, 1962).

[5]The term "delegation" will be used throughout these pages to include both delegates and alternates.

The fact that there was no contest between rival party factions in the June 1960 presidential primary, that there was only one authentic party slate presented to the Democratic voters, meant that no group of party leaders was excluded from the delegation through defeat at the polls.[6] But the primary served more to confirm than to cause the cross-sectional nature of the California contingent to the Democratic convention. A delegation selection committee had met four months earlier, in February, and had drawn up the slate of delegates pledged to the "favorite son," Governor Edmond G. Brown, which was subsequently presented to the Democratic primary voters. There was no domination of that committee by a particular party group or faction.[7] Nor was there a com-

mitment to any bona fide candidate to give his supporters inordinate preferential treatment, or to exclude his opponents from consideration in the selection of the delegation members.[8] Indeed, the selection committee—with all deliberateness—attempted to design a delegation slate on which every leadership element within the party was represented and from which no party group was seriously omitted.

---

[6]A delegation slate pledged to George McLain, old-age pension promoter, managed to attract some 646,387 votes in the Democratic presidential primary—almost half the number of votes given to the slate pledged to Governor Brown. However, by no stretch of the imagination can the McLain slate be considered to have been a repository of state Democratic leadership.

The 1960 situation stands in marked contrast to those of 1952 and 1956. In 1952 a delegation slate largely composed of political unknowns and pledged to Senator Estes Kefauver carried the presidential primary after the last-minute withdrawal of President Truman from the race had left the "regular" slate without its candidate. In 1956 California Democrats were treated to a primary contest between two real contenders for the presidential nomination—Kefauver and Adlai Stevenson. Each was represented by a reasonably strong delegation slate; neither had a monopoly of state party leadership supporting him.

In both 1952 and 1956, then, primary contests meant that the delegations sent by California to the Democratic national conventions were something less than cross sections of state party leadership. Despite the McLain phenomenon, this was not true in 1960.

[7]The ten-member selection committee included: the chairman and vice-chairman of the Democratic State Central Committee, the chairman of the Women's Division of the Democratic State Central Committee, the Democratic national committeeman and committeewoman from California, the president of the California Democratic Council, the dean of the California Democratic delegation to the U.S. Congress, a second congressman designated by U.S. Senator

Clair Engle, the speaker of the state Assembly, and the president pro tempore of the state Senate.

Additionally, a twenty-nine-member Advisory Committee was appointed to assist the selection committee in its duties. This included representatives of each of the following groups: Democrats holding elective office in the state and national governments; officers of the official party machinery, i.e., of state and county central committees; and officers of the unofficial "citizen" wings of the party, principally of the California Democratic Council. While the Advisory Committee never met, some of its members did submit lists of names for the consideration of the delegation selection committee.

[8]Paul David has recently written that in preprimary negotiations in California Senator John F. Kennedy successfully "pressed for the inclusion of a substantial number of his own supporters in the Brown delegation." See "The Presidential Nomination," in Paul David (ed.), *The Presidential Election and Transition, 1960–1961* (Washington, Brookings, 1961), p. 9. There is little evidence, however, that there was any pressure from the Kennedy organization which significantly affected the delegation selection committee in its deliberations, or, indeed, that the committee was even concerned with the presidential preference of those people whom it was considering for a place on the delegation. In fact, late February, when the delegation members were chosen, was somewhat early for presidential preferences to be developed among party leaders. The Kennedy objective of the moment was achieved nonetheless, a consequence of the decision to construct a delegation broadly representative of party leadership throughout the state: a fair sample of California Democrats was bound to include "a substantial number" of Kennedy supporters.

The charge sometimes heard among California Democrats that the selection committee was biased against Stevenson and toward Kennedy seems particularly questionable in view of the fact that, in the final analysis, only three of its members voted for Kennedy at the national convention, while six of the remaining seven voted for Stevenson.

Success in this attempt, it was felt, would effectively discourage any challenge in the primary by a rival slate pledged to a bona fide presidential aspirant. A costly fratricidal contest would thus be averted, while, at the same time, a delegation which in effect was uncommitted would presumably maximize California's influence at the Democratic national convention.[9]

In sum, a thoroughgoing and conscious attempt was made to construct a delegation which was as representative of all leadership elements within the party as possible.[10] And there is every reason to

believe that the conclusion of McClosky and his colleagues that national convention delegates represent "as faithful a cross section of . . . party leadership as could be had without an extraordinary expenditure of money and labor"[11] is especially appropriate to California Democrats, 1960.

The decision to make the delegation a repository of as many party leaders in the state as possible was an opportune one for the purposes of this study; and it involved two fortunate ancillary consequences. Coupled with the amplitude of the delegation's membership—there were 162 delegate and 80 alternate posts to fill —it meant that official status at the national convention was to be extended to 74 Democratic congressmen and state legislators and to 8 elected officials of the state executive branch.[12] This extraordinary representation of elected officeholders serves further to commend the California delegation to the 1960 Democratic national convention as the focal point for a study of attitude conflict between differentiated groups of party leaders.

The second fortunate consequence of the desire to create a broadly representative delegation was the adoption of the caucus nominee system. Caucuses of local party leaders were called by the delegation selection committee in each of the state's thirty congressional districts to nominate candidates for positions on the

---

[9]In 1960 the California *Election Code* required not only that each delegation slate entered in the presidential primary be committed to a particular candidate, but that that slate have the endorsement of its candidate before presentation to the primary voters. Thus a commitment to Governor Brown as a "favorite son" was the nearest possible thing to an "uncommitted delegation." Thus, too, Senator Kennedy, or any other candidate, would have had to approve explicitly any attempt to challenge the Governor and his "strong" delegation in the primary.

[10]This cross-sectional nature of the California delegation was achieved at a high price. As Eugene Lee and William Buchanan conclude: "Forestalling a primary contest by selecting a delegation on which every faction was represented made it impossible for the delegation to act in a unified and coherent fashion." "The 1960 Election in California," *Western Political Quarterly*, XIV (March 1961), p. 312. Thus, by convention-time the unity achieved at the primary had been completely dissipated. So, too, had been the hopes that the state might play a decisive role at Los Angeles.

The California vote at the Democratic convention for the various presidential aspirants serves as the most obvious demonstration of the delegation's divisiveness: 67 of the delegates voted for Kennedy, 63 for Stevenson, 16 for Symington, 15 for Johnson, and one for Governor Brown. In only four other instances did delegations fail to give a particular candidate a majority of their respective votes; and the combined vote of these delegations—those of Hawaii, Idaho, Nevada and South Dakota—was only a little over half that of California. Indeed, no delegation had so wide a discrepancy between potential and performance, between sanguine hopes for political influence and the disappointing reality of political effeteness.

But the practitioner's bane is the analyst's boon, and it is this very conflict within the

delegation—born of the cross-sectional nature of its membership—which makes it particularly interesting for the student of party leadership.

[11]Herbert McClosky *et al.*, p. 408. [Also on p. 295 in this text]

[12]Thus, over 80 per cent of those Democrats holding such office were on the delegation. The selection committee did not follow a policy of deliberately excluding any Democratic officeholder for personal or political reasons. The fact that 17 of them were not on the delegation is attributable to other considerations, principally their own decision not to serve and the fact that the state Senate is apportioned in such a way that there were more legislators in some rural congressional districts than were permitted on the delegation.

delegation.[13] These caucuses were instructed not to include elected state or national government officials among their nominees, because the delegation selection committee was to consider them separately. Indeed, the approximately 300 men and women nominated by the caucuses were by and large voluntary contributors of time and energy to party endeavors whose personal political ambitions were limited in nature. Their partisan activities tended to be focused more on their localities and less on Sacramento, California in general, or Washington than those of the other Democratic leaders considered in this paper. Again more than these other leadership groups, the caucus nominees tended to play active roles in the California Democratic Council, the unofficial, mass-membership arm of the state's Democratic party.[14] Francis Carney describes the motives of men and women such as

these when he discusses those who attend annual C.D.C. conventions: "The overwhelming majority of them have no personal or financial interest in politics, no ambitions to be served, no enemies whose jugulars must be pierced."[15] But however limited the focus of political activity and the motives of the caucus nominees, they can nevertheless be considered party leaders. The recognition extended by their fellow partisans at the local nominating caucuses serves as testimony to that fact. And for some—86 of the approximately 300—recognition was further extended by the top party leadership in the state when they were selected as members of the delegation.[16]

Thus, the California delegation to the 1960 Democratic national convention is a particularly appropriate focus for a study of attitude conflict between differentiated groups of party leaders. (1) Unlike many other delegations, it was, by conscious design and a series of circumstances, the repository of top leaders from all elements within the party. (2) It was unusual in that it included among its members a large number of elected government officials, the traditional object of analysis for students of party leadership. (3) It was unusual in that a finite group of "grass roots" party leaders was specifically considered and in substantial part deliberately rejected for membership on the delegation.

Substantial as its advantages are, however, our focus is clearly a limited one. And the distinctive characteristics of California politics—the heritage of nonpartisanship and of weak party discipline, the tradition of progressivism and of the political maverick, the strength and nature

---

[13]The following were invited to attend these caucuses: (1) all members of the Democratic State Central Committee from within the Congressional District; (2) all members of Democratic County Central Committees from within the district; (3) all Democrats holding elective office as mayor, city councilman or county supervisor within the district; (4) all Assembly District, Congressional District, and County Council officers from within the district; (5) one delegate for every twenty members of each club within the district chartered by the Democratic County Central Committee or the California Federation of Young Democrats, or authorized to participate in the 1960 convention of the California Democratic Council.

[14]Of the 141 caucus nominees responding to questionnaires sent in connection with this study, 110 (77 per cent) claimed to be active members of the California Democratic Council, with 50 of these saying that they were officeholders in the organization. Eight of the remaining 31 failed to respond to this particular question, 3 denied membership, and 20 claimed that they were not very active members.

In contrast, only 39 (48 per cent) of the 81 respondents who were on the delegation but who were not caucus nominees claimed to be active in the C.D.C., and only five of these said they held official status in the organization. Fourteen of the remaining 42 failed to respond to this particular question, 10 denied membership, and 18 claimed that they were not very active members.

---

[15]Francis Carney, *The Rise of Democratic Clubs in California,* Eagleton Foundation Case Studies in Practical Politics (New York: Holt, 1958), p. 12.

[16]Each caucus could nominate up to 10 names, of which the delegation selection committee was pledged to select at least 2 for delegate or alternate status.

of the Democratic club movement, the power limitations of the governorship, the extraordinarily high esteem with which Adlai Stevenson is held, etc.—were all reflected in the story of the California delegation to the 1960 Democratic national convention. Certainly this study should be seen in terms of the context of California politics. And certainly its findings are, at best, suggestive rather than validating, heuristic rather than conclusive.

PROCEDURES

Questionnaires designed for self-administration were sent to all delegation members, with 99 of the 162 delegates (61 per cent) and 59 of the 80 alternates (74 per cent) responding. Additionally, questionnaires were sent to 115 of the 203 congressional district caucus nominees who had been denied a place on the delegation by the selection committee (hereafter referred to as "rejected caucus nominees"). Some 67 (58 per cent) of these were returned. Virtually all of the transactions— remission and receipt of the questionnaires—occurred during the two months immediately preceding the national convention at Los Angeles in July 1960.

The questions with which this discussion will be concerned relate to the political attitudes of the respondent. (1) He was asked to evaluate his own position within the party on a five-point liberal– conservative scale. (2) He was asked to register a preference for the Democratic presidential nomination. Six candidates were listed for his consideration, and although he was permitted to write in another choice the respondent was specifically requested to exclude Governor Brown, the favorite son candidate whom each member of the delegation was formally pledged to support. (3) He was asked, finally, to express his attitudes toward each of nine national issues by indicating whether he was "very much," "somewhat," "very little," or "not at all"

favorably disposed toward the proposed policy.

To analyze the latter data a technique very similar to the "ratio of support score" used by McClosky and his colleagues has been adopted, the principal difference being a consequence of the fact that McClosky used a three-point scale—"increase," "remain as is," and "decrease"—as opposed to the four-point scale herein employed. Table 4 does more than merely present the percentage of each leadership group favoring each proposed policy "very much," "somewhat," etc. For ease of analysis it also presents a single statistic for each policy proposal—a "ratio of support"—which simultaneously takes account of all four percentages of policy acceptance or rejection among the members of the party group being considered. The "ratio of support" was arrived at by assigning a weight of 1.000 to each "very much" response, 0.667 to each "somewhat" response, 0.333 to each "very little" response, and 0.000 to each "not at all" response. Thus, it may vary from zero to unity, with support for a proposed policy increasing as the score approaches unity.

It should be noted that in all of the groupings used for this analysis our Democratic respondents registered larger support ratios on each issue than did a sample of delegates and alternates from California to the 1960 Republican national convention.[17] Thus, the higher the support

---

[17] Unfortunately, the Republican respondents cannot be grouped in a manner corresponding to that in which the Democrats have been grouped (see pp. 323–24). There were few (less than 20) elected government officials on the Republican delegation; and there were no congressional district caucuses called to nominate possible delegation members. Indeed, even differentiating delegates from alternates seems unjustified because of the small size of the delegation and the consequent small number of respondents in each category. For these reasons, and for others, an analysis of data arising from questionnaires sent to the members of the Republican delegation will not be presented in this paper. Footnote 20, however, presents the ratio of support scores for the (*Footnote continued on next page*)

TABLE 1

Relationship Between Candidate Preference and Liberal-Conservative Self-Evaluation:
All Respondents (Delegation Members and Rejected Caucus Nominees)
(in percentages)

Self-evaluation	Candidate Preference					
	Bowles $(N = 18)$	Humphrey $(N = 13)$	Stevenson $(N = 97)$	Johnson $(N = 10)$	Kennedy $(N = 32)$	Symington $(N = 24)$
Very liberal $(N = 58)$	39	31	41	...	6	21
Somewhat liberal $(N = 94)$ ...	44	61	43	20	59	46
Middle-of-the-road $(N = 35)$..	11	8	12	50	25	25
Somewhat conservative $(N = 13)$	6	...	3	30	9	8
Very conservative $(N = 0)$ ...	...	...	...	...	...	...
Liberalism Ratio	0.790	0.808	0.810	0.475	0.650	0.700

ratios for the Democratic groups here being considered the greater their "radicalism" or their deviation from the mean score of the two rival delegations. In view of the nature of our two parties, of the policies being proposed, and of the relationship between the policy questions and the other attitude questions under consideration, we shall also speak of a higher ratio of support score as indicating a more "liberal" orientation. The terminology is not as important as the direction and magnitude of attitude differences between different respondent groupings.

A technique similar to the ratio of support score is used to evaluate the response of the question regarding liberal–conservative self-evaluation. By assigning a weight of 1.00 to each "very liberal" response, 0.75 to each "somewhat liberal" response, 0.50 to each "middle of the road" response, 0.25 to each "somewhat conservative" response, and 0.00 to each "very conservative" response a single statistic is derived which, for simplicity's sake, shall be termed a "liberalism ratio."

To evaluate the question relating to

Republican respondents in the aggregate. Suffice it to say at this point that their issue posture is substantially different from that of the Democrats. In fact, there was no issue on which the mean Republican score was even two-thirds the magnitude of the mean Democratic score.

candidate preference the political facts of the pre-convention presidential sweepstakes among California Democrats are assessed in the following manner: Bowles, Humphrey, and Stevenson tended to be the candidates of "liberals"; Johnson, Kennedy, and Symington tended to be the candidates of "conservatives." The relationship between the candidate preference and liberal–conservative self-evaluation of our Democratic respondents is shown in Table 1, and it would seem to support this contention. Between 30 and 40 per cent of those who preferred either Bowles, Humphrey, or Stevenson considered themselves to be very liberal. On the other hand, 20 per cent of those enamored of Symington, and 7 per cent of the Kennedy supporters, claimed to be very liberal. Not one Johnson supporter so evaluated himself. Applying the liberalism ratio technique, we find that Bowles, Humphrey, and Stevenson supporters achieved liberalism ratios of 0.790, 0.808, and 0.810 respectively, as contrasted to the 0.475, 0.650, and 0.700 for the supporters of Johnson, Kennedy, and Symington, respectively.

FINDINGS

For each of the three sets of questions (candidate preference, liberal–conservative self-evaluation, issue orientation), the respondents are grouped in three ways. First, differences between delegates, alternates, and rejected caucus nominees are distinguished. Second, elected state and national government officials on the delegation are compared with the remainder of the delegation and with the rejected caucus nominees. Third, those members of the delegation who were not caucus nominees are compared with those that were and, again, with the rejected caucus nominees. Given the nature of the total sample under consideration, these three groupings would seem to be the most appropriate for an analysis of the attitudes of differentiated levels of party leadership. The distinctions may be diagrammatically represented as in the accompanying illustration.

place on the political spectrum, we find that 23 per cent of the delegates, 27 per cent of the alternates, and 36 per cent of the rejected caucus nominees consider themselves "very liberal" (see Table 2).[18] The delegates register a liberalism ratio of 0.715, the alternates, 0.728, and the rejected caucus nominees, 0.792.

A similar relationship prevails for these three groups on the question of candidate preference. The delegates divided in half in their support of the three liberal versus the three conservative candidates (see Table 3). In contrast, two-thirds of the alternates preferred the three liberal candidates. And of the group farthest removed from top party leadership—the rejected caucus nominees—more than four-fifths preferred the three liberal candidates. In respect to four of the six candi-

High-level leadership	Delegates	Elected government officials (state and national) on delegation	Non-caucus nominees on delegation
Middle-level leadership	Alternates	Members of delegation who were not elected government officials	Caucus nominees on delegation
Low-level leadership			Rejected caucus nominees

The results of the questionnaire analysis clearly sustain our basic hypothesis. In each case, the group which tends to include the superstructure of party leadership in California (delegates, government officials, non-caucus nominees on the delegation) is less "radical" or "liberal" than the groups beneath it in the party edifice. The group which most nearly represents the sub-structure of party leadership (rejected caucus nominees) is consistently more "radical" or "liberal" than the groups above it in the party edifice.

1. In differentiating delegates, alternates and rejected caucus nominees in terms of their own assessment of their

dates, the progression conforms to the hypothesized pattern. That is, the higher the place of the group in the party hierarchy the more the conservative candidate is preferred and the less the liberal candidate is preferred. In one of the other two cases the alternates evince a greater preference for a liberal candidate (Bowles) than do the rejected caucus nominees, and in the other case the alternates evince a lesser preference for a liberal candidate (Humphrey) than do the delegates.

With reference to issue orientation, again our basic hypothesis is supported:

---

[18]No answer responses are excluded from consideration in all of this paper's tabulations.

TABLE 2
Liberal–Conservative Self-Evaluation of Various Leadership Groups
(in percentages)

Self-evaluation	Delegates ($N = 94$)	Alternates ($N = 55$)	Elected Government Officials ($N = 42$)	Other Delegation Members ($N = 107$)	Non-caucus Nominees on Delegation ($N = 77$)	Caucus Nominees on Delegation ($N = 77$)	Rejected Caucus Nominees ($N = 66$)
Very liberal	23	27	17	28	21	30	36
Somewhat liberal	48	44	40	49	42	51	50
Middle-of-the-road	22	22	36	17	30	14	9
Somewhat conservative ...	6	7	7	6	8	6	5
Very conservative	...	...	...	...	...	...	...
Total	99	100	100	100	101	100	100
Liberalism Ratio ...	0.715	0.728	0.668	0.748	0.695	0.768	0.792

TABLE 3
Candidate Preference of Various Leadership Groups
(in percentages)

	Delegates ($N = 84$)	Alternates ($N = 55$)	Elected Government Officials ($N = 39$)	Other Delegation Members ($N = 100$)	Non-caucus Nominees on Delegation ($N = 71$)	Caucus Nominees on Delegation ($N = 65$)	Rejected Caucus Nominees ($N = 64$)
Bowles	5	15	5	10	6	12	11
Humphrey	5	2	...	5	3	5	14
Stevenson	40	51	44	45	38	51	58
Three Candidate Total ...	50	68	49	60	47	68	83
Johnson	8	5	13	5	10	5	2
Kennedy	23	15	18	20	20	18	12
Symington	19	13	20	15	24	9	2
Three Candidate Total ...	50	33	51	40	54	32	16

the lower the respondent's status in the leadership hierarchy the more "radical" or "liberal" he tends to be (see Table 4). That is, he tends to accentuate the differences between the top leadership of the two parties and to have a programmatic posture which would generally be considered more liberal. For seven of the nine issues presented in our questionnaire, the highest ratio of support score is achieved by the rejected caucus nominees, and in

five of these the alternates register the next highest ratio of support score. The mean support ratios for the nine issues clearly conform to the hypothesized pattern: delegates have a mean score of 0.714, alternates, 0.726, and rejected nominees, 0.798.

2. In comparing incumbent elected state and national government officials with the rest of our respondents on the delegation, we find that this top leader-

ship group stands in the same relationship —although the hypothesized differences are even more exaggerated—to the groups lower in the party hierarchy as did the delegates in relation to alternates and rejected caucus nominees.[19] The officials consider themselves less liberal than the other members of the delegation; and the latter, in turn, feel they are less liberal than the rejected caucus nominees (see Table 2). Thus 17 per cent of the officials evaluate themselves as very liberal, as opposed to 28 per cent of the other delegation members, and, as indicated, 36 per cent of the rejected caucus nominees. The liberalism ratio for the government officials is 0.668, while the others on the delegation achieved 0.748 and the rejected caucus nominees 0.792.

On candidate preference and on issue orientation our hypothesis is again sustained. Less than one-half of the elected government officials prefer the three liberal candidates, as contrasted with three-fifths of the other delegation members, and, as indicated, more than four-fifths of the rejected caucus nominees (see Table 3). For five of the six candidates, the higher the place in the party hierarchy the more the conservative candidate is preferred and the less the liberal candidate is preferred. In the other case the non-government officials on the delegation indicate a preference for a conservative candidate (Kennedy) which surpasses that of the government officials.

At the same time, on six of the nine issues the hypothesized differences prevail, with the support ratios progressing in magnitude from government officials on the delegation, to others on the dele-

---

19Thirty-two respondents were elected state or national government officials with delegate status at Los Angeles; fourteen were alternates. Forty-one of the forty-six officials were state legislators or congressmen, and three of the remaining five neglected to indicate whether they were in the state executive or legislative branch. As indicated, none of the rejected caucus nominees were state or national government officials.

gation, to rejected caucus nominees (see Table 4). Indeed, the mean support ratios for the nine issues conform to this progression as follows: 0.649 for the government officials, 0.747 for the other delegation members, and, again, 0.798 for the rejected caucus nominees. On no issue do the government officials register a higher support ratio than the rejected caucus nominees.

3. The same general relationships hold true in our final rearrangement of Democratic leadership groups in California. Those members of the delegation who were selected from lists submitted by congressional district caucuses tend to be more "radical" or "liberal" than those who were appointed directly by the delegation selection committee, i.e., than the group which is largely composed of heavy financial contributors, interest group representatives, high party functionaries, and government officials. At the same time, the caucus nominees on the delegation are less "radical" or "liberal" than the rejected caucus nominees, i.e., than those who were nominated by the same congressional district caucuses but who were rejected by the selection committee. It will be recalled that more than 35 per cent of those in the latter group evaluate themselves as very liberal. In contrast, approximately 20 per cent of the non-caucus nominees on the delegation and 30 per cent of the caucus nominees on the delegation make such a claim (see Table 2). As for comparative liberalism ratios, the non-caucus nominees on the delegation compile a mean ratio of 0.695, the caucus nominees on the delegation, 0.768, and the rejected caucus nominees, 0.792.

Similarly, somewhat less than half the non-caucus nominees on the delegation prefer one of the three liberal candidates, whereas over two-thirds of the selected caucus nominees and over four-fifths of the rejected caucus nominees are so inclined (see Table 3). In the case of only one candidates does the pattern of sup-

TABLE 4
Issue Orientation of Various Leadership Groups
(in percentages)

	Delegates	Alternates	Elected Government Officials	Other Delegation Members	Non-Caucus Nominees on Delegation	Caucus Nominees on Delegation	Rejected Caucus Nominees
For recognition of Communist China	(N = 85)	(N = 50)	(N = 39)	(N = 96)	(N = 74)	(N = 69)	(N = 58)
Not at all	39	34	54	30	46	25	17
Very little	18	24	15	22	16	25	19
Somewhat	34	26	23	34	29	34	40
Very much	9	16	8	14	9	16	24
Support Ratio	0.377	0.413	0.283	0.440	0.337	0.470	0.570
For abolition of the House Committee on Un-American Activities	(N = 87)	(N = 51)	(N = 39)	(N = 99)	(N = 67)	(N = 69)	(N = 65)
Not at all	15	20	23	14	19	13	11
Very little	15	14	20	12	19	9	3
Somewhat	25	16	36	16	29	15	20
Very much	45	51	20	58	33	63	66
Support Ratio	0.667	0.663	0.507	0.727	0.587	0.760	0.803
For nationalization of selected basic industries	(N = 84)	(N = 48)	(N = 41)	(N = 91)	(N = 67)	(N = 63)	(N = 62)
Not at all	63	58	66	59	61	60	37
Very little	26	21	22	25	24	25	27
Somewhat	5	13	2	10	7	8	18
Very much	6	8	10	5	7	6	18
Support Ratio	0.180	0.237	0.187	0.200	0.197	0.197	0.390
For increasing the federal minimum wage from $1.00 to $1.25	(N = 89)	(N = 52)	(N = 43)	(N = 98)	(N = 71)	(N = 67)	(N = 67)
Not at all	2	2	5	1	3	1	1
Very little	9	2	7	6	7	4	1
Somewhat	13	25	19	17	21	15	10
Very much	75	71	70	76	69	79	87
Support Ratio	0.867	0.883	0.850	0.893	0.853	0.903	0.940

	(N = 93)	(N = 53)	(N = 43)	(N = 103)	(N = 74)	(N = 69)	(N = 66)
For a medical-aid-to-the-aged act tied to the social security program							
Not at all	4	2	5	3	4	3	...
Very little	1	2	2	1	3	...	2
Somewhat	22	21	21	21	23	19	17
Very much	73	75	72	75	70	78	82
Support Ratio	0.880	0.897	0.867	0.893	0.863	0.907	0.940

	(N = 91)	(N = 53)	(N = 43)	(N = 101)	(N = 72)	(N = 69)	(N = 66)
For power projects entirely developed with federal funds over those developed through federal-private partnership							
Not at all	7	6	9	5	8	4	3
Very little	10	9	9	10	11	9	6
Somewhat	22	21	30	18	26	17	24
Very much	62	64	51	67	54	70	67
Support Ratio	0.800	0.810	0.740	0.823	0.750	0.843	0.850

	(N = 92)	(N = 51)	(N = 44)	(N = 99)	(N = 73)	(N = 68)	(N = 65)
For greater economic aid to under-developed countries							
Not at all	3	2	7	1	5	...	3
Very little	7	2	11	2	10	...	5
Somewhat	28	22	39	20	32	21	22
Very much	62	75	43	77	53	79	71
Support Ratio	0.830	0.903	0.727	0.910	0.777	0.930	0.873

	(N = 93)	(N = 53)	(N = 44)	(N = 102)	(N = 74)	(N = 69)	(N = 67)
For federal aid to school construction							
Not at all	1	6	4	2	4	1	1
Very little	2	4	9	...	5	...	3
Somewhat	12	13	14	12	14	12	12
Very much	85	77	73	86	77	87	84
Support Ratio	0.937	0.870	0.853	0.940	0.880	0.950	0.930

	(N = 90)	(N = 52)	(N = 41)	(N = 101)	(N = 71)	(N = 68)	(N = 66)
For a federal Fair Employment Practices Commission							
Not at all	4	2	7	2	6	1	2
Very little	3	8	2	6	6	4	5
Somewhat	12	21	24	12	21	10	20
Very much	80	69	66	80	68	84	74
Support Ratio	0.890	0.857	0.827	0.900	0.840	0.920	0.890
Mean Support Ratio for Nine Issues	0.714	0.726	0.649	0.747	0.676	0.764	0.798

TABLE 5

Issue Orientation—Rank Order of Differences in Support Scores
for Low-Level versus High-Level Leadership Groups

Rejected caucus nominees versus delegates

1.	Nationalization of selected basic industries	0.210
2.	Recognition of Communist China	0.193
3.	Abolition of House Committee on Un-American Activities	0.136
4.	Increasing federal minimum wage to $1.25	0.073
5.	Medical aid to the aged tied to social security program	0.060
6.	Federal development of power projects	0.050
7.	Greater economic aid to under-developed countries	0.043
8.	Federal Fair Employment Practices Commission	0.000
9.	Federal aid to school construction	−0.007
	Difference in Mean Support Ratios	0.084

Rejected caucus nominees versus elected government officials

1.	Abolition of House Committee on Un-American Activities	0.296
2.	Recognition of Communist China	0.287
3.	Nationalization of selected basic industries	0.203
4.	Greater economic aid to under-developed countries	0.146
5.	Federal development of power projects	0.110
6.	Increasing minimum wage to $1.25	0.090
7.	Federal aid to school construction	0.077
8.	Medical aid to the aged tied to social security program	0.073
9.	Federal Fair Employment Practices Commission	0.063
	Difference in Mean Support Ratios	0.149

Rejected caucus nominees versus non-caucus nominees on delegation

1.	Recognition of Communist China	0.233
2.	Abolition of House Committee on Un-American Activities	0.216
3.	Nationalization of selected basic industries	0.193
4.	Federal development of power projects	0.100
5.	Greater economic aid to under-developed countries	0.096
6.	Increasing federal minimum wage to $1.25	0.087
7.	Medical aid to the aged tied to social security program	0.077
8.	Federal Fair Employment Practices Commission	0.050
9.	Federal aid to school construction	0.050
	Difference in Mean Support Ratios	0.122

port fail to conform to the hypothesized pattern: Bowles is preferred by a greater proportion of caucus nominees on the delegation than of rejected caucus nominees.

On six of the nine issues the hypothesized progression prevails (see Table 4). And again, on no issue do the rejected caucus nominees achieve a lower ratio of support score than the top leadership group—the non-caucus nominees on the delegation. It will be recalled that for the former group the mean support score is

0.798. For the latter group it is 0.676. As before, our middle-level leadership group —in this case, the caucus nominees on the delegation—falls between the other two leadership groups under consideration, its mean support ratio being 0.764.

4. Table 5 presents a partial recapitulation of the data developed on the issue orientation of the various groups under consideration. It compares low-level leadership with high-level leadership in terms of the ratio of support scores achieved on each issue. The issues are ranked in order

of the magnitude of the differences between each pair of groups. The rejected caucus nominees are treated as the lowest level of party leadership in each of the three sets of comparisons. The highest levels are alternately the members of the delegation who had delegate status, the elected government officials on the delegation, and the members of the delegation who had not previously been nominated by congressional district caucuses. Inasmuch as there are nine issues and three groupings, there are twenty-seven comparisons made. Three features of the comparisons summarized in Table 5 might be noted.

In the first place, in twenty-five of the twenty-seven comparisons the basic hypothesis of this paper is sustained, i.e., the low-level leadership group has a higher ratio of support score than each of the high-level leadership groups with which it is compared. Additionally, taking the differences in average support scores between the groups, we find that the hypothesized relationship applies in all three instances.

In the second place, three issues clearly stand out in terms of the magnitude of differences in support scores between high-level and low-level leadership groups. On these issues—the recognition of Communist China, the nationalization of selected basic industries, and the abolition of the House Committee on Un-American Activities—intraparty conflict is greatest, and the willingness of the rejected caucus nominees to support the proposed policies, while less than in the case of the other issues, is markedly higher than that of the delegates, government officials, and non-caucus nominees on the delegation. What can be said about the nature of these issues? (1) Unlike the others, they do not stand in any clear relationship to the established position of the Democratic party. The proponent of recognition, of abolition, or of nationalization is not acting on the basis of any

authoritative pronouncement by the national party. And the opponent is not acting in violation of party norms or expectations. (2) Unlike the others, these three issues are of such a nature as to make any public approval of the proposed policies an act of political courage. Such approval would probably be unpopular in the general community and might even inspire public ridicule. (3) These three policy proposals are precisely those to which a sample of the California delegation to the Republican national convention is most markedly opposed.[20] On none of the other proposals do the Republican respondents so nearly approach a posture of total rejection.

In sum, of the nine issues presented to the Democrats considered in this study, those dealing with Communist China, the House Committee on Un-American Activities, and nationalization of basic industries seem to involve the most critical tests of political radicalism—most critical in the sense that support of the suggested policies would be derived independent of the guidance of official party pronouncement, would be in least conformance with community norms, and would be most at odds with the virtually unanimous opposition of the Republican party. It is on these very three issues that the lowest

---

[20]The Republican ratio of support scores follows:
1. Recognition of Communist China
   (N = 54) 0.047
2. Abolition of the House Comm. on
   Un-American Activities (N = 53) 0.033
3. Nationalization of selected basic
   industries (N = 53) 0.020
4. Increasing the federal minimum wage
   to $1.25 (N = 50) 0.353
5. Medical aid to the aged tied to the social
   security program (N = 51) 0.280
6. Federal development of power projects
   (N = 52) 0.170
7. Greater economic aid to underdeveloped countries (N = 50) 0.527
8. Federal aid to school construction
   (N = 52) 0.493
9. Federal Fair Employment Practices
   Commission (N = 50) 0.427
        Mean Support Ratio 0.261

level leadership group—the rejected caucus nominees—differs most markedly from the high-level leadership.

The third feature which might be noted from the comparisons summarized in Table 5 is that the elected government officials are the least "radical" top leadership group. In fact, Table 4 indicates that of the seven leadership groupings considered, the elected government officials achieve the lowest support ratio on seven of the nine issues, and in each of the other two instances their support ratio is slightly higher than that of only one other group. Similarly, on the self-evaluation question, the officials score the lowest liberalism ratio and have the smallest percentage of "very liberal" respondents. The officials also least prefer two of the liberal presidential candidates, Bowles and Humphrey. To the extent that the government officials stand as the most conservative leadership group under consideration, this study serves to support the specific hypothesis proffered by David Butler.

SUMMARY AND CONCLUSIONS

The research described in this paper was principally designed to apply a limited empirical test to a hypothesis regarding the relationship between two rather obvious facts of American political life: political party leadership is, in the first place, stratified, and, in the second place, heterogeneous in attitudes. Questionnaires were sent to approximately 350 Democratic leaders from California, selected for study because they were either delegates and alternates to their party's 1960 national convention or had been specifically considered but then rejected for delegation membership. The resulting sample of approximately 225 was grouped according to status within the party leadership hierarchy. The groups, in turn, were compared in terms of their responses to questions regarding certain political attitudes, i.e., questions regarding selected policy

proposals, presidential preference, and liberal–conservative self-evaluation. All of these comparisons supported the original hypothesis: the superstructure of party leadership tends to be more "moderate" and "centrist" than the substructure.

Is this finding applicable to other parties in other places at other times? A substantial body of literature has been developed concerning very much the same phenomenon within British political parties. Further inquiry into the extent of its incidence in this country would seem to be in order, for such an inquiry would have considerable bearing on questions to which students of American politics have long been addressing themselves.

One of these questions concerns the extent to which the leaders of the two parties have tended to ignore the cleavages in attitude and programmatic demands within the electorate and between their respective followers. For some, the Tweedledum and Tweedledee character of party leadership has had salutary effects. To Clinton Rossiter, for example, the essence of American political history is that "the parties have been the peacemakers of the American community, the unwitting but forceful suppressors of the 'civil war potential' we carry always in the bowels of our diverse nation."[21] To Pendleton Herring, "the accomplishment of party government [in the United States] lies in its demonstrated ability for reducing warring interests and conflicting classes to cooperative terms."[22] Similarly, John Fischer, in defending the American party system, has concluded: "The purpose of European parties is, of course, to divide men of different ideologies into coherent and disciplined organizations. The historic role of the American party, on

---

[21]Clinton Rossiter, *Parties and Politics in America* (Ithaca: Cornell University Press, 1960), p. 59.

[22]Pendleton Herring, *The Politics of Democracy* (New York: Holt, Rinehart & Winston, 1940), p. 132.

the other hand, is not to divide but to unite."[23]

For others, the mitigation of ideological divisions within the electorate by party leaders is cause for concern and reason for reform. More than fifty years have elapsed since James Bryce critically characterized American political parties as two empty bottles differing only in their labels and suggested that "a time for a reconstruction of parties is approaching."[24] Since then many observers have repeated Bryce's characterization in one form or another, and have sought to encourage and hasten the ever-approaching "time for a reconstruction." Stephen K. Bailey, for example, has recently advocated a program of political readjustment which would allow the parties "to appeal to the natural ideological divisions within the population and within us as individuals."[25]

Certainly many of the salient features of American politics seem to have been conducive to the rise and perpetuation of programmatically similar party leaders. And yet, put to an empirical test, the notion that these leaders tend to mitigate ideological divisions within the electorate seems unfounded: Professor McClosky and his colleagues have demonstrated that the party leader is less "moderate" or "centrist" than the party follower, that

the ideological differences that exist between the rank-and-file supporters of the two parties are, in fact, magnified by their leaders. The McClosky study concludes the description of its findings by stating: "Little support was found for the belief that deep cleavages exist among the electorate but are ignored by the leaders. One might, indeed, more accurately assert the contrary, to wit: that the natural cleavages between the leaders are largely ignored by the voters."[26] It would seem, then, that American party leaders tend to divide rather than to unite.

To the extent that the findings of this study have bearing beyond the California Democracy of 1960, they indicate that the leader–follower dichotomy adopted by McClosky may conceal significant aspects of the complex pattern of clash and counterpoint within a political party. These findings suggest an explanation of the magnification of inter-follower cleavage by the top party leaders which would stand in addition to those appearing in McClosky's catalogue of causative factors: the top leaders may be drawn to less centrist positions by the radicalism of lower-level leaders. Or, to put it somewhat differently, the radicalism of lower-level leaders may serve as a counterforce to the "natural" tendency of top leaders to gravitate toward the political center as a consequence of their public responsibilities and of the overriding objective of electoral success.

While the top party leader may be less moderate than his followers—as McClosky's evidence indicates—the present findings suggest that he may still be an ideological intermediate within his party. That is, he may be faced not only with a more moderate followership but with a more radical lower-level leadership. As V. O. Key, Jr., has concluded, "the top party leadership must try to restrain the extremists within the party ranks. . . . Lower-

[23]John Fischer, "Unwritten Rules of American Politics," *Harper's*, 197 (November, 1948), p. 32.

[24]James Bryce, *The American Commonwealth* (rev. ed.; New York: Macmillan, 1910), Vol. II, p. 29. The characterization and prediction both first appeared in the 1910 edition, although their spirit was evident in earlier editions.

[25]Stephen K. Bailey, *The Condition of Our National Political Parties* (The Fund for the Republic, 1959), p. 4. It must be noted, however, that Bailey insists that the needed "political reform does not include making the parties any more ideological than they are now." The problem is not one of ideological effeteness but rather "that neither party has a sufficiently unified structure to enable it to dramatize its program around its ideology; neither has the power, even if it had the right structure, to carry out the program; neither has sufficiently clear and unambiguous lines of political accountability running to the voters."

[26]Herbert McClosky *et al.*, *op. cit.*, p. 426.

level leaders may flourish by the fanning of extremist and particularist emotions, but the top echelon must seek to hold together divergent and often conflicting elements."[27] In sum, it is possible that the

[27]V. O. Key, Jr., *Politics, Parties and Pressure Groups* (4th ed.; New York: Crowell, 1958), p. 241.

top party leaders of the two parties at once magnify the ideological differences between their respective followers and blunt the differences between their respective lower-level leaders. If top party leaders divide, as Herbert McClosky so well demonstrates, they may also unify, as John Fischer believes.

THE IDEOLOGICAL STRUCTURE OF THE PARTY*

Samuel J. Eldersveld

American politics has for some time been characterized as "nonprogrammatic." The "end of ideology" for the American political scene has often been proclaimed. Yet, every practitioner of politics knows the ideologue in party activity, the militant who fervently holds definite political views and is involved in party work solely for the purpose of implementing those convictions. A set of important empirical questions confronts us in the study of party ideology. Has the alleged hushing of ideological warfare discouraged the ideologue from joining the party, muted the issue enthusiasm of those already in the party, and produced a leadership organizationally conscious but indifferent to issue controversies? Or is the American party a structure which comprehends ideologues as well as those apathetic on the issues of the day, and is thus a sound balance of idealistic fervor and realism? And what is the pattern of ideological conviction in the party structure—are there significant differences by echelon, by subcoalitional interest groups, and by career status? Is the party clearly fractionated ideologically according to internal structural differences—by hierar-

*From Samuel J. Eldersveld, *Political Parties: A Behavioral Analysis* (Chicago: Rand McNally & Co., 1964). Reprinted by permission of Rand McNally & Company.

chical level or by socio-political interests, or is the party a melange of ideological divergencies which are not neatly structured and highly irregular? A survey of the ideological *direction* of party leaders, the *intensity* of their issue positions, and the *congruence* of ideology within the hierarchies of the parties will suggest answers to these questions.

In determining ideological direction at all leadership levels, we used in our interviews a series of questions touching on significant policy matters. The three areas most frequently used were: aid to foreign countries "even if they are not as much against communism as we are," civil rights, and governmental assistance in helping people "get doctors and hospital care at low cost." We probed to discover whether the respondent had an opinion, whether he thought the government should act, and whether the level of governmental action at present was adequate or not. There were other questions concerning campaign issues and the issue differences between the parties which were designed, however, and here utilized, for different analytical objectives.

HIERARCHICAL VARIATIONS IN IDEOLOGY

At the apex of the local party machines, the Republican chairmen were consistent-

TABLE 1

Ideological Direction by Hierarchy Level

	Republicans (Percentage Liberal)		Democrats (Percentage Liberal)		Party Difference	
	Executive Board	Precinct	Executive Board	Precinct	Executive Board	Precinct
Civil rights	36%	41%	61%	57%	25%	16%
Foreign aid	54	37	74	59	20	22
Medical aid	22	28	69	76	47	48

ly more conservative on these issues than the Democrats. Only one Republican district chairman was a thoroughgoing liberal on all three issues, while five of the six Democratic chairmen showed this attitude. There was somewhat more liberalism in the Republican top leadership on the civil rights question, and somewhat less Democratic liberalism, but differences at this level of the party, in the elite nucleus, were striking and consistent. This is not to say that the district chairmen were rabid ideologues. A minority of one-third in each party was quite outspoken and articulate about issue positions and the need of the party to fight its battles in ideological terms. The majority, however, were by no means forceful and forthright crusaders. But when the interviewer pushed beyond the generalities about "rugged individualism," "free enterprise," "government for the common man" and pressed for specific opinion on controversial issues, it was clear that they had opinions, and fairly consistent ones in an ideological sense. These chairmen, holding considerable influence and control over their respective organizations, were not operating in an ideological vacuum. The Republican elite consisted of committed conservatives; the Democratic elite were committed liberals.

Among the secondary leadership cadre in each party, the executive board members, there was somewhat less consistency and uniformity in outlook, but the ideological direction was the same (Table 1). One-fifth of the Republicans and three-

fifths of the Democrats were consistent liberals on domestic policy questions. The important difference appeared in the issue of foreign aid. Here the Republicans showed much more liberalism in the middle ranks than at the top, with over half of the executive board members supporting foreign aid. There was more Democratic liberalism on this issue also, three out of four secondary-level leaders giving their support. The medical aid question received the least Republican support among executive board members, while civil rights received the lowest Democratic support.

On all issues the Democratic executive board was considerably more liberal than the Republican group, with a marked contrast on the question of medical aid—only 22 per cent of the Republicans in support, but 69 per cent of the Democrats in support, a 47 percentage-point differential. Yet, it appeared that the middle cadre of Republicans was definitely more liberal than the top level; for the Democrats, if any difference was discernible, it was that the middle-level Democratic leader was inclined to be somewhat less liberal than the top echelon of the organization. These differences were not great for the Democrats, however, and one must be cautious about developing a thesis of hierarchical retrogression in liberalism until the precinct leadership data are seen.

A sizeable number of ideological dissenters appeared within each party at the middle level of leadership. About one in

TABLE 2

Attitudes within the Hierarchy on Two Issues, Domestic and Foreign Policy

	Republicans		Democrats	
	Executive Board	Precinct	Executive Board	Precinct
"The U.S. should give help to foreign countries, even if they are not as much against communism as we are."				
Agree strongly	33%	5%	61%	12%
Agree	21	32	13	47
Unsure	18	8	4	4
Disagree	28	27	4	12
Disagree strongly	0	8	0	10
No opinion and not ascertained	0	20	18	15
"The government ought to help people get doctors and hospital care at low cost."				
Agree strongly	11	11	65	51
Agree	11	17	4	25
Unsure	18	11	4	4
Disagree	61	31	9	11
Disagree strongly	0	22	0	4
No opinion and not ascertained	0	8	18	5

four Republican executive board members was a consistent liberal, and about 10 per cent of the Democrats were conservative, especially on domestic issues. The split in Republican ranks was more in terms of domestic versus foreign policy issues. The vast majority of Republican leaders were decidedly against governmental aid in the medical and public housing fields, but less opposed to foreign aid to countries, even though they might be in the communist orbit of influence, or tending in that direction, or neutralist. Yet, despite this sharp contrast with Democratic leaders, ideological factionalism existed in each party. This was no monolithic ideological party structure.

These observations of party differences and hierarchical diversity are re-enforced by the attitudes of precinct leaders. Fewer precinct leaders than middle-level cadres, in both parties, had strong, positive, liberal views on foreign aid and med-

ical assistance. Thus, only 12 per cent of the Democratic precinct leaders agreed strongly on the foreign aid question, compared to 61 per cent of the executive board members; the parallel Republican percentages are 5 and 33 per cent. The Republicans were a relatively nonliberal group at the precinct level, especially on the medical aid question. Apparent, too, was the wide range and diversity in attitudes among precinct leaders of both parties, particularly in the Republican party. No Republican executive board members disagreed strongly on either the foreign aid or medical aid issues, but extreme conservatism was found among Republican *precinct* leaders. (See, for example, the distribution of opinion on the medical aid issue.) The same tendency, to a lesser degree, was found among the Democrats, suggesting that the upper echelons of the two parties were more homogeneous in ideology.

An intensive analysis such as this reveals striking differences within the local party structures on critical policy issues. Democrats were indeed much more liberal, significantly so, than were Republicans, at all echelons of the hierarchy, even in a city like Detroit, where since 1950 there had been a movement away from conservative policy positions in both parties, encouraged by liberal state chairmen. And precinct leaders re-enforced this condition of ideological distinctiveness, rather than diluted it. As a consequence, although a certain amount of ideological factionalism existed in both parties, particularly at the precinct level, there was remarkable like-mindedness in both hierarchies, from top to bottom.

Precinct leaders in these two structures were, thus, not the most liberal contingent. In fact, the middle-level cadre was most liberal on the Republican side, and the middle and top levels appeared most liberal on the Democratic side. This raises questions about the thesis proposed by Herbert McClosky to the effect that lower-echelon Republican leadership is more liberal than the upper echelons, and practically as liberal as the Democrats.[1] The McClosky thesis is not completely refuted by these data, since the top Republican leadership was, indeed, the most conservative element of either party. But there is no evidence here that the Republican party became more liberal as one proceeds down the hierarchy, nor that Republican party leadership at the grass roots was essentially as liberal as the Democratic. The rank order of party leadership in descending order of liberalism suggested by our data is:

Most liberal	Democratic chairman
	Democratic secondary cadre
	Democratic precinct
	Republican secondary cadre
	Republican precinct
Least Liberal	Republican chairmen

Two other aspects of leadership ideology can be measured with these data. One is homogeneity of leadership attitudes at any hierarchical level; the other is congruence of attitudes between levels (see Table 3). Our indices measure homogeneity in three ways. First, in terms of *range of opinion* on the three issues we used, the index shows considerable similarity in outlook, with the exception of the middle-level Republican cadre, where relatively great diversity existed. Otherwise the scores were low. Second, the *amount of extremism* (in *content* of opinion, not intensity, or affect) was measured. Our data indicate that the Democratic chairmen were highest in this respect (all but one were ultra-liberals), while the Republican executive board was lowest (less than 10 per cent extremism). There was considerably more extremism in Democratic leadership groups than in Republican. Thus, the Democratic precinct leaders included 58 per cent who held extreme positions, compared to 37 per cent of the Republican precinct leaders. Third, the *factionalism score* indicates more homogeneity in Democratic ranks. Smaller percentages of Democrats at each leadership level deviated from the majority ideological position at that level than among the Republicans. In sum, Democrats and Republicans revealed about the same range in opinion, but the Democrats took more extreme (liberal) positions on issues, while the Republicans revealed more factionalism in the distribution of opinion.

The congruence indices show that the two lower echelons of the party structure were extremely close in ideological viewpoints. The district chairmen were more distant ideologically from the middle-level cadre than the middle was distant from the precinct level. But there was much more congruence in the Republican structure—in fact, relatively, the latter gave

---

[1] "Issue Conflict and Consensus Among Party Leaders and Followers," *American Political Science Review*, Vol. LIV, No. 2 (June 1960), 406–

27. Editor's note: This article is reproduced earlier in this text.

TABLE 3
Indices of Ideological Consensus
(in percentages)

	Republicans			Democrats		
	Chairman	Executive Board	Precinct	Chairman	Executive Board	Precinct
Ideological direction*						
Liberalism (means)						
All respondents	28	37	35	89	68	64
Those with opinions	28	40	39	89	79	71
Conservatism (means)						
All respondents	67	49	47	11	13	27
Those with opinions	67	52	53	11	16	26
Homogeneity						
Range in percentages of liberalism on three issues	17	39	16	17	13	18
Amount of extremism—percentage with 2 extreme positions (medical aid) ...	34	9	37	83	72	58
Factionalism—percentage deviating from majority on medical aid	17	22	30	0	14	15
Congruence between levels (percentage point difference on liberal mean)						
Between chairmen and executive board ..		9			21	
Between executive board and precinct ...		2			4	
Between chairmen and precinct		7			25	

*These percentages are averages of the proportions which are liberal or conservative.

the appearance of a tightly knit group in issue positions as compared to the Democrats. It is particularly interesting that the Republican chairmen were closer to the precinct leaders than were the Democratic chairmen. There was a great gap between the positions of the Democratic top nucleus and both the middle cadre and the precinct. Although there was some distinctiveness of the same order for the Republicans, the latter had a more unified, essentially conservative, state of organizational consensus.

IDEOLOGICAL CONGRUENCE— LEADERS AND FOLLOWERS

Significant findings emerge when the condition of public opinion in the Detroit area on the issues of medical assistance, foreign aid, and civil rights is examined. The "public" was divided into the following sectors:

Loyal Republicans
Loyal Democrats
(self-identified partisans who had consistently voted for their party) 33 per cent

Other Republicans
Other Democrats
(self-identified partisans who had not, however, consistently voted or voted for their party) 47 per cent

Independents and others
(did not consider themselves partisans and revealed no consistent voting behavior) 20 per cent

The total population varied in the extent of its "liberalism" on these issues, ranging from 33 per cent supporting foreign aid programs, through 54 per cent liberal in the civil rights controversy, to a high of 62 per cent agreeing that the government

TABLE 4

Congruence of Leadership Opinion with Public Opinion

(percentage "liberal" on each of three issues)

	Republicans					Democrats					Independents	Population
	Chairman	Executive Board	Precinct	Loyalists	Others*	Chairman	Executive Board	Precinct	Loyalists	Others*		
Medical aid ..	17%	22%	28%	40%	48%	100%	69%	76%	87%	67%	55%	62%
Foreign aid ...	34	54	37	39	37	100	74	59	26	35	31	33
Civil rights ...	34	36	41	53	59	67	61	57	55	51	51	54

*"Other" Republicans or Democrats who claimed to be partisans but did not vote consistently for their party.

should provide aid in securing low-cost hospital and medical care programs.

Most critical in the study of party leadership is the analysis of the division of opinion within the five sectors, and the relation of sector opinion to the issue positions of the party leadership. How close to, or removed from, public opinion is a party's leadership structure?

The answer certainly depends on the type of public policy question involved. In the Republican party, for example (see Table 4), on the question of foreign aid, the leadership (with the exception of the executive board) was very close to the incidence of "liberalism" among its own loyal supporters, other Republicans who were not too loyal, the independents, and the population generally. But the reaction to the question of medical aid under government sponsorship is quite different, with a great deal more acceptance of the idea appearing among the public sectors than among the Republican leaders. The Republican precinct leaders were only 28 per cent "liberal" on this issue, while the loyal Republican voters were 40 per cent, other Republicans 48 per cent, independents 55 per cent, and the general population as a whole 62 per cent. Similarly, the Democratic leadership was close to the public sectors in its opinion on civil rights, but far removed ideologically on the issue of foreign aid.

Despite these differences in relationships in terms of the type of issue, a com-

posite analysis reveals certain uniform relationships between party leadership and its publics. If the leaders are viewed as a single category, our data reveal the Republicans to be a more like-minded group than the Democrats, but the leadership tended to be more conservative than the followers. The "mean" or "average" liberalism scores are as follows:

	Republicans	Democrats
All leaders	33%	74%
Loyalists	44	56
Others	48	51
All followers	46	54

The only Republican leadership group which surpassed the Republican followers in liberalism was the executive board contingent, on the issue of foreign aid. The opposite is true for the Democrats: only one instance occurred of "followers" surpassing the Democratic leaders in liberalism, and this was the Democratic loyalist group, on the question of medical aid. The Republicans, thus, were fairly like-minded, with a leadership lagging behind the liberal opinion movement in its supporter ranks. The Democrats were less well-knit, but the leadership group, together with party supporters, were moving in more liberal directions.

A second concern is the precise leadership level most representative of the party rank-and-file. Is it true that precinct lead-

TABLE 5

Ideological Gaps Between Leadership Levels and Followers

(average of differences on three issues*)

	Chairmen and		Executive Board and		Precinct and	
	Loyalists	Others	Loyalists	Others	Loyalists	Others
Republicans	16	20	17	23	9	13
Democrats	33	38	24	17	15	13

*Two computations are possible here. The one used is the average of differences on each issue, whatever the ideological direction of the difference. Another measure, the "average size of the liberal gap," not used in this table, would slightly alter the figures, since pluses and minuses on liberal direction would cancel each other out. Using such a measure would make the Democratic precinct leaders slightly closer to the party loyalists.

ers are closest, while district chairmen, entrenched over time in their power positions, are more distant? Our data suggest that the latter is indeed clearly true, while at the same time noting that the top elite is not necessarily the most conservative. The Republican precinct leaders were on balance closer than their Democratic counterparts to the rank-and-file. The Democratic district chairmen were the most unrepresentative and ideologically removed. Table 5 indicates these differences in relationship.

The ideological distance of Democratic chairmen from the loyalists on this liberalism index is more than twice as great as the distance of precinct leaders, while executive board members are only moderately distant. The Democratic party thus exhibits a neat descending order of ideological relationships, while the Republican party reveals small gaps and less hierarchical orderliness in attitude structures. The Republican leadership appears, therefore, to be more "representative" of the attitudes of its loyal and consistent supporters than the Democratic leadership. The evidence is not as clear that the Republican leadership is more representative of the "other Republicans" who are less loyal to the party in terms of self-perception and voting behavior. The theory of oligarchy holds that the top elite nucleus of the organization will be unrepresenta-

tive of the rank-and-file, *and* more conservative. Although these data tend to confirm the unrepresentativeness of the so-called oligarchs, an increasing conservatism is not demonstrable in our data. The Democratic top elite is much more liberal than the party's rank-and-file, and, even in the Republican party, the precinct leadership is clearly very conservative and highly congruent ideologically with the Republican top elite.

A third problem and type of analysis is thereby suggested. In the study of the party we are interested in the ideological relationship between the leadership (and party structure proper) and those to whom the party must appeal for support —the irregular partisans and the independents. How congruent are the attitudes of leadership with the "floating voters"? In a metropolitan area such as Detroit this is an especially critical problem for the Republicans, as the minority party. But with 20 per cent of the adult population classifiable as "independents," probably a minimal figure, this is a concern of the majority party as well.

The independents in the Detroit area tended to be less liberal than the population generally on these three issues, and less liberal than the Republican followers on all issues except medical aid. Yet the greatest ideological gap between Republican leaders and independents occurred on the issue of medical aid. The Republican leadership was actually more liberal than the independents on the foreign aid issue, although remote and more conservative on the other two issues, the extreme case being medical aid.

The Democratic organization, on the other hand, from chairmen down to loyal supporters, was generally more liberal than the independents, the gap widening as one moves up the Democratic hierarchy. The closest congruence existed on the civil rights question, and the least on the foreign aid issue.

Though a minority party, the Republican leadership was not competing ideologically for the independent vote as realistically as the Democratic leadership. This was true particularly on domestic issues. Although it is apparent that the Democratic machine's top nucleus was far too liberal for the independents, the grassroots leadership of the Democratic party was closer to, and more representative of, the attitude directions of independents on domestic issues. Their support potential among the independents was, thus, greater, even though they needed such support less urgently than did the Republican leadership. The latter, a fairly like-minded conservative hierarchy, despite differentials in conservatism within leadership ranks, not only lagged slightly behind the liberals in its own loyalist ranks, and among those predisposed to be Republican supporters, but lagged behind the liberal tendencies of independents as well. The Republican leadership thus tended to live in relative ideological isolation.

SALIENCY OF IDEOLOGY

So far we have dealt with the *direction* of ideology (defined as particular or patterned attitudes toward public policy questions). Since party leaders differ also in the *saliency* of ideology (the extent to which they think in terms of party ideol-

ogy, and the importance they attach to attitude differences in political perceptions), it is also necessary to examine the echelons of the party hierarchies in this respect. In which party and at which hierarchical level does ideology seem to be most salient?

Different measures of the phenomenon of "saliency" were used: perception of differences between the parties, motivations for political activity, basis of interest in politics, and perception of own role in the party. For illustrative purposes, we will use only the first of these approaches (Table 6).

TABLE 6

Ideological Saliency of Party Leaders and Their Publics
(percentage perceiving party differences in issue terms)

	Republicans	*Democrats*
Chairman	33%	83%
Executive board	69	76
Precinct	29	17
Loyalists	26	8
Others	17	7
Independents	14%	

In both parties the precinct leaders seemed less ideologically conscious than the upper echelons. This is particularly true for Democratic precinct leaders, who typically explained the differences between the two parties in terms of the constituency they represented: "The Republicans are the party of the rich," "The Republicans represent the business people," "The Democratic party is the party of the working man." Though more liberal, lower-echelon Democrats were less inclined to articulate issue difference, while the conservative Republican grassroots activists were more articulate. These differences corresponded also to the extent of saliency found in the immediate support groups of the parties. The Republican loyalists differed considerably from the Democrats, and were only slightly less ideologically conscious than the Republican precinct activists. The "other," less loyal, Republicans also exceeded the Democratic irregular party followers. The latter were certainly less ideologically involved, and there was less pressure on the party leadership to emphasize its issue image in competing with the Republicans.

This resulted in a strange paradox for the Democrats. The top and middle-level leadership was very "salient" on ideological differences. Though not rabid ideologues, as pointed out above, the top Democrat leaders were articulate and conscious of issue positions. Having a follower base with negligible ideological saliency means that it was difficult to maximize support primarily by issue appeals. It may also mean that moving upward in the Democratic party hierarchy was an educational experience so far as exposure to public policy positions of the party were concerned. Those at the lower reaches of the Democratic structure had little ideological intensity. In fact, the independents showed as much saliency as the Democratic precinct workers, and more than the Democratic loyal supporters. It may be that in both parties, but particularly the Democratic, career continuity and mobility could result in more awareness of party issue differences.

The two top leadership groups presented a study in contrasts, the Republicans conservative, and not ideologically involved, the Democrats quite liberal, and heavily involved with the issue differences between the parties. Only at the top echelon of the Democratic party and in the middle-level cadre of both parties did we find substantial ideological awareness. The basic direction of ideology was different in each party, but there was a great range in the extent to which the party's position on policy issues was of first importance in the thinking of the leaders.

IDEOLOGICAL DIFFERENCES IN LOCAL PARTY ORGANIZATIONS

In the description of the parties as ideological structures, we have suggested by implication that the direction of a party leader's (or follower's) thinking on public-policy questions, as well as the importance of ideological differences to him, is partly a product of the party to which he belongs, and the echelon at which he is working. That is, of course, only part of the story; other major types of explanations require investigation. One of these is the internal characteristics of the particular party structure and certain conditions of party life, especially conditions of party competition, which are relevant to the development of ideological conviction in the party leader.

District organizations within the same political party varied remarkably in the ideological relationships between leadership and followers. This emerges clearly from Tables 7 and 8. Leaders were not always more conservative, or more liberal, than the supporters. As a matter of fact, three distinct types of relationships for each party may be observed.

There was the district (X and A, for the Republicans) in which the leadership was very conservative and unrepresentative of the followers, with extreme cases showing for the Republicans on both the civil rights and medical aid issues. The majority of Republican followers, two-thirds or more, were liberal, while the chairman was a conservative, and the precinct leadership was overwhelmingly conservative. This occurred in less extreme form on the Democratic side (districts A and B).

The second type occurred in the district where the leadership was much more liberal than the followers. Sometimes only the chairman was a liberal, while the precinct leaders were conservative (Repub-

TABLE 7

Ideological Gaps and Congruence—Three Districts
(percentage liberal on the civil rights issue)

	District X		District Y		District Z	
	Republican	Democratic	Republican	Democratic	Republican	Democratic
Chairman	Con*	Pro*	Pro*	Pro*	Unsure	Con*
Precinct	11%	89%	35%	62%	46%	40%
Loyalists	66†	70†	41	61	58	42
Irregulars			53	61	39	54
Independents	59		59		46	

*Con = conservative; Pro = liberal.
†The loyal and irregular supporters were combined because there were too few cases for separate analysis.

TABLE 8

Ideological Gaps and Congruence—Three Districts
(percentage liberal on the medical aid issue)

	District A		District B		District C	
	Republican	Democratic	Republican	Democratic	Republican	Democratic
Chairman	Con*	Pro*	Unsure	Pro*	Con*	Pro*
Precinct	6%	53%	55%	47%	27%	98%
Loyalists	72†	77†	78†	75†	50	95
Irregulars					47	75
Independents	71		71		62	

*Con = conservative; Pro = liberal.
†The loyal and irregular supporters were combined because there were too few cases for separate analysis.

licans, District Y). In other cases there was a split in the follower group, although the differences in this respect were not usually great. An example of this may be found in the overwhelming support of medical aid by the Democratic leadership and loyal supporters in District C, with somewhat less liberalism among the irregular Democrats.

The third basic type was the district organization in which there was fairly close congruence between the opinions of the leadership and the followers. In one case the chairman might be ambivalent on the issue in the face of a decided split within the ranks (Republicans, District Z). In another case the chairman might take a conservative position in the face of a split in the ranks (Democrats, District Z; Republicans, District C). In this case the ideological position of the precinct leadership might be the controlling factor for the chairman, or vice versa.

The striking fact which emerges from a district-by-district analysis of the data is that a political party is a composite of significantly varying ideological types. Each district structure may be characterized as an ideological entity. The Republican precinct leaders in District A were extremely different in their attitudes on medical aid from those in District B—the one group was only 6 per cent liberal on this question, the second group 55 per cent liberal—while both the precinct leadership cadres, Republican and Democratic, differed radically in Districts X and Z. There did not appear to be as much difference, however, in the attitude distributions of the "loyalists" and irregular sup-

TABLE 9

Range of Liberalism within Six District Party Structures
(percentage-point spread in liberal positions from the lowest
percentage of liberalism in a district to the highest)

	Precinct Leaders		All Followers		
	Republican	Democratic	Republican	Democratic	Independents
Civil rights	59	49	35	26	18
Medical aid	64	51	59	15	34
Foreign aid	38	41	16	14	20

porters of the parties by district, although differences did exist. The range in liberalism for all of the six congressional districts in our study is shown in Table 9, revealing that, on each issue, the precinct leaders as groups were more dispersed and the followers more homogeneous from district to district. There is a strong suggestion here that rank-and-file partisan supporters and independents were relatively stable throughout the metropolitan area in their political opinions, but activists varied greatly in their attitudes from one party structure to the next. One primary reason for this is that the party as a group influences and conditions ideological position, making the activist more conservative in the Republican case, or more liberal (though there are exceptions to this, too) in the Democratic case. A second reason with some probability is that the party attracts (or recruits) as activists from its support group individuals who were ideologically predisposed to follow the attitude positions of those already in the hierarchy, at the same time discouraging those perceived to be too liberal or conservative, as the case might be. No doubt both factors operated together; the evidence is too clear and the variations too striking to indicate otherwise. A party structure is constantly struggling, in its subtle relationships with the environment, to maintain itself as a viable ideological entity. The potential supporters of the party structure are constantly evaluating the ideological position of the party ma-

chine, and if inclined to political activity, calculating their chances for ideological survival and career mobility if they assume activist responsibilities.

In this two-way flow of contacts between the party leadership and its publics, the Democrats seemed to have developed a more successful set of relationships. The job of the Democrats had been abetted, of course, by the existence of a majority liberalism among its followers in these districts. With the exception of perhaps two districts, there was less range in the extent of liberal support among Democrats, and, too, they seemed to have done a better job of inducting liberals in the constituent groups into precinct work. The exception was District B. The Republicans in some districts had done fairly well in this respect also, notably Districts Y and Z, thus maintaining a proper equilibrium in ideological position between leaders and followers. But generally the Republican leadership had inducted conservatives into the hierarchy, leaving a follower remnant at odds, in attitude, with the leadership. Third, the Democrats in four of the districts had developed a leadership structure conforming more closely to the ideology of independents than had the Republican party.

PARTY COMPETITION AND THE IDEOLOGY OF THE ACTIVISTS

The competitive context and status of the two parties differed greatly among districts. There were three basic types:

1. Conservative Republican leaders faced relatively conservative Democratic leaders (Districts Z and B)
2. Conservative Republicans faced liberal Democrats (Districts X, Y, and A)
3. Liberal Democrats and Republicans faced each other in the same district (a district not included in the above tables, where, for example, 70 per cent of the Republican precinct leaders were liberal on civil rights and medical aid issues, and 89 and 78 per cent of the Democratic leaders were liberal, respectively, on each of these issues).

Now, three of these districts were overwhelmingly Democratic, and three were somewhat more competitive, though still voting Democratic. In the "sure Democratic" districts the Republican leadership was of all three types noted above, while in the more "marginal" districts were only Republican conservatives, opposing either Democratic liberals or moderate conservatives.

Clear-cut ideological struggles, therefore, appeared in three of the districts, with liberals opposing conservatives on most issues. This conflict occurred primarily in marginal districts; in fact, in the most marginal district in the area one found the most highly conservative Republicans arrayed against the most liberal Democrats. The Republicans and Democrats had diversified their organizational "battle plans," but moderation in ideological position did not characterize those areas with the greatest potential in party competition. The Republicans did not appear to be making much progress in those sure Democratic districts where they were either as conservative as the Democrats, or almost as liberal as the Democrats. And, in a sense, Republican liberalism was wasted in the sure Democratic district where this held, but they had waged battle in marginal areas by remaining conservative in the face of Democratic liberalism. Whether this was wise in the long run, in the face of considerable liberalism among their followers and the independents, is a difficult question to answer. These marginal districts were becoming less marginal over time, and more Democratic. Witness the 17th District, which was only 52 per cent Democratic in the congressional election of 1954, but in 1958 was 60 per cent Democratic. This was apparently the manner in which the Republicans sought to battle in marginal districts, by maintaining a distinctive ideological position in the hierarchy, in contrast to their diversified approaches in sure Democratic areas. This technique was probably not sufficiently adaptive to the types of constituency to which they must appeal, for example, barely 10 per cent of the Republican precinct leaders were liberal on the civil rights issue in a Negro congressional district organization. But, realistic or not, it produced party conflict situations which were more clearcut than one would expect in a two-party system under which both parties were seeking *presumably* to maximize their appeal to "potential clienteles" in a metropolitan electorate.

There is evidence here, then, of three organizational conditions which influence the ideological character of the leadership structure of the party. One is the tendency for the leadership to maintain itself as a viable ideological structure. Another is the tendency of certain types of people to be attracted to party leadership. The third is the character of the competitive struggle in the district, with marginal competitive conditions finding conservatives in the Republican organization, and liberals in the Democratic. Thus, with district party structures varying greatly in ideological composition, the type of district organization to which the activist is recruited may have a great deal to do with his subsequent ideology. He may be conservative or liberal at the time he is recruited, but certainly the indoctrination process commences as soon as he has joined the party machine.

TABLE 10

Ideological Differences for Precinct Leaders by Precinct Type

	Sure Democratic Precincts		Marginal Precincts		Sure Republican Precincts	
	Republican	Democratic	Republican	Democratic	Republican	Democratic
Medical aid						
Liberal	39%	67%	18%	100%	20%	76%
Conservative	35%	20%	80%	0%	60%	13%
Index*		43		162		103
Civil Rights						
Liberal	48%	58%	31%	53%	40%	62%
Conservative	49%	33%	69%	47%	51%	34%
Index*		26		44		39
Foreign aid						
Liberal	29%	48%	36%	80%	54%	62%
Conservative	28%	23%	53%	20%	28%	24%
Index*		24		77		12

*The index score is a computation of party differences, including both the liberal and conservative percentages. Unless indicated otherwise, it represents the extent to which the Democrats were more liberal than the Republicans.

Confirmation of this last finding is found by detailed analysis of the ideological position of precinct leaders in relation to the competitive status of the 87 precincts included in the study (Table 10). Of the Republican leaders, 80 per cent were opposed to medical aid in the marginal precincts, while 60 per cent were opposed in the sure Republican precincts, and only 35 per cent were opposed in the sure Democratic precincts. In contrast, none of the Democratic precinct leaders in the marginal precincts was opposed to medical aid, while 13 per cent and 20 per cent were opposed in the sure Republican and sure Democratic precincts, respectively. The opinions on the other issues bear out this finding that the party leadership structures were strikingly opposed to each other ideologically in marginal districts. Index scores also indicate that the greatest ideological distance between Republican and Democratic leaders was found in these marginal precincts.

While the Republicans competed as conservatives in marginal precincts, they tended to be more liberal in sure Democratic precincts. Not a majority, to be true,

and not extremists, but this was where they appeared to be concentrated. Since the lowest Democratic liberal tendencies appeared in the sure Democratic precincts, it may be that the Republicans saw this as the best tactic to win back some support from the complacent, and less liberal, Democrats. The rationale may also have been that these were precincts where the Republicans could afford to be relatively liberal, and precincts in which liberal Republicans could infiltrate as activists without too much competition.

The most fundamental observation from these data is that where there was the most intense party competition, conservatives sought, or were selected, for Republican precinct leadership posts, and liberals sought, or were selected for, the Democratic posts. This, of course, contradicts much impressionistic observation about American politics, particularly the view that the parties moderate and mute ideological differences in order to maximize their votes in the most competitive areas. So far as the precinct leaders were concerned, the battle forces in highly competitive areas were ideologically distinctive.

SOCIAL STRUCTURE AND LEADERSHIP IDEOLOGY

The three social factors of race, religion, and nationality affect the interrelationship between ideology and the social stratum of the individual party leader. These differences cut across party lines and in each case Negro precinct leaders tended to be more liberal that whites, Protestants than Catholics, and those with eastern and southern European nationality backgrounds more liberal than those from northwestern or central Europe. These elements in positions of leadership constitute an ideological continuum undergirding the party organization and provide an ideological integration for the party system.

This was not true of the ideological tendencies of income groups, educational groups, or age groups. The lower-income groups were the most liberal on the Republican side; the higher income groups liberal for Democrats (very liberal on civil rights, moderately liberal on medical aid). The college-educated Republican precinct leader was the least liberal, while the college-educated Democratic leader was rather liberal. Nor did union affiliation relate to more liberalism among Democratic party leaders, although it did seem to be associated with liberalism among Republicans.

Two striking results from this analysis are the differences between parties in the ideology of women and Catholics. Less than 10 per cent of female Republican precinct leaders, but over 70 per cent of female Democrats, were consistent liberals. Democratic Catholic party leaders were considerably more liberal than Republican.

The ideological differences between the parties, as a matter of fact, for these different demographic groups were very consistent. In Table 11 out of 36 comparisons which could be made between the liberalism of Democratic and Republican party leaders for these personal characteristics, only three instances emerged in which the Republican subgroup exceeded the Democratic subgroup in liberalism. These were all on the civil rights issue for the lowest social-status groups—those with an elementary-school education, and the two lowest income groups—otherwise the Democrats were invariably more liberal. We checked this finding on the foreign aid issue and for other demographic categories, and found that in 88 per cent of the comparisons the Democratic leadership subgroups were more liberal.

This suggests strongly that ideology is a party-related phenomenon on the leadership level, even though there seem to be consistent differences in terms of race, religion, and nationality which cut across party lines. The liberal ideologues were Democrats, whatever their social stratum. The Republicans could increase their liberalism by recruiting more Negroes, and perhaps also by attracting certain nationality groups, Protestants, and certain lower social-status groups. These people eventually proved to be less liberal than their counterparts in the Democratic party, the product again, no doubt, of the two-way interaction between party and potential clientele groups. The party selectively recruits; the potential activists selectively choose sides.

Analysis of the personal characteristics of liberals and conservatives on the executive boards of the two parties (though the number of cases for each demographic and social subgroup is, of course, small) suggests certain distinctions in the precinct leadership. Thus, the Republicans had slightly more female, Catholic, college-educated liberals on the executive boards than in the precincts. The Democrats had fewer female, Negro, college-educated liberals on their executive boards. In both parties uniformly, Catholics were less conservative and Protestants more conservative on the executive boards than in the precincts. It may be

TABLE 11

Ideological Direction by Personal Characteristics
(precinct leaders only—percentage of demographic category
liberal on each issue)

	Republicans		Democrats	
	Civil Rights	Medical Aid	Civil Rights	Medical Aid
Race				
White	36%	23%	52%	78%
Negro	70	61	78	72
Sex				
Male	50	33	54	77
Female	4	11	81	71
Religion				
Catholic	21	24	48	66
Protestant	52	29	63	82
Education				
Elementary or less	70	31	45	08
High school	47	49	54	80
College	31	14	73	65
Nationality				
Northwestern European	36	22	51	78
Central European	29	18	41	76
Eastern and Southern European	50	33	100*	90
Income				
Under $5,000	58	50	41	88
$5–7,000	47	19	44	74
$7–10,000	22	39	79	82
Over $10,000	36	20	70	61
Union affiliation				
Yes	53	49	58	77
No	36	20	58	74

*Too few cases for reliable analysis.

that the parties could, or must, tolerate more liberalism, or conservatism, in the upper echelons. The Republicans found themselves with more liberal Catholics on executive boards, for example, while the Democrats encountered a rather conservative-minded group of women on their boards. This tendency may have been the product of recruitment deficiencies at the precinct level or an indication that individuals change ideologically as they move up the party hierarchy. In any case, both parties faced ideological factionalism among the same social-group memberships at two different levels of the organization.

THE IDEOLOGY OF THE SUBCOALITIONS

Party subcoalitions can vary widely in ideological direction. If we look at the ideological position of those structural subgroups described in Chapter 4,[2] party differences existed, clearly, but subcoalitional differences also appeared (Table 12). The medical aid and foreign aid issues were selected as illustrative, although other issues revealed the same tendencies. In both party structures the degree of

[2] In Samuel J. Eldersveld's *Political Parties: A Behavioral Analysis* (Chicago: Rand McNally & Co., 1964).

TABLE 12
The Ideology of the Subcoalitions and the "Deviants"
(percentage of subgroup liberal on each issue)

	Medical Aid		Foreign Aid	
Democrats	Precinct Leaders	Loyal Followers	Precinct Leaders	Loyal Followers
Subcoalitions:				
Negroes	69%	88%	50%	21%
Poles	94	100	56	19
Irish	67	88	39	41
Other labor	76	81	62	21
Business and professional whites	86	71	79	35
Southern blue collar	*	100	*	6
All CIO	*	95	*	30
All AFL	*	73	*	13
"Deviants":				
Germans	55	53†	100	26†
English	91	78†	91	27†
Business-managerial group	74	69†	84	31†

	Medical Aid		Foreign Aid	
Republicans	Precinct Leaders	Loyal Followers	Precinct Leaders	Loyal Followers
Subcoalitions:				
Business-managerial whites	11%	30%	50%	35%
Other white collar (northwestern European)	35	27	53	50
Nonlabor blue collar whites	*	38†	*	33†
Labor (whites)	44	53†	18	34†
Negroes	61	93†	17	13†
All Germans	22	24	30	59
All English, Welsh, and Scottish	29	35	36	39
"Deviants":				
Irish and Poles	11	62†	39	29†
Other southern, central, and eastern Europeans	32	74†	84	42†
Semi- and unskilled	43	58†	43	25†

*Too few cases, or analysis was not possible.
†Based on all followers, since there were too few cases of "loyal" followers.

liberalism or conservatism varied by subcoalitional issue orientation. Among Democratic subgroups the least conflict appeared on medical aid (all were over 60 per cent liberal); yet subcoalitional precinct representatives varied from two-thirds to almost 100 per cent support. On foreign aid there was much more difference in ideological conviction in the Democratic structure: only 39 per cent of the Irish precinct leaders were liberal, 50 per cent of the Negroes, while 79 per cent of the "business-professional whites" were

liberal. In the Republican party there was extreme subcoalitional variation in ideology. On medical aid, 61 per cent of the Negro Republican precinct leaders were liberal, but only 11 per cent of the business-managerial class, and 22 per cent of the Germans. Conversely, 50–53 per cent of the white-collar and business-managerial precinct leaders were liberal in foreign aid, but only 17 per cent of the Negro leaders (and 18 per cent of the "labor whites").

Ideological disagreement by subcoali-

TABLE 13

Variation among Democratic Loyal Followers on
Civil Rights Issue

Loyal Followers Subcoalition	Percentage Liberal on Civil Rights Issue	Number of Cases
Negroes	85%	52
Poles	43	21
Irish	47	17
Business and professional whites	29	17
Southern blue collar migrants	44	16
All CIO	42	73
All AFL	45	40

tions among precinct leaders was greater among the loyal followers. The Republican party was a structure which had to reconcile a subgroup of Negro supporters (93 per cent of whom were liberal) with a subgroup of upper-status businessmen who were 30 per cent (or 32 per cent if all followers were used) liberal. The "ideological spread" in the Democratic structure was not as great, but on the issue of civil rights, for example, the variation shown in Table 13 appeared among loyal Democratic supporters.

The ideological distance between Negro loyal Democrats and the rest of the party, particularly the business-professional group, is obvious. One wonders, indeed, whether a serious effort at compromising these groups at the top level of the party structure could even be attempted!

We have included in Table 12 some of the "deviant" social categories for each party previously used.[3] The purpose here is twofold—to reveal the party differences for each "deviant" group, and to test the proposition that open recruitment can result in ideological disjunction in the party structure. Although Negroes have an ideology which tends to be homogeneous regardless of party, the same cannot be said for other categories. Irish and Polish precinct leaders in the Republican party, for example, were overwhelmingly con-

servative, while in the Democratic party they were generally liberal. The same finding, in reverse, exists for the German and English Democratic precinct leaders, who were very liberal contrasted to the Republican Germans and English, only one-fifth to one-third of whom were liberal. Similarly the "business-managerial" class in the Democratic party was over 70 per cent liberal, while the same class in the Republican party was very conservative on medical aid, and 50 per cent liberal on foreign aid. Here is clear evidence again of the probability that a precinct leader in the Democratic party, rather than the Republican party, was *either* a liberal at the beginning, *or* that the party had a real influence on his ideology after he joined. In fact, the hypothesis that recruitment of "deviants," as precinct leaders or as followers, attracts people at ideological odds with the rest of the party, is not generally supported by data on the Democratic party. Only the German Democrats pose a problem as a conservative force. The hypothesis does seem to be true for the Republican party's socially "deviant" followers, however, though not for their "deviant" precinct leaders. The "deviant" precinct leaders were not particularly liberal, but 62 per cent of the Irish and Polish followers and 58 per cent of the semi- and unskilled laborers *were* liberal on the issue of medical aid. While Democratic "deviants" seemed to have re-

---

[3] Samuel J. Eldersveld, *op. cit.*, chap. 3.

TABLE 14

Career Background and Status as Related to Ideology

(precinct leaders only)

(percentage of career category liberal on each of three issues)

	Republicans			Democrats		
	CR^*	MA^*	FA^*	CR^*	MA^*	FA^*
Career origin						
1956	49%	22%	22%	59%	38%	31%
1952–55	50	22	72	69	83	83
1940–51	41	38	30	43	97	77
1932–39	40	47	40	41	78	59
Before 1932	24	19	14	85	90	35
Father's preference						
Democratic	40	40	40	53	81	58
Republican	45	27	28	79	86	57
Father politically active						
Yes	36	24	23	53	87	67
No	44	32	36	60	70	54
Father's preference and activity						
Republican						
Active	32	27	47	‡	‡	‡
Inactive	49	27	29	80†	90†	50†
Democratic						
Active	45†	18†	45†	46	85	65
Inactive	38	50	38	56	79	54

*CR—civil rights; MA—medical aid; FA—foreign aid.
†Small number of cases: R, 11; D, 10.
‡Too few cases for analysis.

linquished their conservative leanings, Republican "deviants" still clung to liberal attitudes.

CAREER STATUS AND IDEOLOGY

The question of the role of career background and status in ideological perspective deserves special analysis since ideology appears strongly related to selection of party. Is there evidence that career pattern variables are related to the ideological structure of the party? Or does party career origin and process have nothing to do with ideology?

The time of origin of political career is a related factor to ideology in both parties (Table 14). The latecomers in the Republican party, and those who began their careers before 1932, were the most

conservative (though the latecomers were relatively liberal on civil rights). Among Republican precinct leaders, therefore, the ideological conflict arrayed the newest members and the oldest members against those who entered the party in the thirties and the forties.

It is interesting that recent Democratic entrants were also quite conservative, and in sharp contrast to the liberalism of those who began Democratic careers prior to 1932. These findings suggest that there may have been a movement toward ideological moderation in both parties in 1956.

The family political context in which the individual was "socialized" for politics also bears some relationship to ideological direction among activists. Democratic fathers sired more conservative Republican activists than liberals; Republican

TABLE 15
Career Status and Ideological Direction
(precinct leaders)
(percentage of career category liberal on each issue)

	Republicans				Democrats			
	CR^*	FA^*	MA^*	In-dex†	CR^*	FA^*	MA^*	In-dex†
Top mobiles	21%	46%	21%	29	65%	80%	83%	76
Informal influentials	53	26	63	47	60	57	90	69
Nonmobile regulars	23	28	16	22	57	71	90	73
Potentials	60	33	35	43	56	25	78	53
Noncareerists	63	75	25	54	52	60	36	49

*CR—civil rights; MA—medical aid; FA—foreign aid.
†The index score is a simple mean of the three percentages.

fathers produced more Democratic liberal activists than conservatives, *and* a larger proportion of liberals than did Democratic fathers! A "rebel reaction" seems to be indicated here. It is indeed significant that 86 per cent of the offspring of Republican fathers who served as Democratic precinct leaders in 1956 favored medical aid programs, but only 40 per cent of the offspring of Democratic fathers who were in the Republican camp in 1956 favored medical aid programs. The data reveal that the political activity of the father is also an important variable—Republicans with active fathers were more conservative, while Democrats with active fathers were generally more liberal. Yet, a combined analysis (though the cases are few) indicates that there may be some validity in the "rebel reaction" theory. Active Democratic fathers produced a preponderance of conservative Republicans, though greater conservatism resulted from having an active Republican father. And active Republican fathers contributed liberals to the Democratic camp. This finding emphasizes again the fluidity of the American party affiliation structure, and hints at an alienation tendency at home combined with an indoctrination process in the party, which together may have much to do with the ideological position of the activist.

On the question of career status, and using the same career categories employed in Chapter 6, we are able to see whether position in the party hierarchy is related to ideology (Table 15).

There is an obvious and clear connection between career continuity, mobility, and aspiration on the one hand, and ideological direction on the other. The "top organization mobiles" and the "regulars" (who had been in the organization a long time even though nonmobile) were fairly distinctive groups. They were the most conservative in the Republican organization, and the most liberal in the Democratic. Only one-fifth of these took a liberal position on medical aid and civil rights questions in the Republican party, while from 60 to 90 per cent did in the Democratic party. The "potential careerists" (who aspired but had not served long or continuously) tended to be more liberal in the Republican party (particularly on foreign aid). This may have resulted from basic differences with the hierarchy, or misperceptions as to the ideological conditions under which one moved upward, or evidence that they had not been subjected to the indoctrination process of the party. In any event, they constituted an ideological challenge in both parties, much more so than the "noncareerists" (the irregular activists who come and go and have no organizational aspirations). The latter were also rather liberal in the Republican party, and somewhat conservative in the Democratic party (particularly on the question of medical aid).

Three major observations emerge from this analysis of career status. One is that there is clear evidence that length of tenure in the party machine and movement upward, combined with aspiration to be influential, inclined the party activist to an ideology which is conformist. He was less likely to be a liberal in the Republican party machine under such conditions, and less likely to be a conservative in the Democratic party. (The only exception to this was the group of Republican "informal influentials" who had held no formal position beside precinct leader, but who seemed to have many contacts in the hierarchy. This group tended to be rather liberal in the Republican party, just as it did in the Democratic party.)

A second basic observation is that the nonmobile and irregular activists, who constituted 40 per cent of the precinct leadership cadre, were least conformist—more liberal in the Republican party, and more conservative in the Democratic party. The party relied heavily on these newcomers and irregulars, not all of whom aspired to position in the party, and there was a latent dysfunctional aspect in their relationship to the party. The party might have to capitulate to them or modify its position on key policy issues if it wished to maximize the support and efforts of these precinct leaders.

Third, although the top mobiles in the precinct cadre were inclined to be congruent attitudinally with the top executive nucleus (the chairmen and executive board members), one-fourth of them were noncongruent. And they were no more congruent than the nonmobile regulars, a finding which raises questions again as to the acceptability of the theory of oligarchy.

CONCLUSIONS

This chapter has discussed party leadership as a structure of ideological perspectives, presumably shared within the hierarchy. We have been interested in the ideological basis of party organization and the ideological conditions under which the parties compete in the precincts. We examined the extent of ideological dissensus and unity in the party machine, and how monolithic, incoherent, or balanced ideologically the party structure was. We sought to assemble and study the available evidence concerning the problem of ideological indoctrination and the role of the party structure in determining the attitudes of its leadership on public policy questions.

Some observers assert that it is ideological homogeneity which makes a party structure viable, but examination of party structures discloses, in fact, considerable ideological diversity, by echelon, by subcoalition, by career status.

We found that the Republican and Democratic hierarchies varied considerably in ideological direction, at all echelons —the Republicans conservative, the Democrats much more liberal. These differences were striking at the top leadership level, but were significant at the precinct level as well. Yet, there were sizeable dissenting groups in each party—from 10 to 25 per cent of the leadership, depending on the leadership echelon. In neither party was the precinct leadership the most liberal, a finding which is possibly at odds with general impressions and other research.

Our indices of the amount of extremism in attitudes, the extent of factionism, intraparty attitudinal congruence, and the relationship between leadership and followers reveal a lack of homogeneity in both parties. Republican leadership tended to lag considerably behind the Republican rank-and-file in liberalism; Democratic leaders were also ideologically distant from their follower base. It seems clear that the Republicans were not competing realistically for independent voters, who were much more liberal than the Republican leadership groups. These descriptive differences seem most important in ideological direction, even though in both parties there was a low level of ideological awareness and saliency, particularly at the precinct level.

In probing for explanations and relationships, certain factors seemed to be working together to produce these differences. The type of party organization in which the leader is active seemed of considerable importance. District organizations developed, over time, their own distinctive ideological directions, and the activists seemed to vary from one district to another, even though the follower groups and the public generally were rather consistent and stable in their opinion directions. Another factor, the competitive character of the district and precinct (whether it be sure or doubtful) revealed ideological differences in leadership. This was particularly noticeable for marginal districts, where the Republican leadership fought as conservatives, while the Democrats fought as liberals.

Thirdly, there were differences in ideology by the personal and social backgrounds of the leaders, religion, race, and nationality appearing to have the greatest cross-cutting relevance. Within each party, also, there were certain social backgrounds which correlated with liberal or conservative ideology. The subcoalitional differences were particularly significant, revealing a 40 per cent difference for Democratic precinct leaders from its subgroups, and a 50 per cent Republican subcoalitional difference. Finally, career background and career status were factors related to differences in ideological direction. Those with career origins prior to 1932, as well as the more recent entrants, seemed to be most distinctive in ideology.

Father's political preference and activity were also relevant, with considerable "rebel reaction" in evidence.

A prominent and consistent finding, with explanatory power, is that ideology is a phenomenon related to party organization. There were major differences between the two parties' leadership structures, at all leadership levels. The type of district organization in which the activist was recruited or found himself, the competitive nature of the precinct, and the career status of the individual activist in the party—all made important contributions, it appears, to the ideology of the leader. This configuration of factors operated with a variety of processes for which one might be tempted to accept simply this explanatory image: The would-be activist has a perception of the leadership ideological structure, makes the decision to join, or is involuntarily "recruited." The party, on the other hand, endeavors to recruit a selective leadership. Subsequently, the party socializes this leadership in terms of its own ideological position, indoctrinates the party "line" through overt or informal and indirect processes, and "promotes" a majority of those with conformist tendencies to upper-echelon tasks and responsibilities. Thus, in this image, induction into the party structure and indoctrination following induction are twin re-enforcing processes with great potential for ideological control.

Countervailing forces and evidence reveal, however, that there are serious limits to ideological control, particularly by the top elite nucleus. It is quite apparent that large minorities of leaders at the executive board level did not know or follow the "party line"—from 20 to 40 per cent. It is also obvious that even the top executives were not all liberals or conservatives. Further, sizeable numbers of precinct leaders continued in their posts even though, theoretically, their ideological position must have been anathema to top leadership—from 30 to 40 per cent. Again, though conformity to the party line may seem to have had value, the "deviants" were tolerated and nonconformists promoted. Approximately 30 per cent of the Republican "top mobiles" in the precinct cadre were liberals and 25 per cent of the Democratic "top mobiles" were conservatives. Apparently, the top elite nucleus could not obstruct their mobility aspirations despite ideological nonconformity. Above all, the subcoalitional diversity in ideology which the party must and did tolerate is obvious. We have here, then, concomitant with evidence that ideology is influenced by party associations, evidence also of great ideological diversity, autonomy, nonsocialization, dilution, and dissent. The party machine is no monolith, co-opting and coercing a homogeneous and unique ideological leadership. Pressure to conform exists. But the party gladly embraces, and freely associates with, a most ideologically conglomerate set of potential supporters and activists. From the bottom to the top, the party welcomes, and rewards, the ideological deviant.

PATTERNS OF LEADERSHIP POLICY PREFERENCE:
A STUDY OF SOME ASSUMPTIONS IN COMMUNITY RESEARCH

Norman R. Luttbeg

For some time the focus of community research has been: Who governs. This question and the controversy surrounding it have certainly revitalized interest in community politics. Unfortunately this interest has not resulted in an empirically substantiated theory of community politics. A controversy rages; and because the opposing schools of thought disagree on not one but several important matters, many of their findings about the community have been thrown into question. The schools find different concepts useful in understanding community politics; they value different research techniques; finally, they sharply disagree on their preconceived biases as to the true nature of American community politics. This last area of disagreement is evident as both seek to generalize beyond the communities studied.

To the first group—the pluralists—the actors in community decision making vary greatly between issues, since those who participate in one decision seldom act in others with the exception of political leaders, especially the mayor. The pluralists' emphasis of political leaders' activity would seem to reflect their belief that only these leaders can rise above economic interests. Using their preferred research technique, the study of participation in community decisions, Robert A. Dahl has lent support to this argument in a study of New Haven, Connecticut.[1]

The opposing school might be called the social stratificationists. Although they do not seem so conscious of their shared orientation as do the pluralists, Nelson Polsby makes a good case for identifying them as a group.[2] The name social stratifi-

---

[1] Robert A. Dahl, *Who Governs?* (New Haven, Conn.: Yale University Press, 1961), p. 183.

[2] Nelson W. Polsby, *Community Power and Political Theory* (New Haven, Conn.: Yale University Press, 1963).

cationist, used in this article, derives from his work. This school conceives the political stratification of society as less basic than its social stratification; consequently, they argue, those within the highest social stratum govern even though they may not hold public office. The best known study of the social stratificationists is Floyd Hunter's *Community Power Structure*, a study of Atlanta, Georgia. He asked informants: "Who is most influential?" This technique has been broadly adopted by this school. Again, the findings of the social stratificationists substantiate their preconception of community politics. Consequently Dahl's New Haven and Hunter's Atlanta, as reported, differ greatly.

The explanation of the differences between these two communities has focused on the differences in research methods used.[3] Although this focus has greatly benefited the development of research techniques, the channeling of extensive energies into this effort has been at the expense of broadening our understanding of community politics. Rather than concluding that different research techniques explain the differences in the two communities, a simpler explanation seems more likely and constructive—namely that the communities themselves differ. Indeed, more recent studies of other communities with both methods have discovered that the methods do not bias the results to the degree previously suggested in the more polemic discussions.[4] If communities differ in the nature of their politics, we must conceive of the possible range of their variation. Perhaps the two types of communities suggested by these schools—elite and pluralist—may serve as a first attempt

to define a continuum of variability in community politics.[5]

Dampening the fires raging around research methods would hopefully lead to the broadening of the range of research interests in the community political process. Rather than asking "who governs?" future research might investigate why one community's leadership approximates an elite while another tends to be pluralistic. Also, we might ask what are the policy implications of finding different types of men governing the community. Does an elite enact policies different than a more pluralistic group of leaders? Hopefully, these and other second-generation questions will supplement the continued investigation of who governs. This study makes a first attempt to answer one such question.

The study concentrates on the political attitudes of leaders and followers. If the same political values and policy preferences were shared by the entire public, it would not matter which individuals led and which followed. But even the most insensitive observer of American society must appreciate the absence of such a pervasive consensus.[6]

Thus, as long as some men lead and policy preferences and values are not consensually held, public policy may differ from public preference. While one would certainly expect the wants and desires of those who exercise leadership to affect decisions more substantially than those of

---

[3]See Nelson W. Polsby for the clearest statement of this in *ibid.*, chaps. ii and iii.

[4]Robert Presthus, *Men at the Top* (New York: Oxford University Press, 1964), p. 424; M. Kent Jennings, *Community Influentials: The Elite of Atlanta* (New York: The Free Press of Glencoe, 1964), p. 198; and Robert E. Agger *et al.*, *The Rulers and the Ruled* (New York: John Wiley & Sons, Inc., 1964), p. 331.

[5]Thomas R. Dye suggests such a continuum in his review of Aaron Wildavsky, *Leadership in a Small Town*, in "Book Notes and Bibliography," The *American Political Science Review*, Vol. 59 (March 1965), p. 173. Also see Jennings, *op. cit.*, p. 201.

[6]V. O. Key, Jr. has an excellent discussion of the concept of consensus and what little we know of it. *Public Opinion and American Democracy* (New York: Alfred A. Knopf, Inc., 1961). chap. ii. He suggests in a footnote, p. 36, that consensus is more likely in small communities, presumably because it is easier to find agreement among a few people than among many.

the less active, we have an incomplete understanding of how leaders' preferences differ from those of their constituents.[7]

Certainly we would expect other variables to affect the impact of any bias among leaders. For example, institutional devices may afford the public a better opportunity to affect policy, and some political leaders may be motivated to enact policies they think are desired by the public rather than their own personal preferences.

Given their disagreement in other areas, both schools somewhat surprisingly share many expectations about the nature of the modern American community. They both accept the existence of some structuring of influence in the community, preference differences between social classes, and the strong tendency for the influential to be drawn from the upper social classes. But are such assumptions correct?

The social stratificationists, of course, see the structuring of influence as coincident with social stratification, stressing the important roles played by persons of high social status in the community's decision making. But is it sufficient to show that persons of high social status dominate a community's decision making in order to conclude that policy reflects upper class preferences? Are there always identifiable social class positions; do influential persons of higher social status hold attitudes typical of their class; even if so, do they act entirely on these attitudes?[8] These questions have not been thoroughly researched.

Because the public officeholder frequently does not belong to the community's upper social classes, the social strati-

ficationists often discount his importance in local decision making. Not being independently influential, he is seen as subject to the influence of the social and economic notables.[9] Often, they argue, he may be their pawn.

The pluralists also distinguish between publicly elected leaders and persons whose influence derives from social and economic stature, but they do not find the public leaders so ineffectual. In fact, they find he plays a central role in community decision making.[10] While they share the social stratificationists' belief that economic notables would govern in their own interest if given the opportunity, they stress the political leader's activity in decision making, clearly not perceiving him as a pawn of the economic notables. Presumably the political leaders' activities in community decision making move public policy away from being entirely an expression of economic interest. The pluralists seem to assume that political leaders act on attitudes more nearly in line with those of the public. The battle thus waxes over who governs and not over the implication to governmental policy in finding a community dominated by political leaders as opposed to economic leaders. This is assumed.

Any effort to synthesize the essential differences between two positions, especially those involving strong emotional commitment, entails potential criticism from the adherents of the positions who may protest their having been misrepresented. So it is with my effort to portray differences between the schools of community research. They may insist that I have grossly oversimplified their argument; but since I intended to identify the essence of their disagreement, simplification is necessarily involved. Certainly both

---

[7]*Ibid.*, p. 184. This of course assumes that leaders' personal attitudes affect their actions more than other factors.

[8]Peter Rossi long ago stressed the lack of concern with these assumptions, but to my knowledge there has been little or no follow-up. See Peter Rossi, "Community Decision-Making," *Administrative Science Quarterly*, Vol. 1 (March 1957), p. 419.

[9]Robert S. Lynd and Helen Merrel Lynd, *Middletown in Transition* (New York: Harcourt, Brace, 1937), p. 89; Hunter, *Community Power Structure* (Chapel Hill, N.C.: The University of North Carolina Press, 1953), p. 248.

[10]Dahl, *op. cit.*, p. 183.

positions have subtleties and nuances difficult, if not impossible, to conceive in a measurable form; yet the acceptance or rejection of the theories cannot proceed until they are subjected to empirical testing.

This presentation of the argument between the two schools facilitates empirical evaluation as it implies that the personal attitudes of leaders directly affect their actions as rulers. Some may protest that actions may not reflect attitudes, and much research supports this wariness. But some evidence indicates a very strong, though not perfect, relationship between attitudes and actions in just this area of leader behavior.[11] The linkage between actions taken and personal attitudes among leaders is commonly accepted in our literature. Its virtue comes from its economy and simplicity in explaining leadership behavior, but it has been insufficiently examined.

PROCEDURES

Two communities in the Northwest served as a setting for this study. In each community a probability sample of the public and a leadership sample responded to questions concerning their approval or disapproval of programs or proposed innovations at issue in the community at the time.[12] The leaders were identified by

[11]Warren E. Miller and Donald E. Stokes, "Constituency Influence in Congress," *The American Political Science Review*, Vol. LVII (March 1963), pp. 45–56.

[12]The Springfield sample included every seventh household on a list provided by a local utility of residential installations. In Eugene, blocks were randomly chosen at a constant density (13 percent) from districts thought to reflect similar socioeconomic characteristics. Once the blocks were chosen, the interviewers were told to start at the northeast corner on the first block given them and to proceed in a systematic sampling throughout the blocks assigned to them. Approximately 1 in every 28 households were sampled. Interviewers were instructed to interview 50 percent males.

An extensive analysis of these samples by members of the Institute for Community Studies at the University of Oregon, comparing the

reputational technique.[13] Although many may protest the use of this method of identifying leaders, its continued use seems justified for several reasons. Despite the extensive theoretical criticism of this method, simplicity and the consistency between findings in using it as compared to the more expensive and complicated techniques remain its virtue.[14] Also in this specific study I am interested in assessing the correctness of the implications to policy suggested by the social stratificationists, and since they nearly exclusively use this method it would seem most appropriate. Finally I wish to compare politically elected leaders and economic notables, and both can be identified within such a sample.

Among other items on a lengthy questionnaire, the public respondents answered questions that permitted them to be stratified both socially and politically.[15] The

samples with population parameter from the 1960 census and local party registration roles, has shown the samples to be highly representative. The Eugene sample does slightly overrepresent the better educated and aged.

The issues studied in these two communities were: attracting industry to the community, annexation of suburban areas, providing public parking lots in central shopping areas, expansion of special education in the schools, fluoridating the city's water supply, public housing, urban renewal, constructing a metropolitan park along the Willamette River and between two cities, and provision of public kindergartens in the local school system. All these were judged by the researchers to be important in at least one of the communities.

[13]Two randomly and independently selected samples of officers of formally organized voluntary associations and elected or appointed officials of local government were used as informants in identifying leaders. A panel of 20 persons constructed a list of potential leaders. A second panel of 17 indicated the 20 or 25 "most important" persons in "community policy making." The procedures were the same in both communities.

[14]This consistency in results was noted earlier. The reader is referred to footnote 4.

[15]Political stratification is assessed by a person's discussion of local issues with others, his attendance at meetings in which local issues were discussed, and his taking an active part in a local government or community issue. If he indicated that he "once in a while" or "often"

TABLE 1

Comparison of Leaders' and Followers' Attitudes in the Two Communities

Issues	Leaders	Springfield Followers	Differ- ence†	Leaders	Eugene Followers	Differ- ence†
Attraction of industry ...	3.82(44)*	3.49(433)	.33†	3.71(73)	3.44(509)	.27
Annexation	3.17(42)	2.61(400)	.56	3.58(73)	2.74(451)	.84
Parking lots	3.14(44)	2.58(411)	.56	2.55(71)	2.55(470)	.00†
Special education	2.93(44)	2.81(429)	.12	2.86(72)	2.84(502)	.02†
Fluoridation	3.24(42)	2.27(420)	.97	2.86(65)	2.18(492)	.68
Public housing	1.98(44)	2.44(417)	−.46	1.97(70)	2.43(483)	−.46
Urban renewal	3.02(44)	2.22(409)	.80	2.93(73)	2.40(406)	.53
Metropolitan park	3.35(43)	2.75(411)	.60	3.39(72)	2.75(467)	.64
Public kindergartens ...	2.18(44)	1.94(433)	.24	1.80(71)	1.99(496)	−.19

*The values given are the means of the opinion distributions on the specific issue for leaders and for followers. A score of 0 was assigned to "strongly disapprove" responses, 1 to "disapprove," 2 to "undecided," 3 to "approve," and 4 to "strongly approve." The number in parentheses is the number of persons answering.
†Difference is equal to the leaders' mean less that of the followers. Note the sign of the difference.
‡Not statistically significant.

samples include a total of 73 leaders and 526 followers in Eugene, Oregon, and 44 leaders and 448 followers in Springfield, Oregon.

The analysis consists of comparing the mean approval on each issue of various strata and subgroups within both samples. A value of four was assigned to the "strongly approve" response, three to an "approve" response, two to an "undecided" response, one to a "disapprove" re-

discussed local matters, he received a high score. Similarly a "yes" response on taking part or attending meetings was scored high. The three measures were combined into a four-value indicator with the following n's:

	Eugene	Springfield
Low 0	158	159
1	274	236
2	63	32
High 3	21	15

The social stratification index was similarly constructed, using income, education, and occupational status as measures. Twelve years of schooling or more, $5000 or more total family income, and white-collar occupations were taken as indicators of higher social class. The members in each stratum are:

	Eugene	Springfield
Low 0	58	67
1	81	129
2	119	109
High 3	142	63

sponse, and zero to a "strongly disapprove" response. Therefore a mean greater than two indicates approval. Leaders better reflect or attitudinally represent followers if their means are quite close.

Although the public sample is unbiased, the leaders can in no way be viewed as a probability sample of all community leadership. This sample is perhaps best viewed as the universe of all persons with at least a certain level of reputation for influence. Since only the public sample introduces sampling error, one can evaluate a null hypothesis that the public exactly shares the leaders' opinions on the issues. This would of course imply that the differences noted in this study are purely those of sampling variations in the public sample. A comparison of their means showed all but two differences between leaders and followers are statistically significant $(z > 2.00)$. Table 1 indicates this finding.

With samples as large as these, differences as small as .04 are sufficiently great to be not accountable by sampling error. Thus the reader in his interest for meaningful findings should not be lulled into accepting statistical significance as the sole criterion for judging the importance of the findings. He is urged, rather, to consider the consistency of the findings across issues.

THE FINDINGS

The followers generally approve of the nine innovations of issue in the two communities, and disapprove of only one—public kindergartens. Moreover, the two communities' publics vary similarly in the degree of their approval (r Spearman $= +.983$). Surprisingly, although the two communities differ greatly in terms of sociological variables and traditions of municipal programs, they respond quite similarly to these issues. The leaders also show this similarity in responses to the issues (r Spearman $= +.833$). But how do the attitudes of leaders and followers compare?

Given the errors caused by the crudeness of the measuring instrument and simple chance, one might expect differerences between the leaders' and the public's opinions. Of concern here, however, are the consistent or systematic biases among leaders' attitudes. Table 1 shows that differences between the opinions of leaders and followers in both communities vary from very slight in Eugene on the parking lot issue to quite substantial in Springfield on fluoridation. But more notable, leaders express greater approval on all but two issues in Eugene and one in Springfield. The factors that politically stratify individuals into leaders and followers consistently cause leaders to favor the adoption of these programs more so than the followers.

The communities vary in the representativeness of their leadership. With the exception of the annexation issue, Eugene leaders more closely reflect the opinions of their community; even including the strongly deviant annexation issue the average discrepancy between Eugene leaders' opinions and those of Eugene followers is .40 versus .52 for Springfield. Eugene leaders better reflect their community's opinions.

Before exploring possible explanations

of this bias, we must change our focus to the patterns of social class and political stratum attitude differences within these communities. Although the lower class consistently shows itself liberal on national issues, numerous researchers have found conservatives among this class at the community level.[16] The two communities studied support this finding, since higher classes are less approving on only the public housing question.[17] Two other issues—parking lots and the metropolitan park—showed no relationship. If disapproval of new programs or the expansion of old programs indicates conservatism, lower social strata in these communities are more conservative.

Just as individuals within the public can be classed socially, so can they be stratified in terms of their local political involvement. Thus far society has been divided into only two political strata—leaders and followers—but what is the relationship between approval of the programs and the level of political involvement within the public? The relationship is not so clear as with social stratification. On seven of the nine issues in Springfield and six in Eugene, approval increases with increasing political involvement. Once again the public housing issue runs counter to the overall trend, and the other issues show no linear relationship.

In addition to the weak pattern for the politically involved to show greater support for the issue, they are also more intense in their opinions, tending either to approve or disapprove strongly. While 19 percent of the lowest political stratum give these more intense answers, more than 40 percent of the highest political stratum give them. One might expect politically active persons to have developed rather definite opinions on issues facing

---

[16]Key, *op. cit.*, p. 143.

[17]On this relationship and that for political stratification the tables are too cumbersome to include in this article.

TABLE 2

Comparison of the Direction of Social Status Bias among Springfield and
Eugene Leaders on the Basis of a Comparison of Means

	Springfield		Eugene	
Issues	Social Status Level* Best Reflected	Social Status Level* Least Reflected	Social Status Level* Best Reflected	Social Status Level* Least Reflected
Attraction of industry 3	0	1	0	
Annexation 3	0	3	0	
Parking lots 2	0	0	1	
Special education 2	1	2	0	
Fluoridation 3	0	3	1	
Public housing 3	0	3	1	
Urban renewal 3	1	3	2	
Metropolitan park 2	0	0	2	
Public kindergartens 3	1	0	2	

*Social Status is measured on a scale varying from a low value of 0 to a high value of 3.

the community with the certainty of their decision reflected in less qualified responses.

Having thus evaluated the distribution of public opinion, it is possible to determine the social and political stratum bias in leaders' opinions. If they better reflect the opinions of those with higher social status or political involvement, the mean of the leaders' opinions should lie closer to that of higher political and social strata and further from lower strata. Table 2 shows the data for social stratification and Table 3 for political stratification.

Springfield leaders better reflect the opinions of higher social strata. In every case in Springfield, leaders give better expression to a higher social stratum's opinions than that they most poorly reflect; and four issues show a perfect relationship in which they best reflect the opinions of the highest social stratum (3) and least reflect those of the lowest social stratum (0). Eugene leaders, however, show much less of this bias because only six of the nine issues lend any support to it; and only one is the perfect, highest best–lowest poorest pattern. Looking only at the best represented column, Eugene leaders give expression to the lower two socioeconomic strata nearly as frequently

as the higher two strata. Although Springfield leaders evidence a social status bias, the social distinction seems much less useful in understanding the public or leaders in Eugene.

In seeking an explanation of community differences, the reader should recall that the relationship between social status and approval is not so evident among Eugene's public as Springfield's and that leaders in the two communities respond similarly to the issues. These facts would suggest that the weakness of the social status bias among Eugene leaders is not caused by their being different from Springfield leaders but is the result of weak social class positions among the public. In conclusion, one community, Eugene, shows a very weak relationship between class and preference, and little leadership social class bias.

Before focusing on the relationship between political stratification and approval in Table 3, we should again recall that this relationship shows none of the clarity of that for social status. This weak relationship would seem sufficient grounds to question the relevance of speaking of the leaders' bias toward the policy preferences of the more politically active. In part, the argument that such a bias exists fails

TABLE 3

Comparison of the Direction of Leadership Bias toward the Opinions of the
Political Activists on the Basis of a Comparison of Means

| | Springfield | | Eugene | |
| | Political Stratum* Best Reflected | Political Stratum* Least Reflected | Political Stratum* Best Reflected | Political Stratum* Least Reflected |
Issues				
Attraction of industry	3	0	2	0
Annexation	2	0	2	3
Parking lots	1	2	3	0
Special education	1	0	1	3
Fluoridation	3	0	2	3
Public housing	2	0	3	0
Urban renewal	3	1	0	3
Metropolitan park	3	0	3	0
Public kindergartens	2	0	0	2

*Political Stratum is measured on a scale varying from the lowest stratum of political activity with a value of 0 to the highest with a value of 3.

from the lack of a clear political activist's position on many issues.

But the data show that Springfield leaders again more clearly evidence a bias in the hypothesized direction than do Eugene leaders. In eight of the nine issues Springfield leaders better reflect the opinions of a higher political stratum than that they least reflect. They best reflect the opinions of the most active stratum (3) on only four issues.

Surprisingly, Eugene leaders *least* reflect the opinions of the highest political stratum. On five issues they better reflect the opinions of a lower stratum than the stratum they least reflect. They best reflect the opinions of the highest political stratum (3) on three issues and least reflect it on four issues; thus while leaders in Springfield show a bias toward the opinions of the more active, those in Eugene do not.

The leaders' opinions show none of the division into the strong approval and strong disapproval categories that characterize the public's highest political stratum. Thus, although leadership tends to better reflect the opinions of the highest political stratum, those activists who strongly disapprove are unrepresented.

The absence of leadership for those opposing the issues not only indicates the weakness of the bias toward the opinions of the higher political strata but also highlights potential threats to the stability of community leadership and of the community itself.

Although Springfield leaders fail to accurately reflect their community's popular preference, showing both social and political bias, Eugene leaders only weakly manifest the anticipated biases. Unrepresentativeness due to social class bias is not a universal characteristic of American community leaders, and both schools would therefore seem advised to test leadership's attitudinal bias rather than presuming it on the basis of class bias. But the question of the political leaders' attitudinal uniqueness remains unanswered.

DISTINCTIONS AMONG LEADERS

Community studies have discovered leadership to be a diverse group. As noted above, an important distinction among leaders is that between political and economic leaders, since control of a community's economic resources and popular support appear to be the two most important bases of influence.[18]

It is likely, therefore, that the two most common leadership subgroups will belong to the highest political and social strata. As this analysis focuses on the pluralistic claim of the political leaders' distinctiveness, they are identified and labeled "vulnerable." This concept denotes the fact that such leaders are subject to popular rejection—vulnerable to public displeasure.[19] All elected officeholders and candidates for public office are classed as vulnerable. In the few cases where social and economic leaders held public office they are classed as vulnerable because this is the particular attribute to be analyzed.

Economic dominants—a select group of leaders whose influence derives from their control of the major business or financial resources of the community—could also be distinguished as a subgroup within our leadership sample, leaving a group of leaders who do not fall in either category. The implication to community policy, however, of dominance by economically influential individuals is not contingent on their being the "top" economic leaders, because dominance by nonvulnerable leaders opens the possibility of community policy based on unrepresentative attitudes with no available public recourse. All leaders other than the vulnerable are classed as "less vulnerable"; no claim is

[18]Presthus, op. cit., p. 410.

[19]Vulnerability is not necessarily a dichotomized variable, but given our present crude measurements, it is dichotomized in this analysis. Some economic leaders may be more susceptible to public expression of dissatisfaction than others. For example, the public may boycott the merchant, but it can do little against the manager of a large corporation, especially one producing a basic material, such as steel, rather than a finished commodity. Similarly some political leaders may be more insulated, such as by having longer terms of office. Also, subjective assessment of vulnerability by the leaders rather than objective assessment by the researcher may be more important.

made that this category consists entirely of high social status, economic leaders.

The two communities vary greatly in the percentage of vulnerable leaders, since only 7 percent of Springfield's leaders are vulnerable as compared with 29 percent of Eugene's. In addition it should be recalled that Eugene leaders somewhat better reflect their community's opinions. And, finally, the above analysis stressed the absence of social and political bias among Eugene leaders. These relationships might be taken as evidence that a large percentage of vulnerable leaders among a community's leadership will cause its leadership to better represent popular opinion. But in Table 4 an issue-by-issue comparison of vulnerable and less vulnerable leaders in both communities fails to support this conclusion. In both communities vulnerable leaders *less* accurately reflect community opinions than do the less vulnerable leaders. This is true on six of the nine issues in both communities.

The reader is cautioned that the number of vulnerable leaders in Springfield is only three, and thus the findings would change greatly were one leader to switch his opinions. Therefore the findings for Eugene are most important; the consistent pattern in Springfield lends some additional confidence.

Although differentiating between vulnerable and less vulnerable leaders does manifest their attitudinal distinctiveness, for the most part this intraleader difference is small in comparison with leader–follower differences. In only three instances—one issue in Springfield and two in Eugene—are leadership differences sufficient for either the vulnerable or the less vulnerable to be less conservative than the public while the other is more liberal. On these programs the holders of and candidates for public office do not hold opinions that better reflect public opinion; therefore this distinction does not help us

TABLE 4

Comparison of Vulnerable and Less Vulnerable Leaders in the Two Communities on the
Basis of the Differences between Their Means and Those of the Communities

| | Differences from the Public* | | | |
| | Springfield | | Eugene | |
Issues	Vulnerable Leaders	Less Vulnerable Leaders	Vulnerable Leaders	Less Vulnerable Leaders
Attraction of industry	.51(3)†	.31(41)	.32(20)	.25(51)
Annexation	1.06(3)	.52(39)	1.02(20)	.76(51)
Parking lots	.42(3)	.57(41)	−.05(19)	.02(50)
Special education	.19(3)	.11(41)	.16(19)	−.03(51)
Fluoridation	1.07(3)	.97(39)	.88(15)	.62(48)
Public housing	−.44(3)	−.47(41)	−.16(18)	−.56(50)
Urban renewal	1.45(3)	.76(41)	1.03(20)	.33(51)
Metropolitan park	.92(3)	.58(40)	.58(20)	.66(50)
Public kindergartens	−.27(3)	.28(41)	−.09(19)	−.23(50)

*Difference is equal to the leaders' means less that of the public.
†The number in parentheses is the number of leaders answering.

to understand which leaders represent the public most adequately. The value of having publicly vulnerable leaders in terms of the desirability of a more representative leadership seems exaggerated.

CONCLUSIONS

Of course data from medium-sized communities in the Northwest may not reflect what is true throughout the United States or the world. But the lack of a social bias among Eugene leaders and the failure of vulnerable leaders to prove more representative of the public should demonstrate the need to assess this attitudinal dimension prior to judging community leaders. Attributing attitudes to them on the basis of their social class or occupation can lead to great inaccuracies.

Should these findings prove true in other communities, the social stratification

theorists would seem to err in assuming that finding (1) persons of higher socioeconomic status have atypical attitudes and (2) persons of higher socioeconomic status are over represented in community leadership implies that persons of atypical attitudes dominate community politics. Furthermore, the pluralists probably err in assuming that the devices of democracy—especially popular election—function effectively. It would seem there has been too much acceptance of the belief that community dominance by certain types of leaders has unequivocal policy implications. The overall conclusion of this study implies that additional research needs to be completed on leadership selection, leaders' personal opinions, the process of their deciding how they will act in making decisions, and the relationships between the above and their actual behavior.

CONSENSUS AND IDEOLOGY IN AMERICAN POLITICS*

Herbert McClosky

The belief that consensus is a prerequisite of democracy has, since deTocqueville, so often been taken for granted that it is refreshing to find the notion now being challenged. Prothro and Grigg,[1] for example, have questioned whether agreement on "fundamentals" actually exists among the electorate, and have furnished data which indicate that it may not. Dahl,[2] reviewing his study of community decision makers, has inferred that political stability does not depend upon widespread belief in the superiority of Democratic norms and procedures, but only upon their *acceptance*. From the findings turned up by Stouffer,[3] and by Prothro and Grigg, he further conjectures that agreement on

democratic norms is greater among the politically active and aware—the "political stratum" as he calls them—than among the voters in general. V. O. Key,[4] going a step further, suggests that the viability of a democracy may depend less upon popular opinion than upon the activities and values of an "aristocratic" strain whose members are set off from the mass by their political influence, their attention to public affairs, and their active role as society's policymakers. "If so, any assessment of the vitality of a democratic system should rest on an examination of the outlook, the sense of purpose, and the beliefs of this sector of society."

Writers who hold consensus to be necessary to a free society have commonly failed to define it precisely or to specify what it must include. Even Tocqueville[5] does not go deeply enough into the matter

---

*Reprinted from the *American Political Science Review,* Vol. LVIII (June 1964) pp. 361–82. Copyright 1964, American Political Science Association.

This is a revised version of a paper initially prepared for delivery at the Annual Meeting of the American Political Science Association, Washington, D.C., September 1962. The research on which it is based has been processed and analyzed through the Survey Research Center, University of California, Berkeley. Major support for the research was made available by the Social Science Research Council; supplementary support was given by the Rockefeller Foundation and the Institute of Social Sciences, University of California. I am indebted to my research assistant, Beryl L. Crowe, for assistance in the preparation of the research materials. This article may be referred to as number A22 in the Survey Research Center's publication series.

[1]James W. Prothro and C. W. Grigg, "Fundamental Principles of Democracy: Bases of Agreement and Disagreement," *Journal of Politics,* Vol. 22 (Spring 1960), pp. 276–94.

[2]Robert A. Dahl, *Who Governs?* (New Haven, 1961), ch. 28.

[3]Samuel A. Stouffer, *Communism, Conformity, and Civil Liberties* (New York, 1955).

---

[4]V. O. Key, "Public Opinion and the Decay of Democracy," *Virginia Q. Rev.,* Vol. XXXVII (Autumn 1961), pp. 481–94. See also David B. Truman, "The American System in Crisis," *Political Science Quarterly,* Vol. LXXIV (Dec. 1959), pp. 481–97. John Plamenatz, "Cultural Prerequisites to a Successfully Functioning Democracy: a Symposium," *American Political Science Review,* Vol. 50 (March 1956), p. 123.

[5]Alexis de Tocqueville, *Democracy in America* (ed. Phillips Bradley, New York, 1945), II, p. 8; I, pp. 392, 322. The difficulty of specifying the values which underly democracy, and on which consensus is presumed to be required, is illustrated in the exchange between Ernest S. Griffith, John Plamenatz, and J. Roland Pennock, cited above, pp. 101–37. The problem of certifying the "fundamentals" of democratic consensus is directly discussed by Pennock, pp. 132–33. See also Peter Bachrach, "Elite Consensus and Democracy," *Journal of Politics,* Vol. 24 (August 1962), pp. 449–52.

to satisfy these needs. He tells us that a society can exist and, *a fortiori,* prosper only when "the minds of all the citizens [are] rallied and held together by certain predominant ideas; . . . when a great number of men consider a great number of things from the same aspect, when they hold the same opinions upon many subjects, and when the same occurrences suggest the same thoughts and impressions to their minds"—and he follows this pronouncement with a list of general principles he believes Americans hold in common. Elsewhere, he speaks of the "customs" of the American nation (its "habits, opinions, usages, and beliefs") as "the peculiar cause which renders that people able to support a democratic government." But nowhere does he set forth explicitly the nature of the agreement upon which a democratic society presumably depends.

Later commentators have not clarified matters much. Some, like A. Lawrence Lowell,[6] have avoided Tocqueville's emphasis upon shared ideas, customs, and opinions in favor of the less demanding view that popular government requires agreement mainly "in regard to the legitimate character of the ruling authority and its right to decide the questions that arise." Consensus, in this view, becomes merely a synonym for legitimacy. Others speak of consensus as a sense of solidarity or social cohesion arising from a common ethos or heritage, which unites men into a community.[7] Political scientists have most frequently employed the term to designate a state of agreement about the "fundamental values" or "rules of the game" con-

sidered essential for constitutional government. Rarely, however, have writers on consensus attempted to state what the fundamentals must include, how extensive the agreement must be, and *who* must agree. Is agreement required among all men or only among certain of them? Among the entire electorate or only those who actively participate in public affairs? Is the same type of consensus essential for all democracies at all times, or is a firmer and more sweeping consensus needed for periods of crisis than for periods of calm, for newer, developing democracies than for older stable ones?

While certain of these questions are beyond the scope of this paper (no one, in any event, has done the systematic historical and comparative research needed to answer them satisfactorily), something might be learned about the relation of ideological consensus to democracy by investigating the subject in at least one major democracy, the United States. In the present paper I wish to explore further some of the questions raised by the writers I have cited and to present research findings on several hypotheses relating to those questions.

I. HYPOTHESES AND DEFINITIONS

We expected the data to furnish support for the following hypotheses, among others:

That the American electorate is often divided on "fundamental" democratic values and procedural "rules of the game" and that its understanding of politics and of political ideas is in any event too rudimentary at present to speak of ideological "consensus" among its members.

That, as Prothro and Grigg report for their samples, the electorate exhibits greater support for general, abstract statements of democratic belief than for their specific applications.

That the constituent ideas of American democratic ideology are principally held by

[6] A. L. Lowell, *Public Opinion and Popular Government* (New York, 1926), p. 9.

[7] *Cf.,* for example, Louis Wirth, *Community Life and Social Policy* (Chicago, 1956), pp. 201–3, 381–82. For a critique of "consensus theory" and the several definitions of consensus see Irving L. Horowitz, "Consensus, Conflict, and Cooperation: a Sociological Inventory," *Social Forces,* Vol. 41 (Dec. 1962), pp. 177–88.

the more "articulate" segments of the population, including the political influentials; and that people in these ranks will exhibit a more meaningful and far reaching consensus on democratic and constitutional values than will the general population.

That consensus is far from perfect even among the articulate classes, and will be evidenced on political questions more than on economic ones, on procedural rights more than on public policies, and on freedom more than equality.

That whatever increases the level of political articulateness—education, S.E.S., urban residence, intellectuality, political activity, etc.—strengthens consensus and support for American political ideology and institutions.

Whether a word like ideology can properly be employed in the American context depends, in part, on which of its many connotations one chooses to emphasize. Agreement on the meaning of the term is far from universal, but a tendency can be discerned among contemporary writers to regard ideologies as *systems* of belief that are elaborate, integrated, and coherent, that justify the exercise of power, explain and judge historical events, identify political right and wrong, set forth the interconnections (causal and moral) between politics and other spheres of activity, and furnish guides for action.[8] While liberal democracy does not fulfill perfectly the terms of this definition, it comes close enough, in my opinion, to be considered an ideology.[9] The elements of liberal dem-

ocratic thought are not nearly so vague as they are sometimes made out to be, and their coalescence into a single body of belief is by no means fortuitous. American democratic "ideology" possesses an elaborately defined theory, a body of interrelated assumptions, axioms, and principles, and a set of ideals that serve as guides for action. Its tenets, postulates, sentiments, and values inspired the great revolutions of the seventeenth and eighteenth centuries, and have been repeatedly and explicitly set forth in fundamental documents, such as the Constitution, the Declaration, and the Federalist Papers. They have been restated with remarkable unanimity in the messages of Presidents, in political speeches, in the pronouncements of judges and constitutional commentators, and in the writings of political theorists, historians, and publicists. They are so familiar that we are likely to see them not as a coherent union of ideas and principles embodying a well-defined political tendency, but as a miscellany of slogans and noble sentiments to be trotted out on ceremonial occasions.

Although scholars or Supreme Court justices might argue over fine points of interpretation, they would uniformly recognize as elements of American democratic ideology such concepts as consent, accountability, limited or constitutional government, representation, majority rule, minority rights, the principle of political opposition, freedom of thought, speech, press, and assembly, equality of opportunity, religious toleration, equality before the law, the rights of juridical defense, and individual self-determination over a broad range of personal affairs. How widely such elements of American liberal democracy are approved, by whom and with what measure of understanding, is another question—indeed, it is the central question to be addressed in this paper. But that they form an integrated body of ideas which has become part of the

---

[8] *Cf.* Daniel Bell, *The End of Ideology* (Glencoe, 1960), pp. 369–75; Edward Shils, "Ideology and Civility: on the Politics of the Intellectual," *Sewanee Review*, Vol. 66 (Summer 1958), pp. 450–51; Louis Wirth, *op. cit.*, pp. 202–3.

[9] A persuasive case for considering liberal democracy as an ideology is made by Bernard Williams, "Democracy and Ideology," *Political Science Quarterly*, Vol. 32 (October–December 1961), pp. 374–84. The nature of ideology in America and some of the other questions addressed in the present paper are discussed by Robert G. McCloskey, "The American Ideology," in Marian D. Irish (ed.), *Continuing Crisis in American Politics* (Englewood Cliffs, N.J., 1963), pp. 10–25.

American inheritance seems scarcely open to debate.[10]

The term consensus will be employed in this paper to designate a state of agreement concerning the aforementioned values. It has principally to do with shared beliefs and not with feelings of solidarity, the willingness to live together, to obey the laws, or to accept the existing government as legitimate. Nor does it refer to an abstract or universal state of mind, but to a measurable state of concurrence around values that can be specified. Consensus exists in degree and can be expressed in quantitative form. No one, of course, can say how close one must come to unanimity before consensus is achieved, for the cutting point, as with any continuous variable, is arbitrary. Still, the term in ordinary usage has been reserved for fairly substantial measures of correspondence, and we shall take as a minimal requirement for consensus a level of agreement reaching 75 per cent. This figure, while also arbitrary, recommends itself by being realistically modest (falling as it does midway between a bare majority and unanimity), and by having been designated in this country and elsewhere as the extraordinary majority required for certain constitutional purposes.

Since I shall in subsequent pages frequently (and interchangeably) employ such terms as the "articulate minority," the "political class," the "political elite," the "political influentials," and the "politi-

cal stratum," I should also clarify what they are intended to signify. I mean them to refer to those people who occupy themselves with public affairs to an unusual degree, such as government officials, elected office holders, active party members, publicists, officers of voluntary associations, and opinion leaders. The terms do not apply to any definable social class in the usual sense, nor to a particular status group or profession. Although the people they designate can be distinguished from other citizens by their activity and concerns, they are in no sense a community, they do not act as a body, and they do not necessarily possess identical or even harmonious interests. "Articulates" or "influentials" can be found scattered throughout the society, at all income levels, in all classes, occupations, ethnic groups, and communities, although some segments of the population will doubtless yield a higher proportion of them than others. I scarcely need to add that the line between the "articulates" and the rest of the population cannot always be sharply drawn, for the qualities that distinguish them vary in form and degree and no single criterion of classification will satisfy every contingency.

The data for the present inquiry have been taken from a national study of political actives and supporters carried out in 1957–58. I have in a previous paper described the procedures of that study in some detail,[11] and will not trouble to repeat that description here. Perhaps it will suffice for present purposes merely to note the following: national surveys were carried out on two separate samples, the first a sample of over 3,000 political "actives" or "leaders" drawn from the delegates and alternates who had attended the Democratic and Republican conventions of

---

[10]See Gunnar Myrdal, *An American Dilemma: The Negro Problem and American Democracy* (New York, 1944), ch. 1. For a comprehensive review of the American value system and evidence concerning its stability over time, see Clyde Kluckhohn, "Have There Been Discernible Shifts in American Values during the Past Generation?" in E. E. Morison (ed.), *The American Style: Essays in Value and Performance* (New York, 1958), pp. 145–217. Kluckhohn concludes (p. 152) that despite some changes, the American value system has been "remarkably stable" since the 18th century and remains "highly influential in the life of the United States."

[11]Herbert McClosky, Paul J. Hoffmann, and Rosemary O'Hara, "Issue Conflict and Consensus Among Party Leaders and Followers," *American Political Science Review*, Vol. LIV (June 1960), pp. 406–27.

1956; the second a representative national sample of approximately 1,500 adults in the general population drawn by the American Institute of Public Opinion (Gallup Poll). Gallup interviewers also delivered and introduced the questionnaire to all respondents, discussed its contents with them, and furnished both oral and written instructions for its self-administration and completion. (For sample characteristics, see Appendix B.)

The party actives may be considered an especially pure sample of the "political stratum," for every person in the sample has marked himself off from the average citizen by his greater political involvement. Although the general population sample may be regarded as a sample of "inarticulates," to be compared with the sample of leaders, there are within it, of course, many persons who by virtue of education, profession, organizational activities, etc. can be classified as "articulates." We shall for certain purposes consider them in this light in order to provide further tests for our hypotheses.

Both samples received the same questionnaire—a lengthy instrument containing questions on personal background, political experience, values, attitudes, opinions, political and economic orientation, party outlooks, and personality characteristics. Many of the questions were direct inquiries in the standard form, but most were single sentence "items" with which the respondent was compelled to express his agreement or disagreement. While each of these items can stand alone and be regarded in its own right as an indicator of a person's opinions or attitudes, each of them is simultaneously an integral element of one of the 47 "scales" that was expressly fashioned to afford a more refined and reliable assessment of the attitude and personality predispositions of every respondent. Each of the scales (averaging approximately nine items) has been independently validated either by empirical validation procedures employ-

ing appropriate criterion groups, or by a modified Guttman reproducibility procedure (supplemented, in some instances, by a "face validity" procedure utilizing item ratings by experts).

Data on the *scale* scores are presented in Table 4 and are to be distinguishable from the "percentage agree" scores for *individual items* presented in the remaining tables.

FINDINGS

"Rules of the Game" and Democratic values

Although the so-called "rules of the game" are often separated from other democratic values, the distinction is to some extent arbitrary. One might, for example, reasonably regard as "rules of the game" many of the norms governing free speech, press, social and political equality, political toleration, and the enforcement of justice. For convenience, nevertheless, we shall treat separately those responses that stand out from the general body of democratic attitudes by their particular emphasis upon fair play, respect for legal procedures, and consideration for the rights of others. A sample of items expressing these values is presented in Table 1.

The responses to these items show plainly that while a majority of the electorate support the "rules of the game," approval of such values is significantly greater and more uniform among the influentials. The latter have achieved consensus (as we have defined it) on eight of the twelve items and near consensus on three of the remaining four items. The electorate, by contrast, does not meet the criterion for consensus on a single item.

Although the *scales* (as distinguished from individual *items*) cannot appropriately be used to measure *consensus*, comparison of the scores on those scales which most nearly embody the "rules of the game" furnishes additional evidence that

TABLE 1

Political Influentials vs. the Electorate: Response to Items Expressing "Rules of the Game"*

Items	Political Influentials (N = 3020)	General Electorate (N = 1484)
	% Agree	
There are times when it almost seems better for the people to take the law into their own hands rather than wait for the machinery of government to act.	13.3	26.9
The majority has the right to abolish minorities if it wants to.	6.8	28.4
We might as well make up our minds that in order to make the world better, a lot of innocent people will have to suffer.	27.2	41.6
If congressional committees stuck strictly to the rules and gave every witness his rights, they would never succeed in exposing the many dangerous subversives they have turned up.	24.7	47.4
I don't mind a politician's methods if he manages to get the right things done.	25.6	42.4
Almost any unfairness or brutality may have to be justified when some great purpose is being carried out.	13.3	32.8
Politicians have to cut a few corners if they are going to get anywhere.	29.4	43.2
People ought to be allowed to vote even if they can't do so intelligently.	65.6	47.6
To bring about great changes for the benefit of mankind often requires cruelty and even ruthlessness.	19.4	31.3
Very few politicians have clean records, so why get excited about the mudslinging that sometimes goes on?	14.8	38.1
It is all right to get around the law if you don't actually break it.	21.2	30.2
The true American way of life is disappearing so fast that we may have to use force to save it.	12.8	34.6

*Since respondents were forced to make a choice on each item, the number of omitted or "don't know" responses was, on the average, fewer than one percent, and thus has little influence on the direction or magnitude of the results reported in this and subsequent tables.

the political class responds to such norms more favorably than does the electorate. The proportion scoring high[12] on a scale of "faith in direct action" (a scale measuring the inclination to take the law into one's own hands) is 26.1 per cent for the

active political minority and 42.5 per cent for the general population. On a scale assessing the willingness to flout the rules of political integrity, the proportions scoring high are 12.2 per cent and 30.6 per cent respectively. On "totalitarianism," a scale measuring the readiness to subordinate the rights of others to the pursuit of some collective political purpose, only 9.7 per cent of the political actives score high compared with 33.8 per cent of the general population.

These and other results which could be cited support the claim advanced by ear-

---

[12]"High" refers to a score made by the upper third of the popular distribution on the scale in question. For example, in the case of the "political indulgence" scale approximately one-third (actually 30.6%) received scores of five or above. Hence, anyone making a score of five or above on this scale is considered to have scored high on "political indulgence." "Low" refers to scores made by the lower third of the distribution.

TABLE 2

Political Influentials vs. the Electorate: Responses to Items Expressing
Support for General Statements of Free Speech and Opinion

Items	Political Influentials $(N = 3020)$	General Electorate $(N = 1484)$
	% Agree	
People who hate our way of life should still have a chance to talk and be heard.	86.9	81.8
No matter what a person's political beliefs are, he is entitled to the same legal rights and protections as anyone else.	96.4	94.3
I believe in free speech for all no matter what their views might be..	89.4	88.9
Nobody has a right to tell another person what he should and should not read.	81.4	80.7
You can't really be sure whether an opinion is true or not unless people are free to argue against it.	94.9	90.8
Unless there is freedom for many points of view to be presented, there is little chance that the truth can ever be known.	90.6	85.2
I would not trust any person or group to decide what opinions can be freely expressed and what must be silenced.	79.1	64.6
Freedom of conscience should mean freedom to be an atheist as well as freedom to worship in the church of one's choice.	87.8	77.0

lier investigators like Prothro and Grigg, and Hyman and Sheatsley,[13] that a large proportion of the electorate has failed to grasp certain of the underlying ideas and principles on which the American political system rests. Endorsement of these ideas is not unanimous among the political elite either, but is in every instance greater than that exhibited by the masses.

The picture changes somewhat when we turn from "rules of the game" to items which in a broad, general way express belief in freedom of speech and opinion. As can be seen from Table 2, support for these values is remarkably high for both samples. Both groups, in fact, respond so overwhelmingly to abstract statements about freedom that one is tempted to conclude that for these values, at least, a far-

reaching consensus has been achieved.[14] These results become even more striking when we consider that the items in the table are not mere clichés but statements which in some instances closely paraphrase the arguments developed in Mill's essay, On Liberty. We cannot, therefore, dismiss them as mere responses to familiar, abstract sentiments which commit the respondent to nothing in particular.

Still, as can readily be discerned from the items in Table 3, previous investigators have been partially correct, at least, in observing that the principles of freedom and democracy are less widely and enthusiastically favored when they are confronted in their specific, or applied, forms.[15] As Dahl remarks, it is a "common tendency of mankind . . . to qualify uni-

[13]Prothro and Grigg, loc. cit.; Herbert Hyman and Paul B. Sheatsley, "The Current Status of American Public Opinion," in Daniel Katz et al. (eds.), Public Opinion and Propaganda (New York, 1954), pp. 33–48.

[14]Cf. Robert Lane's report on his "Eastport" sample, in Political Ideology (New York, 1962), pp. 461–62.
[15]See Hyman and Sheatsley, op. cit., pp. 40–42; Prothro and Grigg, op. cit.

TABLE 3

Political Influentials vs. the Electorate: Response to Items Expressing
Support for Specific Applications of Free Speech and Procedural Rights

Items	Political Influentials ($N = 3020$)	General Electorate ($N = 1484$)
	% Agree	
Freedom does not give anyone the right to teach foreign ideas in our schools.	45.5	56.7
A man oughtn't to be allowed to speak if he doesn't know what he's talking about.	17.3	36.7
A book that contains wrong political views cannot be a good book and does not deserve to be published.	17.9	50.3
When the country is in great danger we may have to force people to testify against themselves even if it violates their rights.	28.5	36.3
No matter what crime a person is accused of, he should never be convicted unless he has been given the right to face and question his accusers.	90.1	88.1
If a person is convicted of a crime by illegal evidence, he should be set free and the evidence thrown out of court.	79.6	66.1
If someone is suspected of treason or other serious crimes, he shouldn't be entitled to be let out on bail.	33.3	68.9
Any person who hides behind the laws when he is questioned about his activities doesn't deserve much consideration.	55.9	75.7
In dealing with dangerous enemies like the Communists, we can't afford to depend on the courts, the laws and their slow and unreliable methods.	7.4	25.5

versals in application while leaving them intact in rhetoric."[16] This observation, of course, also holds for the political articulates, but to a lesser degree. Not only do they exhibit stronger support for democratic values than does the electorate, but they are also more consistent in applying the general principle to the specific instance.[17] The average citizen has greater difficulty appreciating the importance of certain procedural or juridical rights, especially when he believes the country's internal security is at stake.

---

[16]Robert A. Dahl. *loc. cit.* For data on the failure of some people to perceive the relevance of democratic principles for concrete situations see G. D. Wiebe, "The Army-McCarthy Hearings and the Public Conscience," *Public Opinion Quarterly*, Vol. XXII (Winter 1958–59), pp. 490–502.

[17]See also Stouffer, *op. cit.*, ch. 2.

Findings which underscore and amplify these conclusions are yielded by a comparison of the scale scores. The data presented in Table 4 confirm that the influentials not only register higher scores on all the pro-democratic scales (faith in freedom, faith in democracy, procedural rights, tolerance), but are more likely to reject antidemocratic sentiments as well. Although they are themselves an elite of a sort, they display greater faith in the capacity of the mass of men to govern themselves, they believe more firmly in political equality, and they more often disdain the "extreme" beliefs embodied in the Right Wing, Left Wing, totalitarian, elitist, and authoritarian scales. Their repudiation of anti-democratic attitudes is by no means unanimous either, but their responses are more uniformly democratic

TABLE 4

Political Influentials vs. the Electorate: Percentages Scoring High and
Low on Democratic and Anti-Democratic Attitude Scales*

Scale	Political Influentials ($N = 3020$)	General Electorate ($N = 1484$)	Scale	Political Influentials ($N = 3020$)	General Electorate ($N = 1484$)
	(%s down)			(%s down)	
Faith in democracy			Elitism		
% High* 40.1		18.5	% High 22.8		38.7
% Low 14.4		29.7	% Low 41.0		22.4
Procedural rights			Totalitarianism		
% High 58.1		24.1	% High 9.7		33.8
% Low 12.3		31.3	% Low 60.1		28.4
Tolerance			Right wing		
% High 61.3		43.1	% High 17.5		33.1
% Low 16.4		33.2	% Low 45.3		28.9
Faith in freedom			Left wing		
% High 63.0		48.4	% High 6.7		27.8
% Low 17.1		28.4	% Low 68.7		39.3
Ethnocentrism			California F-scale		
% High 27.5		36.5	% High 14.7		33.5
% Low 46.9		36.3	% Low 48.0		23.5

*For explanation of % High and Low see footnote 12. The middle group has been omitted from this table. Differences between the influentials and the electorate on all the scales in this table are, by Kolmogorov-Smirnov and chi-square tests, statistically significant at or beyond the .01 percent level of significance.

than are those expressed by the electorate.

Equalitarian Values

If Americans concur most strongly about liberty in the abstract, they disagree most strongly about equality. Examples of equalitarian values are presented in Table 5. Both the political stratum and the public divide sharply on these values, a finding which holds for political, as well as for social and economic equality. Both are torn not only on the empirical question of whether men are *in fact* equal but also on the normative issue of whether they should be *regarded* as equal. Neither comes close to achieving consensus on such questions as the ability of the people to rule themselves, to know their best interests in the long run, to understand the issues, or to pick their own leaders wisely. Support for these equalitarian features of "popular" democracy, however, is greater among the elite than among the masses.

The reverse is true for the values of economic equality. Among the political stratum, indeed, the weight of opinion is against equality—a result strongly though not exclusively influenced by the pronounced economic conservatism of the Republican leaders in the sample. Support for economic equality is only slightly greater among the electorate. The pattern, furthermore, is extremely spotty, with some policies strongly favored and others as strongly rejected. Thus approval is widespread for public policies (such as social security) that are designed to overcome gross inequalities, but is equally strong for certain features of economic life that promote inequality, such as private enterprise, economic competition, and unlimited pursuit of profit.[18] On social and ethnic equality, both samples are deeply split.

[18] These inferences are drawn not only from the few items presented in Table 5, but from data previously reported by H. McClosky, P. J.
(*Footnote continued on next page*)

TABLE 5

Political Influentials vs. the Electorate: Responses to Items
Expressing Belief in Equality

Items	Political Influentials ($N = 3020$)	General Electorate ($N = 1484$)
	% Agree	
Political equality		
The main trouble with democracy is that most people don't really know what's best for them.	40.8	58.0
Few people really know what is in their own best interest in the long run.	42.6	61.1
"Issues" and "arguments" are beyond the understanding of most voters.	37.5	62.3
Most people don't have enough sense to pick their own leaders wisely.	28.0	47.8
It will always be necessary to have a few strong, able people actually running everything.	42.5	56.2
Social and ethnic equality		
We have to teach children that all men are created equal but almost everyone knows that some are better than others.	54.7	58.3
Just as is true of fine race horses, some breeds of people are just naturally better than others.	46.0	46.3
Regardless of what some people say, there are certain races in the world that just won't mix with Americans.	37.2	50.4
When it comes to the things that count most, all races are certainly not equal.	45.3	49.0
The trouble with letting certain minority groups into a nice neighborhood is that they gradually give it their own atmosphere.	49.8	57.7
Economic equality		
Labor does not get its fair share of what it produces.	20.8	44.8
Every person should have a good house, even if the government has to build it for him.	14.9	28.2
I think the government should give a person work if he can't find another job.	23.5	47.3
The government ought to make sure that everyone has a good standard of living.	34.4	55.9
There will always be poverty, so people might as well get used to the idea.	40.4	59.4

In short, both the public and its leaders are uncertain and ambivalent about equality. The reason, I suspect, lies partly in

Hoffmann, and R. O'Hara, *op. cit.*, p. 413; and from the responses to dozens of items in the present study that express attitudes and opinions toward the private enterprise system, taxes, private property, profits, socialism, etc. On the whole, little enthusiasm is registered among either the elite or the masses for a drastic revision of the economy or a major redistribution of the wealth.

the fact that the egalitarian aspects of democratic theory have been less adequately thought through than other aspects, and partly in the complications connected with the concept itself. One such complication arises from the historical association of democracy with capitalism, a commingling of egalitarian and inegalitarian elements that has never been (and perhaps never can be) perfectly reconciled. Another complication lies in the diffuse and variegated nature of the concept, a result of its application to at least four separate domains: political (*e.g.,* universal suffrage), legal (*e.g.,* equality before the law), economic (*e.g.,* equal distribution of property or opportunity), and moral (*e.g.,* every man's right to be treated as an end and not as a means). Accompanying these are the confusions which result from the common failure to distinguish equality as a *fact* from equality as a *norm.* ("All men are created equal," for example, is taken by some as an empirical statement, by others as a normative one.) Still other complications arise from the differential rewards and opportunities inevitable in any complex society, from the differences in the initial endowment individuals bring into the world, and from the symbolism and fears that so often attend the division of men into ethnic compartments. All these confound the effort to develop a satisfactory theory of democratic equality, and further serve to frustrate the realization of consensus around egalitarian values.

Faith in the Political System

Another perspective on the state of ideology and consensus in America may be obtained by observing how people respond to the political system. How do Americans feel about the political and social institutions by which they are ruled? Do they perceive the system as one they can reach and influence? Are they satisfied that it will govern justly and for the common good?

Sample items relating to these questions are contained in Tables 6 and 7. An assessment of the other responses, however, is confounded by an ambivalence in our tradition. Few will question that Americans are patriotic and loyal, that they accept the political system as legitimate, and that they are inclined to shy away from radical or extreme movements which aim

to alter or to overthrow the constitutional foundations of the system. Yet Americans are also presumed to have a longstanding suspicion of government—a state of mind which some historians trace back to the depredations of George III and to the habits of self-reliance forced upon our ancestors by frontier life.[19]

It is possible in the present context to determine the extent to which the scores contained in these tables signify genuine frustration and political disillusionment and the extent to which they represent familiar and largely ritualistic responses. It is plain, however, that Americans are, verbally at least, both confused and divided in their reactions to the political system. Many feel themselves hopelessly ineffectual politically. Approximately half perceive government and politicians as remote, inaccessible, and largely unresponsive to the electorate's needs or opinions.[20] About the same proportion regard politics as squalid and seamy, as an activity in which the participants habitually practice deception, expediency and self-aggrandizement. Yet by a curious inconsistency which so frequently frustrates the investigator searching the data for regularities, 89.6 per cent express confidence that the government will do what is right. However strongly they mistrust the men and the procedures through which public policies are fashioned, most voters seem not to be greatly dissatisfied with the outcome. They may be cynical about the

[19]Evidence is accumulating that the distrust of politics, often thought to be peculiar to the United States, is also found in many other countries. In fact, Gabriel Almond and Sidney Verba report in their cross-cultural study of citizenship that political interest is higher in the United States than it is in the four other countries they studied (United Kingdom, West Germany, Italy, and Mexico); and that Americans, if anything, are less negative toward politics than are the citizens of the other countries. See *The Civic Culture* (1963), chs. III–IV.

[20]See also the Michigan data on voters' sense of "political efficacy" in Angus Campbell, Gerald Gurin, and Warren E. Miller, *The Voter Decides* (Evanston, 1954), pp. 187–94.

TABLE 6

Political Influentials vs. the Electorate: Responses to Items
Expressing Cynicism toward Government and Politics

Items	Political Influentials (N = 3020)	General Electorate (N = 1484)
	% Agree	
Most politicians are looking out for themselves above all else.	36.3	54.3
Both major parties in this country are controlled by the wealthy and are run for their benefit.	7.9	32.1
Many politicians are bought off by some private interest.	43.0	65.3
I avoid dealing with public officials as much as I can.	7.8	39.3
Most politicians can be trusted to do what they think is best for the country.	77.1	58.9
I usually have confidence that the government will do what is right.	81.6	89.6
The people who really "run" the country do not even get known to the voters.	40.2	60.5
The laws of this country are supposed to benefit all of us equally, but the fact is that they're almost all "rich-man's laws."	8.4	33.3
No matter what the people think, a few people will always run things anyway.	30.0	53.8
Most politicians don't seem to me to really mean what they say. . .	24.7	55.1
There is practically no connection between what a politician says and what he will do once he gets elected.	21.4	54.0
A poor man doesn't have the chance he deserves in the law courts. . .	20.3	42.9
Most political parties care only about winning elections and nothing more.	28.3	46.2
All politics is controlled by political bosses.	15.6	45.9

operation of the political system, but they do not question its legitimacy.[21]

Although the influentials do not unanimously endorse American political practices either, they are substantially less suspicious and cynical than is the electorate. Indeed, they have achieved consensus or come close to achieving it on most of the items in the two tables. These results are further borne out by the *scale* scores: only 10.1 per cent of the articulates score "high" on the political cynicism scale, as contrasted with 31.3 per cent of

the general population; on political suspiciousness the scores are 9.0 per cent high versus 26.7 per cent; on pessimism they are 12.6 per cent versus 26.7 per cent; and on sense of political futility the influentials score (understandably enough) only 3.1 per cent high compared with 30.2 per cent high for the electorate. The active minority also exhibits a stronger sense of social responsibility than the people do (their respective percentage high scores are 40.7 per cent versus 25.8 per cent) and, as previously noted, they are less tolerant of infractions against ethical political procedures.

Should we not, however, have expected

---

[21]For other data on ambivalent attitudes toward government, see Hyman and Sheatsley, *op. cit.*

TABLE 7

Political Influentials vs. the Electorate: Responses to Items
Expressing a Sense of Political Futility

Items	Political Influentials $(N = 3020)$	General Electorate $(N = 1484)$
	% Agree	
It's no use worrying my head about public affairs; I can't do anything about them anyhow.	2.3	20.5
The people who really "run" the country do not even get known to the voters.	40.2	60.5
I feel that my political leaders hardly care what people like myself think or want.	10.9	39.0
Nothing I ever do seems to have any effect upon what happens in politics.	8.4	61.5
Political parties are so big that the average member hasn't got much to say about what goes on.	37.8	67.5
There doesn't seem to be much connection between what I want and what my representative does.	24.0	43.7
It seems to me that whoever you vote for, things go on pretty much the same.	21.1	51.3

these results as a matter of course, considering that the influentials were selected for study precisely because of their political experience and involvement? Possibly, except that similar (though less pronounced) differences emerge when we distinguish articulates from inarticulates by criteria other than actual political activity. Voters, for example, who have been to college, attained high status occupations or professions, or developed strong intellectual interests are, by a significant margin, also likely to possess more affirmative attitudes toward government, politics, and politicians.[22] They display a greater sense of social and political responsibility, are more optimistic, and are less indulgent of shoddy political methods. The political actives who are highly educated exhibit

these attitudes even more strongly. Familiarity, it seems, far from breeding contempt, greatly increases respect, hope and support for the nation's political institutions and practices. Inferential support for this generalization is available from the findings turned up by Almond and Verba in all five countries they investigated in their comparative study of citizenship.[23]

Coherence and Consistency of Attitudes

So far we have explored the question of ideology and consensus mainly from the point of view of agreement on particular values. This, however, is a minimum criterion. Before one can say that a class or

[22]Similar findings are reported by Robert E. Agger, Marshall N. Goldstein and Stanley A. Pearl, "Political Cynicism: Measurement and Meaning," *Journal of Politics,* Vol. 23 (1961), pp. 477–506.

[23]Almond and Verba, *op. cit.,* ch. IV. One can, of course, imagine circumstances, such as political disorganization or revolutionary crises, in which the generalization would not hold—in which, indeed, the political elite might lead the struggle *against* the existing governing institutions. I am speaking, in the present context, of politics under "normal" conditions in established democracies.

group or nation has achieved consensus around an ideology, one should be satisfied that they understand its values in a coherent and correct way. It is a poor consensus in which generalities and slogans are merely echoed with little appreciation of their significance. It seemed appropriate, therefore, to compare the influentials and voters concerning their information and understanding, the relation of their opinions to their party preferences, and the consistency of their views on public affairs.

To begin with, the influentials are more likely than the electorate to have opinions on public questions. For example, 28 per cent of the public are unable (though a few may only be *unwilling*) to classify themselves as liberal, middle of the road, or conservative; while only 1.1 per cent of the articulates fail to make this classification. Forty-eight per cent of the voters, compared to 15 per cent of the actives, do not know in which direction they would turn if the parties were reorganized to reflect ideological differences more clearly. Forty-five per cent of the electorate but only 10.2 per cent of the influentials cannot name any issue that divides the parties. By ratios of approximately three or four to one the electorate is less likely to know which level of government they are mainly interested in, whether they prefer their party to control Congress or the presidency, whether they believe in party discipline and of what type, whether control of the parties should rest at the national or local levels, and so on.

As these and other of our findings suggest, active political involvement heightens one's sense of intellectual order and commitment. This inference is further supported by the data on partisanship. One example may suffice to illustrate the point: when the articulates and the electorate are ranged on a scale assessing their orientation toward 14 current liberal–conservative issues, the political actives

tend to bunch up at the extreme ends of the distribution (the Democratic actives at the "liberal" end, the Republican actives at the "conservative" end), while the rank-and-file supporters of both parties fall more frequently into the middle or conflicted category. The political influentials, in short, display issue orientations that are more partisan and more consistent with their party preferences.

Essentially the same effect is achieved among the general population by increases in education, economic status, or other factors that raise the level of articulateness. College-educated Democrats and Republicans, for example, disagree more sharply on issues than grade school Democrats and Republicans do. Partisan differences are greater between the informed than between the uninformed, between the upper-class supporters of the two parties than between the lower-class supporters, between the "intellectuals" in both parties than between those who rank low on "intellectuality."

Increases in political knowledge or involvement, hence, cause men not so much to waver as to choose sides and to identify more unswervingly with one political tendency or its opposite. Inarticulateness and distance from the sources of political decision increase intellectual uncertainty and evoke political responses that are random rather than systematic. We are thus led by the findings to a pair of conclusions that may at first appear contradictory but that in reality are not: the political class is more united than the electorate on fundamental political values but divides more sharply by party affiliation on the issues which separate the two parties.[24] Both facts—the greater consensus in the one instance and the sharper cleavage in the other—testify to its superior ideological sophistication.

---

[24]See also V. O. Key, *Public Opinion and Democracy* (New York, 1961), pp. 51–52.

Not only are the articulates more partisan, but they are also more consistent in their views. Their responses to a wide range of political stimuli are to a greater extent intellectually patterned and informed. They are, for example, better able to name reference groups that correspond with their party affiliation and doctrinal orientation: approximately twice as many active Democrats as ordinary Democratic voters name liberal, Democratically oriented organizations as groups they would seek advice from (e.g., trade unions, Farmers Union, etc.); and by equally large or larger ratios they *reject* as sources of advice such conservative or Republican oriented organizations as the NAM, the Farm Bureau, and the Chamber of Commerce. With some variations, similar findings emerge when Republican leaders are compared with Republican voters. If we also take into account the liberal or conservative issue-orientation of the respondents, the differential ability of party leaders and followers to recognize reference groups becomes even more pronounced. Clearly, the political stratum has a better idea than the public has of who its ideological friends and enemies are. The capacity to recognize sympathetic or hostile reference groups is not highly developed among the public at large.

Compared with the individuals, ordinary voters show up poorly in their ability to classify themselves politically. For example, among Democratic actives who score as "liberals" in their views on issues, 82.2 per cent correctly describe themselves as "liberals," while 16.7 per cent call themselves "middle of the roaders" and only 1.1 per cent misclassify themselves as "conservatives." Among Democratic *voters* who actually hold liberal views, only 37.0 per cent are able to label themselves correctly. The disparity is less striking between Republican leaders and followers but bears out no less conclusively that most voters lack the sophistication to rec-

ognize and label accurately the tendency of their own political views. Even their choice of party is frequently discrepant with their actual ideological views: as we reported in a previous paper,[25] not only do Democratic and Republican voters hold fairly similiar opinions on issues, but the latter's opinions are closer to the opinions of Democratic leaders than to those of their own leaders.

Data we have gathered on patterns of support for individual political leaders yield similar conclusions: the articulates are far better able than the electorate to select leaders whose political philosophy they share. Often, in fact, voters simultaneously approve of two or more leaders who represent widely different outlooks—for example, Joseph McCarthy and Dwight D. Eisenhower. In a similar vein, a surprisingly large number of voters simultaneously score high on a Right Wing scale and a liberal issues scale, or hold other "discrepant" outlooks. Such inconsistencies are not unknown among the political actives either, but they are much less frequent. Not only does the public have less information than the political class but it does not succeed as well in sorting out and relating the information it does possess.[26]

Most of the relationships reported in the foregoing have been tested with education, occupation, and sometimes with other demographic variables controlled, but the introduction of these factors does not change the direction of the findings, although it sometimes affects the magnitude of the scores.

Comparisons of scores for the two samples have also been made with "acquiescent" response-set controlled. Acquies-

---

[25] McClosky, Hoffmann, and O'Hara, *op. cit.*

[26] For other findings on the state of ideological development among the electorate, see Angus Campbell, Philip E. Converse, Warren E. Miller and Donald E. Stokes, *The American Voter* (New York, 1960), chs. 8–10.

cence affects the results, but does not eliminate the differences reported or alter the direction or significance of the findings. (See Appendix A.)

III. SUMMARY AND DISCUSSION

Several observations can be offered by way of summarizing and commenting upon the data just reported.

1. American politics is widely thought to be innocent of ideology, but this opinion more appropriately describes the electorate than the active political minority. If American ideology is defined as that cluster of axioms, values and beliefs which have given form and substance to American democracy and the Constitution, the political influentials manifest by comparison with ordinary voters a more developed sense of ideology and a firmer grasp of its essentials. This is evidenced in their stronger approval of democratic ideas, their greater tolerance and regard for proper procedures and citizen rights, their superior understanding and acceptance of the "rules of the game," and their more affirmative attitudes toward the political system in general. The electorate displays a substantial measure of unity chiefly in its support of freedom in the abstract; on most other features of democratic belief and practice it is sharply divided.

The political views of the influentials are relatively ordered and coherent. As liberals and conservatives, Democrats and Republicans, they take stands on issues, choose reference groups, and express preferences for leaders that are far more consistent than the attitudes and preferences exhibited by the electorate. The latter's opinions do not entirely lack order but are insufficiently integrated to meet the requirements of an ideology.[27] In contrast to the political elite, which tends to be united on basic values but divided on issues by party affiliation (both of which testify to a measure of ideological sophistication), the voters divide on many basic political values and adopt stands on issues with little reference to their party affiliation.

The evidence suggests that it is the articulate classes rather than the public who serve as the major repositories of the public conscience and as the carriers of the Creed. Responsibility for keeping the system going, hence, falls most heavily upon them.[28]

2. Why should consensus and support for democratic ideology be stronger among the political stratum than among the electorate? The answer plainly has to do with the differences in their political activity, involvement and articulateness.

Some observers complain that Americans have little interest in political ideas because they are exclusively concerned with their own personal affairs. Evidence is becoming available, however, that political apathy and ignorance are also widespread among the populations of other countries and may well be endemic in all societies larger than a city-state. It is difficult to imagine any circumstance, short of war or revolutionary crisis, in which the mass of men will evince more interest in the community's affairs than in their own concerns. This is not because they are selfish, thoughtless, or morally deficient, but because the stimuli they receive from public affairs are relatively remote and intangible. One can scarcely expect ordinary men to respond to them as intensely as

---

[27]For a similar conclusion on this point, see V. O. Key, *Public Opinion and American Democracy* (New York, 1961), pp. 41, 49. The second chapter of this volume contains an excellent discussion of opinion consensus among the electorate, and touches on a number of the points dealt with in this paper. Evidence on the infrequency of "ideological" thinking among the voters is presented in Campbell, Converse, Miller and Stokes, *op. cit.*, p. 249. By the criteria used the authors were able to classify only 3.5% of the voters as "ideologues" and 12% as "near-ideologues."

[28]V. O. Key, "Public Opinion and the Decay of Democracy," *loc. cit.*

they respond to the more palpable stimuli in their own everyday lives, which impinge upon them directly and in ways they can understand and do something about. The aphorism which holds man to be a political animal may be supportable on normative grounds but is scarcely defensible as a description of reality. Political apathy seems for most men the more "natural" state. Although political matters are in a sense "everyone's concern", it is just as unreasonable to hope that all men will sustain a lively interest in politics as it would be to expect everyone to become addicted to chamber music, electronics, poetry, or baseball. Since many voters lack education, opportunity, or even tangible and compelling reasons for busying themselves with political ideas, they respond to political stimuli (if they respond at all) without much reflection or consistency. Their life-styles, furthermore, tend to perpetuate this state of affairs, for they are likely to associate with people like themselves whose political opinions are no more informed or consistent than their own. As inarticulates, they are also inclined to avoid the very activities by which they might overcome their indifference and develop a more coherent point of view.

Many voters, in addition, feel remote from the centers of political decision and experience, an acute sense of political futility. They know the political world only as a bewildering labyrinth of procedures and unceasing turmoil in which it is difficult to distinguish the just from the wicked, the deserving from the undeserving. The political questions about which they are asked to have opinions are complex and thorny; every solution is imperfect and exacts its price; measures that benefit some groups invariably aggrieve others. The principles which govern the political process seem vague, recondite and impossible to relate to actual events. All this obviously deters voters from developing ideologically, from acquiring insights into the subtleties of the democratic process, and from achieving consensus even on fundamental values.

Although the influentials face some of the same obstacles, they are better able to overcome them. As a group they are distinguished from the mass of the electorate by their above-average education and economic status, their greater political interest and awareness, and their more immediate access to the command posts of community decision. Many of them participate not only in politics but in other public activities as well. This affords them, among other benefits, a more sophisticated understanding of how the society is run and a more intimate association with other men and women who are alert to political ideas and values. Political concepts and abstractions, alien to the vocabulary of many voters, are for the elite familiar items of everyday discourse.

Consider also that the political stratum is, by almost every social criterion we have examined, more homogeneous than the electorate. This promotes communication among them and increases their chances of converging around a common body of attitudes.[29] As Newcomb[30] has remarked, "The actual consequences of communication, as well as the intended ones, are consensus—increasing." Among many segments of the general population, however, communication on matters of political belief either occurs not at all or is so random and cacophonous as to have little utility for the reinforcement of political values. If Louis Wirth is correct in observing that "the limits of consensus are marked by the range of effective communication,"[31] it

---

[29]For additional data on the homogeneity of social characteristics and values among American elite groups, see James N. Rosenau, "Consensus-Building in the American National Community: Hypotheses and Supporting Data," *Journal of Politics*, Vol. 24 (November 1962), pp. 639–61.

[30]Theodore M. Newcomb, "The Study of Consensus," in R. K. Merton *et al.* (eds.), Sociology Today (New York, 1959), pp. 277–92.

[31]*Op. cit.*, p. 201.

becomes easier to understand why the active minority achieves consensus more often than the voters do.

Compared with the electorate, whose ordinary members are submerged in an ideological babble of poorly informed and discordant opinions, the members of the political minority inhabit a world in which political ideas are vastly more salient, intellectual consistency is more frequently demanded, attitudes are related to principles, actions are connected to beliefs, "correct" opinions are rewarded and "incorrect" opinions are punished. In addition, as participants in political roles, the actives are compelled (contrary to stereotype) to adopt opinions, to take stands on issues, and to evaluate ideas and events. As *articulates* they are unavoidably exposed to the liberal democratic values which form the main current of our political heritage. The net effect of these influences is to heighten their sensitivity to political ideas and to unite them more firmly behind the values of the American tradition. They may, as a result, be better equipped for the role they are called upon to play in a democracy than the citizens are for *their* role.

The findings furnish little comfort for those who wish to believe that a passion for freedom, tolerance, justice and other democratic values springs spontaneously from the lower depths of the society, and that the plain, homespun, uninitiated yeoman, worker and farmer are the natural hosts of democratic ideology. The mystique of the simple, unworldly, "natural" democrat has been with us since at least the rise of Christianity, and has been assiduously cultivated by Rousseau, Tolstoy, Marx, and numerous lesser writers and social reformers. Usually, the simpler the man, the lower his station in life, and the greater his objective need for equality, the more we have endowed him with a capacity for understanding democracy. We are thus inclined to give the nod to the farmer over the city man, the unlearned

over the educated, the poor man over the man of wealth, the "people" over their leaders, the unsophisticated over the sophisticated. Yet every one of these intuitive expectations turns out, upon investigation, to be questionable or false. Democratic beliefs and habits are obviously not "natural" but must be learned; and they are learned more slowly by men and women whose lives are circumscribed by apathy, ignorance, provincialism and social or physical distance from the centers of intellectual activity. In the absence of knowledge and experience—as we can readily observe from the fidgety course of growth in the newly emerging nations— the presuppositions and complex obligations of democracy, the rights it grants and the self-restraints it imposes, cannot be quickly comprehended. Even in a highly developed democratic nation like the United States, millions of people continue to possess only the most rudimentary understanding of democratic ideology.

3. While the active political minority affirms the underlying values of democracy more enthusiastically than the people do, consensus among them is far from perfect, and we might well inquire why this is so.

Despite the many forces impelling influentials toward agreement on basic ideological values, counteracting forces are also at work to divide them. Not all influentials are able to comprehend democratic ideas, to apply them to concrete contexts, or to thread their way through the complexities of modern political life. Nor is communication perfect among them either, despite their greater homogeneity. Many things divide them, not least of which are differences in education, conflicting economic and group interests, party competition, factional cleavages and personal political ambitions.

In demonstrating that the influentials are better prepared than the masses to receive and reflect upon political ideas, we run the risk of overstating the case and of exaggerating their capacity for ideological reasoning. Some members of the political class obviously have no more intellectual concern with politics than the masses do; they are in it for "the game," for personal reasons, or for almost any reason except ideology.

Then, too, while most democratic ideas are in their most general form simple enough for almost all members of the elite to understand, they become considerably more puzzling when one sets out to explicate them, to relate them to each other, or to apply them to concrete cases. Only a few of the complications need to be cited to illustrate the point: several of the ideas, such as equality, are either inherently vague or mean different things in different contexts. Some democratic (or constitutional) values turn out in certain situations to be incompatible with other democratic values (*e.g.*, the majority's right to make and enforce the laws at times clashes with individual rights, such as the right to stand on one's religious conscience). As this suggests, democratic ideas and rules of the game are ordinarily encountered not in pure form or in isolation but in substantive contexts that are bound to influence the ways in which we react to them.[32] Many businessmen who consider the regulation of business as an unconstitutional invasion of freedom look upon the regulation of trade unions as a justifiable curb upon lawlessness; trade unionists, needless to say, lean to the opposite view.

Consider, too, what a heavy burden we place upon a man's normal impulses by asking him to submit unconditionally to democratic values and procedures. Compliance with democratic rules of the game often demands an extraordinary measure of forbearance and self-discipline, a willingness to place constraints upon the use of our collective power and to suffer opinions, actions, and groups we regard as repugnant. The need for such self-restraint is for many people intrinsically difficult to comprehend and still more difficult to honor. Small wonder, then, that consensus around democratic values is imperfect, even among the political influentials who are well situated to appreciate their importance.

4. We turn now to the most crucial question suggested by the research findings, namely, what significance must be assigned to the fact that democratic ideology and consensus are poorly developed among the electorate and only imperfectly realized among the political influentials?

Our first and most obvious conclusion is that, contrary to the familiar claim, a democratic society can survive despite widespread popular misunderstanding and disagreement about basic democratic and constitutional values. The American political system survives and even flourishes under precisely these conditions, and so, we have reason to think, do other viable democracies. What makes this possible is a more conjectural question, though several observations can be offered by way of answering it.

Democratic viability is, to begin with, saved by the fact that those who are most confused about democratic ideas are also likely to be politically apathetic and without significant influence. Their role in the nation's decision process is so small that their "misguided" opinions or non-opinions have little practical consequence for stability. If they contribute little to the vitality of the system, neither are they likely to do much harm. Lipset[33] has pointed out that "apathy undermines consensus," but to this one may add the corollary observation that apathy also furnishes its own partial corrective by keeping the

[32]For a discussion of this point, see Peter Bachrach, "Elite Consensus and Democracy," *Journal of Politics,* Vol. 24 (August 1962), pp. 439–52.

[33]Seymour Martin Lipset, *Political Man* (New York, 1960), p. 27. Chapter I of this volume provides a stimulating and valuable discussion of the relation of conflict and consensus to the operation of democracy.

doubters from acting upon their differences. In the United States, at least, their disagreements are *passive* rather than *active*, more the result of political ignorance and indifference than of intellectual conviction or conscious identification with an "alien" political tendency. Most seem not even to be aware of their deviations from the established values. This suggests that there may, after all, be some utility in achieving agreement on large, abstract political sentiments, for it may satisfy men that they share common values when in fact they do not. Not only can this keep conflicts from erupting, but it also permits men who disagree to continue to communicate and thus perhaps to convert their pseudo-consensus on democratic values into a genuine consensus.

I do not mean to suggest, of course, that a nation runs no risk when a large number of its citizens fail to grasp the essential principles on which its constitution is founded. Among Americans, however, the principal danger is not that they will reject Democratic ideals in favor of some hostile ideology, but that they will fail to understand the very institutions they believe themselves to be defending and may end up undermining rather than safeguarding them. Our research on "McCarthyism," for example, strongly suggests that popular support for the Senator represented less a conscious rejection of American democratic ideals than a misguided effort to defend them. We found few McCarthy supporters who genuinely shared the attitudes and values associated with his name.[34]

Whether consensus among the influentials is either a necessary or sufficient condition for democratic stability is not really known. Since the influentials act, make public decisions, are more organized, and take political ideas more seriously, agree-

ment among them on constitutional values is widely thought to be essential for viability. At present, however, we do not have enough information (or at least we do not have it in appropriately organized form) to state with satisfactory precision what the actual relation is between elite consensus and democratic stability. Some democratic governments, *e.g.*, Weimar Germany, crumbled when faced with ideological conflicts among their political classes; others, *e.g.*, post-war Italy and France, have until now managed to weather pronounced ideological cleavages. The opinion has long prevailed that consensus is needed to achieve stability, but the converse may be the more correct formulation, *i.e.*, that so long as conditions remain stable, consensus is not required; it becomes essential only when social conditions are disorganized. Consensus may strengthen democratic viability, but its absence in an otherwise stable society need not be fatal or even particularly damaging.

It should also be kept in mind that the existence of intellectual disagreements—even among the influentials—does not necessarily mean that they will be expressed or acted upon. In the United States (and doubtless elsewhere as well), numerous influences are at work to prevent ideological cleavages from assuming an important role in the nation's political life. This is certainly the tendency of such political institutions as federalism, checks and balances, separation of powers, bicameralism, the congressional committee system, the judiciary's practice of accommodating one discrepant law to another, and a system of elections more often fought around local issues and personalities than around urgent national questions. Our two-party system also functions to disguise or soften the genuine disagreements that distinguish active Democrats from active Republicans. The American social system contributes to the same end, for it is a model of the pluralistic society, a profuse collection of diverse groups, interests and

---

[34]Herbert McClosky, "McCarthyism: The Myth and the Reality," unpublished paper delivered at the American Psychological Association, New York, September 1957. See also Wiebe, *loc. cit.*

organizations spread over a vast and variegated territory. Consensus in such a society becomes difficult to achieve, but by the same token its absence can also more easily be survived. The complexities of a highly pluralistic social and political order tend to diminish the impact of intellectual differences, to compel compromise, and to discourage the holders of divergent views from crystalizing into intransigent doctrinal camps. Thus it seems, paradoxically enough, that the need for consensus on democratic rules of the game increases as the conflict among competing political tendencies becomes sharper, and declines as their differences becomes more diffused. Italy, by this reasoning, has greater need of consensus than the United States, but has less chance of achieving it. A democratic nation may wisely prefer the American model to the Italian, though what is ideally desired, as Lipset observes,[35] is a balance between cleavage and consensus —the one to give reality and force to the principle of opposition, the other to furnish the secure framework within which that principle might be made continuously effective. Countervailing power within a structure of shared political values would, by this logic, be the optimal condition for the maintenance of a democratic society.

5. But even giving this much weight to consensus may exaggerate the role which intellectual factors play in the attainment of democratic stability. The temptation to assign a controlling influence to the place of ideas in the operation of democracy is very great. Partly this results from our tendency to confuse the textbook model of democracy with the reality and to assume the high order of rationality in the system that the model presupposes (*e.g.*, an alert citizenry aware of its rights and duties, cognizant of the basic rules, exercising consent, enjoying perfect information and choosing governers after carefully weighing their qualifications, deliberating over the issues, etc.). It it not my

purpose to ridicule this model but to underscore the observation that it can easily mislead us into placing more weight than the facts warrant upon cognitive elements —upon ideas, values, rational choice, consensus, etc.—as the cementing forces of a democratic society. An *ad hominem* consideration may also be relevant here: as intellectuals and students of politics, we are disposed both by training and sensibility to take political ideas seriously and to assign central importance to them in the operation of the state. We are therefore prone to forget that most people take them less seriously than we do, that they pay little attention to issues, rarely worry about the consistency of their opinions, and spend little or no time thinking about the values, presuppositions, and implications which distinguish one political orientation from another. If the viability of a democracy were to depend upon the satisfaction of these intellectual activities, the prognosis would be very grim indeed.

Research from many different lines of inquiry confirms unequivocally that the role heretofore assigned to ideas and to intellectual processes in general has been greatly exaggerated and cannot adequately explain many political phenomena which, on *a priori* grounds, we have expected them to explain. Witness, for example, the research on the non-rational factors which govern the voting decision, on the effects—or rather the non-effects—of ideology on the loyalty and fighting effectiveness of German and American soldiers, on the differences between the views of party leaders and followers, on the influence of personality on political belief, and on group determinants of perception.[36]

---

[36]*Cf.*, for example, Campbell *et al.*, *op. cit.*; Bernard R. Berelson, Paul F. Lazarsfeld, and William N. McPhee, *Voting* (Chicago, 1954), especially ch. 14; Edward A. Shils and Morris Janowitz, "Cohesion and Disintegration in the German Wehrmacht in World War II," *Public Opinion Quarterly*, Vol. XII (1948), pp. 280–315; Herbert McClosky, "Conservatism and Personality," *American Political Science Review*, (*Footnote continued on next page*)

---

[35]Lipset, *op. cit.*, pp. 21–22.

We now have evidence that patriotism and the strength of one's attachment to a political community need not depend upon one's approval of its intellectual, cultural, or political values. Indeed, our present research clearly confirms that the men and women who express "patriotism" in extreme or chauvinistic form usually have the least knowledge and understanding of American democratic ideals, institutions, and practices.

Abundant anecdotal data from the observation of dictatorial and other nations further corroborates the conclusion that men may become attached to a party, a community, or a nation by forces that have nothing to do with ideology or consensus. Many of these forces are so commonplace that we often neglect them, for they include family, friends, home, employment, property, religion, ethnic attachments, a common language, and familiar surroundings and customs. These may lack the uplifting power of some political doctrines, but their ability to bind men to a society and its government may nevertheless be great. This observation, of course, is less likely to hold for the intelligentsia than for the inarticulates, but even the political behavior of intellectuals is never governed exclusively by appeals to the mind.

The effect of ideas on democratic viability may also be diminished by the obvious reluctance of most men to press their intellectual differences to the margin and to debate questions that may tear the community apart. So long as no urgent reason arises for bringing such differences to the surface, most men will be satisfied to have them remain dormant. Although there are men and women who are exceptions to this generalization, and who cannot bear to leave basic questions unre-

solved, they are likely to be few, for both the principles and practices of an "open society" strongly reinforce tolerance for variety, contingency and ambiguity in matters of belief and conscience. As our data on freedom of opinion suggest, few Americans expect everyone to value the same things or to hold identical views on public questions. The tendency to ignore, tolerate, or play down differences helps to create an illusion of consensus which for many purposes can be as serviceable as the reality.[37]

6. To conclude, as we have in effect, that ideological awareness and consensus are overvalued as determinants of democratic viability is not to imply that they are of no importance. While disagreements among Americans on fundamental values have tended to be passive and, owing to apathy and the relative placidity of our politics, easily tolerated; while they do not follow party lines and are rarely insinuated into the party struggle; and while no extremist movement has yet grown large enough to challenge effectively the governing principles of the American Constitution, this happy state of affairs is not permanently guaranteed. Fundamental differences could *become* activated by political and economic crises; party differences could *develop* around fundamental constitutional questions, as they have in France and other democra-

---

Vol. LII (March 1958), pp. 27–45; T. W. Adorno *et al., The Authoritarian Personality* (New York, 1950), ch. XVII; Richard Crutchfield, "Conformity and Character," *American Psychologist,* Vol. X (1955), pp. 191–98.

[37]Robert G. McCloskey, *loc. cit.,* suggests that the American political tradition is marked by "ambivalence" toward certain of our fundamental values and that this may discourage the achievement of "consensus" in the usual sense. He believes, however, that Americans have learned to live with, and even to ignore, inconsistencies in the value system, in keeping with our "pragmatic spirit." Whether this ability is uniquely American or whether it is characteristic of all "open," democratic societies is a question well worth investigating. It could, conceivably, be a natural outgrowth of democratic ideology itself, no element of which can be conceived and enforced absolutely without infringing other elements. On this last point, see Sidney Hook, *The Paradoxes of Freedom* (Berkeley, 1962), pp. 14–62.

cies; and powerful extremist movements are too familiar a phenomenon of modern political life to take for granted their eternal absence from the American scene.

Obviously a democratic nation also pays a price for an electorate that is weakly developed ideologically. Lacking the intellectual equipment to assess complex political events accurately, the unsophisticated may give support to causes that are contrary to their own or to the national interest. In the name of freedom, democracy, and the Constitution, they may favor a McCarthy, join the John Birch Society, or agitate for the impeachment of a Supreme Court Justice who has worked unstintingly to uphold their constitutional liberties. They may also have difficulty discriminating political integrity from demagoguery, maturity and balanced judgment from fanaticism, honest causes from counterfeits. Our findings on the attitudes shown by ordinary Americans toward "extreme" political beliefs (Left Wing beliefs, Right Wing beliefs, totalitarianism, isolationism, etc.) verify that the possibilities just cited are not merely hypothetical. Those who have the least understanding of American politics subscribe least enthusiastically to its principles, and are most frequently "misled" into attacking constitutional values while acting (as they see it) to defend them.

There is, however, reason to believe that ideological sophistication and the general acceptance of liberal democratic values are increasing rather than declining in the United States. Extreme ideological politics of the type associated with Marxism, facsism and other doctrinaire networks of opinion may be waning, as many sociologists believe,[38] but the same observation does not hold for the influence of democratic ideas. On the contrary, democratic ideology in the United States, linked

as it is with the articulate classes, gives promise of growing as the articulate class grows. Many developments in recent American life point to an increase in "articulateness": the extraordinary spread of education, rapid social mobility, urbanization, the proliferation of mass media that disseminate public information, the expansion of the middle class, the decline in the size and number of isolated rural groups, the reduction in the proportion of people with submarginal living standards, the incorporation of foreign and minority groups into the culture and their increasing entrance into the professions, and so on. While these developments may on the one side have the effect of reducing the tensions and conflicts on which extreme ideologies feed, they are likely on the other side to beget a more articulate population and a more numerous class of political influentials, committed to liberal democracy and aware of the rights and obligations which attend that commitment.

APPENDIX A. THE EFFECT OF ACQUIESCENCE OR "RESPONSE-SET"

Because responses to scale items are subject to a response-set known as acquiescence, *i.e.*, a tendency to agree (or disagree) with items regardless of what the items say, all procedures in the present study have routinely been run with acquiescence controlled. For this purpose we employed a specially constructed acquiescence scale, consisting of 19 pairs of contradictory or near-contradictory items. Each respondent received an acquiescence score of 0 to 38, depending upon the number of "agree" and "disagree" responses he registered on the scale. For convenience we have divided our sample into those who scored high, middle, or low on acquiescence, and have compared the influentials and electorate within each acquiescence level.

As accompanying Table 8 shows, vari-

TABLE 8

Influentials vs. the Electorate: Percentages Scoring High–Low on Selected.
Scales with Acquiescent Response-Set Controlled

| | *%'s Down* | | | | | |
| | *Low Acq.* | | *Mid Acq.* | | *High Acq.* | |
	Infl. $N = 1,369$	*Elect.* 453	*Infl.* 1,159	*Elect.* 520	*Infl.* 492	*Elect.* 471
Faith in Procedural Rights						
High	70	35	56	28	32	10
Low	6	21	13	27	28	45
Faith in Democracy						
High	50	29	36	21	22	6
Low	8	19	16	28	28	42
Tolerance						
High	66	57	62	48	45	27
Low	13	21	15	29	29	48
Faith in Freedom						
High	64	45	63	50	59	50
Low	17	32	15	27	20	26
Totalitarianism						
High	2	11	9	26	35	63
Low	80	52	54	30	21	5
F-Authoritarianism						
High	4	9	14	24	46	67
Low	70	48	38	22	10	2
Political Cynicism						
High	2	9	10	24	31	60
Low	74	51	47	25	20	6
Elitism						
High	12	21	27	35	45	60
Low	53	37	36	23	20	8

ations in acquiescence have a powerful effect on the scale scores (and implicitly the item scores) of both the political elite and the public. It is equally plain, nevertheless, that the differences between the two samples on democratic and related ideological values remain large and statistically significant even when acquiescence is held constant; they cannot, therefore, be explained as mere artifacts of response-set. Then, too, although one cannot discern it from these tables, acquiescence functions in the case of some items to reduce rather than to enlarge the "actual" differences between the influentials and the electorate.

The question might also be raised whether we are doing the inquiry a disservice by conceiving acquiescence *entirely* as a response-set which artificially inflates or deflates the scores registered by respondents on certain items or scales. Our research has yielded a vast amount of data on acquiescence which suggests that the tendency to agree or disagree with items indiscriminately reflects personality and cognitive capacities that are strongly associated with the ability to sort out, understand, relate, and internalize norms. Conceivably, therefore, the electorate demonstrates a weaker grasp of democratic and constitutional principles not only because its members are more prone than the influentials to response-set

TABLE 9
Characteristics of McClosky National General Population Sample and Selected Other Samples (in Percent)

	AIPO Samples* (Jan. 1958) (N = 3024)	Michigan SRC Sample† (1956 Presidential Election) (N = 1,762)	McClosky-PAB General Population Sample (Jan. 1958) (N = 1,484)	Others
Sex				
Men	48.0	44.7	51.0	48.4
Women	52.0	55.3	49.0	51.6
				(1960 Census)
Age (1)				
21–29	16.5	...	17.3	...
30–49	45.5	...	44.5	...
50 +	37.0	...	37.9	...
Undesignated	1.0	...	.3	...
Age (2)				
Under 35	...	30.2	28	...
35–44	...	25.6	23.6	...
45–54	...	19.1	20.6	...
55 +	...	25.0	27.7	...
Race				
White	...	91.3	93.1	...
Negro	...	8.3	6.5	...
Rural-Urban				(1960 Census)
Urban (over 2,500)	...	68.0	72.2	71.5
Rural (farm-nonfarm under 2,500)	...	32.0	27.8	28.5
Region				PAB (Adjusted)
East	28	25.7	27.7	24.8‡
Midwest	32	34.4	35.7	35.7
South	25	26.7	19.7	22.8
West	15	13.3	16.9	16.9
Education				
College	15.5	18.7	27.2	...
High School	51.5	50.6	51.2	...
Grade School	33.0	30.7	21.6	...
Religion				
Catholic	...	21.1	21.9	...
Jew	...	3.2	2.5	...
Prot., Other, & NA	...	75.7	75.6	...
Income				
Under $3000	...	24.3	20.4	...
$3000–5000	...	28.8	34.0	...
$5000–7500	...	25.6	26.6	...
$7500–10,000	...	10.8	9.4	...
$10,000 +	...	7.6	5.7	...
Refuse, NA, Dk	...	3.6	3.8	...
				(Actual Congressional Vote, November, 1958)§
Party Preference				
Democrat	56.0§	57.1	56.9‖	56.6
Republican	44.0	42.9	43.1	43.4

*The figures for the AIPO sample are averages computed from two national surveys conducted by the Gallup Poll in January 1958. The information on the characteristics of these samples was supplied by the AIPO in a letter to the author.

†In most cases, the figures from the Michigan SRC sample are computed from the information supplied in the codebook for Deck 6 of Study 417, September 1956. Urban rural figures are computed from a table in *The American Voter*, p. 454. Criteria for urban-rural are set out on p. 406.

‡Michigan SRC included Md. and W. Va. in the South, while we had classified these states as Eastern. This column shows the PAB figures with Md. and W. Va. classified as Southern. SRC regional figures combine data from 1952 and 1956 (See *The American Voter*, p. 158.)

§Data on party preference for the AIPO and the national congressional elections of 1958 are taken from a Gallup news release, May 24, 1959.

‖Two-party vote only. PAB sample contained 821 Democrats, 623 Republicans, and 40 Independents, Other, and DK's.

(which means that they say yes to items that happen *in this case* to express undemocratic and "unconstitutional" sentiments), but also because they characteristically lack the habits, skills, or capacities for thinking about these matters in a coherent and sophisticated way. It appears, in short, that the correlation between acquiescence and the expression of certain poorly valued sentiments results not entirely from the influence of the former upon the latter, but also from the influence upon *both* of a common, underlying, mental state.*

APPENDIX B. CHARACTERISTICS OF THE PAB GENERAL POPULATION SAMPLE

Because the self-administration and return of questionnaires left with respondents by interviewers represents a somewhat unorthodox sampling procedure, the accompanying Table 9 presents a description of the PAB general population sample utilized in this paper. For purposes of comparison, the table also includes the characteristics of two AIPO (Gallup) samples, interviewed in January–February, 1958; the September–November sample employed by the Survey Research Center, University of Michigan, in its study of the 1956 presidential election; and, where comparable, census and voting data.

---

*The full presentation and explication of our findings on acquiescence cannot be accommodated within the limitations of the present paper, and I have put the matter aside for presentation in a separate paper.

As the figures make plain the PAB sample closely resembles in its social characteristics both the AIPO and Michigan SRC samples. Although some of the differences among the samples doubtless arise from the differences in response rate, other differences may be due to the differences in the time of polling as well as differences in the coding criteria employed.

In only one characteristic does the PAB sample deviate substantially from the other samples, namely, in the overrepresentation of the college-educated strata and the corresponding underrepresentation of the grade school educated. This, of course, was to be expected, in light of the length and complexity of the PAB questionnaire and the difficulty associated with its self-administration. It should, however, be kept in mind that oversampling the upper educated has tended to flatten rather than to accentuate the differences between the influentials and the electorate reported in this paper. Since the highly educated tend to embrace democratic values and the "rules of the game" more frequently than the less educated do, the item and scale scores we have reported for the general population of voters are doubtless slightly inflated. In other words, the differences in ideological outlook between the political stratum and the electorate are probably even a bit larger than we have reported. Hence, correcting for the educational bias in the sample would strengthen rather than weaken the conclusions of this paper.

SECTION VI

The Role-Playing Model

In a study of the legislatures of California, New Jersey, Ohio, and Tennessee, Eulau, Wahlke, Buchanan, and Ferguson find that legislators disagree on whether they should voice their constituencies' opinions, be their own men, or balance these alternative roles depending on the situation. Although these different legislator roles relate to the competitiveness of their districts, no inquiry is made about whether the delegates—those who believe they should follow the instructions of their constituency—succeed in reflecting their constituencies' opinions better than other legislators. This of course would be expected if the role-playing model were an effective linkage.

But in a study of congressmen, Warren Miller and Donald Stokes find, ". . . the Congressman's own convictions and his perceptions of district opinion make a distinct contribution to his roll call behavior." They divide policy matters into three classes, and find that in the area of civil rights congressmen vote their perception of constituency opinion. This pattern is much less important in the foreign policy and social welfare areas, and we do not know whether congressmen feel forced to vote this way in civil rights or whether they feel they should do so. But clearly perceptions of constituency opinions effect public policy in all areas and strongly so in civil rights.

Even if the representative seeks to voice the opinion of those he leads, his success is contingent on his having an accurate idea of what they want. The correlation between constituency's attitudes and the representative's perception of their attitudes is only .19 in the area of social welfare, which should indicate extensive misperception. Even in civil rights the .63 correlation denotes substantial inaccuracy. How does a leader form his perception of follower attitudes?

Certainly elections, interest groups, and political parties can provide information about what public opinion is. This information may or may not be correct, and judging from the findings above it seems inaccurate. But public opinion can also be assessed by more direct public expressions, such as letters written directly to leaders. In trying to understand the failure of the 1964 Goldwater election strategy, Converse, Clausen, and Miller found that those who write letters present a biased expression of public opinion.

If our understanding of leadership behavior and political linkage is to improve, we need to gain a more complete understanding of the opinions leaders have toward their job and its responsibilities, and of their perceptions of public opinion. The evidence we have suggests that many leaders are motivated to voice their constituency's opinions, and a good part of public policy is an attempt to reflect public opinion as the leaders perceive it.

THE ROLE OF THE REPRESENTATIVE: SOME EMPIRICAL OBSERVATIONS ON THE THEORY OF EDMUND BURKE*

Heinz Eulau, John C. Wahlke, William Buchanan, Leroy C. Ferguson

The problem of representation is central to all discussions of the functions of legislatures or the behavior of legislators. For it is commonly taken for granted that, in democratic political systems, legislatures are both legitimate and authoritative decision-making institutions, and that it is their representative character which makes them authoritative and legitimate. Through the process of representation, presumably, legislatures are empowered to act for the whole body politic and are legitimized. And because, by virtue of representation, they participate in legislation, the represented accept legislative decisions as authoritative. But agreement about the meaning of the term "representation" hardly goes beyond a general consensus regarding the context within which it is appropriately used. The history of political theory is studded with definitions of representation,[1] usually embedded in ideological assumptions and postulates which cannot serve the uses of empirical research without conceptual clarification.[2]

---

*Reprinted from The American Political Science Review, Vol. LIII (September 1959), pp. 742–56. Copyright 1959, The American Political Science Association.

This study was made possible by grants from the Political Behavior Committee of the Social Science Research Council. Neither the Committee nor the Council is responsible for what we have written.

[1] For a convenient and comprehensive summary of definitions, see John A. Fairlie, "The Nature of Political Representation," American Political Science Review, Vol. XXXIV (April–June 1940), pp. 236–48; 456–66.

[2] An effort at conceptual clarification is made by Alfred De Grazia, Public and Republic— Political Representation in America (New York, 1951).

I

Many familiar formulations treat representation in a non-functional fashion, viewing it as something valuable in itself, as an ultimate end, and seek to discover or specify its "nature" or "essence." Functional theory, on the other hand, deals with representation from the point of view of the political system as a whole or its component units. Herman Finer, for instance, has suggested that "responsibility is the chief and wider aim, and representativeness merely a convenient means to attain this. . . . The desire for responsible government is paramount; people not merely wish to represent their views, but actually to make and unmake governments."[3] But while functional formulations treat representation as a means for the attainment of some other political objective, failure to test functional propositions by way of empirical research leaves the problems raised by theory in the realm of hypothesis rather than reliable knowledge. In connection with Finer's proposition, for example, there has been little, if any, empirical analysis of the extent to which the represented do, in fact, want to enforce political responsibility, and how capable they are, under modern conditions, of exercising the necessary control. Nevertheless, once relevant concepts are clarified, a functional formulation of representation can open up areas of research which, in

---

[3] Herman Finer, The Theory and Practice of Modern Government (New York, rev. ed., 1949), p. 219.

turn, may contribute to theoretical cumulation.

The relationship between the representative and the represented is at the core of representational theory. The term "representation" directs attention, first of all, to the attitudes, expectations and behaviors of the represented—to their acceptance of representatives' decisions as legitimate and authoritative for themselves. More particularly, representation concerns not the mere fact that they do accept such decisions, but rather the reasons they have for doing so, their rationalizations of the legitimacy and authority of the decisions made by their representatives.

Sometimes the adjective "representative" denotes nothing more than the publicly approved process by which representatives are to be chosen—as when a distinction is made between a "representative body" (meaning a group of men elected by specific modes of popular election) and a "non-representative body" (meaning a group of men selected by royal or executive appointment, entailed inheritance, or some other non-electoral process). Such usage implies that citizens' attitudes and expectations include, and may extend no farther than, the belief that representatives' decisions must be accepted as legitimate and authoritative *if* the representatives have been selected in the approved manner. In other words, elected officials are called "representatives" primarily because of the way they have been chosen. Even in a looser usage an appointed commission may be approvingly called a body of "representative" citizens, or may be attacked as "unrepresentative," depending on whether its members might conceivably have been chosen had they been subject to election rather than appointment; and their views will correspondingly be accorded or denied a measure of authority and legitimacy.

But the appropriate process of selecting public decision-makers has never been the really fundamental question for theories of representation. Behind every proposal for altering the method of selecting officials is some assumption, at least, about the effect of such changes on what decision-makers or decision-making institutions do, and how they do it. Proposals for reform must assume or show that the proposed change will bring it about that *what* representatives decide and *the way* they reach decisions is more nearly in accord with expectations and demands of the represented than has been in the case under the system to be reformed. The various defenses of existing systems of selection which postulate "virtual representation" have in common some shading of the belief that the process of selection is not of major significance in determining what representatives do or how they do it, or that decisions made by representatives can be brought in harmony with public expectations, without altering whatever process of selection is being defended by the advocacy of virtual representation.

The relationship between the process of selection of legislators and the modes and consequences of legislative behavior, or the relationship between public expectations and legislative decisions, offer wide and fertile fields for empirical research. Our purpose here, however, is less ambitious than a full-scale investigation of such relationships. It is to eliminate those particular ambiguities in the concept of representation which concern the actions or behavior of representatives, by use of the concept or "role," and to demonstrate the utility of this approach for further research relevant to the theory of representation.

II

A convenient and useful starting point in theoretical clarification is Edmund Burke's theory of representation. For, in following his classic argument, later theorists have literally accepted Burke's formulation and ignored its contextual basis and polemical bias. Burke ingeniously combined two notions which, for analytical purposes, should be kept distinct. In effect, he combined a conception of the *focus* of representation with a conception of the *style* of representation. Parliament, Burke said in a famous passage,[4]

is not a *congress* of ambassadors from different and hostile interests; which interests each must maintain, as an agent and advocate, against other agents and advocates; but parliament is a *deliberative* assembly of *one* nation, with *one* interest, that of the whole; where, not local purposes, not local prejudices ought to guide but the general good, resulting from the general reason of the whole.

The sentence indicates that Burke postulated two possible foci of representation: local, necessarily hostile interests, on the one hand; and a national interest, on the other hand. He rejected the former as an improper and advocated the latter as the proper focus of the representative's role. But in doing so, he also linked these foci of representation with particular representational styles. If the legislature is concerned with only one interest, that of the whole, and not with compromise among diverse interests, it follows that the representative cannot and must not be bound by instructions, from whatever source, but must be guided by what Burke called "his unbiased opinion, his mature judgment, his enlightened conscience." Moreover, Burke buttressed his argument by emphasizing the deliberative function of the legislature—presumably in contrast to its representational function. Yet if one rejects his notion of the legislature as only a deliberative body whose representational focus is the whole rather than its constituent parts, the logic of Burke's formulation is no longer necessary or relevant.

Today, many "publics" constitute significant foci of orientation for the representative as he approaches his legislative task. Under the conditions of a plural political and social order, these foci of representation may be other than geographical interests, be they electoral districts or the larger commonwealth. The modern representative faces similar choices concerning the style of his representational role not only *vis-à-vis* his constituency or state and nation, but *vis-à-vis* other clienteles, notably political parties, pressure groups and administrative agencies. From an analytical point of view—though not, of course, from an empirical standpoint—the style of the representative's role is neutral as far as these different foci of representation are concerned. Regardless of his focus of representation—a geographical unit, a party, a pressure group, or an administrative organization—he is not committed to take either the role of free agent, following his own convictions, or the role of delegate, bound by instructions. In other words, Burke's linkage of a particular areal focus of representation with a particular representational style constitutes only a special case in a generic series of empirically viable relationships between possible and different foci of representation and appropriate styles of representation.

Of course, different foci of representation need not be mutually exclusive. They may occur simultaneously, and appropriate role orientations may be held simultaneously. For instance, a party may be so strong in a district that, in the representative's mind, the interests of district and party are identical. Or a pressure group may have such pervasive influence —as, for example, the Farm Bureau in a predominantly agricultural constituency, or the AFL–CIO in a predominantly working class district—that, again, the interests of district and pressure group become identified. Moreover, it is possible that different focal role orientations are activated *seriatim* as circumstances require. In particular, one may assume that on matters of no relevance to the representative's district, roles oriented towards party

[4]In his "Speech to the Electors of Bristol" (1774), *Works,* Vol. II, p. 12.

or lobby as foci of representation may serve as major premises of choice.

The generic extension of Burke's special case, broken down into analytic components, suggests that the focal and stylistic dimensions of representation must be kept separate in empirical research. Burke combined them for polemical reasons: he was writing in opposition to the idea of mandatory representation which had much popular support in the middle of the eighteenth century.[5] The result of this polemical commitment was that the problem of *how* the representative should behave *vis-à-vis* his clienteles became a substantive problem—*what* he should do for the clienteles. But the fact that a representative sees himself as reaching a decision by following his own convictions or judgment does not mean that the content of his decisions is necessarily oriented towards a general rather than a particular interest, just as his acceptance of instructions from a clientele group does not necessarily mean that he is oriented towards a special rather than the public interest. A representative may base his decisions on his own conscience or judgment, but the cause he promotes may be parochial. Or he may follow instructions, but the mandate may be directed towards the realization of the general welfare.

The distinction between the focal and stylistic dimensions of the representative's role allows us to suggest that representation is not concerned with what decisions should be made, but with how decisions are to be made. Now, it is axiomatic that decisions made in institutional contexts, such as legislatures provide, are made in terms of a set of premises which guide the behavior of decision-makers. The notion—explicit in Burke and other traditional formulations—that legislative decisions can be purely rational is not tenable in view of the fact that rationality, while not altogether absent, is invariably bounded by the legislature's institutional environment.[6] One of these boundaries is the representational fabric of the legislature. The representative system provides the representative with some of the assumptions in terms of which he defines his role. The roles he takes, in turn, whether in the focal or stylistic dimensions of representation, provide the premises for decision.

Premises underlying decisions made by legislatures, then, may be of two kinds: (1) they may be premises relevant to the focus of representation; and (2) they may be relevant to the style of representation. With regard to the first kind, for instance, a representative may be guided by premises such as that legislation should benefit either his district or the state, that it should be "liberal" or "conservative," that it should or should not favor special interests, that it should or should not be in performance of his party's campaign pledges, and so on. With regard to the second kind of premises, the representative's choices may be circumscribed by his stylistic role orientation, whether he sees himself following his own conscience or instructions. In this dimension the premises involved in his decisional behavior refer not to the focus but to the style of his role as representative.

III

The issue of styles of representation—free agency versus mandate—has been confounded by the fact that the enabling source of a representative's power is the

---

[5] *Cf.* Samuel H. Beer, "The Representation of Interests in British Government," *American Political Science Review*, Vol. LI (Sept. 1957), p. 613, who points out how little general legislation was proposed or enacted in those days.

[6] For the conception of "bounded rationality" as well as the notion that roles constitute some of the premises of decision-making behavior, we are indebted to Herbert A. Simon's writings, notably *Models of Man* (New York, 1957). Our own formulations of the concept of role are developed in John C. Wahlke and Heinz Eulau, *Legislative Behavior: A Reader in Theory and Research* (Glencoe, 1959).

electorate of a geographical district. Representation of geographical areas introduces a certain amount of ambiguity into the relationship between representative and represented which is likely to be absent under schemes of proportional or vocational representation.[7] Part of this ambiguity is the widely held expectation, contested by Burke but shared by many citizens and politicians alike, that the representative is a spokesman of the presumed "interests" of the area from which he has been elected. Of course, implicit in this expectation is the assumption that a geographical unit has interests which are distinct and different from those of other units, and which should be represented in public decision-making. This assumption has been challenged on a variety of grounds: that the geographical area as such, as an electoral unit, is artificial; that it cannot and does not generate interests shared by its residents; that it has no unique interests; and so on. Schemes of proportional or vocational representation have been advanced to make possible the representation of allegedly more "natural" interest groupings, such as minority groups, skill groups or economic groups.[8]

The assumption that geographical districts have particular characteristics—such as population attributes and industrial, agricultural or commercial properties—and hence, unique interests which are, or ought to be, factors influencing the direction of public decisions continues to be shared not only by voters, politicians and others involved in policy-making, but also by scientific students of the political process. It underlies many studies which seek to relate legislative roll-call votes to the socio-economic characteristics of electoral districts,[9] as well as those studies which analyze the socio-economic composition of legislatures.[10]

It is a further assumption of these studies that legislators, having lived in their districts for all or substantial parts of their lives, share the values, beliefs, habits and concerns of the people who elected them and whom they presumably represent. Indeed, a literal interpretation of "represent" is to make something present that is not actually present. But this interpretation is most tenuous under modern conditions. Electoral districts tend to be so heterogeneous in population attributes, so pluralistic in the character of their group life, so diverse in the kinds of values and beliefs held, that whatever measures of central tendency are used to classify a district are more likely to conceal than to reveal its real character. The notion that elections are held as a method to discover persons whose attributes and attitudes mirror those most widely shared by people in their district appears to be of dubious validity.

This does not mean, of course, that the geographical district is dysfunctional from the point of view of maintaining the political system. The very circumstance of heterogeneity in the district tends to free the representative from being readily bound by a mandate, to make for discretion and political responsibility, and to enable him to integrate conflicting de-

---

[7] For a perspicacious discussion of ambiguities in representation, see Harold F. Gosnell, *Democracy—The Threshold of Freedom* (New York, 1948), pp. 124–42.

[8] Most theories of functional or proportional representation are motivated or supported by tacit and untested assumptions about the relationship of legislators' behavior to the process by which they are selected. This is merely a special case of the general democratic assumption that political responsibility is the mechanism *par excellence* for bringing legislators' actions in line with the expectations of the represented.

[9] See, for instance, Julius Turner, *Party and Constituency: Pressures on Congress* (Baltimore, 1951); or Duncan MacRae, Jr., *Dimensions of Congressional Voting* (Berkeley, 1958).

[10] See, for instance, Donald R. Matthews, *The Social Background of Political Decision-Makers* (Garden City, 1954); or Charles S. Hyneman, "Who Makes Our Laws?" *Political Science Quarterly*, Vol. 55 (December 1940), pp. 556–81.

mands. The function of representation in modern political systems is not to make the legislature a mathematically exact copy of the electorate.

But the difficulty of finding an identity between representative and represented does not also mean that a representative's point of reference in making decisions cannot be his district. It may or may not be, and whether it is or not is a matter of empirical inquiry. We merely doubt that what orients a representative towards his district rather than some other focus of attention is the similarity between his district's characteristics and his own. We cannot assume, therefore, that even if a representative incorporates in himself the characteristics of his district—which, for argument's sake, may be admitted when he comes from a relatively homogeneous area—he will be more oriented towards the district than a representative who, from the point of view of district characteristics, is a deviant. In fact, the latter may be more concerned with his district and seek to discover its "interests," if they are discoverable, than the former. And if a district interest, so-called, can be specifically singled out, it is more likely to be the interest of a politically salient group in the district than of the district as an undifferentiated entity.

In so far as the district rather than some other unit, such as the entire commonwealth, is at the representative's focus of attention, it is more likely to be a function of political than of demographic or socio-economic variables. The problem is one of discovering under what conditions the representative can afford to disregard the district and still hope to maintain the confidence of his constituents. We might speculate, for instance, that in so far as he cherishes the position of power he holds, he is unlikely to ignore his district. We should expect, therefore, that representatives from districts where competition between the parties is keen are more district-

oriented than representatives from one-party districts. Yet, we also know that competitive districts are more likely to be found in the heterogeneous metropolitan areas where district "interests" are difficult to ascertain.[11] In other words, what tends to orient the representative towards his district is likely to be the mechanism of political responsibility effectuated by political competition. District-oriented representatives from metropolitan areas where party competition is strong are, therefore, likely to rely on their own judgment, for a mandate must yield here to discretion to satisfy the demands of political responsibility. Discretion, of course, does not mean that the representative is wholly free to act as he pleases. On the contrary, it means that he will have due regard for all the considerations relevant in the making of legislative decisions. And among these considerations, certainly, the "interests" of his electorate or segments of the electorate, as well as his own estimate of the limits which these interests set to his actions, are important. As Burke admitted,

it ought to be the happiness and glory of a representative to live in the strictest union, the closest correspondence, and the most unreserved communication with his constituents. Their wishes ought to have great weight with him; their opinion high respect, their business unremitted attention. . . .

Though analytically the foci and the style of the representative's role are distinct, they can be expected to be related empirically in a system of mutually interpenetrating orientations. In other words, just as we need not assume that a commitment to district invariably involves the representative's following instructions from his district (the role orientation of Delegate), or that a commonweal-oriented

---

[11]See Heinz Eulau, "The Ecological Basis of Party Systems: The Case of Ohio," *Midwest Journal of Political Science*, Vol. 1 (August 1957), pp. 125–35.

representative is invariably a free agent (the role orientation of Trustee), so also we need not assume that the foci of a representative's role are invariably unrelated to his representational style. In fact, it is the functionally related network of roles which makes for a representational *system*. We can assume, for instance, that a representative who is highly sensitive to the conflict of pressure groups, but not committed to any one, is more likely to be a Trustee in his representational role than the representative who feels close to a particular group and, consequently, is more likely to be a Delegate. Similarly, we might expect that a representative not strongly attached to a party, but not independent of it, is likely to shift between his own judgment and instructions (the role orientation of Politico).

<h2 style="text-align:center">IV</h2>

An opportunity to test the validity of the theoretical distinction here made, between the focus and style of representation, as well as of the representative's role, was afforded in connection with a comparative research project undertaken by the authors during the 1957 sessions of the state legislatures in California, New Jersey, Ohio and Tennessee.[12] State legislators in these four states were asked the following question, among others: "How would you describe the job of being a legislator—what are the most important things you should do here?" Of the 474 respondents, 295 gave answers relevant to the stylistic dimension of the representa-

tive's role, and 197 of these gave additional answers referring to the areal focus of their role.[13]

Responses concerning the stylistic dimension yielded three major representational role types: Trustee, Delegate, and Politico.[14] These types may be described as follows:

1. *Trustee:* This role finds expression in two major conceptions which may occur separately or jointly. First, a moralistic interpretation: the representatives is a free agent, he follows what he considers right or just—his convictions or principles, the dictates of his conscience. Second, a rational conception: he follows his own judgments based on an assessment of the facts in each case, his understanding of the problems involved, his thoughtful appraisal of the sides at issue.

The orientation of Trustees derives not only from a purely normative definition, but is often grounded in conditions which make it functionally necessary. The represented may not have the information to give intelligent instructions; the representative is unable to discover what his clienteles want; preferences remain unexpressed; there is no need for instructions because of a presumed harmony of interests between representative and represented—all of these circumstances may be cited as sources of the role orientation of Trustee.

2. *Delegate:* Just as the Trustee is by no means an empirically pure type, the orienta-

---

[12]The samples for the four legislatures are 91 per cent in Tennessee, 94 per cent in California and Ohio, and 100 per cent in New Jersey. The four states composing the total sample represent different regions of the country, different ratios of metropolitan and non-metropolitan population, and different degrees of party competition. The interviews, using fixed schedules, uniform in all four states and including both open-ended, focused-type questions as well as closed, or fixed-answer type questions, averaged about two hours.

[13]The reduction in the number of respondents from the total samples is, of course, due to the open-endedness of the question. Hence not all respondents could be used in the construction of the role types as they emerged from representatives' own definitions, and in the analysis.

[14]In constructing stylistic and areal-focal role orientation types, the responses to the question were coded in terms of (a) characterization of job; (b) objectives of job; and (c) criteria of decision. Each total answer was broken up into individual statements and coded in terms of manifest content rather than latent meanings, though meaning was taken into consideration in locating manifest statements. Role orientation types were constructed by combining relevant manifest statements which seemed to make for a major orientational dimension. In general, data concerning criteria of decision yielded the stylistic orientation, and data concerning the objectives of the job yielded the areal orientation.

tion of Delegate allows for a number of conceptions. All Delegates are, of course, agreed that they should *not* use their independent judgment or convictions as criteria of decision-making. But this does not mean that they feel equally committed to follow instructions, from whatever clientele. Some merely speak of consulting their constituents, though implying that such consultation will have a mandatory effect on their behavior. Others frankly acknowledge their direct dependence on instructions and accept them as a necessary or desirable premise for their decisions. Some may even follow instructions counter to their own judgment or principles. In other words, the possibility of conflict in role orientations is clearly envisaged and resolved in favor of subordinating one's independence to what is considered a superior authority.

3. *Politico:* The classical dichotomization of the concept of representation in terms of free agency and mandate was unlikely to exhaust the possibilities of representational styles. Depending on circumstances, a representative may hold the Trustee orientation at one time, and the Delegate orientation at another time. Or he might seek to reconcile both in terms of a third. One can think of representation as a continuum, with the Trustee and Delegate orientations as poles, and a midpoint where the orientations tend to overlap and, within a range, give rise to a third role. Within this middle range the roles may be taken simultaneously, possibly making for conflict, or they may be taken serially, one after another as conditions call for.

Because the data do not permit sharp discrimination between the two possibilities, we shall speak of representatives who express both orientations, either simultaneously or serially, as Politicos. In general, then, the Politico as a representational role type differs from both the Trustee and the Delegate in that he is more sensitive to conflicting alternatives in role assumption, more flexible in the way he resolves the conflict of alternatives, and less dogmatic in his representational style as it is relevant to his decision-making behavior.

The spell of the Burkean formulation on the interpretation of representation tended to create reactions which, it seems, are almost as arbitrary as Burke's formula

itself. In particular, the functional notion, itself quite realistic under modern conditions, that the legislature is an agency for the coordination and integration of diverse social, economic and political interests makes apparent the simple-mindedness of Burke's theory, now as then. Carl J. Friedrich, for instance, has pointed out that "the pious formula that representatives are not bound by mandate, that they are subject only to their conscience and are supposed to serve the common weal, which is repeated in so many European constitutions, while significant as a norm, may lead to differentiating as well as to integrating results."[15] Yet, in concentrating on the multiplicity of potential representational foci, Friedrich went too far in his rejection of Burke. For, once the distinction is made between the style of the representative's role and its focus, Burke's "pious formula" is still relevant. Both the focus and the style are likely to be influenced by the character of politics at a given time and by the demands of contemporary political circumstances on the representative as a decision-maker. Functional analysis cannot limit itself to the foci of representation alone, but must also pay attention to those political requirements which may be relevant to the representative's style.

Our hypothesis may be stated as follows: the exigencies of modern government, even on the relatively low level of state government, are exceedingly complex. Taxation and finance, education and public welfare, legal reform, licensing and regulatory problems, transportation, and so on, are topics more often than not, beyond the comprehension of the average citizen. Unable to understand their problems and helpless to cope with them, people are likely to entrust the affairs of government to the elected representatives who, presumably, are better informed than their constituents. People may pay

---

[15]*Constitutional Government and Democracy* (Boston, rev. ed., 1950), p. 297.

TABLE 1

Distribution of Representational Role Orientations in Four States

Representational Role Orientation	Calif. $(N = 49)$	N.J. $(N = 54)$	Ohio $(N = 114)$	Tenn. $(N = 78)$	Total $(N = 295)$
Trustee	55%	61%	56%	81%	63%
Politico	25	22	29	13	23
Delegate	20	17	15	6	14
Total	100%	100%	100%	100%	100%

lip service to the notion that a representative should *not* use his independent judgment,[16] but in fact they are unable, or do not care, to give him instructions as may once have been possible when the tasks of government were comparatively simpler. It is likely, therefore, that the representative has become less and less a Delegate and more and more a Trustee as the business of government has become more and more intricate and technical. Rather than being a "pious formula," the role orientation of Trustee may be a functional necessity, and one should expect it to be held by state legislators more frequently than that of Politico, and the latter more frequently than that of Delegate.

A test of this general proposition is possible by way of comparative analysis of the distribution of representational role styles in the four states. As Table 1 indicates the role orientation of Trustee is held by a greater number of legislators than that of either Politico or Delegate. In all four states it appears more frequently, and significantly more frequently, than the other two. Moreover, the Politico appears somewhat more frequently in all states than the Delegate.

The Trustee orientation appears significantly more frequently in Tennessee than in the other three states, a fact that seems to contradict the proposition that the orientation of Trustee varies with the complexity of governmental affairs. As Tennessee is less urbanized and industrialized than the other states, one should expect Tennessee legislators to be less often Trustees and more often Delegates than legislators in California, New Jersey or Ohio. But it may also be that "complexity" is a function of perceptions, regardless of the real situation. If so, then to Tennesseans the relatively less complex character of socio-economic life may appear more complex than it actually is, compared with the other states. The more frequent appearance of the Trustee orientation there may only be symptomatic of an even greater feeling of helplessness and inefficacy on the part of people *vis-à-vis* governmental problems, as it is perceived by state representatives. Such perceptions may be a reflection of the lower educational level in Tennessee; but to demonstrate this is beyond the limits of this analysis.[17]

---

[16]In the years before the second World War, public opinion polls several times sampled expectations in this regard. Relevant poll questions were: (1) Do you believe that a Congressman should vote on any question as the majority of his constituents desire or vote according to his own judgment? (2) Should members of Congress vote according to their own best judgment or according to the way the people in their district feel? (3) In cases when a Congressman's opinion is different from that of the majority of the people in his district, do you think he should usually vote according to his own best judgment, or according to the way the majority of his district feels? In three of four polls, 61, 63 and 66 per cent, respectively, of the respondents said the Congressman should vote the way people feel. In the fourth poll, only 37 per cent gave this answer. See Hadley Cantril, ed., *Public Opinion, 1935–1946* (Princeton, 1951), p. 133.

---

[17]As the Trustee orientation includes responses stressing traditional moral values, it might be assumed that these virtues—such as following one's conscience or what one feels to

V

If, as suggested earlier, a representative's areal-focal orientation does not automatically derive from ascertainable district interests or from personal characteristics he may share with his constituents, the question arises where such orientations do come from, and how they intrude on the representative's conception of his role. For the purposes of this study, it was possible to delineate three areal-focal orientations which may be described as follows:

1. *District-orientation:* District-oriented representatives had essentially two alternatives: either they could simply mention their districts or counties as being relevant in their conception of their jobs, or they could explicitly place their districts as being above the state as an important factor in their legislative behavior. Among the former, the most frequent responses suggested that it is the representative's job to take care of his district's needs and pass legislation which will benefit his district or county. Others emphasized the policy problems involved in legislation and the necessity to protect what they considered district interests from the policy point of view. Or the emphasis was on the services which these representatives think they are expected to render for their district. Another group of district-oriented representatives specifically pointed to the importance of placing the interests of their district above those of the state, though they usually admitted that state concerns should also be given consideration.

2. *State-orientation:* As in the case of the district-oriented respondents, state-oriented representatives may either mention the state alone as the salient focus, or they may also mention the district, but clearly tend to place

state above district. Some emphasized the need of state policy or state programs as an overriding consideration. A second group pointed to both state and district as relevant foci, but tended to give the benefit of doubt to the state. Finally, some state-oriented representatives explicitly emphasized the desirability of overcoming parochial considerations in favor of the state.

3. *District-and-state-orientation:* A third major group of respondents who spontaneously concerned themselves with the areal focus of their role mentioned both district and state, but, apparently, did not envisage a possibility of conflict and thought that they could attend to both foci without undue difficulty. Yet, the generality of the responses given in this connection may be deceptive, and coding them under this rubric may have been somewhat arbitrary in a number of cases. Though the actual language used tended in the direction of the state as the focus of role orientation, the tone often appeared to be more indicative of a latent district orientation. One should expect these hyphenated representatives to resemble district- more than state-oriented representatives.

Areal role orientations may be assumed to be a function of the dynamics of the democratic political system with its emphasis on the responsibility of the representatives to the represented. Political responsibility—a set of relationships in which the elected are sensitive to the power of the electors over them, and in which the elected are aware of the sanctions which make responsibility a reality —is predicated on the existence of a competitive political system where constituents have a genuine choice, *i.e.*, where the representatives are periodically confronted with the real possibility of removal from office. The sanction of removal inherent in a competitive party system serves to focus representatives' attention on their district rather than the state as the crucial point of reference. Representatives from competitive areas are more likely to be district-oriented than representatives from one-party areas, while representatives from one-party areas are

---

be "right"—are more valued in rural Tennessee than in the three more urbanized states. But inspection of the frequency with which this attitude appears in Tennessee as against the other states does not reveal significantly different distributions of relevant responses: California—18%; New Jersey—8%; Ohio—28%; and Tennessee—23%.

TABLE 2
Distribution of Areal Role Orientations in Four States

Areal Role Orientation	California $(N = 113)$	New Jersey $(N = 79)$	Ohio $(N = 162)$	Tennessee $(N = 120)$	Total $(N = 474)$
District	35%	27%	28%	21%	27%
District-and-State	14	28	25	8	19
State	20	14	16	9	15
No mention	31	31	31	62	39
Total	100%	100%	100%	100%	100%

more likely to be state-oriented than those from competitive areas.

An initial, though crude, test of this hypothesis is possible by examining the distribution of areal role orientations in the four states. Tennessee representatives might be expected to be less district-oriented than representatives in the other states, in view of the predominant one-party character of Tennessee politics. As Table 2 indicates, the data support this hypothesis. Though the percentage differences are small and statistically not significant, except in the California-Tennessee contrast, only 21 per cent of the Tennessee representatives are district-oriented as against 35 per cent in California, 27 per cent in New Jersey, and 28 per cent in Ohio. But the most noticeable aspect of Table 2 is the fact that Tennessee representatives in significantly greater proportion failed to express themselves spontaneously in this connection. Why this is so can, at this point, be only a matter of speculation. Tennessee representatives may take whatever areal foci they have so much for granted that they feel no need to mention them, or they may simply be less articulate than representatives elsewhere. Finally, while there is a somewhat sharper differentiation between district and state role orientations in California than in New Jersey and Ohio (where the combined category figures more prominently), relatively few representatives in all states mentioned the state alone as the focus of their areal orientation.

A more severe test of the hypothesis

is possible by relating areal role orientations to the political character of representatives' home districts. Because party competition as an independent variable has no room for operation in predominantly one-party Tennessee,[18] Table 3 presents the combined data for California, New Jersey and Ohio alone.[19] As Table 3 shows, 53 per cent of the representatives from competitive districts were district-oriented, while only 33 per cent of those from one-party districts were so classified. On the other hand, one-party district representatives held in significantly greater proportion a state orientation than those from competitive districts.[20] The data support the hypothesis that areal orientation varies with the political character of the district in which representatives are elected.[21]

[18]Of the 46 Tennessee respondents who mentioned an areal orientation, only four came from competitive and five from semi-competitive districts.

[19]Competition in district was severally defined in the four states on the basis of past election returns. Space limitations prevent us from specifying the criteria here. They may be obtained from the authors.

[20]$\chi^2 = 9.238$ for the entire array, where d.f. = 4, p $\geq$ .05. If the middle categories are omitted and only competitive and one-party districts are compared with respect to state and district orientation alone, $\chi^2 = 7.12$; d.f. = 1; p < .01.

[21]However, this finding may be spurious. It might be less a function of the political character of the district than of its ecological character. Competitive districts are, more often than not, located in metropolitan areas, while one-party districts are more frequent in non-metropolitan areas. It seemed advisable, therefore, to control the districts' political character by their ecological

TABLE 3
Political Character of Electoral Districts and Areal
Role Orientations in Three States*

Areal Role Orientation	Political Character of District		
	Competitive $(N = 72)$	Semi-competitive $(N = 77)$	One-party $(N = 96)$
District	53%	48%	33%
District-and-State	28	34	33
State	19	18	34
Total	100%	100%	100%

*California, New Jersey and Ohio. "Non-respondents" on the areal dimension have been omitted.

VI

The analytical distinction between the foci and the style of representation is helpful in dissecting the representative's role. Actual behavior is not a function of discrete role orientations, however, but of a system of such orientations. It is the network of interpenetrating roles which gives pattern and coherence to the representational process. It is essential, therefore, to relate areal and stylistic role orientations to each other in terms of significant hypotheses about conditions of their co-variation in the representational system.

It has been suggested earlier that, analytically, stylistic role orientations are neutral. What correlation may be found

character. For this purpose, the districts were divided on the basis of the 1950 Census specifications. The hypothesis concerning the relationship between political character of district and areal orientation was clearly maintained in both metropolitan and non-metropolitan districts. However, while the pattern proved similar in both ecological categories, a greater proportion of of district-and-state-oriented representatives appeared in the non-metropolitan than in the metropolitan areas, suggesting a pull towards greater dichotomization of areal orientations in the metropolitan environment. In view of the intimate connection in industrialized states between metropolitan and state-wide problems, this result is not surprising. It seems that the state is more salient as a focus of attention for representatives from metropolitan districts (no matter what their political character) than from non-metropolitan districts.

empirically, therefore, should depend on some crucial attribute in the independent variable—in this connection the areal role orientation. It may be suggested that this crucial attribute is the condition of effective political responsibility. In so far as they differ, district-oriented representatives are ultimately responsible for their constituents, while state-oriented representatives are not responsible to an equivalent state-wide constituency. The state-oriented representative cannot point to a state-wide clientele from which he could possibly receive a mandate.[22] Hence the hypothesis may be advanced that state-oriented representatives are more likely to be Trustees than district-oriented representatives, whereas the latter are more likely to be Delegates than the former. As Table 4 demonstrates, this is in fact the case. While 84 per cent of the state-oriented representatives are Trustees, only 37 per cent of the district-oriented and 55 per cent of the district-and-state-oriented representatives are so. And while 36 per cent of the district-oriented representatives are Delegates, only 8 per cent of the district-and-state-oriented and none of the state-oriented hold a mandatory view of their representational role.

[22]He might, of course, receive instructions from a state-wide clientele such as a pressure group or political party, but these constitute other dimensions of his attention foci.

TABLE 4
Areal-Focal and Representational Role Orientations in Four States*

Representational Role Orientation	District oriented ($N = 89$)	State-District-oriented ($N = 64$)	State-oriented ($N = 44$)
Trustee	37%	55%	84%
Delegate	36	8	—
Politico	27	37	16
Total	100%	100%	100%

* χ^2 for the entire array $= 37.759$; d.f. $= 4$; $p < .001$.

Moreover, Table 4 supports some corollary hypotheses. In the first place, because a representative is district-oriented, he need not be a Delegate any more frequently than a Trustee. This simply means that though a representative may clearly have his district at his focus of attention, he may nevertheless act on behalf of the district, in his own conception, as a free agent. Such a representative will say that he knows and understands what the district needs and wants, and he rejects the notion that anybody in the district can tell him what to do. As Table 4 shows, among the district-oriented representatives, almost equal proportions, 37 per cent and 36 per cent respectively, are Trustees and Delegates. On the other hand, state-oriented representatives are more likely to be Trustees than anything else. This hypothesis is based on the assumption that the state-oriented representatives do not and cannot recognize a state-wide areal clientele which could give them instructions. As Table 4 indicates, none of the state-oriented representatives is a Delegate, and only 16 per cent are Politicos.

Finally, if the representative's areal focus is both his district and the state, one should expect that he will take the role of Politico more frequently than either the district- or the state-oriented representative. For, because he stresses both foci, he is likely to be subject to cross-pressures: as a district-oriented representative he will take the role of Delegate at least as frequently as that of Trustee; as a state-oriented representative he will take the role of Trustee more frequently than any other. We should expect, therefore, that this representative will not only be a Politico more frequently than the other two areal-orientational types, but also that he will take the Trustee role more frequently than the Delegate role. Both hypotheses find support in the data reported in Table 4. While the differences are small, 37 per cent of the district-and-state-oriented representatives are Politicos, while only 16 per cent and 27 per cent of the other two groups admit to this representational style. Moreover, a majority are also Trustees, while only 8 per cent are Delegates —evidence of the differential effect of areal orientations on the particular stylistic roles which seem most appropriate.

This analysis supports the notion that the areal-focal and stylistic dimensions of representation give rise to role orientations which, though analytically distinct, constitute a role system, and that this system gives the process of representation both its structure and its function.

CONSTITUENCY INFLUENCE IN CONGRESS*

Warren E. Miller and Donald E. Stokes

Substantial constituency influence over the lower house of Congress is commonly thought to be both a normative principle and a factual truth of American government. From their draft constitution we may assume the Founding Fathers expected it, and many political scientists feel, regretfully, that the Framers' wish has come all too true.[1] Nevertheless, much of the evidence of constituency control rests on inference. The fact that our House of Representatives, especially by comparison with the House of Commons, has irregular party voting does not of itself indicate that Congressmen deviate from party in response to local pressure. And even more, the fact that many Congressmen *feel* pressure from home does not of itself establish that the local constituency is performing any of the acts that a reasonable definition of control would imply.

I. CONSTITUENCY CONTROL IN THE NORMATIVE THEORY OF REPRESENTATION

Control by the local constituency is at one pole of *both* the great normative controversies about representation that have arisen in modern times. It is generally recognized that constituency control is opposite to the conception of representation associated with Edmund Burke. Burke wanted the representative to serve the constituency's *interest* but not its *will*, and the extent to which the representative should be compelled by electoral sanctions to follow the "mandate" of his constituents has been at the heart of the ensuing controversy as it has continued for a century and a half.[2]

Constituency control also is opposite to the conception of government by responsible national parties. This is widely seen, yet the point is rarely connected with normative discussions of representa-

---

*Reprinted from the *American Political Science Review*, Vol. LVII (March 1963), pp. 45–56. Copyright 1963, The American Political Science Association.

The research reported here was made possible through grants of the Rockefeller Foundation and the Social Science Research Council, whose support is gratefully acknowledged. The authors are indebted also to Ralph Bisco and Gudmund R. Iversen for invaluable assistance.

[1] To be sure, the work of the Federal Convention has been supplemented in two critical respects. The first of these is the practice, virtually universal since the mid-19th Century, of choosing Representatives from single-member districts of limited geographic area. The second is the practice, which has also become virtually universal in our own century, of selecting party nominees for the House by direct primary election.

---

[2] In the language of Eulau, Wahlke *et al.*, we speak here of the "style," not the "focus," of representation. See their "The Role of the Representative: Some Empirical Observations on the Theory of Edmund Burke," *American Political Science Review*, Vol. LIII (September 1959), pp. 742–756. An excellent review of the mandate–independence controversy is given by Hanna Fenichel Pitkin, "The Theory of Representation" (unpublished doctoral dissertation, University of California, Berkeley, 1961). For other contemporary discussions of representation, see Alfred de Grazia, *Public and Republic* (New York, 1951), and John A. Fairlie, "The Nature of Political Representation," *American Political Science Review*, Vol. XXXIV (April–June 1940), pp. 236–48, 456–66.

tion. Indeed, it is remarkable how little attention has been given to the model of representation implicit in the doctrine of a "responsible two-party system." When the subject of representation is broached among political scientists the classical argument between Burke and his opponents is likely to come at once to mind. So great is Burke's influence that the antithesis he proposed still provides the categories of thought used in contemporary treatments of representation despite the fact that many students of politics today would advocate a relationship between representative and constituency that fits *neither* position of the mandate-independence controversy.

The conception of representation implicit in the doctrine of responsible parties shares the idea of popular control with the instructed-delegate model. Both are versions of popular sovereignty. But "the people" of the responsible two-party system are conceived in terms of a national rather than a local constituency. Candidates for legislative office appeal to the electorate in terms of a *national* party program and leadership, to which, if elected, they will be committed. Expressions of policy preference by the local district are reduced to endorsements of one or another of these programs, and the local district retains only the arithmetical significance that whichever party can rally to its program the greater number of supporters in the district will control its legislative seat.

No one tradition of representation has entirely dominated American practice. Elements of the Burkean, instructed-delegate, and responsible-party models can all be found in our political life. Yet if the American system has elements of all three, a good deal depends on how they are combined. Especially critical is the question whether different models of representation apply to different public issues. Is the saliency of legislative action to the public so different in quality

and degree on different issues that the legislator is subject to very different constraints from his constituency? Does the legislator have a single generalized mode of response to his constituency that is rooted in a normative belief about the representative's role or does the same legislator respond to his constituency differently on different issues? More evidence is needed on matters so fundamental to our system.

II. AN EMPIRICAL STUDY OF REPRESENTATION

To extend what we know of representation in the American Congress the Survey Research Center of The University of Michigan interviewed the incumbent Congressman, his non-incumbent opponent (if any), and a sample of constituents in each of 116 congressional districts, which were themselves a probability sample of all districts.[3] These in-

---

[3]The sampling aspects of this research were complicated by the fact that the study of representation was a rider midway on a four-year panel study of the electorate whose primary sampling units were not congressional districts (although there is no technical reason why they could not have been if the needs of the representation analysis had been foreseen when the design of the sample was fixed two years before). As a result, the districts in our sample had unequal probabilities of selection and unequal weights in the analysis, making the sample somewhat less efficient than an equal-probability sample of equivalent size.

It will be apparent in the discussion that follows that we have estimated characteristics of whole constituencies from our samples of constituents living in particular districts. In view of the fact that a sample of less than two thousand constituents has been divided among 116 districts, the reader may wonder about the reliability of these estimates. After considerable investigation we have concluded that their sampling error is not so severe a problem for the analysis as we had thought it would be. Several comments may indicate why it is not.

To begin with, the weighting of our sample of districts has increased the reliability of the constituency estimates. The correct theoretical weight to be assigned each district in the analysis is the inverse of the probability of the district's selection, and it can be shown that this weight

terviews, conducted immediately after the congressional election of 1958, explored a wide range of attitudes and perceptions held by the individuals who play the reciprocal roles of the representative relation in national government. The distinguishing feature of this research is, of course, that it sought direct information from both constituent and legislator (actual and aspiring). To this fund of comparative interview data has been added information about the roll call votes of our sample of Congressmen and the political and social characteristics of the districts they represent.

Many students of politics, with excellent reason, have been sensitive to possible ties between representative and constituent that have little to do with issues of public policy. For example, ethnic identifications may cement a legislator in the affections of his district, whatever (within limits) his stands on issues. And many Congressmen keep

their tenure of office secure by skillful provision of district benefits ranging from free literature to major federal projects. In the full study of which this analysis is part we have explored several bases of constituency support that have little to do with policy issues. Nevertheless, the question how the representative should make up his mind on legislative issues is what the classical arguments over representation are all about, and we have given a central place to a comparison of the policy preferences of constituents and Representatives and to a causal analysis of the relation between the two.

In view of the electorate's scanty information about government it was not at all clear in advance that such a comparison could be made. Some of the more buoyant advocates of popular sovereignty have regarded the citizen as a kind of kibitzer who looks over the shoulder of his representative at the legislative game. Kibitzer and player may dis-

---

is approximately proportional to the number of interviews taken in the district. The result of this is that the greatest weight is assigned the districts with the largest number of interviews and, hence, the most reliable constituency estimates. Indeed, these weights increase by half again the (weighted) mean number of interviews taken per district. To put the matter another way: the introduction of differential weights trades some of our sample of congressional districts for more reliable constituency estimates.

How much of a problem the unreliability of these estimates is depends very much on the analytic uses to which the estimates are put. If our goal were case analyses of particular districts, the constituency samples would have to be much larger. Indeed, for most case analyses we would want several hundred interviews per district (at a cost, over 116 districts, of several small nuclear reactors). However, most of the findings reported here are based not on single districts but on many or all of the districts in our sample. For analyses of this sort the number of interviews per district can be much smaller.

Our investigation of the effect of the sampling variance of the constituency estimates is quite reassuring. When statistics computed from our constituency samples are compared with corresponding parameter values for the constituencies, the agreement of the two sets of figures is quite close. For example, when the proportions

voting Democratic in the 116 constituencies in 1958, as computed from our sample data, are compared with the actual proportions voting Democratic, as recorded in official election statistics, a product moment correlation of 0.93 is obtained, and this figure is the more impressive since this test throws away non-voters, almost one-half of our total sample. We interpret the Pearsonian correlation as an appropriate measure of agreement in this case, since the associated regression equations are almost exactly the identity function. The alternative intraclass correlation coefficient has almost as high a value.

Although we believe that this analysis provides a textbook illustration of how misleading intuitive ideas (including our own) about the effects of sampling error can be, these figures ought not to be too beguiling. It is clear that how close such a correlation is to 1.0 for any given variable will depend on the ratio of the between-district variance to the total variance. When this ratio is as high as it is for Republican and Democratic voting, the effect of the unreliability of our constituency estimates is fairly trivial. Although the content of the study is quite different, this sampling problem has much in common with the problem of attenuation of correlation as it has been treated in psychological testing. See, for example, J. P. Guilford, *Fundamental Statistics in Psychology and Education* (New York, 1956), pp. 475–78.

agree as to which card should be played, but they were at least thought to share a common understanding of what the alternatives are.

No one familiar with the findings of research on mass electorates could accept this view of the citizen. Far from looking over the shoulder of their Congressmen at the legislative game, most Americans are almost totally uninformed about legislative issues in Washington. At best the average citizen may be said to have some general ideas about how the country should be run, which he is able to use in responding to particular questions about what the government ought to do. For example, survey studies have shown that most people have a general (though differing) conception of how far government should go to achieve social and economic welfare objectives and that these convictions fix their response to various particular questions about actions government might take.[4]

What makes it possible to compare the policy preferences of constituents and Representatives despite the public's low awareness of legislative affairs is the fact that Congressmen themselves respond to many issues in terms of fairly broad evaluative dimensions. Undoubtedly policy alternatives are judged in the executive agencies and the specialized committees of the Congress by criteria that are relatively complex and specific to the policies at issue. But a good deal of evidence goes to show that when proposals come before the House as a whole they are judged on the basis of more general evaluative dimensions.[5] For example, most Congressmen, too, seem to have a general

conception of how far government should go in the area of domestic social and economic welfare, and these general positions apparently orient their roll call votes on a number of particular social welfare issues.

It follows that such a broad evaluative dimension can be used to compare the policy preferences of constituents and Representatives despite the low state of the public's information about politics. In this study three such dimensions have been drawn from our voter interviews and from congressional interviews and roll call records. As suggested above, one of these has to do with approval of government action in the social welfare field, the primary domestic issue of the New Deal–Fair Deal (and New Frontier) eras. A second dimension has to do with support for American involvement in foreign affairs, a latter-day version of the isolationist–internationalist continuum. A third dimension has to do with approval of federal action to protect the civil rights of Negroes.[6]

Because our research focused on these

[4]See Angus Campbell, Phillip E. Converse, Warren E. Miller, and Donald E. Stokes, *The American Voter* (New York, 1960), pp. 194–209.

[5]This conclusion, fully supported by our own work for later Congresses, is one of the main findings to be drawn from the work of Duncan MacRae on roll call voting in the House of Representatives. See his *Dimensions of Congressional Voting: A Statistical Study of the House of Representatives in the Eighty-First Congress* (Berkeley and Los Angeles: University of California Press, 1958). For additional evidence of the existence of scale dimensions in legislative behavior, see N. L. Gage and Ben Shimberg, "Measuring Senatorial Progressivism," *Journal of Abnormal and Social Psychology*, Vol. XLIV (January 1949), pp. 112–17; George M. Belknap, "A Study of Senatorial Voting by Scale Analysis" (unpublished doctoral dissertation, University of Chicago, 1951), and "A Method for Analyzing Legislative Behavior," *Midwest Journal of Political Science*, Vol. II (1958), pp. 377–402; two other articles by MacRae, "The Role of the State Legislator in Massachusetts," *American Sociological Review*, Vol. XIX (April 1954), pp. 185–94, and "Roll Call Votes and Leadership," *Public Opinion Quarterly*, Vol. XX (1956), pp. 543–58; Charles D. Farris, "A Method of Determining Ideological Groups in Congress," *Journal of Politics*, Vol. XX (1958), pp. 308–38; and Leroy N. Rieselbach, "Quantitative Techniques for Studying Voting Behavior in the U.N. General Assembly," *International Organization*, Vol. XIV (1960), pp. 291–306.

[6]The content of the three issue domains may be suggested by some of the roll call and interview items used. In the area of social welfare these included the issues of public housing, public power, aid to education, and government's role in maintaining full employment. In the area

three dimensions, our analysis of constituency influence is limited to these areas of policy. No point has been more energetically or usefully made by those who have sought to clarify the concepts of power and influence than the necessity of specifying the acts *with respect to which* one actor has power or influence or control over another.[7] Therefore, the scope or range of influence for our analysis is the collection of legislative issues falling within our three policy domains. We are not able to say how much control the local constituency may or may not have over *all* actions of its Representative, and there may well be pork-barrel issues or other matters of peculiar relevance to the district on which the relation of Congressman to constituency is quite distinctive. However, few observers of contemporary politics would regard the issues of government provision of social and economic welfare, of American involvement in world affairs, and of federal action in behalf of the Negro as constituting a trivial range of action. Indeed, these domains together include most of the great issues that have come before Congress in recent years.

In each policy domain we have used the procedures of cumulative scaling, as

developed by Louis Guttman and others, to order our samples of Congressmen, of opposing candidates, and of voters. In each domain Congressmen were ranked once according to their roll call votes in the House and again according to the attitudes they revealed in our confidential interviews. These two orderings are by no means identical, nor are the discrepancies due simply to uncertainties of measurement.[8] Opposing candidates also were ranked in each policy domain according to the attitudes they revealed in our interviews. The nationwide sample of constituents was ordered in each domain, and by averaging the attitude scores of all constituents living in the same districts, whole constituencies were ranked on each dimension so that the views of Congressmen could be compared with those of their constituencies.[9] Fi-

---

of foreign involvement the items included the issues of foreign economic aid, military aid, sending troops abroad, and aid to neutrals. In the area of civil rights the items included the issues of school desegregation, fair employment, and the protection of Negro voting rights.

[7]Because this point has been so widely discussed it has inevitably attracted a variety of terms. Dahl denotes the acts of *a* whose performance *A* is able to influence as the *scope* of *A's* power. See Robert A. Dahl, "The Concept of Power," *Behavioral Science*, Vol. II (July 1957), pp. 201–15. This usage is similar to that of Harold D. Lasswell and Abraham Kaplan, *Power and Society* (New Haven: Yale University Press, 1950), pp. 71–73. Dorwin Cartwright, however, denotes the behavioral or psychological changes in *P* which *O* is able to induce as the *range* of *O's* power: "A Field Theoretical Conception of Power," *Studies in Social Power* (Ann Arbor: Research Center for Group Dynamics, Institute for Social Research, The University of Michigan, 1959), pp. 183–220.

---

[8]That the Representative's roll call votes can diverge from his true opinion is borne out by a number of findings of the study (some of which are reported here) as to the conditions under which agreement between the Congressman's roll call position and his private attitude will be high or low. However, a direct confirmation that these two sets of measurements are not simply getting at the same thing is given by differences in attitude–roll call agreement according to the Congressman's sense of how well his roll call votes have expressed his real views. In the domain of foreign involvement, for example, the correlation of our attitudinal and roll call measurements was .75 among Representatives who said that their roll call votes had expressed their real views fairly well. But this correlation was only .04 among those who said that their roll call votes had expressed their views poorly. In the other policy domains, too, attitude–roll call agreement is higher among Congressmen who are well satisfied with their roll call votes than it is among Congressmen who are not.

[9]During the analysis we have formed constituency scores out of the scores of constituents living in the same district by several devices other than calculating average constituent scores. In particular, in view of the ordinal character of our scales we have frequently used the *median* constituent score as a central value for the constituency as a whole. However, the ordering of constituencies differs very little according to which of several reasonable alternatives for obtaining constituency scores is chosen. As a result, we have preferred mean scores for the greater number of ranks they give.

nally, by considering only the constituents in each district who share some characteristic (voting for the incumbent, say) we were able to order these fractions of districts so that the opinions of Congressmen could be compared with those, for example, of the dominant electoral elements of their districts.

In each policy domain, crossing the rankings of Congressmen and their constituencies gives an empirical measure of the extent of policy agreement between legislator and district.[10] In the period of our research this procedure reveals very different degrees of policy congruence across the three issue domains. On questions of social and economic welfare there is considerable agreement between Representative and district, expressed by a correlation of approximately 0.3. This coefficient is, of course, very much less than the limiting value of 1.0, indicating that a number of Congressmen are, rela-

tively speaking, more or less "liberal" than their districts. However, on the question of foreign involvement there is no discernible agreement between legislator and district whatever. Indeed, as if to emphasize the point, the coefficient expressing this relation is slightly negative (-0.09), although not significantly so in a statistical sense. It is in the domain of civil rights that the rankings of Congressmen and constituencies most nearly agree. When we took our measurements in the late 1950s the correlation of congressional roll call behavior with constituency opinion on questions affecting the Negro was nearly 0.6.

The description of policy agreement that these three simple correlations give can be a starting-point for a wide range of analyses. For example, the significance of party competition in the district for

---

[10] The meaning of this procedure can be suggested by two percentage tables standing for hypothetical extreme cases, the first that of full agreement, the second that of no agreement whatever. For convenience, these illustrative tables categorize both Congressmen and their districts in terms of only degrees of favor and assume for both a nearly uniform distribution across the three categories. The terms "pro," "neutral," and "con" indicate a relative rather than an absolute opinion. In Case I, full agreement, all districts relatively favorable to social welfare action have Congressmen who are so too, etc.; whereas in Case II, or that of no agreement, the ordering of constituencies is independent in a statistical sense of the ranking of Congressmen: knowing the policy orientation of a district gives no clue at all to the orientation of its Congressman. Of course, it is possible for the orders of legislators and districts to be *inversely* related, and this possibility is of some importance, as indicated below, when the policy position of non-incumbent candidates as well as incumbents is taken into account. To summarize the degree of congruence between legislators and voters, a measure of correlation is introduced. Although we have used a variety of measures of association in our analysis, the values reported in this article all refer to product moment correlation coefficients. For our hypothetical Case I a measure of correlation would have the value 1.0; for Case II, the value 0.0. When it is applied to actual data this convenient indicator is

likely to have a value somewhere in between. The question is where.

Case I: Full Policy Agreement

Constituencies:

	Pro	Neutral	Con	
Congressmen:				
Pro	33	0	0	33
Neutral	0	34	0	34
Con	0	0	33	33
	33	34	33	100%

Correlation $= 1.0$

Case II: No Policy Agreement

Constituencies:

	Pro	Neutral	Con	
Congressmen:				
Pro	11	11	11	33
Neutral	11	12	11	34
Con	11	11	11	33
	33	34	33	100%

Correlation $= 0.0$

policy representation can be explored by comparing the agreement between district and Congressman with the agreement between the district and the Congressman's non-incumbent opponent. Alternatively, the significance of choosing Representatives from single-member districts by popular majority can be explored by comparing the agreement between the Congressman and his own supporters with the agreement between the Congressman and the supporters of his opponent. Taking *both* party competition and majority rule into account magnifies rather spectacularly some of the coefficients reported here. This is most true in the domain of social welfare, where attitudes both of candidates and of voters are most polarized along party lines. Whereas the correlation between the constituency majority and congressional roll call votes is nearly $+0.4$ on social welfare policy, the correlation of the district majority with the non-incumbent candidate is -0.4. This difference, amounting to almost 0.8, between these two coefficients is an indicator of what the dominant electoral element of the constituency gets on the average by choosing the Congressman it has and excluding his opponent from office.[11]

These three coefficients are also the starting-point for a causal analysis of the relation of constituency to representative, the main problem of this paper. At least on social welfare and Negro rights a measurable degree of congruence is found between district and legislator. Is this agreement due to constituency influence in Congress, or is it to be attributed to other causes? If this question is to have a satisfactory answer the conditions that are necessary and sufficient to assure constituency control must be stated and compared with the available empirical evidence.

III. THE CONDITIONS OF CONSTITUENCY INFLUENCE

Broadly speaking, the constituency can control the policy actions of the Representative in two alternative ways. The first of these is for the district to choose a Representative who so shares its views that in following his own convictions he does his constituents' will. In this case district opinion and the Congressman's actions are connected through the Representative's own policy attitudes. The second means of constituency control is for the Congressman to follow his (at least tolerably accurate) perceptions of district attitude in order to win re-election. In this case constituency opinion and the Congressman's actions are connected through his perception of what the district wants.[12]

These two paths of constituency control are presented schematically in Figure 1. As the figure suggests, each path has two steps, one connecting the constituency's attitude with an "intervening" attitude or perception, the other connecting this attitude or perception with the Representative's roll call behavior. Out of re-

---

[11] A word of caution is in order, lest we compare things that are not strictly comparable. For obvious reasons, most non-incumbent candidates have no roll call record, and we have had to measure their policy agreement with the district entirely in terms of the attitudes they have revealed in interviews. However, the difference of coefficients given here is almost as great when the policy agreement between the incumbent Congressman and his district is also measured in terms of the attitudes conveyed in confidential interviews.

[12] A third type of connection, excluded here, might obtain between district and Congressman if the Representative accedes to what he thinks the district wants because he believes that to be what a representative *ought* to do, whether or not it is necessary for re-election. We leave this type of connection out of our account here because we conceive an influence relation as one in which control is not voluntarily accepted or rejected by someone subject to it. Of course, this possible connection between district and Representative is not any the less interesting because it falls outside our definition of influence or control, and we have given a good deal of attention to it in the broader study of which this analysis is part.

FIGURE 1

Connections between a Constituency's Attitude and
Its Representative's Role Call Behavior

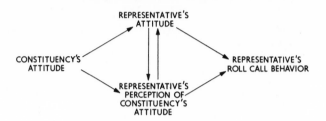

spect for the processes by which the human actor achieves cognitive congruence we have also drawn arrows between the two intervening factors, since the Congressman probably tends to see his district as having the same opinion as his own and also tends, over time, to bring his own opinion into line with the district's. The inclusion of these arrows calls attention to two other possible influence paths, each consisting of *three* steps, although these additional paths will turn out to be of relatively slight importance empirically.

Neither of the main influence paths of Figure 1 will connect the final roll call vote to the constituency's views if either of its steps is blocked. From this, two necessary conditions of constituency influence can be stated: *first*, the Representative's votes in the House must agree substantially with his own policy views or his perceptions of the district's views, and not be determined entirely by other influences to which the Congressman is exposed; and, *second*, the attitudes or perceptions governing the Representative's acts must correspond, at least imperfectly, to the district's actual opinions. It would be difficult to describe the relation of constituency to Representative as one of control unless these conditions are met.[13]

Yet these two requirements are not sufficient to assure control. A *third* condition must also be satisfied: the constituency must in some measure take the policy views of candidates into account in choosing a Representative. If it does not, agreement between district and Congressman may arise for reasons that cannot rationally be brought within the idea of control. For example, such agreement may simply reflect the fact that a Representative drawn from a given area is likely, by pure statistical probability, to share its dominant values, without his acceptance or rejection of these ever having been a matter of consequence to his electors.

IV. EVIDENCE OF CONTROL: CONGRESSIONAL ATTITUDES AND PERCEPTIONS

How well are these conditions met in the relation of American Congressmen to their constituents? There is little question that the first is substantially satisfied; the evidence of our research indicates that members of the House do in fact vote both their own policy views and their perceptions of their constituents' views, at least on issues of social welfare, foreign involvement, and civil rights. If these two intervening factors are used to predict roll call votes, the prediction is quite successful. Their multiple correlation with roll call position is 0.7 for social welfare, 0.6

---

[13]It scarcely needs to be said that demonstrating *some* constituency influence would not imply that the Representative's behavior is *wholly* determined by constituency pressures. The legislator acts in a complex institutional setting in which he is subject to a wide variety of influences. The constituency can exercise a genuine

measure of control without driving all other influences from the Representative's life space.

for foreign involvement, and 0.9 for civil rights; the last figure is especially persuasive. What is more, both the Congressman's own convictions and his perceptions of district opinion make a distinct contribution to his roll call behavior. In each of the three domains the prediction of roll call votes is surer if it is made from both factors rather than from either alone.

Lest the strong influence that the Congressman's views and his perception of district views have on roll call behavior appear somehow foreordained—and, consequently, this finding seem a trivial one —it is worth taking a sidewise glance at the potency of possible other forces on the Representative's vote. In the area of foreign policy, for example, a number of Congressmen are disposed to follow the administration's advice, whatever they or their districts think. For those who are, the multiple correlation of roll call behavior with the Representative's own foreign policy views and his perception of district views is a mere 0.2. Other findings could be cited to support the point that the influence of the Congressman's own preferences and those he attributes to the district is extremely variable. Yet in the House as a whole over the three policy domains the influence of these forces is quite strong.

The connections of congressional attitudes and perceptions with actual constituency opinion are weaker. If policy agreement between district and Representative is moderate and variable across explained much more in terms of the second condition of constituency control than the first. The Representative's attitudes and perceptions most nearly match true opinion in his district on the issues of Negro rights. Reflecting the charged and polarized nature of this area, the correlation of actual district opinion with perceived opinion is greater than 0.6, and the correlation of district attitude with the Representative's own attitude is nearly 0.4, as shown by Table 1. But the com-

TABLE 1
Correlations of Constituency Attitudes

Policy Domain	Correlation of Constituency Attitude with	
	Representative's Perception of Constituency Attitude	Representative's Own Attitude
Social welfare	.17	.21
Foreign involvement	.19	.06
Civil rights	.63	.39

parable correlations for foreign involvement are much smaller—indeed almost negligible. And the coefficients for social welfare are also smaller, although a detailed presentation of findings in this area would show that the Representative's perceptions and attitudes are more strongly associated with the attitude of his electoral *majority* than they are with the attitudes of the constituency as a whole.

Knowing this much about the various paths that may lead, directly or indirectly, from constituency attitude to roll call vote, we can assess their relative importance. Since the alternative influence chains have links of unequal strength, the full chains will not in general be equally strong, and these differences are of great importance in the relation of Representative to constituency. For the domain of civil rights Figure 2 assembles all the intercorrelations of the variables of our system. As the figure shows, the root correlation of constituency attitude with roll call behavior in this domain is 0.57. How much of this policy congruence can be accounted for by the influence path involving the Representative's attitude? And how much by the path involving his perception of constituency opinion? When the intercorrelations of the system are interpreted in the light of what we assume its causal structure to be, it is influence passing through the Congressman's perception of the district's views that is found

FIGURE 2
Intercorrelations of Variables Pertaining to
Civil Rights

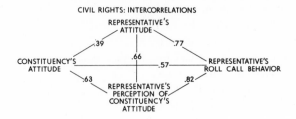

to be preeminently important.[14] Under the

14We have done this by a variance-component technique similar to several others proposed for dealing with problems of this type. See especially Herbert A. Simon, "Spurious Correlation: A Causal Interpretation," *Journal of the American Statistical Association*, Vol. 49 (1954), pp. 467–79; Hubert M. Blalock, Jr., "The Relative Importance of Variables," *American Sociological Review*, Vol. 26 (1961), pp. 866–74; and the almost forgotten work of Sewall Wright, "Correlation and Causation," *Journal of Agricultural Research*, Vol. 20 (1920), pp. 557–85. Under this technique a "path coefficient" (to use Wright's terminology, although not his theory) is assigned to each of the causal arrows by solving a set of equations involving the correlations of the variables of the model. The weight assigned to a full path is then the product of its several path coefficients, and this product may be interpreted as the proportion of the variance of the dependent variable (roll call behavior, here) that is explained by a given path.

A special problem arises because influence may flow in either direction between the Congressman's attitude and his perception of district attitude (as noted above, the Representative may tend both to perceive his constituency's view selectively, as consistent with his own, and to change his own view to be consistent with the perceived constituency view). Hence, we have not a single causal model but a whole family of models, varying according to the relative importance of influence from attitude to perception and from perception to attitude. Our solution to this problem has been to calculate influence coefficients for the two extreme models in order to see how much our results could vary according to which model is chosen from our family of models. Since the systems of equations in this analysis are linear it can be shown that the coefficients we seek have their maximum and minimum values under one or the other of the limiting models. Therefore, computing any given coefficient for each of these limiting cases defines an interval in which the true value of the coeffi-

least favorable assumption as to its importance, this path is found to account for

cient must lie. In fact these intervals turn out to be fairly small; our findings as to the relative importance of alternative influence paths would change little according to which model is selected.

The two limiting models with their associated systems of equations and the formulas for computing the relative importance of the three possible influence paths under each model are given below.

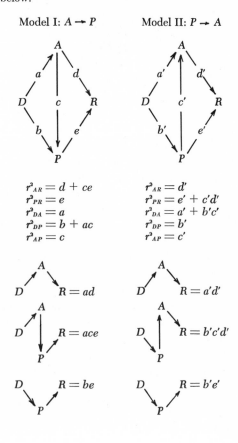

more than twice as much of the variance of roll call behavior as the paths involving the Representative's own attitude.[15] However, when this same procedure is applied to our social welfare data, the results suggest that the direct connection of constituency and roll call through the Congress man's own attitude is the most important of the alternative paths.[16] The reversal of the relative importance of the two paths as we move from civil rights to social welfare is one of the most striking findings of this analysis.

V. EVIDENCE OF CONTROL: ELECTORAL BEHAVIOR

Of the three conditions of constituency influence, the requirement that the electorate take account of the policy positions of the candidates is the hardest to match with empirical evidence. Indeed, given

---

[15]By "least favorable" we mean the assumption that influence goes only from the Congressman's attitude to his perception of district attitude (Model I) and not the other way round. Under this assumption, the proportions of the variance of roll call behavior accounted for by the three alternative paths, expressed as proportions of the part of the variance of roll call votes that is explained by district attitude, are these:

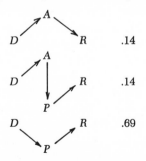

Inverting the assumed direction of influence between the Congressman's own attitude and district attitude (Model II) eliminates altogether the effect that the Representative's attitude can have had on his votes, independently of his perception of district attitude.

[16]Under both Models I and II the proportion of the variance of roll call voting explained by the influence path involving the Representative's own attitude is twice as great as the proportion explained by influence passing through his perception of district attitude.

the limited information the average voter carries to the polls, the public might be thought incompetent to perform any task of appraisal. Of constituents living in congressional districts where there was a contest between a Republican and a Democrat in 1958, less than one in five said they had read or heard something about both candidates, and well over half conceded they had read or heard nothing about either. And these proportions are not much better when they are based only on the part of the sample, not much more than half, that reported voting for Congress in 1958. The extent of awareness of the candidates among voters is indicated in Table 2. As the table shows, even of

TABLE 2
Awareness of Congressional Candidates among Voters, 1958

		Read or Heard Something About Incumbent*		
		Yes	No	
Read or Heard Something About Non-Incumbent	Yes	24	5	29
	No	25	46	71
		49	51	100%

*In order to include all districts where the House seat was contested in 1958 this table retains ten constituencies in which the incumbent Congressman did not seek re-election. Candidates of the retiring incumbent's party in these districts are treated here as if they were incumbents. Were these figures to be calculated only for constituencies in which an incumbent sought re-election, no entry in this four-fold table would differ from that given by more than two percent.

the portion of the public that was sufficiently interested to vote, almost half had read or heard nothing about either candidate.

Just how low a hurdle our respondents had to clear in saying they had read or heard something about a candidate is indicated by detailed qualitative analysis of the information constituents *were* able to associate with congressional candidates. Except in rare cases, what the voters "knew" was confined to diffuse evaluative judgments about the candidate: "he's a good man," "he understands the problems," and so forth. Of detailed information about policy stands not more than a chemical trace was found. Among the comments about the candidates given in response to an extended series of free-answer questions, less than two percent had to do with stands in our three policy domains; indeed, only about three comments in every hundred had to do with legislative issues of *any* description.[17]

This evidence that the behavior of the electorate is largely unaffected by knowledge of the policy positions of the candidates is complemented by evidence about the forces that *do* shape the voters' choices among congressional candidates. The primary basis of voting in American congressional elections is identification with party. In 1958 only one vote in twenty was cast by persons without any sort of party loyalty. And among those who did have a party identification, only one in ten voted against their party. As a result, something like 84 percent of the vote that year was cast by party identifiers voting their usual party line. What is more, traditional party voting is seldom connected with current legislative issues. As the party loyalists in a nationwide sample of voters told us what they liked and disliked about the parties in 1958, only a small fraction of the comments (about 15 percent) dealt with current issues of public policy.[18]

Yet the idea of reward or punishment at

the polls for legislative stands is familiar to members of Congress, who feel that they and their records are quite visible to their constituents. Of our sample of Congressmen who were opposed for re-election in 1958, more than four-fifths said the outcome in their districts had been strongly influenced by the electorate's response to their records and personal standing. Indeed, this belief is clear enough to present a notable contradiction: Congressmen feel that their individual legislative actions may have considerable impact on the electorate, yet some simple facts about the Representative's salience to his constituents imply that this could hardly be true.

In some measure this contradiction is to be explained by the tendency of Congressmen to overestimate their visibility to the local public, a tendency that reflects the difficulties of the Representative in forming a correct judgment of constituent opinion. The communication most Congressmen have with their districts inevitably puts them in touch with organized groups and with individuals who are relatively well informed about politics. The Representative knows his constituents mostly from dealing with people who *do* write letters, who *will* attend meetings, who *have* an interest in his legislative stands. As a result, his sample of contacts with a constituency of several hundred thousand people is heavily biased: even the contacts he apparently makes at random are likely to be with people who grossly overrepresent the degree of political information and interest in the constituency as a whole.

But the contradiction is also to be explained by several aspects of the Representative's electoral situation that are of great importance to the question of constituency influence. The first of these is implicit in what has already been said. Because of the pervasive effects of party loyalties, no candidate for Congress starts from scratch in putting together an electoral majority. The Congressman is a

---

[17]What is more, the electorate's awareness of Congress as a whole appears quite limited. A majority of the public was unable to say in 1958 which of the two parties had controlled the Congress during the preceding two years. Some people were confused by the coexistence of a Republican President and a Democratic Congress. But for most people this was simply an elementary fact about congressional affairs to which they were not privy.

[18]For a more extended analysis of forces on the congressional vote, see Donald E. Stokes and Warren E. Miller, "Party Government and the Saliency of Congress," *Public Opinion Quarterly*, Vol. 26 (Winter 1962), pp. 531–46.

dealer in increments and margins. He starts with a stratum of hardened party voters, and if the stratum is broad enough he can have a measurable influence on his chance of survival simply by attracting a small additional element of the electorate—or by not losing a larger one. Therefore, his record may have a very real bearing on his electoral success or failure without most of his constituents ever knowing what that record is.

Second, the relation of Congressman to voter is not a simple bilateral one but is complicated by the presence of all manner of intermediaries: the local party, economic interests, the news media, racial and nationality organizations, and so forth. Such is the lore of American politics, as it is known to any political scientist. Very often the Representative reaches the mass public through these mediating agencies, and the information about himself and his record may be considerably transformed as it diffuses out to the electorate in two or more stages. As a result, the public—or parts of it—may get simple positive or negative cues about the Congressman which were provoked by his legislative actions but which no longer have a recognizable issue content.

Third, for most Congressmen most of the time the electorate's sanctions are potential rather than actual. Particularly the Representative from a safe district may feel his proper legislative strategy is to avoid giving opponents in his own party or outside of it material they can use against him. As the Congressman pursues this strategy he may write a legislative record that never becomes very well known to his constituents; if it doesn't win votes, neither will it lose any. This is clearly the situation of most southern Congressmen in dealing with the issue of Negro rights. By voting correctly on this issue they are unlikely to increase their visibility to constituents. Nevertheless, the fact of constituency influence, backed by potential sanctions at the polls, is real enough.

That these potential sanctions are all too real is best illustrated in the election of 1958 by the reprisal against Representative Brooks Hays in Arkansas' Fifth District.[19] Although the perception of Congressman Hays as too moderate on civil rights resulted more from his service as intermediary between the White House and Governor Faubus in the Little Rock school crisis than from his record in the House, the victory of Dale Alford as a write-in candidate was a striking reminder of what can happen to a Congressman who gives his foes a powerful issue to use against him. The extraordinary involvement of the public in this race can be seen by comparing how well the candidates were known in this constituency with the awareness of the candidates shown by Table 2 above for the country as a whole. As Table 3 indicates, not a

TABLE 3

Awareness of Congressional Candidates among Voters in Arkansas Fifth District, 1958

		Read or Heard Something about Hays		
		Yes	No	
Read or Heard Something about Alford	Yes	100	0	100
	No	0	0	0
		100	0	100%

single voter in our sample of Arkansas' Fifth District was unaware of either candidate.[20] What is more, these interviews

[19]For an account of this episode see Corinne Silverman, "The Little Rock Story," Inter-University Case Program series, reprinted in Edwin A. Bock and Alan K. Campbell, eds., *Case Studies in American Government* (Englewood Cliffs, 1962), pp. 1–46.

[20]The sample of this constituency was limited to twenty-three persons of whom thirteen voted. However, despite the small number of cases the probability that the difference in awareness between this constituency and the country generally as the result only of sampling variations is much less than one in a thousand.

show that Hays was regarded both by his supporters and his opponents as more moderate than Alford on civil rights and that this perception brought his defeat. In some measure, what happened in Little Rock in 1958 can happen anywhere, and our Congressmen ought not to be entirely disbelieved in what they say about their impact at the polls. Indeed, they may be under genuine pressure from the voters even while they are the forgotten men of national elections.[21]

V. CONCLUSION

Therefore, although the conditions of constituency influence are not equally satisfied, they are met well enough to give the local constituency a measure of control over the actions of its Representatives. Best satisfied is the requirement about motivational influences on the Congressman: our evidence shows that the Representative's role call behavior is strongly influenced by his own policy preferences and by his perception of preferences held by the constituency. However, the conditions of influence that presuppose effective communication between Congressman and district are much less well met. The

---

[21]In view of the potential nature of the constituency's sanctions, it is relevant to characterize its influence over the Representative in terms of several distinctions drawn by recent theorists of power, especially the difference between actual and potential power, between influence and coercive power, and between influence and purposive control. Observing these distinctions, we might say that the constituency's influence is *actual* and not merely *potential* since it is the sanction behavior rather than the conforming behavior that is infrequent (Dahl). That is, the Congressman is influenced by his calculus of potential sanctions, following the "rule of anticipated reactions" (Friedrich), however oblivious of his behavior the constituency ordinarily may be. We might also say that the constituency has *power* since its influence depends partly on sanctions (Lasswell and Kaplan), although it rarely exercises *control* since its influence is rarely conscious or intended (Cartwright). In the discussion above we have of course used the terms "influence" and "control" interchangeably.

Representative has very imperfect information about the issue preferences of his constituency, and the constituency's awareness of the policy stands of the Representative ordinarily is slight.

The findings of this analysis heavily underscore the fact that no single tradition of representation fully accords with the realities of American legislative politics. The American system *is* a mixture, to which the Burkean, instructed-delegate, and responsible-party models all can be said to have contributed elements. Moreover, variations in the representative relation are most likely to occur as we move from one policy domain to another. No single, generalized configuration of attitudes and perceptions links Representative with constituency but rather several distinct patterns, and which of them is invoked depends very much on the issue involved.

The issue domain in which the relation of Congressman to constituency most nearly conforms to the instructed-delegate model is that of civil rights. This conclusion is supported by the importance of the influence-path passing through the Representative's perception of district opinion, although even in this domain the sense in which the constituency may be said to take the position of the candidate into account in reaching its electoral judgment should be carefully qualified.

The representative relation conforms most closely to the responsible-party model in the domain of social welfare. In this issue area, the arena of partisan conflict for a generation, the party symbol helps both constituency and Representative in the difficult process of communication between them. On the one hand, because Republican and Democratic voters tend to differ in what they would have government do, the Representative has some guide to district opinion simply by looking at the partisan division of the vote. On the other hand, because the two parties tend to recruit candidates who

differ on the social welfare role of government, the constituency can infer the candidates' position with more than random
accuracy from their party affiliation, even
though what the constituency has learned
directly about these stands is almost nothing. How faithful the representation of
social welfare views is to the responsible-
party model should not be exaggerated.
Even in this policy domain, American
practice departs widely from an ideal conception of party government.[22] But in this
domain, more than any other, political
conflict has become a conflict of national
parties in which constituency and Representative are known to each other primarily by their party association.

It would be too pat to say that the domain of foreign involvement conforms to
the third model of representation, the con-

ception promoted by Edmund Burke.
Clearly it does in the sense that the Congressman looks elsewhere than to his district in making up his mind on foreign
issues. However, the reliance he puts on
the President and the Administration suggests that the calculation of where the
public interest lies is often passed to the
Executive on matters of foreign policy.
Ironically, legislative initiative in foreign
affairs has fallen victim to the very difficulties of gathering and appraising information that led Burke to argue that Parliament rather than the public ought to
hold the power of decision. The background information and predictive skills
that Burke thought the people lacked are
held primarily by the modern Executive.
As a result, the present role of the legislature in foreign affairs bears some resemblance to the role that Burke had in mind
for the elitist, highly restricted *electorate*
of his own day.

---

[22]The factors in American electoral behavior
that encourage such a departure are discussed
in Stokes and Miller, *loc. cit.*

CAMPAIGN STRATEGY: THE SOUTH AS REPUBLICAN TARGET*

Philip E. Converse, Aage R. Clausen, Warren E. Miller

The strategy of the Goldwater camp for
a November victory was both simple and
relatively selective. Goldwater felt, to begin with, that he could hold on to essentially the same states that Nixon had won
in 1960. This meant a clean sweep of the
populous states of the Pacific Coast, most
of the Mountain and Plains states, and a
scattering east of the Mississippi. To reap
the additional electoral votes for victory,

---

*Philip Converse, Aage R. Clausen, Warren
Miller, "Electoral Myth and Reality: The 1964
Election," reprinted from the *American Political
Science Review*, Vol. LIX (June 1965), pp. 327–
36. Copyright 1965, The American Political Sci-
ence Association.

Goldwater believed that the way lay
open, under proper circumstances, for the
Republican Party to make further major
inroads in the once solidly Democratic
South. The plan implied that Goldwater
could largely afford to write off the populous industrial states of the Northeast and
some, if not all, of the Midwest—a matter
which greatly reduced the importance of
the dissident liberal Republican bloc. And
it represented a dramatic departure from
any past Republican strategy in making
of the South a fulcrum for victory.

Such a strategy was not only unusual
but, against the long sweep of American
electoral history, it might even be thought

of as implausible. Yet it was no hastily devised scheme. For years Goldwater had participated in the Congressional coalition between conservative Republicans and Southern Democrats. The same drive for ideological neatness that led him to call for the reorganization of American politics into "Conservative" and "Liberal" parties impressed upon him the grotesque incongruity of a Democratic South. The South had no reason to be a Democratic bastion; by all of its affinities and traditions, it should long since have become Republican. Part of the problem lay with the national Republican Party, which, in the control of the Northeastern bloc, had failed to present national-level candidates making clear that Republicanism was the natural home of the Southern voter. This had been a frustrating fact since Goldwater's entry into national politics—a period during which political observers had frequently predicted an imminent partisan realignment of the South; but gains in the region, while very obvious, had remained rather modest. In discussions of Republican difficulty in recapturing majority status in the land, Goldwater had opined that the Party had to learn to "go hunting in the pond where the ducks are"—the South. As bitterness began to mount in that region toward the civil rights pressures of the Kennedy Administration, the time seemed more ripe than ever for the presentation of a purely conservative Republican candidate who could appeal to the Southern ethos in a most direct way, thereby breaking the Democratic hold on the region in one dramatic and decisive stroke.

This long-planned strategy had suffered two temporary but alarming setbacks. The assassination of President Kennedy suddenly placed a Southerner in the White House, and removed from power the most feared personal symbols of federal intrusion. The continuation of the Kennedy beginnings by the Johnson Administration, however—particularly in the 1964 Civil

Rights bill—helped to reset the stage. So did the increased signs of Negro unrest, and the new element of "white backlash" in the North as well as the South that seemed apparent in the spring primaries. The capping touch was Goldwater's vote against the Civil Rights bill. This vote, to be sure, represented no condoning of segregationism *per se*, but rather a blow for states' rights against the encroachment of the federal government. Nevertheless, white supremacists in the South had so long paraded under the states' rights banner as to leave little room for fear lest the Goldwater gesture go unappreciated. The liberal wing of the Republican Party, having worked for years to prevent the Democrats from "gaining position" on the civil rights issue, was further horrified as it envisioned the G.O.P. suddenly transformed into "the party of the white man" at just the moment when the Negro vote was becoming effectively mobilized.

The second setback threatened when Governor Wallace of Alabama decided to enter the presidential race as a states' rights candidate. This was especially alarming, for Wallace would have competed for exactly the same votes that Goldwater had been wooing toward the Republican column. However, Wallace's subsequent withdrawal left the field open again for the original victory blueprint, and the implementation began in force. Mid-campaign accounts of the Goldwater organizational efforts spoke of a high-powered, modernistic campaign apparatus in the South stocked with volunteer labor in numbers that would have been unbelievable for the earlier Eisenhower and Nixon campaigns. While the machine had been humming efficiently from the start, the Goldwater organization in the West was described as effective but less advanced; in the Midwest it was chaotic, and in the Northeast next to non-existent. At few if any points in recent political history have so many campaign resources —in both issue positions taken and organizational efforts made—been devoted to the cultivation of a single region. The first discordant note came when, during the campaign and apparently as the result of new poll data, Goldwater remarked to reporters that he was not as strong in the South as everybody seemed to think.

After the votes were counted, what was the success of this strategy? The verdict must come in two halves. From one point of view, the strategy was a brilliant success, and it left its imprint on the geographical voting returns with greater strength than any other of what we have called "short-term forces" in the 1964 election. One crude way of separating these immediate or new effects from those better attributable to long-term standing loyalties is to create a different kind of electoral map, entering state by state or region by region the departure of a particular presidential vote in a more Republican or more Democratic direction than the normal voting of the area involved. A map so constructed for 1964, with pro-Goldwater deviations regarded as "high ground" and pro-Johnson deviations as "low," would show one primary "tilt" or gradient across the nation. The very lowest ground would appear in the northern reaches of New England, and the gradient would move upward with fair regularity all the way west to the Pacific Coast. The same gradient would appear, but much more sharply tilted still, as one moved southward to the Gulf of Mexico. In other words, Goldwater's regional emphases were indeed profoundly reflected in the vote.

As soon as one leaves the relative question of the regional and the geographic, however, the strategy was a dismal failure. For while the whole continent tilted in the expected direction, the strong Democratic tide nationally left virtually all of the country submerged under what from a Goldwater point of view was "sea level" —the 50–50 mark in popular votes. In terms of electoral votes, Goldwater was

stranded on a few islands which remained above the tide on the outer Southern and Southwestern fringe of the continent. These islands represented stunning "firsts" or dramatic historic reversals in states like Georgia, Alabama, Mississippi and South Carolina. But their historic interest did not bring Goldwater any closer to the presidency.

Indeed, while Goldwater scored sharp Republican gains through the "Black Belt" of the deepest South, his assault on the South as a whole produced rather pathetic results. All observers agree, for example, that the South has been drifting away from its old status as a one-party Democratic bastion for at least two decades, if not for five or more. Hence Goldwater could have hoped to profit from four years more of this drift than Nixon, and a decade more than Eisenhower. Secondly, all observers are equally agreed that not only in the Black Belt but well north into the Border States of the South, civil rights was the prime political issue, and there is no doubt where the mass white population stood on the matter. Our data from the late 1950s and the early 1960s have consistently made clear that the potential of this issue for dramatic partisan realignment in the South had been muffled because of lack of clarity in the eyes of the mass population, prior to 1964, that either of the two major national parties offered much hope to the Southern white. It was exactly this ambiguity that Goldwater set out to remove by providing a clear party differentiation on civil rights at the national level. Putting these two ingredients together, the actual 1964 election results from the South as a whole might seem astonishing. For Goldwater actually did less well in the region than either Nixon in 1960 or Eisenhower in 1952 and 1956. One has to return at least to 1948 to find a comparably poor showing for a Republican presidential candidate; and there are reasonable treatments of the 1948 Thurmond vote which would send one back to 1944 for a parallel. Given the fact that Goldwater wooed the South so straightforwardly, and injected the new and potent ingredient of clear party differentiation on civil rights into the 1964 picture, this retrogression of Republican popular voting strength for a presidential candidate back to levels of the 1940s may seem quite incomprehensible.

A possible explanation, although one that we can summarily reject, would be that the clear party differentiation on civil (or "states'") rights which Goldwater tried to communicate failed to come across to the mass voters.[1] Perhaps to the dismay of the liberal wing of the Republicans, however, the communication was near-perfect. In our 1960 election study, a measure of association between the two parties and the policy extremes of the civil rights controversy showed values of .02 and .05 (the Democrats only very slightly associated with a pro-civil rights position) on two different civil rights policy items.[2] In 1964, the perceived association in the same terms on the same two items had risen to values of .54 and .50. The change in *volunteered* identifications of the two parties with the issue, among the much smaller subset of people so concerned that they brought the matter up themselves, showed even more dramatic change. In 1960 these civil rights-concerned people

had tended to associate Kennedy somewhat with a pro-civil rights position, and Nixon with more of a "go-slow" approach (an association of .30). For Johnson and Goldwater in 1964, the association had mounted to .84, approaching consensus. The same volunteered materials include images of the parties, as well as of the candidates, and it is a matter of some interest to know in what measure Goldwater's 1964 position "rubbed off" on the Republican Party as a whole. In 1960, the civil rights association appeared to lie more clearly with the Kennedy–Nixon pairing (.30) than with any differences between the two parties, for these volunteered references to the parties showed only an association of .08. The comparable figure for the two parties in 1964 was .86. In short, we cannot explain why Goldwater produced a retrogression of Republican presidential voting strength in the South by suggesting that his key civil rights position failed to get across.

The Southern vote for Goldwater becomes intelligible if we add three elements to the consideration. First, while civil rights lent an important new pro-Goldwater force to the situation, various strong short-term forces which had pushed the Southern electorate in a pro-Republican direction in 1952, 1956 and 1960 were no longer present. We have argued elsewhere that the popular vote for Eisenhower and Nixon in the South was a very misleading index of the degree of solid Republican advance there.[3] While our data do show the Republican Party inching forward in the affections of mass Southern voters, the pace has been slow; the South remains a preponderantly Democratic region. In 1952 and 1956, the Southern presidential vote swung far to the Republican side of normal for the region, just as it did in all other parts of

---

[1] We have examined this possibility in some seriousness simply because often in the past we have found public perceptions of party differences on major issues totally confused and muddy. Even on issues where the politically sophisticated see marked party differences, general public inattention and the ambiguities which politicians exploit to blur the edges of their positions combine to produce either lack of recognition of differences, or very conflicting impressions of what those differences are at any given point. See Campbell *et al., The American Voter* (New York, 1960), pp. 179ff.

[2] The statistic is such that if all citizens in the sample agreed that the Democrats represented one side of the issue and the Republicans the other, the figure would be 1.00 (perfect association). A figure of .00 represents the case of no aggregate association whatever.

[3] Philip E. Converse, "A Major Political Realignment in the South?" in Allan P. Sindler, ed., *Change in the Contemporary* South (Durham, N.C.: Duke University Press, 1963).

the United States. In 1960, with the Eisenhower appeal gone, most other regions moved back toward the Democrats as we expected. This return toward normal was almost invisible in the South, since a new and offsetting short-term force—Kennedy's Catholicism—had arisen which was peculiarly repugnant to the Southern population with its concentration (Louisiana excepted) of devout and fundamentalist Protestants.[4] Thus if any other of the Republican aspirants had run in 1964, we might have expected a delayed return toward a much more normally Democratic vote in the South. From this point of view, the injection of a new civil rights differentiation by Goldwater did not occur in a void, but was something of a replacement for other forces which had kept the Southern vote extended in a remarkably pro-Republican direction for three consecutive presidential elections.

Once we take this into account, the Republican retrogression is less perplexing, although intuitively we would expect civil rights to have an impact on the Southern voter more potent than either Eisenhower's appeal or fear of a Catholic president. It is here that the second and third considerations enter. While Goldwater's civil rights position drew Southern whites toward the Republicans, Negroes both South and North moved monolithically toward the Democrats. Although Southern Negro voting was still limited by registration difficulties, it increased over 1960 and was almost unanimously Democratic for the first time.[5] If this sudden new increment of Negro votes could be removed from the Southern totals, the Goldwater

vote proportion would undoubtedly appear to be a slight progression, rather than a retrogression, over the Eisenhower and Nixon votes.

Finally, it must be recognized that civil rights, while the primary issue in the South, was not the only one. Beyond civil rights, Southerners reacted negatively to the Goldwater positions much as their fellow citizens elsewhere. Many Southern white respondents said in effect: "Goldwater is right on the black man, and that is very important. But he is so wrong on everything else I can't bring myself to vote for him." From this point of view, the civil rights issue did indeed have a powerful impact in the South: without it, the 1964 Goldwater vote probably would not only have slipped to normal Republican levels, but would have veered as elsewhere to the pro-Democratic side. The more general ideological appeal to what Goldwater saw as Southern "conservatism" aside from the Negro question, did not have major impact.

Much the same comments hold for the failure of "white backlash" to develop in the way many expected outside the South. Our data show that civil rights feeling did not lack impact elsewhere. But for many non-Southern whites who resented the advance of the Negro cause and the summer of discontent, the election involved other important issues as well; and Goldwater's positions on them struck such voters very negatively. Thus "white backlash" feelings were translated into Goldwater votes by Democrats only where fear of the Negro was so intense as to blot out virtually all other considerations. Voters fitting this description existed in fair number and geographic concentration in the deepest latitudes of the South. Elsewhere, they were thinly scattered.

IV. THE ELECTION "POST-MORTEM"

Up to this point we have referred only vaguely to the many negative reactions

---

[4]These religious effects were described in Converse et al., "Stability and Change in 1960: a Reinstating Election," *American Political Science Review*, Vol. LV (June 1961), pp. 269–80.

[5]In our data, expressions of party loyalty from the South which had been slowly losing Democratic strength throughout the 1950s show a sudden rebound in 1964. However, all of the rebound can be traced to Southern Negroes; the downward trend among Southern whites continued and at about the same pace.

Goldwater occasioned in all sectors of the country, which tended to dim out isolated attractions he did present. The Goldwater "image" was indeed phenomenally unfavorable. We have measured such images in the past, among other ways, by tallying the simple number of favorable and unfavorable references made by respondents to broad questions inviting them to say what they like and dislike about each of the candidates. Typically, American voters have tended on balance to speak favorably, even about candidates they were about to send down to defeat. The least favorable image we have seen—in Adlai Stevenson's second try in 1956—involved only about 52 percent of all responses that were favorable. Less than 35 percent of the Goldwater references were favorable.

Just after the election, Goldwater observed that "more than 25 million people" voted "not necessarily for me, but for a philosophy that I represent. . . ." At another time, in assessing the magnitude of his defeat, he chastised himself for having been a personally ineffective spokesman for that philosophy. This seemed particularly odd against the descriptions of Goldwater before his nomination, in which even opponents concurred that at long last the right wing had found an articulate spokesman with a magnetic personality.

The candidate references we collect are a mixture of observations concerning the personality and leadership qualities of the individuals themselves as well as reactions to policy positions they represent in the public eye. Ideally, we could take this image material and split it cleanly into references to personal attributes as opposed to policy positions, in order to judge the accuracy of the proposition that what the public repudiated was the spokesman, and not the philosophy. Practically speaking, such divisions present many difficult coding decisions.[6]

---

[6]Take, for example the charge hung on Goldwater by Democrats and some Republicans that he was "impulsive." This allegation reverberated

Nevertheless, we have sifted Johnson and Goldwater references into categories more or less purely reflecting "policy" as opposed to "personality" significance. Among the most pure policy references, Johnson's were favorable by an 80–20 margin, visibly ahead of the 69–31 balance of his total image. Mentions of Goldwater policies ran less than 30–70 favorable, thereby trailing the rest of his image slightly. In general, the farther one moves from pure policy to pure personality, Johnson's advantage declines. His "wheeler-dealer" style and the aura of conflicts-of-interest which dogged him during the campaign came through to dilute his attractiveness. Against this backdrop, Goldwater's personal "integrity" and "sincerity" drew praise. Throughout, the data suggest that Johnson was carried along to an image nearly as positive as Eisenhower's best, less by his personal characteristics than by the policies with which he was associated (many of them identified by respondents as continuations from the Kennedy Administration). For Goldwater, if anything, the reverse was true.

Aside from civil rights and a faint flutter of approval brought by Goldwater's latter-day stand against immorality, none of his major positions was attractive to voters outside the most hard-core Republican ranks. In general, the mass of public opinion has been quite unsympathetic to traditional Republican thinking in areas of social welfare and other domestic problems for several decades. A major Goldwater theme involved attacks against the increasingly heavy hand of "big government," yet this struck little in the way of

---

in the public and came to make up one of our largest single categories of negative references to Goldwater. "Impulsiveness" is a personality trait that on one hand might have been less plausible for some other right-wing leader. Yet the charge took roots and began to flourish with respect to a cluster of policies that Goldwater shared with other Republican leaders of similar persuasions. It seems quite arbitrary to decide that it is exclusively either the person or the policy which is "impulsive."

TABLE 1

Perceptions as to the Party Most Likely to Keep the United States
out of War in the Ensuing Four Years

	1956	1960	1964
	(%)	(%)	(%)
Democrats would handle better	7	15	38
No party difference	45	46	46
Republicans would handle better	40	29	12
Don't know, not ascertained	8	10	4
	100	100	100

a responsive chord. Most Americans in the more numerous occupational strata do not appear to feel the governmental presence (save for local civil rights situations) in any oppressive or day-to-day manner, and as a consequence simply have no reactions to the area which have any motivational significance. Among those more aware of the practices and potentials of federal government, a slight majority feels that if anything, governmental services and protections are inadequate rather than overdone. Thus for better or for worse, such contentions on Goldwater's part had little popular resonance.

Goldwater's failure to make much capital of domestic policy was not uncharacteristic of a Republican presidential candidate. What was new for a Republican, however, was his performance in the area of foreign policy. In a degree often overlooked, the 1950s were a period during which, from the point of view of many Americans inattentive to the finer lines of politics and reacting to the parties in terms of gross associations and moods, something of an uneasy equilibrium prevailed between the two major parties. Much more often than not, for these Americans the Democratic Party was the party of prosperity and good times, but also the party more likely to blunder into war. The Republican Party, conversely, was more skilled in maintaining peace, but brought with it depression and hard times.

The foreign policies proposed by Gold-

water and refracted through the press and other commentators, shifted this image more dramatically than one might have thought possible (Table 1). Setting aside the large mass of voters who throughout the period did not see any particular differences between the parties in foreign policy capability, the balance of expectations in the area favored the Republicans by better than a 5–1 margin in 1956. This margin deteriorated somewhat in the late stages of the Eisenhower Administration, but remained at an imposing 2–1 edge. During the Goldwater campaign it reversed itself to a 3–1 margin favoring the Democrats.

Thus to the many ways of describing the public's repudiation of the Goldwater candidacy, another may be added: between a party of prosperity and peace, as against a party of depression and war, there is little room for hesitation.

V. LEVELS OF PUBLIC OPINION AND THE BASES FOR MISPERCEPTION

From at least one point of view, it is less interesting that Goldwater lost the 1964 election than that he thought he had a chance to win. What most of our descriptions of the election year have had in common is a sort of chronic miscalculation of electoral reality: miscalculations of standing strength, of new strength that might be won, and of what appeals were necessary to win that new strength. Since "electoral reality" is at many points a nest of uncertainties, and since we are told that in the face of uncertainty personal needs are likely to color perceptions the more strongly, there is little surprising in the fact that Goldwater overestimated his strength and drawing power. But as these misperceptions of Goldwater and his aides went grossly beyond what many observers felt were the margins of uncertainty, they deserve closer comment.

Rather than write off these perceptions as figments of imagination, let us suppose that to persist in the way many electoral misperceptions of the right wing have persisted, there must be some sustaining reality bases; and let us ask instead what such bases might be. For "public opinion" is a protean thing, and we shall discover that there are perfectly sound ways of measuring public opinion during the 1964 campaign which, instead of illustrating Johnson's towering lead in the opinion polls, would actually have shown Goldwater enjoying a slight margin.

As is well known, public opinion was spoken of and roughly gauged long before the operations of public opinion polling were developed. What was gauged was opinion from a variety of kinds of sources: informal reactions to events among ancillary elites around the centers of government; the writings of intellectuals and newspaper editors; representations from leaders of interest groups, and the like. While it was apparent that this conglomerate of opinion came disproportionately from relatively elite and informed sources and hence need not have coincided with what the "real public" thought, beyond mass elections themselves there were (and *are,* for those who totally distrust the polls) few further ways of understanding what the public below an elite level was thinking. One of those few ways of "digging down" into the real population was letters of opinion: letters sent from unassuming constituents to public officials, "letters to the editor" composed by nonprofessional writers reacting to daily

events and even, in no few cases, to the opinions of the editor himself. This was one level of public opinion that seemed to be generated below the elite level and that, for the observer interested in opinion beyond the localisms of municipal government, could be monitored regularly on a wide geographic base.[7]

In our 1964 interview schedule we spent some time investigating the behavior of our respondents with respect to the writing of politically relevant letters. We ascertained first whether or not they had ever written such a letter either to any kind of public official, or to the editor of a newspaper or magazine. Then, among the minority who could recall ever writing such a letter, we went on to ask about the frequency of such activity—whether any of the letters had been written in the past four years, and if so, roughly how many letters the respondent would estimate he had written to each of the two types of targets over that recent period.

Many aspects of these data remain intriguing despite their general predictability. Thus, for example, the materials demonstrate handsomely that the large bulk of letters to public officials or the printed media come from a tiny fraction of the population, which tends to write very repetitively. Thus, in the data summarized in Figure 1, we find that only about 15 percent of the adult population reports ever having written a letter to a public official, and of the total stream of such letters from the grass-roots, two-thirds are composed by about 3 percent of the population. Where letters to newspapers or magazines are concerned, the constituency is even more restrictive still: only about 3

---

[7]Undoubtedly, for such an observer, letters were not weighted equally in his impressions as to how opinion stood: some were more cogent than others, some were more distressed, and so on. But as a rough first approximation, one can imagine that what registered as "public opinion" on a particular issue in the mind of such an observer was closely related to the simple frequency of letters pro and con.

FIGURE 1
Letters to Public Officials and Letter-Writers
within the Electorate

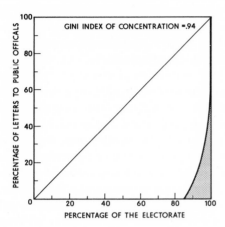

percent of the population recalls ever having written such a letter, and two-thirds of such letters are turned out by not more than half of one percent of the population.[8] Needless to say, there is fair overlap between those who write to the printed media and those writing to public officials, so that the observer monitoring both lines of communication would tend to count the same people twice.

Furthermore, as these few people write more and more letters over time, they are counted again and again, and this of course is the phenomenon that interests us. What we have done is to reconstruct our data on various preferences relevant to the 1964 election *not* by a raw head-count, which is what a mass election measures, but rather with each individual's preference on an item weighted by the number of letters that he has reported writing to either target in the four preceding years. This provides a basis, within

reasonable limits, for a fair replication of the different kind of "public opinion" as it might be assessed by a hypothetical observer.[9]

Figure 2 contrasts "public opinion" in the head-count sense, with that form of public opinion as measured by letter-writing. We suggest that this figure may usher us into the reality world on which many of Goldwater's assessments and stratagems were based. This is not to say that Goldwater had no other bases from which to calculate public opinion. He had, among other things, public opinion as measured by the polls, and he did not entirely discredit this information. Yet as we have noted there was evidence that poll data perplexed him, not simply because they customarily brought bad news, but also because they failed to square with all of his other intuitive impressions as to what the public was thinking. In the measure that these impressions came from a variety of sources not very different from the letter-writers among the public (*i.e.*, from party activists, from campaign personnel and from informal associations), it is not hard to believe that they may have been displaced from the head-count of public opinion in much the same ways.

If we accept letter-writing for the moment then as a relevant indicator of public opinion, we see a rather marvelous change in the state of political affairs. In Figure 2(a), instead of trailing Johnson sadly in

---

[8]Data on letters to the news media are not presented graphically, in part because the inequality is so complete that there is little one can discriminate in the figure. The Gini index of concentration for the newspaper and magazine letters is .99. See H. Alker and B. Russett, "On Measuring Inequality," *Behavioral Science*, Vol. IX, No. 3 (July 1964), pp. 207–18.

[9]We wish to stress that it remains a crude approximation, in part because we do not know, letter by letter, what political opinions the respondent was expressing. Conceivably in many cases they lay outside the range of any of our items. But the exercise is worth completing in part because it is likely that our hypothetical observer generalizes beyond the specific content of letters ("if ultra-conservative opinion on issue *x* is running about 30 percent, then it is likely that ultra-conservative opinion on issue *y* would run about the same level if something made that issue salient"); and in part because the systematic lines of displacement of "letter opinion" from "public opinion" in the mass electoral sense are undoubtedly valid in their general direction, whatever the details.

FIGURE 2
Public Opinion as Measured by
People or Political Letters

MASS OPINION   **"LETTER" OPINION**

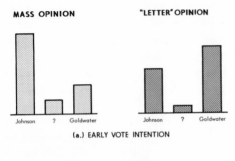

Johnson   ?   Goldwater   Johnson   ?   Goldwater

(a.) EARLY VOTE INTENTION

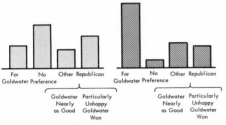

For   No   Other Republican   For   No   Other Republican
Goldwater Preference   Goldwater Preference

Goldwater   Particularly   Goldwater   Particularly
Nearly   Unhappy   Nearly   Unhappy
as Good   Goldwater   as Good   Goldwater
            Won   Won

(b.) REPUBLICAN CONVENTION PREFERENCE
(Among Independents and Republicans Only)

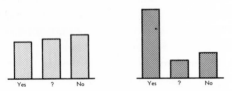

Yes   ?   No   Yes   ?   No

(c.) FEDERAL GOVERNMENT GETTING TOO STRONG?

Pro   ?   Anti   Pro   ?   Anti

(d.) NEGOTIATION WITH COMMUNISTS

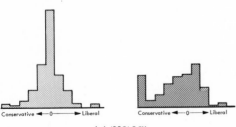

Conservative ◄—0—► Liberal   Conservative ◄—0—► Liberal

(e.) IDEOLOGY

the anonymous crowd in mid-campaign, Goldwater holds a visible lead. Moving back to the time of the San Francisco convention (b), Goldwater is no longer the candidate of a small minority among Republicans and Independents, but rather is the toast of an absolute majority, even counting "no preferences" against him. In (c), we discover that not only is a vast majority of the public interested in the problem of the growing strength of the federal government,[10] but those upset by this growing strength outnumber their opponents by a ratio approaching 3 to 1! In Figure 2(d), the displacement of "letter opinion" from public opinion is much less, in part because the item wording brought a relatively consensual response. However, it is clear that Goldwater's "hard" inclinations in foreign policy are somewhat over-represented as well in the letter-writing public.

In some ways, Figure 2(e) contains more grist than any of the others, however. First, the very form of the distributions of ideological preference differs rather dramatically. Where "public opinion" is concerned, nearly half the population falls in the "zero" category, making no affective distinction whatever between conservatives and liberals.[11] In addition, the clus-

---

[10] The wordings of the issue items involved in Figure 2(c) and (d) were as follows:

(For 2c) "Some people are afraid the government in Washington is getting too powerful for the good of the country and the individual person. Others feel that the government in Washington has not gotten too strong for the good of the country. . . . What is your feeling?"

(For 2d) "Some people think our government should sit down and talk to the leaders of the Communist countries and try to settle our differences, while others think we should refuse to have anything to do with them. . . . What do you think?"

Figure 2(e) is based on a set of questions that asked people to indicate their affective reactions toward a variety of groups, including "conservatives" and "liberals." The scores for the figure are based on the difference in reaction to the two stimuli.

[11] It is likely that this contingent is roughly coterminous with that 40–50 percent of the Ameri-

tering around this zero-point is very tight: over three-quarters of the population is located within one category of the zero-point. The distribution of "letter opinion," however is quite different. The central mode of indifference or ignorance shrinks dramatically, and voices from more extreme positions on the continuum gain in strength. Other analyses show that virtually all letter-writers rank very high on measures we have used of ideological sensitivity. Hence those who remain toward the middle of the continuum in the right half of Figure 2(e) are not there through indifference or ignorance: they understand the ideological alternatives and place themselves toward the middle of the road with forethought. And, as the bimodal shape of the distribution suggests, political discourse becomes most notably a dialogue between very mild liberals and ultra-conservatives.

It is to the world of letter opinion or one like it that the Goldwater campaign, in its original design, was addressed. At least until its late stages, it assumed an electorate with near-total ideological comprehension and sensitivity. The appeal to the Southern conservative tradition in any abstract vein was indeed joyfully received in the South, and created great ferment among a part of the Southern population. Except as this theme became concretized in day-to-day problems with Negroes, however, the part of the population affected was tiny, even though in the letter-writing and related senses it was so visible as to appear to be "most of the South," politically speaking.

can electorate which we have described elsewhere as having no impression as to what such terms as "conservative" and "liberal" mean. See Philip E. Converse, "The Nature of Belief Systems in Mass Publics," in David E. Apter, ed., *Ideology and Discontent* (New York, 1964), pp. 206–61. The data presented there were gathered in 1960. In the 1964 study we collected the same data on recognition of ideological terms, thinking that perhaps the nature of the Goldwater campaign might render these terms and meanings more salient to a wider public. The data show that it did not.

Similarly, the distribution of the population in this world of letter opinion helped maintain persistent overestimations of strength. Empirically speaking, the center of Goldwater support lay roughly in the third bar of the figure on the conservative side. It weakened rapidly with any further steps toward the center, and was relatively solid in the outer two bars of the graph. If one looks at "letter opinion" with this zone in mind, it would appear that the base of standing Goldwater support was very substantial. Goldwater hoped to firm up the support on his side of the center sufficiently to create a majority, and in this figure it would have taken only a modest extension of influence to achieve this. In the world of public opinion relevant for mass elections, however, the distribution of actual and potential support was radically different. Rather than starting from a solid base of support on the conservative wing, the initial springboard was scarcely populated at all. To win a majority, a much deeper penetration into the center would have been required.

In the measure that we have delineated in Figure 2(e), the kind of political environment familiar to many practicing politicians, we can also better understand the first of our puzzles, the myth of the stay-at-home Republicans. For ultra-conservatives who found a wide measure of social support and resonance for their views in the world of public opinion which they understood, it must indeed have been perplexing that uniquely at election time, and uniquely in vote totals, this vigorous support had a habit of evaporating. How could one interpret this gross discrepancy between what one heard and read about public sentiments and what happened at the polls? The easiest explanation was that strong conservatives in large numbers simply refused to go to the polls, however vigorously they would express themselves otherwise. And as soon as a useful reason was worked out as to why this willful non-voting should occur, a theory was born.

It persisted in part because it was a handy tactical weapon; but it persisted in some part as well because the discrepant realities which helped to catalyze the theory also persisted. For its proponents, the election of 1964 was a sobering reality test.

VI. CONCLUSIONS

It should be apparent that the phenomena we have examined in this paper have a significance that stretches considerably beyond the 1964 election, or questions of the credibility of public opinion polls, or the playing of games with the epistemologies of practicing politicians fascinating though each of these subjects may be.

But the more important implications flow from the reflection that while these opinion worlds may be discrepant from one another in many regards, and it behooves us not to confuse them, it is not a simple matter of fact *vs.* fantasy: both worlds are real, and have real effects on the political process. Save for the obvious fact that the reality of "one man, one vote," governs the mass election with

greater or lesser modification, while other public-opinion realities like the letter-writing world tend to hold sway otherwise, we know all too little empirically about the counterpoint between the two in actual political systems, and the normative significance of motivation-weighted votes is largely unexamined.

However this may be, if the reality of one of these worlds was manifest on Election Day, 1964, then the reality of the other was equally apparent in the San Francisco convention. For it is obvious that the intense levels of political motivation which underlie the letter-writing of the ultra-conservative wing are part and parcel of the ingredients which led to a Republican convention delegation so markedly discrepant from either the rank-and-file of the Party or its customary leadership. What had been lacking around the country in bodies was made up for in dedication; but the outcome of the convention was in no sense the less real for it. And from this juxtaposition of two worlds, the oddities of the 1964 election grew.

SECTION VII

Failures in the Process: Instability and Civil Strife?

Does the public in any way react to the decisions made by leaders? More specifically, does the public judge leadership performance by whether or not leaders satisfy public wants? Surprisingly we have very little evidence that they do. As you have already read, V. O. Key, Jr. suggests that leaders operate within the confines of permissive dikes of public opinion; and only a leader who violates these dikes is likely to draw a public reaction. Miller and Stokes' discussion in Section VI, of Representative Brooks Hays' defeat suggests a public capable of enforcing its opinions, at least in certain sensitive areas. But other manifestations of public dissatisfaction might well indicate the public's desire to show the failure of political linkage. Are the so-called alienated voters in the United States and those who vote Communist in Italy and France doing so as an expression of dissatisfaction with leadership behavior, which in turn is caused by linkage failure?

Both Gans and Cantril suggest that unhappiness with public decisions underlies the anger of Boston's West Enders and Italy's Communist voters. Whether this unhappiness with leadership decisions reflects an accurate assessment is not systematically treated in either study, but in the case of the West Enders it seems justified. Furthermore, it is evident from Cantril's study that if this sentiment grows sufficiently common it can threaten the stability of the system.

Earlier Herbert McClosky suggested the importance of attitudes of political futility and cynicism. What attitudes might we expect among those experiencing the failure of all types of political linkage? Using a measure of political cynicism, Luttbeg finds those whose opinions are most poorly represented in community decision making are more cynical and otherwise aware of their situation.

These studies offer only the most crude support for the theory that failures in the processes of political linkage can lead to public dissatisfaction, which in turn frequently results in an unstabilizing attempt to correct the situation.

THE POLITICIANS: AMBASSADORS TO THE OUTSIDE WORLD*

Herbert J. Gans

GOVERNMENT AND THE CITIZEN

The West Enders become most suspicious of, and hostile toward, the outside world when they must deal with government and the law. Most West Enders are convinced that the police, the government bureaucracy, the elected officials, and the courts are corrupt and are engaged in a never-ending conspiracy to deprive the citizens of what is morally theirs. Although suspicion of government and politics can be found among all social strata, in smaller communities as well as in the city, the West Enders' feelings on this subject are more intense and less open to change. Consequently, they try to have as little to do with government as possible and pass on to the area politician the task of dealing with it in their behalf.

By government, West Enders mean city government. There is almost no interest in state government, even though the State House is located less than half a mile from the West End, and even though an Italian occupied the governor's chair during the time of my study.[1] There is even less interest in the doings of the federal government. In 1958, the local congressman was an Irishman who lived in East Boston and paid little attention to the West End. At that time, John F. Kennedy was a United States Senator, and even though people

sometimes mentioned that he was a West End boy—because he had attended the parish church as a child—he was too far removed from the area by his high office and took no direct interest in it. There was occasional criticism of the then President Eisenhower, but the comments were much like those made about mass media personalities, and dealt with rumors about his personal life. State and federal government are far removed from the concerns of most West Enders; their existence is noticed only when some issue develops with relevance to them.[2]

The West Enders' conception of government and its officials also sheds further light on the dominating role of the peer group society. As already noted, West Enders think of government primarily as an agency that should be an arm of the peer group society to satisfy their needs. Moreover, they conceive the governmental process to be much like personal relationships in the peer group society. Thus, government agencies are identified with the individuals who run them, and agency behavior is explained in terms of their personal motives. During the time of my study, for example, West Enders were naturally concerned with redevelopment, which brought the Housing Authority and the Mayor into their view. The West Enders, however, spoke not of agencies but of individuals in them, notably one leading Authority official and the Mayor. They felt that these two men were in the

*Reprinted with permission of The Macmillan Company from *Urban Villagers* by Herbert J. Gans. Copyright © The Free Press of Glencoe, a Division of The Macmillan Company 1962.

[1]He was not, however, of working-class origins.

[2]These observations were made during a time in which there were no major elections; interest undoubtedly rises somewhat during a presidential vote.

pay of the private redevelopers, and were tearing down the West End for personal gain.

Government agencies have no reality; the city is seen as a congeries of individuals, most of whom are corrupt. Although West Enders know bribery to be wrong, for instance, they do not hesitate to bribe a policeman to prevent a traffic ticket. They believe that in either case the money they pay goes into someone's pocket. To them, there is thus no difference between the payoff to the policeman and the fine that is paid to the traffic court, and both go to the outside world.

The personalization of government operations stems in part from the West Enders' inability to recognize the existence of object-oriented bureaucracies. The idea that individual officials follow rules and regulations based not on personal morality but on concepts of efficiency, order, administrative hierarchy, and the like, is difficult to accept. For example, when the redevelopment agency initiated its procedures for taking title to the West End properties, and for relocating people and demolishing houses, West Enders refused to believe that these procedures were based on local and federal regulations. They saw them only as individual, and individually motivated, acts. Taking title to the land was described as a land grab to benefit the redeveloper. Relocation was explained in terms of the desire of the redeveloper and his governmental partners to push West Enders out of their homes as quickly as possible, so that the new buildings could be put up. The protests of redevelopment officials that they were only following standard operating procedures went unheeded.

Since the government is viewed as consisting of individual actors, West Enders evaluate it on the basis of the same moral code that they apply to each other. Government officials are expected to act on the basis of absolute and unvarying principles, to treat West Enders as equals,

and to respect the patterns of mutual obligation that operate in the peer group. As a result, West Enders hold to a conception of "good government" that is as strict if not stricter than that of the middle-class reformer. Their conception differs only in substance. Middle-class reformers define good government by the extent to which it follows business concepts of efficiency, fairness and honesty in contractual relations, and the allocation of resources by middle-class priorities—be these liberal or conservative in ideology. West Enders judge good government by peer group rules and by the extent to which its allocation policies fit their interests. Thus, they described middle-class reform movements in Boston as nothing more than a shifting of the graft from the pockets of politicians to those of bankers and businessmen.[3] Conversely, the regime of Mayor James Curley, long considered as one of the most corrupt by the middle class, was generally praised by the West Enders because it respected and benefited the poor people. Evidence of graft and corruption in his administration were not denied; they were simply compared to the much larger amounts of profit made in the assignment of contracts to private business when government was run by businessmen. This they called "legal graft." Since West Enders judge the law by the extent to which it benefits or hurts them, the fact that the business reform administration acted within the limits of the written law was not considered relevant.

West Enders see that, most of the time, government does not act as they would wish it to and that it is exploiting or depriving them of their rights. This, they also explain in peer group society terms. Thus, the people who conduct government business are individuals gone wrong, motivated by greed and ambition, and unable

---

[3] It should be noted that the reform movement which flourished briefly in Boston during the first half of the 1950's was dominated by business elements more than by the liberals.

to control their desires. They have been corrupted by the object-goals of the outside world. West Enders are disappointed that individuals in government do not act like peer group members, and they express great admiration for the honest cop or government official. Such individuals are rare, however, for few can act as West Enders would wish them to.

Since West Enders think that the majority of government officials are out to exploit them, they feel justified to do likewise if and when the need arises. They avoid contact with the government as much as they can, but should it threaten to exploit them, they feel free to retaliate. For example, when the city took over the West End and, in effect, became its landlord, West Enders demanded that redevelopment officials rehabilitate buildings that had just been declared a slum. Some refused to pay rent in order to get even with the city.

Such a conception of the governmental process, and of government–citizen relationships, may indeed seem irrational to the middle-class person who learns early in life to understand bureaucratic organization and behavior.[4] And, as I have already noted, it also may appear to be paranoid. Only a clinician can make judgments about individual pathology. But given the West Enders' status in the larger society, their view of the outside world is neither irrational nor a sign of group paranoia. No group can long retain a conceptual system that does not stand up against experience. For while the West Enders' explanation of governmental behavior may be distorted, it fits the phenomena they observe more often than not.

There are several reasons for the "fit" of the West Enders' theory. In the first place, most of them have had little direct experience with bureaucratic organizations.

---

[4]Daniel B. Miller and Guy E. Swanson, *The Changing American Parent* (New York: Wiley and Sons), 1958.

Few of them work in offices, either in private industry or in the government. Moreover, since Boston's political life is still firmly in the control of the Irish population, few Italians have even tried to find jobs in government offices. They described sardonically the experience of a North Ender who had tried and failed for years to get a job in a city department—until he changed his long Sicilian name to Foley. Consequently, West Enders see the bureaucracy only from the position of the client. And, since bureaucracies do not generally explain the reasons for their actions to clients, there is little opportunity to learn how they work.

In addition, many of the actions of the government do tend, whether intentionally or not, to hurt them and to benefit the more well-to-do citizens. The clearest case in point is the redevelopment of the West End itself, which took their homes to construct apartments for the wealthy few. In earlier years, West Enders could see that the city tore down part of the nearby North End—where some West Enders had grown up—in order to build an expressway that aided the suburban residents who drove downtown to work or shop. They also saw that the quality of municipal services on Beacon Hill was much better than in the West End. In 1958 they had only to read the papers to learn that the Mayor was planning to accept a well-paying position with a local insurance company after his retirement, and that this company, which was planning a huge redevelopment project elsewhere in Boston, had been able to get a liberal tax reduction as an incentive.

Moreover, despite the inroads of civil service, city governments still are run to a considerable extent by methods that seem to validate the West Ender's conceptions. This is particularly true in Boston, where traditional political machine methods have not given way to reform, and where nepotism and graft are still accepted as normal and inevitable. Even where reform movements have taken over control of government operations, they rarely have time to do more than make changes at the higher echelons. West Enders, however, come into contact with only the lowest echelons of the government. Whereas they do not know department heads or police commissioners, they do know, or know of, policemen, building inspectors, and laborers who work for the city. For example, many West Enders play the numbers, and since "policy" is controlled by Italian elements, they have fairly reliable evidence that payoffs are made to allow the policy wheels to operate. Also, they know that some policemen sell parking spaces on downtown streets at regular monthly rates. Consequently, it is not difficult to understand why they believe the police can be "legal racketeers" who take payoffs whenever they can. The final proof of the correctness of their view is that the higher graft payoffs go to the top police echelons, and that the men who walk the beat get little or nothing from the large amounts of money that are distributed. In government, as in business, the big money goes not to the little man but to the boss.[5]

Middle-class people have a much different type of contact with their city governments. They rarely find themselves inside a police station, and, if they work for the city, they are employed in the middle or higher levels of the bureaucracy. Most of the time, they see only the performance of civic progress and democracy that the government puts on for their benefit. Rarely do they go behind the scenes where the operations that actually keep the city running are taking place. Even when they do, they are able to maintain the kind of detachment that allows them to pay small bribes to a traffic policeman without feeling guilty or outraged about corruption. Not only do they have little direct contact

with corruption, but most important, their contact is limited to those times when they are the beneficiaries.

The West Enders more often are found behind the scenes, either as employees, or as friends and relatives of employees. They are hired or turned down for patronage jobs, and may work on city construction projects. Thus, when bribes are passed, illegal influence employed, and shoddy materials used in construction, they are closer to the evidence than the middle-class person. They confront corruption every day, and see others gain by it, without reaping any benefit from it themselves.

Consequently, the West Enders' theory of government is frequently supported because they are closer to the seamy side of city operations. Nevertheless, they also hold to the theory even in the absence of such evidence. Thus, they not only expect to find corruption and wrongdoings before the evidence is available, but may reject contrary evidence even when it is available. For example, the city's decision to give the aforementioned insurance company a tax reduction was an incentive to still the company's doubt about proceeding with the project—not a result of the job offer made to the Mayor. Likewise, most of the city's actions in the redevelopment process reflected federal and local regulations, rather than the immoral motives of city officials.

As a result, the belief that the outside world is harmful can blind the West Enders to its beneficial acts. In the West End for example, they failed to see that the police often kept adolescent misbehavior off the police blotter, and that caretakers genuinely wanted to be of assistance. Nor did they see, during the redevelopment, that relocation officials sometimes went out of their way to help people who could not help themselves. This blindness has had undesirable consequences for both parties. The West Enders play it safe by minimizing relationships with government

---

[5] I am reporting what West Enders told me. I did not check on the validity of the stories or of the motives that were attributed.

officials. The latter interpret this hesitancy —and the distorted view of motives—as insult or personal rejection, and consider West Enders to be ungrateful citizens.[6]

Middle-class people may be equally sensitive to the corruption of government and the dishonesty of its representatives, but they can be convinced by evidence to the contrary. Moreover, they believe in the possibility that government and politics can be reformed. The West Enders, on the other hand, are nigh well certain that one cannot fight—or change—city hall.

THE POLITICIANS: AMBASSADORS TO THE OUTSIDE WORLD

If the government is run, or thought to be run, by universally known and publicly visible rules, the citizen need only to know these rules and deduce from them his rights, obligations, and the proper posture toward its officials. When the government is, or its thought to be, personalized, capricious, and depriving, however, the citizen feels helpless, and must call on an influential person who can intervene in the government on his behalf. For the West Ender, this person is the politician.

The major functions of the "pol"—as West Enders call him—are to do favors for his constituency, to keep them informed of what is going on, and to represent their point of view in the legislative and executive chambers. For this functions, West Enders turned to the state representative—the "state rep"—and the city councilor. Until 1950, city councilors in Boston were elected from wards, and thus functioned as local politicians. Since then, they have been elected at large, and no longer represent any single ward. But West Enders were still able to contact one of the city councilors, because he lived in the West End, and had his political

roots in that area and the nearby North End. As a result—and because he was an Italian—West Enders continued to consider him their local politician, and used him for this purpose. He was available to do favors, and could function as an informant, but since he was elected at large and had to represent the entire city, he could no longer think purely of his home ward when it came to legislation.

With the change in the city council, the representative to the State House, who is still elected by wards, became more important as a local politician. Consequently, West Enders treated their two "state reps" as their representatives to the city, even though the two men had no official standing at City Hall. They did, however, have some political influence. Moreover, since Boston does not have home rule, a considerable amount of municipal legislation is enacted in the State legislature. As a result, the state representatives could act as local politicians.

Doing favors is the local politician's most important function. And since this is his most frequent reason for contact with his constituents, it is their most important index for evaluating him. Should the politician be unwilling to do favors or unable to obtain what he has promised, he will lose the confidence and the votes of those who asked him for favors. In addition, he will get a reputation for being unable "to produce." Such a reputation can mean loss of an election.

In a government that is perceived as a system in which selfish individuals seek to maximize their takings, favors are viewed as a normal device by which constituents get their rightful share. Most of the favors are requests for jobs and for welfare payments. But these are usually covered respectively by civil service regulations and eligibility criteria over which the politician has no control. He can only find out the results of bureaucratically made decisions, and transmit these to his constituents. The politician thus functions mostly as an am-

---

[6]The communication problems between government officials and the West Enders are considered in more detail in Gans' *Urban Villagers* (Glencoe, Ill.: Free Press Div. Macmillan Company, 1962), Chapters 13 and 14.

bassador to the outside world. He handles the West Enders' dealings with an impersonal bureaucracy which they cannot understand, or are afraid to face. Moreover, by acting as a go-between, he allows his constituents to retain their personalized image of government. He does not do this purposely, however. In fact, he wishes he did not have to do it at all. Politicians often complain about the amount of time they must spend on what to them are time-consuming and superfluous errands, although they also realize that doing such favors raises their batting average for being able to produce.

The politician is also asked to do favors that require the application of his political influence. The most common request is for jobs that are not covered or only partially covered by civil service. For example, when a number of men have made equal scores on a civil service test, political influence can evidently help to place a constituent at the top of his equals. It also can help to get one of several equally qualified applicants into a public housing project, especially one with a long waiting list.

Although the social welfare functions have shrunk considerably since the days of the New Deal, the politician is still, to some extent, a caretaker. He offers advice on how to deal with the outside world, and acts as a middleman between the external caretaker and the client. He has retained a caretaking function partially because he is market-oriented, and because he abstains from missionary activities. He provides a service to voters in exchange for political loyalty. In return, he is able to spare them contact with missionary caretakers who want to change their behavior, or who ask questions which imply to West Enders that they ought to change their behavior. Thus, he shelters them from discomfort and rejection by the outside world.

Another of the politician's important functions is that of providing reliable information. West Enders often do not believe much of what they read in the newspapers. They consider the press to be an agency of the outside world that usually defends, and sometimes fronts for, the city government—a belief for which there is some justification. Newspapers, at least in Boston, seem to be written on the assumption that poor people, like the West Enders, do not read them. They either present the news from a middle-class perspective or leave out the kinds of information that would be of most interest to the West Enders. For example, the Boston press not only favored the redevelopment of the West End in repeated and enthusiastic editorials, but also covered the news only from the point of view of the Redevelopment Authority. Press releases or interviews with officials about the West End were never complemented by the West Enders' version of the situation, or, indeed, by their feelings about the matter. Features, moreover, depicted the West End as a vice-ridden set of hovels in which respectable human beings could not be expected to live, thus insulting the West Enders and making them feel like outcasts.[7] As stories about redevelopment or relocation procedures generally were written from the point of view of the casual bystander, West Enders had difficulty in understanding what was happening next.

The press bias was not necessarily intentional, except in the editorial columns which generally reflected the businessman's point of view on most topics. The newspages were written by people who simply expressed their preconceptions about slum areas—often of a quite falsely stereotyped nature—and who then applied them to the West End. The West Enders, of course, were convinced that the distortions were intentional, and had been dictated by City Hall in order to discredit and drive them out of the West End. They were not surprised by the patterns of news

---

[7] See Gans, *op. cit.*, Chapter 13.

coverage. This is what they expected from the outside world.

Because of such situations as these, the politician is asked to provide information, not only to fill the news vacuum, but to deliver unpublished information about behind-the-scenes activities and about motivations so that West Enders may interpret the news according to their own theory of government. Since politicians operate on the basis of a similar theory to explain City Hall politics, they have no difficulty in providing the desired facts, rumors, motives, and interpretations.[8] During the tense period preceding the start of redevelopment, however, some politicians tried to scotch the more outrageous rumors and interpretations when they had facts to the contrary. By this time, however, they had little success, for the West Enders were ready always to believe the worst and, since the redevelopment officials did not understand the informational role of the local politicians, and often failed to keep them abreast of events, the politicians frequently knew little more than did their constituents.

The politician's third major function is that of representation. Not only must he vote according to local directives, he must also carry out what middle-class people call citizen participation, and develop a public image of the West Enders for the outside world. As already noted, West Enders are not given to political participation any more than to other forms of civic activity. Their only personal participation in the political process is to ask for favors, to express occasional opinions to politicians if they happen to run into them, and to vote. Any other political duties are expected to be carried out by elected officials; after all, that is what they were elected for. Thus West Enders did not protest the redevelopment to City Hall more systematically because, among other things, they conceived this to be the job of their elected politicians.

This apparent passivity carries over from Italian society, for the West Enders' ancestors were not encouraged to participate politically. Among the immigrant generation, moreover, there was no incentive for change in the tradition, because from about 1900 to 1925 the West End literally ran the city. During this time a political machine headed by Martin Lomasney, which represented a ward consisting of the North, West, and South Ends, had its headquarters in the West End. Lomasney, then the most powerful figure in Boston politics, was thus able to see that his constituents received their share, or more, of the political spoils. He also passed out the jobs, the loans, the welfare, and the Christmas baskets that his constituents needed.[9] Even had the West End not been so well represented, it is doubtful whether the immigrant generation would have become politically active. For neither they nor the second generation seemed willing or able to participate effectively in politics as a group, and could not carry the ward even though they outnumbered the Irish population in later years. Shortly after Lomasney's death the machine began to break up—thanks partly to the welfare measures of the New Deal. But his Irish followers continued to retain control over its remains throughout the 1930's and 1940's. Even though the North End section of the ward had long been predominantly Italian, Irish candidates still stood regularly for election, and, more often than not, they won.[10] I was told that

---

[9]For a description of Lomasney's organization, see Lincoln Steffens, *The Autobiography of Lincoln Steffens* (New York: Harcourt, Brace, and World, 1931), chap. 36. Steffens used Lomasney and his organization as the model in his arguments in behalf of political machines.

[10]The Irish nominees, of course, were frequently tied in with Italian political groups, and even controlled by powerful Italian figures. For an analysis of one of the Irish victories in the North End during the 1930's, see William F. Whyte, Jr., *Street Corner Society* (Chicago: University of Chicago Press, 1943; 2nd ed., 1955), chap. 6.

---

[8]See p. 442.

the Irish domination had finally been eliminated when quarreling Italian factions realized that until they made peace, they would never elect someone of Italian origin to city office. Italian politicians—most of them from the North End—finally took over the ward after World War II.

The rarity of participant motivations and skills among the West Enders has meant, among other things, that the politician who represents them does not have the benefit of citizen groups that can demonstrate to his legislator colleagues or to the Mayor the extent of his political influence. In short, he is required to be his own pressure group—a fact that does not enhance his political effectiveness. In addition, West Enders expect their politician to develop a public image of them, depicting them as proud citizens fighting for their rights against the hostile outside world. He is encouraged to make fiery speeches that condemn the powerful for criminal or negligent behavior, and threaten them with violence or political reprisals by an aroused electorate. Luckily for the politician, West Enders are more interested in having this image presented to themselves than to his colleagues or superiors. Nevertheless, as I suggested earlier, political speeches in the West End appeared to the outside world as demagoguery and rabble-rousing. The more successful politicians learn to make speeches that will satisfy their constituents without alienating the powerful agencies or individuals with whom they must work.

What little political activity there was took place mainly before elections. West Enders are Democrats, and, however skeptical they may be of that party, they would not think of voting Republican. Consequently, local elections in the West End were decided in the Democratic primary. The election for city councilor and for state representatives that took place during my study created little interest. The candidates put up posters, gave a few

speeches before the remaining social clubs, and made themselves generally visible at church and in the neighborhood. The most effective campaigning, however, was done through word-of-mouth, as families and friends of the candidates tried to get support for them from the neighborhood—exploiting the system of obligations within the peer group society, and promising favors when they were needed. In the election campaign which I observed, there was, of course, only one issue—redevelopment—and all the candidates opposed it strongly. The major emphasis in the campaign was on the moral and cultural attributes of the candidates themselves, especially on their honesty and their ability to fight on behalf of the West End.[11] The two major opponents represented the routine-seeking and the action-seeking points of view, respectively. Both candidates vowed to fight City Hall. But whereas one implied that he would use his intelligence, citing his college education, the other stressed his ability to defend himself and his constituents against exploitation and his willingness to use his fists if necessary. The college-educated candidate also appealed to the lower-class group by playing down his educational achievements in his campaign literature.

Once a candidate is elected, he is relatively independent of his constituents. As long as he is willing to do favors and to vote properly on the few issues that concern them, he is free to act as he sees fit. He can vote his conscience, and make alliances that will help him politically and financially. At the same time, however, people soon begin to wonder about his activities in the outside world, and before long he is suspected of acting like an outsider. If his votes hurt any West Enders

———

[11]I was told that in past decades, candidates campaigned largely by "mudslinging"—casting doubt on their opponents' honesty and qualifications with slanderous, and often fictional, details of their personal and political misdeeds.

or noticeably benefit some persons or areas outside the West End, he is suspected of having been "bought." If he fails to attend a local meeting, people wonder if he has deserted them or has sold out to an enemy. Once the suspicion arises—and it always does—even his actions in behalf of his constituents may be explained as an attempt to seek personal gain.

The voters' suspicions stem in part from the fact that politicians use their office to enhance their business activities or law practices. Since salaries paid to municipal and state lawmakers are low, the elected official needs an additional source of income. Success in business or legal practice, therefore, can quickly lead to suspicions that political influence has been used or that the politician has been corrupted. Given Boston politics, the suspicions were sometimes justified. Even if they are not, they would be bound to crop up anyway, simply because the politician's work takes him into the outside world—tacit evidence that he has adopted its exploitative behavior patterns. Moreover, as the politician moves into the outside world, his activities do change, if only because he must adopt some of its styles in order to function effectively. This in turn increases the social distance between him and his constituents. If he is elected on an at-large basis, and must represent interests other than those of his home district, suspicion develops almost automatically that he has become a renegade.

Thus the politician is caught between conflicting pressures. On the one hand, he must participate in the outside world in order to be effective, even if only in the service of his constituents. On the other hand, as his constituents display little interest in his activities, he cannot explain them fully. As a result, he is suspected of having deserted the peer group and of having become a crook. Moreover, since the suspicion exists regardless of whether or not he has done anything to deserve them he may himself become cynical, and conclude that he should use his office to advance his own fortunes. This does not necessarily hurt his political future. Voters who are convinced that he is dishonest simply because he was elected may not cast their ballot for him again anyway. Conversely, others will vote for him either because they believe all candidates to be dishonest, or because he is an Italian or a "neighborhood boy," or simply because they think that the outside world deserves to be exploited by a self-seeking politician.

The image of the working-class politician as a beloved neighborhood figure is largely fiction. West Enders feel that politics is intrinsically and inevitably corrupt, and that few politicians can resist the temptations. Consequently, they must be watched so that the constituents come out ahead in the exchange of votes and favors. I was told that this view had prevailed also in the days when Martin Lomasney was the boss of the West End and when his organization had a much more frequent, direct, and visible impact on the voters' everyday life. Although Lomasney's contributions to the area's economic welfare were freely acknowledged and his personal honesty rarely questioned, informants agreed that he had been ruthless in manipulating his constituents for his own political needs. It was said that young men who were interested in a political career had to join his organization and that if they refused, he would see to it that they were politically blacklisted. Sometimes, a fledgling politician's first assignment was to run as a dummy opposition candidate to the organization nominee. If he performed that service properly, he then would be rewarded by nomination as an organization candidate in a subsequent election. Although Lomasney was reported to have been very generous in helping people in need, he did dictate in turn how they should vote. He was respected because he could produce, and many West Enders felt sure that had he still been alive, the area would never have been proposed for redevelopment.

PERSONAL CHARACTERISTICS OF THE POLITICIAN

Voter suspicions—and the social distance between citizens and politicians—are supported by the fact that the local politician is often socially mobile. Political life has traditionally served as a channel for social mobility to ethnic group members who lack the social background and investment capital necessary to success in other occupations. Thus, it is not surprising to find that many of the local politicians who served the West End were mobile people. This was not true of all of them. Some were in politics because it had become a family occupation, or because it was a useful adjunct to business activities. For example, among Italians, funeral directors often will enter politics because their work provides them with the necessary free time, and because it is good advertising for their establishment. This was true also in the West End.

Even so, three of the four local politicians with whom I talked were using their political careers to move themselves or their children into the middle class.[12] One of them was the man who, under the pseudonym of Chick Morelli, played a central role in Whyte's *Street Corner Society.*[13] An ambitious young man when

Whyte knew him in the North End, his political fortunes had risen when I met him to the point where some West Enders thought that he might someday become Boston's first mayor of Italian background.

The three men, Chick Morelli included, were quite ambivalent, however, about their mobility. Two had married women from middle-class families, but they themselves retained considerable allegiance to the peer group society in which they had grown up. The wives were uncomfortable in their surroundings, and put considerable pressure on the men to leave the ward, so that their children could be raised in higher status surroundings—a move the men resisted, both for personal and political reasons. The clearance of the West End did provide one of the men with an excuse to move into a middle-class neighborhood, but since he left somewhat earlier than the rest of the population, the West Enders interpreted his move as a sign that he had sold them out. Although the other man did not have to move right away, he did not know how long he could hold out against his wife's insistence that they leave the area. Both men liked the neighborhood, and were reluctant to give up the peer group ties, although they also enjoyed their contacts with the middle-class world. The wives, however, who were not raised in the peer group society, wanted their husbands to spend more time with them and the children, and resented the childhood friends and other men who invaded the household almost nightly. The third of the mobile politicians was torn between his enjoyment of politics and the low status of his position. Having at one time considered becoming a doctor, he was now sorry that he had not entered the medical profession, because of the higher prestige and respect accorded it.

The politicians' status ambivalence also

---

[12]I interviewed only about a third of the dozen or so men who were politicians in the ward in which the West End was located. I suspect that the majority of those to whom I did not talk were less mobile than my respondents.

[13]Whyte, *op. cit.,* especially chap. 2, and Appendix, pp. 344–49. The fact that he was Morelli came out one evening at his house when he asked me my opinion of *Street Corner Society.* Subsequently, I learned that during one of his previous election campaigns, a Boston newspaper had reported that "his struggles to overcome boyhood disadvantages . . . are pictured in a well-known college textbook entitled *Street Corner Society.*" The story was given to the paper by one of his associates the day before

election. Many of Morelli's companions in *Street Corner Society* were still his friends, and functioned as his political advisors.

reflected itself in their political behavior. When I talked with them, for example, two of the men were struggling to decide what to do after the loss of their West End constituents—whether to continue as working-class politicians in other parts of the district, or to become reformers and serve a more middle-class group of voters. One of the men had already begun to take the latter path. Consequently, he adopted two political styles, one for West Enders and other Italian voters, another for the middle-class reform groups. In the privacy of his own home, however, he has remained a West Ender. While his speeches and some of his actions are cued to middle-class reform, his thinking about city problems differs little from that of other West Enders. Favoring impulsive action at the expense of analysis, he still talks about resorting to violence to get things done, and his solutions tend to be authoritarian, with little concern for the rights of those who disagree. His proposals for reform call not for structural changes in city government, but for moralistic crusades against the men whom he believes to be corrupt.

As his political career advances, he has moved into the powerful and statusful sectors of city life, but he is still quite insecure about mixing with upper-middle-class people. His reports of his social activities to the peer group, for example, are full of anecdotes in which he confronts prominent people with the fact that he is now their equal despite his lowly origins in the Boston slums. He enjoys such encounters, and feels that he is making fools of high-status individuals. In short, although he has entered the outside world and has become successful within it, he has retained the peer group society's hostility toward it.

In many ways the politicians' own view of the power structure coincides with the peer group society's person-orientation. Politicians see issues in terms of their appeal to voters, and the power structure as a group of individuals competing for personal political advantage. They describe the decision-making process, whether in politics or in government, in terms of the goals of the competing decision-makers: power, money, and prestige. These are traced in turn to motives of political ambition and greed. The goals and motives are, moreover, interpreted in moral terms, and political life is thus evaluated as a struggle between heroes and villains. The local politicians fail to see that many of their own actions and those of their colleagues are determined by the requirements of the political party system and by the diverse demands of their respective constituencies. In short, the "pols" interpret political events with the same theory of government as their West End constituents and lack the detachment and insight that is common among the party leaders. This is probably one reason that they are local politicians.

THE COMMUNIST PROTEST VOTER AS A HUMAN BEING*

Hadley Cantril

"I want a good life, that's all."

Aldous Huxley has noted that "you could make a roaring farce" out of Oedipus, or Lear, or even Jesus or Gandhi. "It's just a question of describing your characters from the outside, without sympathy and in violent but unpoetical language. In real life, farce exists only for spectators, never for the actors. What *they* participate in is either a tragedy or a complicated and more or less painful psychological drama."[1]

The object of our inquiry has been to understand from the inside, and with sympathy and compassion, the psychological characteristics of the reality world the protest voter fashions with all of its complication and all of its more or less painful psychological drama. Unless we are able to see things the way the protest voter sees them and feels things as he feels them, we will never be able to understand a situation fraught with the imminent danger that he might vote himself into a Communist state with the evils he believes it involves and which he himself does not want.

What seems to be the upshot of our study?

The protest voter—like every other human being everywhere—wants to experience more frequently and in new ways what he senses is *potentially* available out there in the world around him to be ex-

perienced and enjoyed. What the protest voter, like all other people, believes *is* potentially out there is, of course, what he has learned are satisfactions that might some day be his and that constitute his own particular bundle of hopes and aspirations.

In France, all the feelings symbolized by the revered slogans of *Liberté-Egalité-Fraternité* are an inseparable part of the workers' reality world. And he is aware that French tradition in all classes of society shares his own sense of the value of what these words stand for. The fact that he, the worker, doesn't yet have more *egalité* and *fraternité* produces in him another feeling—one of inferiority, resentment, isolation. In Italy, there are constant historical reminders of the country's glorious past which are in sharp contrast to its international position today. Since the Italian citizen had little experience with democracy until after World War II, the concepts of "democracy" and "freedom" are equated in his mind with what he has experienced politically in recent years, experiences which have left him, too, with a sense of injustice and resentment.

The gripes, frustrations, and insecurities of the protest voter are very real for him. They are part of his reality world. They are, he figures, due to "The System," "The State," "The Ruling Class," "The Government." His frustrating experiences are entirely consistent with what he has come to believe are the values these abstract symbols represent and stand for. He has it drilled into him that the present "system" just won't work. And, more impor-

---

*From *The Politics of Despair,* by Hadley Cantril, © 1958 by Basic Books, Inc., New York.

[1] *The Genius and the Goddess* (New York: Harper, 1955), p. 132.

tant, he feels that he is experiencing the consequences of the "system's" values as they operate in the concreteness of the here and now of his own living: that these values are depriving him of what he thinks he could and ought to have and of what he could and ought to become. In his eyes, they are negating, thwarting, stifling the kinds of satisfactions he wants more of.

He will not try to make these symbols work. He will oppose them—try to get rid of what they refer to.

The Communist Party also wants to get rid of them. Party opposition is intense, bold, systematic, continuous. The protest voter, too, will show his opposition to the system by voting for the Communist Party. It stands unequivocally for the left. It is trying to help him and his fellow workers. While he would not exactly feel that he would be a traitor to the working class, as would the Communist Party member, if he voted anything but Communist, still the protest voter does not want his fellow workers to take him for a reactionary supporting the present system. So he continues his political heresy.

Unlike the Communist Party member, the protest voter has as yet found nothing to substitute for the symbols he is against. And unlike the voter who does not vote Communist because he has for one reason or another acquired a sense of self-reliance within the context of the present "system," the protest voter craves some value standards he can enthusiastically identify himself with and some effective political organization in which he can be an active participant with others who share his aspirations and who, by their common strivings, would bolster his own faith in the worthwhileness and attainability of his goals.

Yet, while the protest voter is against the "system," he is not too unhappy within it. His conditions are not desperate. There are many things about his personal world that give him satisfaction and happiness: his family, some aspects of his job, his freedom to join his friends at the bistro and express his gripes, his privacy, his social security benefits, his personal responsibilities, and his sense of importance in his neighborhood. He thinks that his boss is not such a bad fellow and that he is making only normal profits, even though he could pay higher wages. He has respect for his superiors; on the whole, he considers them able and efficient.

He values these satisfactions, these rewards, and these relationships, small and inadequate as they may be. They correspond to some of the values which he has learned intellectually are good and which are represented by such concepts as "Egalitarianism," "Liberty," "Socialism," "Democracy."

And his reality world also corresponds to some of the feelings he shares with other workers: feelings that feel right and good to him—a sense of personal dignity and pride; a certain independence; the potential satisfaction of sharing the comforts, opportunities, and status of the middle-class bourgeoisie. He experiences what these abstractions refer to in enough occasions of living so that their reality and significance are maintained. He wants to hang on to them. He could be a lot worse off.

He sees from the goings-on around him in his own country and from what he learns about some other parts of the world that more and more people like him are enjoying more and more comforts and opportunities. He learns that working people *can* become more secure, more like the middle class in their way of life, in their educational opportunities, in their identifications. The French worker senses that *Egalité* and *Fraternité* can become even more alive as functioning realities; the Italian worker senses that independence, security, and freedom *can* become more meaningful in his own experience.

The protest voter has a hunch that if he were to join the Communist Party, he would have to submerge himself in a revolutionary movement and that many of the standards he now uses to judge worthwhileness and progress would be thrown overboard. He senses that if political liberty disappeared, then liberty in other forms would probably disappear, too. He knows that severe Communist Party discipline means he would lose his valued privacy, would not be left alone, would not dare express his gripes freely.

He refuses to take seriously the attempts at indoctrination by a party he feels would, once in power, humiliate him, a human being who prides himself on his independence, his worth, his integrity.

He doesn't want that. He doesn't want to give up what he has and what he might might have. He doesn't want to give up what he is and what he might become.

He also senses the inconsistencies between Communist preaching and what goes on behind the Iron Curtain. He notices the strife within the Communist Party and the occasional prolonged periods of silence on the party of Party leaders when certain events that people like him don't approve of are announced by the non-Communist press and radio. He has become suspicious of the Communist Party's closed system and its professed idealism, which has seemed more and more hollow in recent years. The Party has made itself ineligible for his wholehearted consideration and his complete confidence.

But while he is properly described as cautious and conservative, as reformist rather than revolutionary, still the most effective way he can find to show his resentment against the way the institutions he dislikes are holding him back—are not changing economic and social conditions swiftly enough to keep up with his own changed expectations, are not delivering the goods—is to vote for the Communist Party despite all its shortcomings. For it does share *some* of his goals. And it has the most efficient political organization. He chooses it to represent him politically just the way he would choose an able lawyer to represent him in court, even though he may not necessarily share all the lawyer's views. He is not a Communist between elections. But he will vote Communist until something better comes along.

What seems most painfully lacking in the reality world of the protest voter is some encompassing set of abstractions that represent values he can really be enthusiastically *for,* in the way the Communist Party member is enthusiastically for the abstractions the Party has provided him. The protest voter wants abstractions that will be consistent with his goals and aspirations for greater social justice and for a decent life, that could be represented by symbols he could rally around and communicate to others, that would assure both freedom *and* change as personal experience gave them the blood of life and made them real. For he senses that the political and social change he wants to participate in will involve responsibilities and that responsibilities, in turn, involve and require freedom of choice and action.

No formation of acceptable and plausible abstractions can be expected to take hold and become a reality for protest voters until something happens by way of broadly based political-socio-economic reforms—reforms aimed at bringing about *personal* psychological consequences that must be consistently felt if a solid confidence, a new hope, and a sustaining faith are to be generated. In brief, the new abstractions must operate in such a way that they satisfy what is often called the spiritual side of human life, but a side of life often only dimly perceived by those who talk most about man's spiritual make-up and who often fail to see where it is, how to find it, or what to do about it.

Only then will new abstractions and symbols take hold. Only when the protest voter has some sustaining faith he can believe in will he refuse to condone in his vote the abuses of freedom and personal independence he now senses are integral aspects of Communism. However, if his frustrations should become more intense, if he is unable to achieve the self-confidence of his compatriot who does not vote Communist and who feels no need to resort to potentially revolutionary collective action because the values of the present system provide him sufficient bases for action, then there is the real possibility that he might himself become a party member in sheer desperation. This eventuality is especially likely if the Communist Party should manage to identify itself in his mind with middle-class respectability and with the social mobility which educational and other opportunities might bring to him and his children.

Only when the protest voter begins to experience in his own life the psychological consequences of new value-symbols which he can accept, value-symbols which are congenial to his whole being, will the abstractions he now blames for his troubles really become insignificant, really lose their reality.

And only when their reality disappears will the protest voter also disappear.

We can sense all this in the robust expression of Monsieur Paul Dumard, the French tool- and die-maker who votes Communist. . . .[2]

"Hell, I have to work under any system. I got my family to think of. The kids need shoes and the wife needs a coat. Where the hell do you think I can get the money? What the workers want is a standard of living and more opportunities for themselves and their kids.

I don't care if the workers get a good standard of living under capitalism or socialism. It doesn't make any difference to me. I don't want a revolution; I just want change. It's none of my business what workers do in other countries. They don't concern themselves about me; why the hell should I concern myself about them? Let them fight their own battles, and I'll fight mine.

But nothing I say is going to make any difference.

All I want is to enjoy myself in this life. For all I know it may be the only one I have. When you're dead, maybe you've had it. Hell, I don't know. All I want is to have a good life, that's all. Is that too much?"

---

[2]For more on Dumard see Hadley's, *The Politics of Despair* (New York: Basic Books, Inc., 1958), pp. 50–52, 213–4.

AWARENESS ON THE PART OF THE UNREPRESENTED CITIZEN*

Norman R. Luttbeg

The literatures dealing with political alienation and leader–follower differences both have grown in recent years. The alienation literature documents Americans' suspicion and distrust for authority, especially politicians and the belief that such

---

*Once again I would like to thank Robert E. Agger for his generosity in allowing me to make use of his data.

leaders are not responsive to the public. Often researchers view this response as unrealistic or even irrational, but perhaps it isn't. The leader–follower studies have often, but not always, shown leaders to hold opinions not entirely consistent with popular preferences. If these differences find expression in public policy, as the Miller and Stokes study of congressional

TABLE 1

Attitudes on Issues and Number of Persons Identified as Unrepresented in
Each of the Issues in Both Communities

Issue	Number of Persons Unrepresented	Their Attitudes on the Issue
Springfield		
Attraction of industry	18	Uncertain, disapprove, strongly disapprove
Annexation	12	Strongly disapprove
Parking lots	12	Strongly disapprove
Special education	12	Strongly disapprove
Fluoridation	64	Strongly disapprove
Public housing	0	
Urban renewal	0	
Metropolitan park	45	Disapprove, strongly disapprove
Public kindergartens	0	
Eugene		
Attraction of industry	29	Uncertain, disapprove, strongly disapprove
Annexation	39	Disapprove, strongly disapprove
Parking lots	0	
Special education	20	Strongly disapprove
Fluoridation	0	
Public housing	0	
Urban renewal	27	Strongly disapprove
Metropolitan park	53	Disapprove, strongly disapprove
Public kindergartens	0	

behavior strongly suggests, it may well mean alienation is a response to leadership behavior.[1]

This article assesses the responses of persons who are unrepresented in their community's leadership. Do they show evidence of alienation?

THE UNREPRESENTED CITIZEN

In 1958 both leader and public samples in Eugene and Springfield, Oregon, responded to a lengthy questionnaire assessing their attitudes on several questions of political participation. Among these questions were nine dealing specifically with issues of concern in both communities at the time. Since both leaders and the public answered the same questions it is possible to compare leaders' attitudes with those of the public. Persons whose attitudes on any of the issues were not

held by any leader were identified as "unrepresented citizens" in Springfield, but because of the few persons so identified in Eugene a less rigorous criterion was used there. If less than 5 percent of the leaders in Eugene shared an attitude with an individual, he was identified as unrepresented. Table 1 shows the number of persons so identified in each community and their attitudes.

Strikingly, the table shows the unrepresented consistently disapprove of the issue on which they are unrepresented. No one who favors the programs suffers from lack of leadership.

The unrepresented seldom find themselves not represented on more than one issue, as Table 2 shows. Only 24 percent of the unrepresented citizens in both communities receive little or no representation or more than one issue. If dissatisfaction and alienation derive from the state of being unrepresented, we would certainly expect the intensity of reaction to increase with the number of issues on which the

[1]Warren E. Miller and Donald E. Stokes, "Constituency Influence in Congress," *The American Political Science Review*, 57 (March 1963).

TABLE 2

Number of Issues on Which Unrepresented Citizens Are Unrepresented

	Number of Issues on which Unrepresented			
Community	One	Two	Three	Four
Springfield	95	21	8	1
Eugene	99	27	5	

TABLE 3

Comparison of General Political Involvement of Unrepresented and Represented Citizens

	General Political Involvement					
	(0) Low	(1)	(2)	(3) High	Total %	N
Springfield						
Represented	34.8%	53.6	7.8	3.8	100.0	319
Unrepresented	39.0	52.8	5.7	2.5	99.9	123
Eugene						
Represented	32.1	51.8	12.2	3.9	100.0	386
Unrepresented	26.2	56.9	12.3	4.6	100.0	130

individual lacks representation. Thus in one sense both Springfield and Eugene would have to be judged favorably because so few people are unrepresented on more than one issue. But the number of issues on which an individual lacks leadership, the generality of his unrepresentativeness, is an important dimension in the following analysis.

Having identified unrepresented citizens, we now turn to their other characteristics. Tables 3 and 4 show them not to be atypical of others in the community, at least in terms of general political involvement and social status.[2]

An analysis of the relationship between degree of approval and social and political status shows political and high social status persons tend to give greater approval on eight of the nine issues presented. But despite this relationship and

the fact that the unrepresented generally do not favor these issues, being unrepresented is not a social class or political strata characteristic.

AWARENESS OF BEING UNREPRESENTED

The unrepresented citizens in both communities show awareness of their situation, although they seem to perceive it as typical of all voters. They do not see themselves as an unjustly treated minority. Unrepresented citizens of both communities show a statistically significant pattern of seeing city officials as not acting consistently with the public's will. Table 5 shows this relationship. Furthermore this belief is neatly continuous and quite strong when run against the number of issues on which they are unrepresented, as shown in Table 6. And this table shows another interesting relationship.

Not only do the unrepresented manifest an awareness of their situation, but in the two communities they differ on whose policy preferences they believe are best represented. Those in Springfield see city officials responding to the preferences of

---

[2]Chi square was used to evaluate the statistical significance of relationships presented in this article unless otherwise noted. When a relationship is noted, it is statistically significant; when I speak of no relationship being evident, as in Tables 3 and 4, the Chi square is not statistically significant.

TABLE 4

Comparison of Social Status of Unrepresented Citizens and Represented Citizens

	Social Status					
	(0) Low	(1)	(2)	(3) High	Total %	N
Springfield						
Represented	17.2	34.3	29.9	18.6	100.0	274
Unrepresented	21.3	37.2	28.7	12.8	100.0	94
Eugene						
Represented	13.4	20.2	31.3	35.2	100.1	307
Unrepresented	18.3	20.4	24.7	36.6	100.0	93

TABLE 5

Comparison of How Unrepresented and Represented Citizens View Activities of City Officials

	City Officials Do:			
	Pretty Much What Citizens Want	What Some More Influential People Want	What They Themselves Think Best	N
Springfield				
Represented	52.4%	26.0	21.6	273
Unrepresented	35.5	34.5	30.0	110
Eugene				
Represented	41.1	34.2	24.8	319
Unrepresented	26.3	45.8	28.0	118

the more influential. Such perceptions would be accurate if an elite controlled the community's political process. In contrast, Eugene's unrepresented citizens show less certainty than their Springfield counterparts on whose policy preference they think influences the city officials. Their response that city officials do what they themselves think best could mean they also think the local government is dominated by an elite, but in this case city officials are the elite. Or it could mean that they see city officials as motivated by technical or other opinions apart from what the community's influentials might want.

That another alternative answer to the question—an elite controls the community—was available and that many did choose to answer in this way would seem to belie the first interpretation, because persons who believe city officials are the commu-

nity's elite would be expected to answer with the response that indicates this.

THE ACCURACY OF THE PERCEPTIONS OF THE UNREPRESENTED CITIZENS

If we accept the public's responses in Table 6 as indicating that in Springfield the unrepresented see city officials responding to the desires of the influentials, while the unrepresented in Eugene see the city officials as biased but not necessarily in the direction of what the influentials might want, there is some cause to doubt the accuracy of these perceptions from the data gathered about the community's leaders. It is true that not one of Springfield's city officials was identified as a community leader, which suggests that political leaders either are the ministers of the community's nonofficial leaders or play no role at all in that community's

TABLE 6

Comparison of Unrepresented and Represented Citizens' View of Activities of City Officials,
Controlling for Number of Issues on Which Unrepresented Citizen Is Not Represented

| | City Officials Do: | | | |
	Pretty Much What Citizens Want	What Some More Influential People Want	What They Themselves Think Best	N
Springfield				
Represented	52.4%	26.0	21.6	273
Unrepresented				
(1)	39.0	30.5	30.5	82
(2)	31.6	42.1	26.3	19
(3)	12.5	62.5	25.0	8
(4)	0.0	100.0	0.0	1
Eugene				
Represented	41.1	34.2	24.8	310
Unrepresented				
(1)	31.5	46.1	22.5	89
(2)	12.0	44.0	44.0	25
(3)	0.0	50.0	50.0	4

decision making.[3] Furthermore Springfield's community leaders have many of the characteristics of an elite. They are rather consensual in their policy preferences and tend to reflect the preferences of higher social status levels. These facts would tend to confirm the Springfield unrepresented citizens' perceptions.

But the cities differ only in degree, because Eugene shows the same relationships shown in Springfield but more weakly. Only two of the city officials in Eugene —the mayor and a councilwoman—are among the community's leaders. The other publicly elected officials among Eugene's community leaders are county officials. Eugene leaders also tend to reflect upper class policy preferences and are more consensual in their policy preferences than is their public. And more tellingly, the data in no way indicate that the political process in Eugene is a contest between city officials and the public. If this were true, more city officials would be expected among the community's leaders. In sum-

mary then, the relationships found in Eugene differ only insignificantly from those in Springfield.

Thus it appears that the unrepresented citizens' perceptions of the nature of the community political process are correct in the sense that they see community leaders as less than accurately reflecting the public's policy preference. But they err in the sense that community officials in one city are seen as acting at the behest of influence and in the other city as merely acting independently. No such distinctions appear in the data.

IMPACT OF THE REALIZATION OF ONE'S UNREPRESENTATIVENESS

It is strongly apparent in the preceding analysis as well as in Table 7 that the unrepresented citizens do not view themselves as atypical. They believe they share with their fellow citizens their difficulties in getting the community political process to respond to their needs. There is little reason to feel personally disenfranchised if everyone shares your situation, and indeed Table 8 shows only a slight, not

---

[3]See the earlier article, "Patterns of Leadership Policy Preferences," for a description of the techniques used in identifying community leaders.

TABLE 7

Comparison of Unrepresented and Represented Citizens' View of Their Personal Influence

		Personal Influence			
	Very Influential	More Influential than Most	Average in Influence	Less Influence than Most People	N
Springfield					
Represented	0.0	4.7	54.1	41.3	320
Unrepresented	0.0	2.6	54.7	42.7	117
Eugene					
Represented	.5	5.3	49.2	44.9	376
Unrepresented	.8	5.6	46.8	46.8	126

TABLE 8

Comparison of Unrepresented and Represented Citizens' Sense of Efficacy

		Sense of Efficacy				
	(4) Low	(3)	(2)	(1)	(0) High	N
Springfield						
Represented	12.0%	23.5	28.9	12.0	23.5	166*
Unrepresented	12.9	35.7	21.4	12.9	17.1	70
Eugene						
Represented	12.1	26.8	15.8	16.2	29.0	272
Unrepresented	13.8	34.5	18.4	9.2	24.1	87

*Data derived from mail-back questionnaires. The low N's are a result of the failure of some respondents to return the questionnaires and of the nonscale types, which were excluded from the table.

statistically significant, tendency for the unrepresented to see themselves as less efficacious.[4] Another measure of alienation —distrust and cynicism about political leaders—would be expected to be common among persons who felt that they were personally denied representation in the community.[5] Cynicism does indeed seem to be related to unrepresentativeness, as shown in Table 9. The more unrepresented the citizen, the more cynical he is about his community political leaders.

This suggestive data implies that the unrepresented do manifest awareness of their situation in the form of increased

cynicism, and because of their continued sense of political efficacy they may well act at the polls on the basis of this cynicism. We might indeed conclude that their actions would be indistinguishable from the actions of those we have heretofore labeled alienated.

CONCLUSIONS

In my reading of the alienated voter literature, I was struck by the lack of empirical evaluation on whether this means of response to the political system derived from personality factors or whether it was a response that would be understandable in terms of social-psychological positions of persons who show alienation. My personal research bias is to exhaust a social-psychological type of explanation before seeking personality explanations.

[4]Robert E. Agger, Marshall N. Goldstein, Stanley A. Pearl, "Political Cynicism: Measurement and Meaning," *Journal of Politics*, 23 (August 1961), pp. 477–506.

[5]Angus Campbell, Gerald Gurin, and Warren E. Miller, *The Voter Decides* (Row, Peterson and Co., Evanston, Ill., 1954), pp. 187–99.

TABLE 9

Comparison of Unrepresented and Represented Citizens' Cynicism toward Local Politicians,
Controlling for Number of Issues on Which Unrepresented Citizen Is Not Represented

	Cynicism			
	High (0, 1)	Medium (2, 3, 4)	Low (5, 6)	N
Springfield				
Represented	22.7%	52.5	35.0	154
Unrepresented				
(1)	29.2	35.5	35.4	48
(2)	12.5	37.5	50.0	8*
(3)	66.6	33.3	0.0	6
Eugene				
Represented	17.0	42.4	40.7	248
Unrepresented				
(1)	28.2	40.7	31.2	64
(2)	50.0	33.3	16.6	12*
(3)	100.0	0.0	0.0	1

*The small N's in this table would suggest the collapsing of categories. This was done because of the importance of showing the consistency of the relationship.

My concern with discovering whether alienated voting behavior is explainable as an act of an individual who somehow correctly perceives that leadership fails to reflect his preferences. I have not sought to explain all the alienated voter behavior but rather have focused on those who might be expected to rationally reflect alienated voting because of the nature of their role in the community's political process.

Several facts seem evident in this analysis. First, the unrepresented, at least in these two Northwestern communities, generally disapprove of the expansion of community political programs. Second, they seem aware of their situation but do not seem to conceive of it as a personal problem but rather as one common to all voters in the community. Finally, their awareness is manifested by increased cynicism with continued high efficacy. What would happen if the unrepresented conceived of their situation as a personal disenfranchisement is important and certainly would seem to justify additional research.

SECTION VIII

Difficulties in Making Policy Recommendations

Having read the material thus far reproduced, the reader must be conscious of the differing reactions to findings of the rank-and-files' limited ability to play a participatory role in modern democracies. Many authors can find beneficial aspects of such findings in the autonomy thereby granted leaders and in the reduction of a possible source of instability to what they view as desirably performing examples of democracy. But others find the facts alarming. Jack Walker stresses the desirability of individual participation and derides the stress on stability he finds so common in the writings of those offering empirical information on mass participation. Originally, this reading was followed by a rather intemperate rebuttal by Robert A. Dahl in which, among other things, he stressed the distinction between description of facts and prescription of values. This in turn prompted a "Communication to the Editor" by Professor Walker, which is reproduced here.

Although this exchange focuses solely on the participant models, Rational-Activist and Political Parties, their arguments would apply equally if we found that none of the models account for the direction of public policy. Finding a failure of political linkage, should we pursue the question of what does account for the perpetuation of democratic societies supposedly dependent on such linkage, or would we direct our inquiry into what the repercussions of linkage failure are for the society and the individual? I personally see no reason why both paths cannot be taken, but I grant that as a profession we flow in clearly marked channels of what is accepted as legitimate research. Professor Walker's critique of the study of stability might well be viewed as an attempt to alter the channel or at least open another.

But even more importantly, we are frequently guilty of concluding that because something *is*, it *should be*. Thus those who continue to research the basis of a society's stability may be unwarrantedly accused of believing that society should, above all else, be stable. Similarly those who study the repercussions of political linkage failure will be accused of implying that political linkage is of preeminent normative importance. And unfortunately many will read such work in just that manner, even if the researcher is quite cautious in what he says.

People feel quite intensely about democracy, and there is anything but agreement on what is important in achieving it. Given this condition, far more rigorous research will be required before we can as a science make recommendations on how to better implement democracy. We can only hope that society can wait!

A CRITIQUE OF THE ELITIST THEORY OF DEMOCRACY*

Jack L. Walker

During the last thirty years, there have been numerous attempts to revise or re-constitute the "classical" theory of democracy: the familiar doctrine of popular rule, patterned after the New England town meeting, which asserts that public policy should result from extensive, informed discussion and debate.[1] By extending general participation in decision-making the classical theorists hoped to increase the citizen's awareness of his moral and social responsibilities, reduce the danger of tyranny, and improve the quality of government. Public officials, acting as agents of the public at large, would then carry out the broad policies decided upon by majority vote in popular assemblies.

Although it is seldom made clear just which of the classical democratic theorists is being referred to, contemporary criticism has focused primarily on the descriptive elements of the theory, on its basic conceptions of citizenship, representation and decision-making.[2] The concept of an

active, informed, democratic citizenry, the most distinctive feature of the traditional theory, is the principal object of attack. On empirical grounds it is argued that very few such people can be found in Western societies. Public theory is not the expression of the common good as conceived of by the citizenry after widespread discussion and compromise. This description of policy making is held to be dangerously naive because it overlooks the role of demagogic leadership, mass psychology, group coercion, and the influence of those who control concentrated economic power. In short, classical democratic theory is held to be unrealistic; first because it employs conceptions of the nature of man and the operation of society which are utopian, and second because it does not provide adequate, operational definitions of its key concepts.

Since contemporary scholars have found the classical theory of democracy inadequate, a "revisionist" movement has developed, much as it has among contemporary Marxists, seeking to reconstitute the theory and bring it into closer correspondence with the latest findings of empirical

*Reprinted from *The American Political Science Review*, Vol. LX (June 1966), pp. 285–95. Copyright 1966, The American Political Science Association.

[1]For discussions of the meaning of the classical theory of democracy see: George Sabine, "The Two Democratic Traditions," *The Philosophical Review*, 61 (1952), 451–74; and his *A History of Political Theory* (New York, 1958), especially chs. 31 and 32. Also see J. Roland Pennock, *Liberal Democracy: Its Merits and Prospects* (New York, 1950); and Sheldon Wolin, *Politics and Vision* (Boston, 1960), especially chs. 9 and 10.

[2]Criticism of the descriptive accuracy of the classical theory has been widespread in recent years. The best statement of the basic objections usually made is Joseph Schumpeter, *Capitalism, Socialism and Democracy* (New York, 1942), Part IV. See also Bernard Berelson *et al.*, *Voting*

(Chicago, 1954), chap. 14; articles by Louis Hartz and Samuel Beer in W. N. Chambers and R. H. Salisbury (eds.), *Democracy in the Mid-20th Century* (St. Louis, 1960); Seymour Martin Lipset, *Political Man* (New York, 1960); Robert Dahl, *A Preface to Democratic Theory* (Chicago, 1956), and *Who Governs?* (New Haven, 1961), especially pp. 223–325; V. O. Key, *Public Opinion and American Democracy* (New York, 1961), especially Part VI; Lester W. Milbrath, *Political Participation* (Chicago, 1965), especially chap. VI; and for a general summary of the position: Henry Mayo, *An Introduction to Democratic Theory* (New York, 1960).

research. One major restatement, called the "elitist theory of democracy" by Seymour Martin Lipset,[3] is now employed in many contemporary books and articles on American politics and political behavior and is fast becoming part of the conventional wisdom of political science.

The adequacy of the elitist theory of democracy, both as a set of political norms and as a guide to empirical research, is open to serious question. It has two major shortcomings: first, in their quest for realism, the revisionists have fundamentally changed the normative significance of democracy, rendering it a more conservative doctrine in the process; second, the general acceptance of the elitist theory by contemporary political scientists has led them to neglect almost completely some profoundly important developments in American society.

I. NORMATIVE IMPLICATIONS OF THE ELITIST THEORY

At the heart of the elitist theory is a clear presumption of the average citizen's inadequacies. As a consequence, democratic systems must rely on the wisdom, loyalty and skill of their political leaders, not on the population at large. The political system is divided into two groups: the *elite*, or the "political entrepreneurs,"[4] who possess ideological commitments and manipulative skills; and the *citizens at large*, the masses, or the "apolitical clay"[5] of the system, a much larger class of passive, inert followers who have little knowledge of public affairs and even less interest. The factor that distinguishes democratic and authoritarian systems, according to this view, is the provision for limited, peaceful competition among members of the elite for the formal positions

of leadership within the system. As Joseph Schumpeter summarized the theory; "the democratic method is that institutional arrangement for arriving at political decisions in which individuals acquire the power to decide by means of a competitive struggle for the people's vote."[6]

Democracy is thus conceived primarily in procedural terms; it is seen as a method of making decisions which insures efficiency in administration and policy making and yet requires some measure of responsiveness to popular opinion on the part of the ruling elites. The average citizen still has some measure of effective political power under this system, even though he does not initiate policy, because of his right to vote (if he chooses) in regularly scheduled elections. The political leaders, in an effort to gain support at the polls, will shape public policy to fit the citizen's desires. By anticipating public reaction the elite grants the citizenry a form of indirect access to public policy making, without the creation of any kind of formal institutions and even in the absence of any direct communication. "A few citizens who are non-voters, and who for some reason have no influential contact with voters, have no indirect influence. Most citizens, however, possess a moderate degree of indirect influence, for elected officials keep the real or imagined preferences of constituents constantly in mind in deciding what policies to adopt or reject."[7] An ambiguity is created here because obviously leaders sometimes create opinions as well as respond to them, but since the leaders are constantly being challenged by rivals seeking to gain the allegiance of the masses it is assumed that the individual citizen will receive information from several conflicting sources, making it extremely difficult for any one group to "engineer consent" by manipulating public opinion. As Lipset puts it: "Representation is neither simply a means of

[3]Introduction by Lipset to the Collier Books paperback edition of Robert Michel's *Political Parties* (New York, 1962), 33.

[4]The phrase is Dahl's in *Who Governs?* *op. cit.*, p. 227.

[5]*Ibid.*, p. 225.

[6]Schumpeter, *op. cit.*, p. 269.

[7]Dahl, *Who Governs?* *op. cit.* p. 164.

political adjustment to social pressures nor an instrument of manipulation. It involves both functions, since the purpose of representation is to locate the combinations of relationships between parties and social bases which makes possible the operation of efficient government."[8]

There has been extensive research and speculation about the prerequisites for a democratic system of this kind. There is general agreement that a well developed social pluralism and an extensive system of voluntary groups or associations is needed, along with a prevailing sense of psychological security, widespread education and limited disparities of wealth. There must be no arbitrary barriers to political participation, and "enough people must participate in the governmental process so that political leaders compete for the support of a large and more or less representative cross section of the population."[9]

Elitist theory departs markedly from the classical tradition at this point. Traditionally it was assumed that the most important prerequisite for a stable democracy was general agreement among the politically active (whose who vote) on certain fundamental policies and basic values, and widespread acceptance of democratic procedures and restraints on political activity. Political leaders would not violate the basic consensus, or "democratic mold," if they wished to be successful in gaining their objectives, because once these fundamental restraints were broken the otherwise passive public would become aroused and would organize against the offending leaders. Elitist theorists argue instead that agreement on democratic values among the "intervening structure of elites," the very elements which had been seen earlier as potential

threats to democracy, is the main bulwark against a breakdown in constitutionalism. Writing in 1959 David Truman discards his notion of "potential groups," a variation of the traditional doctrine of consensus, and calls instead for a "consensus of elites," a determination on the part of the leaders of political parties, labor unions, trade associations and other voluntary associations to defend the fundamental procedures of democracy in order to protect their own positions and the basic structure of society itself from the threat of an irresponsible demagogue.[10] V. O. Key, in his *Public Opinion and the American Democracy*, concludes that "the critical element for the health of a democratic order consists in the beliefs, standards, and competence of those who constitute the influentials, the opinion-leaders, the political activists in the order.[11] Similarly, Robert Dahl concludes in his study of New Haven that the skillful, active political leaders in the system are the true democratic "legitimists."[12] Since democratic procedures regulate their conflicts and protect their privileged positions in the system the leaders can be counted on to defend the democratic creed even if a majority of the voters might prefer some other set of procedures.[13]

---

[10]David Truman, "The American System in Crisis," *Political Science Quarterly* (December 1959), 481–97. See also a perceptive critique of Truman's change of attitude in Peter Bachrach, "Elite Consensus and Democracy," *The Journal of Politics*, XXIV (1962), 439–52.

[11]Key, *op. cit.*, p. 558. See also Key's "Public Opinion and the Decay of Democracy," *The Virginia Quarterly Review*, XXXVII (1961), 481–94.

[12]Dahl's position on this issue seems to have undergone a transformation somewhat similar to Truman's. Compare Dahl and Lindblom, *op. cit.*, ch. 11 with Dahl, *Who Governs?* *op. cit.*, Books IV, V, VI.

[13]Dahl, *Who Governs?* pp. 311–25. It is important to note that these conclusions about the crucial function of an elite consensus in democracy were based on little empirical evidence. Truman, Key and Dahl seem to rely most heavily on Samuel Stouffer, *Communism, Conformity, and Civil Liberties* (New York, 1955), a study based on national opinion surveys which was

---

[8]Lipset, Introduction to Michels, *op. cit.*, p. 34.

[9]Robert Dahl and Charles Lindblom, *Politics, Economics and Welfare* (New York, 1953), p. 309.

It has also been suggested by several elitist theorists that democracies have good reason to fear increased political participation. They argue that a successful (that is, stable) democratic system depends on widespread apathy and general political incompetence.[14] The ideal of democratic participation is thus transformed into a "noble lie" designed chiefly to insure a sense of responsibility among political leaders. As Lester Milbrath puts it:

. . . it is important to continue moral admonishment for citizens to become active in politics, not because we want or expect great masses of them to become active, but rather because the admonishment helps keep the system open and sustains a belief in the right of all to participate, which is an important norm governing the behavior of political elites.[15]

If the uninformed masses participate in large numbers, democratic self-restraint will break down and peaceful competition among the elites, the central element in the elitist theory, will become impossible.

The principal aim of the critics whose views we are examining has been to make the theory of democracy more realistic, to bring it into closer correspondence with empirical reality. They are convinced that the classical theory does not account for "much of the real machinery"[16] by which the system operates, and they have expressed concern about the possible spread among Americans of either unwarranted anxiety or cynical disillusionment over the condition of democracy. But it is difficult to transform a utopian theory into a realistic account of political behavior without changing the theory's normative foundations. By revising the theory to bring it into closer correspondence with reality, the elitist theorists have transformed democracy from a radical into a conservative political doctrine, stripping away its distinctive emphasis on popular political activity so that it no longer serves as a set of ideals toward which society ought to be striving.[17]

---

concerned with only one issue (McCarthyism) and did not investigate the relationship between the expressed opinions of its subjects and their behavior under stress; and James Prothro and Charles Grigg, "Fundamental Principles of Democracy: Bases of Agreement and Disagreement," *Journal of Politics*, XXII (1960), 276–94, a study of attitudes in two small cities. More recently, however, Herbert McClosky has produced more convincing data in his "Consensus and Ideology in American Politics," *American Political Science Review*, LVIII (1964), 361–82. On page 377 McClosky concludes that widespread agreement on procedural norms is not a prerequisite to the success of a democratic system: "Consensus may strengthen democratic viability, but its absence in an otherwise stable society need not be fatal, or even particularly damaging." McClosky's conclusions are called into question by data presented by Samuel Eldersveld, *Political Parties: A Behavioral Analysis* (Chicago, 1964), 183–219; and Edmund Constantini, "Intra-party Attitude Conflict: Democratic Party Leadership in California," *Western Political Quarterly*, 16 (1963), 956–72.

[14]See Bernard Berelson *et al.*, *op. cit.*, ch. 14; Lipset, *op. cit.*, pp. 14–16; W. H. Morris-Jones, "In Defense of Apathy," *Political Studies*, II (1954), 25–37.

[15]Milbrath, *op. cit.*, p. 152.

[16]Louis Hartz, "Democracy: Image and Reality," in Chambers and Salisbury (eds.), *op. cit.*, p. 26.

[17]Several articles have recently appeared which attack the elitist theory on normative grounds. The best and most insightful is Lane Davis, "The Cost of Realism: Contemporary Restatements of Democracy," *Western Political Quarterly*, XVII (1964), 37–46. Also see: Graeme Duncan and Steven Lukes, "The New Democracy," *Political Studies*, XI (1963), 156–77; Steven W. Rousseas and James Farganis, "American Politics and the End of Ideology," *British Journal of Sociology*, XIV (1963) 347–60; and Christian Bay, "Politics and Pseudopolitics," *American Political Science Review*, LIX (1965), 39–51. The subject is also treated in: Henry Kariel, *The Decline of American Pluralism* (Stanford, 1961), chs. 9 and 11; T. B. Bottomore, *Elites and Society* (London, 1964), 108-10; Robert Presthus, *Men at the Top* (New York, 1964), 3–47; and Robert Agger, Daniel Goldrich and Bert Swanson, *The Rulers and the Ruled* (New York) (1964), 93–99, 524–32. For an insightful critique of the work of Dahl and Mills, conceived of as opposing ideological positions see: William E. Connolly, *Responsible Political Ideology: Implications of the Sociology of Knowledge for Political Inquiry* (unpublished doctoral dissertation, University of Michigan, 1965), 18–39. This section of this article depends heavily on Lane Davis' analysis.

The most distinctive feature, and the principal orienting value, of classical democratic theory was its emphasis on individual participation in the development of public policy. By taking part in the affairs of his society the citizen would gain in knowledge and understanding, develop a deeper sense of social responsibility, and broaden his perspective beyond the narrow confines of his private life. Although the classical theorists accepted the basic framework of Lockean democracy, with its emphasis on limited government, they were *not* primarily concerned with the *policies* which might be produced in a democracy; above all else they were concerned with *human development*, the opportunities which existed in political activity to realize the untapped potentials of men and to create the foundations of a genuine human community. In the words of John Stuart Mill:

. . . the most important point of excellence which any form of government can possess is to promote the virtue and intelligence of the people themselves. The first question in respect to any political institutions is how far they tend to foster in the members of the community the various desirable qualities, . . . moral, intellectual, and active.[18]

In the elitist version of the theory, however, emphasis has shifted to the needs and functions of the system as a whole; there is no longer a direct concern with human development. The central question is not how to design a political system which stimulates greater individual participation and enhances the moral development of its citizens, but how "to combine a substantial degree of popular participation with a system of power capable of governing *effectively* and *coherently?*"[19]

The elitist theory allows the citizen only a passive role as an object of political activity; he exerts influence on policy making only by rendering judgments after the fact in national elections. The safety of contemporary democracy lies in the high-minded sense of responsibility of its leaders, the only elements of society who are actively striving to discover and implement the common good. The citizens are left to "judge a world they never made, and thus to become a genteel counter-part of the mobs which sporadically unseated aristocratic governments in eighteenth- and nineteenth-century Europe."[20]

The contemporary version of democratic theory has, it seems, lost much of the vital force, the radical thrust of the classical theory. The elitist theorists, in trying to develop a theory which takes account of the way the political system actually operates, have changed the principal orienting values of democracy. The heart of the classical theory was its justification of broad participation in the public affairs of the community; the aim was the production of citizens who were capable enough and responsible enough to play this role. The classical theory was not meant to describe any existing system of government; it was an outline, a set of prescriptions for the ideal polity which men should strive to create. The elitist theorists, in their quest for realism, have changed this distinctive prescriptive element in democratic theory; they have substituted stability and efficiency as the prime goals of democracy. If these revisions are accepted, the danger arises that in striving to develop more reliable explanations of political behavior, political scientists will also become sophisticated apologists for the existing political order. Robert Lane, in concluding his study of the political ideologies of fifteen "common men" in an Eastern city, observes that they lack a utopian vision, a well-defined sense of social justice that would allow them to

---

[18]John Stuart Mill, *Considerations on Representative Government* (New York, 1862), 39–40.

[19]Samuel Beer, "New Structures of Democracy: Britain and America," in Chambers and Salisbury (eds.), *op. cit.*, p. 46.

[20]Davis, *op. cit.*, p. 45.

stand in judgement on their society, and its institutions.[21] To some degree, the "men of Eastport" share this disability with much of the American academic elite.

II. THE ELITIST THEORY AS A GUIDE FOR RESEARCH

The shortcomings of the elitist theory are not confined to its normative implications. Serious questions also arise concerning its descriptive accuracy and its utility as a guide to empirical research. The most unsatisfactory element in the theory is its concept of the passive, apolitical, common man who pays allegiance to his governors and to the sideshow of politics while remaining primarily concerned with his private life, evenings of television with his family, or the demands of his job. Occasionally, when the average citizen finds his primary goals threatened by the actions or inactions of government, he may strive vigorously to influence the course of public policy, but *"Homo Civicus"* as Dahl calls him, "is not, by nature, a political animal."[22]

It was the acceptance of this concept that led the elitist theorists to reject the traditional notion of consensus. It became implausible to argue that the citizenry is watchful and jealous of the great democratic values while at the same time suggesting that they are uninvolved, uninformed and apathetic. Widespread apathy also is said to contribute to democratic stability by insuring that the disagreements that arise during campaigns and elections will not involve large numbers

of people or plunge the society into violent disorders or civil war.

No one can deny that there is widespread political apathy among many sectors of the American public. But it is important to ask why this is so and not simply to explain how this phenomenon contributes to the smooth functioning of the system. Of course, the citizens' passivity might stem from their satisfaction with the operation of the political system, and thus they would naturally become aroused only if they perceived a threat to the system. Dahl, for one, argues that the political system operates largely through "inertia," tradition or habitual responses. It remains stable because only a few "key" issues are the objects of controversy at any one time, the rest of public policy having been settled and established in past controversies which are now all but forgotten. Similarly, Nelson Polsby argues that it is fallacious to assume that the quiescent citizens in a community, especially those in the lower income groups, have grievances unless they actually express them. To do so is to arbitrarily assign "upper and middle-class values to all actors in the community."[23]

But it is hard to believe, in these days of protest demonstrations, of Black Muslims and the Deacons of Defense and Justice, that the mood of cynical apathy toward politics which affects so many American Negroes is an indication of their satisfaction with the political system, and with the weak, essentially meaningless alternatives it usually presents to them. To assume that apathy is a sign of satisfaction in this case is to overlook the tragic history of the Negroes in America and the system of violent repression long used to deny them any entrance into the regular channels of democratic decision-making.

Students of race relations have concluded that hostile attitudes toward a racial group do not necessarily lead to hos-

---

[21]Robert Lane, *Political Ideology* (New York, 1962), 475. See also Donald Stokes' comments on the same topic in "Popular Evaluations of Government: An Empirical Assessment," in Harlan Cleveland and Harold Lasswell (eds.), *Ethics and Bigness* (published by the Conference on Science, Philosophy and Religion in their relation to the Democratic Way of Life, 1962), p. 72.

[22]Dahl, *Who Governs?* *op. cit.*, p. 225.

[23]Nelson Polsby, *Community Power and Political Theory* (New Haven, 1963), p. 117.

tile actions, and amicable feelings do not ensure amicable actions. Instead "it is the social demands of the situation, particularly when supported by accepted authority figures, which are the effective determinants of individual action. . . ."[24] This insight might apply to other areas besides race relations. It suggests that a society's political culture, the general perceptions about the nature of authority and the prevailing expectations of significant reference groups, might be a major influence on the political behavior of the average citizen regardless of his own feelings of satisfaction or hostility. There have been sizable shifts in rates of political participation throughout American history which suggests that these rates are not rigidly determined. A recent analysis indicates that rates of voter participation are now *lower* than they were in the nineteenth century even though the population is now much better educated and the facilities for communication much better developed.[25] Other studies indicate that there are marked differences in the political milieu of towns and cities which lead citizens of one area to exhibit much more cynicism and distrust of the political system than others.[26] Although the studies showed no corresponding changes in feelings of political competence, cynical attitudes might inhibit many forms of participation and thus induce apathy.

---

[24]Herbert Blumer, "Recent research [on race relations in the] United States of America," *International Social Science Bulletin* (UNESCO), 10 (1958), 432. Similar arguments concerning the relationship of beliefs and action can be found in J. D. Lohman and D. C. Reitzes, "Deliberately Organized Groups and Racial Behavior," *American Sociological Review*, 19 (1954), 342-44; and in Earl Raab (ed.), *American Race Relations Today* (Garden City, 1962).

[25]Walter Dean Burnham, "The Changing Shape of the American Political Universe," *American Political Science Review*, 59 (1965), 7-28.

[26]Robert Agger, Marshall Goldstein and Stanley Pearl, "Political Cynicism: Measurement and Meaning," *The Journal of Politics*, 23 (1961), 477-506; and Edgar Litt, "Political Cynicism and Political Futility," *The Journal of Politics*, 25 (1963) 312-23.

Political apathy obviously has many sources. It may stem from feelings of personal inadequacy, from a fear of endangering important personal relationships, or from a lack of interest in the issues; but it may also have its roots in the society's institutional structure, in the weakness or absence of group stimulation or support, in the positive opposition of elements within the political system to wider participation; in the absence, in other words, of appropriate spurs to action, or the presence of tangible deterrents.[27] Before the causes of apathy can be established with confidence much more attention must be directed to the role of the mass media. How are the perceptions of individual citizens affected by the version of reality they receive, either directly or indirectly, from television, the national wire services, and the public schools[28]—and how do these perceptions affect their motivations? Political scientists have also largely neglected to study the use of both legitimate and illegitimate sanctions and private intimidation to gain political ends. How do the activities of the police,[29] social workers, or elements of organized crime affect the desires and the opportunities available for individual political participation?

Certainly the apparent calm of American politics is not matched by our general social life, which is marked by high crime rates, numerous fads and crazes, and much intergroup tension.[30] One recent study

---

[27]For a brief survey of findings on this subject, see Milbrath, *op. cit.*; and for a clear, brief summary, see: Morris Rosenburg, "Some Determinants of Political Apathy," *Public Opinion Quarterly*, XVIII (1954-55), 349-66. Also see David Apter (ed.), *Ideology and Discontent* (New York, 1964), especially chapters by Converse and Wolfinger *et al.*

[28]A major study of the influence of secondary schools on political attitudes is underway at the University of Michigan under the direction of M. Kent Jennings.

[29]An extensive investigation of the role of the police and the courts in city politics is being conducted at Harvard University by James Q. Wilson.

[30]It is very difficult to compare crime rates or other indications of social disorganization in the

showed that during the civil rights protests in Atlanta, Georgia, and Cambridge, Maryland, crime rates in the Negro communities dropped substantially.[31] A finding of this kind suggests that there is some connection between these two realms of social conflict and that both may serve as outlets for individual distress and frustration. High crime (or suicide) rates and low rates of voting may very well be related; the former may represent "leakage" from the political system.[32]

Once we admit that the society is not based on a widespread consensus, we must look at our loosely organized, decentralized political parties in a different light. It may be that the parties have developed in this way precisely because no broad consensus exists. In a fragmented society which contains numerous geographic, religious and racial conflicts, the successful politician has been the man adept at negotiating and bargaining, the man best able to play these numerous animosities off against each other, and thereby build *ad hoc* coalitions of support for specific programs. Success at this delicate business of coalition-building depends on achieving some basis for communication among the leaders of otherwise antagonistic groups and finding a formula for compromise. To create these circumstances sharp conflicts must be avoided; highly controversial, potentially explosive issues shunned. Controversy is shifted to other issues or the public authorities simply refuse to deal with

the question, claiming that they have no legitimate jurisdiction in the case or burying it quietly in some committee room or bureaucratic pigeonholes.[33]

In other words, one of the chief characteristics of our political system has been its success in suppressing and controlling internal conflict. But the avoidance of conflict, the suppression of strife, is *not* necessarily the creation of satisfaction or consensus. The citizens may remain quiescent, the political system might retain its stability, but significant differences of opinion remain, numerous conflicts are unresolved and many desires go unfulfilled. The frustrations resulting from such deprivations can create conflict in other, nonpolitical realms. Fads, religious revivals, or wild, anomic riots such as those which occurred in the Negro ghettos of several large American cities during the summers of 1964 and 1965, phenomena not directly related to the achievement of any clearly conceived political goals, may be touched off by unresolved tensions left untended by the society's political leaders.

The American political system is highly complex, with conflicting jurisdictions and numerous checks and balances. A large commitment in time and energy must be made, even by a well-educated citizen, to keep informed of the issues and personalities in all levels of government. Most citizens are not able or willing to pay this kind of cost to gain the information necessary for effective political participation.

United States with those in other countries. For a discussion of some of the difficulties see: UNESCO 1963 *Report on the World Social Situation* (New York, 1963).

[31]Fredric Solomon, Walter L. Walker, Garrett O'Connor and Jacob Fishman, "Civil Rights Activity and Reduction of Crime Among Negroes," *Archives of General Psychiatry*, XII (March 1965), 227–36.

[32]For an excellent study of the Black Muslims which portrays the movement as a nonpolitical outlet for the frustration and bitterness felt by many American Negroes see the study by an African scholar: E. V. Essien-Udom, *Black Nationalism: A Search for an Identity in America* (Chicago, 1962).

---

[33]Herbert Agar makes a similar analysis and argues for the retention of the system in *The Price of Union* (Boston, 1950). On page 689 he states:

The lesson which Americans learned [from the Civil War] was useful: in a large federal nation, when a problem is passionately felt, and is discussed in terms of morals, each party may divide within itself, against itself. And if the parties divide, the nation may divide; for the parties, with their enjoyable pursuit of power, are a unifying influence. Wise men, therefore, may seek to dodge such problems as long as possible. And the easiest way to dodge them is for both parties to take both sides.

This may be especially true in a political system in which weak or unclear alternatives are usually presented to the electorate. For most citizens the world of politics is remote, bewildering, and meaningless, having no direct relation to daily concerns about jobs or family life. Many citizens have desires or frustrations with which public agencies might be expected to deal, but they usually remain unaware of possible solutions to their problems in the public sphere. This group within our political system are citizens only from the legal point of view. If a high degree of social solidarity and sense of community are necessary for true democratic participation, then these marginal men are not really citizens of the state. The polity has not been extended to include them.[34]

For the elitist theorist widespread apathy is merely a fact of political life, something to be anticipated, a prerequisite for democratic stability. But for the classical democrat political apathy is an object of intense concern because the overriding moral purpose of the classical theory is to expand the boundaries of the political community and build the foundations for human understanding through participation by the citizens in the affairs of their government.

III. LEADERS AND FOLLOWERS

While most elitist theorists are agreed in conceiving of the average citizen as politically passive and uncreative, there seems to be a difference of opinion (or at least of emphasis) over the likelihood of some irrational, anti-democratic outburst from the society's common men. Dahl does not dwell on this possibility. He seemingly conceives of *homo civicus*, the average citizen, as a man who consciously chooses to avoid politics and to devote

himself to the pleasures and problems of his job and family:

Typically, as a source of direct gratifications political activity will appear to *homo civicus* as less attractive than a host of other activities; and, as a strategy to achieve his gratifications indirectly political action will seem considerably less efficient than working at his job, earning more money, taking out insurance, joining a club, planning a vacation, moving to another neighborhood or city, or coping with an uncertain future in manifold other ways.[35]

Lipset, on the other hand, seems much more concerned with the danger that the common man might suddenly enter the political system, smashing democratic institutions in the process, as part of an irrational, authoritarian political force. He sees "profoundly anti-democratic tendencies in lower class groups,[36] and he has been frequently concerned in his work with Hitler, McCarthy and other demagogic leaders who have led anti-democratic mass movements.

Although there are obviously some important differences of opinion and emphasis concerning the political capacities of average citizens and the relative security of democratic institutions, the elitist theorists agree on the crucial importance of leadership in insuring both the safety and viability of representative government. This set of basic assumptions serves as a foundation for their explanation of change and innovation in American politics, a process in which they feel creative leadership plays the central role.

Running throughout the work of these writers is a vision of the "professional" politician as hero, much as he is pictured in Max Weber's essay, "Politics as a Vocation." Dahl's Mayor Lee, Edward Banfield's Mayor Daley, Richard Neustadt's ideal occupant of the White House all possess great skill and drive, and are engaged in the delicate art of persuasion

---

[34]For a study of several important factors affecting the degree of participation in American politics see: E. E. Schattschneider, *The Semi-Sovereign People* (New York, 1960), especially chs. 5 and 6.

[35]Dahl, *Who Governs?* p. 224.
[36]Lipset, *op cit.*, p. 121.

and coalition-building. They are actively moving the society forward toward their own goals, according to their own special vision. All of them possess the pre-eminent qualities of Weber's ideal-type politician: "passion, a feeling of responsibility, and a sense of proportion."[37] As in Schumpeter's analysis of capitalism, the primary source of change and innovation in the political system is the "political entrepreneur"; only such a leader can break through the inherent conservatism of organizations and shake the masses from their habitual passivity.

It is obvious that political leaders (especially chief executives) have played a very important role in American politics, but it is also clear that the American system's large degree of internal bargaining, the lack of many strong hierarchical controls and its numerous checks and balances, both constitutional and political, place powerful constraints on the behavior of political executives. American presidents, governors and mayors usually find themselves caught in a web of cross pressures which prevent them from making bold departures in policy or firmly attaching themselves to either side of a controversy. The agenda of controversy, the list of questions which are recognized by the active participants in politics as legitimate subjects of attention and concern, is very hard to change.

Just as it can be argued that the common citizens have a form of indirect influence, so it can also be argued that the top leaders of other institutions in the society, such as the business community, possess indirect influence as well. As Banfield suggests in his study of Chicago, the top business leaders have great potential power: "if the twenty or thirty wealthiest men in Chicago acted as one and put all their wealth into the fight, they could

easily destroy or capture the machine."[38] The skillful politician, following Carl Friedrich's "rule of anticipated reactions,"[39] is unlikely to make proposals which would unite the business community against him. The aspiring politician learns early in his career, by absorbing the folklore which circulates among the politically active, which issues can and cannot be exploited successfully. It is this constellation of influences and anticipated reactions, "the peculiar mobilization of bias" in the community, fortified by a general consensus of elites, that determines the agenda of controversy.[40] The American political system, above all others, seems to be especially designed to frustrate the creative leader.

But as rigid and inflexible as it is, the political system does produce new policies; new programs and schemes are approved; even basic procedural changes are made from time to time. Of course, each major shift in public policy has a great many causes. The elitist theory of democracy looks for the principal source of innovation in the competition among rival leaders and the clever maneuvering of political entrepreneurs, which is, in its view, the most distinctive aspect of a democratic system. Because so many political scientists have worn the theoretical blinders of the elitist theory, however, we have overlooked the importance of broadly based social movements, arising from the public at large, as powerful agents of innovation and change.

The primary concerns of the elitist the-

[37]Hans Gerth and C. Wright Mills (eds.), *From Max Weber: Essays in Sociology* (New York, 1946), 115.

[38]Edward Banfield, *Political Influence* (New York, 1961), 290.

[39]Carl Friedrich, *Constitutional Government and Politics* (New York, 1939) 17–18.

[40]This point is made persuasively by Peter Bachrach and Morton Baratz, "The Two Faces of Power," *American Political Science Review*, LVI (1962), 947–52. Also see their "Decisions and Nondecisions: An Analytical Framework," *American Political Science Review*, LVII (1963), 632–42; and Thomas J. Anton, "Power, Pluralism and Local Politics," *Administrative Quarterly*, VII (1963), 425–57.

orists have been the maintenance of democratic stability, the preservation of democratic procedures, and the creation of machinery which would produce efficient administration and coherent public policies. With these goals in mind, social movements (if they have been studied at all) have usually been pictured as threats to democracy, as manifestations of "political extremism." Lipset asserts that such movements typically appeal to the "disgruntled and the psychologically homeless, to the personal failures, the socially isolated, the economically insecure, the uneducated, unsophisticated, and authoritarian persons at every level of the society."[41] Movements of this kind throw the political system out of gear and disrupt the mechanisms designed to maintain due process; if the elites were overwhelmed by such forces, democracy would be destroyed. This narrow, antagonistic view of social movements stems from the elitist theorists' suspicion of the political capacities of the common citizens,[42] their fear of instability and their failure to recognize the elements of rigidity and constraint existing in the political system. But if one

holds that view and at the same time recognizes the tendency of the prevailing political system to frustrate strong leaders, it becomes difficult to explain how significant innovations in public policy, such as the social security system, the Wagner Act, the Subversive Activities Control Act of 1950, or the Civil Rights Bill of 1964, ever came about.

During the last century American society has spawned numerous social movements, some of which have made extensive demands on the political system, while others have been highly esoteric, mystical, and apolitical. These movements arise because some form of social dislocation or widespread sense of frustration exists within the society. But dissatisfaction alone is not a sufficient cause; it must be coupled with the necessary resources and the existence of potential leadership which can motivate a group to take action designed to change the offending circumstances.[43] Often such movements erupt along the margins of the political system, and they sometimes serve the purpose of encouraging political and social mobilization, of widening the boundaries of the polity.[44] Through movements such as the

---

[41]Lipset, op. cit., p. 178.

[42]Ruth Searles and J. Allen Williams, in a study of Negro students who took part in the sit-in demonstrations, found no evidence that they were authoritarian or posed threats to democracy. "Far from being alienated, the students appear to be committed to the society and its middle class leaders": "Negro College Students' Participation in Sit-ins," Social Forces, XL (1962), p. 219. For other studies of this particular social movement see: Robert Coles, "Social Struggle and Weariness," Psychiatry, XXVII (1964), 305–15; and three articles by Frederic Solomon and Jacob Fishman; "Perspectives on Student Sit-in Movement," American Journal of Ortho-psychiatry, 33 (1963), 872–82; "Action and Identity Formation in First Student Sit-in Demonstration," Journal of Social Issues, XX (1964), 36–45; and "Psycho-social Meaning of Nonviolence in Student Civil Rights Activities," Psychiatry, XXVII (1964), 91–99. Also see the October 1964 issue of The Journal of Social Issues, entitled "Youth and Social Action," edited by Fredric Solomon and Jacob Fishman; and Jack L. Walker, "Protest and Negotiation: A Case Study of Negro Leaders in Atlanta, Georgia," Midwest Journal of Political Science, VII (1963), 99–124.

[43]Sociologists usually study social movements under the rubric of collective behavior. For general treatments see: Herbert Blumer, "Collective Behavior" in J. B. Gittler (ed.), Review of Sociology (New York, 1957); Rudolph Heberle, Social Movements, (New York, 1951); Lewis Killian, "Social Movements" in Robert Faris (ed.), Handbook of Modern Sociology (Chicago, 1964); Charles King, Social Movements in the United States (New York, 1956); Karl Lang and Gladys Lang, Collective Dynamics (New York, 1961); Neil Smelser, Theory of Collective Behavior (New York, 1963); Ralph Turner and Lewis Killian, Collective Behavior (Englewood Cliffs, N.J., 1957). For a brief historical sketch of some American social movements see: Thomas Greer, American Social Reform Movements: Their Pattern Since 1865 (Englewood Cliffs, N.J., 1946).

[44]For a book which investigates social movements which have served this function among Italian peasants see: E. J. Hobsbawn, Primitive Rebels (Manchester, 1959). See also: Vittorio Lanternari, The Religions of the Oppressed (New York, 1964) for a study of the relationship of Messianic cults and revolutionary movements on five continents; and George Ruth, The Crowd

Negroes' drive for civil rights, or the midwestern farmers' crusade for fair prices in the 1890's, the Ku Klux Klan, or the "radical right" movements of the 1960's, "*pre-political* people who have not yet found, or only begun to find, a specific language in which to express their aspirations about the world"[45] are given new orientation, confidence, knowledge, sources of information and leadership.

Social movements also serve, in Rudolf Heberle's words, as the "creators and carriers of public opinion."[46] By confronting the political authorities, or by locking themselves in peaceful—or violent[47]—conflict with some other element of the society, social movements provoke trials of strength between contending forces or ideas. Those trials of economic, political or moral strength take place in the court of public opinion and sometimes place enormous strain on democratic institutions and even the social fabric itself. But through such trials, as tumultuous as they may sometimes be, the agenda of controversy, the list of acceptable, "key" issues may be changed. In an effort to conciliate and mediate, the political leaders fashion new legislation, create unique regulatory bodies and strive to establish channels of communication and accommodation among the combatants.

Of course, members of the political elite

may respond to the movement by resisting it, driving it underground or destroying it; they may try to co-opt the movement's leaders by granting them privileges or by accepting parts of its program, or even by making the leaders part of the established elite; they may surrender to the movement, losing control of their offices in the political system in the process. The nature of the political leader's response is probably a prime determinant of the tactics the movement will adopt, the kind of leadership that arises within it, and the ideological appeals it develops. Other factors might determine the response of the leadership, such as the existence of competing social movements with conflicting demands, the resources available to the political leaders to satisfy the demands of the movement, the social status of the participants in the movement, the presence of competing sets of leaders claiming to represent the same movement, and many other elements peculiar to each particular situation. In this process social movements may be highly disruptive and some institutions may be completely destroyed; the story does not always have a happy ending. But one major consequence (function, if you will) of social movements is to break society's log jams, to prevent ossification in the political system, to prompt and justify major innovations in social policy and economic organization.[48]

This relationship of challenge and response between the established political system and social movements has gone without much systematic study by political scientists. Sociologists have been concerned with social movements, but they have directed most of their attention to

---

in History (New York, 1964) for a study of popular uprisings in England and France from 1730–1848.

[45]Hobsbawn, *op. cit.*, p. 2.

[46]Heberle, *op. cit.*, pp. 417–18.

[47]American political scientists have not been sufficiently concerned with the role of violence in the governmental process. Among all the articles published in *The American Political Science Review* between 1906 and 1963, there was only one whose title contained the word "violence," only one with the word "coercive" (it concerned India), and none with the word "force." During the same period there were forty-nine articles on governmental reorganization and twenty-four on civil service reform. See Kenneth Janda (ed.), *Cumulative Index to The American Political Science Review* (Evanston, 1964). Efforts to retrieve this situation have begun in: Harry Eckstein (ed.), *Internal War* (New York, 1964).

---

[48]Lewis Coser has discussed the role of conflict in provoking social change in his *The Functions of Social Conflict* (Glencoe, 1956); and in his "Social Conflict and the Theory of Social Change" *British Journal of Sociology*, IX (1957) 197–207. See also Irving Louis Horowitz, "Consensus, Conflict and Cooperation: A Sociological Inventory," *Social Forces*, XLI (1962), 177–88.

the causes of the movements, their "natural history," and the relationship between leaders and followers within them.[49] Historians have produced many case studies of social movements but little in the way of systematic explanation.[50] This would seem to be a fruitful area for investigation by political scientists. But this research is not likely to appear unless we revise our concept of the masses as politically inert, apathetic and bound by habitual responses. We must also shift our emphasis from theories which conceive of the "social structure in terms of a functionally integrated system held in equilibrium by certain patterned and recurrent processes," to theories which place greater emphasis on the role of coercion and constraint in the political system and which concentrate on the influences within society which produce "the forces that maintain it in an unending process of change."[51] The greatest contribution of Marx to the understanding of society was his realization that internal conflict is a major source of change and innovation. One need not accept his metaphysical assumptions to appreciate this important insight.

IV. CONCLUSION

In a society undergoing massive social change, fresh theoretical perspectives are essential. Political theorists are charged

___

[49]For an insightful and stimulating example, see Joseph Gusfield, *Symbolic Crusade* (Urbana, 1963), which makes an excellent analysis of the causes of the Temperance movement and changes in its leadership but makes only brief mention of the movement's impact on the government and the responses of political leaders to its efforts.

[50]John Higham is somewhat of an exception of this generalization. See his *Strangers in the Land: Patterns of American Nativism 1860–1925* (New York, 1963). Also see his: "Another Look at Nativism," *Catholic Historical Review*, XLIV (1958), 147–58; and his "The Cult of the 'American Consensus': Homogenizing Our History," *Commentary* (February 1959), 159.

[51]Ralf Dahrendorf, *Class and Class Conflict in Industrial Society* (Stanford, 1959), 159.

with the responsibility of constantly reformulating the dogmas of the past so that democratic theory remains relevant to the stormy realities of twentieth century American society with its sprawling urban centers, its innumerable social conflicts, and its enormous bureaucratic hierarchies.

In restating the classical theory, however, contemporary political scientists have stripped democracy of much of its radical *élan* and have diluted its utopian vision, thus rendering it inadequate as a guide to the future. The elitist theorists generally accept the prevailing distribution of status in the society (with exceptions usually made for the American Negro), and find it "not only compatible with political freedom but even . . . a condition of it."[52] They place great emphasis on the limitations of the average citizen and are suspicious of schemes which might encourage greater participation in public affairs. Accordingly, they put their trust in the wisdom and energy of an active, responsible elite.

Besides these normative shortcomings the elitist theory has served as an inadequate guide to empirical research, providing an unconvincing explanation of widespread political apathy in American society and leading political scientists to ignore manifestations of discontent not directly related to the political system. Few studies have been conducted of the use of force, or informal, illegitimate coercion in the American political system, and little attention has been directed to the great social movements which have marked American society in the last one hundred years.

If political science is to be relevant to society's pressing needs and urgent problems, professional students of politics must broaden their perspectives and become aware of new problems which are in need

___

[52]Sabine, "The Two Democratic Traditions," *op. cit.*, p. 459.

of scientific investigation. They must examine the norms that guide their efforts and guard against the danger of uncritically accepting the value of the going system in the name of scientific objectivity. Political scientists must strive for heightened awareness and self-knowledge; they must avoid rigid presumptions which diminish their vision, destroy their capacities for criticism, and blind them to some of the most significant social and political developments of our time.

A REPLY TO "FURTHER REFLECTIONS ON 'THE ELITIST THEORY OF DEMOCRACY'"*

Jack L. Walker

Attempts to identify the dominant themes implicit in the work of any political theorist is a difficult and risky enterprise and, as Professor Dahl himself admits, efforts to show that common tendencies are present in several writers are even more hazardous. After reading Professor Dahl's rejoinder, I am convinced that it was a mistake to use the label "The Elitist Theory of Democracy" (even though it came directly from Lipset) to describe the doctrines with which I tried to deal. The word "theory" gives a false precision to what would be more properly identified as a prevailing attitude toward the American political process. The word "elitist" apparently carries, at least in Dahl's view, some objectionable anti-democratic connotations. My intent was not to question Dahl's, or anyone else's democratic *bona fides*. My article was intended as a critique of the prescriptive implications of a set of ideas concerning democratic political systems which can be found, in varying degrees of prominence, in the writings of many contemporary students of politics—Dahl among them.

The doctrines with which I was concerned were: (1) the belief that the political inactivity of the average citizen is a more or less permanent aspect of his behavior, not an artifact of the social and political systems; (2) the related belief that political inactivity is a sign of satisfaction with the operation of the political system, a form of passive consent; (3) the belief that political apathy is not seriously dysfunctional in a democratic system and, on the part of some writers, the belief that widespread apathy may be a prerequisite for the successful functioning of the system; (4) the belief that agreement on democratic norms among political leaders is more important than consensus among the common citizens for achieving political stability; and (5) an overriding concern with maintaining the stability of democratic systems. I meant to analyze this set of ideas and its consequences; I did not set out to write a comprehensive appraisal of the political theory of Professor Dahl, or any other single writer.

Since my principal concern was with the prescriptive implications which I believe have been drawn from these five

*Reprinted from *The American Political Science Review*, Vol. LX (June 1966), pp. 391–92. Copyright 1966, The American Political Science Association.

beliefs, Professor Dahl misses the point when he complains that I have not dealt with his own normative model, "polyarchal democracy." I never intended to deal with his normative theory; instead, my intention was to analyze the normative consequences of the descriptive and explanatory efforts of Professor Dahl, and several other contemporary political scientists. Ideas and beliefs have manifold consequences, some intended and others wholly unexpected; writings meant by their author to be purely descriptive may still lead their readers to draw normative conclusions, and it is quite possible to study these conclusions without violating the logical distinction between descriptive and prescriptive statements. It would be extremely difficult, perhaps impossible, for any single writer to describe every aspect of the American political system. Each writer must choose among innumerable phenomena which could conceivably be studied. Regardless of the writer's intention, I would argue that the facts he presents and the explanations he proposes may prompt his readers to make certain normative inferences. In the case of the beliefs I considered in my article, the normative impact has been to reduce the urgency of the need to extend the limits of the active political community; and as I argued further, this has tended to divert the attention of political scientists from such phenomena as social movements which appear on the periphery of the organized political system.

Since I was primarily concerned with the normative consequences of contemporary political theory, I had no need to discover the personal values of each writer I studied. But when Americans write about their own political system they frequently reveal the normative implications of their own work. Professor Dahl, in *A Preface to Democratic Theory*, concludes his chapter, "The American Hybrid" with these words:

. . . the normal American political system . . . appears to be a relatively efficient system for reinforcing agreement, encouraging moderation, and maintaining social peace in a restless and immoderate people operating a gigantic, powerful, diversified, and incredibly complex society. This is no negligible contribution, then, that Americans have made to the arts of government—and to that branch, which of all the arts of politics is the most difficult, the art of democratic government.[1]

I do not believe I would be alone in asserting that there are normative criteria implicit in these sentences (criteria not analyzed or discussed in Dahl's chapter on "Polyarchal Democracy") which might guide us in evaluating the performance of the political system he has so brilliantly described.

Perhaps the most significant point upon which Professor Dahl and I differ is this final question of the criteria to be used in evaluating the performance of a democratic political system. Professor Dahl places great value on the capacities of a system "for reinforcing agreement, encouraging moderation, and maintaining social peace." The examples of political disaster that spring readily to his mind are the collapse of the Weimar Republic and the Kerensky regime, the awful bloodshed and senseless chaos of the Spanish civil war, and the grotesque displays of mass obedience and total political involvement in Hitler's Germany and Mussolini's Italy. He is part of a generation which has experienced a series of savage attacks on political democracy and his concern with political stability, in light of all that has happened, is certainly understandable. Political stability is indeed a precious commodity; I do not wish to create the impression that I reject its obvious importance. But I do think that both the discipline of political science and American society have suffered from our exces-

[1] *Robert Dahl*, A Preface to Democratic Theory (Chicago, 1956), p. 151.

sive concern with the protection and maintenance of our political system. I believe that the time has come to direct our attention to the infinitely more difficult task of involving larger and larger numbers of people in the process of government. The theory of democracy beckons us toward an ancient ideal: the liberation of the energies of all our citizens in the common pursuit of the good society.